LIABILITY

of

CORPORATE OFFICERS

and

DIRECTORS

FOURTH EDITION

---

by

WILLIAM E. KNEPPER and DAN A. BAILEY

partners in

Arter & Hadden

Cleveland, Columbus, Washington, Dallas & Canton

THE MICHIE COMPANY
Law Publishers
CHARLOTTESVILLE, VIRGINIA

TABLE OF CONTENTS

Chapter 1

BASIC DUTIES

Chapter 2

DUTY OF DILIGENCE

TABLE OF CONTENTS

Chapter 5

LIABILITY FOR DEBTS AND TO CREDITORS AND THIRD PERSONS

Chapter 6

BUSINESS JUDGMENT RULE

TABLE OF CONTENTS

Chapter 7

STATE LEGISLATION LIMITING LIABILITY

Chapter 8

CRIMINAL LIABILITY

Chapter 9

LIABILITY UNDER ERISA

Chapter 10

ENVIRONMENTAL, SAFETY, AND EMPLOYMENT-RELATED LIABILITY

Chapter 11

ACCOUNTANTS, ATTORNEYS, BROKERS AND DEALERS

TABLE OF CONTENTS

Chapter 12

FINANCIAL INSTITUTIONS AND THEIR MANAGEMENT

Chapter 13

NONPROFIT AND CHARITABLE ORGANIZATIONS

TABLE OF CONTENTS

Chapter 14

FEDERAL SECURITIES LAWS

Chapter 15

LIABILITY IN TAKEOVERS, MERGERS AND BUYOUTS

Chapter 16

DISCLOSURE AND MISUSE OF BUSINESS INFORMATION

Chapter 17

LEGAL REPRESENTATION; CONDUCTING THE DEFENSE

Chapter 18

CLASS, DERIVATIVE AND DIRECT ACTIONS

Chapter 19

DEFENSES AND PROTECTIVE MEASURES

TABLE OF CONTENTS

Chapter 20

INDEMNIFICATION

Chapter 21

LIABILITY INSURANCE

Chapter 22

LIABILITY AND FIDUCIARY SURVEYS

APPENDICES

Appendix A

SELECTED STATE STATUTES

TABLE OF CONTENTS

Appendix B-1

STATUTES LIMITING DIRECTOR LIABILITY

Appendix B-2

INDEMNIFICATION STATUTES

Appendix C

SELECTED INSURANCE FORMS

TABLE OF CONTENTS

Appendix D-1

SAMPLE CHARTER OR BYLAW INDEMNIFICATION PROVISION

Appendix D-2

SAMPLE INDEMNITY AGREEMENT

Appendix E

SAMPLE STATEMENT OF SELF-INSURANCE

Chapter 1

BASIC DUTIES

§ 1.01. Public scrutiny of corporate boards.

The spate of litigation against corporate officers and directors since 1968[1] has brought the integrity of corporate managements and their boards of directors under public scrutiny. Although some reforms have been instituted and much has been written on the subject, the torrent of lawsuits against corporate directors and officers flows on apace.

Judicially identified wrongdoing by corporate officers and directors lends credence to the belief that directors are disinclined to criticize managements and are disposed to criticize managements' decisions with a minimum of delay and unpleasantness. Because of frequent disapproval of such complacent relationships by the courts, directors have become

---

1. E.g., Escott v. BarChris Constr. Corp., 283 F. Supp. 643 (S.D.N.Y. 1968); Gould v. American-Hawaiian S.S. Co., 535 F.2d 761 (3d Cir. 1976); Panter v. Marshall Field & Co., 646 F.2d 271 (7th Cir.), cert. denied, 454 U.S. 1092 (1981); Joy v. North, 692 F.2d 880 (2d Cir. 1982), cert. denied, 460 U.S. 1051 (1983); Smith v. Van Gorkom, 488 A.2d 858 (Del. 1985); Hanson Trust PLC v. ML SCM Acquisition, Inc., 781 F.2d 264 (2d Cir. 1986).

increasingly vulnerable to liability for management of the corporations left in their charge.[2]

It is common knowledge that many corporations under pressure of the SEC, the courts, and private litigants have increased the proportion of their outside directors, made more use of board committees, particularly audit committees, and improved the flow of information from managements to their boards. But directors with limited time to devote to their directorial duties and dependent upon management for access to administration can do little to guide or direct corporate policies in many instances.

Even in specific cases where judicially mandated institutional reform was intended to change corporate governance,[3] the difference between what the restructured boards did and what hypothetical insider boards would have done was probably imperceptible.

Numerous devices for creating a truly "independent" board have been suggested,[4] but experience discloses that in most cases the board will conform to and acquiesce in management's proposals.[5]

Whether the law should impose more or less control on corporate governance depends on the outcome of debates between two competing ideologies.[6] The interest of the federal government in controlling corporations was demonstrated in the Foreign Corrupt Practices Act,[7] but the commentators report that "market theory as an efficient regulator of economic institutions" is becoming widely accepted.[8]

---

2. See Solomon, "Restructuring the Corporate Board of Directors: Fond Hope — Faint Promise?," 76 Mich. L. Rev. 581 (1979).

3. Id. at 591-610, discussing the results of such court orders in the Mattel, Inc., Northrup Corp., and Phillips Petroleum Co. litigation.

4. Brudney, "The Independent Director — Heavenly City or Potemkin Village?," 95 Harv. L. Rev. 507, 598 n.3 (1982).

5. Note, "The Propriety of Judicial Deference to Corporate Boards of Directors," 96 Harv. L. Rev. 1894, 1902 (1983).

6. Goldstein, "Future Articulation of Corporation Law," 39 Bus. Law. 1541 (1984).

7. 15 U.S.C. §§ 78a, 78m, 78dd-1, 78dd-2, 79ff.

8. Goldstein, supra note 6, at 1541.

Permeating both ideologies is the business judgment rule.[9] Where it applies, courts will not disturb a transaction or find liability unless directors have abused their discretion. But the commentators are concerned with the definition of a director's "duty of care" as it is now spelled out,[10] and suggest that it may need restructuring if increased burdens on directorships are to be avoided.[11]

Public pressure and scrutiny, and significant court decisions, have brought significant changes and reforms into corporate boardrooms. Courts, governmental agencies, and the investing public are no longer content to accept corporate management by directors who do not direct. Proof of that statement is found in the "apparently unending stream of cases, administrative decisions, rulings and private settlements" during the past two decades, by which corporate "directors and officers have been held financially accountable for what they have done, what they have undone, and what they have failed to do."[12]

§ 1.02. Management of corporate business.

Today's director no longer has a sinecure. He holds a job.

Most state corporation statutes provide that the business and affairs of a corporation shall be managed by or under the direction of its board of directors.[13] Under Delaware law the business judgment rule is the offspring of that fundamental principle.[14] That rule presumes that in making a business decision, the directors acted on an informed basis, in good

---

9. See discussions infra in section 1.13 and Chapter 6.

10. Manning, "The Business Judgment Rule and the Director's Duty of Attention: Time for Reality," 39 Bus. Law. 1477, 1478 (1984).

11. Id. at 1492-1501.

12. Schaeftler, The Liabilities of Office: Indemnification and Insurance of Corporate Officers and Directors (1976), comment of Prof. Stanley Siegel in Foreword, p. ix.

13. E.g., Del. Code Ann. tit. 8, § 141; N.Y. Bus. Corp. Law § 701; Ohio Rev. Code Ann. § 1701.59.

14. Smith v. Van Gorkom, 488 A.2d 858, 872 (Del. 1985).

faith, and in the honest belief that the action taken was in the best interests of the company.[15]

The structure of a corporation's management is pyramidal in form.[16] At the apex are the executive officers who, in theory, have some discretion but in general are deemed to execute policies formulated by the board. Such officers are nominally selected by the board of directors, which prescribes their duties and fixes their compensation.

Although the law charges the board with selection of the officers, a chief executive officer usually has much to say about the designation of his successor,[17] and boards are generally reluctant to oppose his recommendation.[18] Certainly, the chief executive officer plays a prominent role in choosing his subordinates, albeit those who are corporate officers in theory will be selected and elected by the board.[19]

At the base of the pyramid are the shareholders to whom corporation law grants the power to elect directors and vote on major corporation actions.[20] As a matter of practice, directors are elected by the shareholders, but are usually selected by management, particularly the chief executive officer.[21] Except in relatively rare instances, the chief executive officer is able to direct the operations of the proxy system to elect his choices of directors when contests arise.[22] Such directors often

---

15. Aronson v. Lewis, 473 A.2d 805, 812 (Del. 1984); Unocal Corp. v. Mesa Petroleum Co., 493 A.2d 946, 954 (Del. 1985). See discussion infra in section 1.13 and Chapter 6.

16. Eisenberg, "Legal Models of Management Structure in the Modern Corporation: Officers, Directors and Accountants," 63 Calif. L. Rev. 375, 376 (1975).

17. Bacon & Brown, "Corporate Directorship Practices: Role, Selection and Legal Status of the Board" 26 (Conference Board Report No. 646, 1975). See also, e.g., Businessmen in the News, "My Scenario for Disaster," Fortune, July, 1977, at 18.

18. Zald, "Who Shall Rule? A Political Analysis of Succession in a Large Welfare Organization," Pac. Soc. Rev. Spring, 1965, at 58-59.

19. Mace, Directors: Myth and Reality 65-68, 70-71 (1971).

20. Eisenberg, supra note 16, at 376.

21. Mace, supra note 19, at 94.

22. Schaeftler, supra note 12, at 46.

are reluctant to challenge the chief executive officer who selected them.[23]

It seems likely that a director who would otherwise oppose the chief executive will usually keep silent or resign from the board. Otherwise, he risks loss of his seat as a consequence of his opposition. This dilemma poses some difficult questions as to the personal liability of such a director if he remains silent against his better judgment.

§ 1.03. Board functions.

What does the board do? Under statutes such as those mentioned above,[24] the board exercises all of the corporate powers and directs the management of the business and affairs of the corporation. It has been said that "the ultimate obligation of directors is to represent the company's shareholders."[25] Also, a prime responsibility of directors is to act as a check and a balance on management.

Directors are not expected to conduct a "hands on," day-by-day actual management of the corporation; that is customarily done by the executive officers.[26] But the concept of managing involves something more than mere monitoring. Among board functions generally considered to be essential are:

(1) Authorization of major corporation actions. This is an obligation customarily imposed by state statutes.[27]

(2) Advice and counsel to the corporation's management, especially to its chief executive officer.[28]

(3) Providing effective auditing procedures so that the board will be adequately informed of the corporation's financial status. In addition to selecting inde-

---

23. Eisenberg, supra note 16, at 383.

24. Supra note 13.

25. Caldwell, "Generally Accepted Rules and Key Functions of the Board," Handbook for Corporate Directors 10.1 (1985).

26. Eisenberg, supra note 16, at 376.

27. See Eisenberg, "The Legal Roles of Shareholders and Management in Modern Corporate Decisionmaking," 57 Calif. L. Rev. 1, 60-68 (1969).

28. E.g., Mace, supra note 19, at 13-22.

pendent auditors, this function also entails establishing uniformly organized audit committees manned by outside directors. The Commission on Auditors' Responsibilities has concluded that "the board of directors, with outside members and an audit committee when appropriate, is the best vehicle for achieving and maintaining balance in the relationship between the independent auditor and management."[29] The board has the responsibility for adopting sound accounting policies[30] and insisting upon their execution. The board's audit committee may have the primary charge of nominating or recommending dismissal of the independent auditor and of directing its activities.[31]

(4) Serving as a facility or mechanism, which may be used to provide access to corporate decision-making for others than the personnel included in management.[32] Thus employees, suppliers, consumers, financial advisers, social groups, and other client groups may be given representation on a corporation's board.[33]

(5) Review of the corporation's investments at regular intervals, at least annually, to ensure that they com-

---

29. The Commission on Auditors' Responsibilities: Report, Conclusions, and Recommendations 106 (1978).

30. Grady, "Inventory of Generally Accepted Accounting Principles for Business Enterprises," 12 AICPA Accounting Research Study No. 7 (1965).

31. See "AICPA Executive Committee Statements on Audit Committees of Boards of Directors," 124 Journal of Accountancy 10 (Sept. 1967); SEC Accounting Services Release No. 123 (March 23, 1972); "Recommendations and Comments on Financial Reporting to Shareholders and Related Matters," 6 New York Stock Exchange (1973); SEC Securities Act of 1933 Release No. 5550 (Dec. 20, 1974); Farrell, "Audit Committee: A Lawyer's View," 28 Bus. Law. 1089 (1973). Cf. Hawes, "Stockholder Appointment of Independent Auditors: A Proposal," 74 Colum. L. Rev. 1, 37 (1974).

32. Eisenberg, supra note 16, at 393, denominates this function as "A Modality for Exercising Influence or Control."

33. Blumberg, "Reflections on Proposals for Corporate Reform Through Change in the Composition of the Board of Directors: 'Special Interest' or 'Public' Directors," 53 B.U.L. Rev. 547 (1973).

ply with all applicable provisions of law. This function may well include approval of written guidelines for such policies, including types of securities, general mix of securities, maximum underwriting positions, reporting of losses, valuation procedures, forbidden transactions, and approvals and review of transactions.

(6) Monitoring the performance of management, setting objectives and measuring management's results against them, evaluating the accomplishments of management and their results, and being responsible for the selection and removal of the chief executive officer.

Although certainly not exclusive, the foregoing list suggests the scope of the functions of a corporate board of directors in today's legal climate.

In the broad context of corporate governance, a board of directors is not a passive instrumentality.[34]

§ 1.04. Duties, in general.

The duties that a corporate officer or director owes to his corporation are rooted not only in the elementary rules of equity, but also in business morality and public policy. They include undivided, unselfish, and unqualified loyalty, unceasing effort never to profit personally at corporate expense, and unbending disavowal of any opportunity which would permit the director's private interests to clash with those of his corporation.[35]

Directors must use reasonable care and diligence[36] and must act within the scope of the authority conferred upon them.[37] The standards of conduct for directors are imposed

---

34. Unocal Corp. v. Mesa Petroleum Co., 493 A.2d 946, 954 (Del. 1985).

35. Patient Care Servs., S.C. v. Segal, 32 Ill. App. 3d 1021, 337 N.E.2d 471 (1975). See also Bartle v. Markson, 423 F.2d 637 (2d Cir. 1970); Borden v. Sinskey, 530 F.2d 478 (3d Cir. 1976).

36. See 2 Model Bus. Corp. Act Ann. 934-37 (3d ed. 1985).

37. General Rubber Co. v. Benedict, 215 N.Y. 18, 109 N.E. 96 (1915); Selheimer v. Manganese Corp. of Am., 423 Pa. 563, 224 A.2d 634 (1966).

both by statutes and by court decisions. The powers of a board of directors may be limited by express provisions of the articles of incorporation.

It is the consensus of authorities that directors must keep themselves informed as to the general type of business in which the corporation is engaged and be knowledgeable as to the corporation's business activities.[38] Their failure to attend directors' meetings does not excuse their failure to supervise the corporation's affairs.[39] Of course, the mere fact that a person accepts a corporate office and directorship does not necessarily impute to him full knowledge of all the corporate business.[40]

Directors have a duty to see that their corporation obeys the law and confines its activities within the limits of its corporate powers.[41] That is, directors may be held accountable for their corporation's ultra vires or otherwise unauthorized acts. Where the directors are guilty of neglect of their duties and the corporation suffers loss as a direct result, the directors may be held liable to the corporation, which may recover damages. Such an action may be brought by the corporation itself or by the stockholders in a derivative action for the corporation's benefit.

Under Delaware law, directors are required to act in an informed and deliberate manner and may not delegate their responsibility to management or abdicate it to the shareholders.[42] The duty of directors to inform themselves in preparation for a decision derives from the fiduciary capacity in which they serve the corporation and its shareholders.[43]

Corporate directors, acting as a board, also derive their powers from statutes such as those dealing with management

---

38. See Barnes v. Andrews, 298 F. 614 (S.D.N.Y. 1924).

39. Dinsmore v. Jacobson, 242 Mich. 192, 218 N.W. 700 (1928).

40. Berg v. King-Cola, Inc., 227 Cal. App. 2d 338, 38 Cal. Rptr. 655 (1964).

41. Diedrick v. Helm, 217 Minn. 483, 14 N.W.2d 913 (1944).

42. Smith v. Van Gorkom, 488 A.2d 858, 873 (Del. 1985).

43. See infra section 1.06.

of the corporation[44] and those authorizing it to deal in its own stock.[45]

In addition, a board's power to act in defense of its corporation results from the fundamental duty and obligation to protect the corporate enterprise, including shareholders, from harm reasonably perceived, regardless of source.[46] Such powers are not absolute. The board's actions must stand the test of judicial examination, and defensive measures must be reasonable in relation to a threat posed.

§ 1.05. Three basic duties.

Corporate officers and directors owe three basic duties to the corporations they serve: obedience, diligence, and loyalty.[47]

As to "obedience," directors and officers must contain their activities within the powers conferred upon their corporation by its charter and within the powers conferred upon them or as restricted by the articles of incorporation, code of regulations, and bylaws. If a director's behavior exceeds his authority conferred by the state corporation statutes, it may be challenged.

While directors have been absolved from liability for permitting their corporation to engage in ultra vires acts,[48] the duty of "obedience" contemplates that ultra vires corporate activities should be avoided. Some of the same considerations discussed in connection with the business judgment rule[49] may also apply in deciding whether an action is ultra vires.

---

44. E.g., Del. Code Ann. tit. 8, § 141.

45. E.g., id. § 160(a).

46. Unocal Corp. v. Mesa Petroleum Co., 493 A.2d 946, 954 (Del. 1985).

47. Gearhart Indus., Inc. v. Smith Int'l, Inc., 741 F.2d 707, 719 (5th Cir. 1984).

48. See Sutton v. Reagan & Gee, 405 S.W.2d 828 (Tex. Civ. App. 1966), and cf. Litwin v. Allen, 25 N.Y.S.2d 667 (1940).

49. For discussion of business judgment rule, see infra section 1.13 and Chapter 6.

9

For willful violation of the duty of obedience[50] and for negligence resulting in harm,[51] directors and officers may be held liable to their corporation.

The duty of "diligence," sometimes stated as the standard of care to be exercised, has been the subject of statutory enactment in most states. More than thirty jurisdictions follow the pattern of the Model Business Corporation Act.[52] Such enactments require the director to discharge his duties:

(1) in good faith;
(2) with the care that an ordinarily prudent person in a like position would exercise under similar circumstances; and
(3) in a manner he reasonably believes to be in the best interests of the corporation.[53]

The third duty is "loyalty." It contemplates that a director must refrain from engaging in his own personal activities in such a manner as to injure or take advantage of his corporation. Later chapters will deal with specific examples of disloyalty; but as a general proposition, it may be stated that directors may not make secret or private profits out of their official positions, and must give to the corporation the benefit of any advantages they obtain in their official positions. Once self-dealing or bad faith is demonstrated, the duty of loyalty supersedes the duty of diligence, and the directors must prove that the transaction was fair and reasonable to the corporation.[54]

§ 1.06. Directors as fiduciaries.

Directors of a corporation occupy a special fiduciary relationship to the corporation and its shareholders as a class

---

50. Leppaluoto v. Eggleston, 57 Wash. 2d 393, 357 P.2d 725 (1960).
51. Gottfried v. Gottfried Baking Co., 1 A.D.2d 993, 151 N.Y.S.2d 583 (1956).
52. See 2 Model Bus. Corp. Act Ann. 934-37 (1985).
53. Revised Model Bus. Corp. Act § 8.30.
54. Norlin Corp. v. Rooney, Pace, Inc., 744 F.2d 255, 265 (2d Cir. 1984); Diamond v. Oreamuno, 24 N.Y.2d 494, 301 N.Y.S.2d 78, 248 N.E.2d 910 (1969).

similar to that of a trustee. The foundation of that rule was laid in 1939, in *Pepper v. Litton*,[55] when Justice Douglas wrote:

> A director is a fiduciary.... So is a dominant or controlling stockholder or group of stockholders.... Their powers are powers in trust.... Their dealings with the corporation are subjected to rigorous scrutiny....

Under Delaware law, "directors are charged with an unyielding fiduciary duty to the corporation and its shareholders."[56] Cases decided in 1985 by the Delaware Supreme Court[57] examined the fiduciary duty of directors in takeovers and reaffirmed earlier decisions holding that defensive actions by directors will be protected by the business judgment rule absent a showing of bad faith, overreaching, self-dealing, or fraud on the part of the directors.

In New York, a director's obligation to the corporation and its shareholders, as a corporate fiduciary, is to use at least that degree of diligence that an "ordinarily prudent" person under similar circumstances would use.[58]

The Model Business Corporation Act and the corporation statutes of most states make no reference to fiduciary responsibilities.[59] Most states, however, have established the fiduciary status of directors in their case law. There are, of course, variations in terminology. In New York[60] and Michigan[61] "a high fiduciary duty of honesty and fair dealing" has

---

55. 308 U.S. 295, 306, 84 L.Ed. 281, 60 S.Ct. 238, 245 (1939).

56. Guth v. Loft, Inc., 2 A.2d 225 (Del. Ch. 1938), aff'd, 5 A.2d 503 (Del. 1939).

57. Smith v. Van Gorkom, 488 A.2d 858, 872 (Del. 1985); Unocal Corp. v. Mesa Petroleum Co., 493 A.2d 946 (Del. 1985); Moran v. Household Int'l, Inc., 500 A.2d 1346 (Del. 1985).

58. Hanson Trust PLC v. ML SCM Acquisition, Inc., 781 F.2d 264, 273 (2d Cir. 1986).

59. Statutes which designate directors as fiduciaries include: La. Rev. Stat. Ann. § 12.91, N.C. Gen. Stat. § 55-35; 42 Pa. C.S.A. 8363.

60. ChrisCraft Indus., Inc. v. Piper Aircraft Corp., 480 F.2d 341 (2d Cir.), cert. denied sub nom. Bangor Punta Corp. v. ChrisCraft Indus., Inc., 414 U.S. 910 (1973).

61. Berman v. Gerber Prod. Co., 454 F. Supp. 1310 (W.D. Mich. 1978).

been imposed; in Florida[62] "strict fiduciary duties"; in Kansas[63] "very strict fiduciary responsibilities"; and in others "fiduciary duty" or "fiduciary relationship".[64]

The law of the state of incorporation is controlling with respect to the fiduciary duties of directors.[65]

Corporate directors and officers are frequently treated as agents of the corporation,[66] but they are not considered agents of the individual shareholders who elect them. In so holding, the federal court for the Southern District of New York stated that a stockholder's profit interest in a particular corporate transaction was only "a remote proprietary interest." The court emphasized that while the shareholders "indirectly own the corporation, they do not manage it, and the acts of management are not attributed to them individually."[67]

Whether considered trustees or agents, the fiduciary relation requires that directors act in good faith on all occasions and give their conscientious care and best judgment to their

---

62. City of Miami Beach v. Smith, 551 F.2d 1370 (5th Cir. 1978).

63. Mid-West Underground Storage, Inc. v. Porter, 717 F.2d 493 (10th Cir. 1983); Delano v. Kitch, 542 F.2d 550 (10th Cir. 1976), opinion clarified, 554 F.2d 1004 (10th Cir. 1977), appeal after remand, 663 F.2d 990 (10th Cir. 1981), cert. denied, 456 U.S. 946 (1982).

64. E.g., DePinto v. Landoe, 411 F.2d 297 (9th Cir. 1969); Jewel Cos. v. Pay Less Drug Stores Northwest, Inc., 741 F.2d 1555 (9th Cir. 1984); United States v. Gates, 396 F.2d 65 (10th Cir. 1967); Kidwell ex rel. Penfold v. Meikle, 597 F.2d 1273 (9th Cir. 1979); Treco, Inc. v. Land of Lincoln Sav. & Loan, 749 F.2d 374 (7th Cir. 1984); Robinson v. Watts Detective Agency, Inc., 685 F.2d 729 (1st Cir. 1982), cert. denied sub nom. Consolidated Serv. Corp. v. Robinson, 459 U.S. 1105 (1983); Ohio Drill & Tool Co. v. Johnson, 625 F.2d 738 (6th Cir. 1980); Gearhart Indus., Inc. v. Smith Int'l, Inc., 741 F.2d 707 (5th Cir. 1984); Knauff v. Utah Constr. & Mining Co., 408 F.2d 958 (10th Cir.), cert. denied, 396 U.S. 831 (1969).

65. McDermott, Inc. v. Lewis, 531 A.2d 206 (Del. 1987); Treco, Inc. v. Land of Lincoln Sav. & Loan, supra note 64; Davis & Cox v. Summa Corp., 751 F.2d 1507 (9th Cir. 1985).

66. Sequoia Vacuum Sys. v. Stransky, 229 Cal. App. 2d 281, 40 Cal. Rptr. 203 (1964).

67. Popkin v. Dingman, 366 F. Supp. 534, 539 (S.D.N.Y. 1973).

tasks.[68] The fiduciary relation has been held applicable even
to a dummy director, who was a mere figurehead and discharged no duties.[69]

§ 1.07. Shareholders as fiduciaries.

A majority stockholder is subject to the same fiduciary obligations as a director, because he may control the directors.[70]
He may not misuse his power to promote his personal interests at the expense of the corporation's interests.[71] To the
minority stockholders, he owes a duty to exercise good faith,
reasonable care, and due diligence. When minority shareholders have no voice in management, the majority shareholders have a duty to protect the interests of the minority.[72]

Majority shareholders owe to each other and to the minority shareholders fiduciary duties to limit their capacity to
convert corporate property to their own individual pursuits.[73]

Dominant or controlling stockholders or groups of shareholders may also occupy a similar fiduciary relationship.
Their dealings with the corporation are subject to rigorous
scrutiny. Where a shareholder's contract or engagement with
the corporation is challenged, the burden is on the shareholder not only to prove the good faith of the transaction but
also to show its inherent fairness from the viewpoint of the
corporation and those interested in it.[74]

---

68. See Schildberg Rock Prods. Co. v. Brooks, 258 Iowa 759, 140 N.W.2d
132 (1966).

69. Gabelli & Co. Profit Sharing Plan v. Liggett Group, Inc., 444 A.2d
264 (Del. Ch. 1982); Burton v. Exxon Corp., 583 F. Supp. 405, 414 (S.D.N.Y.
1984).

70. Perlman v. Feldmann, 219 F.2d 173 (2d Cir.) cert. denied, 349 U.S.
952 (1955).

71. United States v. Byrum, 408 U.S. 125, 33 L.Ed.2d 238, 92 S.Ct. 2382,
reh'g denied, 409 U.S. 898 (1972).

72. See Pepper v. Litton, 308 U.S. 295, 84 L.Ed. 281, 60 S.Ct. 238 (1939);
Mason v. Pewabic Mining Co., 133 U.S. 50, 33 L.Ed. 524, 10 S.Ct. 224
(1890).

73. Silverman & Sons Realty Trust v. Commissioner, 620 F.2d 314, 318
(1st Cir. 1980).

74. Pepper v. Litton, supra note 72; Hyams v. Calumet & Hecla Mining
Co., 221 F. 529, 537 (6th Cir. 1915); Gerstle v. Gamble-Skagmo, Inc., 298 F.

A corporation which owned seventy-four percent of the stock of a subsidiary owed a fiduciary duty to the subsidiary and to the minority shareholders of the parent to protect them from domination and overreaching by the controlling parent. This obligation was extended to the members of the board of directors of the subsidiary who were also officers of the parent.[75]

Minority shareholders have been permitted to sue in tort for fraudulent breach of fiduciary duty by a corporation officer and majority shareholder.[76] And it is well established that the corporation itself may maintain an action against its directors and officers for mismanagement, waste of corporate assets, or derelictions of duty.[77]

When the claim by minority shareholders is for mismanagement of the corporation by directors-shareholders who constitute a controlling majority, it must generally be pursued on a derivative basis. The claim belongs to the corporation. If it recovers, the shareholders will benefit in proportion to their equity ownerships. Such actions are discussed in Chapter 18. Where there is a special injury to a shareholder independent of the fiduciary duties owed to the corporation, the shareholder may maintain a direct action.[78]

Supp. 66, 99 (E.D.N.Y. 1969), modified, 478 F.2d 1281 (2d Cir. 1973). See also Comment, "Fiduciary Duties of Majority of Controlling Stockholders," 44 Iowa L. Rev. 734 (1959); Comment, "Fiduciary Duty of Controlling Shareholders," 7 W. Res. L. Rev. 467 (1956); Wolff v. Arctic Bowl, Inc., 560 P.2d 758 (Alaska 1977).

75. Valente v. Pepsico, Inc., 68 F.R.D. 361, 364 (D. Del. 1975). Cf. Unocal Corp. v. Mesa Petroleum, Inc., 493 A.2d 946, 958 (Del. 1985).

76. Jacobson v. Yaschik, 249 S.C. 577, 155 S.E.2d 601 (1967). See also Jones v. H.F. Ahmanson & Co., 1 Cal. 3d 93, 81 Cal. Rptr, 592, 460 P.2d 464 (1969), as to directors' duty to protect minority shareholders.

77. Platt Corp. v. Platt, 21 A.D.2d 116, 249 N.Y.S.2d 75 (1964), aff'd, 15 N.Y.2d 705, 256 N.Y.S.2d 335, 204 N.E.2d 495 (1965), distinguishing Capitol Wine & Spirit Corp. v. Pokrass, 277 A.D. 184, 98 N.Y.S.2d 291 (1950), aff'd, 302 N.Y. 734, 98 N.E.2d 704 (1951).

78. Cowin v. Bresler, 741 F.2d 410, 414 (D.C. Cir. 1984); see also Bokat v. Getty Oil Co., 262 A.2d 246, 249 (Del. 1970), and Elster v. American Airlines, Inc., 100 A.2d 219, 222 (Del. Ch. 1953).

Promoters are held to be fiduciaries in transactions with their corporate instrument, and may be required to account for stock issued to them without payment and in excess of the value of their promotional services.[79]

§ 1.08. Officers other than directors.

The statutes of all states provide for corporate officers, usually elected or appointed by its board of directors.[80] Most state statutes provide that duties of officers shall be prescribed in the bylaws, or by resolution of the board of directors.[81]

The Revised Model Business Corporation Act states that nondirector officers with discretionary authority must discharge their duties with the same standards of care imposed upon directors.[82] However, they may be more limited in reliance upon information, reports, or statements because they have better opportunities for first-hand knowledge of corporate affairs than do directors who are not officers.[83]

Nondirector officers and inside directors who are also officers are usually the real managers of the organization. The standards applied to them are high and reflect their greater responsibilities and their obligation of greater familiarity with the affairs of the corporation.

Most of the cases concern the liability of directors as such, rather than their liabilities arising out of the holding of particular corporation offices. Sometimes an officer who is not a director may be held liable, and it is certainly true that corporate officers, as such, are personally liable for actionable tort in the fraudulent violation of their fiduciary duties.[84] It has been said that the liability of a corporation's president may

---

79. Whaler Motor Inn, Inc. v. Parsons, 363 N.E.2d 493 (Mass. 1977). See also 84 A.L.R.3d 162 (1978) regarding recovery from a promoter for secret profits in sale of property to a corporation.

80. Cf. Kan. Stat. Ann. § 17-6302; N.C. Gen. Stat. § 55-34(d).

81. E.g., Del. Code Ann. tit. 8, § 142; N.Y. Bus. Corp. Law § 715; Ohio Rev. Code Ann. § 1701.64.

82. Revised Model Bus. Corp. Act § 8.42. See infra section 2.06.

83. Masonic Bldg. Corp. v. Carlsen, 128 Neb. 108, 258 N.W. 44 (1934).

84. Price v. Hibbs, 225 Cal. App. 2d 209, 37 Cal. Rptr. 270 (1964).

be more extensive than that of a mere director, because of his greater participation in the corporation's management as its chief executive officer.[85] And there are occasions when a corporation's president, as president, may be held liable where he might not be liable as a mere director.[86]

The scope of authority of a corporation's officers is not easily defined.[87] It may not be the same for all purposes. The difference between the actual authority of an officer and his apparent authority may become important when the reliance of an outsider on the officer's authority is involved.[88] It has been held that the powers of a general manager may be coextensive with the powers of the corporation.[89]

In recent years it has become common for the chairman of the board to be the chief executive officer of a corporation and the president its chief administrative officer. Whether outsiders may assume this to be the fact has not yet been established by the court decisions.

The limit of an officer's powers is the measure of his liability. He is expected to stay within the limits of his authority and may be held liable to his corporation if he violates those limits.[90] In addition, a corporation officer who exceeds his

---

85. Brown v. Farmers & Merchants Nat'l Bank, 88 Tex. 265, 31 S.W. 285 (1895).

86. See, e.g., Bates v. Dresser, 251 U.S. 524, 64 L.Ed. 388, 40 S.Ct. 247 (1920).

87. See, e.g., Note, "Corporations — Inherent Power of President to Bind Pennsylvania Corporation by Virtue of his Office," 36 Temp. L.Q. 353 (1963); Note, "Inherent Power as a Basis of a Corporate Officer's Authority to Contract," 57 Colum. L. Rev. 868 (1957). See also Pettit v. Doeskin Prods., Inc., 270 F.2d 95 (2d Cir. 1959), cert. denied, 362 U.S. 910 (1960).

88. Cf. Geyer v. Walling Co., 175 Neb. 456, 122 N.W.2d 230 (1963); Piening v. Titus, Inc., 113 Ohio App. 532, 179 N.E.2d 374 (1960); Mid-Continent Constr. Co. v. Goldberg, 40 Ill. App. 2d 251, 188 N.E.2d 511 (1963).

89. See, e.g., Memorial Hosp. Ass'n v. Pacific Grape Prods. Co., 45 Cal. 2d 634, 290 P.2d 481 (1955).

90. Restatement (Second) of Agency §§ 383(e), 399 (1958). For exculpation by ratification, see Bennett v. Corporation Fin. Co., 258 Mass. 306, 154 N.E. 835 (1927), and Hennessey v. Nelen, 299 Mass. 569, 13 N.E.2d 431 (1938).

16

powers and authority may be held liable to an injured outsider, unless his corporation duly ratifies his unauthorized actions and thereby assumes corporate liability for them.[91]

Because specific management functions and most decision-making are left to the corporation's full-time officers and executive employees, it is appropriate for standards of care to reflect that they are the real managers. The growth and complexity of corporate activities, the increase in environmental problems, the energy crisis, products liability, civil rights issues, employee welfare, and consumer protections, for example, raise questions of accountability which must be met in the first instance by the corporation's active management.

Of course, the ultimate policy decisions are for the board, but the corporate course may already have been set before the board can take considered action. Even then, the board's decision will probably be based on materials supplied by the management personnel who set the course in the first instance; and the board's decision may have little real significance.[92]

The fiduciary obligations of corporate officers are often identical to those of directors.[93] In an Eighth Circuit case the father of Marlon Brando, the actor, was president and manager of a ranch corporation whose stock was owned by the son. In denying secured claim status to mortgages given by the corporation to Brando at the father's behest, the court found a violation of the fiduciary duties imposed by law upon such officers. The Eighth Circuit affirmed, citing *Pepper v. Litton*.[94]

---

91. Vulcan Corp. v. Cobden Mach. Works, 336 Ill. App. 394, 84 N.E.2d 173 (1949); Allen v. Morris Bldg. Co., 360 Mich. 214, 103 N.W.2d 491 (1960). See also Claman v. Robertson, 164 Ohio St. 61, 128 N.E.2d 429 (1955).

92. "One executive ... remarked that he did not care who formulated the policy so long as he was left to carry it out, because he knew that by the time the operating organization had modified the ... policy decision to meet realities, he would have pretty much his own way." Copeland & Towle, The Board of Directors and Business Management 66 (1942).

93. Gearhart Indus., Inc. v. Smith Int'l, Inc., 741 F.2d 707, 719 (5th Cir. 1984).

94. In re Black Ranches, Inc., 362 F.2d 19 (8th Cir.), cert. denied sub nom. Black v. Brando, 385 U.S. 990 (1966).

The fiduciary capacity in which a corporate officer functions permits him to deal with the corporation but not to profit at its expense.[95] That capacity dictates undivided loyalty by the officer and prohibits neglect of the corporation's business and activities detrimental to the corporation's best interests.[96]

Generally, claims against corporate officers for failing to perform their fiduciary duties arise under state law in the absence of manipulation, misrepresentations, deception, or nondisclosure which would violate federal securities laws.[97]

§ 1.09. Inside directors.

While state corporation laws do not distinguish between inside and outside directors, courts and commentators are beginning to look at them differently from the standpoint of liability. If, as noted in section 1.08, nondirector officers are expected to assume responsibilities commensurate with their familiarity with the corporation's affairs, the same rule should apply to inside directors who are officers or employees of the corporation.[98]

Officers who are appointed to the board of directors usually have gone through the chairs of corporate office and demonstrated their skills and abilities. They are more deeply involved in the corporation's affairs and usually have better access to information than other board members. They are at some disadvantage because they are subordinates of the chief executive officer and may find it awkward to disagree with or criticize his views.[99]

There is reason to believe that management directors may contribute more to decision making when their access to the

---

95. Smith v. Robinson, 343 F.2d 793, 797 (4th Cir. 1965). See also Belcher v. Birmingham Trust Nat'l Bank, 348 F. Supp. 61 (N.D. Ala. 1968).

96. Franklin Music Co. v. American Broadcasting Cos., 616 F.2d 528 (3d Cir. 1980).

97. Vaughn v. Teledyne, Inc., 628 F.2d 1214, 1222 (9th Cir. 1980).

98. Estes, "Outside Directors: More Vulnerable Than Ever," 51 Harv. Bus. Rev. 107, 112 (Jan.-Feb., 1973).

99. Schaeftler, supra note 12, at 74.

18

board as directors enables their views to be aired at board level. A chief executive who is the only management representative on the board can present his views as having total management support. A nondirector executive, speaking in opposition, may be accused of going behind his chief's back. Thus "the degree of freedom of management directors from domination by the chief executive ... may depend to some extent on the composition of the board."[100]

Nonemployee directors such as outside legal counsel, the corporation's banker or investment banker, retired executives of the corporation, or representatives of major corporate suppliers or customers should be treated as inside directors because of their lack of independence. They probably hold their seats on the board economically or psychologically through friendship, prior employment, or the fact that they have been selected and indoctrinated by the chief executive.[101] Sometimes their familiarity with the corporation's affairs may be insufficient to justify imposing on them the same responsibilities as on employee-officer-directors. In other cases they may be involved as deeply as the officers and employees.

In a situation where the liability of directors under the federal securities laws is in issue, the decision of the Second Circuit in *Lanza v. Drexel & Company*[102] needs careful study. While the majority opinion exonerated the underwriter-director for wrongdoing, the case plainly suggests that directors may be judged in the light of their experience, knowledge, intimacy of involvement in the corporation's affairs, and awareness of the consequences of complaints of corporate acts.[103]

When the corporation's lawyer is also a director, he is confronted with special problems whether his position is house

---

100. Letts, "Corporate Governance: A Different Slant," 35 Bus. Law. 1505, 1511 (1980), hereafter Letts article.

101. See Eisenberg, supra note 16, at 404.

102. 479 F.2d 1277 (2d Cir. 1973) (en banc).

103. Sommer, "Directors and the Federal Securities Laws," Fed. Sec. L. Rep. (CCH) ¶79,669, at 83,806 (1974).

counsel or outside legal counsel. The board needs his judgment and advice. His comprehensive knowledge of the corporation's legal problems enables him to provide clear and persuasive legal opinions.[104] On the other hand, a lawyer's role as the corporation's legal advisor and his duties as a corporate director may conflict.[105] To the extent that his position as legal adviser causes other directors to give particular weight to his views, the lawyer-director probably will be held to a higher standard of care than other directors less knowledgeable in the law.[106]

§ 1.10. Outside directors.

One result of the increased public scrutiny of corporate boards has been an increase in the number of outsiders holding membership on the boards of most public corporations. Since about 1978, with that trend, many such boards have a majority of outside directors. To the extent that a board monitors the corporation management, it is generally recognized that those to be monitored cannot perform the monitoring function.

An outside director's independence should be his most distinguishing characteristic. Such independence does not require an outside director to take an adversary attitude toward management, to characteristically dissent from management's proposals, or to assume without proof that management is not dealing in good faith.[107] An outside director should be vigilant and questioning in an effort to learn what is in the corporation's best interests.[108] He is expected to exer-

---

104. See Hinsey IV, Coombe, Jr., Harris, Ruder, Schauer, "Lawyers as Directors, A Panel," 30 Bus. Law. (Special Issue) 41, 58-59 (1975).

105. Cf. Gartner, "Guest Opinion: Are Outside Directors Taking Outside Chances," Juris Doctor 4 (March, 1973).

106. Escott v. BarChris Constr. Corp., 283 F. Supp. 643, 690 (S.D.N.Y. 1968). See also Knepper, "The Lawyer-Director," Handbook for Corporate Directors 26.1 (1985).

107. Leech & Mundheim, "The Outside Director of the Publicly Held Corporation," 31 Bus. Law. 1799, 1830 (1976).

108. Id. at 1805.

cise "a healthy skepticism" and an alertness to possible wrongdoing on the part of corporate insiders.[109]

While "monitoring" is seen by some as the principal role of outside directors,[110] they should expect to perform all tasks assigned to them by state law, federal law and sound business practices. Successful corporations are finding new ways to improve their performance by creative use of their outside directors' abilities.[111]

Although independent outside directors should undertake active and vigorous scrutiny of corporate activities,[112] they should not attempt to run the corporation or arbitrarily to substitute their judgment for that of management. Courts will probably give great weight to their actions on the assumption that their sole interest is the furtherance of the corporate enterprise.[113]

The role and value of interested outside directors continues to receive attention of the commentators. Lawyers, brokers, customers and others who might be characterized as "suppliers" to the corporation fall into this category.[114] Should they be excluded from board memberships?[115] Or does the very interest which renders them subject to question enhance their value as corporate directors?[116] Their perspectives, experience and sophistication may provide expertise which is unavailable to the corporation from any other source. However, it is not easy to know when the outsider becomes an insider; when the person brought in to solve a problem becomes a part of the problem.

---

109. See Sommer, supra note 103, at 83,806.

110. Leech & Mundheim, supra note 107, at 1804-06.

111. See, e.g., Schaeftler, supra note 12, at 44; Leech & Mundheim, note 107, at 1809-10.

112. Gould v. American Hawaiian S.S. Co., 351 F. Supp. 853, 859 (D. Del. 1972).

113. See, e.g., Puma v. Marriott, 283 A.2d 693, 696 (Del. Ch. 1971).

114. Knepper, "Liability of Lawyer-Directors," 40 Ohio St. L.J. 341, 352 (1978); Riger, "The Lawyer-Director — 'A Vexing Problem'," 33 Bus. Law. 2381 (1978).

115. See Williams, "Corporate Accountability and the Lawyer's Role," 34 Bus. Law. 7, 10 (1978).

116. Letts article, supra note 100, at 1513.

Disinterested outside directors probably qualify as corporate watchdogs better than any other class of directors. However, unless they are truly professional directors, it is likely that their relative unfamiliarity with the details of the corporation's affairs may make them less valuable than interested outsiders. Also, the extent of their economic dependency on their directorships may impair their usefulness as monitors of the management team.[117] Job security and compensation may be critical to an outside director's independence. If he believes he owes his position to the chief executive officer, or if his compensation is materially important to him and either the chief executive officer or corporate insiders have the dominant voice in its establishment and continuation,[118] such a director may become subservient to management.

No director can function effectively without an adequate and continuing flow of information to him about the corporation, its goals, programs and activities. This is especially true of outside directors. Hence, a complete orientation program for the new director is essential.[119] It is the responsibility of the corporation to provide such a program and to emphasize to each new director the importance of the job he has undertaken.[120]

During the course of directors' service on the board, they must be furnished appropriate information relating to all matters upon which the board acts. Court decisions hold that a director's fiduciary capacity imposes a duty to inform himself in preparation for a business decision. There is no protection for directors who have made "an unintelligent or ill-advised judgment."[121] Such decisions require directors to follow methods and procedures that provide for adequate identification and study of all elements of matters to be decided.

---

117. Id. at 1514-15.
118. Leech & Mundheim, supra note 107, at 1830.
119. Schaeftler, supra note 12, at 51; Leech & Mundheim, supra note 107, at 1811-14; Corporate Director's Guidebook, 33 Bus. Law. 1590 (1978).
120. See infra section 19.06 for orientation of outside directors.
121. Smith v. Van Gorkom, 488 A.2d 858, 872 (Del. 1985).

There must also be sufficient information that directors may monitor the company's progress in the light of its goals and objectives, without imposing so much material upon them that they do not have time to absorb it. As a minimum, such information should encompass:

(1) internal financial statements, structured in a way that presents a meaningful breakdown of the enterprise's activities and summarized in a way that permits ready comprehension and reasonable analysis;

(2) periodic reporting dealing with various areas of compliance;

(3) periodic briefing by senior executives concerning developments affecting the business and affairs of the enterprise; in some cases, this dimension of reporting will be effectively accomplished by a memorandum from the chief officer distributed to the board members in advance of each meeting;

(4) forward planning, including critical issues facing the enterprise and new directions appropriate for board consideration in the context of corporate policy.[122]

Although restraints on time and information may limit the participation of outside directors in corporate affairs, some of their most important services may be rendered in dealing with audits: the financial audit[123] and the audit of management. Also, outside directors have a particular role in special litigation committees created in relation to derivative actions.

Regular evaluation of management performance, in which outside directors are effectively involved, is the type of an "audit of management" being given increasing attention as corporations look for ways to improve their performance.[124] Such an evaluation process probably should involve not only

---

122. Corporate Director's Guidebook, supra note 119, at 1608.

123. Audit committees, which deal with financial auditors, are discussed infra section 1.11.

124. Leech & Mundheim, supra note 107, at 1824.

an adequate flow of information between management and the board, but also personal contacts between outside directors and management personnel.[125] The outside directors need to measure management performance against stated goals, to be acquainted with specific problems which they should consider, and to consult with each other as to their information, conclusions, and recommendations. As mentioned above, the performance of this part of the monitoring function does not mean that the outside directors are to be hands-on managers of the corporation. Institutional processes that provide for such evaluation of management with regularity, according to an established plan, will help to develop an effective working relationship between management and the board,[126] which is certain to redound to the benefit of the enterprise.

§ 1.11. Committees of the board.

All state statutes provide for committees to be appointed by a corporation's board of directors. In ten states only an executive committee is named. The other statutes refer to other committees also.[127]

This section deals with the so-called "overview committees": the nominating committee, the compensation committee and the audit committee,[128] and also briefly discusses the executive committee. Because state law governs the delegation of board powers to committees, each case must be considered in the light of the particular state statutes under which the corporation exists. As a general rule, however, all such statutes will be interpreted to deny a director the right to rely

---

125. Id. at 1825-26.

126. Id. at 1827.

127. A list of such statutes appears in 2 Model Bus. Corp. Act Ann. 916-17 (1985).

128. Report of Committee on Corporate Laws, American Bar Association, Section of Corporation, Banking and Business Law, "The Overview Committees of the Board of Directors," 35 Bus. Law. 1335 (1980), hereafter Overview Committees.

on committee reports, if he has knowledge that makes such reliance unwarranted.[129]

Nominating Committee

This committee should have responsibility for recommending nominees to fill board vacancies and for bringing to the full board recommendations for the membership of board committees. When a vacancy occurs in the office of chief executive, this committee should recommend a successor.[130]

A nominating committee can help to establish an overall board environment conducive to objective decision making, bring about board involvement in determining board and committee composition and management succession, and enhance the likelihood of judicial approval when decisions affecting individual director interests are subjected to scrutiny in the courts.[131]

Among other responsibilities of this committee may be establishing (1) a procedure for identifying potential nominees, (2) criteria for board membership, (3) criteria for determining whether directors should be continued in office, (4) a mandatory retirement age for directors, (5) length of terms for directors, and (6) other factors relating to effective directorial performance. This committee may also make recommendations to the full board as to board size, committee structure, committee membership, and, particularly, management succession.[132]

The nominating committee would be expected to work closely with the corporation's chief executive officer, but there are strong views pro and con as to whether anyone in management should serve on this committee.[133]

---

129. See infra section 2.05, "Reliance on reports of committees."
130. Corporate Director's Guidebook, supra note 119, at 1626.
131. Overview Committees, supra note 128, at 1342.
132. Id. at 1344-45.
133. Id. at 1342.

Compensation Committee

The compensation committee should have responsibility for approving (or recommending to the full board) the compensation arrangements for the corporation's senior management, as well as the adopting of any compensation plans (including the granting of stock options) in which officers and directors are eligible to participate.[134]

By delegating such duties to a committee the board may obtain a forum with independent judgment as to the fairness of such arrangements. Obviously, no inside director should serve on this committee. In addition, this procedure may avoid the burden, imposed by most state statutes, of proving the fairness of his compensation by a director who participates in fixing it.[135]

Among other responsibilities of this committee may be (1) administering stock option plans and incentive compensation plans, (2) administering ERISA plans and benefit programs, (3) functioning, when appropriate, as a committee to determine whether indemnification should be provided in a particular case, and (4) periodically reviewing and making recommendations as to compensation and benefit plans generally.[136]

Audit Committee

An audit committee functions as the communication link between the board of directors, as representatives of the shareholders, on one hand, and the corporation's independent auditors, on the other hand.[137] It will usually recommend what auditors should be employed, review the intended scope of the independent audit, and review and discuss the results of the audit. In addition, it may help the independent auditors to be insulated from undue management influence which

---

134. Corporate Director's Guidebook, supra note 119, at 1626.
135. Overview Committees, supra note 128, at 1347.
136. Id. at 1350.
137. Corporate Director's Guidebook, supra note 119, at 1626.

may result from the auditors' close working relationship with management.[138]

Other responsibilities of the audit committee may include (1) dealing with the scope of the independent auditors' work, (2) reviewing fees of the auditors, (3) reviewing with management and the auditors financial reports, 10-K reports to the SEC, and similar publicly filed documents, (4) reviewing periodically the adequacy of the company's accounting and financial personnel, and (5) paying close attention to the details of the independent auditors' reports and consulting regularly with respect thereto.[139]

In 1940 the SEC recommended that a publicly held corporation establish an independent audit committee "to make all company or management nominations of auditors and ... [to recommend] the details of the engagement".[140] The American Institute of Certified Public Accountants spoke favorably of audit committees in 1967.[141] A study in 1984 disclosed that 99.2 percent of the nation's 1000 largest corporations had established audit committees.[142] Since June 30, 1978, the New York Stock Exchange has required all listed companies to have audit committees.

It has been recommended that an audit committee be composed of individuals who have "curiosity and impatience with obscurity" and that it be "a small effective working unit of from three to four directors." This recommendation continues: The audit committee may find it desirable to meet at least twice a year with the outside auditors; a significant part of those meetings should be without management present. The first meeting should be used to review the proposed scope of the audit. A second meeting should be held at the completion of the audit but prior to the release of the financial state-

---

138. Leech & Mundheim, supra note 107, at 1814-15.

139. Overview Committees, supra note 128, at 1354-55.

140. In the Matter of McKesson & Robbins, Inc. — Summary of Findings and Conclusions, Accounting Series Release No. 19 (Dec. 5, 1940).

141. "AICPA Executive Committee Statement on Audit Committees of Boards of Directors," Journal of Accountancy 10 (Sept. 1967).

142. Korn/Ferry, "Board of Directors Eleventh Annual Study" 14 (1984).

ments. At this meeting, the following items should be reviewed: problems identified during the audit; approval of format and content of the year's audit report. The independent auditors will not only deliver their opinion on the financial statements but will also make recommendations concerning the company's internal accounting practices. The audit committee should review both aspects of the work of the independent auditors and report on them to the board. Areas of major disagreement between management and the auditors should be identified and reviewed by the committee. The audit committee will also want to understand the significance of any departures in the company's accounting practices from those used by others in comparable businesses. Further, the committee should inquire into the prospective impact of newly emerging accounting principles on the company's accounts.[143]

Constraints of time and other factors suggest that audit committees should not assume too extensive a list of duties. In this respect, the corporate documents should clearly specify the assigned duties for the protection of committee members and the board as a whole.

Executive Committee

An executive committee can take a significant role in the functioning of a board of directors. Typically, it will deal with important corporate matters on an ongoing basis and exercise the board's authority between board meetings. It may handle numerous routine tasks and is available to act on a short-time, emergency basis.

Most state statutes permit boards to delegate many of their powers to committees, usually excepting such as:

- adopting, amending or repealing bylaws;
- taking action to amend the corporate charter;[144]
- filling vacancies among directors or in a board committee;

---

143. Leech & Mundheim, supra note 107, at 1815.
144. See Del. Code Ann. tit. 8, § 141(c).

• fixing directors' compensation.[145]

However, a few state statutes contain an unusually large number of express restrictions,[146] so it is prudent to deal with this subject on a state-by-state basis. In most states, however, the board may make an extensive delegation of powers to an executive committee. Consequently, an executive committee has great potential power and should not be utilized as a substitute for the full board.[147]

Generally

The District of Columbia Circuit has taken the position that the "existence of an audit committee" implies a "structured investigation and analysis of a company's fiscal welfare" and that "committees create at least the impression of great care and precision through detailed review and oversight."[148] In that light a board member serving on a board committee may expect to have a higher standard of care imposed upon him with respect to matters of which he has, or should have, special knowledge as a committee member.[149]

§ 1.12. State and federal control.

Fiduciary responsibilities are imposed upon corporate directors under both state laws and federal laws. It is difficult to compare state law on fiduciary matters with federal law on the same subject. State law varies among the fifty states. Federal law varies from circuit to circuit, except in areas where the Supreme Court has spoken decisively. Even then a

---

145. See N.Y. Bus. Corp. Law § 712(a).

146. McMullen, "Committees of the Board of Directors," 29 Bus. Law. 755, 767 (1974). See also Revised Model Bus. Corp. Act § 8.25 (1985).

147. Cf. "Report of Investigation in the Matter of Stirling Homex Corporation," Securities Exchange Act Release No. 11, 516 (July 2, 1975), stating that the board of directors seldom met and "the real decision-making body for the company was the Executive Committee."

148. SEC v. Falstaff Brewing Corp., 629 F.2d 62, 75 (D.C. Cir. 1980).

149. See discussion supra in section 1.09 at note 98.

comparison of such decisions as the *Blue Chip Stamps* case[150] and *Superintendent of Insurance of New York v. Bankers Life and Casualty Company*[151] suggests that the Court may not yet have spoken finally on some aspects of federal securities law.[152]

Treating state jurisprudence in the corporate field in the aggregate, it is important to note that state court decisions are either extending or vigorously confirming the character of fiduciary obligations of corporate directors and the means by which they may be enforced.[153]

In light of the circumstance that state statutes confer the power of incorporation, prescribe corporate structures, and purport to fix the parameters for enforcing management accountability,[154] it would appear that corporate law reform should be accomplished at the state level. However, some commentators[155] find the state statutes inadequate as instruments of corporate control and suggest that their trend toward "ever greater permissiveness" may be "irreversible absent some presently unforeseeable changes in the basic structure of the American economy."[156] There have been significant proposals for a Federal Corporate Minimum Standards

---

150. Blue Chip Stamps v. Manor Drug Stores, 421 U.S. 723, 44 L.Ed.2d 539, 95 S.Ct. 1917 (1975).

151. 404 U.S. 6, 30 L.Ed.2d 128, 92 S.Ct. 165 (1971).

152. A consideration of deficiencies in the Delaware decisions is treated extensively in Cary, "Federalism and Corporate Law: Reflections upon Delaware," 83 Yale L.J. 663 (1974).

153. E.g., Aronson v. Lewis, 473 A.2d 805 (Del. 1984); Smith v. Van Gorkom, 488 A.2d 858 (Del. 1985); Moran v. Household Int'l, Inc., 500 A.2d 1346 (Del. 1985); Unocal v. Mesa Petroleum Co., 493 A.2d 946 (Del. 1985); Auerbach v. Bennett, 47 N.Y.2d 619, 419 N.Y.S.2d 920, 393 N.E.2d 994 (1979); Diamond v. Oreamuno, 24 N.Y.2d 494, 301 N.Y.S.2d 78, 248 N.E.2d 910 (1969); Jones v. H.F. Ahmanson & Co., 1 Cal. 3d 93, 81 Cal. Rptr. 592, 460 P.2d 464 (1969).

154. Jennings, "Federalization of Corporation Law: Part Way or All the Way," 31 Bus. Law. (Special Issue) 991 (1976).

155. Id. See articles cited in n.1, at 991-92.

156. Folk, "Some Reflections of a Corporation Law Draftsman," 42 Conn. B.J. 409, 410 (1968).

Act,[157] that the progress made under Rule 10b-5[158] and Section 14(a) of the 1934 Securities Exchange Act[159] be carried forward in further federalizing our corporation law,[160] and that the state chartering of major corporations be replaced with a system of federal chartering.[161] Such proposals have not met with enthusiastic acceptance in most quarters.

§1.13. Presumption of sound business judgment.

A board of directors enjoys a presumption of sound business judgment.[162] The rationale for this presumption is that in order for a corporation to be managed properly and efficiently, directors must be given wide latitude in their handling of corporate affairs.[163] The doctrine that bars judicial inquiry into directorial actions taken in good faith and in honest pursuit of the legitimate purposes of the corporation is called the "business judgment doctrine."[164]

There are five preconditions to the application of this doctrine:

(1) A business decision.[165]

(2) Disinterestedness (i.e., the absence of personal interest or self-dealing).[166]

---

157. Cary, "A Proposed Federal Minimum Standards Act," 29 Bus. Law. 1101 (1974).

158. 17 C.F.R. § 240.10b-5.

159. 15 U.S.C. § 78n(a).

160. Jennings, supra note 154, at 1021.

161. Schwartz, "A Case for Federal Chartering of Corporations," 31 Bus. Law. (Special Issue) 1125 (1976). See also Nader, "The Case for Federal Chartering," Corporate Power in America 67 (1973).

162. Sinclair Oil Co. v. Levien, 280 A.2d 717, 720 (Del. 1971).

163. Cramer v. General Tel. & Elec. Corp., 582 F.2d 259, 274 (3d Cir. 1978).

164. Galef v. Alexander, 615 F.2d 51, 57 (2d Cir. 1980), applying Ohio law.

165. Aronson v. Lewis, 473 A.2d 805, 813 (Del. 1984).

166. Auerbach v. Bennett, 47 N.Y.2d 619, 631, 419 N.Y.S.2d 920, 927, 393 N.E.2d 994, 1001 (1979).

    (3) Due care (i.e., an informed decision following a rea-
sonable effort to become familiar with the relevant
and available facts).[167]

    (4) No abuse of discretion (i.e., a reasonable belief that
the best interests of the corporation and its stockholders are being served).[168]

    (5) Good faith.[169]

Related to the "business judgment doctrine" is the "business judgment rule." The courts use both terms sometimes
without distinction. As suggested by one commentator,[170] the
term "doctrine" is used here in a more generic sense, whereas
the word "rule" is used in the context of defensive application
of the doctrine to shield directors from personal liability.[171]

When the foregoing preconditions have been established,
the business judgment rule will be applied, unless it can be
shown that the directors acted with a primary objective of
accomplishing some impermissible purpose.[172] The courts
generally apply this principle.[173] If director self-interest is
demonstrated, the burden of proof shifts to the directors to
prove that the "transaction was fair and reasonable to the
corporation."[174]

There are three significant reasons for the business judgment doctrine and rule:

---

167. See infra Chapter 2.

168. Auerbach v. Bennett, supra note 166.

169. Hanson Trust PLC v. ML SCM Acquisition, Inc., 781 F.2d 264, 275
(2d Cir. 1986).

170. Veasey, "New Insights into Judicial Deference to Directors' Business Decisions: Should We Trust the Courts?," 39 Bus. Law. 1461, 1462 n.2
(1984).

171. For a full discussion of the business judgment rule and doctrine, see
infra Chapter 6.

172. See Johnson v. Trueblood, 629 F.2d 287, 292 (3d Cir. 1980), under
Delaware law, imposing a burden upon the plaintiff to show "that the sole
or primary motive of the defendant was to retain control."

173. Treco, Inc. v. Land of Lincoln Sav. & Loan, 749 F.2d 374, 379 (7th
Cir. 1984).

174. Norlin Corp. v. Rooney, Pace, Inc., 744 F.2d 255, 265 (2d Cir. 1984);
Treadway Cos. v. Care Corp., 638 F.2d 357, 382 (2d Cir. 1980).

(1) If management were liable for mere good faith errors in judgment, few capable individuals would be willing to incur the financial and emotional risk of serving as a director or officer. Competent persons should be encouraged rather than deterred from seeking to serve as corporate managers.

(2) Courts are generally ill-equipped to evaluate business judgments or to second guess the validity of a business decision.

(3) Corporate managers should be encouraged to efficiently manage the corporation by taking reasonable risks and by being allowed wide discretion in the handling of corporate affairs.

In this connection, the Second Circuit recognized the problems inherent in permitting courts to second-guess business decisions, stating:

> [C]ourts recognize that after-the-fact litigation is a most imperfect device to evaluate corporate business decisions. The circumstances surrounding a corporate decision are not easily reconstructed in a courtroom years later, since business imperatives often call for quick decisions, inevitably based on less than perfect information. The entrepreneur's function is to encounter risks and to confront uncertainty, and a reasoned decision at the time made may seem a wild hunch viewed years later against a background of perfect knowledge.[175]

Notwithstanding the foregoing, the business judgment rule will not insulate directors whose decisions breach their fiduciary obligations imposed by statutes or public policy. Thus, the doctrine does not supersede the strict fiduciary obligations imposed by ERISA.[176]

---

175. Joy v. North, 692 F.2d 880, 886 (2d Cir. 1982), cert. denied, 460 U.S. 1051 (1983).

176. Leigh v. Engle, 727 F.2d 113, 125 (7th Cir. 1984). See also infra Chapter 9.

§ 1.14. Liability to indemnify corporation for tortious acts.

A right to indemnity among tortfeasors may arise out of contract or from equitable considerations. Generally, such a right does not exist where the parties are in pari delicto; that is, where the fault of each is of equal grade and similar in character. The right to indemnity depends upon the principle that everyone is responsible for the consequences of his own wrong, and if others have been compelled to pay damages which ought to have been paid by the wrongdoer, they may recover from him.[177] Thus, an employer may have indemnity from his employee where the employer is held vicariously liable to a third person injured by the negligence of his employee and the employer is not himself negligent.[178]

Under the rule that one secondarily liable may have indemnity from the one primarily liable, the terms primary and secondary are not based on a difference in degrees of care or on any concept of comparative negligence, but on a difference in the character or kind of wrong which caused the injury, and in the nature of the legal obligation owed by each wrongdoer to the claimant.[179]

The liability of corporate officers and directors to indemnify their corporation for losses caused by their negligent or unauthorized acts rests upon the foregoing principles. Directors and officers are liable to their corporation in cases of fraud, misappropriation of corporate property to their own use, and culpable negligence.[180]

---

177. Herrero v. Atkinson, 227 Cal. App. 2d 69, 38 Cal. Rptr. 490 (1964); Home Ins. Co. v. Atlas Tank Mfg. Co., 230 So.2d 549 (Miss. 1970).

178. Fireman's Fund Am. Inc. Cos. v. Turner, 260 Ore. 30, 488 P.2d 429 (1971).

179. Builders Supply Co. v. McCabe, 366 Pa. 322, 77 A.2d 368 (1951).

180. Briggs v. Spaulding, 141 U.S. 132, 35 L.Ed. 662, 11 S.Ct. 924 (1891). See also Stern v. Lucy Webb Hayes Nat'l Training School for Deaconesses and Missionaries, 381 F. Supp. 1003 (D.D.C. 1974), and DSG Corp. v. Anderson, 754 F.2d 678, 682 (6th Cir. 1985).

COROLLARY REFERENCES

Arsht, "The Business Judgment Rule Revisited," 8 Hofstra L. Rev. 93 (1979).

Brudney, "Corporate Governance, Agency Costs, and the Rhetoric of Contract," 85 Colum. L. Rev. 1403 (1985).

Brudney, "The Independent Director — Heavenly City or Potemkin Village?," 95 Harv. L. Rev. 597 (1982).

Hinsey, "Business Judgment and the American Law Institute's Corporate Governance Project: the Rule, the Doctrine, and the Reality," 52 Geo. Wash. L. Rev. 609 (1984).

Knauss, "Corporate Governance — A Moving Target," 79 Mich. L. Rev. 478 (1981).

Letts, "Corporate Governance: A Different Slant," 35 Bus. Law. 1505 (1980).

Manning, "Life in the Boardroom After Van Gorkom," 41 Bus. Law. 1 (1985).

Manning, "The Business Judgment Rule and the Director's Duty of Attention: Time for Reality," 39 Bus. Law. 1477 (1984).

McDaniel, "Bondholders and Corporate Governance," 41 Bus. Law. 413 (1986).

Ubelaker, "Director Liability Under the Business Judgment Rule," 35 Sw. L.J. 775 (1981).

Veasey, "New Insights Into Judicial Deference to Directors' Business Decisions: Shall We Trust the Courts?," 39 Bus. Law. 1461 (1984).

Veasey, "Seeking a Safe Harbor from Judicial Scrutiny of Directors' Business Decisions — An Analytical Framework for Litigation Strategy and Counseling Directors," 37 Bus. Law. 1247 (1982).

Williamson, "Corporate Governance," 93 Yale L.J. 1197 (1984).

"Overview Committees of the Board of Directors," a report by the ABA Committee on Corporate Laws, 35 Bus. Law. 1335 (1980).

Note, "Personal Liability of Directors of Federal Government Corporations," 30 Case W. Res. L. Rev. 733 (1980).

Note, "The Propriety of Judicial Deference to Corporate Boards of Directors," 93 Harv. L. Rev. 1894 (1983).

Chapter 2.

DUTY OF DILIGENCE

§ 2.01. Exercise of care.

Under the law of most jurisdictions, the exercise of care requires a director to be diligent and prudent in managing the corporation's affairs. Usually, the question of a director's negligence is a question of fact to be decided on a case-by-case basis.[1] It is settled that where directors make decisions likely to affect shareholder welfare, the duty of due care requires that the decisions be made on the basis of "reasonable diligence" in gathering and considering material information. A director's decisions must be informed ones.[2]

A director's "unyielding fiduciary duty to the corporation and its shareholders"[3] does not tolerate faithlessness or self-dealing. It requires the director to recognize that he acts on

---

1. Gearhart Indus., Inc. v. Smith Int'l, Inc., 741 F.2d 707, 720 (5th Cir. 1984).

2. Hanson Trust PLC v. ML SCM Acquisition, Inc., 781 F.2d 264, 274 (2d Cir. 1986); Smith v. Van Gorkom, 488 A.2d 858, 872 (Del. 1985).

3. Loft, Inc. v. Guth, 2 A.2d 225 (Del. Ch. 1938), aff'd, 5 A.2d 503 (Del. 1939).

37

behalf of others. Representation of the financial interests of others imposes an affirmative duty to protect those interests.[4]

A director's duty to exercise an informed business judgment is in the nature of a duty of care.[5] Its elements are defined both by statute and by court decisions, as sections 2.02 and 2.03 illustrate. However, most of the rules describe the manner in which directors should perform their duties; there is little, if anything to define the duties.[6]

One commentator points out that the cases which have been litigated have concerned "discrete judgments by boards" and the court's responses have been "addressed to individual discreet events."[7] As a consequence, the decisions do not spell out what directors should do or not do, when they exercise due care. The decisions merely state that what was done, or not done, in a particular situation did, or did not, constitute such care. The statutes and rules merely reflect the court decisions rendered to date.

§ 2.02. Statutory standards.

Section 8.30 of the Revised Model Business Corporation Act is not the enactment of any legislature but reflects several statutory enactments.[8] It is based on former Section 35 of the 1969 Model Act,[9] a number of state statutes and on judicial statements as to the duty of care applicable to corporate directors.[10] State statutes generally contain part or all of the provisions of this model section.

The basic requirement of Section 8.30 is:

---

4. Smith v. Van Gorkom, supra note 2.

5. Id. at 872-73.

6. E.g., Revised Model Bus. Corp. Act § 8.30; Principles of Corporate Governance: Analysis and Recommendations (ALI) (Tent. Draft No. 3, 1984) § 4.01.

7. Manning, "The Business Judgment Rule and the Director's Duty of Attention: Time for Reality," 39 Bus. Law. 1477, 1494 (1984).

8. E.g., Cal. Corp. Code §§ 309, 316; Fla. Stat. Ann. § 607.111; Ohio Rev. Code Ann. § 1701.59(B); Wash. Rev. Code §§ 23A.08.343, 23A.08.345.

9. See 30 Bus. Law. 501 (1975).

10. See 2 Model Bus. Corp. Act. Ann. 936-44 (3d ed. 1985).

(A) A director shall discharge his duties as a director, including his duties as a member of a committee:
(1) in good faith;
(2) with the care an ordinarily prudent person in a like position would exercise under similar circumstances; and
(3) in a manner he reasonably believes to be in the best interests of a corporation.

In California, Pennsylvania and Washington, "reasonable inquiry" is required by statute.[11] Nonetheless, all directors are required to be adequately informed when making decisions.

The statutory requirements reflect the "good faith" concept embodied in the business judgment doctrine and a well-established definition of ordinary care taken from the common law.[12] The Model Act does not use the term "fiduciary" on the premise that it could be confused with the unique attributes and obligations of a fiduciary established in the law of trusts.[13]

The Model Act provides no guidelines as to what a director should consider in determining what he reasonably believes to be in the best interests of the corporation. A 1985 amendment to the Ohio statute requires a director to consider the interests of the corporation's shareholders and permits him to consider any of:

(1) The interests of the corporation's employees, suppliers, creditors, and customers;
(2) The economy of the state and nation;
(3) Community and societal considerations;
(4) The long-term as well as short-term interests of the corporation and its shareholders, including the possi-

---

11. Cal. Corp. Code § 309(a); 42 Pa. C.S.A. § 8363; Wash. Rev. Code 23A.08.343.
12. See discussion infra section 6.07.
13. Comment on Amendments to Section 35 of the Model Bus. Corp. Act, 32 Bus. Law. 42, 44 (1976).

bility that those interests may be best served by the continued independence of the corporation.[14]

It may be questioned whether such statutory provisions provide greater protection for directors or impose greater potential liabilities. The language may afford enforceable rights to the expanded constituencies and may charge the directors with the responsibility of acting in the light of such rights.

The second and third parts of Section 8.30 relate to reliance by a director on information received from others and are discussed infra in sections 2.05 and 2.06.

The concluding provision of Section 8.30 attempts to exonerate directors from liability if they performed their duties in compliance with the section. Such exoneration would be automatic and would not require invocation of the business judgment rule.[15]

Statutes imposing specific liability on directors have been enacted in some states. In Ohio, for example, there are express provisions relating to false reports or statements about the corporation or its business and false entries in the corporate records;[16] failure to maintain and furnish certain records;[17] unlawful dividends, distributions of assets and loans to officers, directors, or shareholders;[18] and the exercising of corporate powers or authority after the articles have been canceled, or the corporation has been dissolved.[19]

The Delaware statutes and those of most other states contain express provisions relating to unlawful dividends and unlawful stock purchases or redemptions,[20] purchasing the

---

14. Ohio Rev. Code Ann. § 1701.59(E). See also comparable statutes: Ind. Code § 23-1-35-1(d); Me. Rev. Stat. tit. 13A, § 716; Minn. Bus. Corp. Act § 302A.251, subd. 5; Mo. Bus. Corp. Law § 351.347; N.Y. Bus. Corp. Law § 717; 42 Pa. C.S.A. § 8363(b). See also discussion infra section 7.08.

15. 2 Model Bus. Corp. Act Ann. 932 (3d ed. 1985).

16. Ohio Rev. Code Ann. § 1701.93.

17. Id. § 1701.94.

18. Id. § 1701.95.

19. Id. § 1701.97.

20. Del. Code Ann. tit. 8, § 174; Fla. Stat. § 607.144; Ill. Bus. Corp. Act § 8.65; Ind. Code § 23-1-35-4; Md. Corps. & Ass'ns Code Ann. § 2-315; Me.

corporation's own shares when its capital is impaired, failure to publish notice of reduction of capital, willful refusal or neglect to produce a list of stockholders, and payment of the corporation's debts.[21]

Beginning in 1986 several state legislatures enacted statutes limiting the civil liability of corporate directors in light of the crisis which had occurred in the areas of liability and insurance for such persons. Chapter 7 discusses the nature and scope of such legislation. However, even in the states adopting the new liability limitations, there are areas which are not covered and to which the statutes discussed here still apply. Typical examples are equitable relief, including injunction and rescission, and claims arising out of unlawful dividends, distributions and stock purchases.

Because of recent developments, it is necessary to emphasize the importance of knowing and understanding the federal statutes and rules of federal regulatory bodies. Recent court decisions of particular significance, arising under the federal laws and regulations, are discussed in Chapters 14, 15 and 16, and only brief reference is made here to the important provisions of the various federal securities laws and regulations promulgated thereunder. Of course, the new state statutes cannot affect federal liabilities.

The Securities Act of 1933,[22] the Securities Exchange Act of 1934,[23] the Public Utility Holding Company Act of 1935,[24] the Trust Indenture Act of 1939,[25] the Investment Company Act

---

Rev. Stat. tit. 13A, § 720; Mich. Comp. Laws §§ 450.1551 and 450.1552; N.J. Stat. § 14A:6-12(1); N.Y. Bus. Corp. Law § 719; Pa. Stat. tit. 15 § 1707; Va. Code § 13.1-692; Tex. Bus. Corp. Act art. 2.41; Wash. Rev. Code Ann. § 23A.08.450.

21. Del. Code Ann. tit. 8, §§ 160, 219, 244 and 325.

22. Act of May 27, 1933, ch. 38, Title I, § 1, 48 Stat. 74, 15 U.S.C. § 77a et seq.

23. Act of June 6, 1934, ch. 404, Title I, § 1, 48 Stat. 881, 15 U.S.C. § 78a et seq.

24. Act of Aug. 26, 1935, ch. 687, Title I, § 33, 49 Stat. 838, 15 U.S.C. § 79 et seq.

25. Act of May 27, 1933, ch. 38, Title III, § 301, as added Aug. 3, 1939, ch. 411, 52 Stat. 1149, 15 U.S.C. § 77aaa et seq.

of 1940,[26] and the Investment Advisers Act of 1940[27] all have as their fundamental purpose the substitution of "a philosophy of full disclosure for the philosophy of caveat emptor" and thus the achievement of "a high standard of business ethics in the securities industry."[28] The recent amendments, especially those amendments of the Securities Exchange Act of 1934 made in 1964 and 1966,[29] relate to special protection for investors. Requirements of the amended federal laws dealing with registration of securities,[30] periodical and other reports,[31] solicitation and use of proxies,[32] registration of over-the-counter brokers and dealers and information and reports required of certain issuers,[33] filings by insiders (directors, officers, and principal shareholders) and reports of changes in their holdings,[34] and liabilities imposed upon officers and directors of insurers (and owners of their securities) for hindering, delaying, or obstructing the filing of documents, reports, or information[35] are of concern to all officers and directors of corporations affected by those statutes.

Section 11 of the Securities Act of 1933[36] served as the basis for the *BarChris* case,[37] which emphasizes the heavy responsibilities imposed on corporate directors and officers in using "due diligence" in securities matters. The case is also

---

26. Act of Aug. 22, 1940, ch. 686, Title I, § 1, 54 Stat. 789, 15 U.S.C. § 80a-1 et seq.

27. Act of Aug. 22, 1940, ch. 686, Title II, § 201, 54 Stat. 847, 15 U.S.C. § 80b-1 et seq.

28. Justice Goldberg, delivering the opinion of the court, in SEC v. Capital Gains Research Bur., Inc., 375 U.S. 180, 186, 11 L.Ed.2d 237, 243, 84 S.Ct. 275 (1963).

29. Act of Aug. 20, 1964, Pub. L. 88-467, 78 Stat. 565, 15 U.S.C. § 78a et seq.; Act of Nov. 3, 1966, Pub. L. 89-754, Title V, § 504(b), 80 Stat. 1278, 15 U.S.C. § 77ddd.

30. 15 U.S.C. § 78l.

31. Id. § 78m.

32. Id. § 78n.

33. Id. §§ 78o.

34. Id. § 78p.

35. Id. § 78t.

36. Id. § 77k.

37. Escott v. BarChris Constr. Corp., 283 F. Supp. 643 (S.D.N.Y. 1968).

valuable for its discerning analysis of the somewhat elaborate scheme of defenses in Section 11, especially in connection with the standard of care required of persons who seek to rely on those defenses. No student of the liabilities of corporate officers and directors can ignore the significance of *BarChris,* even though it went no further than the district court and was settled without rulings from higher tribunals.

The enlargement of the liability of corporate officers and directors imposed under Section 10(b) of the Securities Exchange Act of 1934, and the implementing Rule 10b-5, is discussed in Chapter 16. It is of particular significance to note that the Supreme Court has shown reluctance to expand the scope of such liability beyond the clear language of the statutes. In cases where "the cause of action [was] one traditionally relegated to state law," the court refused to apply the federal statute and the SEC rule.[38]

§ 2.03. Common-law standards.

Corporations are "creatures of state law"[39] and state law "is the font of corporate directors' powers."[40] Accordingly, state court decisions or federal court decisions under state law provide the sources for determining the common-law standard of care for directors.

In Delaware a leading case holds that "directors of a corporation in managing corporate affairs are bound to use that amount of care which ordinarily careful and prudent men would use in similar circumstances."[41] Although that is similar to the "ordinary negligence" rule stated in the Model

---

38. See, e.g., Cort v. Ash, 422 U.S. 66, 78, 45 L.Ed.2d 26, 95 S.Ct. 2080 (1975); Piper v. ChrisCraft Indus., Inc., 430 U.S. 1, 51 L.Ed.2d 125, 97 S.Ct. 926, reh'g denied, 430 U.S. 976 (1977); Santa Fe Indus., Inc. v. Green, 430 U.S. 462, 51 L.Ed.2d 480, 97 S.Ct. 1292 (1977).

39. Cort v. Ash, supra note 38, 442 U.S. at 84.

40. Burks v. Lasker, 441 U.S. 471, 478, 60 L.Ed.2d 404, 99 S.Ct. 1831 (1979).

41. Graham v. Allis-Chalmers Mfg. Co., 41 Del. Ch. 89, 188 A.2d 125, 130 (1963).

Business Corporation Act,[42] later Delaware decisions have held that "under the business judgment rule director liability is predicated upon gross negligence."[43] Unfortunately, the cases contain no clear definition of "gross negligence" that could be applied to a variety of situations. In fact some jurisdictions do not recognize degrees of negligence.[44] For purposes of this discussion, gross negligence may be defined as more than ordinary negligence but different in kind from wanton or willful misconduct.[45]

In New York a board member's duty of care requires him to exercise, in the performance of his tasks, the care that a reasonably prudent person in a similar position would use under similar circumstances.[46] Questions of policy of management, expediency of contracts or action, adequacy of consideration, and lawful appropriation of corporate funds to advance corporate interests are left solely to the "honest and unselfish decision" of the corporate directors.[47]

Under Colorado law directors are liable for losses of the corporation caused by their bad faith or willful and intentional departure from duty, their fraudulent breaches of trust, their gross or willful negligence, or their ultra vires acts.[48]

Obviously, the courts have articulated different formulations of the liability rules applicable to a director's duty of care. That is due, at least in part, to the concept that the degree of care required depends upon the circumstances under which the director acted.[49] Thus, a director of a bank may

---

42. See supra section 2.02.

43. Aronson v. Lewis, 473 A.3d 805, 812 (Del. 1984); Smith v. Van Gorkom, 488 A.2d 858, 873 (Del. 1985).

44. 57 Am. Jur. 2d Negligence § 94.

45. Id. § 99.

46. Norlin Corp. v. Rooney, Pace, Inc., 744 F.2d 255, 264 (2d Cir. 1984).

47. Auerbach v. Bennett, 47 N.Y.2d 619, 419 N.Y.S.2d 920, 393 N.E.2d 994, 1000 (1979).

48. Christy v. Cameron, 710 F.2d 669 672 (10th Cir. 1983), citing Colorado decisions.

49. Briggs v. Spaulding, 141 U.S. 132, 35 L.Ed. 662, 11 S.Ct. 924 (1891).

owe a greater duty than directors of other types of corpora-tions.[50] A leading text states:

> Directors and officers are not insurers, nor are the direc-tors and managing officers of a corporation, as a rule, liable to stockholders for slight omissions from which a loss which results to the corporation could not reasonably have been expected. It is generally agreed that directors are liable for losses or injury resulting from their gross negligence.[51]

If a director engages in an activity that is fraudulent, if he violates his duties of obedience, diligence, and loyalty to the corporation and its shareholders, if he acts to further his own interests at the expense of the corporation or its shareholders, he must anticipate that liability will be imposed upon him under both state and federal laws.

Conversely, if a director meets his duties to the corpora-tion, if he performs his duties in good faith and in a manner he reasonably believes to be in the best interests of the corpo-ration, and if he exercises free and independent business judgment,[52] it is likely that neither state courts nor federal courts will impose liability upon him because of erroneous judgment. But the state of the law is uncertain, and the wise corporate director or officer will not seek to act as his own lawyer.[53]

Under the common law courts are disposed to give directors a wide latitude in the management of a corporation's affairs, as long as they reasonably exercise an honest, unbiased judg-ment.[54] This is often referred to as the "business judgment rule."

There are instances in which the courts have placed limita-tions on the "business judgment rule." Specifically, when

---

50. Gadd v. Pearson, 351 F. Supp. 895, 903 (M.D. Fla. 1974).
51. 18B Am. Jur. 2d Corporations § 1696.
52. Corporate Director's Guidebook, 33 Bus. Law. 1590, 1599-1600 (1978), discussed infra section 19.04.
53. See Report of The Committee on Corporate Law Departments on Corporate Director's Guidebook, 32 Bus. Law. 1841, 1845-46, 1849 (1977).
54. Casey v. Woodruff, 49 N.Y.S.2d 625, 643 (1944).

complaints have asserted losses to the corporation from refusal to register with the Securities and Exchange Commission,[55] or from a violation of antitrust laws,[56] or from a violation of the National Labor Relations Act,[57] the courts have ruled that they stated actionable causes.

The 1973 decision of the Second Circuit in *Lanza v. Drexel and Company*[58] has raised some questions as to the extent of supervision of corporate affairs required of directors. While the majority of the court absolved the defendant-directors of responsibility to search out the misconduct of other officers and directors, a strong dissenting opinion suggests some significant guidelines that bear careful consideration. The *Lanza* case arose under the securities laws, but its analysis of directors' obligations is so thorough that it must be noted in the general common law of corporations.[59] Perhaps the most significant of the suggested guidelines are those which impose upon a director the obligations to maintain an awareness of corporate developments, to consider any material adverse developments which may come to his attention, and to investigate when his knowledge and experience warn him that certain events or circumstances known to him require that further inquiry be made. Decisions imposing criminal liability upon accountants and attorneys[60] for closing their eyes to the obvious suggest that the above guidelines merit careful consideration.

When a secret profit has been obtained, the good faith of the officer who obtains it does not diminish his liability,[61] and

---

55. Downing v. Howard, 162 F.2d 654 (3d Cir.), cert. denied, 332 U.S. 818 (1947).

56. Knopfler v. Bohen, 15 A.D.2d 922, 225 N.Y.S.2d 609 (1962).

57. Halpern v. Pennsylvania R.R., 178 F. Supp. 494 (E.D.N.Y. 1960).

58. 479 F.2d 1277 (2d Cir. 1973) (en banc).

59. See SEC v. Frank, 388 F.2d 486 (2d Cir. 1968); United States v. Cooperative Grain & Supply, 476 F.2d 47, 60 (8th Cir. 1973).

60. United States v. Benjamin, 328 F.2d 854, 863 (2d Cir. 1964); United States v. Natelli, 527 F.2d 311 (2d Cir. 1975), cert. denied, 425 U.S. 934 (1976).

61. Western States Life Ins. Co. v. Lockwood, 166 Cal. 185, 135 P. 496 (1913). Cf. Bromschwig v. Carthage Marble & White Lime Co., 334 Mo. 319, 66 S.W.2d 889 (1933).

this is true even though what he did may have actually benefited his trust.[62] Whenever self-dealing has been shown, the
directors have the burden of proving good faith,[63] although
this burden may be shifted by exculpatory provisions in the
relevant corporate documents.[64] A director or officer cannot
take for himself or give to another the property or assets of a
corporation for any purpose except those of the corporation or
to pay a just debt.[65]

§ 2.04. Reliance on advice of counsel or experts.

Evidence of reliance on advice of counsel is admissible to
prove that a director acted in good faith or with due care, but
is not an absolute defense. And the advice relied upon must
have been legal advice.[66] When asserted defensively, there
must be proof that the defendant (1) made a complete disclosure to counsel, (2) requested counsel's advice as to the legality of the proposed action, (3) received advice that the action
would be lawful, and (4) proceeded in reliance on that advice.[67]

The elements of this defense rest upon good faith and due
care, and import that counsel providing the advice was com-

---

62. See Keely v. Black, 90 N.J. Eq. 439, 107 A. 825 (1919), rev'd, 91 N.J.
Eq. 520, 111 A. 22 (1920). Cf. State ex rel. Hayes Oyster Co. v. Keypoint
Oyster Co., 64 Wash. 2d 375, 391 P.2d 979 (1964).

63. Geddes v. Anaconda Copper Mining Co., 254 U.S. 590, 65 L.Ed. 425,
41 S.Ct. 209 (1921); Ripley v. International Rys. of Cent. Am., 8 A.D.2d
310, 188 N.Y.S.2d 62 (1959), aff'd, 8 N.Y.2d 430, 209 N.Y.S.2d 289, 171
N.E.2d 443 (1960).

64. Everett v. Phillips, 288 N.Y. 227, 43 N.E.2d 18, reargument denied,
289 N.Y. 625, 43 N.Y.2d 841, 289 N.Y. 675, 45 N.E.2d 176 (1942).

65. See N.Y. Bus. Corp. Law § 719(a)(1).

66. Draney v. Wilson, Morton, Assaf & McElligott, 592 F. Supp. 9, 11 (D.
Ariz. 1984).

67. SEC v. Savoy Indus., Inc., 665 F.2d 1310, 1314 n.28 (D.C. Cir. 1981);
SEC v. Scott, 565 F. Supp. 1513, 1534 (S.D.N.Y. 1983), aff'd sub nom. SEC
v. Cayman Islands Reinsurance Corp., 734 F.2d 118 (2d Cir. 1984). See also
Citronelle-Mobile Gathering, Inc. v. Herrington, 826 F.2d 16, 26 (Em.
App.), cert. denied sub. nom. Chamberlain v. United States, 98 L.Ed.2d 355
(1987).

petent to do so and sufficiently unbiased to make the advice reliable.[68]

Section 8.30(b) of the Revised Model Business Corporation Act offers some explicit guidelines and also deals with reliance upon the advice of experts other than legal counsel, as follows:

> (b) In discharging his duties a director is entitled to rely on information, opinions, reports, or statements and other financial data, if prepared and presented by:
> (1) ...
> (2) legal counsel, public accountants, or other persons as to matters the director reasonably believes are within the person's professional or expert competence; ...

This entitlement is restricted by the condition that the director is not acting in good faith if he has knowledge concerning the matter in question that makes such reliance unwarranted.[69] Thus, knowledge of incompetency or conflict of interest or knowledge that there was incomplete disclosure of facts to the expert, or knowledge that the advice was contrary to law would, for example, cause reliance to be unwarranted.

Inherent in the concept of good faith is the requirement that in order to be entitled to such reliance a director must have read any such statement or report, or must have been present when it was orally presented, or must have taken other steps to become generally familiar with its contents.[70]

The Model Act permits reliance upon outside advisers, in addition to lawyers and accountants, such as engineers, geologists, investment bankers, management consultants, actuaries, and appraisers. In this respect it goes beyond any exist-

---

68. Longstreth, "Reliance on Advice of Counsel as a Defense to Securities Law Violations," 37 Bus. Law. 1185, 1191 (1982). See also Arthur Lipper Corp. v. SEC, 547 F.2d 171, 181-82 (2d Cir. 1976).

69. Revised Model Bus. Corp. Act § 8.30(c).

70. Official Comment to Section 8.30(b), 2 Model Bus. Corp. Act Ann. 1930 (3d ed. 1985).

ing state statute, although some state statutes expressly permit reliance upon reports of appraisers.[71]

The concept of "expert competence" is not limited to a narrow interpretation such as is contained in the Securities Act of 1933, but is intended to include all fields of expertise involving special experience and skills. The question of competence will probably depend on the facts in each case, but it is necessary that the director, in good faith and in the exercise of due care, "reasonably believe" that the subject-matter of the information or advice is within the area of the expert's professional competence.[72]

The requirement that directors' decisions must be informed ones[73] means that before acting they must consider all material information reasonably available to them.[74] When the advice of legal counsel or experts is reasonably available, directors may be less than diligent if they fail to obtain it.[75]

In *Smith v. Van Gorkom* (the Trans Union case) and the *Unocal/Mesa Petroleum* case, decided within a period of five months, the Delaware Supreme Court reviewed the acts of corporate directors and their consultation of legal advisors and experts. In *Unocal*[76] the directors were upheld; in *Van Gorkom* their actions were struck down, and the directors held liable in damages.[77]

A Second Circuit decision under New York law shed further light on the right of directors to rely on the advice and reports of experts. It invoked the struggle for control of SCM, a large public corporation.[78] The directors had advice from a

---

71. Id.; Del. Code Ann. tit. 8, § 141(e); see also Cal. Corp. Code § 309; N.Y. Bus. Corp. Law § 717; Ohio Rev. Code Ann. §§ 1701.59(B)(2), 1702.30(B)(2); 17B Am. Jur. 2d Corporations § 1702.

72. Hawes & Sherrard, "Model Act Section 35 — New Vigor for the Defense of Reliance on Counsel," 32 Bus. Law. 119, 142 (1976).

73. See supra section 2.01.

74. Kaplan v. Centrex Corp., 284 A.2d 119, 125 (Del. Ch. 1981); Smith v. Van Gorkom, 488 A.2d 858, 872 (Del. 1985).

75. 12 Ohio Jur. 3d Business Relationships § 414.

76. Unocal Corp. v. Mesa Petroleum Co., 493 A.2d 946 (Del. 1985).

77. Smith v. Van Gorkom, supra note 74.

78. Hanson Trust PLC v. ML SCM Acquisition, Inc., 781 F.2d 264 (2d Cir. 1986).

leading law firm and a prominent firm of investment bankers. However, the court found that the directors "failed to take many of the affirmative directorial steps that underlie the finding of due care" and that they "apparently contented themselves with their financial advisor's conclusory opinion" as to fair value of option prices without learning that the advisor "had not calculated a range of fairness."[79] Other instances of lack of diligence by the directors are recited in the opinion. The court found sufficient evidence of the breach of a duty of care to shift the burden of justification.[80] It concluded that the burden was not sustained and held that injunctive relief was warranted.[81] Of particular significance is the statement in the concurring opinion of Judge James L. Oakes:

> Due care requires full inquiry. To obtain the benefit of the business judgment rule, then, the directors must make certain that they are fully informed, and, to the extent that they are relying on advisers, that the advisers are fully informed and in turn fully inform the directors.[82]

In order to rely on outside advice it is a pre-condition that directors must avail themselves of material information and oversee the outside advisors to be sure that they are adequately informed and prepared.[83]

§ 2.05. Reliance on reports of committees.

All of the state corporation codes permit a corporation's board to appoint committees of directors and delegate board powers to them.[84] Many of the statutes follow the Model Business Corporation Act which, in its revised Section 8.25,

---

79. Id. at 275.
80. Id. at 277.
81. Id. at 283.
82. Id. at 284.
83. Id. at 276.
84. E.g., Cal. Corp. Code, §§ 307(c), 311; Del. Code Ann. tit. 8, §§ 141(b), 141(c); N.Y. Bus. Corp. Law §§ 708(b), 708(c), 712; Ohio Rev. Code Ann. § 1701.63.

makes explicit the power of the directors to act through committees and specifies powers which are nondelegable.[85]

With respect to reliance on a committee of the board by a
nonmember director, Section 8.30(b)(3) of the Revised Model
Business Corporation Act provides:

> (b) In discharging his duties a director is entitled to rely
> on information, opinions, reports, or statements, in-
> cluding financial statements and other financial
> data, if prepared or presented by:
>
> (1) ...
>
> (2) ...
>
> (3) a committee of the board of directors of which he
> is not a member if the director reasonably be-
> lieves the committee merits confidence.

This entitlement is restricted by the provision that a director is not acting in good faith if he has knowledge concerning
the matter in question that makes such reliance unwarranted.[86] Also, it is inherent in the concept of good faith that
the director will have become generally familiar with the
contents of such a report or statement.

The appointment of board committees should be provided
for in the corporation's articles of incorporation or bylaws,
and board action to do so should be by resolution adopted by a
majority of the full board of directors.[87]

Although the board may delegate the authority to act to a
committee, neither the designation of that committee, delegation of such authority, nor action by the committee will constitute compliance by a non-committee board member with
his responsibility to act in good faith, and with such care as
an ordinarily prudent person in a like position would use
under similar circumstances, in what he reasonably believes

---

85. See also supra section 1.11.

86. Revised Model Bus. Corp. Act § 8.30(c).

87. Some state statutes, such as Mass. Gen. Laws Ann. ch. 156B, §§ 55,
59; Mich. Comp. Laws Ann. § 450.1521(3) — 450.1528; and Ohio Rev. Code
Ann. § 1701.63, permit such action by a majority vote of the directors
present.

to be the best interests of the corporation. A non-committee member's right to rely upon a committee of the board can be affected by the care used in delegation to and surveillance over the committee, which includes appraisal of the capabilities and diligence of the directors-members of the committee in the light of the subject, and its relative importance. It can also be affected by the amount of knowledge of the particular subject that the non-committee director has available to him.

It is to be expected that each director will receive copies of minutes of all meetings of the full board and of each board committee, whether or not he is a committee member. If a director seeks to rely on a particular committee, he should be expected to review its minutes and any other reports it may issue.

The draftsmen of the Revised Model Business Corporation Act had in mind two general categories of committee activity that might be relied upon by non-committee directors: first, the work product resulting from a more detailed investigation undertaken by such a committee and reported to the full board, which forms the basis for board action; and second, where a committee performs an ongoing role of oversight or surveillance, such as (i) an audit committee with respect to accounting and audit functions, or (ii) a committee commissioned to maintain surveillance at a policy level over compliance with antitrust laws or environmental matters.[88]

Of course, directors cannot escape liability by delegating their responsibilities to a committee, and blame for fraudulent corporate action may not be avoided merely by asserting ignorance of facts they had a duty to know and should have known.[89]

§ 2.06. Reliance on corporate officers and employees.

As a general rule corporate directors are entitled to rely in good faith on reports made by corporate officers and em-

---

88. Official Comment to Section 8:30(b), 2 Model Bus. Corp. Act Ann. 931 (3d ed. 1985).

89. Fowler v. Elm Creek State Bank, 198 Neb. 631, 254 N.W.2d 415 (1977).

ployees, especially competent persons who are in immediate charge of the corporation's business.[90] A Delaware statute says that a director in the performance of his duties shall be "fully protected" in relying in good faith upon reports made to the corporation by any of the officers.[91]

Section 8.30(b)(1) of the Revised Model Business Corporation Act provides:

> (b) In discharging his duties a director is entitled to rely on information, opinions, reports, or statements, including financial statements and other financial data, if prepared or presented by:
> (1) one or more officers or employees of the corporation whom the director reasonably believes to be reliable and competent in the matters presented;
> ...

This entitlement is restricted by the condition that the director is not acting in good faith if he has knowledge concerning the matter in question that makes such reliance unwarranted.[92] As noted above,[93] it is inherent in the concept of good faith that the director will have become generally familiar with the contents of such a report or statement.

Corporate directors are often required to make decisions involving complex and sophisticated questions. Usually they have no staff of their own to gather information for them or to evaluate the information they receive. Outside directors serve on a part-time basis. Because most directors are not involved in the day-to-day operations of the business, they are dependent upon officers and other employees for information and guidance. Under these circumstances they should be entitled to rely upon such information and guidance as long as they act in good faith and with due care.

---

90. 18B Am. Jur. 2d Corporations § 1701.

91. Del. Code Ann. tit. 8, § 141(e).

92. Revised Model Bus. Corp. Act § 8.30(c). See also Federal Deposit Ins. Corp. v. Lauterbach, 626 F.2d 1327 (7th Cir. 1980).

93. See discussion supra in section 2.04.

As in the case of experts, a director may rely on a corporate officer or employee's information or guidance only if the director "reasonably believes" the officer or employee to be reliable and competent in the matters presented. There are no guidelines to detail the factors a director should consider in reaching that conclusion. Accordingly, it is for the trier of the facts to decide if a conclusion was arrived at in good faith and in the exercise of due care. A director may not close his eyes to what is going on about him in the conduct of the corporate business. If he learns of suspicious circumstances, he must make such inquiries as an ordinarily prudent person would make under the same or similar circumstances.[94]

The Trans Union litigation in 1985 provided some illustrations of the responsibilities of directors who rely on reports and statements of corporate officers. In that case the Delaware court imposed personal liability upon the outside directors of Trans Union when they approved a cash-out merger at a per-share price over current market price but without any valuation study to determine what would be a "fair price."[95]

Trans Union was a large, publicly traded, diversified holding company. It was having difficulty in generating sufficient taxable income to offset increasingly large investment tax credits. Seeking a solution to this problem, Van Gorkom, the company's longtime chairman and CEO, approached Pritzker, a takeover specialist, and proposed a cash-out merger at a price of $55 per share. Pritzker accepted but insisted that the Trans Union board act on the proposal within three days.[96] The board met and recommended the proposal, for submission to the shareholders, relying primarily on a twenty-minute oral presentation by Van Gorkom, a supporting presentation by the company's president, an oral statement by the chief financial officer (who had learned of the proposal that day), a statement of an attorney retained by

---

94. Cf. Lanza v. Drexel & Co., 479 F.2d 1277, 1306 (2d Cir. 1973) (en banc).

95. Smith v. Van Gorkom, 488 A.2d 858 (Del. 1985).

96. Id. at 867.

the CEO to advise on legal aspects of the merger,[97] and other knowledge of the market history of the company's stock.[98]

The court concluded that the board "was grossly negligent in that it failed to act with informed reasonable deliberation in agreeing to the Pritzker merger proposal" on that occasion.[99] Approximately five months later the board's recommendation was submitted to a vote of the shareholders who "overwhelmingly" approved it.[100] However, the court found that the shareholders were not fully informed of all facts material to their vote on the merger.[101] And the court held that various activities engaged in by the board after its original approval were not adequate to cure the infirmities in that action.[102]

Among the factors recited by the court in holding the Trans Union directors grossly negligent were the following:

(1) The officers did not "come up with" a price for the stock. They merely "ran the numbers" to calculate a possible cost of a leveraged buy-out.[103]

(2) Van Gorkom proposed a $55 price to Pritzker with no evidence that it represented the intrinsic value of the company.[104]

(3) Van Gorkom did not consult Trans Union's general counsel or a director who was its former general counsel.[105]

(4) Van Gorkom called a board meeting on one day's notice, a meeting of senior management one hour earlier, told only two officers the purpose of the

---

97. He reportedly advised that the board members might be sued if they failed to accept the offer, and that a fairness opinion was not required as a matter of law. Id. at 868, 880-81.
98. Id. at 869.
99. Id. at 881.
100. Id. at 889.
101. Id. at 890.
102. Id. at 874, 881, 888.
103. Id. at 865.
104. Id. at 866.
105. Id. at 867.

meetings, and did not invite the company's investment banker or its Chicago-based partner to attend.[106]

(5)   No copies of the proposed merger agreement were furnished to senior management.[107]

(6)   The chief financial officer's study for an LBO was not made available for the board meeting.[108]

(7)   Van Gorkom did not consider opposition of senior management but proceeded with the board meeting.[109]

(8)   Van Gorkom did not disclose how he arrived at the $55 figure.[110]

(9)   The board ignored the chief financial officer's report that $55 was only "at the beginning of a fair price."[111]

(10) No director read the merger agreement before Van Gorkom signed it without reading it himself.[112]

(11) Van Gorkom executed amendments to the merger agreement without telling the board they changed the agreement from what the directors understood it to be.[113]

(12) No board member was an investment banker or a trained financial analyst.[114]

(13) Van Gorkom and the board members knew that the market had consistently undervalued Trans Union stock. They admitted they could not rely on the stock price as evidence of its value.[115]

---

106. Id.
107. Id.
108. Id.
109. Id. at 868.
110. Id.
111. Id. at 869.
112. Id.
113. Id. at 870.
114. Id. at 868, 877.
115. Id. at 876.

(14) The board had no information on which to base a valuation of the company as a going concern.[116]

(15) The board did not request its chief financial officer to make any valuation study.[117]

(16) The board accepted without scrutiny Van Gorkom's representation as to the fairness of the $55 price.

(17) The board did not take more time to elicit more information as to the sufficiency of the offer.[118]

The court remanded the case for an evidentiary hearing to determine the fair value of the shares represented by the plaintiff's class as of the date of the board meeting when the proposal of merger was accepted.[119]

§ 2.07. Reliance on corporate books and records.

In addition to the reliance provisions discussed supra in sections 2.04, 2.05 and 2.06, there are some general provisions contained in the statutes of some states which permit directors to rely in good faith on any records of their corporation, and afford them full protection in so doing. Such provisions are contained in Section 141(e) of the Delaware Corporation Code,[120] which states:

A member of the board of directors of any corporation organized under this chapter, or a member of any committee designated by the board of directors shall, in the performance of his duties, be fully protected in relying in good faith upon the books of account or reports made to the corporation by any of its officers, or by an independent certified public accountant, or by an appraiser selected with reasonable care by the board of directors or

---

116. Id.

117. Id. at 877.

118. Id.

119. Subsequently, an agreement was reached to settle the litigation by a payment of $23.5 million to the plaintiff class. See Manning, "Reflections and Practical Tips on Life in The Boardroom After Van Gorkom," 41 Bus. Law. 1, at "Editor's Note" (1985).

120. Del. Code Ann. tit. 8, § 141(e).

by any such committee, or in relying in good faith upon other records of the corporation.[121]

As in Section 8.42 of the Revised Model Business Corporation Act, this protective provision does not extend to officers who are not also directors. The Official Comment to the Model Act states that the ability of a nondirector to rely on information, reports, or statements may, depending on the circumstances of a particular case, "be more limited than in the case of a director in view of the greater obligation he may have to be familiar with the affairs of the corporation."[122]

§ 2.08. Ignorance of corporate books and records.

A corporate director has a right to inspect all books and records of the corporation, and to receive copies of all minutes of the board of directors and of its committees. He has a duty to maintain an awareness of significant corporate developments and to consider material developments which come to his attention.[123]

There is substantial authority that the directors and managing officers of a corporation will be presumed to have knowledge of information contained in the corporation's books and records.[124] In some of the decisions, particularly those under the Securities Act of 1933,[125] the courts have been critical of corporate officers and directors who failed to look at the books to verify oral information received from others. Some of the older cases display a tendency to restrict the above rule so as to charge the directors only with a rea-

---

121. See also, e.g., Ohio Rev. Code Ann. § 1701.59(B).

122. Official Comment to Section 8.42, 2 Model Bus. Corp. Act Ann. 1067 (3d ed. 1985).

123. Federal Deposit Ins. Corp. v. Lauterbach, 626 F.2d 1327, 1334 (7th Cir. 1980); cf. Lanza v. Drexel & Co., 479 F.2d 1277, 1306 (2d Cir. 1973) (en banc).

124. Myzel v. Fields, 386 F.2d 719 (8th Cir. 1967), cert. denied, 390 U.S. 951 (1968); Redstone v. Redstone Lumber & Supply Co., 101 Fla. 226, 133 So. 882 (1931).

125. E.g., Escott v. BarChris Constr. Corp., 283 F. Supp. 643 (S.D.N.Y. 1968).

sonable amount of knowledge of what is apparent in the corporation's books,[126] but such rulings will probably not be followed in cases involving profit taking by insiders.

Several states have statutory requirements compelling dissenting directors to make sure that their dissents are set forth in the minutes or to file them in writing with the corporation's secretary.[127] It has been suggested that this elementary precaution "has an important psychological effect upon the other directors" and that it "forces directors to pay attention to the accuracy of the minutes, a responsibility otherwise likely to be neglected."[128]

Directors are clothed with the power to control their corporation's property and to manage its affairs. As to third persons, they are the corporation's agents,[129] as to the corporation, they are at least quasi trustees.[130] Thus, although they are not expected to be accountants or bookkeepers,[131] their failure to examine the books and records of the corporation has been held sufficient to impose liability upon them.

§ 2.09. Shirking responsibility; inexperience.

By accepting office, a corporate director or officer undertakes to give his best judgment to the venture and is presumed to have a competent knowledge of the duties entered upon.[132] His responsibility includes dedication of his uncorrupted business judgment for the sole benefit of the corpora-

---

126. E.g., Mason v. Moore, 73 Ohio St. 275, 76 N.E. 932 (1906); F.H. Hill Co. v. Barmore, 220 Ill. App. 222 (1920); Goff v. Emde, 32 Ohio App. 215, 221, 167 N.E. 699 (1928).

127. See infra section 4.03.

128. 1 Hornstein, Corporation Law and Practice § 432 (1959).

129. Cornell v. Seddinger, 237 Pa. 389, 85 A. 446 (1912).

130. E.g., Beach v. Williamson, 78 Fla. 611, 83 So. 860 (1919). See also supra section 1.06.

131. Ford v. Taylor, 176 Ark. 843, 4 S.W.2d 938 (1928); Sternberg v. Blaine, 179 Ark. 448, 17 S.W.2d 286 (1929); Dinsmore v. Jacobson, 242 Mich. 192, 218 N.W. 700 (1928).

132. 18B Am. Jur. 2d Corporations § 1695.

tion in any dealings which may adversely affect it.[133] Neglect of a corporation's affairs is a basis for imposing liability upon a director.[134] Thus, a director is not insulated from liability because he was ignorant of wrongdoing by other insiders if his ignorance was the result of shirking responsibility, inattention, or negligence.[135] For example, a director who ignored newspaper attacks upon the integrity of his corporation's management, and paid no attention to weekly reports sent to his office, was held liable despite his protestations of good faith.[136]

In the *DePinto* litigation, a director was held liable for failing to resist a raid on his corporation's assets. He resigned his directorship and thereby incapacitated himself from effectively opposing the raid.[137] The Ninth Circuit held this to be a "violation of duties under an implied or constructive trust."[138]

The Nebraska Supreme Court has held that directors of a profitable insurance company violated their fiduciary duties by approving a sale of the company to an investment company without first informing themselves of the complete terms of sale.[139] The court stated that where the duty to know exists, ignorance because of negligence by a director creates the same liability as actual knowledge and failure to act on that knowledge.

Directors act at their peril when they ignore the corporation's activities and leave its operations entirely to others. If

---

133. Perlman v. Feldmann, 219 F.2d 173 (2d Cir.), cert. denied, 349 U.S. 952 (1955).

134. Mann v. Commonwealth Bond Corp., 27 F. Supp. 315 (S.D.N.Y. 1938).

135. Olin Mathieson Chem. Corp. v. Planters Corp., 236 S.C. 318, 114 S.E.2d 321 (1960).

136. Virginia-Carolina Chem. Co. v. Ehrich, 230 F. 1005 (E.D.S.C. 1916).

137. DePinto v. Provident Sec. Life Ins. Co., 323 F.2d 826 (9th Cir. 1963); DePinto v. Provident Sec. Life Ins. Co., 323 F.2d 839 (9th Cir. 1963), cert. denied, 376 U.S. 950 (1964); DePinto v. Provident Sec. Life Ins. Co., 374 F.2d 37 (9th Cir.), cert. denied, 389 U.S. 822 (1967).

138. DePinto v. Landoe, 411 F.2d 297, 300 (9th Cir. 1969).

139. Doyle v. Union Ins. Co., 202 Neb. 599, 277 N.W.2d 22, 36 (1979).

a director could discover with reasonable care whether certain activities are inimical to the corporation's welfare, he may be held negligent for his failure to do so.[140]

Just as ignorance is not a valid excuse for a director's neglect of his duties, he also cannot absolve himself of responsibility by pleading inexperience. If he is not capable of performing the duties of a corporate director, he should refrain from taking the job. He is bound to exercise ordinary skill and judgment, and he cannot excuse himself by setting up his lack of them.[141]

The acceptance of an uncompensated corporate directorship of a "dummy" or "outside" type nevertheless implies a certain competence and knowledge of the duties of the position.[142] Even though such a director is a mere figurehead who actually performs none of those duties, he nonetheless occupies a fiduciary relationship to the corporation and its shareholders.[143] While he may have accepted his position as an "accommodation" to the corporation with the advance understanding that he would perform no duties, he is not relieved of all responsibility. In fact, the habitual failure to attend directors' meetings and to pay attention to the corporation's affairs may itself constitute negligence.[144] A director may not assert his ignorance as an excuse for his nonfeasance.[145]

The mere fact that directors may have received no pay for their services will not relieve them of their responsibilities, although it has been suggested that the payment of an officer's salary to a director will cause his responsibilities to

---

140. DePinto v. Provident Sec. Life Ins. Co., supra note 137, at 43-44.

141. Hun v. Cary, 82 N.Y. 65, 59 How. Prac. 439 (1880); New Haven Trust Co. v. Doherty, 74 Conn. 353, 50 A. 887 (1902).

142. Godbold v. Branch Bank, 11 Ala. 191 (1847). See also King v. Livingston Mfg. Co., 192 Ala. 269, 68 So. 897 (1915).

143. Golden Rod Mining Co. v. Bukvich, 108 Mont. 569, 92 P.2d 316 (1939).

144. Martin v. Hardy, 251 Mich. 413, 232 N.W. 197 (1930). Cf. Darling & Co. v. Petri, 138 Kan. 666, 27 P.2d 255 (1933), and Medford Trust Co. v. McKnight, 292 Mass. 1, 197 N.E. 649 (1935).

145. Bowerman v. Hamner, 250 U.S. 504, 63 L.Ed. 1113, 39 S.Ct. 549 (1919).

approach those of a trustee.[146] There are some old cases which suggest that if the director is not compensated,[147] or if the compensation is nominal,[148] these facts may affect the standard of care imposed upon him by the common law. However, later decisions indicate that the rule of ordinary care will probably be applied even in such instances.[149] There also seems to be a definite trend to impose a higher standard of care upon directors who are highly paid professional directors[150] or who hold corporate offices paying substantial salaries.[151]

§ 2.10. Supervision of officers and employees.

Corporate directors must exercise ordinary care and prudence, which includes the duty of reasonable supervision of officers and employees.[152] They are responsible for not knowing that of which they had the means of knowledge, and may be held liable for ignorance of what could have been discovered by good business diligence.[153]

A director cannot escape liability for acts of subordinates by abandoning his duties as a director.[154] If he has recklessly reposed confidence in an obviously untrustworthy employee, or has ignored danger signs of employee wrongdoing, he may be held liable for losses resulting therefrom.[155]

Directors may commit the details of the corporate business to subordinate officers, but they may not thereby divest

---

146. Bates v. Dresser, 251 U.S. 524, 64 L.Ed. 388, 40 S.Ct. 247 (1920).

147. Briggs v. Spaulding, 141 U.S. 132, 35 L.Ed. 662, 11 S.Ct. 924 (1891); Jones v. Johnson, 86 Ky. 530, 6 S.W. 582 (1888).

148. Dunn v. Kyle, 77 Ky. (14 Bush) 135 (1878).

149. See Bowerman v. Hamner, supra note 145.

150. E.g., Escott v. BarChris Constr. Corp., 283 F. Supp. 643 (S.D.N.Y. 1968).

151. E.g., Bates v. Dresser, supra note 146.

152. Briggs v. Spaulding, 141 U.S. 132, 35 L.Ed. 662, 11 S.Ct. 924 (1891).

153. O'Connor v. First Nat'l Invs.' Corp., 163 Va. 907, 177 S.E. 852 (1935).

154. Allied Freightways, Inc. v. Cholfin, 325 Mass. 630, 91 N.E.2d 765 (1950).

155. Graham v. Allis-Chalmers Mfg. Co., 41 Del. Ch. 89, 188 A.2d 125 (1963).

themselves of their duty of general supervision and control. When defalcations occur, courts will treat directors with more leniency with respect to a single isolated act of fraud on the part of a subordinate than where the practice appears to have been habitually and openly committed so as to have been easily detected upon proper supervision.[156]

Directors do not warrant the skill or fidelity of the corporation's employees and are not insurers.[157] Directors of a business corporation, other than a bank, will ordinarily not be held liable for mere errors of judgment.[158] However, negligence or the lack of it is usually a question of fact, depending upon a circumstance under which the directors acted.[159]

A director's liability for negligence in permitting mismanagement or defalcations by officers or employees may be determined by the standard of care of (1) a reasonably prudent man under similar circumstances,[160] or (2) an ordinary director,[161] or (3) a prudent man in the conduct of his own business affairs.[162] The type of corporation involved may be significant.[163]

In the supervision of corporate affairs, the duty of a director to exercise due care includes a duty to investigate the veracity of information furnished the director by subordinates. The duty to investigate is only a "reasonable" one, but it may require affirmative action beyond a mere oral inquiry of management. For example, a director has been held liable to his corporation for his failure to make a reasonable investigation

---

156. Lowell Hoit & Co. v. Detig, 320 Ill. App. 179, 50 N.E.2d 602, 603 (1943).

157. Briggs v. Spaulding, supra note 152.

158. Allied Freightways, Inc. v. Cholfin, supra note 154, 91 N.E.2d at 768.

159. Wallach v. Billings, 277 Ill. 218, 115 N.E. 382, cert. denied, 244 U.S. 659 (1917).

160. E.g., Harman v. Willbern, 374 F. Supp. 1149 (D. Kan. 1974), aff'd, 520 F.2d 1333 (10th Cir. 1975).

161. E.g., Allen v. Roydhouse, 232 F. 1010 (E.D. Pa. 1916).

162. E.g., Bynum v. Scott, 217 F. 122, 124 (E.D.N.C. 1914); Wallace v. Lincoln Sav. Bank, 89 Tenn. 630, 653, 15 S.W. 448 (1891).

163. E.g., Lippett v. Ashley, 89 Conn. 451, 94 A. 995 (1915).

to determine whether a proposed share exchange would be in his corporation's best interests and his failure to argue for those best interests.[164]

Although a corporate employer was legally liable only for the payment of worker's compensation to the next of kin of a deceased employee, its vice-president and superintendent was held personally liable for wrongful death where he negligently ordered the movement of a crane, the boom of which struck a power line causing decedent's electrocution.[165] In another similar action in Louisiana a construction corporation's building superintendent was held to be an executive officer of his corporation and was declared guilty of personal negligence that caused deaths and bodily injuries at the construction site.[166] And corporate officers who failed to exercise due care to prevent injury to a corporate employee were held personally liable to him for allowing the removal of a protective screen from the engine fan of a dragline.[167]

While the foregoing Louisiana cases involved direct actions against the insurer under that state's unique statute, they are indicative of a trend to impose personal tort liability upon corporate officers who fail to exercise reasonable care for the safety of corporate employees.

§ 2.11. Participating in or causing corporate tort or crime.

It is a well-established rule that a corporation will be held liable for the torts and wrongful acts of its directors, officers, and employees within the scope of their authority.[168] Thus, a

---

164. DePinto v. Provident Sec. Life Ins. Co., 374 F.2d 37 (9th Cir.), cert. denied, 389 U.S. 822 (1967).

165. Jones v. Brupbacher, 242 So. 2d 627 (La. App. 1970). See also Canter v. Koehring Co., 267 So. 2d 270 (La. App. 1972), rev'd, 283 So. 2d 716 (La. 1973).

166. Strickland v. Transamerica Ins. Co., 481 F.2d 138 (5th Cir. 1973).

167. Saucier v. United States Fid. & Guar. Co., 280 So. 2d 584 (La. App. 1973). Cf. Willis v. Stauffer Chem. Co., 348 So. 2d 158 (La. App.), modified, 349 So. 2d 1390 (La. App. 1977).

168. See UMW v. Coronado Coal Co., 259 U.S. 344, 66 L.Ed. 975, 42 S.Ct. 570 (1922).

corporation has been held criminally liable for the acts of an agent who committed a criminal offense within the authority vested upon him and within the scope of the corporate business.[169]

Just as a corporation may not escape liability merely because its agent's act was criminal,[170] so the individual who commits a tortious or criminal act may not escape personal liability on the ground that he was acting as a corporate officer or agent.[171] Under proper circumstances, both the individual and the corporation may be jointly liable.[172] A director who actually voted for the commission of a tort was held personally liable, even though the wrongful act was performed in the name of the corporation.[173]

That principle has been carried forward in court decisions imposing liability on corporate officers and directors on a "central figure theory." The Temporary Emergency Court of Appeals termed this theory "specific language of the corporate-director realm" and applied it to hold liable for restitution an oil company officer and director who was the "central figure" in an alleged willful scheme to overcharge gasoline customers during the 1973 Arab oil embargo.[174] The court determined that his misconduct brought about violations by his corporation of crude oil pricing laws. Citing earlier decisions to support its position, the court declared:

---

169. Standard Oil Co. v. United States, 307 F.2d 120, 127 (5th Cir. 1962). See also discussion infra Chapter 8.

170. Bourgeois v. Commonwealth, 217 Va. 268, 227 S.E.2d 714 (1976); State ex rel. Taylor v. American Ins. Co., 355 Mo. 1053, 200 S.W.2d 1 (1946).

171. Aetna Life Ins. Co. v. Brewer, 12 F.2d 818 (D.C. Cir. 1926). See also Scribner v. O'Brien, Inc., 169 Conn. 389, 363 A.2d 160 (1975); Chandler v. Hunter, 340 So. 2d 818 (Ala. App. 1976).

172. Russell v. American Rock Crusher Co., 181 Kan. 891, 317 P.2d 847 (1957); Bishop v. Readsboro Chair Mfg. Co., 85 Vt. 141, 81 A. 454 (1911).

173. Tillman v. Wheaton-Haven Rec. Ass'n, 517 F.2d 1141 (4th Cir. 1975).

174. Citronelle-Mobile Gathering, Inc. v. Herrington, 826 F.2d 16 (Em. App.) cert. denied sub nom. Chamberlain v. United States, 98 L.Ed.2d 355 (1987).

> [T]he sum of the holdings of these cases is that personal
> responsibility for corporate liability may attach when the
> individual's wrongful conduct causes the violation of a
> statute and accompanying regulations such as the crude
> oil pricing laws.[175]

In denying certiorari the Supreme Court did not accept
contentions of the officer and of the Chamber of Commerce of
the United States and American Corporate Counsel, in amici
curiae briefs, that corporate officers "by definition of their
position, will always be central figures responsible for their
corporation's compliance with regulatory statutes."[176] The
Court of Appeals held that a finding of liability on this
ground should be conditioned "on the particular circumstances and equities of each case."[177]

A corporate officer is individually liable for injuries to a
third party when the corporation owes a duty of care to the
third party, the corporation delegates that duty to the officer,
the officer breaches that duty through personal fault
(whether by malfeasance, misfeasance, or nonfeasance) and
the third party is injured as a proximate result of the officer's
breach of that duty.[178] Under New York law "a corporate
officer who controls corporate conduct and thus is an active
participant in that conduct is liable for the torts of the corporation.[178a]

As a general rule, a director or officer must have participated in the wrongdoing or have directed the tortious act in
order to be personally liable. That is particularly true when
the actual wrongdoer is a subordinate employee.[179]

---

175. Id. at 25.

176. Chamberlain v. United States, U.S. Supreme Court, October term,
No. 87-140.

177. 826 F.2d at 25.

178. Schaefer v. D & J Produce, Inc., 62 Ohio App. 2d 53, 403 N.E.2d
1015 (1978); Bowes v. Cincinnati Riverfront Coliseum, Inc., 12 Ohio App.
3d 12, 465 N.E.2d 904 (1983).

178a. New York v. Shore Realty Corp., 759 F.2d 1032, 1052 (2d Cir.
1985).

179. 17B Am. Jur. 2d Corporations §§ 1880 and 1893. See also Graham
v. Allis-Chalmers Mfg. Co., 188 A.2d 125 (Del. 1963).

Directors and officers may be held liable civilly and criminally under various statutes, such as the National Banking Act,[180] the Federal Food and Drug Act,[181] the Sherman Anti-Trust Act[182] and RICO,[183] where their involvement in the offenses warrants such liability.

When a corporate officer went to Erie, Pennsylvania, and executed a contract there, she was held amenable to jurisdiction in Pennsylvania in an action alleging breach of confidential relationship, borrowing of trade secrets, unfair competition, and patent infringement.[184] The court said that "a corporate officer who personally commits a tort in his capacity as an officer of the corporation can be held along with the corporation."[185]

One who participated in forming a corporation and participated with it in activities constituting patent infringement was held liable for the infringement upon a showing that he was cognizant of it.[186]

A case of first impression, decided by the Supreme Court of Washington in 1980, considered the proper test for imposing liability upon a corporate officer for tortious interference with his corporation's contractual relations.[187] Olympic contracted to purchase roe herring from Yankee. Glenovich, an officer and director of Yankee, was sued by Olympic for inducing Yankee to breach the contract. He moved for summary judg-

---

180. 12 U.S.C. § 21 et seq.; see del Junco v. Conover, 682 F.2d 1338 (9th Cir. 1982), cert. denied, 459 U.S. 1146 (1984).

181. 21 U.S.C. § 301(k); see United States v. Park, 421 U.S. 658, 44 L.Ed.2d 489, 95 S.Ct. 1903 (1975).

182. 15 U.S.C. § 1 et seq.; see United States v. American Radiator & Std. San. Corp., 433 F.2d 174 (3d Cir. 1970).

183. 18 U.S.C. § 1964(c); see Lode v. Leonardo, 557 F. Supp. 675 (N.D. Ill. 1982).

184. Lighting Systems, Inc. v. International Merchandising Assocs., Inc., 464 F. Supp. 601 (W.D. Pa. 1979).

185. Id. at 604.

186. Universal Athletic Sales Co. v. American Gym, 480 F. Supp. 408, 417 (W.D. Pa. 1979).

187. Olympic Fish Prod., Inc. v. Lloyd, 93 Wash. 2d 596, 611 P.2d 737 (1980) (en banc).

ment on the ground that, as an officer of Yankee, he was immune from such liability.[188] The motion was denied. The court held that his immunity must be based on a showing of good faith which required him to prove that he acted with the intent to benefit his corporation and not for personal gain.[189]

A corporation's president who permitted it to sell financed property "out of trust" without forwarding the proceeds pursuant to the security agreement for payment of outstanding and then overdue loans was held personally liable in an action in the Eastern District of New York.[190]

§ 2.12. Misuse of corporate funds; waste.

Misuse of their corporation's funds is a violation of fiduciary duty which will subject corporate directors to personal liability.[191] Such liability may be enforced by the corporation[192] or on its behalf, by derivative action.[193] In a proper case such liability may also be enforced by the corporation's creditors[194] or its trustee in bankruptcy.[195]

---

188. A party to a contract cannot be liable for inducing its own breach. Houser v. City of Redmond, 16 Wash. App. 743, 559 P.2d 577 (1977), aff'd, 91 Wash. 2d 36, 586 P.2d 482 (1978).

189. Olympic Fish Prod., Inc. v. Lloyd, supra note 187, 611 P.2d at 739.

190. Birmingham Small Arms Co. v. Brooklyn Cycle, Inc., 408 F. Supp. 707 (E.D.N.Y. 1976). See also Scriven v. Maple Knoll Apts., Inc., 46 A.D.2d 210, 361 N.Y.S.2d 730 (1974); Norton Refrigerated Express, Inc. v. Ritter Bros. Co., 552 S.W.2d 910 (Tex. Civ. App. 1977). Cf. Cane River Needle Art v. Reon, Inc., 335 So. 2d 751 (La. App. 1976).

191. E.g., Goff v. Emde, 32 Ohio App. 216, 167 N.E. 699 (1928); Dome Realty Co. v. Rottenberg, 285 Mass. 324, 189 N.E. 70 (1934); Ryan v. Robert Ryan Hotels, 198 Ore. 133, 255 P.2d. 130 (1953).

192. Garden Hill Estates, Inc. v. Bernstein 24 A.D.2d 512, 261 N.Y.S.2d 648 (1965), aff'd, 17 N.Y.2d 525, 267 N.Y.S.2d 906, 215 N.E.2d 163 (1966).

193. See Lawson v. Baltimore Paint & Chem. Corp., 347 F. Supp. 967 (D. Md. 1972); Ludlam v. Riverhead Bond & Mtg. Corp., 244 A.D. 113, 278 N.Y.S. 487 (1935). Cf. Marcone v. Mott, 33 A.D.2d 919, 307 N.Y.S.2d 517 (1970).

194. Wortham v. Lachman-Rose Co., 440 S.W.2d 351 (Tex. Civ. App. 1969); Klein v. Benaron, 247 Cal. App. 2d 607, 56 Cal. Rptr. 5 (1967).

195. Gray v. Sutherland, 124 Cal. App. 2d 280, 268 P.2d 754 (1954). See also infra Chapter 5.

Several of the questions frequently presented in such cases were involved in a Seventh Circuit decision.[196] It was claimed that the directors had wasted corporate assets by canceling and reissuing stock options at lower exercise prices. The court held that:

(1) Ordinarily, employee compensation and other corporate payments are not a waste or gift of assets as long as their consideration is returned to the corporation.

(2) The question of the adequacy of consideration is committed to the sound business judgment of the corporation's directors;

(3) A plaintiff attacking a corporate payment has the heavy burden of demonstrating that no reasonable businessman could find that adequate consideration had been supplied for the payment;

(4) But where the directors have a personal interest in the application of the payments (such as where they are fixing their own compensation), the business judgment rule no longer applies and the burden shifts to the directors to demonstrate affirmatively that the transactions were engaged in with good faith and were fair, i.e., that adequate consideration had been supplied.

In this case the transactions were effectively ratified by the shareholders. The court found no evidence to demonstrate that the transactions were unfair and rendered summary judgment for the directors.

When corporate property was wasted or applied in payment of claims which the directors had no authority to pay,[197] when a director gave away corporate assets,[198] when an officer paid unwarranted personal expenses,[199] or when the corporation

---

196. Cohen v. Ayers, 596 F.2d 733 (7th Cir. 1979).

197. Lake Harriet State Bank v. Venie, 138 Minn. 339, 165 N.W. 225 (1917).

198. Cahall v. Burbage, 14 Del. Ch. 55, 121 A. 646 (1923).

199. Nanikian v. Mattingly, 265 Mich. 128, 251 N.W. 421 (1933).

paid office rent for its president's law firm,[200] liability was imposed. But directors could properly use corporate funds to resist the appointment of a receiver for the corporation,[201] and the use of corporate funds to buy off union racketeers to avoid a crippling strike was held to be a proper corporate expenditure.[202]

§ 2.13. Nonuse or misuse of computers.

Computer systems, commonly referred to as EDP ("electronic data processing"), are in common use today in American business and industry. They are indispensable in modern business life. With their increased availability have come new legal problems, not only for computer manufacturers, service centers, operators and programmers, but also for officers and directors of corporations which use or should use EDP services.[203]

Among the questions which corporate management and their legal counsel may be called upon to answer are:

(1) What areas of the law deal with computer liability
(2) Does their corporation have a duty to avail itself of EDP?
(3) May a business organization incur liability for losses resulting from its failure to keep pace with technological advances in its industry?
(4) When losses result from misuse of EDP, upon whom will the loss come to rest?

Computer fraud and breaches of EDP security are becoming increasingly frequent and present additional sources of

---

200. McMahon v. Burdette, 106 N.J. Eq. 79, 150 A. 12 (1930), modified, 109 N.J. Eq. 84, 156 A. 420 (1931).

201. Godley v. Crandall & Godley Co., 181 A.D. 75, 168 N.Y.S. 251 (1917), aff'd, 228 N.Y. 656, 125 N.E. 908 (1930).

202. Hornstein v. Paramount Pictures, 22 Misc. 2d 996, 37 N.Y.S.2d 404 (1942), aff'd, 266 A.D. 659, 41 N.Y.S.2d 210 (1943), 292 N.Y. 468, 55 N.E.2d 740 (1944).

203. Lundell & Bride, Computer Use — An Executive's Guide (1973); Awalt, "Corporate Legal Problems Associated with Computers," 1965-66 Modern Uses of Logic in Law.

potential liability for corporate officers and directors. In a 1981 discussion of this topic, one authority notes that "the very characteristics that make computers so useful can also be the prime sources of fraud."[204] These are identified as the accelerating use of low-cost computers, central computers that may be accessed by telephone or tapping into transmission lines, remote access terminals, the soaring number of people learning to operate computers, and programmers and the programming process.

Among the kinds of losses that may result are fraud losses, program errors delaying the issuance of statements or invoices, keypunching errors which result in issuance of incorrect statements or invoices, and similar matters which cause substantial, unnecessary expenditures of a corporation's time and money.

Senior executives and the board itself may be charged with responsibility for failure to recognize that "data is a corporate asset" like plant and equipment and money.[205]

Top management has the ultimate responsibility for EDP security, and such responsibility must be specifically and precisely defined.[206]

Just as the failure to make proper use of radar may impose liability on its owner,[207] so the nonuse or misuse of EDP may impose liability upon a corporation[208] and, perhaps, on its directors and officers. The books are full of "horror stories" resulting from computer malfunction and consequent puni-

---

204. "'EDP Security' What's Behind Those Headlines," Coopers & Lybrand Newsletter, Vol. 23, No. 9, at 8, Sept. 1981.

205. Id. at 9.

206. Id. at 10. See also booklets covering some aspects of computer security: "Contingency Planning: A Discussion of Strategies" and "EDP Security — A Management Responsibility," available by writing c/o Coopers & Lybrand, P.O. Box 682, Times Square Station, New York, N.Y. 10108.

207. See White Stack Towing Corp. v. Bethlehem Steel Co., 279 F.2d 419 (4th Cir. 1960); Pocahontas S.S. Co. v. The Esso Aruba, 94 F. Supp. 486, 490 (D. Mass. 1950), aff'd sub nom. Standard Oil Co. v. Pocahontas S.S. Co., 197 F.2d 422 (1st Cir. 1952).

208. E.g., Burnett v. Westminster Bank, Ltd., 3 All. E.R. 81 (Q.B. 1965); Neal v. United States, 402 F. Supp. 678 (D.N.J. 1975).

tive damage awards to automobile owners because their property was repossessed when they are not actually in default.[209] Undue reliance upon a computer for decision making has been strongly criticized in most such cases. In the words of one court, "the law must require that men in the use of computerized data regard those with whom they are dealing as more important than a perforation on a card."[210]

In a Michigan case an attorney was criticized for not making use of information which was available to lawyers generally through a computerized legal research service.[211]

In a Minnesota case an EDP service bureau made broad representations as to the effectiveness of its inventory-control system. In reliance thereon, a wholesaler purchased an inventory-control service from the defendant. The system failed because the plaintiff's personnel made mistakes in preparing input for the defendant's computer. Under the "GIGO Rule of Computers," the EDP system reflected these errors in its output. Here, the plaintiff prevailed because the defendant had overstated the capabilities of its computer and had misrepresented the effectiveness of its inventory-control system.[212]

The scope of EDP use is constantly expanding. Tasks of varying complexity now assigned to computers may involve preparing tax returns and checking them, inventory control, maintaining bank accounts, routing telephone calls, maintaining circulation control for periodicals, design and engineering of new automobiles, processing orders of customers, operating chemical plants and oil refineries, flying and landing aircraft, legal and medical research, switching railroad cars in train yards, and many more. As corporate directors

---

209. E.g., Ford Motor Credit Co. v. Hitchcock, 116 Ga. App. 563, 158 S.E.2d 468 (1967); Ford Motor Credit Co. v. Swarens, 447 S.W.2d 53 (Ky. App. 1969); Price v. Ford Motor Credit Co., 530 S.W.2d 249 (Mo. App. 1975). See also Davis v. Nash Cent. Motors, 332 S.W.2d 475 (Mo. App. 1960); Beggs v. Universal C.I.T. Credit Corp., 409 S.W.2d 719 (Mo. 1966).

210. Ford Motor Credit Co. v. Swarens, supra note 209, at 57.

211. Holt v. Whelan, 388 Mich. 50, 199 N.W.2d 195 (1972).

212. Clements Auto Co. v. Service Bur. Corp., 298 F. Supp. 115 (D. Minn. 1969), modified, 444 F.2d 169 (8th Cir. 1971).

and officers place more reliance on EDP services in such areas, they must not abdicate their fiduciary responsibilities to a machine no matter how sophisticated it may be.

§ 2.14. Directors' liability as shareholders.

Although directors are fiduciaries "with duties running primarily to the corporation," they are not agents of the shareholders who elect them. A shareholder's profit interest in a particular corporate transaction is "a remote proprietary interest."[213] The Southern District of New York has emphasized that while the shareholders "indirectly own the corporation, they do not manage it, and the acts of management are not attributed to them individually."

Directors who are also shareholders are nonetheless subject to liability as shareholders. Thus, directors may be liable as shareholders when they receive unlawful dividends. There is a common-law liability[214] as well as liability imposed by statute.[215] Some statutes make such liability absolute.[216] Under others, shareholders are held liable only to the extent that the loss may not be recouped from the errant directors.[217] There is also some authority that if the shareholder received the dividend in good faith, believing it was paid from surplus, he is relieved from liability for paying it back,[218] although there are other decisions to the contrary.[219] An action to re-

---

213. Popkin v. Dingman, 366 F. Supp. 534 (S.D.N.Y. 1973).
214. Wood v. National City Bank, 24 F.2d 661 (2d Cir. 1928).
215. E.g., Ohio Rev. Code Ann. § 1701.95(D); Wash. Rev. Code Ann. § 23A.08.450. And see Comment, "Federal Control of Corporate Distributions to Stockholders Under the Public Utility Holding Company Act," 49 Yale L.J. 492 (1940).
216. Mich. Comp. Laws § 450.1551.
217. Cf. Alliegro v. Pan Am. Bank, 136 So. 2d 656 (Fla. App. 1962), cert. denied, 149 So. 2d 45 (Fla. 1963).
218. See McDonald v. Williams, 174 U.S. 397, 43 L.Ed. 1022, 19 S.Ct. 743 (1899); Bates v. Brooks, 222 Iowa 1128, 270 N.W. 867 (1937).
219. Cf. Detroit Trust Co. v. Goodrich, 175 Mich. 168, 141 N.W. 882 (1913); Mills v. Hendershot, 70 N.J. Eq. 258, 62 A. 542 (1905); Gaunce v. Schoder, 145 Wash. 604, 261 P. 393 (1927).

cover such dividends is brought by or in behalf of the corporation, and statutes commonly so provide.[220]

If the corporation was insolvent when the dividends were declared and paid, the shareholders who received them have little chance of retaining them, regardless of their good faith.[221] The rule in such a case is that the shareholders are constructive trustees of any creditors who are entitled to the money distributed as such dividends.[222] The dividends are in fraud of the creditors because they dispose of assets held in trust to pay corporate debts.[223]

Under Section 719 of the New York Business Corporation Law, however, a creditor cannot maintain an action against a corporate director until he has exhausted his remedies against the corporation itself.[224] Whether this would apply to an action against a shareholder is not settled.

Of course, the shareholder's liability is limited to the amount he received.[225] It would also appear that he is entitled to set off any money that the corporation might owe him.[226]

§ 2.15. Enforcement of liability.

Independent of statutory authorization, a corporation may enforce the liability of its directors, officers and employees for misconduct in the management of its affairs, waste of its assets, or acts in contravention of their duties. Both legal and equitable remedies are available.[227]

Where statutes impose liability upon corporate officers or directors, their common-law liability is not thereby excluded

---

220. Schaefer v. DeChant, 11 Ohio App. 3d 281, 464 N.E.2d 583 (1983), construing Ohio Rev. Code Ann. § 1701.95(E) [now § 1701.95(F)].

221. Wood v. National City Bank, supra note 214.

222. Cf. Bates v. Brooks, supra note 218.

223. Id.

224. Eskimo Pie Corp. v. Whitelawn Dairies Inc., 266 F. Supp. 79 (S.D.N.Y. 1967).

225. Mills v. Hendershot, supra note 219.

226. See Judge Clark's opinion in Brooks v. Buys, 217 Mich. 263, 186 N.W. 472 (1922).

227. Platt Corp. v. Platt, 21 A.D.2d 116, 249 N.Y.S.2d 75 (1964), aff'd, 15 N.Y.2d 705, 707, 256 N.Y.S.2d 335, 204 N.E.2d 95, 496 (1965).

or limited.[228] In some instances the statutes enlarge the directors' common-law liability.[229]

If the corporation fails to take appropriate action, either because it is controlled by the wrongdoers or for other reasons, one or more shareholders may maintain a derivative action to redress the wrong.[230] Such an action is brought for the benefit of the corporation to enforce a corporate right.[231] When a shareholder suffers a loss separate and distinct from that of shareholders generally, an individual action may be brought to redress the loss. If the injury causes loss to a number of shareholders it may be the basis for a class action.[232]

When a statute makes the offending directors liable to creditors, they may bring the action.[233]

The right of a receiver of the corporation to bring such an action is a matter on which the courts are not agreed.[234] A similar conflict exists respecting the right of a trustee in bankruptcy to recover in such a situation.[235] However, there is good authority that condonation of the improper use of corporate funds by the shareholders will not inhibit a receiver in bankruptcy from recovering from directors for the benefit of creditors.[236]

---

228. Id. See also Reilly v. Segert, 31 Ill. 2d 297, 201 N.E.2d 444 (1964), and Manning v. Campbell, 264 Mass. 386, 162 N.E. 770 (1928).

229. E.g., Creamery Package Mfg. Co. v. Wilhite, 149 Ark. 576, 233 S.W. 710 (1921). Cf. Ivy v. Plyler, 246 Cal. App. 2d 678, 54 Cal. Rptr. 894 (1966).

230. See discussion infra Chapter 18.

231. Lewis v. Chiles, 719 F.2d 1044, 1047 (9th Cir. 1983); Adair v. Wozniak, 23 Ohio St. 3d 174, 492 N.E.2d 426 (1986).

232. See discussion infra Chapter 18.

233. Bailey v. Colleen Prods. Corp., 120 Misc. 297, 198 N.Y.S. 418 (1923). Cf. N.Y. Bus. Corp. Law § 720; Steele v. Isman, 164 A.D. 146, 149 N.Y.S. 488 (1914).

234. Hodde v. Nobbe, 204 Mo. App. 109, 221 S.W. 130 (1920); but cf. Stevirmac Oil & Gas Co. v. Smith, 259 F. 650 (E.D. Okla. 1919).

235. Claypoole v. McIntosh, 182 N.C. 109, 108 S.E. 433 (1921); Irving Trust Co. v. Gunder, 234 A.D. 252, 254 N.Y.S. 630 (1932). But cf. Morris v. Sampsel, 224 Wis. 560, 272 N.W. 53 (1937), cert. denied, 305 U.S. 608 (1938).

236. Hux v. Butler, 339 F.2d 696 (6th Cir. 1964). Cf. Buckley Petroleum Prods., Inc. v. Goldman, 28 A.D.2d 640, 280 N.Y.S.2d 876 (1967).

§ 2.16. Extent of liability; damages.

The extent of a director's liability will depend upon the circumstances of a particular case. In actions resulting from unlawful distributions or dividends, the measure of damages varies in the several jurisdictions. In Delaware, for example, the liability is for "the full amount of the dividend unlawfully paid, or to the full amount unlawfully paid for the purchase or redemption of the corporation's stock, with interest from the time such liability accrued."[237] In Ohio the liability is for the amount "in excess of the amount that could have been paid or distributed without violation of law or the articles but not in excess of the amount that would inure to the benefit of the creditors of the corporation if it was insolvent at the time of the payment or distribution or there was reasonable ground to believe that by such action it would be rendered insolvent, plus the amount that was paid or distributed to holders of shares of any class in violation of the rights of holders of shares of any other class."[238]

Other statutes impose liability according to different rules. In some instances the liability is for all corporate debts existing when the dividend was declared or created thereafter during the term of office of the errant directors.[239] In other situations, the rule to be applied either depends on whether the directors did or did not exercise good faith or on whether the directors were or were not free from negligence in declaring the dividends.[240]

In an action to restore assets taken from a surety company by a director's negligence, recovery was limited to the value of the assets.[241] Where officers conspired to wreck a corpora-

---

237. Del. Code Ann. tit. 8, § 174.

238. Ohio Rev. Code Ann. § 1701.95(A)(3).

239. Kehl, Corporate Dividends § 253 (1941); and see McGill's Admx. v. Phillips, 243 Ky. 768, 49 S.W.2d 1025 (1932).

240. City of Franklin v. Coldwell, 123 Ky. 528, 96 S.W. 605 (1906). Cf. Stopford v. Haskell, 147 F. Supp. 509 (D. Conn. 1957), and Cahall v. Lofland, 12 Del. Ch. 299, 114 A. 224 (1921), aff'd, 13 Del. Ch. 384, 118 A. 1 (1922).

241. Hunt v. Aufderheide, 330 Pa. 362, 199 A. 345 (1938).

tion, the measure of damages was held to be the difference between the value of its assets before the wrongdoing and the remaining value at the time of the litigation.[242]

Remote and speculative damages are not recoverable. Generally, punitive damages will not be allowed, yet South Carolina has awarded them for fraudulent failure to disclose relevant facts in a stock purchase.[243]

Interest may be awarded in a proper case, such as wrongful diversion of corporate funds,[244] improper loans,[245] or creating corporate debt in excess of the legal limit.[246] An officer who unlawfully obtained stock has been required to account for dividends paid on it.[247]

---

242. Insuranshares Corp. v. Northern Fiscal Corp., 42 F. Supp. 126 (E.D. Pa. 1941).

243. Jacobson v. Yaschik, 249 S.C. 577, 155 S.E.2d 601 (1967).

244. Prudential Trust Co. v. Brown, 281 Mass. 132, 171 N.E. 42 (1930).

245. Medford Trust Co. v. McKnight, 292 Mass. 1, 197 N.E. 649 (1935).

246. Colcord v. Granzow, 137 Okla. 194, 278 P. 654 (1928).

247. Beaudette v. Graham, 267 Mass. 7, 165 N.E. 671 (1929).

COROLLARY REFERENCES

Adkins & Janis, "Some Observations on Liabilities of Corporate Directors," 20 Bus. Law. 817 (1965).

Berle, "Corporate Powers as Powers in Trust," 44 Harv. L. Rev. 1049 (1931).

Conard, "An Overview of the Laws of Corporations," 71 Mich. L. Rev. 621 (1973).

Douglas, "Directors Who Do Not Direct," 47 Harv. L. Rev. 1305 (1934).

Kaplan, "Fiduciary Responsibility in the Management of the Corporation," 31 Bus. Law. (Special Issue) 883 (1976).

Manning, "The Business Judgment Rule and the Director's Duty of Attention: Time for Reality," 39 Bus. Law. 1477 (1984).

Nimmer & Krauthaus, "Computer Error and User Liability Risk," 35 Def. L.J. 579 (1986).

Nycum, "Liability for Malfunction of a Computer Program," Rutgers J. of Computers, Tech. & Law 1 (1979).

Reece, "Litigation over Faulty Software: Complex and Full of Difficulties," Nat'l L.J., Apr. 20, 1987, at 22, col. 3.

"The Role and Composition of the Board of Directors of the Large Publicly Held Corporation" — Statement of The Business Roundtable, 33 Bus. Law. 2083 (1978).

Vagts, "Directors: Myth and Reality," 31 Bus. Law. (Special Issue) 1227 (1976).

Warden, "The Boardroom as a War Room: The Real World Applications of the Duty of Care and the Duty of Loyalty," 40 Bus. Law. 1431 (1985).

Note, "Corporate Fiduciary Doctrine in the Context of Parent-Subsidiary Relations," 74 Yale L.J. 338 (1964).

Note, "Jones v. Ahmanson: The Fiduciary Obligations of Majority Shareholders," 70 Colum. L. Rev. 1049 (1970).

Note, "The Controlling Influence Standard in Rule 10b-5 Corporate Mismanagement Cases," 86 Harv. L. Rev. 1007 (1973).

Note, "The Federal Common Law," 82 Harv. L. Rev. 1512 (1969).

Annotation, "Liability of corporate directors or officers for negligence in permitting conversion of property of third persons by corporation," 29 A.L.R.3d 660 (1970).

Annotation, "Liability of corporate directors for negligence in permitting mismanagement or defalcations by officers or employees," 25 A.L.R.3d 941 (1969).

Annotation, "Modern status of rule that substantive rights of parties to a tort action are governed by the law of the place of the wrong," 29 A.L.R.3d 603 (1970).

Annotation, "Personal civil liability of officer or director of corporation for negligence of subordinate corporate employee causing personal injury or death of third person," 90 A.L.R.3d 916 (1979).

Annotation, "Personal liability of officers or directors of corporation on corporate checks issued against insufficient funds," 47 A.L.R.3d 1250 (1973).

Annotation, "Right of corporation to indemnity for civil or criminal liability incurred by employee's violation of antitrust laws," 37 A.L.R.2d 1355 (1971).

Chapter 3

DUTY OF LOYALTY

§ 3.01. Loyalty is absolute.

Under Delaware law a director's duty of loyalty requires scrupulous observation of a duty (1) to protect the interests of the corporation and (2) to refrain from doing anything to injure it. A director may not deprive the corporation of profit or advantage which his skill and ability may bring to it or enable it to make, in the reasonable and lawful exercise of its powers. This rule requires "an undivided and unselfish loyalty to the corporation." It "demands that there shall be no conflict between duty and self-interest."[1]

---

1. Guth v. Loft, Inc., 23 Del. Ch. 255, 5 A.2d 503, 510 (1939), reaffirmed in Smith v. Van Gorkom, 488 A.2d 858, 872 (Del. 1985); Weinberger v. UOP, Inc., 457 A.2d 701, 710 (Del. 1983).

81

The duty of loyalty is derived from the prohibition against self-dealing that is inherent in a fiduciary relationship. Once a prima facie showing is made that directors have a self-interest in a particular transaction, the burden shifts to them to demonstrate that the transaction is fair and serves the best interests of the corporation and its shareholders. When self-dealing or bad faith is demonstrated, the duty of loyalty supersedes the duty of care.[2]

In a self-dealing transaction, mere good faith will not preclude a finding of a breach of the duty of loyalty. Such a transaction will be sustained only if it is proved to be objectively or intrinsically fair.[3]

§ 3.02. Conflict of interest.

A conflict of interest transaction is one in which a director of a corporation has a direct or indirect interest, according to the Revised Model Business Corporation Act.[4] The same definition would apply to analogous transactions entered into by officers, employees or dominating shareholders.

Today's approach to the question of loyalty of directors recognizes that most state corporation statutes now allow potential conflicts of interest to exist where directors are interested on both sides of a corporate transaction. The remedy lies in regulation. Interested directors are expected to abstain, and approval by disinterested directors is requisite when inchoate conflicts become choate.

The conduct of directors evidencing any interest adverse to that of their corporation will ordinarily be subjected to the utmost scrutiny, but in the absence of evidence, directors will not be presumed unfaithful to their trust.[5] They are given

---

2. Norlin Corp. v. Rooney, Pace, Inc., 744 F.2d 255, 264-65 (2d Cir. 1984). See also Crouse-Hinds Co. v. Internorth, Inc., 634 F.2d 690, 702 (2d Cir. 1980); Panter v. Marshall Field & Co., 646 F.2d 271, 301 (7th Cir.), cert. denied, 454 U.S. 1092 (1981).

3. A.C. Acquisitions Corp. v. Anderson, Clayton & Co., 519 A.2d 103, 115 (Del. Ch. 1986).

4. Revised Model Bus. Corp. Act § 8.31(a).

5. Atwater v. Wheeling & Lake Erie Ry., 56 F.2d 720, 723 (6th Cir. 1932); Jefferson County Truck Growers Ass'n v. Tanner, 341 So. 2d 485 (Ala. 1977).

wide latitude in the management of the corporate affairs so long as they exercise an honest, unbiased judgment in a reasonable manner.[6]

On the other hand, self-dealing is strictly condemned and is to be avoided. When self-dealing is shown, the burden is upon the interested directors to establish their good faith and the fairness of the transaction to the corporation.[7] Thus, a corporate director may conduct personal transactions with his corporation if he can prove that he did not gain unfair or secret profits and that he dealt openly, honestly and fairly with the corporation and its shareholders.[8]

§ 3.03. Disclosure of material facts.

A significant part of a director's duty of loyalty is to disclose to the decision makers all information in his possession germane to the transaction in issue. In this context, germane information is such as a reasonable person would consider important in deciding how to vote on the transaction.[9] The Delaware court has said that completeness, not mere adequacy, "is both the norm and the mandate."[10]

The Revised Model Business Corporation Act suggests that a conflict of interest transaction should not be voidable solely because of a director's interest in it if the material facts were disclosed to or known by the directors or shareholders and

---

6. Casey v. Woodruff, 49 N.Y.S.2d 625 (1944).

7. Pepper v. Litton, 308 U.S. 295, 84 L.Ed. 281, 60 S.Ct. 238 (1939), citing Geddes v. Anaconda Copper Mining Co., 254 U.S. 590, 65 L.Ed. 425, 41 S.Ct. 209 (1921). See also Ripley v. International Rys. of Cent. Am., 8 A.D.2d 310, 188 N.Y.S.2d 62 (1959), aff'd, 8 N.Y.2d 430, 209 N.Y.S.2d 289, 171 N.E.2d 443 (1960).

8. Simpson v. Spellman, 522 S.W.2d 615 (Mo. App. 1975). The contract must have been fair to the corporation when made. Pederson v. Owen, 556 P.2d 542, 543 (Nev. 1976).

9. Weinberger v. UOP, Inc., 457 A.2d 701, 710 (Del. 1983); TSC Indus., Inc. v. Northway, Inc., 426 U.S. 438, 449, 48 L.Ed.2d 757, 96 S.Ct. 2126, 2132 (1976).

10. Weinberger v. UOP, Inc., supra note 9, at 710.

approved or ratified by one or the other.[11] But such approval or ratification must be with complete information as to all material facts relating to the conflict of interest and the transaction itself.[12]

In some cases the courts have held that a failure of complete disclosure is sufficient to establish a transaction's unfairness.[13] In other decisions the failure of complete disclosure was held to shift the burden of proving fairness to the defendants.[14]

§ 3.04. Statutory provisions.

While there is no "safe harbor" for divided loyalties in Delaware,[15] that state's corporation code[16] and the statutes of thirty-seven other states contain provisions to the effect that transactions between directors and their corporations are not voidable merely because a fiduciary relationship exists between the parties. Most such statutes follow the suggestions contained in the Revised Model Business Corporation Act.[17] The Act relates only to directors, but some state statutes include corporate officers as well.[18]

Generally, the state statutes contain a provision with respect to dealings between a corporation and its directors or officers, or between corporations with common officers. Generally, such a provision provides for upholding such dealings

---

11. Revised Model Bus. Corp. Act § 8.31(a)(i) and (ii). See also infra section 3.18 as to ratification by disinterested directors or shareholders.

12. Weinberger v. UOP, Inc., supra note 9, at 712. See also Del. Corp. Code tit. 8, § 144(a)(2).

13. Weinberger v. UOP, Inc., supra note 9, at 711-12.

14. Shlensky v. South Parkway Bldg. Corp., 19 Ill. 2d 268, 166 N.E.2d 793 (1960); Ohio Drill & Tool Co. v. Johnson, 498 F.2d 186, 195 (6th Cir. 1974).

15. Weinberger v. UOP, Inc., 457 A.2d 701, 710 (Del. 1983).

16. Del. Code Ann. tit. 8, § 144.

17. Revised Model Bus. Corp. Act § 8.31(a) is a simplification of the 1969 Model Bus. Corp. Act § 41.

18. E.g., Ohio Rev. Code Ann. § 1701.60; Wis. Stat. Ann. § 180.355. For a discussion of the various statutes, see 2 Model Bus. Corp. Act Ann. 968-71 (3d ed. 1985).

if (1) the conflict of interest was disclosed to the board and approved by a sufficient vote without counting the votes of involved directors, or (2) if the facts were disclosed and the transaction was approved by a majority vote of the stockholders, or (3) if the transaction is found to be fair and reasonable.[19] The statutes seem to make disclosure an alternative to fairness and reasonableness.

Some statutes validate the transaction if any one of the three alternatives has been satisfied.[20] About an equal number additionally require disclosure of the material facts of the transaction.[21] The difference is important. The earlier form of statute apparently requires only disclosure of the fact of the director's interest, but does not compel him to inform the other directors or shareholders of the material facts of the transaction he seeks to validate. The more recent enactments carry into the statutory language a requirement that the interested directors must disclose the material facts of the transaction. In judicial review, the courts give close scrutiny to such facts.[22]

§ 3.05. Charter and bylaw provisions.

Charter or bylaw provisions to broaden the scope of statutory provisions validating transactions involving interested directors are sometimes included in corporate documents.[23] Such provisions state that contracts or transactions involving directors will not be invalidated because of self-interest or by reason of the fact that the interested director's presence was needed for a quorum or a majority vote.[24] Such special provi-

---

19. Kaplan, "Fiduciary Responsibility in the Management of the Corporation," 31 Bus. Law. (Special Issue) 883, 894 (1976).

20. E.g., Colo. Rev. Stat. § 7-5-114.5; Fla. Stat. Ann. § 607.124; Wis. Stat. Ann. § 180.355.

21. E.g., Del. Code Ann. tit. 8, § 144(a)(1) and (2); N.Y. Bus. Corp. Law § 713; Ohio Rev. Code Ann. § 1701.60.

22. E.g., Weinberger v. UOP, Inc., supra note 15.

23. Marsh, "Are Directors Trustees? Conflict of Interest and Corporate Morality," 22 Bus. Law. 35, 45 (1966).

24. See, e.g., Everett v. Phillips, 288 N.Y. 227, 43 N.E.2d 18, reargument denied, 289 N.Y. 625, 43 N.Y.2d 841, 289 N.Y. 675, 45 N.E.2d 176 (1942).

sions have the effect of shifting the burden of proof of fairness from the directors[25] to the party who questions the contract or transaction.[26] Some charter provisions of the type go so far as to state that a director's interest need not be disclosed,[27] but in the face of statutory requirements to the contrary, they may not be enforceable.

Under such provisions it has been held that a board of directors may authorize the sale of the corporation's authorized but unissued shares to a director, without stockholder approval.[28] However, the burden is placed upon the interested director to show that the transaction was honest, fair and reasonable.[29]

Exculpatory provisions may also be found in the bylaws as, for example, that "no contract or other transaction between this Company and any other corporation shall be affected by the fact that Directors of this Company are interested in, or are directors or officers of, such other corporation."[30]

Of course, such provisions will not exculpate directors who are guilty of fraud, nor will they afford immunity to directors who are guilty of bad faith.[31] And they do not prevent the court from giving rigid scrutiny to the fairness of any given contract or transaction.[32]

---

25. See supra section 3.02.

26. La Vin v. La Vin, 283 A.D. 809, 128 N.Y.S.3d 518, aff'd, 307 N.Y. 790, 121 N.E.2d 620 (1954). Cf. Speigel v. Beacon Participation, Inc., 297 Mass. 398, 8 N.E.2d 895 (1937).

27. See, e.g., Piccard v. Sperry Corp., 48 F. Supp. 465 (S.D.N.Y. 1943), aff'd, 152 F.2d 462 (2d Cir.), cert. denied, 328 U.S. 845 (1946).

28. Pappas v. Moss, 393 F.2d 865 (3d Cir. 1968).

29. Id.

30. Helfman v. American Light & Traction Co., 121 N.J. Eq. 1, 187 A. 540, 546 (1936). See also Sterling Indus. v. Ball Bearing Pen Corp., 298 N.Y. 483, 84 N.E.2d 790 (1949).

31. Sterling v. Mayflower Hotel Corp., 33 Del. Ch. 293, 93 A.3d 107 (1952).

32. Abeles v. Adams Eng'g Co., 35 N.J. 411, 173 A.2d 246 (1961); Knox Glass Bottle Co. v. Underwood, 228 Miss. 699, 89 So. 2d 799 (1956), cert. denied, 353 U.S. 977 (1957).

§ 3.06. Use of corporate powers to maintain control.

Generally, corporate officers and directors may not take advantage of the corporation's procedures, programs and other similar business mechanics to perpetuate their own control or to effectuate a purpose inimical to that of the corporation and its stockholders.[33]

In a leading Delaware case[34] the court set aside a sale of stock to a friendly purchaser, following a threat to present management, on the ground that the sale was for the sole purpose of maintaining control. Most Delaware cases pay obeisance to that rule. However, the spate of litigation in the takeover context has resulted in more strict scrutiny of the actions and motives of corporate directors when corporate control is at stake.

In such cases it is usually alleged that the directors manipulated the internal corporate machinery "for the sole and primary purpose of entrenching themselves in office."[35] Proof of such allegations would show a violation of the duty of loyalty. Accordingly, the loyalty question should be resolved before the court considers whether the directors breached their duty of care in relation to the attempted takeover.[36]

It is established that a board of directors may not use the corporate machinery for the purpose of obstructing legitimate efforts of dissident shareholders to undertake a contest against management.[37] The Second Circuit has held that "decisions affecting a corporation's ultimate destiny are for the shareholders to make in accordance with democratic proce-

---

33. Bennett v. Breuil Petroleum Corp., 34 Del. Ch. 6, 99 A.2d 236 (1953); cf. McPhail v. L.S. Starrett Co., 257 F.2d 388 (1st Cir. 1958), and Condec Corp. v. Lunkenheimer Co., 43 Del. Ch. 353, 230 A.2d 769, 775 (1967).

34. Condec Corp. v. Lunkenheimer Co., supra note 33.

35. E.g., Moran v. Household Int'l, Inc., 490 A.2d 1059, 1071 (Del. Ch.), aff'd, 500 A.2d 1346 (Del. 1985); Hanson Trust PLC v. SCM Corp., 623 F. Supp. 848, 856 (S.D.N.Y. 1985), rev'd sub nom. Hanson Trust PLC v. ML SCM Acquisition, Inc., 781 F.2d 264 (2d Cir. 1986).

36. Aronson v. Lewis, 473 A.2d 805, 812 (Del. 1984).

37. Schnell v. ChrisCraft Indus., Inc., 285 A.2d 437 (Del. 1971).

87

dures" and the responsibility of the courts is "to protect the fundamental structure of corporate governance."[38]

When a court considers the directors' duty of care, the business judgment rule ordinarily provides a presumption in favor of the directors. It affords directors wide latitude in devising strategies to resist unfriendly advances.[39] But in the takeover context, the Delaware court finds "an omnipresent spector that the board may be acting primarily in its own interests, rather than those of the corporation and its shareholders."[40]

In the *Revlon* litigation[41] the court cited the above rule and continued:

> This potential for conflict places upon the directors the burden of proving that they had reasonable grounds for believing there was a danger to corporate policy and effectiveness ... [and] ... that the responsive action taken is reasonable in relation to the threat posed.

In the *Hanson Trust* litigation[42] the Second Circuit emphasized the elements of the duty of loyalty in calling for increased scrutiny of directors' actions because of management's self-interest in the responsive action. This follows the rule in *Norlin* that when self-dealing or bad faith are demonstrated, the duty of loyalty supersedes the duty of care and the burden shifts to the directors to "prove that the transaction was fair and reasonable to the corporation."[43]

The same result was reached by the Delaware court in *Revlon*, which found not only a breach of the duty of loyalty, but also a breach of the duty of care.[44]

---

38. Norlin Corp. v. Rooney, Pace, Inc., 744 F.2d 255, 258 (2d Cir. 1984).
39. Id. at 264.
40. Unocal Corp. v. Mesa Petroleum Co., 493 A.2d 946, 954 (Del. 1985). See also infra Chapter 6.
41. Revlon, Inc. v. MacAndrews & Forbes Holdings, Inc., 506 A.2d 173 (Del. 1986).
42. Hanson Trust PLC v. ML SCM Acquisition, Inc., 781 F.2d 264 (2d Cir. 1986).
43. Norlin Corp. v. Rooney, Pace, Inc., supra note 38, at 265.
44. Revlon, Inc., v. MacAndrews & Forbes Holdings, Inc., supra note 41, at 185.

In the context of a parent-subsidiary cash-out merger the corporate powers were used in a Delaware case to buy out the majority shareholders.[45] The interest of the directors resulted from functioning in dual capacities and invoked the necessity that they establish the "entire fairness" of the transaction.[46] On this point the court held:

> The concept of fairness has two basic aspects: fair dealing and fair price. The former embraces questions of when the transaction was timed, how it was initiated, structured, negotiated, disclosed to the directors, and how the approvals of the directors and stockholders were obtained. The latter aspect of fairness relates to the economic and financial considerations of the proposed merger, including all relevant factors.... All aspects of the issue must be examined as a whole since the question is one of entire fairness.[47]

Part of fair dealing is the duty of candor.[48] Does the transaction carry the earmarks of an arm's length bargain?[49] Did any majority interest use its power to gain undue advantage to itself at the expense of the minority?[50] Under New Jersey law, was the transaction entered into for a proper corporate purpose, and not merely for the directors' selfish purposes?[51] Does the transaction serve the best interests of the corporation and its shareholders?[52] Have the plaintiffs shown that management's sole or primary purpose in taking the challenged action was retention of control?[53] Did anyone possess-

---

45. Weinberger v. UOP, Inc., 457 A.2d 701 (Del. 1983).

46. Id. at 710.

47. Id. at 711.

48. See Lynch v. Vickers Energy Corp., 383 A.2d 278, 281 (Del. 1977), and discussion supra section 3.03.

49. Pepper v. Litton, 308 U.S. 295, 306-7, 84 L.Ed. 281, 60 S.Ct. 238, 245 (1939).

50. Case v. New York Cent. R.R., 15 N.Y.2d 150, 204 N.E.2d 643, 646 (1965).

51. Treadway Cos. v. Care Corp., 638 F.2d 357, 382 (2d Cir. 1980).

52. Howitz v. Southwest Forest Indus., Inc., 604 F. Supp. 1130, 1134 (D. Nev. 1985).

53. Enterra Corp. v. SGS Assocs., 600 F. Supp. 678, 686 (E.D. Pa. 1985).

ing superior knowledge mislead any shareholder by the use of corporate information to which the shareholder was not privy?[54]

All such points may have some relevance in the judicial scrutiny of the transaction. Fairness in this context may be equated to conduct by a theoretical, wholly independent board of directors acting upon a matter before them.[55]

§ 3.07. Use of corporate funds to obtain or maintain control.

Although the courts frequently profess that "actions taken for perpetuation of control are not only suspect but are vulnerable to judicial correction,"[56] the record is less dogmatic.

It is generally recognized that, in the course of defending their position of control, directors may use corporate funds to purchase the corporation's stock and to solicit proxies to be voted in support of management.[57] Such activities are authorized by case law in some jurisdictions[58] and by statutes in others.[59] If, however, the sole and only purpose of the use of

---

54. Lank v. Steiner, 224 A.2d 244 (Del. 1966).

55. Weinberger v. UOP, Inc., supra note 45, at 709, n.7.

56. Kaplan, "Fiduciary Responsibility in the Management of the Corporation," 31 Bus. Law. (Special Issue) 883, 911 (1976).

57. E.g., Rosenfeld v. Fairchild Engine & Airplane Corp., 309 N.Y. 807, 130 N.E.2d 610 (1955).

58. Hall v. Trans-Lux Daylight Picture Screen Corp., 20 Del. Ch. 78, 171 A. 226 (1934); Rosenfeld v. Fairchild Engine & Airplane Corp., supra note 57; Selama-Dindings Plantations, Inc. v. Durham, 216 F. Supp. 104 (S.D. Ohio 1963), aff'd, 337 F.2d 949 (6th Cir. 1964).

59. Del. Code Ann. tit. 8, § 160, provides:

(a) Every corporation may purchase, redeem, receive, take or otherwise acquire, own and hold, sell, lend, exchange, transfer or otherwise dispose of, pledge, use and otherwise deal in and with its own shares; provided, however, that no corporation shall: ...
    (2) Purchase, for more than the price at which they may then be redeemed, any of its shares which are redeemable at the option of the corporation; or, ...
(c) Shares of its own capital stock belonging to the corporation or to another corporation if a majority of the shares entitled to vote in the election of directors of such other corporation is held, directly or indirectly, by the corporation, shall neither be entitled to vote or

corporate funds to purchase stock is to maintain control, that use may be contrary to law.[60] For example, where a board of directors issued shares to its president to pay a debt owed to him and to confer control of the corporation upon him, the then majority shareholder was granted injunctive relief to prevent the transaction.[61]

Despite some earlier cases holding that purchases to maintain control constituted breaches of fiduciary duty and of the corporate power,[62] the recent trend, especially in Delaware and New York, is to recognize management's right to defend its control and its policies at corporate expense.[63] For example, in struggles for corporate control, expenses incurred by management, including such proxy contest expenses as legal fees, proxy solicitors' fees, and public relations fees may be paid by the corporation and constitute "ordinary and necessary expenses of doing business."[64]

---

counted for quorum purposes. Nothing in this section shall be construed as limiting the right of any corporation to vote stock, including but not limited to its own stock, held by it in a fiduciary capacity.

Section 1701.35, Ohio Rev. Code Ann., authorizes a corporation to purchase its own shares under specified circumstances, which must be strictly adhered to. Lowry v. Sunday Creek Coal Co., 2 Ohio App. 2d 260, 207 N.E.2d 678 (1964). See also Ky. Rev. Stat. § 271A.030; Tenn. Code Ann. § 48-16-302.

60. See Hendricks v. Mill Eng'g & Supply Co., 68 Wash. 2d 490, 413 P.2d 811 (1966); Condec Corp. v. Lunkenheimer Co., 43 Del. Ch. 353, 239 A.2d 769 (1967).

61. Chicago Stadium Corp. v. Scallen, 530 F.2d 204 (8th Cir. 1976).

62. E.g., Elliott v. Baker, 194 Mass. 518, 80 N.E. 450 (1907); Andersen v. Albert & M.J. Andersen Mfg. Co., 325 Mass. 343, 90 N.E.2d 541 (1950); Gilchrist v. Highfield, 140 Wis. 476, 123 N.E. 102 (1909).

63. E.g., Hall v. Trans-Lux Daylight Picture Screen Corp., supra note 58; Kors v. Carey, 39 Del. Ch. 47, 158 A.2d 135 (1960); Rosenfeld v. Fairchild Engine & Airplane Corp., 309 N.Y. 168, 127 N.E.2d 291 (1955), reh'g denied, 309 N.Y. 807, 130 N.E.2d 610 (1955); Steinberg v. Adams, 90 F. Supp. 604 (S.D.N.Y. 1950).

64. Locke Mfg. Cos. v. United States, 237 F. Supp. 80, 89 (D. Conn. 1964). Cf. Sutasky v. United States, 325 F.2d 19 (5th Cir. 1963).

Precipitate action to repel a challenger may defeat its purpose. In *Bennett v. Propp*,[65] a corporation's board chairman wasted corporate funds when, in fact, the suspected challenger was not challenging. The Delaware Court of Chancery ruled in this case that the use of the corporate funds was improper. It held the chairman liable for the corporation's loss. However, the court exonerated the other directors on the theory that they had been forced to act in a sudden emergency.

Other significant decisions in this area concern: (1) the use of A company's funds to purchase control of B company for the benefit of C company, when A and C were under common control[66] and (2) use of assets of an acquired corporation to pay the purchase price of the acquisition.[67]

The Second Circuit in New York has approved the use of corporate funds to enjoin the violation of proxy rules by an insurgent group, thereby preventing that group from obtaining a shareholders' list. The theory was that while corporate harm would not necessarily result from a change of control, the corporation itself had an interest in the control transaction.[68]

The Williams Act[69] is important to the use of proxy funds to maintain control since it requires the filing of certain reports and schedules by any person whose acquisition within a given class of stock brings him to the beneficial ownership of more than five percent of that stock class.[70] This statute may have a restraining effect on corporate managers seeking to perpetuate themselves in office. In addition, there is the problem of the disclosure required by Section 10(b) of the Securi-

---

65. 41 Del. Ch. 14, 187 A.2d 405 (1962).

66. Condon v. Richardson, 411 F.2d 489 (7th Cir. 1969).

67. Madigan, Inc. v. Goodman, Fed. Sec. L. Rep. (CCH) ¶93,789 (N.D. Ill. 1972).

68. Studebaker Corp. v. Gittlin, 360 F.2d 692 (2d Cir. 1966).

69. Act of July 29, 1968, Pub. L. 90-439, 82 Stat. 454, 15 U.S.C. §§ 78l(l), 78m(d) to (e), 78n(d) to (f), as amended.

70. E.g., SEC Release 34-8392. See also Bath Indus., Inc. v. Blot, 305 F. Supp. 526 (E.D. Wis. 1969), aff'd, 427 F.2d 97 (7th Cir. 1970).

ties Exchange Act of 1934 and Rule 10b-5 promulgated thereunder. Since the purpose of a transaction is a "material fact,"[71] it is arguable that disclosure of an intention to maintain control will be necessary.[72] And disclosure may well be detrimental to control perpetuating efforts in some instances.

§ 3.08. Sale of corporate control.

Of particular interest in this area are the questions (1) whether a seller of control who sells his shares at a premium is liable to his corporation or its other stockholders for the excess over the current market price of the shares, and (2) whether he owes any obligation to arrange for an equal offer to be made available to minority stockholders.[73]

It is traditional that a controlling block of the shares of a corporation is usually worth more on the market than a noncontrolling block. Thus the sale by a controlling shareholder of his block of control shares at a premium over market value is not necessarily unlawful,[74] but the seller might expect his profit to be scrutinized by the courts if the sale caused corporate harm.[75]

The widely accepted general statement is that the seller of control is not required to share the premium with the minority shareholders.[76] Nonetheless, this subject has produced considerable litigation, and there are numerous court deci-

---

71. Surowitz v. Hilton Hotels Corp., 383 U.S. 363, 370, 15 L.Ed.2d 807, 812, 86 S.Ct. 845, reh'g denied, 384 U.S. 915 (1966).

72. Note, "Rule 10b-5 and Purchase by a Corporation of Its Own Shares," 61 Nw. U.L. Rev. 307 (1966). Cf. Cheff v. Mathes, 41 Del. Ch. 494, 199 A.2d 548 (1964); Lawrence v. Decca Records, Inc., 20 Misc. 2d 424, 195 N.Y.S.2d 431 (1959); Seagrave Corp. v. Mount, 212 F.2d 389 (6th Cir. 1954).

73. Kaplan, "Fiduciary Responsibility in the Management of the Corporation," 31 Bus. Law. (Special Issue) 888, 907 (1976).

74. Cf. Seagrave Corp. v. Mount, 212 F.2d 389, 395 (6th Cir. 1954).

75. See, e.g., Dale v. Thomas H. Temple Co., 186 Tenn. 69, 208 S.W.2d 344 (1947); Gerdes v. Reynolds, 28 N.Y.S.2d 622, 30 N.Y.S.2d 755 (1941).

76. Ruder, "Duty of Loyalty — A Law Professor's Status Report," 40 Bus. Law. 1383, 1394 (1985). See also Doleman v. Meiji Mut. Life Ins. Co., 727 F.2d 1480 (9th Cir. 1984).

sions purporting to carve out exceptions to the general statement. In one frequently cited case,[77] a derivative action by minority shareholders against a controlling shareholder was upheld when the sale of control was for the purpose of transferring a corporate asset made valuable by wartime demand. The seller was barred from appropriating the full value of the monopoly gain.

Another element to be considered in connection with the sale of control is that it is unlawful to buy or sell corporate directorships.[78] Whether a given transaction is a permissible sale of corporate control (with an agreed change in directors), rather than a prohibited sale of a directorship in return for a stock premium, is determined by the percentage of shares transferred. Thus, the payment of a premium for a clear majority of the outstanding shares is entirely proper even though there is an additional agreement containing the typical seriatim-resignation provisions for seating new directors.[79] On the other hand, if the shares sold are less than a controlling block and there is an accompanying transfer of control, or a sale of corporate office, the transfer is unlawful. In such a case a premium paid for the transfer of control is recoverable by the corporation, as is a bribe.[80]

It is generally true, however, that the right of control involves both stock ownership and position. Thus, the power to elect without position, or position alone (enforced by the use of proxy machinery, for example) may not be enough to con-

---

77. Perlman v. Feldmann, 219 F.2d 173, 178 (2d Cir.), cert. denied, 349 U.S. 952 (1955).

78. See, e.g., In re Lionel Corp., 151 N.Y.L.J. No. 24, at 14, col. 3, aff'd sub nom. In re Caplan's Petition, 20 A.D.2d 301, 246 N.Y.S.2d 913, aff'd mem., 14 N.Y.2d 679, 249 N.Y.S.2d 877, 198 N.E.2d 908 (1964), aff'd, 18 N.Y.2d 945, 277 N.Y.S.2d 144, 223 N.E.2d 568 (1966); Gerdes v. Reynolds, supra note 75; Bosworth v. Allen, 168 N.Y. 157, 61 N.E. 163 (1901).

79. E.g., Mayflower Hotel Stockholders Protective Comm. v. Mayflower Hotel Corp., 89 U.S. App. D.C. 171, 193 F.2d 666 (1951). See also Section 14(j) of the Securities Exchange Act of 1934 and SEC Rule 14f-1 as to disclosure before a change in the majority of a board of directors.

80. Haberman v. Murchison, 331 F. Supp. 180, 186 (S.D.N.Y. 1971), aff'd, 468 F.2d 1305 (2d Cir. 1972).

stitute control. The combination of position plus some stock represents control in most large, publicly held corporations.[81]

Among the states, California has taken a leading position where sale of control is involved. A 1969 decision[82] sustained a class action by minority shareholders of a savings and loan association against majority shareholders who were held to have damaged the minority by transferring the majority block to a newly formed holding company in exchange for shares of the holding company, without giving the minority an opportunity to participate in the exchange. The plaintiff contended that the defendants (1) breached the fiduciary duty they owed as controlling shareholders to minority shareholders, (2) used their control of the association for their own advantage to the detriment of the minority, and (3) created a conflict of interest. The defendants contended that as shareholders they owed no fiduciary duty to other shareholders, absent reliance on inside information, use of corporate assets, or fraud. Chief Justice Roger J. Traynor pointed out that California had repudiated that view long ago in favor of the rule that majority shareholders may not use their power or control to cause benefit to themselves or detriment to the minority.[83] He announced a rule of "inherent fairness from the viewpoint of the corporation and those interested therein" which he declared "applies alike to officers, directors, and controlling shareholders in the exercise of powers that are theirs by virtue of their position and to transactions wherein controlling shareholders seek to gain an advantage in the sale or transfer or use of their controlling block of shares."[84]

---

81. Letts, "Sales of Control Stock and the Rights of Minority Shareholders," 26 Bus. Law. 631, 639 (1971).

82. Jones v. H.F. Ahmanson & Co., 1 Cal. 3d 93, 81 Cal. Rptr. 592, 460 P.2d 464 (1969).

83. Citing, inter alia, Pepper v. Litton, 308 U.S. 295, 84 L.Ed. 281, 60 S.Ct. 238 (1939).

84. Jones v. H.F. Ahmanson & Co., note 82 supra, 1 Cal. 3d at 110, 81 Cal. Rptr. at 601, 460 P.2d at 472, citing Remillard Brick Co. v. Remillard-Dandini Co., 109 Cal. App. 2d 405, 420, 241 P.2d 66, 75 (1952); In re Sec. Fin. Co., 49 Cal.2d 370, 317 P.2d 1 (1957).

That decision gives support to the concept of "equal opportunity," which holds that no trading may be done, even among those with equal knowledge, at a price not generally available to other shareholders. At least one commentator[85] has found support for this rule in the *Perlman* case.[86] However, there is a strong indication in the decisions that the concept of equal opportunity, while nice theoretically, is simply not the law.[87]

§ 3.09. Duty to investigate motives of purchaser of controlling stock.

When a majority shareholder sells his shares, and with them transfers control of his corporation to the purchaser, he owes to the corporation a duty of reasonable investigation of the purchaser's motives and intent. In this context the seller's obligations are the same whether an individual owns the majority stock or a group of selling shareholders acts together through an agent.

The majority is not an absolute insurer against any wrongs that may occur after the transfer of control, or against any decisions by the new owners that may not be in the best interests of the minority. But if the seller of control is in a position to foresee the likelihood of fraud on the corporation or on the remaining shareholders, at the hands of the buyer, the seller has "a positive duty to investigate the motives and interest of the would-be purchaser." Unless a reasonable investigation shows that to a reasonable man no fraud is intended or likely to result, the seller may not transfer the control.[88]

---

85. Andrews, "The Stockholder's Right of Equal Opportunity in the Sale of Shares," 78 Harv. L. Rev. 505, 515 (1965).

86. Perlman v. Feldmann, supra note 77.

87. See, e.g., Claggett v. Hutchison, 585 F.2d 1259, 1264 (4th Cir. 1978); McDaniel v. Painter, 418 F.2d 545, 548 (10th Cir. 1969); Zetlin v. Hanson Holdings, Inc., 48 N.Y.2d 684, 421 N.Y.S.2d 877, 397 N.E.2d 387 (1979); Doleman v. Meiji Mut. Life Ins. Co., 727 F.2d 1480, 1483 (9th Cir. 1984).

88. Seinney v. Keebler Co., 480 F.2d 573, 577-78 (4th Cir. 1973); Claggett v. Hutchison, supra note 87; Doleman v. Meiji Mut. Life Ins. Co., supra note 87.

It is not necessary that the seller have actual notice that the buyer intends to loot the corporation. Such a requirement would place a premium on the "head in the sand" approach to corporate sales.[89] If the circumstances surrounding the proposed transfer would arouse the suspicions of a prudent man that the purchaser is irresponsible and apt to loot the corporation, the seller owes a duty to investigate the motives and intent of the purchaser.[90] The Ninth Circuit has upheld a judgment on a jury verdict in a derivative action against a corporate director charged with negligence in failing to investigate whether a change in control of his corporation would be inimical to its best interests. The loss resulted from an exchange of corporate assets for worthless shares of another corporation when the new interests took control.[91] When a seller had actual knowledge that his corporation's assets were used to finance its purchase or as security for the purchase, there was sufficient evidence to put him on notice and require such an investigation.[92] It is proper to apply the tests of common sense and sound business judgment to ascertain if the seller had warning that the corporation was in danger of being looted.[93]

The payment of a premium for the sale of the stock may be considered in determining whether suspicious circumstances existed so that the selling shareholder had a duty to investigate the motives and intent of the purchaser.[94] When it appeared that the premium was paid to obtain an option to require a majority of the directors to replace themselves, it

---

89. Seinney v. Keebler Co., supra note 88, at 577 n.6.

90. Jones v. H.F. Ahmanson & Co., 1 Cal. 3d 93, 110, 81 Cal. Rptr. 592, 460 P.2d 464 (1969); DeBaun v. First W. Bank & Trust Co., 46 Cal App. 3d 686, 120 Cal. Rptr. 354 (1975). Cf. Harman v. Willbern, 374 F. Supp. 1149 (D. Kan. 1974), aff'd, 520 F.2d 1333 (10th Cir. 1975).

91. DePinto v. Provident Sec. Life Ins. Co., 374 F.2d 37 (9th Cir.), cert. denied, 389 U.S. 822 (1967).

92. DeBaun v. First W. Bank & Trust Co., supra note 90.

93. See Levy v. American Beverage Corp., 265 A.D. 208, 38 N.Y.S.2d 517 (1942).

94. Insuranshares Corp. v. Northern Fiscal Corp., 35 F. Supp. 22 (E.D. Pa. 1940).

was held relevant to the question of improper motives for the stock purchase.[95]

§ 3.10. Purchase or sale of stock by directors or officers.

Generally, corporate officers or directors may deal as they please in their corporation's shares. They are not precluded by any fiduciary duty from buying and selling the stock.[96] However, the deal must be made in good faith and not otherwise in violation of any fiduciary duty.[97]

It is the general rule that a corporate officer or director is not prohibited from buying the shares of his own corporation, in a controlling number, even though he does so secretly.[98] The mere fact of such a purchase raises no inference of fraud or unfair dealing.[99] The failure of the officer or director to disclose to the seller inside information, gained by the director or officer in his official capacity, will not taint the transaction so long as he does not actually mislead the seller or perpetrate a fraud upon him.[100]

However, when a director purchases such stock from one of his corporation's shareholders, he may be required to disclose "special facts" of which he has knowledge. This doctrine imposes a limited fiduciary duty which arises when a director possesses special knowledge obtained by reason of his official position.[101] His duty is at least to disclose information relat-

---

95. Essex Universal Corp. v. Yates, 305 F.2d 572 (2d Cir. 1962).

96. SEC v. Chenery Corp., 318 U.S. 80, 88, 87 L.Ed. 626, 63 S.Ct. 454, 459 (1943).

97. Gammon v. Dain, 238 Mich. 30, 112 N.W. 957 (1927).

98. See Vulcanized Rubber & Plastics Co. v. Scheckter, 400 Pa. 405, 162 A.2d 400 (1960); Boss v. Boss, 98 R.I. 146, 200 A.2d 231 (1964).

99. E.g., Shaw v. Cole Mfg. Co., 132 Tenn. 210, 177 S.W. 479 (1915); Guaranty Laundry Co. v. Pulliam, 198 Okla. 667, 171 P.2d 1007 (1947); Voellmeck v. Harding, 166 Wash. 93, 6 P.2d 373 (1931).

100. See List v. Fashion Park, Inc., 340 F.2d 457 (2d Cir.), cert. denied sub nom. List v. Lerner, 382 U.S. 811, reh'g denied, 382 U.S. 933 (1965); Seitz v. Frey, 152 Minn. 170, 188 N.W. 266 (1922); cf. Haverland v. Lane, 89 Wash. 557, 154 P. 1118 (1916).

101. Hobart v. Hobart Estate Co., 26 Cal. 2d 412, 159 P.2d 958 (1945). But cf. James Blackstone Mem. Library Ass'n v. Gulf, M. & O.R.R., 264 F.2d 445 (7th Cir. 1959).

ing to the true financial condition of the corporation[102] and he
may be required to disclose all material facts known to him
which affect the value of the stock.[103]

When a director volunteers information to an owner of the
corporation's stock,[104] or when such owner inquires of him,[105]
the director must speak fully, frankly, and honestly and conceal nothing to the disadvantage of the selling shareholder.[106]
Relief by way of rescission[107] or damages for fraud or concealment[108] may be obtained by a selling shareholder who is a
director.

Directors have been held liable in the purchase of shares
when, at the time of the purchase, the directors knowingly
failed to disclose to the selling shareholders that the corporation, through its directors, was seriously considering the sale
of the entire company.[109]

§ 3.11. Appropriation of corporate opportunity.

A director's fiduciary duty to his corporation requires him
to avoid usurping or misappropriating business opportunities
belonging to the corporation. Thus, a director is obliged to
make a business opportunity available to his corporation
prior to taking it, directly or indirectly, for his own benefit.[110]

---

102. Diamond v. Oreamuno, 24 N.Y.2d 494, 301 N.Y.S.2d 78, 248 N.E.2d
910 (1969).

103. Buckley v. Buckley, 230 Mich. 504, 202 N.W. 955, 956 (1925).

104. See, e.g., Northern Trust Co. v. Essaness Theatres Corp., 348 Ill.
App. 134, 108 N.E. 493 (1952).

105. American Trust Co. v. California W. States Life Ins. Co. 15 Cal. 2d
42, 98 P.2d 497 (1940); Hacker v. Kyle, 211 Wis. 584, 248 N.W. 134 (1933).

106. Low v. Wheeler, 207 Cal. App. 2d 477, 24 Cal. Rptr. 538 (1962).

107. Johnson v. Mansfield Hardwood Lumber Co., 159 F. Supp. 104
(W.D. La. 1958), aff'd, 263 F.2d 748 (5th Cir. 1959).

108. Buckley v. Buckley, supra note 103; Bakus v. Kirsch, 264 Mich. 73,
249 N.W. 469 (1933), aff'd, 264 Mich. 339, 249 N.W. 872 (1933). As to
measure of damages, see Hacker v. Kyle, supra note 105; Hotchkiss v.
Fischer, 139 Kan. 333, 31 P.2d 37 (1934).

109. Dungan v. Colt Indus., Inc., 582 F.2d 832 (N.D. Ill. 1982).

110. Kerrigan v. Unity Sav. Ass'n, 68 Ill. 2d 20, 317 N.E.2d 39 (1974);
Duffy v. Cross Country Indus., Inc., 57 A.D.2d 1063, 395 N.Y.S.2d 852
(1977).

It has been said that while this rule is easy to state, it is difficult to apply, largely because of the problem of determining whether such a business opportunity belonged to the corporation.[111] If there is presented to a corporate officer or director (1) a business opportunity which his corporation is financially able to undertake, (2) from its nature the opportunity is in the line of the corporation's business and of practical advantage to it, (3) the corporation has an interest or a reasonable expectancy in the opportunity, and (4) by embracing the opportunity the self-interest of the officer or director will be brought into conflict with that of his corporation, such officer or director is precluded from seizing the opportunity for himself.[112]

In the various states, greater emphasis may be placed upon different parts of the above tests. The "line of business" test has a substantial following.[113] Other tests often applied are the "interest or expectancy" test,[114] and the "fairness" test.[115] Any test must be applied reasonably and sensibly to the facts and circumstances of a particular case.

New York has held that a director may not exploit an opportunity for himself, even if his corporation is not financially able to undertake it.[116] And Minnesota holds that if a corporation has no interest or expectancy, the opportunity is a personal one, not a corporate one.[117] Delaware decisions

---

111. Miller v. Miller, 301 Minn. 207, 222 N.W.2d 71 (1974).

112. Id., citing Guth v. Loft, Inc., 23 Del. Ch. 255, 271, 5 A.2d 503, 510 (1939). See also Diedrick v. Helm, 217 Minn. 483, 493, 14 N.W.2d 913, 919 (1944).

113. See Annotation, "What business opportunities are in 'line of business' of corporation for purposes of determining whether a corporate opportunity was presented?," 77 A.L.R.3d 961 (1977).

114. E.g., Lagarde v. Anniston Lime & Stone Co., 126 Ala. 496, 28 So. 199 (1900); Cox & Perry, Inc. v. Perry, 334 So. 2d 867 (Ala. 1976).

115. E.g., Durfee v. Durfee & Canning, Inc., 323 Mass. 187, 80 N.E.2d 522 (1948).

116. Irving Trust Co. v. Deutsch, 73 F.2d 121 (2d Cir. 1934), cert. denied, 294 U.S. 708, reargument denied, 294 U.S. 733 (1935). See also infra section 3.13.

117. Diedrick v. Helm, supra note 112. See also Abbott Redmont Thinlits Corp. v. Redmont, 485 F.2d 85, 88 (2d Cir. 1973).

continue to assert that the corporate opportunity doctrine is a manifestation of the general rule that an officer or director owes to his corporation the utmost good faith and individual loyalty.[118]

Commentators have considered whether there should be a different rule as to corporate opportunities applicable to closely held, relatively small corporations as compared to public corporations, especially large ones. Because a corporate opportunity is a corporate asset, the reasons for forbidding its appropriation are the same as those which prohibit corporate agents and fiduciaries from unilaterally taking corporate property for themselves.[119] Some state statutes limit that rule to appropriations which are in violation of a director's duties.[120] Such a limitation appears to conflict with the general principle that under both efficiency in corporate management, and equity, a corporate executive has no right to take a corporation's opportunity for himself.[121]

In the case of public corporations, a categorical rule against a director's self-dealing should apply with the same force as in closely held companies. The considerations of the dependence of shareholders and their necessary reliance upon the loyalty of the directors has been compared with the dependence and reliance by a trust beneficiary upon his trustee.[122]

Only full disclosure to the principal and the informed consent of the principal will allow an agent or a fiduciary to profit from information or resources obtained by him in his position.[123]

---

118. Science Accessories Corp. v. Summagraphics Corp., 425 A.2d 957 (Del. 1980); In re Trim-lean Meat Prods., Inc., 4 B.R. 243 (Bankr. D. Del. 1980).

119. Brudney & Clark, "A New Look at Corporate Opportunities," 94 Harv. L. Rev. 997, 999 (1981).

120. See, e.g., Ga. Code Ann. § 22-714(a)(i)(C) [now Ga. Code Ann. § 14-2-153(a)(1)(C)], construed in Southeast Consultants, Inc. v. McCrary Eng'g Corp., 246 Ga. 503, 273 S.E.2d 112 (1980).

121. Brudney & Clark, supra note 119, at 999.

122. Id. at 1023.

123. See Knauss, "Corporate Governance — A Moving Target," 79 Mich. L. Rev. 478, 496 (1981).

§ 3.12. Value of opportunity to corporation.

One of the elements of the corporate opportunity doctrine is that the opportunity must be one which is of value or importance to the corporation. In applying its "two-step" process for determining the ultimate question of liability for a wrongful appropriation of a corporate opportunity, the Minnesota court inquired whether the business opportunity was of sufficient importance and was so closely related to the existing or prospective activity of the corporation as to warrant judicial sanctions against its personal acquisition by a managing officer or director.[124] Thus, the court recognized the concept of the value of the opportunity to the corporation as an essential element of the problem.

It has been held that the corporate opportunity doctrine should not be used to bar corporate directors from purchasing any property which might be useful to the corporation, but only to prevent their acquisition of property which the corporation needs or is seeking, or which they are otherwise under a duty to the corporation to acquire for it.[125]

Whether the corporation profits or suffers a loss from the appropriation of a corporate opportunity is not controlling. If the opportunity was of value to the corporation and was appropriated, the directors are liable for their gains, despite a corporate profit in the transaction.[126]

§ 3.13. Corporation's inability to accept opportunity.

The trend of the 1980's decisions is that unless a corporation is financially insolvent and not merely unable to obtain credit or pay current bills, its financial inability to take advantage of a business opportunity will not absolve an officer or director of liability for usurping the opportunity.[127] The

---

124. Miller v. Miller, 301 Minn. 207, 222 N.W.2d 71 (1974).

125. Burg v. Horn, 380 F.2d 897 (2d Cir. 1947). See also Johnston v. Greene, 35 Del. Ch. 479, 121 A.2d 919 (1956); Black v. Parker Mfg. Co., 329 Mass. 105, 106 N.E.2d 544 (1952).

126. Farber v. Servan Land Co., 662 F.2d 375 (5th Cir. 1971).

127. Klinicki v. Lundgren, 67 Ore. App. 160, 689 P.2d 1250 (1984), aff'd, 298 Ore. 662, 695 P.2d 906 (1985); Nicholson v. Evans, 642 P.2d 727 (Utah 1982).

director or officer has the burden of proof. Otherwise, said an Oregon court, corporate officers would be encouraged to make inaccurate and self-serving evaluations of the corporation's financial health, which could compromise the duty of loyalty.[128]

If a corporation's directors are uncertain of its ability to undertake an engagement, they need not enter into it; but if they do embark upon the venture, they may not thereafter substitute themselves for the corporation and divert possible benefits into their own pockets.[129] A director's duty of undivided loyalty and his obligation to act with the utmost good faith in his relation to the corporation prevent the exploitation of a corporation's opportunities for the director's personal benefit.[130]

An opportunity ceases to be "corporate" and becomes "personal" to the director or officer, if the corporation is unable to accept the opportunity.[131] Among factors to be considered in determining such inability are the following:

> (1) The corporation may not be able to finance the opportunity. This may arise where the corporation is insolvent,[132] or otherwise lacks the financial ability to undertake the transaction.[133] If the involved director-officer was responsible for his corporation's lack of funds, he could not take advantage of it,[134] but a di-

---

128. Klinicki v. Lundgren, supra note 127.

129. Durfee v. Durfee & Canning, Inc., 323 Mass. 187, 80 N.E.2d 522 (1948).

130. Diedrick v. Helm, 217 Minn. 483, 14 N.W.2d 913 (1944).

131. Schildberg Rock Prods. Co. v. Brooks, 258 Iowa 759, 140 N.W.2d 132 (1966).

132. Hart v. Bell, 222 Minn. 69, 23 N.W.2d 375 (1946); Carper v. Frost Oil Co., 72 Colo. 345, 211 P. 370 (1972). See also Lipkin v. Jacoby, 42 Del. Ch. 1, 202 A.2d 572 (1964).

133. Santarelli v. Katz, 270 F.2d 762 (7th Cir. 1959); Note, "Financial Inability as a Defense Under the Corporate Opportunity Doctrine," 39 Ky. L. Rev. 229 (1951).

134. See Daloisio v. Peninsula Land Co., 43 N.J. Super. 79, 127 A.2d 385 (1956). Cf. Irving Trust Co. v. Deutsch, 73 F.2d 121 (2d Cir. 1934), cert. denied, 294 U.S. 708 (1935).

rector-officer is not compelled to advance his own money to his corporation so it can accept a corporate opportunity.[135]

(2) There may be legal barriers to prevent the corporation from accepting the opportunity.[136] Such barriers might be found in the state law under which the corporation operates.[137]

   (a) The transaction may be ultra vires. However, the director may not assert the claim of ultra vires in order to justify his appropriation of the opportunity.[138]

   (b) The corporation's charter or code of regulations might prevent it from accepting the opportunity.[139] In this connection it should be pointed out that the interested directors act at their peril if they take over a corporate opportunity on the theory that their corporation could not accept it and are later proved wrong.[140]

(3) It may be the settled policy of the corporation not to engage in a particular line of business.[141]

(4) The corporation may have tried without success to obtain the opportunity.[142]

(5) The corporation may have previously rejected the opportunity.[143]

---

135. Urban J. Alexander Co. v. Trinkle, 311 Ky. 635, 224 S.W.2d 923 (1949); Hart v. Bell, supra note 132.

136. Urban J. Alexander Co. v. Trinkle, supra note 135.

137. E.g., Thilco Timber Co. v. Sawyer, 236 Mich. 401, 210 N.W. 204 (1926).

138. Hawaiian Int'l Fin., Inc. v. Pablo, 53 Haw. 149, 488 P.2d 1172 (1971).

139. Cf. Urban J. Alexander Co. v. Trinkle, supra note 135.

140. Durfee v. Durfee & Canning, Inc., 323 Mass. 187, 80 N.E.2d 522 (1948). Cf. Paulman v. Kritzer, 74 Ill. App. 2d 284, 219 N.E.2d 541 (1966), aff'd, 88 Ill. 2d 101, 230 N.E.2d 253 (1967).

141. Urban J. Alexander Co. v. Trinkle, supra note 135.

142. Northwestern Terra Cotta Corp. v. Wilson, 74 Ill. App. 2d 38, 219 N.E.2d 860 (1966).

143. Bisbee v. Midland Linseed Prods. Co., 19 F.2d 24 (8th Cir. 1927). See infra section 3.14.

§ 3.14. Corporation's refusal or failure to accept opportunity.

Where a corporation has declined to avail itself of a business opportunity, or has declined the opportunity for business reasons, a director or officer may take up the opportunity without incurring liability to account to the corporation for his profits.[144]

If it is the settled policy of the corporation not to engage in a particular line of business, the same rule applies. The mere fact that an officer or director learned of the opportunity while in the course of his employment will not bar him from acquiring it for himself.[145] And there is some authority that if the interested directors make a full disclosure and their corporation does not undertake the venture, they may do so.[146] But a significant decision involving a nonprofit corporation indicates that an interested party may not be free to take advantage of the opportunity.[147] Although the trustees of the incorporated nonprofit fishing club had previously decided not to purchase their clubhouse site, the club's president, who did purchase it, was held to be a constructive trustee obligated to account to the club for the property.

§ 3.15. Engaging in competitive enterprise.

Another element of a director's duty of loyalty to the corporation is that he will not engage in business in direct competition with the corporation.[148] Disputes in this area are decided on a case-by-case basis.[149]

---

144. Thilco Timber Co. v. Sawyer, 236 Mich. 401, 210 N.W. 204 (1926). See also supra section 3.13.

145. Cf. Diedrick v. Helm, 217 Minn. 483, 14 N.W.2d 913 (1944).

146. Thilco Timber Co. v. Sawyer, supra note 144. See also Schildberg Rock Prods. Co. v. Brooks, 258 Iowa 759, 140 N.W.2d 132 (1966).

147. Mile-O-Mo Fishing Club, Inc. v. Noble, 62 Ill. App. 2d 50, 210 N.E.2d 12 (1965). See also Knutsen v. Frushour, 92 Idaho 37, 436 P.2d 521 (1968).

148. E.g., Foley v. D'Agostino, 21 A.D. 60, 248 N.Y.S.2d 121 (1964).

149. Burg v. Horn, 380 F.2d 897 (2d Cir. 1967); Johnston v. Greene, 35 Del. Ch. 479, 121 A.2d 919 (1956).

The mere fact of a director's fiduciary relationship to the corporation will not foreclose him from engaging in an independent business in competition with the corporation.[150] If he does, however, he is required to act in good faith[151] and to avoid hindering the corporation's activities.[152]

The organization of a rival company for the express purpose of taking business away from the corporation, or a director's use of his position to prevent his corporation from competing effectively with him, is forbidden by his fiduciary relationship.[153] An officer or director is likewise not allowed to use his official position to make a private or secret profit for himself. If he obtains such an advantage by virtue of his position, he must make the benefit available to his corporation.[154]

When an officer or director is engaged in a competing enterprise, he cannot actively use his position and authority to prevent his corporation from seeking business in competition with his personal enterprise.[155] And he may not go into a competing venture and use it to injure or cripple the business of the corporation in which he is an officer or director.[156] He is not entitled to be compensated by his corporation for services

---

150. See Guth v. Loft, Inc., 23 Del. Ch. 255, 5 A.2d 503 (1939); Tovrea Land & Cattle Co. v. Linsenmeyer, 100 Ariz. 107, 412 P.2d 47 (1966).

151. Raines v. Toney, 228 Ark. 1170, 313 S.W.2d 802 (1958); Hopper v. Western Tablet & Stationery Corp., 66 F.2d 172 (6th Cir. 1933).

152. Patient Care Servs., S.C. v. Segal, 32 Ill. App. 3d 1021, 347 N.E.2d 471 (1975).

153. See, e.g., Storey v. Excelsior Shook & Lumber Co., 198 A.D. 505, 190 N.Y.S. 614 (1921); Singer v. Carlisle, 26 N.Y.S.2d 172 (1940), aff'd, 261 A.D. 897, 26 N.Y.S.2d 320, appeal denied, 261 A.D. 956, 27 N.Y.S.2d 190 (1941); Golden Rod Mining Co. v. Bukvich, 108 Mont. 569, 92 P.2d 316 (1939).

154. Golden Rod Mining Co. v. Bukvich, supra note 153; Rowland v. Kable, 174 Va. 343, 6 S.E.2d 633 (1940); Guth v. Loft, Inc., supra note 150. See also infra section 3.23.

155. See, e.g., Evangelista v. Queens Structure Corp., 28 Misc. 2d 962, 212 N.Y.S.2d 781 (1961); Hall v. Dekker, 46 Cal. App. 2d 783, 115 P.2d 15 (1941).

156. Bancroft-Whitney Co. v. Glen, 64 Cal. 2d 327, 49 Cal. Rptr. 825, 411 P.2d 921 (1966).

performed for it while also engaged in competitive activities antagonistic to the corporate interests.[157]

In connection with activities in competing businesses, it is also appropriate to consider employment contracts which restrict the rights of employees to engage in a competing business after termination of their employment. Here, the reasonableness of such contracts is of prime importance. In each case there must be a determination whether the term of the contract and its area of coverage were too broad and imposed undue hardships.[158]

There would appear to be a plain violation of fiduciary duty when a corporation's business is sold and its officers and directors agree not to compete with the buyer, but then organize a new corporation to be used by them in conducting a competitive enterprise.[159]

§ 3.16. Intercorporate transactions.

When directors of a Delaware corporation are on both sides of a transaction, they are required to demonstrate their utmost good faith and the most scrupulous inherent fairness of the bargain. Such directors have the burden of establishing its entire fairness, sufficient to pass the test of careful scrutiny by the courts.[160]

In the case stating that rule, the Delaware Supreme Court went on to say:

> Thus, individuals who act in a dual capacity as directors of two corporations, one of which is parent and the other subsidiary, owe the same duty of good management to both corporations, and in the absence of an independent negotiating structure or the directors' total abstention

157. Wilshire Oil Co. v. Riffe, 406 F.2d 1061 (10th Cir.), cert. denied, 396 U.S. 843 (1969).

158. Mantek Div. of NCH Corp. v. Share Corp., 780 F.2d 702 (7th Cir. 1986); In re Talmage, 758 F.2d 162 (6th Cir. 1985).

159. United Aircraft Corp. v. Boreen, 413 F.2d 694 (3d Cir. 1969). See also General Bronze Corp. v. Schmeling, 208 Wis. 565, 243 N.W. 469 (1932).

160. Weinberger v. UOP, Inc., 457 A.2d 701, 710 (Del. 1983).

from any participation in the matter, this duty is to be exercised in the light of what is best for both companies.[161]

In any situation where the transacting corporations have one or more common directors, their dealings are subject to judicial scrutiny to determine whether they are fair to both companies. Their contracts may be avoided, but only if unfair. And "the directors who would sustain the challenged transaction have the burden of overcoming the presumption against the validity of the transaction by showing its fairness."[162] If that burden is not sustained, the transaction may be set aside, or it may be held valid with an award of damages for any losses suffered by either corporation.

If an unfair advantage is taken by persons who are directors or officers of both involved corporations, the transaction may be set aside and the errant directors required to account to the corporation which was damaged.[163] The fact that both corporations have common directors is a circumstance to be considered in testing the validity and good faith of the transactions between them.[164]

Because of the closeness with which the courts scrutinize such intercorporate transactions,[165] and because of the difficulty of reconciling some of the cases in this area, several states have statutes which fix guidelines for determining the validity of these dealings. Typical are the California,[166] Dela-

---

161. Id. at 710-11, citing Warshaw v. Calhoun, 221 A.2d 487, 492 (Del. 1966).

162. Shlensky v. South Parkway Bldg. Corp., 19 Ill. 2d 268, 166 N.E.2d 793 (1960); Geddes v. Anaconda Copper Mining Co., 254 U.S. 590, 65 L.Ed. 425, 41 S.Ct. 209 (1921).

163. See Wallace v. Malooly, 4 Ill. 2d 86, 98, 122 N.E.2d 274 (1954); Dixmoor Golf Club v. Evans, 325 Ill. 612, 156 N.E. 785 (1927). Cf. Corsicana Nat'l Bank v. Johnson, 251 U.S. 68, 64 L.Ed. 141, 40 S.Ct. 82 (1919).

164. United States v. Delaware, L. & W.R.R., 238 U.S. 516, 59 L.Ed. 1438, 35 S.Ct. 873 (1915).

165. Swanson v. Tomlinson Lumber Mills, Inc., 239 N.W.2d 216 (Minn. 1976).

166. Cal. Corp. Code § 310.

ware[167] and New York[168] statutes, which provide that a transaction between corporations in which one or more directors have common financial interests will not be void or voidable for this reason alone. In differing language, but with similar effect, such statutes provide for good faith disclosure of the interest, relationship, and transaction, together with authorization, approval, or ratification by disinterested directors or shareholders.

Sections 8 and 10 of the Clayton Act[169] deal with the subject of interlocking directorates. Injunctive relief and actions for damages may result from violations of such provisions.[170]

Also, it has become customary to include provisions relating to interlocking directorates in the articles of incorporation or bylaws of modern corporations. Such provisions usually permit contracts between corporations with common directors and allow interested directors to contract with their corporations and have had favorable treatment by the courts,[171] although they afford no exoneration of directors whose dealings are in bad faith.[172]

§ 3.17. Voting by interested directors.

In conflict of interest transactions[173] the fact that interested directors vote in favor of a contract with their corporation, in which they are personally interested, will not vitiate the contract, if the interested directors' presence was not necessary for a quorum and their votes were not required to

---

167. Del. Code Ann. tit. 8, § 144.

168. N.Y. Bus. Corp. Law § 713.

169. 15 U.S.C. § 19.

170. E.g., United States v. W.T. Grant Co., 345 U.S. 629, 97 L.Ed. 1303, 73 S.Ct. 894 (1953); Klinger v. Baltimore & O.R.R., 432 F.2d 506 (2d Cir. 1970).

171. E.g., Lipkin v. Jacoby, 42 Del. Ch. 1, 202 A.2d 572 (1964); Piccard v. Sperry Corp., 48 F. Supp. 465 (S.D.N.Y. 1943), aff'd, 152 F.2d 462 (2d Cir.), cert. denied, 328 U.S. 845 (1946).

172. See Irwin v. West End Dev. Co., 342 F. Supp. 687 (D. Colo. 1972), modified, 481 F.2d 34 (10th Cir. 1973).

173. See supra section 3.02.

obtain a majority to approve the transaction.[174] This rule may, of course, be varied by any applicable statutory provisions and by the articles of incorporation.[175]

The importance of being aware of the relevant statutory provisions in any given case is emphasized by the trend to include in statutory provisions relating to interested directors such a statement as the following:

> Common or interested directors may be counted in determining the presence of a quorum at a meeting of the board of directors or of a committee which authorizes the contract or transaction.[176]

Even where such statutes are in effect, it appears that there are three principal rules which apply in various jurisdictions. They are:

(1) Such a contract or transaction is voidable at the option of the corporation on the basis of the conflicting interest alone. This appears to be the majority rule.[177]

(2) Such a contract or transaction is voidable at the option of the corporation unless the interested director sustains the burden of proving the good faith of the

---

174. See Rinn v. Asbestos Mfg. Co., 101 F.2d 344 (7th Cir.), cert. denied, 308 U.S. 555 (1939). Cf. Munson v. Syracuse G. & C. Ry., 103 N.Y. 59, 8 N.E. 355 (1886); Everett v. Phillips, 288 N.Y. 227, 43 N.E.2d 18, reargument denied, 289 N.Y. 625, 43 N.Y.2d 841, 289 N.Y. 675, 45 N.E.2d 176 (1942).

175. See, e.g., Piccard v. Sperry Corp., 48 F. Supp. 465 (S.D.N.Y. 1943), aff'd, 152 F.2d 462 (2d Cir.), cert. denied, 328 U.S. 845 (1946); and 19 Am. Jur. 2d Corporations § 1292.

176. Del. Code Ann. tit. 8, § 144(b). See also N.Y. Bus. Corp. Law § 713(c); Ohio Rev. Code Ann. § 1701.60(A)(2).

177. Cases from various states are collected in the footnotes of 6 Cavitch, Business Organizations § 127.05[2] (1969); 19 Am. Jur. 2d Corporations § 1293; 3 Fletcher, Cyclopedia of Corporations § 924 (perm. ed. 1975); see also Point Trap Co. v. Manchester, 98 R.I. 49, 199 A.2d 592 (1964); State ex rel. Hayes Oyster Co. v. Keypoint Oyster Co., 64 Wash. 2d 375, 391 P.3d 979 (1964); Miller v. Ortman, 235 Ind. 641, 136 N.E.2d 17 (1956); Zahn v. Transamerica Corp., 162 F.2d 36, 44 (3d Cir. 1947). But cf. Chelrob, Inc. v. Barrett, 293 N.Y. 442, 57 N.E.2d 825 (1944).

transaction and its fairness from the viewpoint of the corporation.[178]

(3) Such a contract or transaction is void.[179]

In any event and under whichever governing principle, the dealings of directors with the corporation they were elected to serve are subjected to rigorous scrutiny. Where any one of their contracts or engagements with the corporation is challenged, the burden is usually upon the directors to sustain it.[180]

In some instances there is a problem because an interested director is able to dominate the other members of the board. Such dominance may occur even when he abstains from voting.[181] But to vitiate a transaction with him usually requires some evidence of dominance other than the mere fact that he is a majority or controlling shareholder.[182]

§ 3.18. Ratification by shareholders or disinterested directors.

Transactions of officers or directors which are void, illegal or contrary to public policy cannot be ratified.[183] Otherwise,

---

178. Cases from various states are collected in the footnotes of 3 Fletcher, Cyclopedia of Corporations § 931 (perm. ed. 1975); 19 Am. Jur. 2d Corporations § 1291, and 10 C.J.S. Corporations § 781. See also Lipkin v. Jacoby, 42 Del. Ch. 1, 202 A.2d 572 (1964).

179. Cases from the jurisdictions adhering to this rule are collected in the footnotes to 3 Fletcher, Cyclopedia of Corporations § 917 (perm. ed. 1975). See also Comment, "Principal and Agent: Dual Agency Without Knowledge of Either Principal, Rescission of Contract So Entered Into," 14 Calif. L. Rev. 239 (1926).

180. Pepper v. Litton, 308 U.S. 295, 84 L.Ed. 281, 60 S.Ct. 238 (1939), citing Geddes v. Anaconda Copper Mining Co., 254 U.S. 590, 65 L.Ed. 425, 41 S.Ct. 209 (1921). See also Note, "The Fairness Test of Corporate Contracts with Interested Directors," 61 Harv. L. Rev. 335 (1948).

181. Globe Woolen Co. v. Utica Gas & Elec. Co., 224 N.Y. 483, 121 N.E. 378, 380-81 (1918).

182. Blish v. Thompson Automatic Arms Corp., 30 Del. Ch. 538, 64 A.2d 581 (1948). Cf. Fowle Mem. Hosp. Co. v. Nicholson, 189 N.C. 44, 126 S.E. 94 (1925).

183. Sellers v. Head, 261 Ala. 212, 73 So. 2d 747 (1954); Continental Assur. Co. v. Supreme Constr. Corp., 375 F.2d 378 (5th Cir. 1967).

where there is no fraud and the shareholders are supplied with full knowledge of the transaction, they may ratify agreements which would otherwise be voidable at the option of the corporation.[184] It has been pointed out that such a contract is not validated by the ratification, it always was valid unless avoided or repudiated by the corporation.[185]

An Ohio case holds that a disinterested majority of the shareholders has the power to ratify directors' frauds, provided there is no fraud in inducing or effecting such ratification.[186] In the case so holding, Judge James F. Bell went on to state:

> Since a majority of shareholders can ratify the actions of the directors, and since, in the present cause, a majority have so ratified, it is essential that some affirmative action be taken by the plaintiff in order to negate that ratification. [In a derivative suit, such] affirmative action must be in the form of a demand made on the shareholders.

The subject of full disclosure prior to ratification is of major significance. There must have been an intentional relinquishment of known rights if a corporation is to be held to have ratified a breach of fiduciary duties.[187]

A challenged transaction found to be unfair to the corporation may nonetheless be upheld if ratified by a majority of disinterested directors or the majority of the shareholders. An interested director, involved in the challenged transaction, if

---

184. See, e.g., Hodge v. United States Steel Corp., 64 N.J. Eq. 807, 54 A. 1 (1903). Cf. Keenan v. Eshleman, 23 Del. Ch. 234, 2 A.2d 904 (1938); Miller v. Ortman, 235 Ind. 641, 136 N.E.2d 17 (1956); American Timber & Trading Co. v. Niedermeyer, 276 Ore. 1135, 558 P.2d 1211 (1976).

185. Union Pac. R.R. v. Credit Mobilier of America, 135 Mass. 367, 377 (1879).

186. Claman v. Robertson, 164 Ohio St. 61, 128 N.E.2d 429 (1955), citing Foss v. Harbottle [1832], 2 Hare 461 (Eng.) and Hawes v. Oakland, 104 U.S. 450, 26 L.Ed. 827 (1881).

187. State ex rel. Hayes Oyster Co. v. Keypoint Oyster Co., 64 Wash. 2d 375, 391 P.2d 979 (1964).

he is also a shareholder, may vote his shares to ratify his challenged act, under Texas law.[188]

If the board of directors could have authorized a transaction before it occurred, the board may ratify it, but not otherwise.[189] Transactions that shareholders could have authorized in the first instance may be ratified by them.[190]

A corporation may not repudiate a contract involving an interested director and retain the benefits of the contract, unless it was fraudulent or tainted with vice or immorality.[191] However, the retention of proceeds of an authorized transaction does not constitute ratification unless the ratifying body had full knowledge of all material facts of the transaction.[192]

When a director contends that his corporation has ratified a transaction entered into with him, the director has the burden of proving the ratification.[193]

§ 3.19. Contracts encouraging violation of duty.

The fiduciary relationship of corporate directors to their corporation requires them to administer the corporate affairs for the benefit of all the shareholders and to exercise their best care, skill, and judgment in the management of the corporation's business solely in its interest.[194] A director may not bargain away the discretion which he is expected to exercise at board meetings.[195] He has no right to sell his influence in

---

188. Gearhart Indus., Inc. v. Smith Int'l, Inc., 741 F.2d 707, 720 (5th Cir. 1984).

189. Boyce v. Chemical Plastics, 175 F.2d 839 (8th Cir.), cert. denied, 338 U.S. 828 (1949); Best Brewing Co. v. Klassen, 185 Ill. 37, 57 N.E. 20 (1900).

190. Michelson v. Duncan, 407 A.2d 211 (Del. 1979).

191. New York Trust Co. v. American Realty Co., 244 N.Y. 208, 155 N.E. 102 (1926); Keystone Copper Mining Co. v. Miller, 64 Ariz. 544, 164 P.2d 603 (1945).

192. Chesapeake & Potomac Tel. Co. v. Murray, 198 Md. 526, 84 A.2d 870 (1951).

193. Hill Dredging Corp. v. Risley, 18 N.J. 501, 114 A.2d 697 (1955).

194. Western States Life Ins. Co. v. Lockwood, 166 Cal. 185, 190, 135 P. 496, 498 (1913).

195. Seitz v. Michel, 148 Minn. 474, 181 N.W. 106 (1921).

the management of the company, or to enter into any agreement by which his official action would be influenced or controlled.[196] Such contracts have been held to be illegal and void.[197]

A contract in which a corporate director attempts to bind his discretionary vote violates public policy and is void. So directors could not bind themselves in advance to appoint designated persons to fill vacancies on the board.[198] Directors may not divest themselves of their fiduciary obligations in a contract.[199]

Among other contracts of this type which have been struck down by the courts are a contract whereby two directors agree to vote for each other,[200] a contract to resign as a director,[201] a contract, that if a particular officer's salary should be reduced, the directors would purchase his shares in the corporation,[202] and a contract to keep a person permanently in his position as an officer of the corporation.[203]

Such prohibitions grow out of the principle that a corporation is entitled to the uninfluenced judgment and sound discretion of its elected directors.

§ 3.20. Dominating directors or managers.

Dominating directors are common in closely held corporations and are found occasionally in public corporations. The influence and dominance of such a director may effectively control the other directors even though he refrains from voting or absents himself from the meetings when votes are

---

196. Gerdes v. Reynolds, 28 N.Y.S.2d 622, 30 N.Y.S.2d 755 (1941).

197. See, e.g., Ford v. Magee, 160 F.2d 457 (2d Cir. 1947); Odell v. Wells, 183 A.D. 282, 171 N.Y.S. 345 (1918).

198. Chapin v. Benwood Found., 402 A.2d 1205, 1210 (Del. Ch. 1979), aff'd sub nom. Harrison v. Chapin, 415 A.2d 1068 (Del. 1980).

199. Jewel Cos. v. Pay Less Drug Stores Northwest, 741 F.2d 1555 (9th Cir. 1984).

200. Lothrop v. Goudeau, 142 La. 342, 76 So. 794 (1917).

201. Forbes v. McDonald, 54 Cal. 98 (1880).

202. Odell v. Wells, supra note 197.

203. West v. Camden, 135 U.S. 507, 34 L.Ed. 254, 10 S.Ct. 833 (1890).

taken on matters in which he is personally interested.[204] It is
the rule that a dominating director cannot support his conflict-of-interest transaction on the ground that the other directors approved the transaction without his visible participation.[205]

When an interested director is in a position to direct, influence, or even control the action of the board of directors, it
may reasonably be contended that such a director is dealing
with himself.[206] The desires of such a director obviate the
interplay of diverse judgments among several members of the
board.[207]

The authority of the directors is conferred upon them as a
board, their action is expected to be taken as a group and not
individually, and a single director may not act for the corporation unless the board of directors has authorized him to do
so.[208] The circumstance that such a director is the controlling
shareholder does not change the foregoing principle,[209] and an
interested director who is actually the controlling authority
of the corporation cannot engage in self-dealing by transactions between himself and the corporation.[210]

The trend of the decisions since 1968 is to impose liability
upon controlling persons for injuries to those over whom they
are empowered to exercise control, whether the controlling
persons be dominant directors, controlling shareholders or
managing officers. Following *Jones v. H.F. Ahmanson and*

---

204. Cf. Globe Woolen Co. v. Utica Gas & Elec. Co., 170 A.D. 940, 154
N.Y.S. 1123 (1915), aff'd, 224 N.Y. 483, 121 N.E. 378 (1918).

205. Fowle Mem. Hosp. Co. v. Nicholson, 189 N.C. 44, 126 S.E. 94 (1925).
But cf. Deford v. Ballentine Realty Corp., 164 Va. 436, 180 S.E. 164 (1935).

206. Veeser v. Robinson Hotel Co., 275 Mich. 133, 266 N.W. 54 (1936).

207. Bingham v. Bell & Zoller Coal Co., 175 Ill. App. 469 (1912).

208. E.g., Hamlin v. Union Brass Co., 68 N.H. 292, 44 A. 385 (1895);
Dicks v. Clarence L. Boyd Co., 205 Okla. 383, 238 P.2d 315 (1951); Garey v.
Kelvinator Corp., 279 Mich. 174, 271 N.W. 723 (1937); Trethewey v. Green
River Gorge, 17 Wash. 2d 697, 186 P.2d 999 (1943).

209. Danglade & Robinson Mining Co. v. Mexico-Joplin Land Co., 190
S.W. 35 (Mo. App. 1916).

210. Veeser v. Robinson Hotel Co., supra note 206. See also Adams v.
Burke, 201 Ill. 395, 66 N.E. 236 (1903).

Company,[211] a California corporation's president was held liable for compelling his corporation to repay sums it owed him so rapidly as to impair its financial stability.[212] He was the dominant director and manager. The litigation arose out of a marital dispute. The court held he did not act in good faith in a proper fiduciary capacity.

Also following the *Ahmanson* case, Wisconsin has held that directors and managing officers occupy the position of quasitrustees toward all their stockholders and cannot claim that their personal self-interest and self-protection justify them in denying the rights of a minority shareholder.[213]

In the Third Circuit, under Delaware law, it was held that the issue of director "interest" or "domination" was largely a question of fact to be determined from all the relevant facts and circumstances of a particular case.[214] The court found "ample support" in the record for the District Court's conclusion that "Sinskey's domination ... was total, uninterrupted and unchallenged." Under those circumstances the court refused to evaluate Sinskey's transactions under the business judgment rule, but placed the burden upon him to demonstrate the "intrinsic fairness" to the corporation of each transaction.

§ 3.21. Majority shareholders.

A majority shareholder, or a group of shareholders who combine to form a majority, has a fiduciary duty to the corporation and to its minority shareholders if the majority shareholder dominates the board of directors and controls[215] the corporation.[216]

---

211. 1 Cal. 3d 93, 81 Cal. Rptr. 592, 460 P.2d 464 (1969).

212. Thrasher v. Thrasher, 27 Cal. App. 3d 23, 103 Cal. Rptr. 618 (1972).

213. Grognet v. Fox Valley Trucking Serv., 45 Wis. 2d 235, 172 N.W.2d 812 (1969).

214. Borden v. Sinskey, 530 F.2d 478, 495 (3d Cir. 1976), citing Puma v. Marriott, 283 A.2d 693 (Del. Ch. 1971), and Greene v. Allen, 35 Del. Ch. 242, 114 A.2d 916 (1955), rev'd on other grounds, 35 Del. Ch. 479, 121 A.2d 919 (1956).

215. 18 Am. Jur. 2d Corporations § 775.

216. In re Reading Co., 711 F.2d 509, 517 (3d Cir. 1983), construing Delaware law.

The American Law Institute (ALI) project,[217] in the black letter of Section 5.10, employs the term "dominating shareholder" instead of "majority shareholder" and defines it, in Section 1.12:

> "Dominating shareholder" means a shareholder who, either alone or pursuant to an arrangement or understanding with one or more other persons:
>
> (a) owns, and has the unrestricted power to vote, more than 50 percent of the outstanding voting securities of a corporation; or
>
> (b) otherwise in fact exercises control [§ 1.05] over the management of the business of the corporation or the transaction in question. A shareholder who either alone or pursuant to an arrangement or understanding with one or more other persons owns, or has the unrestricted power to vote, 25 percent or more of the outstanding voting securities of a corporation is presumed to exercise control over the management of the business of the corporation.

The ALI Comment on its Section 5.10 points out that the courts have generally taken the view that a dominating shareholder will have the burden of proving that transactions with a dominated corporation are fair.[218] Some decisions have stated that the standard to be applied in cases of self-dealing is "intrinsic fairness".[219] However, the rule of "entire fairness" appears to be the latest expression of the Delaware court.[220]

Self-dealing occurs when the majority shareholder, by virtue of domination, acts in such a way that the dominant party receives something of value to the exclusion of, and detriment

---

217. Principles of Corporate Governance: Analysis and Recommendations (Tent. Draft No. 5, 1986).

218. Id. at 155-56.

219. Borden v. Sinskey, supra note 214.

220. Weinberger v. UOP, Inc., 457 A.2d 701, 710 (Del. 1983). See also supra section 3.06.

to, the minority,[221] or when the minority is denied the right to participate in the benefits of the corporation.[222] A majority shareholder may not misuse his power to promote his personal interests at the expense of the corporation's interests.[223] To the minority shareholders, he owes a duty to exercise good faith, reasonable care and due diligence. When minority shareholders have no voice in management, the majority shareholder has a duty to protect the interests of the minority.[224]

Traditional theories of fiduciary obligations have failed to afford adequate protection to minority shareholders, particularly those in close corporations, whose "precarious position renders them particularly vulnerable to the vagaries of the majority." Hence, in California, a comprehensive rule of good faith and inherent fairness to the minority is the proper guideline for controlling shareholders.[225]

When the controlling shareholder of a closely held corporation acquired stock in another corporation substantially below its fair market value, to the detriment of his own corporation, the Iowa court held him responsible. It stated that its policy was "to put such fiduciaries beyond the reach of temptation and the enticement of illicit profit."[226]

In the Ninth Circuit, under Arizona law, it has been held that management actions which injure minority shareholders will be considered violative of management's fiduciary duties unless a "compelling business reason" for the actions can be shown.[227] In applying this test, the court balanced "the good

---

221. Burton v. Exxon Corp., 583 F. Supp 405, 415 (S.D.N.Y. 1984).

222. Orchard v. Covelli, 590 F. Supp. 1548, 1556 (W.D. Pa. 1984).

223. United States v. Byrum, 408 U.S. 125, 33 L.Ed.2d 238, 92 S.Ct. 2382, reh'g denied, 409 U.S. 898 (1972).

224. See Pepper v. Litton, 308 U.S. 295, 84 L.Ed. 281, 60 S.Ct. 238 (1939); Mason v. Pewabic Mining Co., 133 U.S. 50, 33 L.Ed. 524, 10 S.Ct. 224 (1890).

225. Jones v. H.F. Ahmanson & Co., 1 Cal. 3d 93, 81 Cal. Rptr. 592, 460 P.2d 464 (1969). Cf. Schoenbaum v. Firstbrook, 405 F.2d 215 (2d Cir. 1968), cert. denied, 395 U.S. 906 (1969).

226. Holden v. Constr. Mach. Co., 202 N.W.2d 348 (Iowa 1972).

227. Shivers v. Amerco, 670 F.2d 826, 832 (9th Cir. 1982).

to the corporation against the disproportionate advantage to the majority shareholders and incompetent management."[228]

Failure to establish and maintain an adequate system of internal accounting controls as required by the Foreign Corrupt Practices Act was one of several factors inducing a district court in Georgia to render judgment for the SEC.[229] The action involved the multifarious activities of a "controlling shareholder, chairman of the board, chief executive officer, and president" who played fast and loose with corporate procedures and records. In granting a permanent injunction the court held that the defendants had "exhibited a total disregard for the principles of full and fair disclosure mandated by the federal securities laws."

There is authority that a majority shareholder, acting as a result of his control of corporate functions, is prohibited from pre-empting business opportunities that rightly belong to his corporation. Such a shareholder may not make choices advantageous to himself and contrary to the corporate interest.[230]

§ 3.22. Confidential or inside information.

A corporation is entitled to keep confidential, information obtained and assembled in the course of conducting its business. Such information is a type of property to which the corporation has an exclusive right.[231] A director has a duty to use reasonable diligence to protect and safeguard his corporation's property, and he may not use it in his own personal interests, even if he causes no injury to the corporation.[232] An

---

228. Id. at 834, citing Klaus v. Hi-Shear Corp., 528 F.2d 225, 234 (9th Cir. 1975).

229. SEC v. World-Wide Coin Inv., Ltd., 567 F. Supp. 724 (N.D. Ga. 1983).

230. David J. Greene & Co. v. Dunhill Int'l, Inc., 249 A.2d 427 (Del. Ch. 1968), applying the rule of Guth v. Loft, Inc., 23 Del. Ch., 255, 5 A.2d 503 (1939).

231. Dolgow v. Anderson, 438 F.2d 825 (2d Cir. 1970); B.R. Paulsen & Co. v. Lee, 95 Ill. App. 2d 146, 237 N.E.2d 793 (1968).

232. Diamond v. Oreamuno, 24 N.Y.2d 494, 301 N.Y.S.2d 78, 248 N.E.2d 910 (1969). See also Burg v. Horn, 380 F.2d 897 (2d Cir. 1967).

officer or director[233] may be required to account to the corporation for any profits he derives[234] and may be enjoined from the misuse of such information.[235]

A director, officer, or employee who acquires trade secrets of the corporation during his employment and because of his relationship to the corporation is not permitted to use or disclose such trade secrets to the corporation's detriment.[236] Again, injunctive relief is available to the corporation when the disclosure constitutes an abuse of confidence.[237]

While these rules have been applied in actions involving trade secrets,[238] lists of insurance renewals,[239] and lists of a corporation's customers,[240] inside information as to corporate earnings,[241] a pending merger,[242] or a major ore strike[243] are included in the subjects of extensive federal and state court litigation.

---

233. Or employee, or stockholder. See Douthwaite, Attorney's Guide to Restitution 189, Example B (1977).

234. Diamond v. Oreamuno, supra note 232.

235. Water Servs., Inc. v. Tesco Chems., Inc., 410 F.2d 163 (5th Cir. 1969).

236. A.H. Emery Co. v. Marcan Prods. Corp., 389 F.2d 11 (2d. Cir. 1968), cert. denied, 393 U.S. 835 (1969). Cf. Diodes, Inc. v. Franzen, 260 Cal. App. 2d 244, 67 Cal. Rptr. 19 (1968).

237. See Space Aero Prods. Co. v. R.E. Darling Co., 238 Md. 93, 208 A.2d 74, cert. denied, 382 U.S. 843 (1965). But cf. Bancroft-Whitney Co. v. Glen, 64 Cal. 2d 327, 49 Cal. Rptr. 825, 411 P.2d 921 (1966).

238. E.g., Solo Cup Co. v. Paper Mach. Corp., 240 F. Supp. 126 (E.D. Wis. 1965), modified, 359 F.2d 754 (7th Cir. 1966).

239. Clark-Lami, Inc. v. Cord, 440 S.W.2d 737 (Mo. 1969).

240. Leo Silfen, Inc. v. Cream, 29 N.Y.2d 387, 328 N.Y.S.2d 423, 278 N.E.2d 636 (1972).

241. Diamond v. Oreamuno, 24 N.Y.2d 494, 301 N.Y.S.2d 78, 248 N.E.2d 910 (1969).

242. deHaas v. Empire Petroleum Co., 435 F.2d 1223 (10th Cir. 1970); Mader v. Armel, 402 F.2d 158 (6th Cir. 1968), cert. denied sub nom. Young v. Mader, 394 U.S. 930 (1969), cert. denied, 409 U.S. 1023 (1972). See also infra Chapter 15.

243. SEC v. Texas Gulf Sulphur Co., 401 F.2d 833 (2d Cir. 1968), cert. denied sub nom. Coates v. SEC, 394 U.S. 976 (1969) and 404 U.S. 1005 (1971), reh'g denied, 404 U.S. 1064 (1972).

When a director purchases stock of his corporation from a shareholder, he may be required to disclose "special facts" of which he has knowledge, such as the impending declaration of a large dividend[244] or an anticipated reduction in corporate earnings for the current year.[245]

§ 3.23. Personal advantage; secret profits.

It is a cardinal principle of corporate law that a director cannot, at the expense of the corporation, make an unfair[246] or secret[247] profit from his position. Directors are trustees of the business and property of the corporation for the collective body of the shareholders.[248] They may not misuse their power by promoting their personal interests at the expense of corporate interests.[249]

Obviously, any corporate director or officer will have chances to obtain for himself business opportunities which are offered to or are available to his corporation. If he acts otherwise than in absolute good faith,[250] if he violates business ethics,[251] if he diverts the corporate business opportunity for his own personal gain,[252] he must account to his corpora-

---

244. E.g., Buckley v. Buckley, 230 Mich. 504, 202 N.W. 955 (1925); Hobart v. Hobart Estate Co., 26 Cal. 2d 412, 159 P.2d 958 (1945) Haussler v. Wilson, 164 Cal. App. 2d 421, 330 P.2d 670 (1958).

245. Diamond v. Oreamuno, supra note 241. Cf. Beecher v. Able, 374 F. Supp. 341 (S.D.N.Y. 1974).

246. Remillard Brick Co. v. Remillard-Dandini Co., 109 Cal. App. 2d 405, 241 P.2d 66, 74 (1952).

247. Heit v. Bixby, 276 F. Supp. 217, 225 (E.D. Mo. 1967).

248. Melish v. Vogel, 35 Ill. App. 3d 125, 343 N.E.2d 17, 25 (1976).

249. United States v. Byrum, 408 U.S. 125, 138, 33 L.Ed.2d 238, 248, 92 S.Ct. 2382, reh'g denied, 409 U.S. 898 (1972).

250. Dolese Bros. Co. v. Brown, 39 Del. Ch. 1, 757 A.2d 784 (1960).

251. Note, "Liability of Directors and Other Officers for Usurpation of Corporate Opportunities," 26 Fordham L. Rev. 528 (1957).

252. Hart v. Bell, 222 Minn. 69, 23 N.W.2d 375 (1946); Diedrick v. Helm, 217 Minn. 483, 14 N.W.2d 913 (1944); Tovrea Land & Cattle Co. v. Linsenmeyer, 100 Ariz. 107, 412 P.2d 47 (1966). See also supra sections 3.11-3.14.

tion. The right to an accounting may be enforced in an action by the corporation or in a shareholder's derivative action.[253]

The personal advantage which is prohibited may arise in various ways. For example, it may occur if the corporation's funds are used by the director in buying property which he then re-sells to the corporation at a profit,[254] or if an officer purchases his corporation's own shares which the corporation itself is seeking to acquire under a buy-and-sell agreement,[255] or if officers-directors secretly operate a competing business,[256] or where a director prevents his corporation from going into a business which would be in direct competition with him.[257]

An Idaho court ruled that a corporate manager breached his fiduciary duty in attempting to obtain his employer's leasehold, and in negotiating with other employees to work for a competitor with which he was arranging for his own employment.[258]

When a corporate director in Hawaii represented his corporation as a real estate broker in its purchase of investment real estate, he was not permitted to retain commissions received by him from the vendor's real estate brokers. He claimed the right to do so because his corporation was not

---

253. New v. New, 148 Cal. App. 2d 372, 306 P.2d 987 (1957).

254. Durfee v. Durfee & Canning, Inc., 323 Mass. 187, 80 N.E.2d 522 (1948). And cf. Bubolz v. Burke, 266 F. Supp. 686 (E.D. Mo. 1967); Beury v. Beury, 127 F. Supp. 786 (S.D. W.Va. 1954), appeal dismissed, 222 F.2d 464 (4th Cir. 1955); Vine v. Beneficial Fin. Co., 374 F.2d 627 (2d Cir.), cert. denied, 389 U.S. 970 (1967).

255. Brown v. Dolese, 38 Del. Ch. 471, 154 A.2d 233 (1959), aff'd, 39 Del. Ch. 1, 157 A.2d 784 (1960).

256. See Foley v. D'Agostino, 21 A.D.2d 60, 248 N.Y.S.2d 121 (1964); Twin Falls Farm & City Distrib., Inc. v. D & B Supply Co., 96 Idaho 351, 528 P.2d 1286 (1974).

257. Singer v. Carlisle, 26 N.Y.S.2d 172 (1940), aff'd, 261 A.D. 897, 26 N.Y.S.2d 320, appeal denied, 261 A.D. 956, 27 N.Y.S.2d 190 (1941). See also supra section 3.15.

258. Twin Falls Farm & City Distrib., Inc. v. D & B Supply Co., supra note 256. See also Bancroft-Whitney Co. v. Glen, 64 Cal. 2d 327, 49 Cal. Rptr. 825, 411 P.2d 921, 935-36, 939-40 (1966).

licensed as a real estate broker and could not, itself, lawfully share in the commissions, but this claim was denied.[259]

---

259. Hawaiian Int'l Fin., Inc. v. Pablo, 53 Haw. 149, 488 P.2d 1172 (1971).

COROLLARY REFERENCES

Borden, "Going Private — Old Tort, New Tort, or No Tort," 49 N.Y.U. L. Rev. 987 (1974).

Brudney, "A Note on 'Going Private,'" 61 Va. L. Rev. 1019 (1975).

Brudney & Chirelstein, "Fair Shares in Corporate Mergers and Take-overs," 99 Harv. L. Rev. 297 (1974).

Brudney & Clark, "A New Look at Corporate Opportunities," 94 Harv. L. Rev. 997 (1981).

Cary, "Corporate Standards and Legal Rules," 50 Calif. L. Rev. 408 (1962), reprinted in 40 Harv. Bus. Rev. 53 (1962).

De La Garza, "Conflict of Interest Transactions: Fiduciary Duties of Corporate Directors Who Are Also Controlling Shareholders," 57 Denver L.J. 609 (1980).

Easterbrook & Fischel, "Proper Role of a Target's Management in Responding to a Tender Offer," 94 Harv. L. Rev. 1161 (1981).

Ehrenzweig, "A Counter-Revolution in Conflicts Law? From Beale to Cavers," 80 Harv. L. Rev. 377 (1966).

Goldman, "Self-Dealing by Directors Under Illinois Law: Transactions Between Corporations Having Common Directors," 53 Ill. B.J. 1068 (1965).

Marsh, "Are Directors Trustees? Conflict of Interest and Corporate Morality," 22 Bus. Law. 35 (1986).

Norton, "Relationship of Shareholders to Corporate Creditors Upon Dissolution: Nature and Implications of the 'Trust Fund' Doctrine of Corporate Assets," 80 Bus. Law. 1061 (1975).

O'Neal, Oppression of Minority Shareholders (1975).

Ramsey, "Director's Power to Compete with His Corporation," 18 Ind. L.J. 293 (1943).

Ruder, "Duty of Loyalty — A Law Professor's Status Report," 40 Bus. Law. 1383 (1985).

Slaughter, "The Corporate Opportunity Doctrine," 18 Sw. L.J. 96 (1964).

Walker, "Legal Handles Used to Open or Close the Corporate Opportunity Door," 56 Nw. U.L. Rev. 608 (1961).

Annotation, "Fairness to corporation where 'corporate opportunity' is allegedly usurped by officer or director," 17 A.L.R.4th 479 (1982).

Annotation, "Financial inability of corporation to take advantage of business opportunity as affecting determination whether 'corporate opportunity' was presented," 16 A.L.R.4th 185 (1982).

Annotation, "Purchase of shares of corporation by director or officer as usurpation of 'corporate opportunity,'" 16 A.L.R.4th 784 (1982).

Comment, "Corporate Opportunity," 74 Harv. L. Rev. 765 (1961).

Note, "Protecting Shareholders Against Partial and Two-Tiered Takeovers: The 'Poison Pill' Preferred," 97 Harv. L. Rev. 1964 (1984).

Note, "The Standstill Agreement: A Case of Illegal Vote Selling and Breach of Fiduciary Duty," 93 Yale L.J. 1093 (1984).

Chapter 4
DUTY OF OBEDIENCE

§ 4.01. Unauthorized acts; statutes controlling directors and officers.

Corporate directors and officers are expected to perform their duties in accordance with applicable statutes and the terms of the corporate charter. An act which is beyond the powers conferred upon a corporation by its charter or by the laws of the state of incorporation is "ultra vires."[1] Directors are liable to their corporation for ultra vires acts authorized by the board of directors.[2] A director's duty of obedience requires that he avoid committing ultra vires acts.[3] In some

---

1. Marsili v. Pacific Gas & Elec. Co., 124 Cal. Rptr. 313, 318, 151 Cal. App. 3d 313 (1975); Commmunity Fed. S. & L. Ass'n v. Fields, 128 F.2d 705, 708 (8th Cir. 1942).

2. Small Bus. Admin. v. Segal, 383 F. Supp. 198, 203 (D. Conn. 1974).

3. Gearhart Indus., Inc. v. Smith Int'l, Inc., 741 F.2d 707, 719 (5th Cir. 1984). See also supra section 1.05.

jurisdictions, however, a director will not be held liable for an ultra vires act unless it is also illegal.[4]

All ultra vires acts are not necessarily illegal, although there has been a tendency to confuse the terms in some cases.[5] Some state statutes limit the circumstances under which the doctrine of ultra vires is available, but in actions by corporations against directors or officers this doctrine may be asserted.[6]

There is authority that if an officer enters into a contract for his corporation, which is ultra vires and not binding upon the corporation, he may be held personally liable if the other party is not chargeable with knowledge of the ultra vires character of the transaction.[7]

In support of the general rule of no liability in such instances, it is usually contended that the other contracting party has the same opportunity as the officers to ascertain the extent of the corporation's powers and is thus charged with knowledge.[8] When there is a fraudulent transfer or misappropriation of corporate funds, personal liability will ordinarily be imposed upon the errant directors or officers, and such circumstances overcome the ultra vires rule.[9]

Corporate directors and officers are governed by numerous statutes which command their corporations to carry out specified duties and thereby impose the actual performance of such duties upon the persons through whom the corporation acts. Obedience to such mandates also comes within the scope of this chapter.

---

4. Id., citing Texas law.

5. 18B Am. Jur. 2d 858 Corporations § 2010.

6. See Revised Model Bus. Corp. Act. § 3.04(b)(2); Del. Code Ann., tit. 8, § 124; Cal. Corp. Code § 208; Ohio Rev. Code Ann. § 1701.13(H); N.Y. Bus. Corp. Law § 203.

7. E.g., Lurie v. Arizona Fertilizer & Chem. Co., 101 Ariz. 482, 421 P.2d 330 (1966).

8. Yoakum v. Tarver, 256 Cal. App. 2d 202, 64 Cal. Rptr. 7 (1967); Tennessee Chem. Co. v. Cheatham, 217 Ala. 399, 116 So. 420 (1928).

9. Tennessee Chem. Co. v. Cheatham, supra note 8.

§4.02. Retention of personal profits.

In addition to the rule that directors have no right to divert corporate opportunities and make them their own,[10] the principle here discussed is that any profit derived from an activity engaged in for the corporation's benefit belongs to the corporation. Under such circumstances the corporate officer may be held as a constructive trustee of the profit.[11]

The fiduciary position occupied by corporate officers and directors precludes their retention of personal profits, at least without full disclosure. They may not exercise their directorial powers to serve their own interests at the expense of their corporation and its shareholders. Thus, whatever an officer or director receives resulting from his fiduciary position, except in open dealings with the corporation, belongs to the corporation[12] and must be accounted for.[13]

The good faith in which an officer or director acted will not constitute a defense to an action to recover a commission or fee. A bank president has been held liable for compensation paid him for his effort in arranging a loan,[14] and a director was not permitted to retain a commission paid to him by a third person who sold real estate to his corporation.[15] In the latter case, the Hawaiian Supreme Court held that the "case would have been different" if the director had made advance disclosure of his expectation of the commission.[16] Thus, disclosure may be a factor tending to absolve a director from liability.[17]

---

10. See supra sections 3.11-3.14.

11. Diedrick v. Helm, 217 Minn. 483, 14 N.W.2d 913 (1944).

12. State ex rel. Hayes Oyster Co. v. Keypoint Oyster Co., 64 Wash. 2d 375, 391 P.2d 979 (1964).

13. Guth v. Loft, Inc., 23 Del. Ch. 255, 5 A.2d 503 (1939).

14. Fleishhacker v. Blum, 109 F.2d 543 (9th Cir.), cert. denied, 311 U.S. 665 (1940).

15. Hawaiian Int'l Fin., Inc. v. Pablo, 53 Haw. 149, 488 P.2d 1172 (1971).

16. Id.

17. Morris v. North Evanston Manor Bldg. Corp., 319 Ill. App. 298, 49 N.E.2d 646 (1943).

It is not a defense to such an action that the corporation suffered no damage.[18] Similarly, even if the completed contract is advantageous to the corporation, it may nonetheless recover a commission paid to its director.[19]

§ 4.03. Unlawful distributions.

The Revised Model Business Corporation Act defines a distribution as a direct or indirect transfer of money or other property (except a corporation's own shares) or incurrence of indebtedness by a corporation to or for the benefit of its shareholders in respect of any of its shares.[20] It may be in the form of a declaration or payment of a dividend, a purchase, redemption or other acquisition of shares, a distribution of promissory notes or evidences of indebtedness, or a distribution in voluntary or involuntary liquidation.[21]

The Revised Model Act further declares that a director who votes for or assents to a distribution made in violation of law or the articles of incorporation is personally liable to the corporation for the portion of the distribution that exceeds the maximum amount that could have been lawfully distributed.[22] All state statutes impose liability upon directors for unlawful distributions.[23]

To determine the validity of a distribution it is necessary to consult the statutory law under which the corporation was formed and its articles of incorporation. The various state statutes are in disarray on this subject, and most of them do not follow the Revised Model Business Corporation Act.[24]

Because most statutes impose liability upon directors who vote for or assent to unlawful distributions, it is important to

---

18. See, e.g., Western States Life Ins. Co. v. Lockwood, 166 Cal. 185, 135 P. 496 (1913).

19. Rutland Elec. Light Co. v. Bates, 68 Vt. 579, 35 A. 480 (1896).

20. Revised Model Bus. Corp. Act § 1.40(6).

21. Official Comment, 1 Model Bus. Corp. Act Ann. 76-77 (3d ed. 1985).

22. Revised Model Bus. Corp. Act § 8.33(a).

23. E.g., Cal. Corp. Code §§ 309, 316; Del. Code Ann. tit. 8, §§ 172, 174; N.Y. Bus. Corp. Law §§ 717, 719; Ohio Rev. Code Ann. § 1701.95. See supra section 2.13, as to liability of shareholder receiving unlawful distribution.

24. See discussion in 1 Model Bus. Corp. Act Ann. 489-92 (3d ed. 1985).

note the responsibility imposed upon a director who seeks to dissent or abstain from the action taken. The Revised Model Act states:

> A director who is present at a meeting of the board of directors or a committee of the board of directors when corporate action is taken is deemed to have assented to the action taken unless: (1) he objects at the beginning of the meeting (or promptly upon his arrival) to holding it or transacting business at the meeting; (2) his dissent or abstention from the action taken is entered in the minutes of the meeting; or (3) he delivers written notice of his dissent or abstention to the presiding officer of the meeting before its adjournment or to the corporation immediately after adjournment of the meeting. The right of dissent or abstention is not available to a director who votes in favor of the action taken.[25]

Most state statutes have provisions similar to the above,[26] but differences in language are so significant that particular state statutes should be consulted.[27] The word "assent" used in these statutes includes the approval and ratification of a dividend after it has been declared. It imports the playing of a voluntary part in the declaration or creation of the unlawful distribution.[28]

A director who was absent from the meeting at which the wrongful dividend was declared may be absolved from liability on that account,[29] although some states, such as Delaware, have statutes which require the absent director to cause his dissent to be entered on the books as soon as he has

---

25. Revised Model Bus. Corp. Act § 8.24(d).

26. E.g., Colo. Rev. Stat. §§ 7-5-101, 7-5-106; D.C. Code Ann. §§ 29-336, 29-342; Ohio Rev. Code Ann. § 1701.95(B).

27. Del. Code Ann. tit. 8, §§ 141(b), 174(a); N.Y. Bus. Corp. Law §§ 707, 708(d), 709, 719. And cf. Cal. Corp. Code § 307(a), 316(b).

28. Aiken v. Insull, 122 F.2d 746, 753 (7th Cir.), cert. denied, 315 U.S. 806 (1941).

29. See Hutchinson v. Curtiss, 45 Misc. 484, 92 N.Y.S. 70 (1904). But cf. Williams v. Brewster, 117 Wis. 370, 93 N.W. 479 (1903); City Inv'g Co. v. Gerken, 121 Misc. 763, 202 N.Y.S. 41 (1924).

notice of the action taken.[30] Personal liability may be imposed for failure to attend board meetings when such failure results in waste of corporate assets from the director's failure to exercise his independent supervision and control of the corporation's affairs.[31]

Figurehead or "dummy" directors occupy a dangerous position. There is substantial authority holding such directors liable for their failure to take an active part in the affairs of the corporation by which they are named directors.[32] Such cases have served as the foundation for considerable litigation and have broadened burdens of directors. As a result it is reported that worried directors are showing up more regularly at board meetings.

§ 4.04. Maintaining records.

Because corporate officers and directors are dealing with the property and rights of others, they have the duty to keep accurate books of account and preserve important records.[33] A corporation has only powers granted to it by the state of its incorporation and has a duty to produce its books and records when the interests of justice so require.[34] A corporation ordinarily speaks through its records.[35]

The Revised Model Business Corporation Act contains provisions for keeping and maintaining such records which include (1) minutes of all meetings of shareholders and the board of directors, (2) a record of all actions taken by the shareholders or board of directors without a meeting, and (3) a record of all actions taken by committees of the board of

---

30. Del. Code Ann. tit. 8, § 174.

31. Stern v. Lucy Webb Hayes Nat'l Training School for Deaconesses & Ministers, 381 F. Supp. 1003, 1013 (D.D.C. 1974).

32. E.g., Allied Freightways v. Cholfin, 325 Mass. 630, 91 N.E.2d 765 (1960).

33. Backus v. Finkelstein, 23 F.2d 357, 364 (D. Minn. 1927); cf. National Tube Co. v. Peck, 159 Ohio St. 98, Ill. N.E.2d 11 (1953).

34. In re Greenspan, 187 F. Supp. 177, 178 (S.D.N.Y. 1960).

35. 18A Am. Jur. 2d Corporations § 333.

directors on behalf of the corporation.[36] In addition, appropriate accounting records must be maintained.[37]

All state statutes require the keeping of some corporate records[38] and most of them follow the above provisions of the Revised Model Business Corporation Act. However, other provisions of the Act are not generally followed by the states.[39]

All states have statutes permitting shareholders to inspect corporate records under specified circumstances. The right of shareholders to inspect corporate records existed at common law,[40] and the statutory privileges are considered to be supplemental to the common-law right.[41] Of course, corporate officers and directors also have the right to inspect the corporate books and records.[42]

The Revised Model Act provides penalties or sanctions upon a corporation or its officers for refusing to permit a proper inspection.[43] However, there is little uniformity in state statutes on this point.[44]

An Ohio statute imposes liability upon any officer, director, employee, or agent of a corporation for damages resulting from publication of a false statement or the making of false entries as to the books, records, or accounts of a corporation.[45]

§ 4.05. Dividends: their sources.

Dividends are a return to shareholders on their investment. The term includes money paid out by the corporation

---

36. Revised Model Bus. Corp. Act § 16.01(a).

37. Id. § 16.01(b).

38. E.g., Cal. Corp. Code § 1500; Del. Code Ann. tit. 8, §§ 220, 224; Ohio Rev. Code Ann. § 1701.37; N.Y. Bus. Corp. Law § 624.

39. See discussion in 3 Model Bus. Corp. Act Ann. 1716 (3d ed. 1985).

40. Sarni v. Meloccaro, 324 A.2d 648 (R.I. 1974); G.S. & M. Co. v. Dixon, 220 Ga. 329, 138 S.E.2d 662 (1964).

41. 18A Am. Jur. 2d Corporations § 349.

42. Henshaw v. American Cement Corp., 252 A.2d 125 (Del. Ch. 1969).

43. Revised Model Bus. Corp. Act § 16.04.

44. See, e.g., Cal. Corp. Code §§ 1600, 1603, 1604; Me. Rev. Stat. Ann. tit. 13A, § 626; Del. Code Ann. tit. 8, § 220.

45. Ohio Rev. Code Ann. § 1701.93.

as well as the distribution of additional shares to share-holders.[46] One leading case states that a dividend is a portion of the profits of a corporation declared by its governing body to be set apart and paid to the shareholders ratably according to their respective interests.[47] It has also been said that a dividend is a distribution of assets obtained in excess of capital.[48] In other words, dividends are ordinarily not payable out of capital.[49] However, the dividends paid on liquidation of a corporation are paid as a return of capital and not on account of earnings or profits.[50]

The source of dividends is usually prescribed by statute, and the most common provision is that they be paid out of surplus[51] or net earnings.[52] No dividend may be paid that will impair a corporation's capital,[53] nor while the capital is diminished by depreciation or otherwise.[54] The Federal Bankruptcy Act prohibits the declaration of any dividend that would make a corporation insolvent.[55] In Indiana, unless the articles permit, a distribution may not reduce the assets to less than the liabilities plus an amount necessary to pay off preferential rights upon dissolution.[56]

The origin of the fund out of which dividends are proposed may have a bearing on its availability for the payment of dividends. In Ohio if any portion of a dividend is paid out of

---

46. Liebman v. Auto Strop Co., 241 N.Y. 427, 150 N.E. 505 (1926).

47. Sherman v. Pepin Pickling Co., 230 Minn. 87, 41 N.W.2d 571 (1950).

48. Penington v. Commonwealth Hotel Constr. Corp., 17 Del. Ch. 188, 151 A. 228 (1930), modified, 17 Del. Ch. 394, 155 A. 514, 519 (1931).

49. See, e.g., Berks Broadcasting Co. v. Craumer, 356 Pa. 620, 52 A.2d 571 (1947).

50. Powell v. Madison Safe Deposit & Trust Co., 208 Ind. 432, 196 N.E. 324 (1935).

51. See Model Bus. Corp. Act § 45(a) (1969 revision).

52. Del. Code Ann. tit. 8, § 170(a).

53. N.Y. Bus. Corp. Law § 719.

54. Del. Code Ann. tit. 8, § 170(a).

55. See 11 U.S.C. § 107.

56. Ind. Code Ann. § 23-1-28-3.

capital surplus, the shareholders must be notified of its source.[57] Other states have similar limitations.[58]

§ 4.06. Dividends: duty to pay.

One of the important duties of the board of directors of a corporation is the declaration and payment of dividends. It is through dividends that corporate shareholders derive a return on their investment and are encouraged to continue and to increase their holdings in the corporation.

Directors must exercise their discretion in declaring dividends in an honest manner so as to benefit the corporation and all its shareholders. They must not favor one class of shareholders over another. They must use their power as wisely as possible and must not abuse it since it is well established that the directors and the controlling shareholders stand in fiduciary positions.[59] This rule has its foundation in the principle that one who dominates the rights of others stands as a trustee to them.[60]

Unless directors neglect or refuse to exercise their discretion in declaring dividends, shareholders generally have no power to compel such action.[61] A leading case holds that directors have better opportunities than others of being able to determine whether a declaration of dividends is prudent at a particular time.[62]

Under proper circumstances a corporation may borrow money to pay dividends. This might be appropriate where the corporation had spent its surplus to pay for capital improvements.[63] Of course, there must be the prospect of surplus

---

57. Ohio Rev. Code Ann. § 1701.33(F). See also N.Y. Bus. Corp. Law § 510(c).

58. See, e.g., Iowa Code Ann. § 496A.41(3).

59. Pepper v. Litton, 308 U.S. 295, 84 L.Ed. 281, 60 S.Ct. 238 (1939).

60. Cf. Bloodworth v. Bloodworth, 225 Ga. 379, 169 S.E.2d 150 (1969); Pappas v. Moss, 393 F.2d 865 (3d Cir. 1968).

61. Peabody v. Eisner, 247 U.S. 347, 62 L.Ed. 1152, 38 S.Ct. 546 (1918).

62. New York L.E. & W. R.R. v. Nickals, 119 U.S. 296, 30 L.Ed. 363, 7 S.Ct. 209 (1886).

63. Nebel v. Nebel, 241 N.C. 491, 85 S.E.2d 876 (1955).

earnings to sustain such borrowing. But there is generally no right or duty to declare dividends unless there are earnings or profits from which they can lawfully be paid.[64] The mere fact of a profit does not necessarily mean that a fund is available to pay dividends. It must be set aside as such.[65]

The decision of directors, representing a majority of the shareholders, not to declare dividends may well have the effect of coercing the minority shareholders into disposing of their interest in the corporation; since the purpose of any business corporation is to make a profit, the minority shareholders are thereby discriminated against to their damage. Thus, while the general rule leaves the declaration of dividends to the honest judgment of the board of directors,[66] this principle may not be inflexibly applied, especially in the case of a closely held corporation where a minority shareholder would be unable to sell his shares.[67]

§ 4.07. Dividends: declaration.

Whether or not a dividend should be declared is ordinarily the province of the board of directors, pursuant to statutory authority and subject to any limitations contained in the articles of incorporation or bylaws.[68]

While formal action by directors, duly recorded in the corporate records, is preferable,[69] there is authority that a distribution accepted by the shareholders was a valid dividend even though not authorized by a resolution of the board.[70] It is

---

64. Inscho v. Mid-Continent Dev. Co., 94 Kan. 370, 146 P. 1014 (1915).

65. See Eisner v. Macomber, 252 U.S. 189, 64 L.Ed. 521, 40 S.Ct. 189 (1920).

66. Hornstein, Corporation Law and Practice § 477 (1959). See also infra section 4.10.

67. Note, "Proposals to Help the Minority Stockholder Receive Fairer Dividend Treatment from the Closely Held Corporation," 56 Nw. U.L. Rev. 503 (1961).

68. Hannigan v. Italo Petroleum Corp. of Am., 43 Del. 333, 47 A.2d 169 (1945).

69. Lamb v. Lehmann, 110 Ohio St. 59, 143 N.E. 276 (1924).

70. Gettinger v. Heaney, 220 Ala. 613, 127 So. 195 (1930).

not essential that creditors be notified of a proposed dividend.[71]

Aside from the tax penalties imposed under the Internal Revenue Act,[72] there is no general requirement that corporation directors distribute corporate profits as dividends to shareholders.[73] But the prospect of punitive taxes being imposed because of an unreasonable accumulation of surplus usually has considerable effect on the discretion of corporate directors. In one important case, tax penalties imposed upon a corporation[74] led to a shareholder's derivative suit which resulted in a settlement of more than two million dollars.[75] Directors act in such situations at their peril.

Ordinarily, the courts will not interfere to compel the payment of dividends.[76] It has been said that as long as the corporation's managers act in good faith, they should be left free to deal with the corporation's earnings as their best judgment dictates.[77] This is so because the declaration of dividends involves not only the distribution of earnings, but also a consideration of the business needs of the corporation.

This aspect of directorial responsibility is pointed up in a complaint filed in August, 1987 against directors of A. H. Robins Company, Inc., who were also the company's chairman and CEO, its president and its former president and counsel.[78] In addition to allegations of gross negligence in

71. See Dominguez Land Corp. v. Daugherty, 196 Cal. 468, 238 P. 703 (1925).

72. I.R.C. § 531; Treas. Reg. § 1.531-1 et seq.

73. E.g., Wabash Ry. v. Barclay, 280 U.S. 197, 74 L.Ed. 368, 50 S.Ct. 106 (1930).

74. Trico Prods. Corp. v. McGowan, 67 F. Supp. 311 (W.D.N.Y. 1946), aff'd, 169 F.2d 343 (2d Cir.), cert. denied, 335 U.S. 899 (1948), reh'g denied, 335 U.S. 913 (1949).

75. Mahler v. Oishei, N.Y. S.Ct., N.Y. County No. 28485 (1947), N.Y. Corp. Law Rep. (CCH) ¶10,003.

76. Lamb v. Lehmann, supra note 69.

77. Hayes v. St. Louis Union Trust Co., 317 Mo. 1028, 298 S.W. 91 (1927).

78. In re A.H. Robins Co. (Dalkon Shield Claimants' Comm. v. Robins), Chapter 11, Case No. 85-01307, No. 87-1005R, E.D. Va., Richmond Div.

causing their corporation to commence and continue the manufacturing, marketing, sale and distribution of the Dalkon Shield, knowing it was unsafe for its intended use, the defendants were charged with fraudulent transfers, fraudulent conveyances, and illegal payment of dividends amounting to more than $110 million over a ten-year period during which Dalkon Shield claims aggregating more than $5 billion were filed and pending. The complaint alleged that approximately 50% of each dividend was paid to two of the named defendants.

If directors act arbitrarily, fraudulently or oppressively, in disregard of the rights of shareholders of any status or class, they may be held liable. *Burton v. Exxon Corporation*[79] dealt with a class action by minority shareholders who were protesting a large dividend paid to a subsidiary's parent company, with no dividend to them. Because the directors of the subsidiary were dominated by Exxon, the parent, the court declined to apply the business judgment rule and examined the intrinsic fairness of the transaction. After considering all aspects of the matter the court found that the directors had proceeded in the best interests of all parties and the business needs of the corporations involved. Thus, the directors sustained their burden under the intrinsic fairness test.

§ 4.08. Dividends: charter and contract provisions.

A corporation's articles of incorporation may authorize classes of shares that entitle shareholders to distributions calculated in any manner, including dividends that may be cumulative, noncumulative, or partially cumulative.[80] Under

---

(Aug. 19, 1987). Copy of complaint printed in Corporate Officers & Directors Liability, Lit. Rep. 3,742 (Aug. 26, 1987).

79. 583 F. Supp. 405 (S.D.N.Y. 1984).

80. See Revised Model Bus. Corp. Act § 6.01(c)(3); and, e.g., Cal. Corp. Code §§ 400, 402, 403; Del. Code Ann. tit. 8, § 151; N.Y. Bus. Corp. Law §§ 501, 512, 519; Ohio Rev. Code Ann. §§ 1701.06, 1701.23.

such provisions, dividends may be made mandatory,[81] or may be limited and restricted.[82]

A contract for the declaration and payment of dividends by a corporation made by a director for a consideration personal to himself was held to be against public policy and void. The Ohio court ruled:

> A contract made by a director of a corporation that limits him in the free exercise of his judgment or discretion, or that places him under direct and powerful inducements to disregard his duties to the corporation, its creditors and other stockholders in the management of corporate affairs is against public policy and void.[83]

§ 4.09. Reliance on corporate books or accountant's report.

Most directors are not involved in the day-to-day operations of the business and should be entitled to rely upon the information obtained in good faith from the corporation's books and records.[84] Hence, it is usual for state statutes to absolve a director from liability for wrongfully declared dividends if he, in good faith, relied on the corporate books or the audit of a reputable accountant.[85] These statutes follow the trend of judicial decisions which are inclined to limit the lia-

---

81. Lydia E. Pinkham Med. Co. v. Gove, 303 Mass. 1, 20 N.E.2d 482 (1939).

82. See, e.g., Revised Model Bus. Corp. Act § 6.40.

83. Thomas v. Matthews, 94 Ohio St. 32, 113 N.E. 669 (1916). See also supra section 3.19.

84. Cf. supra sections 2.05 and 2.07.

85. Quintal v. Greenstein, 142 Misc. 854, 256 N.Y.S. 462, aff'd, 236 A.D. 719, 257 N.Y.S. 1034 (1932). See Ohio Rev. Code Ann. § 1701.95(B)(1), providing that a director will not be liable "if, in determining the amount available for any such dividend ... he in good faith relied on a financial statement of the corporation prepared by an officer or employee of the corporation in charge of its accounts or certified by a public accountant or firm of public accountants, or in good faith he considered the assets to be of their book value, or he followed what he believed to be sound accounting and business practice." See also Mich. Stat. Ann. § 21.197(541) and (551).

bility of directors for wrongful declaration of dividends to instances when they have acted negligently or in bad faith.[86]

A Delaware statute fully protects corporate directors who rely in good faith on books of account or reports made by any of the corporate officials or by an independent certified public accountant.[87] Thus, unless circumstances exist to put the directors on inquiry prior to a declaration of dividends, they may rely on statements of competent persons who are in direct control of their corporation's business activities.[88]

When there is no state statute dealing with this subject, the common-law rule allows directors to rely upon the reports of corporate officers, but they have an obligation to determine whether the reports present a true corporate picture and then exercise reasonable judgment as businessmen on the accuracy of the reports.[89]

It is, of course, the duty of the plaintiff, whether he is a creditor or a shareholder, to show the actual wrongfulness of the dividend as well as the participation of the defendant-director therein.[90] The burden of proving the defense of dissent by a particular director in such instances seems to rest on the defendant-director, although there is some authority to the contrary.[91]

§ 4.10. Inadequate dividends; excessive compensation.

Directors have the power to declare dividends or, in their discretion, apply the profits to some other corporate purpose,

---

86. See N.Y. Bus. Corp. Law § 717; Diamond v. Davis, 62 N.Y.S.2d 181 (1945). See also Note, "Reliance on Advice of Counsel," 70 Yale L.J. 978 (1961).

87. Del. Code Ann. tit. 8, § 141(e). See also Prince v. Bensinger, 244 A.2d 89 (Del. Ch. 1968).

88. Savings Bank of Louisville's Assignee v. Caperton, 87 Ky. 306, 8 S.W. 885 (1888).

89. Randall v. Bailey, 23 N.Y.S.2d 173 (1940), aff'd, 262 A.D. 844, 29 N.Y.S.2d 512, appeal denied, 262 A.D. 994, 30 N.Y.S.2d 808 (1941), aff'd, 288 N.Y. 280, 43 N.E.2d 43 (1942).

90. See Scullin v. Mutual Drug Co., 138 Ohio St. 132, 33 N.E.2d 992 (1941).

91. See, e.g., 18B Am. Jur. 2d Corporations § 1339.

as long as they act in good faith.[92] However, if they declare
small dividends and reward themselves with increased fees
and salaries, they may be held liable to shareholders who are
thereby damaged.[93] Such damages may be recovered in a
class action or derivative action.[94]

Excessive compensation paid to directors and officers may
constitute a waste of the corporation's assets. In that event,
the directors and managing officers are responsible.[95] Their
liability may be enforced by a derivative action.[96] But courts
should not interfere with the actions of directors in fixing
their own salaries as officers or corporation employees, in the
absence of fraud or overreaching.[97]

When bonuses are paid to officers instead of dividends to
shareholders, a right of action may exist against the directors. If a bonus payment is unrelated to the value of services
rendered, it constitutes a mere gift and the directors have no
right to give away corporate property over the objections of
minority shareholders.[98]

If compensation is voted by the directors to themselves or to
officers or employees of the corporation, it must be reasonable
and commensurate with the value of the services rendered.[99]
It should be in proportion to the relevant facts and circumstances.[100]

---

92. Wabash Ry. v. Barclay, 280 U.S. 197, 74 L.Ed. 368, 50 S.Ct. 106
(1930).

93. Von Au v. Magenheimer, 126 A.D. 257, 110 N.Y.S. 629 (1908), aff'd,
196 N.Y. 510, 89 N.E. 1114 (1909).

94. Fayard v. Fayard, 293 So. 2d 421 (Miss. 1974).

95. Winkelman v. GMC, 39 F. Supp. 826 (S.D.N.Y. 1940), 44 F. Supp.
960 (S.D.N.Y. 1942).

96. Felsenheld v. Bloch Bros. Tobacco Co., 119 W.Va. 167, 192 S.E. 545
(1937).

97. Spang v. Wertz Eng'g Co., 382 Pa. 48, 114 A.2d 143 (1955).

98. Rogers v. Hill, 289 U.S. 582, 77 L.Ed. 1385, 53 S.Ct. 731 (1933).

99. Hornsby v. Lohmeyer, 364 Pa. 271, 72 A.2d 294 (1950).

100. Glenmore Distilleries Co. v. Seideman, 267 F. Supp. 915, 919
(E.D.N.Y. 1967).

The question of the reasonableness of a corporate officer's compensation is ordinarily a question of fact.[101] In order to come within the rule of reason, such compensation must be in proportion to the officer's ability,[102] services rendered, time devoted to the company, difficulties involved, responsibilities assumed, successes achieved, amounts under his jurisdiction, corporate earnings, profits and prosperity,[103] increase in volume or quality of business or both, and all such relevant facts and circumstances.[104]

In suits by shareholders to recover for the corporation officers' salaries claimed to be excessive, where the officers are also directors and have set their own salaries or their votes were needed to do so, the burden is upon the directors-officers to justify their own salaries and show the reasonableness of them.[105]

Relief may be granted in such cases by enjoining the payment of the unreasonable salaries and adjudging recovery for the excess over reasonable salaries.[106] Also, the court may reduce unreasonable salaries.[107]

An Ohio court has stated that in determining the reasonableness of compensation paid to a director-employee, "all relevant factors should be considered, which would primarily include: (1) whether there has been an increase in the busi-

---

101. Black v. Parker Mfg. Co., 329 Mass. 105, 106 N.E.2d 544 (1952); Luyckx v. R.L. Aylward Coal Co., 270 Mich. 468, 259 N.W. 135 (1935).

102. Poutch v. National Foundry & Mach. Co., 147 Ky. 242, 143 S.W. 1003 (1912).

103. Baker v. Cohn, 42 N.Y.S.2d 159 (1942), modified on other grounds, 266 A.D. 715, 40 N.Y.S.2d 623 (1943), aff'd without opinion, 292 N.Y. 570, 54 N.E.2d 689 (1944); Stearns v. Dudley, 76 N.Y.S.2d 106 (1947), aff'd, 274 A.D. 1028, 86 N.Y.S.2d 478 (1948).

104. Smith v. Dunlap, 269 Ala. 97, 111 So. 2d 1 (1959); Gallin v. Nat'l City Bank, 152 Misc. 679, 273 N.Y.S. 87 (1935); Glenmore Distilleries Co. v. Seideman, supra note 100.

105. Binz v. St. Louis Hide & Tallow Co., 378 S.W.2d 228, 230 (Mo. App. 1964); Fendelman v. Fenco Handbag Mfg. Co., 482 S.W.2d 461 (Mo. 1972).

106. Beha v. Martin, 161 Ky. 838, 171 S.W. 393 (1914); Stratis v. Anderson, 254 Mass. 536, 150 N.E. 832 (1926).

107. Hornsby v. Lohmeyer, supra note 99.

ness of the corporation, (2) the amount of compensation paid to employees for comparable work by similar corporations in the same industries, and (3) whether there has been a proportionate increase in the duties and responsibilities of the directors-employees in connection with the substantial increase in their compensation."[108] The case, which was brought by a minority shareholder who claimed defendants diverted corporate profits to themselves at the expense of the minority, held that the directors-employees did not satisfy their burden of justifying their salaries and the reasonableness thereof and thus required the defendants to repay to the corporation all moneys received as salary or compensation in excess of the amounts approved in the opinion.

§ 4.11. Liability for corporate contract.

Corporate representatives should indicate the representative capacity in which they are executing documents. However, in perhaps the most liberal case decided in the area to date, an Arizona court has ruled that a corporate treasurer who executed a check, but failed to indicate her representative capacity thereon, was not personally liable on the check,[109] notwithstanding a Uniform Commercial Code provision which states that failure to indicate one's representative capacity renders the signer personally liable, particularly as to third-party holders in due course.[110] The court reasoned that the instrument was a routine corporate check which carried the imprinted name of the corporation on the top and just above the place for signing and, therefore, the representative capacity could be inferred even by a third-party holder in due course.

However, in Oklahoma, under the Uniform Commercial Code,[111] a corporate officer who signed checks on the corpo-

---

108. Soulas v. Troy Donut Univ., Inc., 9 Ohio App. 3d 339, 460 N.E.2d 310 (1983).

109. Valley Nat'l Bank v. Cook, 136 Ariz. 232, 665 P.2d 576 (1983).

110. U.C.C. § 3-403(2)(b).

111. Okla. Stat. Ann. tit. 12A, § 3-403.

143

rate account without designating the capacity in which he signed was held personally liable despite the fact that the checks showed the number of the corporate account written in by the officer.[112]

In determining whether it was intended that the agent or officer be bound individually, it is proper to consider all applicable facts and circumstances.[113] If the other party would have learned the facts by reasonable inquiry, the officer may be relieved of liability.[114] Conversely, conduct short of actual fraud will support a finding of personal liability against officers and directors; for example, their use of a thinly capitalized corporation to enter into obligations which it could not perform.[115]

A corporate officer's signature as agent of his corporation does not in and of itself preclude his personal liability on the contract, and this is particularly true where the contract is ambiguous and contains some language suggesting an intent to impose personal liability.[116]

It sometimes happens that the language of a contract is such as to impose personal liability upon a corporate director or officer who acted for his corporation in the transaction. In such a case the director or officer may be sued as a contracting party on the premise that, by its terms, he made the contract his own.[117] More common is the situation where, by carelessness or inadvertence, an officer signs a contract in

112. A.L. Jackson Chevrolet, Inc. v. Oxley, 564 P.2d 633 (Okla. 1977). See also Financial Assocs. v. Impact Mktg., Inc., 90 Misc. 2d 545, 394 N.Y.S.2d 814 (1977); Giacalone v. Bernstein, 348 So. 2d 679 (Fla. App. 1977).

113. Freeport Journal-Standard Pub. Co. v. Frederick W. Ziv Co., 345 Ill. App. 338, 103 N.E.2d 153 (1952).

114. Johnson v. Armstrong, 83 Tex. 325, 18 S.W. 594 (1892). But cf. Special Sections, Inc. v. Rappaport Co., 25 A.D.2d 896, 269 N.Y.S.2d 319 (1966).

115. Kagel v. First Commonwealth Co., 409 F. Supp. 1396 (N.D. Cal. 1973), aff'd, 534 F.2d 194 (9th Cir. 1976).

116. Hokama v. Relinc Corp., 57 Haw. 479, 559 P.2d 279 (1977).

117. See, e.g., J.L. Mott Iron Works v. Clark, 87 S.C. 199, 69 S.E. 227 (1910).

such a manner that it is ambiguous[118] or requires construction and must be interpreted as the personal obligation of the individual who signed it.[119]

A corporate officer who is actually acting for himself will not be relieved of liability merely because he signs his name with a designation such as "director" or "president."[120]

§ 4.12. Loans to directors or officers.

The common law permitted the surplus funds of a corporation to be loaned to its directors or officers, in the absence of fraud,[121] concealment, or unfairness.[122] In most jurisdictions such loans are now more or less regulated by statute.[123]

The Revised Model Business Corporation Act suggests a prohibition against such loans unless (1) approved by a majority vote of the shareholders or (2) determined by the board of directors to be of benefit to the corporation.[124]

The Delaware statute, however, expressly authorizes loans by a corporation to any officer or other employee of the corporation or of its subsidiaries whenever the directors believe such loan may reasonably be expected to benefit the corporation.[125] The very broad provisions of the Delaware statute permit such a loan (or a guaranty or other assistance) to be made with or without interest and secured or unsecured as the directors (who may be the borrowers) shall approve.

---

118. E.g., Denman v. Brennamen, 48 Okla. 566, 49 P. 1105 (1915).

119. See Schwab v. Getty, 145 Wash. 66, 258 P. 1035 (1927). But cf. Salzman Sign Co. v. Beck, 10 N.Y.2d 63, 217 N.Y.S.2d 55, 176 N.E.2d 74 (1961).

120. E.g., Robinson v. Kanawha Valley Bank, 44 Ohio St. 441, 8 N.E. 583 (1886); Braun v. Hess & Co., 187 Ill. 283, 58 N.E. 371 (1900). Cf. Gavazza v. Plummer, 53 Wash. 14, 101 P. 370 (1909).

121. Felsenheld v. Bloch Bros. Tobacco Co., 119 W.Va. 167, 192 S.E. 545 (1937).

122. Paddock v. Siemoneit, 147 Tex. 571, 218 S.W.2d 428 (1929).

123. E.g., Cal. Corp. Code §§ 315, 316; Del. Code Ann. tit. 8, § 143; N.Y. Bus. Corp. Law §§ 714, 719; Ohio Rev. Code Ann. § 1701.95.

124. Revised Model Bus. Corp. Act § 8.32(a).

125. Del. Code Ann. tit. 8, § 143. See also Iowa Code Ann. § 496A.4. Compare Fla. Stat. Ann. § 607.141.

Other less liberal statutes permit loans to corporate directors when approved by the other directors if those who approve and do not participate in the loan constitute a majority of the directors.[126]

New York and Massachusetts provide that loans to directors may be validated only by a vote of disinterested shareholders,[127] Wisconsin prohibits such loans other than in the usual course of business,[128] and North Carolina prohibits loans to directors and officers, and also to any dominant shareholder or any corporation of which such a shareholder is the dominant shareholder.[129]

In Ohio, directors who vote for or assent to loans to an officer, director or shareholder are personally liable for the amount of the loan with interest thereon at six percent per annum until paid.[130] Statutes such as this are typical.[131] The liability of the directors is joint and several.[132] Such liability may be enforced by the corporation itself, by its trustee in bankruptcy, and by its creditors.[133] Such statutes have the purpose of protecting the interests of corporate creditors, preventing the impairment of corporate resources, and prohibiting the use of corporate assets for the private purposes of directors and officers.

Whether such a loan should be treated as a dividend for income tax purposes, rather than a loan, will depend upon the substance of the transaction rather than its form. The intention of the parties,[134] whether notes are given, what occurs with respect to repayment,[135] and whether the borrower is

---

126. E.g., Ga. Code Ann. §§ 14-2-21, 14-5-5.
127. N.Y. Bus. Corp. Law § 714; Mass. Gen. Laws Ann. ch. 156B, § 62.
128. Wis. Stat. Ann. § 180.40(1)(d).
129. N.C. Gen. Stat. § 55-22.
130. Ohio Rev. Code Ann. § 1701.95(A)(3).
131. 3A Fletcher, Cyclopedia of Corporations § 1245 (perm. ed. 1975).
132. Sears v. Weissman, 6 Ill. App. 3d 827, 286 N.E.3d 777 (1972).
133. Cole v. Brandle, 127 N.J. Eq. 31, 11 A.2d 255 (1940).
134. Berthold v. Comm'r, 404 F.2d 119, 122 (6th Cir. 1968).
135. Atlanta Biltmore Hotel Corp. v. Comm'r, 349 F.2d 677, 680 (5th Cir. 1965).

able to pay[136] are some aspects of such transactions that have been given judicial scrutiny.

Because such statutes are usually held to be directory in nature, loans to directors and officers are not void, although they may be ultra vires.[137]

§ 4.13. Loans to corporation by directors or officers.

A director is authorized to make loans to his corporation, and may foreclose, the same as any other creditor, if there is default in repayment. Absent proof of overreaching or lack of good faith, directors, officers, or shareholders who foreclose do not violate any duties which they owe to the corporation or interested party.[138]

In making such a loan, a director acts in a dual capacity so that, if his act is questioned, the burden is upon him to show that he acted in good faith and that the corporation received full value for its obligation.[139] This requirement of good faith exists even when the officer is enforcing a debt admittedly owing to him from the corporation.[140]

A director or officer, like any other creditor, may receive security for his debt, if taken in good faith.[141] However, a corporate director or officer may not take a lien on corporate property while breaching his own duty to the corporation, nor divert corporate property to secure its debt to him.[142]

A creditor is not precluded from exercising his rights as a creditor merely because he is also a director and officer of the

---

136. Estate of Taschler v. United States, 440 F.2d 73, 76 (3d Cir. 1971).

137. See Whitten v. Republic Nat'l Bank, 397 S.W.2d 415 (Tex. 1965).

138. R.J. Enstrom Corp. v. Interceptor Corp., 555 F.2d 277, 283 (10th Cir. 1977).

139. American Exch. Nat'l Bank v. Ward, 111 F. 782 (8th Cir. 1901); Stein v. Gable Park, Inc., 223 Ore. 17, 353 P.2d 1034 (1960); In re Security Fin. Co., 49 Cal. 2d 370, 371, 317 P.2d 1 (1957).

140. See Thrasher v. Thrasher, 27 Cal. App. 3d 23, 103 Cal. Rptr. 618 (1972).

141. Marine & River Phosphate Mining & Mfg. Co. v. Bradley, 105 U.S. 175, 26 L.Ed. 1034 (1882); Jackman v. Nebold, 28 F.2d 107 (8th Cir. 1928); Leister v. Carroll County Nat'l Bank, 199 Md. 241, 86 A.2d 393 (1952).

142. Snyder Elec. Co. v. Fleming, 305 N.W.2d 863 (Minn. 1981).

debtor corporation. But he must take no unfair advantage of the corporation and must see that someone representing the corporation knows what is being done, so that its interests will be protected.[143] The motives and purpose of such a creditor in enforcing repayment of the debt are subject to judicial inquiry.[144]

If the corporation was a going concern at the time the loan was made and the security taken, even though financially embarrassed, its subsequent insolvency will not impair the rights of directors or officers who made loans to it in good faith,[145] especially where the subsequent losses were not attributable to any acts of such creditors-directors.[146]

In most states there are statutory provisions relating to dealings between a corporation and its directors and officers, and between corporations with common directors.[147] Such laws must be considered when a director participates in the corporate proceedings relating to a transaction in which he loans money to the corporation. However, such participation does not, of itself, render the transaction invalid.[148]

§ 4.14. Right to contribution.

Statutes which impose liability upon directors frequently provide that any director against whom a claim is successfully asserted shall be entitled to contribution from the other directors who voted for or concurred in the unlawful transaction. Such statutes also may provide for such director to be subrogated to the rights of the corporation against share-

---

143. Union Ice Co. v. Hulton, 291 Pa. 416, 140 A. 514 (1928). See also Continental Oil Co. v. Zaring, 563 P.2d 964 (Colo. App. 1977).

144. Thrasher v. Thrasher, supra note 140.

145. Illinois Steel Co. v. O'Donnell, 156 Ill. 624, 41 N.E. 185 (1895).

146. Kelly v. Fahrney, 145 Ill. App. 80 (1908), aff'd, 242 Ill. 240, 89 N.E. 984 (1909).

147. E.g., Del. Code Ann. tit. 8, § 144.

148. See, e.g., Schnittger v. Old Home Consol. Mining Co., 144 Cal. 603, 78 P. 9 (1904).

holders who received funds with knowledge of facts indicating illegality.[149]

The Ohio approach is somewhat different. Its statute allows contribution to the director, on equitable principles, from other directors who also are liable. In addition it affords a right of contribution from shareholders, as does the Delaware statute.[150]

In other states still different attitudes prevail.[151] Obviously, it is essential that the applicable statute be consulted in each particular instance.[152]

§ 4.15. Liability under antitrust laws.

Under the antitrust laws, the liability of the participating officers of the offending corporation has long been established.[153] A corporation cannot conspire with its officers or agents to violate the antitrust laws, but a corporate officer or director can be held personally liable for damages arising out of an antitrust violation where he participated in the unlawful acts or acquiesced in or ratified the actions of the officers or agents which were in violation of the antitrust law.[154]

In a civil action for damages for antitrust violations, each defendant is liable for the full amount of the loss and has no right of contribution from any other defendant. There was no contribution between joint tortfeasors at common law, and none exists under the antitrust statutes.[155]

---

149. E.g., Del. Code Ann. tit. 8, § 174(c); Fla. Stat. Ann. § 607.144; Ill. Bus. Corp. Act § 8.65(d); N.Y. Bus. Corp. Law § 719(c); Mich. Comp. Laws § 450.519.

150. Ohio Rev. Code Ann. § 1701.95(E); Del. Code Ann. tit. 8, § 174(c). Reilly v. Folger, 44 Ill. App. 2d 343, 194 N.E.2d 544 (1963), rev'd, 31 Ill. 2d 297, 201 N.E.2d 444 (1964).

151. Cf. Idaho Code Ann. § 30-1-48; Iowa Code Ann. § 491.41; Minn. Stat. Ann. § 301A.559.

152. DePinto v. Landoe, 411 F.2d 297 (9th Cir. 1969).

153. Deaktor v. Fox Grocery Co., 332 F. Supp. 536, 542 (W.D. Pa. 1971), citing Hartford Empire Co. v. United States, 323 U.S. 386 (1945).

154. Higbie v. Kopy-Kat, Inc., 391 F. Supp. 808, 810 (E.D. Pa. 1975).

155. Texas Indus., Inc. v. Radcliff Materials, Inc., 451 U.S. 630, 68 L.Ed.2d 500, 101 S.Ct. 2061 (1981).

A corporate officer who violates the antitrust laws may cause injury to persons affected by his actions. Such a person, if injured "in his business or property," may recover his damages in a civil action under Section 4 of the Clayton Act "and shall recover threefold the damages by him sustained, and the cost of a suit, including a reasonable attorney's fee."[156] The action is in tort[157] and it is not a defense

(a) that the officer was acting as a corporate agent when he performed the wrongful acts,[158] or

(b) that he did not have an intention of violating the statute,[159] or

(c) that he acted in good faith or with good intentions.[160]

Officers, inside directors, and outside directors all may be proper parties to a corporate treble damage suit.[161] Regardless of the outcome of such an action, the cost and wear and tear of the litigation will be troublesome to most defendants.

Section 14 of the Clayton Act also provides that when a corporation violates any of the penal provisions of the antitrust laws, "such violation shall be deemed to be also that of the individual directors, officers, or agents of such corporation who shall have authorized, ordered, or done any of the acts constituting in whole or in part such violation."[162]

Under Section 5(a) of the Clayton Act, the plaintiff in the civil action may put in evidence the judgment or decree in the government's action against the defendant, as prima facie

---

156. 15 U.S.C. § 15.

157. Northwestern Oil Co. v. Socony-Vacuum Oil Co., 138 F.2d 967 (7th Cir. 1943).

158. Kentucky-Tennessee Light & Power Co. v. Nashville Coal Co., 37 F. Supp. 728 (W.D. Ky. 1941), aff'd sub nom. Fitch v. Kentucky-Tennessee Light & Power Co., 136 F.2d 12 (6th Cir. 1943).

159. United States v. Griffith, 334 U.S. 100, 92 L.Ed. 1236, 68 S.Ct. 941 (1948).

160. American Amusement Co. v. Ludwig, 82 F. Supp. 265 (D. Minn. 1949).

161. Cott Beverage Corp. v. Canada Dry Ginger Ale, 146 F. Supp. 300 (S.D.N.Y. 1956), appeal dismissed, 243 F.2d 795 (2d Cir. 1957).

162. 15 U.S.C. § 24.

evidence of the violation,[163] although such evidence may be rebutted by the defendant.[164] Thus, if the decree includes a finding that the defendant violated the antitrust laws upon which the suit against him is based and is final, it will be admissible for the purposes stated.[165]

Generally, a corporate executive will not be held vicariously liable for the torts of his corporation, merely by virtue of his office. Participation is required, which may be found on the basis of direct action or knowing approval or ratification of unlawful acts.[166] The validity of that rule in a Sherman Act case has been put in question by a 1982 decision in which the Supreme Court held a nonprofit association liable for Sherman Act violations upon a showing that its agents had acted within the scope of their apparent authority.[167] Justice Blackmun wrote:

> It is true that imposing liability on ASME's agents themselves will have some deterrent effect, because they will know that if they violate the antitrust laws ... they risk the consequences of personal liability. But if, in addition, ASME is civilly liable for the antitrust violations of its agents acting with apparent authority, it is much more likely that similar antitrust violations will not occur in the future.[168]

The next step may be to hold the corporate executives strictly liable for preventing antitrust violations by subordi-

---

163. Id. § 16(a). This does not apply to consent decrees and to certain other judgments and decrees.

164. Richfield Oil Corp. v. Karseal Corp., 271 F.2d 709 (9th Cir. 1959), cert. denied, 361 U.S. 961 (1960).

165. Proper v. John Bene & Sons, 295 F. 729 (E.D.N.Y. 1923). But cf. International Shoe Mach. Corp. v. United Shoe Mach. Corp., 315 F.2d 449 (1st Cir. 1963).

166. Murphy Tugboat Co. v. Shipowners & Merchants Towboat Co., 467 F. Supp. 841, 852 (N.D. Cal. 1979), aff'd sub nom. Murphy Tugboat Co. v. Crowley, 658 F.2d 1256 (9th Cir.), cert. denied, 455 U.S. 1018 (1981).

167. American Society of Mechanical Eng'rs, Inc. v. Hydrolenel Corp., 456 U.S. 556, 72 L.Ed.2d 330, 102 S.Ct. 1935 (1982).

168. Id. at 572.

nates possessing apparent authority to act for the corporation.[169]

When a corporation suffers loss because of antitrust violations by its directors or officers, it is entitled to indemnity if their violation constituted a breach of their fiduciary duty to the corporation. And this right of indemnity may be asserted in a shareholder's derivative action against the wrongdoing directors and officers.[170]

§ 4.16. Liability for payment of taxes.

Funds collected by a corporation as FICA taxes and withholding taxes must be paid over as provided by law, or the officers responsible for doing so will be held personally liable.[171] This liability is separate from that imposed upon the employer-corporation.[172] The statutes imposing such liability are broad in scope and may be enforced against all officers whose duties relate to this subject matter.[173] The liability is not necessarily limited to taxes, but may include penalty assessments.[174]

Funds collected for such taxes are considered trust funds, and the government may proceed against either the corporation or its responsible officers in the order best suited, in its judgment, to collect the taxes.[175] It is not necessary for the

---

169. Cf. United States v. Wise, 370 U.S. 405, 416, 8 L.Ed.2d 590, 597, 82 S.Ct. 1354 (1962), rev'd, 373 U.S. 29, 9 L.Ed.2d 561, 83 S.Ct. 594 (1963) (criminal prosecution under the Sherman Act).

170. Wilshire Oil Co. v. Riffe, 409 F.2d 1277 (10th Cir. 1969), applying Delaware law. See also Annotation, "Right of corporation to indemnity for civil or criminal liability incurred by employee's violation of antitrust laws," 37 A.L.R.2d 1355 (1971).

171. Liddon v. United States, 448 F.2d 509 (5th Cir. 1971), cert. denied, 406 U.S. 918 (1972); Monday v. United States, 421 F.2d 1210 (7th Cir.), cert. denied, 400 U.S. 821 (1970).

172. See 26 U.S.C. §§ 3403 and 6672.

173. White v. United States, 372 F.2d 513 (Ct. Cl. 1967).

174. Spivak v. United States, 370 F.2d 612 (2d Cir.), cert. denied, 387 U.S. 908 (1967).

175. Liddon v. United States, supra note 171. See also Wilkie v. United States, 279 F. Supp. 671 (N.D. Tex. 1968), in which the government's claim was asserted by third-party complaint.

government to attempt to collect from the corporation before assessing a responsible officer.[176]

In addition to liability to pay such federal taxes and penalties, corporate officers and directors may also be held liable to state authorities under state statutes which make them personally responsible for the payment of corporation taxes.[177]

§ 4.17. Civil liability under RICO.

The expanding use of RICO[178] in civil actions constitutes an additional area in which directors may expect to be subjected to litigation for failure to perform their duties. The stated purpose of this legislation was "the eradication of organized crime in the United States," but its broad provisions extend to many activities formerly treated as simple frauds or business torts. RICO provides civil remedies and criminal penalties.[179] It proscribes (a) deriving income from a "pattern of racketeering activity" or through collection of an unlawful debt and using or investing it or its proceeds in any enterprise engaged in, or whose activities affect, interstate or foreign commerce;[180] (b) acquiring or maintaining any interest in or control of such an enterprise through a pattern of racketeering activity;[181] (c) conducting or participating in the conduct of such an enterprise's affairs (e.g., as an officer or director) through a pattern of racketeering activity;[182] or (d) con-

---

176. Datlof v. United States, 370 F.2d 655 (3d Cir. 1966), cert. denied, 387 U.S. 906 (1967).

177. E.g., Weiss v. Porterfield, 27 Ohio St. 2d 117, 271 N.E.2d 792 (1971), construing Ohio Rev. Code Ann. § 5739.33; State ex rel. Haden v. Calco Awning & Window Corp., 153 W.Va. 524, 170 S.E.2d 362 (1969), applying W. Va. Code Ann. § 11-15-17; Ewing v. Lindley, 23 Ohio St. 3d 222, 492 N.E.2d 435 (1986).

178. The Racketeer Influenced and Corrupt Organizations Act (RICO), enacted in 1970 as part of the Organized Crime Control Act of 1970, 18 U.S.C. §§ 1961-1968.

179. As to criminal RICO, see infra section 8.06.

180. 18 U.S.C. § 1962(a).

181. Id. § 1962(b).

182. Id. § 1962(c).

153

spiring to do any of the above.[183] The four-year statute of limitations applicable to Clayton Act civil enforcement actions applies to RICO civil enforcement actions.[184]

"Racketeering activity" means various state and federal crimes (predicate acts) listed in the statute, including mail fraud, wire fraud, fraud in the sale of securities, and bribery, among others.[185] A "pattern of racketeering activity" requires at least two acts of racketeering activity within ten years, but the implication is that while two acts are required, they may not be sufficient to establish a pattern. However, RICO was not intended to address sporadic activity or an isolated offender. The courts have had some difficulty in determining what relationship between the acts of racketeering is necessary to establish a pattern.[186] The Supreme Court has suggested that in defining "pattern" it may be helpful to note the language used by Congress in 18 U.S.C. § 3575(e), which says that:

> [C]riminal conduct forms a pattern if it embraces criminal acts that have the same or similar purposes, results, participants, victims, or methods of commission, or otherwise are interrelated by distinguishing characteristics and are not isolated events.[187]

An "enterprise" that is the target or instrument of racketeering activity is essential to a RICO violation. An enterprise may be "any individual, partnership, corporation, or other legal entity and any union or group of individuals associated in fact although not a legal entity."[188] That list is illus-

---

183. Id. § 1962(a).

184. Agency Holding Corp. v. Malley-Duff & Assocs., — U.S. —, 97 L.Ed.2d 121, 107 S.Ct. 2759 (1987).

185. 18 U.S.C. § 1961(a).

186. See, e.g., Morgan v. Bank of Waukegan, 804 F.2d 970 (7th Cir. 1986); United States v. Teitler, 802 F.2d 606 (2d Cir. 1986).

187. Sedima, S.P.R.L. v. Imrex Co., 473 U.S. 479, 87 L.Ed.2d 346, 105 S.Ct. 3275, 3285 n.14 (1985) (hereafter "Sedima").

188. 18 U.S.C. § 1961(4).

trative, not exhaustive.[189] Both an enterprise and racketeering activity must be established.[190]

The Act authorizes a person injured in his business or property by a violation of the statute to sue in federal court and recover treble damages and attorneys' fees.[191] A violation may be proved by showing commission of one or more of the predicate acts but a prior criminal conviction is not necessary. In the leading case delineating the procedures to apply RICO in civil actions,[192] Justice White said that racketeering activity "consists of no more and no less than commission of a predicate act."

He went on to point out that Congress wanted to reach both "legitimate" and "illegitimate" enterprises. Those that are legitimate enjoy "neither an inherent incapacity for criminal activity nor immunity from its consequences." He recognized that RICO was being used against respected businesses allegedly engaged in "a pattern of specifically identified criminal conduct", but declared:

> It is true that private civil actions under the statute are being brought almost solely against such defendants, rather than against the archetypal, intimidating mobster. Yet this defect — if defect it is — is inherent in the statute as written, and its correction must lie with Congress. It is not for the judiciary to eliminate the private action in situations where Congress has provided it simply because plaintiffs are not taking advantage of it in its more difficult applications.[193]

Under Section 1964(c) of the statute, a plaintiff must prove that the injury resulted from a pattern of racketeering activity. This invokes the principle of proximate cause which is a

---

189. See, e.g., United States v. Thevis, 665 F.2d 616, 625 (5th Cir.), cert. denied, 456 U.S. 1008 (1982).

190. United States v. Turkette, 452 U.S. 576, 583, 69 L.Ed.2d 246, 101 S.Ct. 2524 (1981).

191. 18 U.S.C. § 1964(c).

192. Sedima, supra note 187, 473 U.S. at 495, 87 L.Ed.2d at 358, 105 S.Ct. at 3285.

193. Id., 473 U.S. at 499-500, 87 L.Ed.2d at 361, 105 S.Ct. at 3287.

fundamental element of a RICO claim. In a Seventh Circuit decision affirmed by the Supreme Court[194] it was so held. And in *Sedima,*[195] Justice White wrote:

> Where the plaintiff alleges each element of the violation, the compensable injury necessarily is the harm caused by the predicate acts sufficiently related to constitute a pattern, for the essence of the violation is the commission of those acts in connection with the conduct of the enterprise.... Any recoverable damages occurring by reason of a violation of § 1962(c) will flow from the commission of the predicate acts.

Many states have enacted their own RICO laws, patterned more or less after the federal act. Some state laws provide injunctive relief and state remedies may be more flexible than those in the federal statute. Some state laws provide no private remedies.[196] Because of the differences among them and their variations from the federal act, each state law should be examined to determine its applicability to a particular situation.

---

194. Haraco, Inc. v. American Nat'l Bank & Trust Co., 747 F.2d 384, 398 (7th Cir. 1984), aff'd, 473 U.S. 606, 87 L.Ed.2d 437, 105 S.Ct. 3291 (1985).

195. Sedima, supra note 187, 473 U.S. at 497, 87 L.Ed.2d at 359, 105 S.Ct. at 3286.

196. E.g., California, Connecticut, Pennsylvania, Puerto Rico.

COROLLARY REFERENCES

Baysinger & Butter, "Antitakeover Amendments, Managerial Entrenchment, and the Contractual Theory of the Corporation," 73 Va. L. Rev. 1257 (1985).

Buxbaum, "The Internal Division of Powers in Corporate Governance," 73 Cal. L. Rev. 1671 (1985).

Cox & Munsinger, "Bias in the Boardroom: Psychological Foundations and Legal Implications of Corporate Cohesion," 48 Law & Contemp. Probs. 83 (1985).

Davis, "Judicial Review of Fiduciary Decisionmaking — Some Theoretical Perspectives," 80 Nw. U.L. Rev. 1 (1985).

"Director Conflict of Interest Under the 1983 B.C.A.: A Standard of Fairness," 1985 U. Ill. L. Rev. 741.

Gates, "Recent Changes to Corporate Capacity and Agency," 15 Fed. L. Rev. 206 (1985).

Painter, "Civil Liability under the Federal Proxy Rules," 64 Wash. U.L.Q. 425 (1986).

Annotation, "Liability of Director or Dominant Shareholder for Enforcing Debt Legally Owed Him by Corporation," 56 A.L.R.3d 212 (1974).

Chapter 5

LIABILITY FOR DEBTS AND TO CREDITORS AND THIRD PERSONS

§ 5.01. Liability for corporate debts.

In view of the oft-stated premise that absent a statutory provision therefor directors are not liable for the debts or obligations of their corporation,[1] statutory provisions are of substantial importance. Delaware law permits a provision imposing liability upon shareholders to be included in the certificate of incorporation.[2] It imposes liability upon directors, jointly and severally, for willful or negligent violation[3] of the statutes relating to purchase, redemption or dealing in their corporation's stock,[4] and to declaration and payments of dividends. Such liability extends to creditors in the event of the corporation's dissolution or insolvency.[5]

Under California law directors who make false reports or entries, or issue or publish false documents, statements, or

---

1. Faulk v. Milton, 25 A.D.2d 314, 268 N.Y.S.2d 844 (1966), aff'd 20 N.Y.2d 894, 285 N.Y.S.2d 864, 232 N.E.2d 860 (1967); Medley Harwoods, Inc. v. Novy, 346 So. 2d 1224 (Fla. App. 1977).

2. Del. Code Ann. tit. 8, § 102(b)(6).

3. Id. § 174.

4. Id. § 160.

5. Id. § 174(a).

159

reports, are liable jointly and severally for all damages to their corporation or to any person injured.[6]

In New York[7] and Ohio,[8] and in several other states,[9] directors who vote for or concur in similar corporate actions are held liable to their corporation for the benefit of its creditors. The statutes vary in different jurisdictions, but the general form is to make directors or officers personally liable for corporate debts if they negligently or willfully fail to perform certain duties, or if they act against specific prohibitions. Some such statutes are "highly penal,"[10] although other statutes which impose liability upon directors to pay corporate debts are merely declaratory of the common law.[11]

It is generally considered that statutes of this type are remedial as to creditors,[12] but there is contrary authority.[13] When remedial, enforcement may be by the corporation itself, by its trustee in bankruptcy, or by its creditors.[14] When a statute creates liability to the corporation and to its creditors, action by the creditors is authorized.[15] California has permitted a direct action by a creditor under its statute.[16] Ordinarily

---

6. Cal. Corp. Code § 1507.

7. N.Y. Bus. Corp. Law § 719.

8. Ohio Rev. Code Ann. § 1701.95(A).

9. E.g., Wisc. Stat. Ann. § 180.40; Ill. Bus. Corp. Act § 8.65(b); Ky. Rev. Stat. Ann. § 271A.240.

10. Broderick v. Marcus, 146 Misc. 240, 261 N.Y.S. 625, aff'd, 239 A.D. 816, 263 N.Y.S. 981 (1933).

11. See Cockrill v. Cooper, 86 F. 7, 12 (8th Cir. 1898). Cf. Underwood v. Stafford, 270 N.C. 700, 155 S.W.2d 211 (1967).

12. Huntington v. Attrill, 146 U.S. 657, 36 L.Ed. 1123, 13 S.Ct. 224 (1892).

13. E.S. Parks Shellac Co. v. Harris, 237 Mass. 312, 129 N.E. 617 (1921); New Jersey Sign Erectors, Inc. v. Cocuzza, 72 N.J. Super. 269, 178 A.2d 111 (1962).

14. Cole v. Brandle, 127 N.J.Eq. 31, 11 A.2d 255 (1940); In re Dalton Elec. Co., 7 F. Supp. 465 (S.D. Miss. 1934).

15. See Seegmiller v. Day, 249 F. 177, 179 (7th Cir. 1918). Cf. N.Y. Bus. Corp. Law § 719, and Cal. Corp. Code § 316.

16. Hoover v. Galbraith, 7 Cal. 3d 519, 102 Cal. Rptr. 733, 498 P.2d 981 (1972); UMP Systems, Inc. v. Eltra Corp., 17 Cal. Rptr. 129, 553 P.2d 225 (1976).

such liability cannot be enforced by an assignee for the benefit of creditors,[17] at least where the statutory liability is not
an asset of the corporation.[18] The same principle appears applicable to a receiver's right to sue a director or officer, viz.,
whether the right belonged to the corporation as part of its
assets.[19]

A Michigan case involved a statute imposing personal liability on corporate officers for debts incurred by the corporation when it was in default for filing its annual report. The
question was whether officers who simply abandoned the corporation without taking any steps to terminate their status
as officers were subject to such liability. The court said, "The
answer must be yes. A position of corporate trust, like a mar-
riage, is not terminated merely by leaving the tent."[20]

Shareholders are liable to creditors of their corporation for
any amount unpaid on their stock. Such liability does not
necessarily depend upon constitutional or statutory provisions, but may be based upon the principle that the corporation's capital is a trust fund for the payment of its creditors.[21]
The law of the state of incorporation controls in determining
such liability,[22] which may be several[23] or joint and several.[24]

---

17. First Nat'l Bank v. Hingham Mfg. Co., 127 Mass. 563 (1879).

18. See McGivern v. Amasa Lumber Co., 77 Wis. 2d 241, 252 N.W.2d 371
(1977).

19. Stevirmac Oil & Gas Co. v. Smith, 259 F. 650 (E.D. Okla. 1919). Cf.
Belmont v. Gentry, 62 S.D. 118, 252 N.W. 1 (1933). See infra section 5.09.

20. Eberts Cadillac Co. v. Miller, 10 Mich. App. 270, 159 N.W.2d 217
(1968).

21. Potts v. Wallace, 146 U.S. 689, 36 L.Ed. 1135, 13 S.Ct. 196 (1892);
State ex rel. Havner v. Associated Packing Co., 210 Iowa 754, 227 N.W. 627
(1929).

22. Edwards v. Schillinger, 246 Ill. 231, 91 N.E. 1048 (1910); Harrigan v.
Bergdoll, 270 U.S. 560, 70 L.Ed. 733, 46 S.Ct. 413 (1926).

23. Edwards v. Schillinger, supra note 22.

24. Bottlers' Seal Co. v. Rainey, 243 N.Y. 333, 153 N.E. 437 (1926).

§ 5.02. Liability to creditors of corporation.

Corporate officers and directors are liable to creditors for damages caused by their fraud or deceit.[25] If they participate in obtaining property of third persons by fraud or misrepresentations, they are liable whether they act with knowledge, or recklessly in the absence of knowledge.[26] False representations may be made in reports, certificates, and the like,[27] in evidences of indebtedness such as corporate bonds,[28] in communications to a credit agency,[29] and in other ways.[30] When a corporate officer made false representations as to his corporation's financial condition which were relied upon, without disclosing his own claims against the corporation, he was held estopped from asserting his claims against persons who extended credit in reliance upon his representations.[31]

A corporation's president actually participated in negligent misrepresentations made by his corporation's agents, and he was held liable for common-law fraud, but his liability was not based on the controlling person theory.[32] The fact that the fraud was perpetrated for the benefit of the corporation will not shield an offending officer or director.[33]

Concealment of material facts or failure to make adequate disclosures to third persons,[34] as well as to fellow directors,[35]

---

25. Bobby Jones Garden Apts., Inc. v. Suleski, 391 F.2d 172 (5th Cir. 1968); Price v. Hibbs, 225 Cal. App. 2d 209, 37 Cal. Rptr. 270 (1964).

26. Citizens Sav. & Loan Ass'n v. Fischer, 67 Ill. App. 2d 315, 214 N.E.2d 612 (1966); Centennial Ins. Co. v. Vic Tanny Int'l, Inc., 46 Ohio App. 2d 137, 346 N.E.2d 330 (1975).

27. E.g., Salmon v. Richardson, 30 Conn. 360 (1862).

28. Bank of Atchison County v. Byers, 139 Mo. 627, 41 S.W. 325 (1897).

29. Forbes v. Auerbach, 56 So. 2d 895 (Fla. 1952).

30. E.g., Atlantic Aluminum & Metal Distribs., Inc. v. Standard Paint & Wallpaper Co., 327 Mass. 415, 198 N.E.2d 307 (1964); Bethesda Salvage Co. v. Fireman's Fund Ins. Co., 111 A.2d 472 (D.C. 1955).

31. Baker v. Seavey, 163 Mass. 522, 40 N.E. 863 (1895).

32. Cameron v. Outdoor Resorts of Am., Inc., 611 F.2d 105 (5th Cir. 1980).

33. Poulsen v. Treasure State Indus., Inc., 626 P.2d 822 (Mont. 1981).

34. E.g., Fowler v. Small, 244 S.W. 1096 (Tex. Civ. App. 1922).

35. W.G. Jenkins & Co., Bankers v. Standrod, 46 Idaho 614, 269 P. 586 (1928).

may constitute actionable fraud.[36] Where a principal shareholder was fraudulently preferred over other creditors by
debts to him that made his corporation insolvent, a tort
claimant was permitted a direct action against the principal
shareholder without first obtaining judgment against the corporation.[37]

Generally speaking the corporate veil will be pierced only
under exceptional circumstances,[38] such as where the corporation is a mere shell serving no legitimate purpose, or where
the corporate structure is illegally or fraudulently used to the
detriment of a third person who is a claimant or a creditor.[39]
Such fraud or illegal use must be proved by the party asserting it; fraud is not presumed.[40]

It is the element of fraud or deceit that differentiates the
cases holding officers and directors liable to creditors from
those which follow the general rule absolving officers and
directors from such liability.[41]

A creditor of a corporation may maintain an action against
the corporation's directors for fraud or mismanagement if the
creditor sustained an identifiable loss peculiar and personal
to itself. But where the misconduct results in loss to the corporation and its creditors generally, the right of action belongs to the corporation and must be maintained by it or by
its receiver.[42]

An Ohio case has held that creditors may not sue directors
of a corporation for violation of a statute prohibiting unlawful

---

36. Hill v. Hicks, 44 Ga. App. 817, 163 S.E. 253 (1932).

37. Sampay v. Davis, 342 So. 2d 1186 (La. App. 1977).

38. Bewigged by Suzzi, Inc. v. Atlantic Dept. Stores, Inc., 49 Ohio App.
2d 65, 359 N.E.2d 721 (1976).

39. Thomas v. Southside Contractors, Inc., 543 S.W.2d 917 (Ark. 1976).
Cf. Lushute v. Diesi, 343 So. 2d 1132 (La. App.), modified, 354 So. 2d 179
(La. 1977).

40. Matassa v. Temple, 346 So. 2d 803 (La. App. 1977).

41. 18B Am. Jur. 2d Corporations § 1842.

42. Ford Motor Credit Co. v. Minges, 473 F.2d 918, 921 (4th Cir. 1973).

distributions of corporate assets. The liability imposed by that statute runs to the corporation.[43]

Under Georgia law an action for mismanagement against corporate directors should be brought by the corporation or for its benefit, and not by a single creditor in its own behalf. The court distinguished an earlier Georgia decision which permitted such an action.[44]

In Alabama it was held that a statute providing that the assets of an insolvent corporation constitute a trust fund for the benefit of corporate creditors did not permit individual creditors to sue the corporation's directors, and did not extend the liability of the directors beyond the duties recognized by the common law.[45]

However, a Minnesota court has held that directors and officers owe a fiduciary duty to creditors, and the sole officer-director-shareholder of a corporation breached this duty by preferring himself as a creditor over the other creditors of the corporation.[46]

§ 5.03. Liability for conversion of property of others.

When a corporation converts property belonging to third persons to its own use, there is some authority that directors or officers of the corporation may be held personally liable for their negligence which directly causes or contributes to such conversion. For such liability to exist, the directors or officers must participate in the transaction or have knowledge amounting to acquiescence, or they must be guilty of negligence in the management of the corporate affairs causing or contributing to the conversion.

Thus, in a case involving the wrongful use of the plaintiff's money and stored grain by a milling company, now bankrupt,

---

43. Schaefer v. DeChant, 11 Ohio App. 3d 281, 464 N.E.2d 583 (1983).

44. Super Valu Stores, Inc. v. First Nat'l Bank, 463 F. Supp. 1183, 1196 (M.D. Ga. 1979).

45. Jefferson Pilot Broadcasting Co. v. Hilary & Hogan, Inc., 458 F. Supp. 310, 313 (M.D. Ala. 1978).

46. Snyder Elec. Co. v. Fleming, 305 N.W.2d 863 (Minn. 1981).

one director, who was president, managing officer, and in active charge of the company's business affairs, was denied a summary judgment. The remaining directors, who had no knowledge of the transactions, were dismissed.[47]

Also, where a defendant neglected her duties as an officer and director of a travel agency, but her neglect was not the cause of the misappropriation of a customer's money, it was held that her negligence was not clear and gross, and judgment against her was reversed.[48]

A New York appellate court has held that a director, who was one of three shareholders of a corporation, was not personally liable for the corporation's conversion of promissory notes where he had no knowledge that proceeds from the sale of the notes had been deposited in the corporation's account. The court stated that even if the director had a duty to investigate, that duty was owed only to the corporation, not the injured third party. The court further noted that mere negligence is not enough to hold a director personally liable in this type of case.[49]

The question of priority may be significant in such cases, although it has been held that a corporation's creditor, reasonably relying on the discharge of their duties by its directors and showing injury because of their neglect to do so, has a remedial right against them personally.[50] The opposite view was taken in an Alabama case wherein the court held that a mere corporate creditor cannot hold a corporate officer liable for neglect, as distinguished from a fraudulent transfer or misapplication of funds derived from the payment of corporate debts; and that corporate directors and officers are trustees for the shareholders but not for the creditors,

---

47. Taylor v. Alston, 79 N.M. 643, 447 P.2d 523 (1967).

48. Dunbar v. Finegold, 501 P.2d 144 (Colo. App. 1972). See also Olin Mathieson Chem. Corp. v. Planters Corp., 236 S.C. 318, 114 S.E.2d 321 (1960).

49. Ecuador Importadora-Exportadora C., L. v. ITF (Overseas) Corp., 94 A.D.2d 113, 463 N.Y.S.2d 208 (1983).

50. Virginia-Carolina Chem. Co. v. Ehrich, 230 F. 1005 (E.D.S.C. 1916). See also Rosebud Corp. v. Boggio, 561 P.2d 367 (Colo. App. 1977).

whether the corporation is solvent or insolvent.[51] That decision does not appear to follow the current weight of authority.

§ 5.04. Liability for corporate checks issued against insufficient funds.

In a few cases corporate officers and directors have been held personally liable for corporate checks issued against insufficient funds. On the basis of a claim for fraud and deceit, a New York court imposed such liability because the corporate officer was chargeable with knowledge of the state of the corporation's bank account, and issuance of the check constituted his representation that it would be paid upon presentation.[52] In a similar case the officer was negligent in failing to determine whether there were sufficient funds.[53] Colorado reached a like result where the trial court found the defendants-directors knew, or should have known, of the falsity of the representations and the consequential damages likely to result therefrom.[54] A famous Kansas decision was to the same effect.[55] And a Georgia case follows the same rule.[56]

"Check-kiting" schemes have imposed liability upon corporate officers in Maine[57] and Louisiana[58] where bank accounts in separate cities were utilized to provide a fictitious cash flow, resulting in losses to the banks.

However, where the payee had actual notice that a corporation's president issued its check in a representative capacity

---

51. Tennessee Chem. Co. v. Cheatham, 217 Ala. 399, 116 So. 420 (1928).

52. Lippman Packing Corp. v. Rose, 203 Misc. 1041, 120 N.Y.S.2d 571 (1953). See also Kilbourn v. Western Sur. Co., 187 F.2d 567 (10th Cir. 1951).

53. Jones v. Freeman's Dairy, Inc., 283 A.D. 667, 127 N.Y.S.2d 200, modified on other grounds, 283 A.D. 806, 129 N.Y.S.2d 498 (1954).

54. Klockner v. Keser, 29 Colo. App. 476, 488 P.2d 1135 (1971).

55. Meehan v. Adams Enter., Inc., 211 Kan. 353, 507 P.2d 849 (1973).

56. Super Valu Stores, Inc. v. First Nat'l Bank, 463 F. Supp. 1183, 1194 (M.D. Ga. 1979).

57. Eastern Trust & Banking Co. v. Cunningham, 103 Me. 455, 70 A. 17 (1908).

58. National Bank of Commerce v. Hughes-Walsh Co., 246 So. 2d 872 (La. App. 1971).

and would not suffer loss in reliance on the check, South Dakota imposed no personal liability on the officer.[59] Likewise, a New York case held that the failure of a corporate officer to ascertain the sufficiency of funds to pay a check constituted only nonfeasance and did not impose liability upon him.[60]

In Utah the evidence disclosed that both the director who issued a corporate check and the payee knew that there were no funds presently available to pay it. The court held the director not liable, the premise being that the instrument was not a check but merely a promise to pay in the future.[61]

§ 5.05. Effects of insolvency.

When a corporation is insolvent, there is a general rule that its directors and officers are to be considered as though trustees of its property for corporate creditors as beneficiaries.[62] This duty arises upon insolvency, under New York law, and not just when liquidation is imminent and foreseeable.[63]

In some states the corporate trust fund doctrine applies.[64] It does not, in fact, involve the application of any "trust," but provides that a court will administer the assets of an insolvent corporation first among its creditors and then among its shareholders. Any controlling person who breaches his "trust" is personally liable for the damage he does.[65]

Because of their position as fiduciaries, directors and officers of an insolvent corporation stand as trustees of the corpo-

---

59. Viajes Iberia, S.A. v. Dougherty, 87 S.D. 591, 212 N.W.2d 656 (1973).

60. Jones v. Freeman's Dairy, Inc., supra note 53.

61. Howells, Inc. v. Nelson, 565 P.2d 1147 (Utah 1977).

62. New York Credit Men's Adjustment Bur. v. Weiss, 305 N.Y. 1, 7, 110 N.E.2d 397 (1953).

63. Clarkson Co. v. Shaheen, 660 F.2d 506, 512 (2d Cir. 1981), cert. denied, 445 U.S. 990 (1982). See also infra section 5.08.

64. E.g., In re Mortgage Am. Corp., 714 F.2d 1266 (5th Cir. 1983); In re Independent Clearing House Co., 41 B.R. 98 (Bankr. D. Utah 1984).

65. In re Mortgage Am. Corp., supra note 64, at 1269.

rate properties for the benefit of creditors first and share-holders second.[66]

§ 5.06. Liability as trustees after dissolution.

Because a corporation is a creature of statute and exists only under the law of the state by which it was created, its dissolution puts an end to its existence. Any prolongation of its life, even for litigation purposes, requires statutory authority.[67] Dissolution may be voluntary or by court action. In most states statutes provide for winding up the affairs of a dissolved corporation and for protecting the rights of creditors and shareholders during the liquidation process.[68]

Liability of directors as trustees after dissolution commonly arises from (1) distribution of assets to shareholders without paying or making adequate provisions to pay all known liabilities of the corporation,[69] and (2) continuing the corporation's business in violation of their statutory duty as trustees to liquidate the corporation and distribute its assets.[70]

Generally, directors, as such trustees, or when appointed by a court for the purpose of corporate liquidation,[71] have the duty to wind up its affairs, and may be held personally liable for debts contracted in continuing the business of the corporation.[72] As such trustees, they may enforce the corporation's contractual rights and pay its debts created prior to its dissolution, although they are not to perform its executory con-

---

66. Bank Leumi-Le-Israel, B.M. v. Sunbelt Indus., Inc., 485 F. Supp. 556, 559 (S.D. Ga. 1980).

67. Chicago Title & Trust Co. v. Forty-One Thirty-Six Wilcox Bldg. Corp., 302 U.S. 120, 125, 82 L.Ed. 147, 58 S.Ct. 125, 127 (1937).

68. 19 Am. Jur. 2d Corporations § 2828.

69. See, e.g., N.Y. Bus. Corp. Law § 719(a)(3); Ohio Rev. Code Ann. § 1701.95(A)(2).

70. See, e.g., Ill. Bus. Corp. Act § 8.65; Del. Code Ann. tit. 8, § 278.

71. E.g., Del. Code Ann. tit. 8, § 279; cf. John Julian Constr. Co. v. Monarch Bldrs., Inc., 324 A.2d 208 (Del. 1974).

72. American Mtg. & Safe Deposit Co. v. Rubin, 168 So. 2d 777 (Fla. App. 1964); First Nat'l Bank v. Silberstein, 398 S.W.2d 914 (Tex. 1966).

tracts beyond the extent necessary or incidental to collection of its assets.[73] Their duties have been compared to those of an administrator or executor of an estate.

The corporation's assets constitute a fund for payment of the corporation's debts and, after dissolution, the surviving directors are charged with managing that fund for the interest of the corporation's creditors until they have been paid.[74] Their liability for breach of their duties is joint and several.[75]

Persons injured by products manufactured by a corporation which dissolved prior to the injury have generally been unsuccessful in recovering from the corporation's directors on the theory that the directors failed to adequately provide for future liabilities upon dissolution.[76] In so holding, courts have recognized a legislative policy to protect shareholders, officers, and directors of a dissolved corporation from prolonged and uncertain liability.

§ 5.07. Actions by creditors.

If corporate managers cause direct loss to particular creditors by such means as fraud, conversion of property, libel, or other civil wrongs, the injured party would have a direct action against the wrongdoer.[77] If, however, the wrong is done to the corporation with resulting insolvency and inability to pay its obligations, the creditors as a class may not usually bring a direct action against the corporate managers. Moreover, the general rule is that creditors may not bring a derivative action on behalf of the corporation, to recoup such a

---

73. See, e.g., Turner v. Browne, 351 Mo. 541, 173 S.W.2d 868 (1943); Young v. Blandin, 215 Minn. 111, 9 N.W.2d 313 (1943).

74. United States Fire Ins. Co. v. Morejon, 338 So. 2d 223 (Fla. App. 1976); Snyder v. Nathan, 353 F.2d 3 (7th Cir. 1965).

75. Leibson v. Henry, 356 Mo. 953, 204 S.W.2d 310 (1947).

76. Blankenship v. Demmler Mfg. Co., 89 Ill. App. 3d 569, 44 Ill. Dec. 787, 411 N.E.2d 1153 (1980); Hunter v. Ft. Worth Capital Corp., 620 S.W.2d 547 (Tex. 1981).

77. Nevada Land & Mtg. Co. v. Lamb, 90 Nev. 249, 524 P.2d 326 (1974); City of Muskegon v. Amec, Inc., 62 Mich. App. 644, 233 N.W.2d 688 (1975).

loss.[78] For example, a creditor lacked standing to assert a claim against its directors and officers for negligence in failing properly to supervise corporate employees. The court ruled that the duty of supervision was owed to the shareholders, not to creditors.[79]

In Wisconsin a creditor holding a corporation's note asserted a claim for "intentional deceit"[80] against the corporation's former president and his wife for inducing the plaintiff to remain a creditor of their lumber company. The court held that the claim was a single and exclusive injury resulting from a direct tort of a director and officer which could be asserted in a direct action against the director and officer. The court distinguished this case from one in which the wrongdoing had caused loss to the corporation, and in which a derivative action was required for the benefit of persons entitled to participate in distribution of the corporation's assets.[81]

To the extent that holders of convertible subordinated debentures are creditors under state laws, rather than security holders under the Securities Exchange Act, there is authority pro[82] and con[83] as to their right to maintain derivative actions.

Creditors, generally, are subject to conflicting decisions in various jurisdictions as to their right to maintain class actions against corporate officers and directors in the absence of specific statutory authorization. A creditors' bill in equity was allowed in Massachusetts.[84] Illinois required a class ac-

---

78. E.g., Dorfman v. Chemical Bank, 56 F.R.D. 363, 364 (S.D.N.Y. 1972); Dodge v. First Wis. Trust Co., 394 F. Supp. 1124 (E.D. Wis. 1975).

79. Ponderosa Dev. Corp. v. Bjordahl, 586 F. Supp. 877 (D. Wyo. 1984).

80. Cf. Stevenson v. Barwineck, 8 Wis. 2d 557, 99 N.W.2d 690 (1959); Whipp v. Iverson, 43 Wis. 2d 166, 168 N.W.2d 201 (1969).

81. McGivern v. Amasa Lumber Co., 77 Wis. 2d 241, 252 N.W.2d 371 (1977).

82. E.g., Hoff v. Sprayregan, 52 F.R.D. 243 (S.D.N.Y. 1971); In re United States Fin. Sec. Litig., 69 F.R.D. 24 (S.D. Cal. 1975).

83. Hariff v. Kerkorian, 324 A.2d 215 (Del. Ch. 1974), modified, 347 A.2d 133 (1975); Brooks v. Welser, 57 F.R.D. 491 (S.D.N.Y. 1972).

84. Burke v. Marlboro Awning Co., 330 Mass. 294, 113 N.E.2d 222 (1953).

tion where directors were held for incurring debts in excess of capital.[85] In New York it appears that a direct action is permitted.[86]

When a creditor is permitted to maintain a derivative action against corporate officers and directors, he may not be required to comply with all of the procedural requirements that must be satisfied by a shareholder bringing such an action,[87] but he must show an endeavor to get redress within the corporation[88] or that such an endeavor would be unavailing as, for example, where the controlling directors or officers are themselves the wrongdoers.[89]

§ 5.08. Liability when corporation is bankrupt or insolvent.

The filing of a bankruptcy petition instantly alters the rights of the corporation's creditors and the obligations of its directors and officers. The assets must then be managed for the benefit of the creditors, not the shareholders.[90] Consequently, the directors and officers may be personally liable to creditors for transactions which damaged them when the corporation was insolvent or when the transactions produced the insolvency. The Supreme Court has imposed such liability when a dominant and controlling shareholder manipulated corporate assets to the injury of creditors prior to the bankruptcy. This rule is not changed by the Bankruptcy Reform Act of 1978 which is the Bankruptcy Code.[91]

---

85. Albert Pick & Co. v. Warshauer, 244 Ill. App. 56 (1927).

86. Whalen v. Strong, 230 A.D. 617, 246 N.Y.S. 40 (1930); Lonas v. Layman Pressed Rod Co., 242 A.D. 444, 275 N.Y.S. 27 (1934), aff'd, 269 N.Y. 529, 199 N.E. 520 (1935).

87. Davis v. Ben O'Callaghan Co., 238 Ga. 218, 232 S.E.2d 53 (1977). See infra Chapter 18.

88. Waters v. Spalt, 22 Misc. 2d 937, 80 N.Y.S.2d 681 (1948).

89. See Creamery Package Mfg. Co. v. Wilhite, 149 Ark. 576, 233 S.W. 710 (1921).

90. Pepper v. Litton, 308 U.S. 295, 306-07, 84 L.Ed. 281, 60 S.Ct. 238 (1939).

91. Id. See also 11 U.S.C. § 510(c).

The overriding nature of the bankruptcy law to void a preferential transfer cannot be circumvented. So the Tenth Circuit held in a case involving Colorado common law which attempted to impose liability on corporate officers and directors who breached their fiduciary duties owed to the company's creditors. No party to the action challenged jurisdiction. The district court entered judgment for the creditor plaintiff. But the Tenth Circuit sua sponte considered the effect of Chapter 11 proceedings commenced prior to the trial. It ruled that the Bankruptcy Code conferred exclusive jurisdiction on the bankruptcy court. The judgment for the creditor was reversed and remanded with instructions to dismiss the action.[92]

When a corporation is insolvent, the duty owed the shareholders is shifted to the creditors, not only as to matters preceding the filing of the petition[93] but also as to subsequent acts.[94] A corporation's redemption of the shares of its sole shareholder was held a fraudulent transfer under the Bankruptcy Code when the corporation was insolvent and bankruptcy was imminent.[95] Not only the Bankruptcy Code[96] but also the Uniform Fraudulent Conveyance Act and the Uniform Fraudulent Transfer Act treat such matters as fraudulent transfers for less than reasonably equivalent value when a corporation is undercapitalized, insolvent or unable to pay its debts as they mature.

In the merger/takeover climate, it is well to bear in mind that if a leveraged buyout is a fraudulent transfer, directors, officers and shareholders may be required to surrender any benefits they receive in the transaction. Extensive litigation in the Third Circuit imposed personal liability on directors and officers of Raymond Corporation who received payment

---

92. Delgado Oil Co. v. Torres, 785 F.2d 857 (10th Cir. 1985).

93. See Clarkson Co. v. Shaheen, 660 F.2d 506 (2d Cir. 1981), cert. denied, 445 U.S. 990 (1982).

94. E.g., In re Happy Time Fashions, Inc., 7 B.R. 665, 671 (Bankr. S.D.N.Y. 1980).

95. Consove v. Cohen (In re Roco Corp.), 701 F.2d 978 (1st Cir. 1983).

96. 11 U.S.C. § 548(a)(2).

for their shares from the assets of a financially insecure company. The courts deemed the payments to be distributions in the nature of dividends to the detriment of creditors.[97]

A reorganization trustee appointed under Chapter X of the Bankruptcy Act was held to be without standing to assert claims against former corporate officers and directors on behalf of the corporation's creditors and debenture purchasers under the former bankruptcy law.[98] In so ruling, the Ninth Circuit followed the Supreme Court's decision in *Caplin v. Marine Midland Grace Trust Company of New York*[99] that a Chapter X reorganization trustee may not assert such claims on behalf of any person or entity other than his debtor corporation. However, a reorganization trustee does have standing to assert the debtor corporation's federal securities law claims against its former officers and directors arising out of the corporation's issuance, reacquisition and resale of its debentures.

Also a reorganization trustee was permitted to invoke the Bankruptcy Act as a means of asserting claims for common-law liability against such officers and directors. By this means he could restore lost corporate assets which, in turn, would be available to pay creditors' claims. Thus the reorganization trustee had standing to sue on behalf of the corporation in at least this instance where the creditors could not do so.[100]

Whether a reorganization trustee is an adequate representative to bring an action in behalf of a class of defrauded shareholders has been answered in the negative in the Second Circuit.[101]

---

97. See United States v. Gleneagles Inv. Corp., 565 F. Supp. 556, 583-85 (M.D. Pa. 1983), aff'd sub nom. United States v. Tabor Court Realty Corp., 803 F.2d 1288 (3d Cir. 1986).

98. 535 F.2d 523 (9th Cir. 1976).

99. 406 U.S. 416, 32 L.Ed.2d 195, 92 S.Ct. 1678 (1974).

100. See also Williams v. Austrian, 331 U.S. 642, 91 L.Ed. 1718, 67 S.Ct. 1443 (1947), rev'g 159 F.2d 67 (2d Cir.) and aff'g 67 F. Supp. 223 (S.D.N.Y. 1946).

101. Bloor v. Carro, Spanbock, Londin, Rodman & Fass, 754 F.2d 57, 62 n.4 (2d Cir. 1985).

173

A trustee in bankruptcy has only the powers conferred upon him by the Bankruptcy Act. He steps into the shoes of the bankrupt and generally has standing to bring any action the bankrupt could have brought if it had remained solvent.[102] But a trustee may not sue upon claims which do not belong to the bankrupt estate that were assigned to him by the bankrupt's creditors.[103] Thus, the Sixth Circuit held that a trustee in bankruptcy had no standing to sue the bankrupt's liability insurance company on a claim of a creditor who had not reduced the claim to judgment against the bankrupt.[104] The court distinguished this case from one in which a trustee in bankruptcy asserted creditors' rights to avoid transactions of the bankrupt corporation on the theory that such transactions were in fraud of its creditors.

§ 5.09. Actions by receiver of corporation.

Since the decision in *Briggs v. Spaulding*[105] it has been established that the common-law liability of a corporate officer or director to his corporation for mismanagement may be enforced by a receiver of the corporation. The corporation's claims against its officers and directors for mismanagement are inchoate assets which may be recovered by its receiver.

When a receiver has the right to enforce such common-law liability, he acts for the benefit of all creditors and stockholders.[106] There is a conflict of authorities as to his right to sue if the corporation, by acquiescence in the acts complained of, could not do so.[107]

Whether a corporation's receiver may enforce claims of statutory liability against its officers and directors depends

---

102. Bayliss v. Rood, 424 F.2d 142 (4th Cir. 1970).

103. In re Petroleum Corp. of Am., 417 F.2d 929 (8th Cir. 1969).

104. Cissell v. American Home Assurance Co., 521 F.2d 790 (6th Cir.), cert. denied, 423 U.S. 1074 (1976).

105. 141 U.S. 132, 35 L.Ed. 662, 11 S.Ct. 924 (1891). See also Michelsen v. Penney, 135 F.2d 409 (2d Cir. 1943).

106. Baker v. Sutton, 47 Ga. App. 176, 170 S.E. 95 (1933).

107. Fordham v. Poor, 109 Misc. 187, 179 N.Y.S. 367 (1919). But see McCullam v. Buckingham Hotel Co., 198 Mo. App. 107, 199 S.W. 417 (1917).

upon the statutory provisions.[108] In particular, if the statute creates a claim in favor of the corporation's creditors, such liability is usually not considered an asset of the corporation and cannot be enforced by its receiver.[109] The scope of the receivership statute may have a bearing on this point. If the receiver represents both the corporation and the creditors,[110] he will be in a better position to assert such claims than if he represents only the corporation.[111]

§ 5.10. Actions involving patent infringement.

Patent infringements have recently become a basis for imposing personal liability upon corporate officers and directors. Until a 1985 decision of the Federal Circuit, there was divergence of opinion among other courts as to the imposition of personal liability upon corporate managers. Now the Federal Circuit has held that one who supervises and directs the infringing activities of his corporation may be liable for inducing infringement under Section 271(b) of the Patent Act.[112]

In that case the Lang company president was notified of a claim of infringement and was offered a license. He responded that before he would pay the patent owner a nickel, he would see it "in the courthouse."[113] The trial court found willfulness and awarded Power Lift attorney fees and costs from both the company and its president. The Federal Circuit affirmed.

---

108. Seegmiller v. Day, 249 F. 177 (7th Cir. 1918); Stevirmac Oil & Gas Co. v. Smith, 259 F. 650 (E.D. Okla. 1919).

109. Fordham v. Poor, supra note 107; Belmont v. Gentry, 62 S.D. 118, 252 N.W. 1 (1933).

110. Folsom v. Smith, 113 Me. 82, 92 A. 1003 (1915); Bowers v. Male, 186 N.Y. 28, 78 N.E. 577 (1906); cf. Ventress v. Wallace, 111 Miss. 357, 71 So. 636 (1916).

111. McCullam v. Buckingham Hotel Co., supra note 107.

112. Power Lift, Inc. v. Lang Tools, Inc., 774 F.2d 478, 481 (Fed. Cir. 1985), construing 35 U.S.C. § 271(b).

113. Id. at 482.

The *Lang Tools* decision was followed by the Federal Circuit in a 1986 decision[114] holding that "corporate officers who actively aid and abet their corporation's infringement may be personally liable for inducing infringement under [35 U.S.C.] § 271(b) regardless of whether the corporation is the alter ego of the corporate officer." The court pointed out that infringement of a patent is a tort. It ruled:

> [O]fficers of a corporation are personally liable for tortious conduct of the corporation if they personally took part in the commission of the tort or specifically directed their officers, agents, or employees of the corporation to commit the tortious act.[115]

In such cases, when there is notice of a claim of infringement, the company's management may be well advised to seek advice of experienced patent counsel, follow such advice, and be certain that the action taken is that of the company and not merely one brought about by an officer as "a moving force."[116]

---

114. Orthokimetics, Inc. v. Safety Travel Chairs, Inc., 806 F.2d 1565 (Fed. Cir. 1986).

115. Id. at 1579.

116. Central Soya Co., Inc. v. Geo. A. Hormel & Co., 723 F.2d 1573, 1577 (Fed. Cir. 1983); Power Lift, Inc. v. Lang Tools, Inc., supra note 112, at 481.

COROLLARY REFERENCES

K. Davis, Jr., "The Status of Defrauded Securityholders in Corporate Bankruptcy," 1983 Duke L.J. 1.

Douglas-Hamilton, "Creditor Liabilities Resulting from Improper Interference with the Management of a Financially Troubled Debtor," 31 Bus. Law. 343 (1975).

Fuld, "Recovery of Illegal and Partial Liquidating Dividends from Stockholders," 28 Va. L. Rev. 50 (1941).

Kempin, "Enforcement of Management's Duties to Corporate Creditors," 6 Am. Bus. L.J. 381 (1968).

Norton, "Relationship of Shareholders to Corporate Creditors upon Dissolution: Nature and Implications of the 'Trust Fund' Doctrine of Corporate Assets," 30 Bus. Law. 1061 (1974).

Note, "Bankruptcy — Corporate Directors' Negligence — Shareholders' Ratification and Creditors' Rights," 35 Tenn. L. Rev. 673 (1968).

Annotation, "Liability of corporate directors or officers for negligence in permitting conversion of property of third persons by corporation," 29 A.L.R.3d 660 (1970).

Annotation, "Personal liability of officers or directors of corporation on corporate checks issued against insufficient funds," 47 A.L.R.3d 1250 (1973).

Annotation, "Personal liability of stockholder, officer or agent for debt of foreign corporation doing business in the state," 27 A.L.R.4th 387 (1984).

Annotation, "Persons liable under statutes imposing, upon directors, officers, or trustees of a corporation, personal liability for its debts on account of their failure to file or publish reports, required by law, as to corporate matters," 39 A.L.R.3d 428 (1971).

Chapter 6

BUSINESS JUDGMENT RULE

§ 6.01. Definition.

The business judgment rule is defined in court decisions. It is a part of the development of legal concepts relating to the control and management of private corporations. The Delaware Supreme Court has said:

> The business judgment rule is an acknowledgment of the managerial prerogatives of Delaware directors under Section 141(a).[1] ... It is a presumption that in making a business decision the directors of a corporation acted on an informed basis, in good faith and in the honest belief that the action taken was in the best interests of the company.[2]

The drafters of the Revised Model Business Corporation Act pointed out in their Official Comment that the "elements of the business judgment rule and the circumstances for its application are continuing to be developed by the courts."

---

1. Del. Code Ann. tit. 8, § 141(a).
2. Aronson v. Lewis, 473 A.2d 805, 812 (Del. 1984).

179

Accordingly, any attempt to codify it was left to the courts and to later revisions of the Model Act.[3] The draftsmen of the American Law Institute's Corporate Governance Project, in their Section 4.01(d), have undertaken to define the business judgment rule, but that draft is still in the tentative form.[4] At this writing the draft language states:

> (d) A director or officer does not violate his duty under this Section with respect to the consequences of a business judgment if he:
> (1) was informed with respect to the subject of the business judgment to the extent he reasonably believed to be appropriate under the circumstances;
> (2) was not interested [§ 1.15] in the subject of the business judgment and made the judgment in good faith; and
> (3) had a rational basis for believing that the business judgment was in the best interests of the corporation.

An oft-cited opinion of the Delaware Supreme Court holds that decisions of a board of directors "will not be disturbed if they can be attributed to any rational business purpose."[5] That language is somewhat less limiting than subparagraph (d)(3) of the ALI draft quoted above.[6] Nonetheless the courts and commentators are in agreement that "a judgment that cannot be sustained on some rational basis falls outside the protection of the business judgment rule."[7]

3. 2 Model Bus. Corp. Act Ann. 928 (3d ed. 1985).

4. ALI, Principles of Corporate Governance: Analysis and Recommendations (Tent. Draft No. 3, April 13, 1984).

5. Sinclair Oil Corporation v. Levien, 280 A.2d 717, 720 (Del. 1971). Accord, Gimbel v. Signal Cos., Inc., 316 A.2d 599, 609 (Del. Ch.), aff'd, 316 A.2d 619 (Del. 1974); Kaplan v. Goldsamt, 380 A.2d 556, 568 (Del. Ch. 1977).

6. See also Block, Barton & Radin, "The Business Judgment Rule-Application, Limitations and the Burden of Proof," Practising Law Institute Course Handbook No. 485 (B4-6718), at 28-29 (1985).

7. Arsht, "The Business Judgment Rule Revisited," 8 Hofstra L. Rev. 93, 122 (1979).

Countless court decisions have described the business judgment rule and have used differing terms to explain it. Among its essential components are:

(1) the absence of personal interest or self-dealing;
(2) an informed decision, attributable to a rational business purpose, based on a reasonable effort to learn the facts;
(3) a reasonable belief that the decision is in the best interests of the corporation; and
(4) good faith.[8]

In the absence of fraud, bad faith, gross overreaching or abuse of discretion, courts will not interfere with the exercise of business judgment by corporate directors.[9]

§ 6.02. Application to action by directors.

The business judgment rule operates in the context of director action. Technically, it has no role where directors either have abdicated their functions or have failed to act, unless the failure to act resulted from a conscious decision not to act.[10] In court opinions describing the rule, the issues presented usually relate to discrete, separate questions presented to and acted upon by a board of directors. But, instead of making such specific decisions, a board may act by selecting which matters to consider and by employing compromise and consensus to reach conclusions.[11] When a negotiated conclusion is not to act on a particular issue, is it "a conscious decision" to refrain from acting to which the business judg-

---

8. See Hinsey, "Business Judgment and the American Law Institute's Corporate Governance Project: The Rule, the Doctrine, and the Reality," 52 Geo. Wash. L. Rev. 609, 610 (1984).

9. Panter v. Marshall Field & Co., 646 F.2d 271, 293 (7th Cir.) cert. denied, 454 U.S. 1092 (1981).

10. Aronson v. Lewis, 473 A.2d 805, 813 (Del. 1984).

11. See, e.g., Manning, "The Business Judgment Rule and the Director's Duty of Attention: Time for Reality," 39 Bus. Law. 1477, 1483 (1984).

ment rule is applicable? One commentator believes that "[t]he most important action is the choice of what to act on."[12]

When the activity in the boardroom is "a continuing flow of supervisory process, punctuated only occasionally by a discrete transactional decision",[13] the business judgment rule may be difficult to apply. For example, it is arguable that no business decision was made by the Trans Union board in *Smith v. Van Gorkom*[14] because the "'directors were so unprepared and acted so quickly that they could not, and did not, really make a judgment."[15] In that case, the business judgment rule provided no defense for the directors. There is precedent for that result in a New York decision which pointed out that "[a] director cannot close his eyes to what is going on about him in the conduct of the business of the corporation and have it said that he was exercising business judgment."[16]

During one National Institute[17] it was noted that no meaningful challenge can be mounted to most routine corporate decisions, the test coming "in the extraordinary transaction, contests for corporate control, and in the handling of derivative suits."[18]

§ 6.03. Policy reasons for rule.

The business judgment rule is grounded, at least in part, in the recognition that courts are ill-equipped and infrequently called on to evaluate what are and must be essentially business judgments. There is no objective standard by which the correctness of every corporate decision may be measured, by the courts or otherwise. The responsibility for business judg-

---

12. Id. at 1485.

13. Id. at 1494.

14. 488 A.2d 858 (Del. 1985).

15. See Manning, "Reflections and Practical Tips for Life in the Boardroom After Van Gorkom," 41 Bus. Law. 1, 4 (1985).

16. Casey v. Woodruff, 49 N.Y.S.2d 265 (1944).

17. Sponsored by the Section of Corporation, Banking and Business Law, American Bar Association, in New York City, December 8-9, 1983.

18. Veasey, "New Insights into Judicial Deference to Directors' Business Decisions: Should We Trust the Courts?," 39 Bus. Law. 1461, 1464 (1984).

ments must rest with corporate directors, because their individual capabilities and experience peculiarly qualify them for the discharge of that responsibility.[19] The business judgment rule applies to protect directors who have performed diligently and carefully and have not acted fraudulently, illegally, or otherwise in bad faith.[20]

Courts recognize that after-the-fact litigation is a most imperfect device to evaluate corporate business decisions. Business imperatives often call for quick decisions, inevitably based on less than perfect information. Corporate directors perform an entrepreneur's function, which involves encountering risks and confronting uncertainty. A reasoned decision at the time may seem "a wild hunch" reviewed years later against a background of perfect knowledge.[21]

The Second Circuit has said that shareholders, to a very real degree, voluntarily undertake the risk of bad business judgment. Moreover, potential profit responds to potential risk, so it is much in the interest of shareholders that the law avoid creating incentives for "overly cautious corporate decisions."[22]

The business judgment rule is intended to prevent "Monday morning-quarterbacking,"[23] encourage initiative in enterprise decisions, encourage qualified persons to serve as directors, encourage decision-making by independent directors, and give directors wide latitude in their handling of corporate affairs.[24]

---

19. Auerbach v. Bennett, 47 N.Y.2d 619, 419 N.Y.S.2d 920, 393 N.E.2d 994, 1000 (1979).

20. Treco, Inc. v. Land of Lincoln Sav. & Loan, 749 F.2d 374, 377 (7th Cir. 1984).

21. Joy v. North, 692 F.2d 880, 886 (2d Cir. 1982), cert. denied, 460 U.S. 1051 (1983).

22. Id. at 885, 886.

23. Panter v. Marshall Field & Co., 646 F.2d 271, 297 (7th Cir.), cert. denied, 454 U.S. 1092 (1981).

24. Cramer v. General Tel. & Elec. Corp., 582 F.2d 259, 274 (3d Cir. 1978).

Nonetheless, the courts recognize that their "most important duty is to protect the fundamental structure of corporate governance." In that context the Second Circuit holds:

> While the day-to-day affairs of a company are to be managed by its officers under the supervision of directors, decisions affecting a corporation's ultimate destiny are for the shareholders to make in accordance with democratic procedures.[25]

§ 6.04. Preconditions to application of rule.

The business judgment rule does not apply when directors are shown to have a self-interest in the transaction at issue.[26] Thus, once self-dealing or bad faith is demonstrated, the duty of loyalty supersedes the duty of care, and the burden shifts to the directors to "prove that the transaction was fair and reasonable to the corporation."[27]

There are five preconditions which must generally be present in order for the business judgment rule to be available to shield directors from liability. They are:

(1) A business decision.

(2) Disinterestedness (i.e., the absence of personal interest or self-dealing).

(3) Due care (i.e., an informed decision following a reasonable effort to become familiar with the relevant and available facts).

(4) No abuse of discretion (i.e., a reasonable belief that the best interests of the corporation and its stockholders are being served).

(5) Good faith.[28]

The court decisions suggest that the primary inquiry should relate to the two elements involved in the duty of loyalty: disinterestedness and good faith. If these hurdles are

---

25. Norlin Corp. v. Rooney, Pace, Inc., 744 F.2d 255, 258 (2d Cir. 1984).
26. Treadway Cos., Inc. v. Care Corp., 638 F.2d 382 (2d Cir. 1980).
27. Norlin Corp. v. Rooney, Pace, Inc., supra note 25, at 265.
28. See also supra sections 1.13 and 6.01.

cleared, the inquiry turns to the duty of due care and the three elements related to it (a) that the decision is a "business decision," (b) that the decision was an informed one made after a reasonable effort to learn the facts, and (c) that there was no abuse of discretion. Actually, "abuse of discretion" may also relate to the duty of loyalty, if it involves fraud or gross overreaching.

§ 6.05. Business decisions.

Application of the business judgment rule depends upon a showing that informed directors did, in fact, make a business decision authorizing the transaction under review.[29] Also, as noted above,[30] the element of action by the directors (distinguished from failure to act) is an aspect of this question. Whether the action taken amounted to a business decision may be a question of fact.[31] The transaction must be one within the corporation's authority.[32] A decision in the lawful and legitimate furtherance of corporate purposes, such as policy of management, expedience of contracts or action, adequacy of consideration, or lawful appropriation of corporate funds to advance corporate interests, is protected by the business judgment rule.[33] When directors are overseeing the activities of the corporate officers instead of making discrete decisions on specific issues, the protection of the business judgment rule may not be available.

§ 6.06. Disinterestedness.

Protection under the business judgment rule may be claimed only by disinterested directors whose conduct meets the tests of business judgment. Directors cannot appear on

---

29. Kaplan v. Centrex Corp., 284 A.2d 119, 124 (Del. Ch. 1971).

30. Supra section 6.02.

31. E.g., Treadway Cos., Inc. v. Care Corp., supra note 26, at 382.

32. Crouse-Hinds Co. v. Internorth, Inc., 634 F.2d 690, 701 (2d Cir. 1980).

33. Auerbach v. Bennett, 47 N.Y.2d 619, 629-31, 419 N.Y.S.2d 920, 926-27, 393 N.E.2d 994 (1979).

both sides of a transaction nor can they expect to derive any personal financial benefit from it without losing the rule's insulation from liability.[34]

Some court decisions have equated disinterestedness with independence.[35] In any event a court's determination that directors who acted on a transaction were interested or not independent may pretermit review of whether the terms of the transaction were fair and reasonable.[36] Especially in cases involving contests for control of a corporation, the courts are becoming more strict in the requirement of disinterestedness.[37]

At a minimum, under Delaware law, directors are deemed to be "interested" not only when they are involved on both sides of a transaction, but also if they expect to derive any personal benefit from it other than the benefit to the corporation or to shareholders generally.[38] Also, "where officers and directors are under any influence which sterilizes their discretion" they are not disinterested. When directors are interested, they are required to demonstrate their utmost good faith and the most scrupulous inherent fairness of the bargain.[39]

By the very nature of corporate life a director has a certain amount of interest in everything he does. The Third Circuit has said:

> The very fact that a director wants to enhance corporate profits is in part attributable to his desire to keep shareholders satisfied so that they will not oust him.[40]

Accordingly, a plaintiff attacking directorial action must allege facts which, if true, support a reasonable doubt that the

---

34. Aronson v. Lewis, 473 A.2d 805, 812 (Del. 1984).

35. E.g., Galef v. Alexander, 615 F.2d 51 (2d Cir. 1980); Abramowitz v. Posner, 513 F. Supp. 120 (S.D.N.Y. 1981), aff'd, 672 F.2d 1025 (2d Cir. 1982).

36. Clark v. Lomas & Nettleton Fin. Corp., 625 F.2d 49, 54 (5th Cir. 1980), cert. denied, 450 U.S. 1029 (1981).

37. See infra section 6.14.

38. Aronson v. Lewis, supra note 34, at 812.

39. Weinberger v. UOP, Inc., 457 A.2d 701, 710 (Del. 1983).

40. Johnson v. Trueblood, 629 F.2d 287, 292 (3d Cir. 1980).

challenged transaction was the product of a valid business judgment.[41] In "rare cases a transaction may be so egregious on its face" that the business judgment rule cannot be applied.[42]

§ 6.07. Exercise of due care; standard.

The duty of corporate officers and directors to exercise care is considered at length in Chapter 2. In the present context the emphasis is upon the requirement that, to invoke the business judgment rule, directors must

(1) inform themselves, prior to making a business decision, of all material information reasonably available to them, and

(2) having become so informed, must then act with requisite care in the discharge of their duties.[43]

A board's decision will not be protected by the business judgment rule if there is proof that the directors "acted so far without information that they can be said to have passed an unintelligent and unadvised judgment."[44] That language was quoted in the opinion in *Smith v. Van Gorkom*,[45] in which the Delaware Supreme Court held that Trans Union's directors breached their fiduciary duty to their shareholders by failing to inform themselves of all information reasonably available to them relative to their decision to recommend a cashout merger at a per-share price less than the "intrinsic value" of the corporation's shares.

The *Van Gorkom* court determined that the Trans Union directors were not entitled to the protection of the business judgment rule and summarized its reasons, as follows:

---

41. Aronson v. Lewis, supra note 34, at 815.

42. Id.

43. Id. at 812.

44. Gimbel v. Signal Cos., Inc., 316 A.2d 599, 615 (Del. Ch.), aff'd, 316 A.2d 619 (Del. 1974), citing Mitchell v. Highland-Western Glass, 167 A. 831, 833 (Del. Ch. 1933).

45. 488 A.2d 858, 872 (Del. 1985).

187

The directors (1) did not adequately inform themselves as to [the CEO's] role in forcing the "sale" of the Company and in establishing the per share purchase price; (2) were uninformed as to the intrinsic value of the Company; and (3) given these circumstances, at a minimum, were grossly negligent in approving the "sale" of the Company upon two hours consideration, without prior notice, and without the exigency of a crisis or emergency.[46]

The *Van Gorkom* decision considered whether the Trans Union directors should be treated as one board or as individuals in terms of invoking the protection of the business judgment rule.[47] Although it is generally the rule that ultimate liability for improper conduct will be considered on an individual basis, the Van Gorkom court concluded:

(1) that since all of the defendant directors, outside as well as inside,[48] take a unified position, we are required to treat all of the directors as one as to whether they are entitled to the protection of the business judgment rule; and (2) that considerations of good faith ... are irrelevant in determining the threshold issue of whether the directors as a Board exercised an informed business judgment.[49]

The subject of adequate information is difficult because there is no practical way to spell out what activities will and will not meet with judicial approval. Some commentators have made suggestions.[50]

Another difficult matter to determine is the standard of care. In cases where the business judgment rule does not apply, the standard is said to be ordinary care, meaning that a director may be held liable for simple negligence.[51] That has also been the standard under most state corporation stat-

---

46. Id. at 874.

47. Id. at 888.

48. Id. at 894. Five were inside directors; five were outside.

49. Id. at 889.

50. E.g., Manning, "Reflections and Practical Tips for Life in the Boardroom After Van Gorkom," 41 Bus. Law. 1 (1985).

51. See supra section 2.03.

utes.[52] When the business judgment rule is available, the Delaware courts apply a "gross negligence" standard[53] and hold that some showing of bad faith on the part of the directors must be made.[54] In a long line of Delaware cases director liability has been predicated on such as "fraud or gross overreaching,"[55] "gross and palpable overreaching,"[56] "bad faith ... or a gross abuse of discretion,"[57] fraud, misconduct or abuse of discretion,[58] or "fraud, self-dealing, gross negligence, waste of corporate assets."[59]

In other states director liability has been imposed under the business judgment rule upon a showing of "fraud, self-dealing and unconscionable conduct,"[60] "bad faith, corrupt motive,"[61] "bad faith, gross abuse of discretion"[62] or "bad faith".[63] California law seems to impose a higher standard of care than Delaware law.[64] In New York the statute sets the standard,[65] but the courts evaluate that standard to require good faith and the exercise of honest judgment in the lawful and legitimate furtherance of corporate purposes.[66]

There is probably no typical corporate director. Just as companies differ in their methods of operation, management

---

52. See supra section 2.02.

53. Aronson v. Lewis, 473 A.3d 805, 812 (Del. 1984); Smith v. Van Gorkom, supra note 45, at 873.

54. Johnson v. Trueblood, 629 F.2d 287, 293 (3d Cir. 1980), decided under Delaware law.

55. Sinclair Oil Corp. v. Levien, 280 A.2d 717, 722 (Del. 1971), rev'g 261 A.2d 911 (Del. Ch. 1969).

56. Getty Oil Co. v. Skelly Oil Co., 267 A.2d 883, 887 (Del. 1970), rev'g 255 A.2d 717 (Del. Ch. 1969).

57. Warshaw v. Calhoun, 221 A.2d 487, 492-93 (Del. 1966).

58. Kors v. Carey, 39 Del. Ch. 47, 158 A.2d 135, 140 (Del. Ch. 1960).

59. Penn Mart Realty Co. v. Becker, 298 A.2d 349 (Del. Ch. 1972).

60. Papalexiou v. Tower West Condominium, 401 A.2d 280 (N.J. 1979).

61. Cramer v. General Tel. & Elec. Corp., 582 F.2d 259 (3d Cir. 1978).

62. Polin v. Conductron Corp., 552 F.2d 797 (8th Cir.), cert. denied, 434 U.S. 857 (1977).

63. Mortgage Brokerage Co. v. Mills, 100 Colo. 267, 67 P.2d 68 (1937).

64. See discussion of Delaware law in Panter v. Marshall Field & Co., 646 F.2d 271, 295 n.7 (7th Cir.), cert. denied, 454 U.S. 1092 (1981).

65. N.Y. Bus. Corp. Law § 717.

66. Norlin Corp. v. Rooney, Pace, Inc., 744 F.2d 255, 264 (2d Cir. 1984).

styles, viewpoints and attitudes, so individual directors differ. The individual capabilities and experience of the directors, which qualify them for their responsibilities, emphasize the difficulty in defining the "ordinarily prudent person" who would serve in directorial capacity.

When that mythical person engages in collegial participation in corporate board functions, such phrases as "under similar circumstances" are employed as guides for action. But few, if any, circumstances are sufficiently similar for the guides to lead to a safe harbor.

§ 6.08. Best interests of corporation and its constituencies.

The business judgment rule may not be invoked to shield directors from liability unless they act in a good faith belief that their business decision is in their corporation's best interests.[67] Under Delaware law the business judgment rule creates a presumption to that effect. The burden is on a party challenging the act of the directors to establish facts rebutting the presumption.[68]

The duty of directors to act in the best interests of the corporation and the shareholders is a fiduciary duty.[69] It extends to protecting the corporation and its shareholders from reasonably perceived harm whether a threat originates from third parties or other shareholders. In the face of a destructive threat, the duty to protect the corporation from threatened harm supervenes the duties of due care and loyalty. The Delaware court has said that directors may reasonably consider the basic shareholder interests at stake, including those of short-term speculators.[70] But consideration of the interests of constituencies other than shareholders is limited by the requirement that there be some rationally related benefit

---

67. Whittaker Corp. v. Edgar, 535 F. Supp. 933, 950 (N.D. Ill. 1982).
68. Aronson v. Lewis, 473 A.2d 805, 812 (Del. 1984).
69. Guth v. Loft, Inc., 23 Del. Ch. 255, 5 A.2d 503, 510 (1939).
70. Unocal Corp. v. Mesa Petroleum Co., 493 A.2d 946, 955, 958 (Del. 1985).

accruing to shareholders. Thus, preferring noteholders to shareholders constituted a breach of the directors' primary duty of loyalty in the *Revlon* case.[71]

The foregoing is based on Delaware law but appears to be fairly representative of the general law on this subject. A Second Circuit decision under New York law follows this pattern,[72] although an earlier District Court decision in New York was more liberal in permitting directors to consider the interests of various corporate constituencies.[73] There is, however, the beginning of a legislative trend to permit corporate directors greater latitude in considering various corporate constituencies, at least in takeover situations.[74]

§ 6.09. Good faith; primary purpose test.

There is a close relationship between the subject of good faith and that discussed in section 6.08: the best interests of the corporation and its constituencies. When directors act "with reckless indifference to" or "in deliberate disregard of" the interests of the shareholders, they cannot be said to be acting in good faith.[75] However, the Delaware courts have ruled that if a board's decision can be attributed to "any rational business purpose," the court will not disturb it.[76]

Between 1977 and 1983 the Delaware courts enforced a business purpose requirement in respect to parent-subsidiary mergers, but it was written out of the Delaware law in favor

---

71. Revlon, Inc. v. MacAndrews & Forbes Holdings, 506 A.2d 173, 176, 182 (Del. 1986).

72. Hanson Trust PLC v. ML SCM Acquisition, Inc., 781 F.2d 264 (2d Cir. 1986).

73. GAF Corp. v. Union Carbide Corp., 624 F. Supp. 1016 (S.D.N.Y. 1985), applying New York law.

74. E.g., Ohio Rev. Code Ann. § 1701.59(E); N.Y. Bus. Corp. Law § 1603(a)(19); Pa. Stat. Ann. § 1408(b). And cf. Cardiff Acquisitions, Inc. v. Hatch, 751 F.2d 906, 912 (8th Cir. 1984).

75. Allaum v. Consolidated Oil Co., 147 A. 257, 261 (Del. Ch. 1929).

76. Sinclair Oil Corp. v. Levien, 280 A.2d 717, 720 (Del. 1971); Unocal Corp. v. Mesa Petroleum Co., supra note 70, at 954.

191

of the fairness test which now obtains.[77] In some jurisdictions, notably California, Arizona and Nevada in the Ninth Circuit, a "compelling business reason" test is still applied, particularly when management actions will injure minority shareholders.[78]

Nearly a century ago the Supreme Court laid the foundation for the business judgment rule and the principle that, absent bad faith or some other corrupt motive, directors are not liable to their corporation for mistakes in judgment.[79] Today it is held that "[a]t a minimum the Delaware cases require that the plaintiff must show some sort of bad faith on the part of the defendant" to overcome the business judgment rule.[80]

Under New York law, however, directors are not immunized merely because they act in good faith without self dealing. To obtain the benefit of the business judgment rule they must exercise their "honest judgment in the lawful and legitimate furtherance of corporate purposes" and make certain that they are fully informed.[81]

The position taken by outside, independent, or "disinterested" directors, "whose sole interest was the furtherance of the corporate enterprise" has been held to support the good faith of a board decision.[82] The structural bias common to corporate boards is sometimes urged against that view.[83]

---

77. Weinberger v. UOP, Inc., 457 A.2d 701, 713 (Del. 1983).

78. See, e.g., Shivers v. Amerco, 670 F.2d 826, 832 (9th Cir. 1982); Klaus v. Hi-Shear Corp., 528 F.2d 225, 233 (9th Cir. 1975); Jones v. H.F. Ahmanson & Co., 1 Cal. 3d 93, 81 Cal. Rptr. 592, 460 P.2d 464 (1969).

79. Briggs v. Spaulding, 141 U.S. 132, 35 L.Ed. 662, 11 S.Ct. 924 (1891).

80. Johnson v. Trueblood, 629 F.2d 287, 293 (2d Cir. 1980).

81. Hanson Trust PLC v. ML SCM Acquisition, Inc., supra note 72, at 274, 284.

82. Puma v. Marriott, 283 A.2d 693, 695-96 (Del. Ch. 1971); Beard v. Elster, 160 A.2d 731, 738 (Del. 1960); Warshaw v. Calhoun, 221 A.2d 487, 493 (Del. 1966); Panter v. Marshall Field & Co., 646 F.2d 271, 294 (7th Cir.), cert. denied, 454 U.S. 1092 (1981). See also Unocal Corp. v. Mesa Petroleum Co., 493 A.2d 946, 955 (Del. 1985), and Moran v. Household Int'l, Inc., 500 A.2d 1346, 1356 (Del. 1985).

83. E.g., Zapata Corp. v. Maldonado, 430 A.2d 779 (Del. 1981); Hasan v. Clevetrust Realty Investors, 729 F.2d 372, 378 (6th Cir. 1984). See also

Also, when a board takes a unified position, a distinction between inside and outside directors may have no bearing.[84]

There is a trend in some cases to employ a "primary purpose" test in scrutinizing a board decision to determine if the directors were in good faith when making it. Thus, the business judgment rule would not insulate directors acting solely or primarily to preserve their positions or otherwise benefit themselves.[85] For example, directors of a Delaware corporation may deal selectively with its shareholders if they have not acted out of a sole or primary purpose to entrench themselves in office. In such a case, however, there is an enhanced duty because of "the omnipresent specter that a board may be acting in its own interests." That enhanced duty calls for judicial examination at the threshold before the protection of the business judgment rule may be conferred.[86]

Where there are no allegations of "fraud, bad faith, or self-dealing, or proof thereof" the business judgment rule supplies a presumption that the directors reached their business judgment in good faith.[87] This presumption is not weakened by the circumstance that control is always arguably a motive in any action taken by a director. To overcome the presumption a plaintiff "must make a showing from which a factfinder might infer that impermissible motives predominated in the making of the decision in question." The showing of a motive to retain control, without more, is insufficient to prove bad faith in this context.[88]

Revlon, Inc. v. MacAndrews & Forbes Holdings, 506 A.2d 173, 176 n.3 (Del. 1986).

84. See Norlin Corp. v. Rooney, Pace, Inc., 744 F.2d 255, 266-67 n.12 (2d Cir. 1984); Smith v. Van Gorkom, 488 A.2d 858, 889 (Del. 1985).

85. Treco, Inc. v. Land of Lincoln Sav. & Loan, 749 F.2d 374 (7th Cir. 1984).

86. Unocal Corp. v. Mesa Petroleum Co., supra note 82, at 954, citing Cheff v. Mathes, 41 Del. Ch. 494, 199 A.2d 548, 554 (Del. 1964), and other authorities.

87. Smith v. Van Gorkom, supra note 84, at 873.

88. Johnson v. Trueblood, supra note 80, at 292. See also Panter v. Marshall Field & Co., supra note 82, at 295 n.7.

Reliance on the advice of experienced and knowledgeable legal counsel shows good faith and a reasonable inquiry in cases where corporate control is an issue.[89]

§ 6.10. Rebutting the presumption.

The burden is on the party challenging a board's decision to establish facts rebutting the presumption supplied by the business judgment rule.[90] The particular circumstances of a case will usually dictate the nature of such facts, but some generalities may be stated. A showing that the directors are actually involved on both sides of a transaction or expect to derive any personal financial benefit from it in the sense of self-dealing, will cause the presumption to fail. Proof of fraud or manifestly oppressive conduct[91] or proof of bad faith or abuse of discretion[92] should suffice. Evidence to show that the sole or primary purpose of the directors was to solidify their control of the corporation is strong proof,[93] but merely showing a motive to retain control, falls short of the requirement.[94]

To rebut the presumption a plaintiff must make a showing from which a fact-finder might infer that impermissible motives predominated in the making of the decision in question.[95] When the "synergies of evidence" make such a prima facie showing, the "burden of justification" shifts to the directors and good faith alone will not preclude a finding of a breach of the duty of loyalty.[96]

---

89. Panter v. Marshall Field & Co., supra note 82, at 277; Grossman v. Johnson, 674 F.2d 115 (1st Cir.), cert. denied, 459 U.S. 838 (1982).

90. Aronson v. Lewis, 473 A.2d 805, 812 (Del. 1984).

91. Northwest Indus., Inc. v. B. F. Goodrich Co., 301 F. Supp. 706, 712 (N.D. Ill. 1969).

92. Whitaker Corp. v. Edgar, 535 F. Supp. 933, 950 (N.D. Ill. 1982).

93. Unocal Corp. v. Mesa Petroleum Co., 493 A.2d 946, 955 (Del. 1985).

94. Johnson v. Trueblood, 629 F.2d 287, 293 (3d Cir. 1980).

95. Panter v. Marshall Field & Co., 646 F.2d 271, 294 (7th Cir.), cert. denied, 454 U.S. 1092 (1981).

96. Hanson Trust PLC v. ML SCM Acquisition, Inc., 781 F.2d 264, 277 (2d Cir. 1986); A.C. Acquisitions Corp. v. Anderson, Clayton & Co., 519 A.2d 103, 115 (Del. Ch. 1986).

194

In a case involving injury to minority shareholders, absence of a compelling business reason for the action taken may rebut the presumption in some jurisdictions.[97]

The business judgment rule can sustain only corporate decisionmaking or transactions that are within the power or authority of the directors.[98] But a procedure, such as a "poison pill," which is authorized and proper under one set of facts may be inappropriate and unauthorized when different circumstances exist.[99]

§6.11. Directors' burden if presumption rebutted.

Under the business judgment rule, directors are called to account for their actions when they are shown to have engaged in self-dealing or fraud, or to have acted in bad faith. Also, if the party contesting the action establishes facts rebutting the business judgment presumption, the burden of proof shifts to the directors. In either event, it is then incumbent upon the directors to "prove that the transaction was fair and reasonable to the corporation." The transaction can only be sustained if it is objectively or intrinsically fair. An honest belief of its fairness is insufficient.[100]

In the takeover context, under Delaware law, the initial burden falls on the directors to show that they had reasonable grounds for believing that a danger to corporate policy and effectiveness existed. They may satisfy that burden "by showing good faith and reasonable investigation."[101] If they undertake a defensive measure, the element of balance will be involved, and the directors must show that it is reasonable in

---

97. E.g., Shivers v. Amerco, 670 F.2d 826 (9th Cir. 1982).

98. Moran v. Household Int'l Inc., 500 A.2d 1346, 1350 (Del. 1985).

99. E.g., Revlon, Inc. v. MacAndrews & Forbes Holdings, Inc., 506 A.2d 173 (Del. 1986).

100. A.C. Acquisitions Corp. v. Anderson, Clayton & Co., supra note 96, at 115; see also Crouse-Hinds Co. v. Internorth, Inc., 634 F.2d 690, 702 (2d Cir. 1980); Treadway Cos., Inc. v. Care Corp., 638 F.2d 357, 382 (2d Cir. 1980); Norlin Corp. v. Rooney, Pace, Inc., 744 F.2d 255, 265 (2d Cir. 1984).

101. Unocal Corp. v. Mesa Petroleum Corp., 493 A.2d 946, 955 (Del. 1985).

relation to the threat posed. Otherwise, the defensive measure may not come within the ambit of the business judgment rule.[102]

Generally, absent a showing of interest or bad faith, the Delaware directors' decision will not be overcome if it can be attributed to "any rational business purpose,"[103] but that rule is subject to qualification under conflicting rules in various jurisdictions and in the takeover context.

The obligation of the directors to sustain their burden of justification is generally recognized in all jurisdictions that have ruled on this point.[104] Nonetheless, the ultimate burden of persuasion is imposed upon the plaintiffs to show a breach of the directors' fiduciary duties.[105]

§ 6.12. Application to "enterprise decisions."

It has been suggested that the business operations issues with which directors regularly deal may be called "enterprise issues" and those relating to the ownership and distribution of the corporation's stock called "ownership claim issues."[106] Closely related to "ownership claim" issues, if not included therein, are those involving corporate control situations.

Decisions relating to "enterprise issues" are of the type that the business judgment rule was originally intended to protect. Commentator Bayless Manning has written:

> A shareholder has an economic stake in major enterprise issues, of course. If a slide rule manufacturer expands its traditional business just as electronic calculators sweep the market, the company will go broke; the result of the board's decision on that enterprise issue will be that shareholders (or some later generation of shareholders) will lose their investment. But that loss to the

---

102. Id.; accord, Moran v. Household Int'l Inc., supra note 98, at 1356.

103. Unocal Corp. v. Mesa Petroleum Corp., supra note 101, at 954, citing Sinclair Oil Corp. v. Levien, 280 A.2d 717, 720 (Del. 1971).

104. See cases cited supra note 100.

105. Moran v. Household Int'l, Inc. supra note 98, at 1356.

106. Manning, "Reflections and Practical Tips on Life in The Boardroom After Van Gorkom," 41 Bus. Law. 1, 5 (1985).

shareholder is a loss in his role as an investor; he bet on the wrong horse that lost, so be it.[107]

Decisions to enter into new fields, to diversify, to enter into contracts, to dispose of or acquire assets, generally to deal with the scope, nature and direction of the business are "enterprise decisions."

In an oft-cited decision concerning the liability of corporate directors for making illegal overseas payments to foreign government officials and private persons, the Third Circuit discussed the reasonableness of a business decision, although the case was dismissed on other grounds.[108] Even the development of the case law relating to the business judgment rule in the context of derivative actions has involved "enterprise decisions."[109]

A leading Delaware case involved a contention that corporate directors had acted without a business purpose and committed waste by approving consulting agreements with a 75-year-old major shareholder.[110] The court thoroughly explored the plaintiff's contention of lack of directorial independence and domination and control of the board by the shareholder. It held the complaint insufficient to raise a reasonable doubt as to the applicability of the business judgment rule.[111]

The Delaware court, in the above case, noted that "certain common principles governing the application and operation of the [business judgment] rule" would come into play "in addressing a demand, in the determination of demand futility, in efforts by independent disinterested directors to dis-

---

107. Id. at 5. Compare Lewis v. S.L. & E., Inc., 629 F.2d 764 (2d Cir. 1980), and Joy v. North, 692 F.2d 880 (2d Cir. 1982), cert. denied, 460 U.S. 1051 (1983).

108. Cramer v. General Tel. & Elec. Corp., 582 F.2d 259 (3d Cir. 1978).

109. See Joy v. North, supra note 107, and cf. United Copper Sec. Co. v. Amalgamated Copper Co., 244 U.S. 261, 61 L.Ed. 1119, 37 S.Ct. 509 (1917); Auerbach v. Bennett, 47 N.Y.2d 619, 419 N.Y.S.2d 920, 393 N.E.2d 994 (1979); Zapata Corp. v. Maldonado, 430 A.2d 779 (Del. 1981).

110. 473 A.2d 805 (Del. 1984).

111. Cf. Clark v. Lomas & Nettleton Fin. Corp., 625 F.2d 49, 52-54 (5th Cir. 1980), cert. denied, 450 U.S. 1029 (1981).

miss the action as inimical to the corporation's best interests, and generally, as a defense to the merits of the suit."[112]

The trend of the cases in the takeover context, to tighten the requirements of the business judgment rule and impose additional restrictions on its application, has not yet related to the "enterprise decisions." The past trend of judicial deference to such decisions continues.[113]

§ 6.13. Application to preplanned strategy.

The "increasing complexity of the tactics employed by contestants vying for corporate control" has caught the attention and aroused the concern of the courts.[114] And the ingenuity of the contestants has encouraged the Delaware court to point out that corporate law is not static. "It must grow and develop in response to, indeed in anticipation of, evolving concepts and needs."[115] In that case, the court declared that "in the broad context of corporate governance, including issues of fundamental corporate change, a board of directors is not a passive instrumentality."

In a contemporaneous Delaware case the directors of a diversified holding company adopted a preferred share purchase rights plan as a preventive mechanism to ward off future advances by corporate raiders. They also retained counsel to formulate a takeover policy which the board approved.[116] The court held:

> [H]ere we have a defensive mechanism adopted to ward off possible future advances and not a mechanism adopted in reaction to a specific threat. This distinguishing feature does not result in the Directors losing the protection of the business judgment rule.

The court went on to say that, to the contrary, preplanning for the contingency of a hostile takeover might reduce the

---

112. Aronson v. Lewis, supra note 110, at 812.
113. See infra section 6.14 on application to corporate control situations.
114. E.g., Norlin Corp. v. Rooney, Pace, Inc., 744 F.2d 255, 269 (2d Cir. 1984).
115. Unocal Corp. v. Mesa Petroleum Co., 493 A.2d 946, 957 (Del. 1985).
116. Moran v. Household Int'l Inc., 500 A.2d 1346, 1348-49 (Del. 1985).

risk that, under the pressure of a takeover bid, management would fail to exercise reasonable judgment. It concluded:

> Therefore, in reviewing a preplanned defensive mechanism it seems even more appropriate to apply the business judgment rule.[117]

§ 6.14. Application to corporate control situations.

The business judgment rule was not developed in the context of defensive tactics in corporate control contests, but it is applicable to them, albeit with the likelihood of some changes in its traditional parameters. As contests for corporate control became "ever more frequent phenomena on the American business scene",[118] and spawned numerous legal controversies, the courts found the business judgment rule a customary defense in litigation over control decisions. Early on, the trend in the federal courts was to sustain any good-faith conclusion that a takeover was not in the best interests of the corporation and its shareholders. Moreover, the trend was to permit a board, after it reached such a conclusion, to exercise unrestrained freedom in choosing defensive tactics to combat the takeover.[119]

Then, a Second Circuit decision under New York law interrupted the trend and turned it in a different direction. Finding evidence of self-dealing in the setting up of an employees' stock option plan in the heat of a contest for corporate control, the court affirmed a preliminary injunction. It concluded that the ESOP was created as part of a management entrenchment effort. In addition the court limited the business judgment rule by declaring that "decisions affecting the corpora-

---

117. Id. at 1350, citing Warner Communications v. Murdoch, 581 F. Supp. 1472, 1481 (D. Del. 1984).

118. Norlin Corp. v. Rooney, Pace, Inc., supra note 114, at 253.

119. E.g., Crouse-Hinds Co. v. Internorth, Inc., 634 F.2d 690 (2d Cir. 1980); Treadway Cos., Inc. v. Care Corp., 638 F.2d 357 (2d Cir. 1980); Panter v. Marshall Field & Co., 646 F.2d 271 (7th Cir.), cert. denied, 454 U.S. 1092 (1981); Buffalo Forge Co. v. Ogden Corp., 717 F.2d 757 (2d Cir.), cert. denied, 464 U.S. 1018 (1983); Gearhart Indus., Inc. v. Smith Int'l, Inc., 741 F.2d 707 (5th Cir. 1984).

199

tion's ultimate destiny are for the shareholders to make in accordance with democratic procedures."[120]

Six months later, in "an unprecedented turnabout in its theretofore passive attitude to takeover defense strategies,"[121] the Delaware court "exploded a bomb."[122] In *Smith v. Van Gorkom* (the Trans Union cash-out merger case)[123] it found the Trans Union directors grossly negligent, denied them the protection of the business judgment rule, imposed personal liability upon them and remanded the case to determine the amount of the damages.[124] The *Van Gorkom* court evidenced its first step in restructuring the business judgment rule when it stated:

> [F]ulfillment of the fiduciary function requires more than the mere absence of bad faith or fraud. Representation of the financial interests of others imposes on a director an affirmative duty to protect those interests and to proceed with a critical eye in assessing information of the type and under the circumstances present here.[125]

Such increased emphasis on the board's duty of care in a corporate control setting is reflected in more careful review of the procedures and decisional processes undertaken by the courts in such cases. This is a significant element of the current refinement of the business judgment rule.

Before the dust had settled from the *Van Gorkom* decision, the Delaware court chose the *Unocal/Mesa Petroleum* case as a vehicle to proclaim some significant changes in the business judgment rule in the context of corporate control situa-

---

120. Norlin Corp. v. Rooney, Pace, Inc., supra note 114, at 258, 267. Cf. Klaus v Hi-Shear Corp., 528 F.2d 225, 233 (9th Cir. 1975).

121. Greene & Palmiter, "Business Judgment Rule Tightened for Takeovers," Legal Times 53 (Jan. 20, 1986).

122. Manning, "Reflections and Practical Tips on Life in the Boardroom After Van Gorkom," 41 Bus. Law. 1 (1985).

123. Smith v. Van Gorkom, 488 A.2d 858 (Del. 1985).

124. The case was settled by a payment of $23.5 million to the plaintiff class, according to Manning, supra note 122, "Editor's note."

125. Smith v. Van Gorkom, supra note 123, at 872.

tions.[126] It first declared that "in the broad context of corporate governance, including issues of fundamental corporate change, a board of directors is not a passive instrumentality." It noted "the omnipresent specter that a board may be acting primarily in its own interests" in addressing a pending takeover bid and found "an enhanced duty which calls for judicial examination at the threshold." This duty required the directors to show that they had reasonable grounds for believing that a danger to corporate policy and effectiveness existed. Proof of good faith and a reasonable investigation would satisfy this obligation.

The next step related to what defensive measures could be invoked. Here, the Unocal court proposed an "element of balance," that the defensive measure must be reasonable in relation to the threat posed. Having thus reconstituted the business judgment rule, the court applied it and held in favor of the directors.

Preplanned strategy was approved in a "poison pill" preferred share rights plan in the next Delaware decision in this series.[127] Citing both the *Unocal* and *Van Gorkom* cases, the *Moran* court found in favor of the directors under the reconstituted business judgment rule. While that case was under consideration, the court heard and decided the *Revlon* action, which involved another "poison pill" defense measure.

The *Revlon* opinion,[128] when it was issued, cited *Unocal*, *Moran* and the *Hanson Trust* case in the Second Circuit,[129] which in turn followed *Norlin Corporation v. Rooney, Pace,*

---

126. Unocal Corp. v. Mesa Petroleum Co., 493 A.2d 946 (Del. 1985). See also Samjieno Partners I v. Burlington Indus., 663 F. Supp. 614 (S.D.N.Y. 1987).

127. Moran v. Household Int'l, Inc., 500 A.2d 1346 (Del. 1985). See also supra section 6.13.

128. Revlon, Inc. v. MacAndrews & Forbes Holdings, Inc., 506 A.2d 173 (Del. 1986).

129. Hanson Trust PLC v. ML SCM Acquisition, Inc., 781 F.2d 264 (2d Cir. 1986).

Incorporated, the case which originally interrupted the trend. Perhaps that completed the circle.[130]

In *Revlon,* the court addressed "for the first time the extent to which a [board] may consider the effect of a takeover threat on constituencies other than shareholders."[131] But the point made in *Revlon* that perhaps most directly affected the business judgment rule was the declaration that when it became apparent that the breakup of the company was inevitable, the board's responsibilities were altered. At that time, said the court as a matter of law, the duty of the board "changed from the preservation of Revlon as a corporate entity to the maximization of the company's value at a sale for the stockholders' benefit."

It had been traditional that the duty of directors to act in the best interests of the corporation and its shareholders was a fiduciary duty.[132] Now the court had severed the interests of the shareholders and given them first priority. The court held:

> The directors' role changed from defenders of the corporate bastion to auctioneers charged with getting the best price for the stockholders at a sale of the company.[133]

The Second Circuit's opinion in *Hanson Trust*[134] made numerous references to the chancellor's opinion in *Revlon.*[135] It faulted the SMC independent directors for inadequately pursuing "their obligations to ensure the shareholders' fundamental right to make the 'decisions affecting [the] corpora-

---

130. See text supra at note 120.

131. Revlon, Inc., supra note 128, at 176. Cf. GAF Corp. v. Union Carbide Corp., 624 F. Supp. 1016 (S.D.N.Y. 1985), applying New York Law. And see discussion supra section 6.08.

132. See Guth v. Loft, Inc., 23 Del. Ch. 255, 5 A.2d 503, 510 (1939), and text at supra section 6.08, note 69.

133. Revlon, Inc., supra note 128, at 182. See also Ivanhoe Partners v. Newmont Mining Co., 535 A.2d 1334 (Del. 1987) as to limitation on *Revlon* rule.

134. Hanson Trust PLC, supra note 129.

135. MacAndrews & Forbes Holdings, Inc. v. Revlon, Inc., 501 A.2d 1239 (Del. Ch. 1985), aff'd, 506 A.2d 173 (Del. 1986).

tion's ultimate destiny'."[136] It criticized the board for deferring to management at the expense of the shareholders and
failing to ensure that bids were negotiated or scrutinized "by
those whose only loyalty was to the shareholders."

In effect, the *Hanson Trust* court followed *Revlon's* path in
finding that the directors breached their duty of care when
they failed "to protect steadfastly shareholders interests in
the face of a management-interested LBO." In such a situation:

> [The] directorial duty of care is heightened because man-
> agement interests are then in direct conflict with those of
> the shareholders of the target corporation to obtain the
> highest price either for their shares or for the company's
> assets.[137]

In light of the trend of the takeover cases to reconstitute or
restructure the business judgment rule in the corporate control context, it is difficult to predict with any certainty the
specific responsibilities of directors in this area. Such a state
of confusion thwarts the policy reasons for the rule and puts
corporate directors in tenuous positions, with their personal
assets at risk, when acting in these cases.

The decisions are reasonably clear in requiring the exercise
of an informed judgment after adequate and documented investigation, and a heightened duty of care when management's interests in defending the corporate bastion conflict
with shareholders' interests in obtaining the highest price for
their shares or the company's assets. But there are few other
guidelines yet available for directors in making decisions relating to corporate control and the ultimate destiny of the
corporation.

§ 6.15. Application to derivative actions.

A derivative action is a suit brought by one or more shareholders to enforce a corporation's cause of action against di-

---

136. Hanson Trust PLC, supra note 129, at 277. See also text supra at
note 120.

137. Id. at 284, Oakes, C.J., concurring.

rectors, officers or third parties.[138] Federal Civil Procedure Rule 23.1 and most state statutes provide that a shareholder must make a demand upon the directors to bring the action, and must afford them a reasonable time to do so, or refuse, unless the demand would be useless or futile. In common parlance a case in which the demand would be useless or futile is termed a "demand-excused" case; that in which the demand must be made is a "demand-refused" case.[139]

In a case in which a demand is required and is refused, the directors' decision refusing to sue will be respected, if it meets the standards of the business judgment rule.[140] Since the Delaware decision of *Aronson v. Lewis,*[141] and to the extent it is followed in other jurisdictions, most cases will fall into this category.[142]

The *Aronson* court held that demand can only be excused "where facts are alleged with particularity which create a reasonable doubt that the directors' action was entitled to the protections of the business judgment rule."[143] The reasonable doubt must relate to whether (1) the directors are disinterested and independent and (2) the challenged transaction was otherwise the product of a valid exercise of business judgment. Specific allegations of fact, not evidence, are required, but mere conclusive allegations will not suffice. Directorial approval of a transaction, in the absence of particularized facts supporting a breach of fiduciary duty claim, or otherwise establishing a lack of independence or disinterestedness of a majority of directors, is insufficient to excuse demand.[144]

---

138. Ross v. Bernhard, 396 U.S. 531, 534, 24 L.Ed.2d 729, 734, 90 S.Ct. 733, 736 (1970). See also infra Chapter 18.

139. See Block & Prussin, "Termination of Derivative Suits Against Directors on Business Judgment Grounds: From Zapata to Aronson," 39 Bus. Law. 1503, 1508 (1984).

140. Zapata Corp. v. Maldonado, 430 A.2d 779, 784 n.10 (Del. 1981).

141. Aronson v. Lewis, 473 A.2d 805 (Del. 1984).

142. Block & Prussin, supra note 139, at 1506.

143. Aronson v. Lewis, supra note 141, at 808.

144. Id. at 817. See also Abramowitz v. Posner, 672 F.2d 1025, 1030-31 (2d Cir. 1982).

The *Aronson* court held that the demand requirement was "a rule of substantive right."[145] As such, it should apply in any forum in which a derivative action is brought against a Delaware corporation.

Another aspect of the derivative action question involves the judicial review of actions of special litigation committees in terminating such actions.[146] There are two lines of decision on this subject. The New York line permits the committee's decision to be sustained if the court finds it to be a good faith business decision that the derivative action is not in the corporation's best interests.[147] A court may inquire only as to the disinterested independence of the members of the committee and as to the appropriateness and sufficiency of its investigative processes.

The Delaware line of authority goes well beyond the business judgment rule in this context. It holds that where a demand is excused and an independent litigation committee seeks dismissal of a derivative action, a two-step test should be applied. The dismissal will be granted only if (1) the court finds that the committee was independent, acted in good faith, and made a reasonable investigation and (2), in the court's independent business judgment as to the corporation's best interests, the action should be dismissed.[148] The second step is to be applied in the court's discretion and may be waived.[149]

In applying this second step the court must carefully consider and weigh how compelling the corporate interest in dis-

---

145. Aronson v. Lewis, supra note 141, at 809.

146. See, e.g., Burks v. Lasker, 441 U.S. 471, 60 L.Ed.2d 404, 99 S.Ct. 1831 (1979); Auerbach v. Bennett, 47 N.Y.2d 619, 419 N.Y.S.2d 920, 393 N.E.2d 994 (1979); Joy v. North, 692 F.2d 880 (2d Cir. 1982), cert. denied, 460 U.S. 1051 (1983).

147. Auerbach v. Bennett, supra note 146; Roberts v. Alabama Power Co., 404 So. 2d 629 (Ala. 1981); Lewis v. Anderson, 615 F.2d 778 (9th Cir. 1979), cert. denied, 449 U.S. 869 (1980); Galef v. Alexander, 615 F.3d 51 (2d Cir. 1980); Genzer v. Cunningham, 498 F. Supp. 682 (E.D. Mich. 1980).

148. Zapata Corp. v. Maldonado, supra note 140; Joy v. North, supra note 146.

149. Kaplan v. Wyatt, 499 A.2d 5 (Del. 1985).

missal is when faced with a nonfrivolous lawsuit, and, when appropriate, give special consideration to matters of law and public policy.[150] Without question, the business judgment rule is ignored when the second step of the test is taken.[151]

§ 6.16. Application to settlement agreements.

A derivative action may be settled with the approval of the court, even over the objection of the plaintiff.[152] Corporate directors have inherent power to settle such actions when it is their business judgment that the claim should not be enforced.[153] The Second Circuit has held in that context that:

> The Court's responsibility at this juncture is to determine whether or not the proposed settlement terms are fair, reasonable and adequate ... when weighed against the probability of recovery at trial .... [T]he recovery of monetary damages from director defendants is not a *sine qua non* to settlement of a derivative action.[154]

However, the power to control corporate litigation presupposes that the directors are not personally interested in its exercise.[155] Hence, it is the court's duty in passing upon the settlement to inquire into the disinterested independence of the directors.[156]

A leading case in the Fifth Circuit refused to approve such a settlement which had been ratified by directors who had

---

150. Zapata Corp. v. Maldonado, supra note 140, at 789.

151. See also Watts v. Des Moines Register & Tribune, 525 F. Supp. 1311, 1326 (S.D. Iowa 1981); Lewis v. Curtis, 671 F.2d 779 (3d Cir. 1981), cert. denied, 459 U.S. 880 (1982); Abella v. Universal Leaf Tobacco Co., 546 F. Supp. 795 (E.D. Va. 1982).

152. Wolf v. Barker, 348 F.2d 994 (2d Cir.), cert. denied sub nom. Wolf v. Blair, 382 U.S. 941 (1965).

153. Clark v. Lomas & Nettleton Fin. Corp., 625 F.2d 49, 52 (5th Cir. 1980), cert. denied, 450 U.S. 1029 (1981), citing United Copper Sec. Co. v. Amalgamated Copper Co., 244 U.S. 261, 263-64, 61 L.Ed. 1119, 37 S.Ct. 509, 510 (1917).

154. Saylor v. Lindsley, 456 F.2d 896 (2d Cir. 1972).

155. Galef v. Alexander, 615 F.2d 51, 58-61 (2d Cir. 1980).

156. See Auerbach v. Bennett, 47 N.Y.2d 619, 419 N.Y.S.2d 920, 393 N.E.2d 944 (1979).

been elected by the votes of the two majority shareholders who were the defendants in the derivative action. Citing the possibility of "structural bias," the court determined that the "board's conflict of interest could not be cured by judicial approval of the settlement terms."[157] It went on to state:

> Our holding pretermits review of whether the terms actually negotiated were "reasonable" in relation to the claims surrendered. That question will arise, if ever, only when this case is settled by parties unbeholden to the alleged wrongdoers.

§ 6.17. Reliance on advice of counsel.

In the appropriate factual context a proper exercise of business judgment may include, as one of its aspects, reasonable reliance on advice of counsel.[158] It has been noted earlier that to be justified in relying on advice of counsel there must be proof that the one so relying (1) made a complete disclosure to counsel, (2) requested counsel's advice as to the legality of the proposed action, (3) received advice that the action would be lawful, and (4) proceeded in reliance on that advice.[159] For example, the mere threat of litigation, acknowledged by counsel, does not constitute legal advice and is not a valid basis upon which to take action.[160]

It has been held that when directors act in good faith reliance on the advice of experienced and knowledgeable counsel they satisfy the requirements of the business judgment rule.[161] Moreover, when advice of legal counsel is readily available, directors may be less than diligent if they fail to obtain it.[162]

---

157. Clark v. Lomas & Nettleton Fin. Corp., supra note 153, at 54.

158. Smith v. Van Gorkom, 488 A.2d 858, 881 n.22 (Del. 1985).

159. See supra section 2.04, at note 67.

160. Smith v. Van Gorkom, supra note 158, at 881.

161. Panter v. Marshall Field & Co., 646 F.2d 271, 297 (7th Cir.), cert. denied, 454 U.S. 1092 (1981).

162. 12 Ohio Jur. 3d Business Relationships § 414.

207

COROLLARY REFERENCES

"Auctioning the Corporate Bastion: Delaware Readjusts the Business Judgment Rule in Revlon, Inc. v. MacAndrews & Forbes Holdings, Inc.," (506 A.2d 173 [Del.]), 40 Sw. L.J. 1117 (1986).

Esterbrook & Fischel, "The Proper Role of Target Management in Responding to a Tender Offer," 94 Harv. L. Rev. 1161 (1981).

Fischel, "The Business Judgment Rule and the Trans Union Case," 40 Bus. Law. 1437 (1985).

Gelfond & Sebastian, "Reevaluating the Duties of Target Management in a Hostile Tender 0ffer," 60 B.U.L. Rev. 403 (1980).

Gerke, "The Business Judgment Rule and Potential Liability for Defensive Takeover Maneuvers by the Board of Directors," 53 UMKC L. Rev. 646 (1985).

Hanson, "The ALI Corporate Governance Project: Of the Duty of Due Care and the Business Judgment Rule, a Commentary," 41 Bus. Law. 1237 (1986).

Hensey, "Business Judgment and the American Law Institute's Corporate Governance Project: The Rule, the Doctrine and the Reality," 52 Geo. Wash. L. Rev. 609 (1984).

Manning, "Life in the Boardroom After Van Gorkom," 41 Bus. Law. 1 (1985).

Manning, "The Business Judgment Rule and the Director's Duty of Attention: Time for Reality," 39 Bus. Law. 1488 (1984).

Manning, "The Business Judgment Rule in Overview," 45 Ohio St. L.J. 615 (1984).

Veasey, "The New Incarnation of the Business Judgment Rule in Takeover Defenses," 11 Del. J. Corp. L. 503 (1986).

Wander & LeCoque, "Boardroom Jitters: Corporate Control Transactions and Today's Business Judgment Rule," 42 Bus. Law. 29 (1986).

Zalecki, "The Duties of Corporate Directors in a Takeover Context: A Rationale for Judicial Focus Upon the Deliberative Process," 17 Toledo L. Rev. 313 (1986).

Chapter 7

STATE LEGISLATION LIMITING LIABILITY

§ 7.01. The need for remedial legislation.

In the summer of 1986, the Delaware General Assembly recognized that "the quality and stability of the governance of Delaware corporations" had been threatened because directors had become unwilling, in many cases, to serve without insurance protection and "may be deterred by the unavailiability of insurance from making entrepreneurial decisions."[1] Delaware took legislative action and amended its Corporation Code.

A few months later, the Ohio General Assembly enacted an emergency measure "necessary for the immediate preservation of the public peace, health and safety" declaring "an urgent need to attract qualified individuals to serve as directors of corporations and to assure that corporations remain incorporated in this state rather than reincorporate in states with laws providing more favorable treatment of directors...."[2] Ohio took legislative action and amended its General Corporation Act as had several other states since the first of that year. These amendments involve the governance

---

1. Synopsis, S.B. No. 533, Del. State Senate, 133rd General Assembly (1986).

2. Sec. 10, Am. Sub. H.B. No. 902, Ohio General Assembly (1986).

209

of corporations for profit, although in some instances the same statutes also relate to nonprofit corporations.[3]

The lack of insurance protection has been termed a symptom of the disease. The availability of D & O insurance serves to help directors insulate their personal assets from total risk, but it does not cure the uncertainty and hazards of exposure to personal liability. Surveys and studies by several state bar associations, Chambers of Commerce, the National Association of Corporate Directors (NACD), and others established the need for state legislation to alleviate the concern of corporate directors over the trend in the courts to second-guess them, not only as to the correctness of their decisions but also as to the quality of their deliberative processes and the sufficiency of their preparation and homework. The enactment of such legislation in several states since 1986 has been the single most important development in the D & O area since the liability crisis surfaced in 1984. It evidences the concern that state governments and the public have toward maintaining an environment in which qualified persons and especially outside directors can afford to serve.

§ 7.02. Proposals for a model bill.

Faced by the rising tide of litigation against directors and officers of public corporations and the resulting difficulty in attracting and retaining experienced and qualified persons to serve in those capacities, various organizations have given attention to the subject of remedial legislation, including the possibility of a model directors' liability statute. Such organizations included bar associations in Boston, Delaware, Ohio and Pennsylvania, the National Association of Corporate Directors (NACD) and others. The American Law Institute (ALI), expressed concern that the threat of liability tends to make directors excessively risk-averse in their decisionmaking, thus injuring shareholders and hampering efficiency.[4] It

---

3. Similar legislation relating to nonprofit corporations is discussed infra section 13.14.

4. ALI, Principles of Corporate Governance and Structure: Restatement and Recommendations, (Tent. Draft No. 6, 1986) comment c, § 7.17.

proposed that directors' liability for due care violations be limited.

The trend of thought has been that model legislation should support sufficiently high awards against wrongdoers to encourage litigation to redress actual breaches of directorial duty yet limit civil recoveries of damages in an effort to reduce the number and frequency of frivolous suits.

Whether the limitation or elimination of certain liabilities of directors should require shareholder approval is another unresolved issue. Several states answered in the affirmative in their 1986 legislation; some other states provided direct statutory relief but left the door open for shareholders to "opt out" to the extent desired.

It has not been proposed that a corporation's liability be affected or that a model bill should relate to criminal violations or actions for damages for bodily injury or death. To date there is no proposal in this area that liability under federal statutes be restricted, except the suggestion of the American Law Institute, in its proposed Federal Securities Code, that there be an arbitrary maximum of $100,000 per individual defendant.[5]

The only model bill given reasonably wide circulation is that proposed in 1987 by the National Association of Corporate Directors, as follows:

MODEL STATUTE

STANDARD OF CONDUCT FOR DIRECTORS

(A) A director shall, based on facts then known to the director, discharge the duties as a director, including the director's duties as a member of a committee:
(1) in good faith;
(2) with the care an ordinarily prudent person in a like position would exercise under similar conditions; and

---

5. Comment to § 1708(c) ALI Fed. Sec. Code, 1980, at pp. 731-31.

(3) in a manner the director reasonably believes to be in, or not opposed to, the best interests of the corporation.

(B) In discharging the director's duties, a director is entitled to rely on information, opinions, reports, or statements, including financial statements and other financial data, if prepared or presented by:

(1) one or more officers or employees of the corporation whom the director reasonably believes to be reliable and competent in the matters presented;

(2) legal counsel, public accountants, or other persons as to matters the director reasonably believes are within the person's professional or expert competence; or

(3) a committee of the board of directors of which the director is not a member if the director reasonably believes the committee merits confidence.

(C) A director is not acting in good faith if the director has actual knowledge concerning the matter in question that makes reliance otherwise permitted by subsection (B) unwarranted.

(D) A director may, but need not, in considering the best interests of the corporation, consider, among others, the effects of any action on employees, suppliers, creditors, and customers of the corporation and communities in which offices or other facilities of the corporation are located.

(E) Unless otherwise provided in the articles of incorporation, a director shall be liable in money damages for any act, or failure to act, as a director, only if it is proved by clear and convincing evidence that:

(1) the director has breached the duties of a director as provided in this section; and

(2) the breach constitutes criminal or willful misconduct or recklessness.[6]

---

6. 11 Director's Monthly, May 1987, at 3, col. 2.

In its commentary on the proposed model provisions, NACD pointed out that it largely follows the approach taken in legislation adopted by Indiana and differs from that adopted by Delaware in a number of important aspects.[7]

Unlike the Delaware statute, the model does not require shareholder action. The NACD suggested that if it is desirable social policy to limit the liability of directors for certain types of misconduct, then that should be a uniform provision applicable across-the-board to corporations and should not depend on the action of the shareholders. A failure by shareholders to approve a limitation of liability might well impede a company from securing independent directors, which would be a harm, not simply to the shareholders of that company, but to the public at large. It was reported that in all cases in which shareholders of Delaware corporations were asked to approve such limitations of liability their vote had been favorable. A provision such as the one proposed would avoid the expense of seeking shareholder approval, a process that for publicly held companies is often accompanied by proxy clearance delays at the Securities and Exchange Commission.

In pointing out that the Delaware statute specifically excludes breaches of the "duty of loyalty" from the liability limitation, NACD referred to Delaware court decisions containing language suggesting that alleged breaches of care would be more aptly characterized as breaches of loyalty.[8]

Calling attention to the model's provision for a higher measure of proof, "clear and convincing" evidence rather than mere preponderance of the evidence, to establish that a director had violated his duty to the corporation, NACD commented that clear and convincing evidence is generally interpreted to mean an intermediate measure of proof between mere preponderance and the certainty, beyond a reasonable doubt, required in criminal cases. In light of the real risk of

---

7. See Gashi, "NACD Drafts Model Legislation Limiting Directors' Monetary Liability," 11 Directors' Monthly, May 1987, at 1, col. 2.

8. E.g., A.C. Acquisitions Corp. v. Anderson, Clayton & Co., 519 A.2d 103 (Del. Ch. 1986).

directors being held personally liable for potentially huge judgments, such a provision seeks greater assurance of directorial wrongdoing before imposing such liability.

§ 7.03. The nature of enacted legislation.

The state legislation enacted since 1986 takes one or both of two approaches: (1) to provide, in varying degrees, relief of directors and, sometimes officers, from civil liability, and (2) expanding the scope and means of corporate indemnification,[9] making the statutes less exclusive in defining rights, and, sometimes, broadening the scope of financial protection by way of insurance or alternatives to insurance.[10] The legislation to provide relief from civil liability involves one or more of (1) authorization for charter provisions eliminating or restricting personal liability for money damages, (2) statutory self-executing elimination or restriction of personal liability, (3) increasing the quality of proof required to impose personal liability; (4) expansion of the criteria and constituencies directors may consider in reaching decisions in control situations and other matters, and (5) enacting or modifying statutory standards of conduct.

In limiting or eliminating directorial personal liability the enacted statutes go from the permissive enabling act, such as that of Delaware, to the automatic limitation unless the corporation "opts out" by way of language in the articles or regulations that specifically refers to the statutory provision and states that it shall not apply, as in the Ohio statute. All statutes exclude some acts and omissions of directors from the liability limitations, but there is wide variance among them. Ohio imposes an evidentiary standard of proof by clear and convincing evidence upon one attempting to prove bad faith or lack of due care of a director. Florida provides statutory definitions of "recklessness" and "improper personal benefit." Missouri details a variety of matters to be considered by directors in dealing with "acquisition proposals." In most in-

---

9. See infra Chapter 20 for a discussion of indemnification statutes.
10. See infra Chapter 19 for alternatives to insurance.

stances, the limitations on liability apply only to directors[11] when acting as directors, and not to officers or other employees or agents.

§ 7.04. Delaware-type statutes.

At least thirty states have followed the lead of Delaware in enacting statutes which authorize their corporations to include in their charters, either originally or by amendment, provisions eliminating or limiting the personal liability of directors for money damages for breach of their duties.[12]

The Delaware legislation

Effective July 1, 1986, Delaware amended its general corporation law by adding a new subsection (7) to Section 102(b) and by amending the indemnification provisions of Section 145.[13] Recommended by the Corporation Law Section and Executive Committee of the Delaware State Bar Association, the legislation expressly referred to the crisis in directors' and officers' liability insurance, the resulting threat to the stability and equality of corporate governance, and the need for Delaware corporations to provide substitute protection, in various forms to their directors and to limit directorial liability under certain circumstances.

New Section 102(b)(7) is an enabling provision to relieve directors of some personal liability for money damages, but it has no effect unless the corporation's original charter or an amendment to the certificate of incorporation, validly approved by shareholders, eliminates such liability for breach of fiduciary duty as a director. Such charter provisions may be written broadly to eliminate the liability of directors, but not officers, for certain breaches of their duty of care, or may be written more narrowly to impose limitations on such liabil-

---

11. Also officers in Louisiana, Maryland, Nevada and New Jersey.

12. See infra Appendix B-1 for a list of the states enacting such laws as of January 1, 1988.

13. See infra Chapter 20 as to the indemnification.

ity. The law does not permit the elimination or restriction of directorial liability in several areas:

(1) Liability for any breach of a director's duty of loyalty to the corporation or its shareholders;

(2) Liability for acts or omissions not in good faith or which involve intentional misconduct or a knowing violation of law;

(3) Liability for the payment of unlawful dividends or unlawful stock purchases or redemptions;

(4) Liability for any transaction from which a director derived an improper personal benefit;

(5) Liability to any person other than the corporation or its shareholders;

(6) Claims for nonmonetary or equitable relief, such as rescission or injunction;

(7) Liability for any act or omission occurring prior to the time when the charter provision became effective; or

(8) Liability for violation of federal statutes, such as RICO and the federal securities laws.

The exclusion of the duty of loyalty from the benefits of the statute restricts the value of its protection substantially. Most lawsuits, especially in change of control situations, will allege a breach of the duty of loyalty. The decision of the Delaware Court in *A.C. Acquisitions Corporation v. Anderson, Clayton & Company*[14] confirms this concern. There, a preliminary injunction enjoined the target company's board from commencing a self-tender because it was "likely" that such action would constitute a breach of the directors' duty of loyalty.

Also, it may be questioned whether the new Delaware statute would protect directors against charges of recklessness. If recklessness involves conscious disregard of a known risk, it

---

14. 519 A.2d 103 (Del. Ch. 1986).

is arguable that the action would not be taken in good faith and thus would constitute a breach of the duty of loyalty.[15]

The commentators agree that the new section does not eliminate or alter a director's fiduciary duty of care. It merely withdraws one remedy for a breach of that duty, and then only if a majority of the shareholders determine that such a withdrawal is in their best interests.[16] In that connection, a survey conducted by the American Society of Corporate Secretaries, Inc. of 310 Delaware corporations disclosed that seventy-five percent planned to ask their shareholders to approve such amendments to their certificates of incorporation.[17]

Other similar legislation

Among the states which enacted statutes following Delaware closely, and in most instances word for word, are Arizona, Arkansas, Colorado, Georgia, Idaho, Iowa, Kansas, Louisiana, Maryland, Massachusetts, Michigan, Minnesota, Montana, Oklahoma, Oregon, Rhode Island, South Dakota, Tennessee, Texas, Utah and Wyoming. New Jersey included officers for a two-year period.[18]

Other states followed the Delaware charter option plan but modified their statutory provisions to deal with some of the problems created by the exceptions to Delaware's limitations on liability. The bill passed in California states that it is not intended "to change case law or statutory law regarding the duty of loyalty of a director.[19] Nevada excludes acts or omissions involving intentional misconduct, fraud, or a knowing

---

15. Veasey, Finkelstein & Bigle, "Delaware Support Directors with a Three-legged Stool of Limited Liability, Indemnification, and Insurance," 42 Bus. Law. 399, 403 (1987).

16. Id. See also Sparks, "Delaware's D & O Liability Law. Other States Should Follow Suit," Legal Times, Aug. 18, 1986, at 10, col. 1, 4.

17. Winston, "Most Delaware firms to limit directors' liability: Survey," Business Insurance, Feb. 9, 1987, at 26, col. 3.

18. See infra Appendix B.

19. Assembly Bill No. 1530, Sec. 14.

violation of law.[20] In North Carolina, good faith is required and the director must have known or believed at the time that the acts or omissions were in conflict with the best interests of the corporation.[21] Pennsylvania excludes acts which constitute self-dealing, willful misconduct or recklessness.[22] New York excludes relief liability if an adverse judgment establishes that the acts or omissions

(1) were in bad faith,
(2) involved intentional misconduct or a knowing violation of law,
(3) that the director gained an unlawful financial profit, or
(4) that his acts violated Section 719 of the Business Corporation Law.[23]

In New Mexico the exclusion relates to negligence, willful misconduct or recklessness.[24] Washington excludes intentional misconduct, a knowing violation of law, and illegal personal benefit.[25] In Georgia a director's liability is not eliminated or limited

(1) for any appropriation, in violation of his duties, of any business opportunity of the corporation;
(2) for acts or omissions not in good faith or which involve intentional misconduct or a knowing violation of law;
(3) for certain statutory violations;
(4) for any transactions from which he received an improper personal benefit.[26]

---

20. Nev. Rev. Stat. 78.036.
21. N.C. Gen. Stat. § 55-7.
22. 42 Pa. C.S.A. § 8364.
23. N.Y. Bus Corp. Law § 402(b).
24. N.M. Stat. Ann. § 53-12-2(E).
25. Wash. Rev. Code § 23A.12.020.
26. Ga. Code Ann. § 14-2-171(b).

§ 7.05. Indiana-type statutes.

The Indiana-type statute is self-executing, does not require shareholder action or any charter provisions or amendment, and does not contain the exception of the duty of loyalty.

The Indiana legislation

Indiana Code Chapter 23-1-35, effective April 1, 1986, was the first of the new legislation and affords broad protection for directors. It details rather typical standards of conduct for directors and then provides that a director (not an officer) is not liable for any action taken as a director unless he (1) failed to conform to the standards of conduct and (2) the breach or failure to perform constituted willful misconduct or recklessness.

Unlike the numerous exceptions to the Delaware law, the only significant exceptions in the Indiana statute are for

> (1) liability for acts or omissions which involve willful misconduct or recklessness;
> (2) liability for federal statutory violations including RICO and the federal securities laws.

The Indiana statute's exemption from liability is not limited to monetary damages and there is no exception for non-monetary claims such as claims for injunction, rescission, or restitution. All are eliminated. There is no express provision for a corporation to opt out of these provisions but presumably it could be done by amending the articles.[27] This type of statute provides the most complete relief from liability for directors of any statute enacted to date with the possible exception of the Ohio statute which became law later in 1986.[28]

Other similar legislation

Florida, Ohio, Virginia and Wisconsin enacted self-executing statutes which require no shareholder action to make

---

27. See Ind. Code § 23-1-38.
28. See infra section 7.08.

219

them effective. However, they are sufficiently different in form and scope from the Indiana law that they will be dealt with separately in the following sections.[29]

§ 7.06. Florida legislation.

Florida's statute limiting directorial liability is self-executing. Effective July 1, 1987, it eliminates the personal liability of a director for monetary damages to the corporation or any other person for any statement, vote, decision or failure to act unless the director breached or failed to perform his duties as a director and:

(1) the breach or failure to act constituted a violation of the criminal law, unless the director reasonably believed his conduct was lawful or had no reasonable cause to believe it was unlawful;

(2) the director either directly or indirectly derived an improper personal benefit;

(3) the liability is based upon improper corporate distributions and other specified corporate statutory violations;

(4) with respect to a proceeding by or in the right of the corporation, the director acted with conscious disregard for the best interests of the corporation or performed willful misconduct; or

(5) with respect to third party litigation, the director acted recklessly or committed acts or omissions in bad faith or with malicious purpose or in a manner exhibiting wanton and willful disregard of human rights, safety or property.[30]

The Florida statute defines several key terms:

(A) "Recklessness" is defined to mean an act or omission in conscious disregard of a risk known or so obvious

---

29. Infra section 7.06, the Florida Statute; section 7.10, the Virginia Statute; section 7.07, the Wisconsin Statute; section 7.08, the Ohio Statute.
30. Fla. Stat. § 607.1645.

that it should have been known to the director and such risk was so great as to make it highly probable that harm would follow from such action or omission.[31]

(B) "Improper personal benefit" does not include a benefit which is not otherwise prohibited by state or federal law or regulation if:

  (1) the transaction and the nature of the personal benefit was disclosed to or known by all directors voting on the matter (except for derivative suits regarding director decisions with respect to takeover bids);

  (2) the transaction and the nature of the personal benefit are disclosed to or known by the shareholders and the transaction was approved by the holders of a majority of the independent shares; or

  (3) the transaction was fair and reasonable to the corporation when authorized.[32]

Florida's legislation contains an unusual reporting requirement requiring D & O insurers providing coverage for officers' and directors' liability to report to the Florida Department of Insurance any claim or action for damages claimed to have been caused by error, omission or negligence in the performance of the officer's or director's services if the claim resulted in a final judgment, settlement or other final disposition. The reports must be filed no later than sixty days following the triggering event and contain, among other things, the following:

- Name, address, and position held by the individual insured and the type of corporation or organization;
- The date of the occurrence which created the claim and when the claim was reported to the insurer;
- The name of the injured person (the statute provides this information shall be privileged, confidential and not subject to disclosure);

---

31. Id.
32. Id. § 607.165.

221

- The names of all defendants involved;
- The date and amount of the judgment or settlement;
- In case of a settlement, information regarding the claimant's anticipated future losses;
- The "loss adjustment expense" paid to defense counsel and others;
- A summary of the occurrence which created the claim, including whether the injuries were the result of the physical damage, damage to reputation or based on self-dealing, a description of the type of activity which caused the injury, and steps taken by the officers and directors to insure that similar occurrences are less likely in the future.[33]

§ 7.07. Wisconsin legislation.

The Wisconsin statute became effective June 13, 1987.[34] It is self-executing. It eliminates the liability of directors and officers to the corporation, its shareholders, or any person asserting rights on behalf of the corporation or its shareholders, for damages, settlements, fees, fines, penalties or other monetary liabilities for breach of or failure to perform any duty arising solely from status as a director, unless the person asserting liability proves that the breach or failure constitutes:

   (1) willful failure to deal fairly with the corporation or its shareholders in a matter in which the director had a material conflict of interest;

   (2) a violation of criminal law unless the director reasonably believed his conduct was lawful or had no reasonable cause to believe it was unlawful;

   (3) deriving an improper personal profit; or

   (4) willful misconduct.

The immunity from liability does not apply to improper corporate distributions and other specific corporate statutory

---

33. Id. § 627.9122.
34. Wis. Stat. § 180.307.

violations. Also, there is a special provision permitting the corporation to opt out of or limit the immunity, but the immunity will nonetheless apply if a cause of action accrued while the immunity was in effect.

§ 7.08. Ohio legislation.

Effective November 22, 1986, Ohio made substantial and significant changes in its general corporation law to provide reduced liability exposure and broader financial protection for corporate directors, but not officers. The new legislation was proposed by the Corporation Law Committee of the Ohio State Bar Association and amended Sections 1701.59 and 1701.60, Ohio Revised Code, to provide considerable protection from monetary and other liability.

The new legislation eliminates liability of a corporate director for money damages unless it is proved by clear and convincing evidence that the director's action or failure to act involved an act or omission undertaken with deliberate intent to cause injury to the corporation or undertaken with reckless disregard for the best interests of the corporation.[35] This exemption from liability will not apply if, and only to the extent that, at the time of the act or omission, the articles or regulations of the corporation state, with specific reference to this provision, that it shall not apply.

Even if a corporation opts out of this new statutory exemption from liability, by such a provision of its articles or regulations, a director can be found to have breached his duties as a director only if it is proved by clear and convincing evidence that the director has not acted in good faith, in a manner he reasonably believed to be in or not opposed to the best interests of the corporation or with the care that an ordinarily prudent person in a like position would use under similar circumstances. This provision expressly includes actions involving or affecting:

(1) a change or potential change in control of the corporation;

---

35. Ohio Rev. Code Ann. § 1701.59(D).

223

(2) a termination or potential termination of the director's service to the corporation as a director;

(3) the director's service in any other position or relationship with the corporation.[36]

In a related amendment it is provided that a director is not
an interested director solely because the subject of a contract,
action or transaction may involve or affect a change in control of the corporation or his continuation in office as a director of the corporation.[37]

The Ohio amendments have also reinforced the power of
directors of Ohio corporations to deal with takeovers and
other change of control situations. New Section 1701.13(F)(7)
authorizes a corporation to resist a change or potential
change in control if the directors by a majority vote of a quorum determine that the change or potential change is opposed to or not in the best interests of the corporation. In
making that determination the directors must consider the
interests of the corporation's shareholders and may consider:

(1) the interests of the corporation's employees, suppliers, creditors and customers;

(2) the economy of the state and nation;

(3) community and social considerations;

(4) the long-term as well as short-term interests of the
corporation and its shareholders, including the possibility that these interests may be best served by the
continued independence of the corporation.[38]

The liability-limiting provisions do not apply to or affect a
director who acts in any capacity other than as a director (i.e.,
as an officer or a shareholder) or for violation of Section
1701.95, Ohio Revised Code, relating to payment of unlawful
dividends or distributions to shareholders or for making un-

---

36. Id. § 1701.59(C), which also applies to claims for nonmonetary relief
whether or not the corporation opts out of the immunity provided by
§ 1701.59(D), supra.

37. Id. § 1701.60(C).

38. See also id. § 1701.59(E).

lawful loans to an officer, director or shareholder of the corporation. Also, none of the protective provisions applies to a director of a corporation with no publicly-traded securities who votes for or against any action that, in connection with a change in control of the corporation, results in a majority shareholder receiving a greater consideration for his shares than other shareholders.[39]

§ 7.09. Retroactive effect.

Some of the statutory provisions discussed in this chapter expressly state that their limitations on liability do not apply to acts or omissions occurring prior to the effective date of the statute[40] or, in the case of some Delaware-type statutes, the date when the amendment of the articles or certificate of incorporation becomes effective.[41] Other statutes are silent on that point.

There is a general rule that the mere fact that a statute applies to a civil action retrospectively does not render it unconstitutional.[42] However, the constitutions of some states prohibit the passage of retroactive laws. In Ohio, for example, that prohibition applies to laws affecting substantive rights but has no reference to laws of a remedial nature.[43] There is also some question whether retroactive application of D & O liability limiting statutes might violate the equal protection or due process clauses of federal or state constitutions. At this writing, there are no definitive court decisions in point.

§ 7.10. Caps on damages.

The only legislation to date attempting to put a statutory cap on the damages recoverable for directorial liability is a

---

39. Id. § 1701.59(F).

40. E.g., Mich. Comp. Laws § 450.1029(c).

41. E.g., Del. Code Ann. tit. 8, § 102(b)(7); Ga. Code Ann. § 14-2-171(b); Iowa Code § 491.5(8); Minn. Stat. § 302A.251(4)(e).

42. Cohen v. Beneficial Indus. Loan Corp., 337 U.S. 541, 554, 93 L.Ed. 528, 69 S.Ct. 1221, 1229 (1949).

43. Kilbreath v. Rudy, 16 Ohio St. 2d 70, 242 N.E.2d 658 (1968).

Virginia statute limiting the damages that may be assessed in a derivative or shareholder's actions against an officer or director, arising out of a single transaction, occurrence or course of conduct, to the lesser of:

(1) The monetary amount specified in the articles or, if approved by the shareholders, in the bylaws, as a limitation on officer or director liability; or

(2) The greater of $100,000 or the amount of cash compensation received by the officer or director during the twelve months immediately preceding the act or omission for which liability was imposed.[44]

The Virginia statute is self-executing and excludes from the cap damages resulting from willful misconduct, a knowing violation of criminal law, or of a federal or state securities law.

In Delaware and Ohio, such proposals for limiting damages were rejected as being arbitrary and unrelated to the wrongdoing involved in the litigation. Moreover, questions have been raised as to the constitutionality of caps on damages.[45]

Statutory limitations on the recovery of damages are new to the D & O area, but have been the subject of much litigation in other fields. The courts have not been in agreement. The Supreme Court upheld the constitutionality of the Price-Anderson Act in placing a dollar limit on the aggregate liability due to a single nuclear incident,[46] and its decision was followed by the Supreme Court of Indiana in upholding a limitation on the amount of recovery under the Indiana Medical Malpractice Act.[47] However, a district judge in the Fourth Circuit, considering the limitation on damages in the Virginia malpractice statute, distinguished the Supreme Court

---

44. Va. Code Ann. § 13.1-692.1.

45. Wagner, "Courts Consider Caps Constitutionality," National L.J., July 20, 1987, at 23, col. 1.

46. Duke Power Co. v. Carolina Envtl. Study Group, 438 U.S. 59, 57 L.Ed. 2d 595, 98 S.Ct. 2620 (1978).

47. Johnson v. St. Vincent Hosp., 404 N.E.2d 585, 599 (Ind. 1980).

decision and struck down the Virginia statute.[48] While the case law is split on the constitutionality of the limitation on damages in the medical malpractice legislation,[49] a 1987 decision of the Florida Supreme Court may shed some light on the validity of Virginia's D & O cap. When Florida's legislature enacted the Tax Reform and Insurance Act of 1986, it placed a cap of $450,000 on damages for noneconomic issues, defined as damages "to compensate for pain and suffering, inconvenience, physical impairment, mental anguish, disfigurement, loss of capacity for enjoyment of life, and other nonpecuniary damages." The cap was attacked as being contrary to Article 1, Section 21, of the Florida Constitution:

> The courts shall be open to every person for redress of any injury, and justice shall be administered without sale, denial or delay.

In *Smith v. Department of Insurance,*[50] the court upheld the challenge and struck down the cap on damages. The per curiam decision stated:

> It is uncontroverted that there currently exists a right to sue and recover noneconomic damages of any amount and that this right existed at the time the current Florida Constitution was adopted.... (W)here such a right has become a part of the common law of the state ... the legislature is without power to abolish such a right with-

---

48. Boyd v. Bulala, 647 F. Supp. 781, 786 (W.D. Va. 1986).

49. Upholding such limitations: e.g., Fein v. Permanente Med. Group, 38 Cal. 3d 137, 211 Cal. Rptr. 368, 695 P.2d 665 (1985); Florida Patient's Comp. Fund v. Von Stelina, 474 So. 2d 783 (Fla. 1985); Johnson v. St. Vincent Hosp., supra note 45, at 591, 597; Prendergast v. Nelson, 199 Neb. 97, 256 N.W.2d 657 (1977); State ex rel. Strykowski v. Wilkie, 81 Wis. 2d 291, 261 N.W. 434 (1978). Cases declaring such limitations unconstitutional: e.g., Wright v. Central Du Page Hosp., 63 Ill. 2d 313, 347 N.E.2d 736 (1976); White v. State, 203 Mont. 363, 661 P.2d 1272 (1983); Carson v. Maurer, 120 N.H. 925, 424 A.2d 825 (1980); Waggoner v. Gibson, 647 F. Supp. 1102 (N.D. Tex. 1986); McGuire v. C & L Restaurant, 346 N.W.2d 605 (Minn. 1984). See also Beatty v. Akron City Hosp., 67 Ohio St. 2d 483, 494, 424 N.E.2d 586, 593 (1981); Jones v. State Bd. of Med., 97 Idaho 859, 555 P.2d 399 (1986).

50. 507 So. 2d 1080 (Fla. 1987).

out providing a reasonable alternative to protect the rights of the people of the state to redress for injuries, unless the legislature can show an overpowering public necessity for the abolishment of such right, and no alternative method of meeting such public necessity can be shown.... Here ... the legislature has provided nothing in the way of an alternative remedy or commensurate benefit and one can only speculate, in an act of faith, that somehow the legislative scheme will benefit the tort victim. We cannot embrace such nebulous reasoning when a constitutional right is involved.

The court went on to point out that no claim had been made that the cap was based on a legislative showing of "an overpowering public necessity for the abolishment of such right."

§ 7.11. Expanded criteria and constituencies.

A few states have enacted new legislation to expand the criteria and the constituencies which directors may consider in arriving at their decisions. Usually such expansion is in the context of determining what directors believe to be in the best interests of the corporation and its shareholders. The language of the Ohio statute is as comprehensive as any. It requires directors to consider the interests of the corporation's shareholders and permits them, in their discretion, to consider any of the following:

(1) The interests of the corporation's employees, suppliers, creditors, and customers;

(2) The economy of the state and nation;

(3) Community and societal considerations;

(4) The long-term as well as the short-term interests of the corporation and its shareholders, including the possibility that these interests may be best served by the continued independence of the corporation.[51]

The New Mexico statute follows the Ohio statute closely.[52]

---

51. Ohio Rev. Code Ann. § 1701.59(E).
52. N.M. Stat. § 53-11-35(D).

Indiana[53] and Pennsylvania[54] enacted substantially identical provisions which permit consideration by directors of the effects of their actions on shareholders, employees, suppliers and customers of the corporation, communities in which offices and other facilities of the corporation are located, and any other pertinent factors.

Missouri limits its expanded criteria and constituencies to the exercise of the board's business judgment concerning any acquisition proposal.[55]

In New York, in taking any action including action which may involve a change or potential change in control of the corporation, a director may consider both the long-term and short-term interests of the corporation and its shareholders.[56]

One commentator has suggested that broadening the factors a board may consider is likely to lead to greater uncertainty over judicial decisions in cases against directors, and possibly may confer on the additional constituencies rights of action against the directors.[57]

---

53. Ind. Code § 23-1-35-1(d).

54. 42 Pa. C.S.A. § 8363(b).

55. Mo. Rev. Stat. § 351.347.

56. N.Y. Bus. Corp. Law § 717(b). See also discussion supra section 2.02.

57. Hanks, "State Legislative Responses to the Director Liability Crisis," 20 Rev. of Sec. & Commodities Req. 23 (1987).

COROLLARY REFERENCES

Block, Barton & Garfield, "Advising Directors on the D & O Insurance Crisis," 14 Sec. Req. L.J. 130 (1986).

"Delaware's Limit on Director Liability: How the Market for Incorporation Shapes Corporate Law," 10 Harv. J.L. & Pub. Pol'y 665 (1987).

"Director Liability: Michigan's Response to Smith v. Van Gorkom [488 A.2d 858 (Del.)]," 33 Wayne L. Rev. 1039 (1987).

Dunlap, "New Protections for Corporate Directors," 44 Wash. St. B. News 25 (Aug. 1987).

Linsley, "Statutory Limitations on Directors' Liability in Delaware: a New Look at Conflicts of Interest and the Business Judgment Rule," 24 Harv. J. on Legis. 527 (1987).

Veasey, Finkelstein & Bigler, "Delaware Supports Directors with Limited Liability, Indemnification, and Insurance," 42 Bus. Law. 399 (1987).

Wander & LeCoque, "Corporate Control Transactions and Today's Business Judgment Rule," 42 Bus. Law. 29 (1986).

Young, "State D & O Liability Legislation: Spotlight on Florida," 11 Director's Monthly 5 (Oct. 1987).

Comment, "1986 Ohio Corporation Amendments: Expanding the Scope of Director Immunity," 56 U. Cin. L. Rev. 663 (1987).

Chapter 8

CRIMINAL LIABILITY

§ 8.01. Crime in the boardroom.

The criminal prosecution of corporations and their executives has increased dramatically in recent years. Between 1970 and 1984 the number of "white collar crimes" pursued by federal authorities increased three-fold. Between 1976 and 1979 there were 574 corporations convicted of federal crimes. In 1985 it was reported that 45 of the 100 largest military suppliers to the federal government were under criminal investigation. Congress has revised the penalty structures in federal criminal statutes[1] and has enacted new legislation directed principally at corporate wrongdoing.[2]

Criminal prosecutions have taken on new and greater significance as mechanisms for controlling the misconduct of corporate officers and directors. Contrary to the concepts prevailing in Great Britain and other European countries, the concept of corporate criminal liability is highly developed in the United States. And the definite trend is to extend this

---

1. E.g., Antitrust Procedures and Penalties Act of 1974, 15 U.S.C. § 3.
2. E.g., Foreign Corrupt Practices Act of 1977, 15 U.S.C. § 78a et seq.

concept to the prosecution of directors and officers charged with the governance and management of their corporation.

Corporations may be held criminally liable for the acts of employees at any level. In 1909, the Supreme Court ruled that a corporation is responsible for acts which an employee has assumed to perform for the corporation, even though not strictly within the powers actually authorized.[3] When the employee's crime occurs during the performance of a job-related activity, the corporation may be held liable. Thus when the managers of an entity are wrongdoers, imposition of responsibility upon the entity is a foregone conclusion.

Because a corporation can act only through individuals, it is generally the case that a corporate crime involves crime of individual agents. The individuals are subject to prosecution despite the fact that they were acting for the corporation in an official capacity.[4] There is also a "collective knowledge doctrine" under which knowledge may be imputed to a corporation on the basis of the aggregate or collective knowledge of the corporation's employees as a group.[5]

§ 8.02. Bases of individual liability.

Corporate officials and agents may be held liable for crimes that they personally commit, for crimes they aid or abet and for crimes they fail to prevent by neglecting to control the misconduct of those subject to their control.

The first category of liability is based on the concept that the corporate official or agent may not hide behind the corporate entity but must answer for his own wrongdoing.[6]

---

3. New York Cent. R.R. v. United States, 212 U.S. 481, 493-94, 55 L.Ed. 613, 29 S.Ct. 304 (1909).

4. E.g., State v. Ralph Williams Northwest Chrysler Plymouth, Inc., 87 Wash. 2d 298, 553 P.2d 423 (1976).

5. See, e.g., Gem City Motors, Inc. v. Minton, 109 Ga. App. 842, 845, 137 S.E.2d 522, 525 (1964).

6. E.g., United States v. American Radiator & Std. San. Corp., 433 F.2d 174 (3d Cir. 1970), cert. denied, 401 U.S. 948 (1971).

The second category, sometimes called "accomplice liability,"[7] exists when a corporate official or agent instructs, counsels or aids someone else to do a criminal act. If the crime is a federal offense, the complicity statute[8] makes the accomplice liable as if he had committed the crime himself. The definition of aiding and abetting requires knowledge of the criminal act and some participation in bringing it to completion.[9] Instructing[10] or authorizing[11] another to commit an offense is all that is required to impose liability.

The third category of liability is based on the "responsible share" concept. In two leading cases the Supreme Court ruled that liability would exist if the defendant "had a responsible relation to the situation."[12] In the *Park* case, the Court found a primary duty "to implement measures that will insure that violations will not occur." An inspector of the Food and Drug Administration found evidence of rodent infestation of food stored in a warehouse. Acme Markets, Incorporated and Park, its president, were charged. Acme pleaded guilty. Park stood trial. The court instructed the jury that the sole question was "whether [Park] held a position of authority and responsibility in the business of Acme Markets" and Park could be found guilty "even if he did not consciously do wrong" and even though he had not "personally participated in the situation" if the jury found that he had a "responsible relation" to the situation.

This line of authority originally developed in cases arising under the Federal Food, Drug and Cosmetic Act. However, it

---

7. 1 K. Brickey, Corporate Criminal Liability §§ 5.08-5.12 (1984).

8. 18 U.S.C. § 2.

9. E.g., United States v. Amrep Corp., 560 F.2d 539 (2d Cir. 1977).

10. United States v. Berger, 456 F.2d 1349 (2d Cir.), cert. denied, 409 U.S. 892 (1972).

11. United States v. Precision Med. Labs., Inc., 593 F.2d 434 (2d Cir. 1978).

12. United States v. Park, 421 U.S. 658, 44 L.Ed.2d 489, 95 S.Ct. 1903 (1975); United States v. Dotterweich, 320 U.S. 277, 88 L.Ed. 48, 64 S.Ct. 134 (1943).

has been extended. Professor Kathleen F. Brickey[13] points out
that the responsible share analysis has been drawn upon under other federal criminal statutes including the Federal
Hazardous Substances Act,[14] the Sherman Act,[15] The Economic Stabilization Act of 1970,[16] the Occupational Safety
and Health Act (OSHA),[17] and the Federal Water Pollution
Act,[18] among others.

§ 8.03. Liability under state statutes.

In the penal laws and corporation laws of every state there
are statutes defining specific offenses which relate to corporate activities and, in many instances, such laws are made
applicable to all persons, whether or not they are officials of
corporations. For example, an Ohio statute prohibits anyone
from exercising or attempting to exercise any rights, privileges, immunities, powers, franchises or authority under the
articles of a domestic corporation after such articles have
been canceled or after the corporation has been dissolved or
after the period of existence of the corporation has expired,
except such acts as are necessary to the winding up of the
affairs of the corporation.[19]

Some state statutes impose criminal liability upon directors and officers for declaring and paying dividends from
sources other than net profits.[20] Generally, good faith is a
defense to such charges unless the director acted recklessly,
or negligently shut his eyes to obvious facts.[21] The offense
may constitute embezzlement.[22]

---

13. Brickey, "Corporate Criminal Liability: A Primer for Corporate
Counsel," 40 Bus. Law. 129, 142-43 (1984).
14. 15 U.S.C. §§ 1261-1276.
15. Id. §§ 1-7.
16. 12 U.S.C. § 1904.
17. 29 U.S.C. §§ 651-678.
18. 33 U.S.C. §§ 1311-1319. See also infra section 8.07.
19. Ohio Rev. Code Ann. §§ 1701.97, 1701.99.
20. E.g., Minn. Stat. Ann. § 300.60.
21. See Cabaniss v. State, 8 Ga. App. 129, 68 S.E. 849 (1910); Mangham
v. State, 11 Ga. App. 440, 75 S.E. 508 (1912). Cf. Guarantee Reserve Life
Ins. Co. v. Holzwarth, 148 Colo. 366, 366 P.2d 377 (1961).
22. Taylor v. Commonwealth, 119 Ky. 731, 75 S.W. 244 (1903).

In New York, a provision of the Penal Law spells out misconduct by a corporate official which constitutes a Class B misdemeanor.[23] The offenses described are the following:

1. A director knowingly concurring in any vote or act of the directors, or any of them, by which it is intended:
   (a) to make a dividend except in the manner provided by law; or
   (b) to divide, withdraw or pay to any stockholder any of the capital stock except in the manner provided by law; or
   (c) to discount or receive a note or other evidence of debt to pay for an installment of capital stock; or
   (d) to discount or receive a note or other evidence of debt to enable a stockholder to withdraw money he had paid for stock; or
   (e) to use corporate funds to purchase its stock except in the manner provided by law.
2. A director or officer:
   (a) issuing, participating in or concurring in issuing an increase in the corporation's capital stock beyond the authorized amount; or
   (b) selling stock he does not own, except as an underwriter or dealer.

The corporation laws of the several states apply penalties for the violation of ministerial duties or obligations imposed on the corporation and its officers.[24]

Violations of Sunday closing laws have resulted in the conviction of corporate officers and employees in several states.[25]

---

23. N.Y. Penal Law § 190.35.

24. E.g., Ohio Rev. Code Ann. § 1701.93, false statements, prospectus or reports by officer, director, employee, or agent of corporation; § 1701.94, corporate officer's liability for failure to keep and produce records; § 1701.95, unlawful loans, dividends or distribution of assets; § 1701.97, exercise of expired powers; § 1701.99, penalties.

25. E.g., State v. Maynard, 1 Ohio St. 2d 57, 203 N.E.2d 332 (1964), cert. denied, 382 U.S. 871 (1965); Bookout v. City of Chattanooga, 59 Tenn. App.

A corporate president and principal shareholder was convicted in New York for nonpayment of money due to pension and welfare funds, where he knew or should have known of the nonpayment.[26] Entertainment of public officials by employees of an Iowa corporation did not violate an Iowa criminal statute prohibiting gifts to influence an officer in the performance of his duty.[27] And a corporate officer was convicted of filing false or misleading statements in connection with the issuance of corporate stock, in violation of a Wisconsin statute.[28]

§ 8.04. Foreign Corrupt Practices Act of 1977.

One of the most important pieces of legislation directed principally at corporate wrongdoing is the Foreign Corrupt Practices Act of 1977.[29] It followed and resulted from the bribery practices of the 1970's, when leading American corporations engaged in and later confessed to worldwide wrongdoing. The SEC's voluntary disclosure program[30] and the IRS's Coordinated Examination Program[31] facilitated such disclosures and led to the legislation.

This act has two segments, each of considerable importance. The antibribery sections prohibit the use of interstate commerce in offering, paying or promising things of value to obtain influence in foreign countries to obtain or retain business or to direct business. Heavy fines and imprisonment are among the penalties and a corporation is proscribed from di-

---

576, 442 S.W.2d 658 (1969); State v. Picheco, 2 Conn. Cir. Ct. 584, 203 A.2d 242 (1964). But cf. State v. Ciminello, 120 Ohio App. 172, 201 N.E.2d 710 (1964).

26. People v. Trapp, 20 N.Y.2d 613, 286 N.Y.S.2d 11, 233 N.E.2d 110 (1967).

27. Dukehart-Hughes Tractor & Equip. Co. v. United States, 341 F.2d 613 (Ct. Cl. 1965), construing Iowa law.

28. State v. Woodington, 31 Wis. 2d 151, 142 N.E.2d 810 (1966).

29. 15 U.S.C. §§ 78a, 78dd-1, 78dd-2, 78m(b), 78ff.

30. Report of the Securities and Exchange Commission on Questionable and Illegal Corporate Payments and Practices (May 12, 1976), reprinted in SEC Reg. & L. Rep. (BNA) No. 353 (May 19, 1976).

31. Internal Revenue Service News Release IR-1945, January 20, 1978.

rectly or indirectly paying any fine imposed upon a director, officer, shareholder or other representative of the corporation.

The second segment of the act contains accounting provisions which require records to be maintained as to corporate financial transactions and resulting disposition of corporate assets. Also accounting controls must be maintained to ensure that (a) management directives will be obeyed, (b) records will provide accountability for corporate assets, (c) access to corporate assets will be controlled, and (d) recorded and existing assets will be compared at reasonable times and discrepancies dealt with.[32] Under the general penalty provision of the Securities Exchange Act of 1934,[33] willful violation of such provisions is a felony.

§ 8.05. Comprehensive Crime Control Act of 1984.

This act creates several new white collar and racketeering offenses, changes law and procedure as to pretrial confinement and revamps federal sentencing of convicted defendants.[34] Among other matters it deals with accessing of certain information by computer, amends the Racketeer Influenced and Corrupt Organizations Act (RICO) to include obscenity offenses as predicate acts and to broaden and strengthen the forfeiture provisions, and extends federal criminal law to payments made to firms holding federal contracts or grants.

An important part of this act is a tough antibribery law applicable to financial institutions.[35] It prohibits officials of such institutions from requesting or receiving anything of value in connection with any transaction of business of the institution. As amended, this law contains an intent element

---

32. For details of the statutory requirements, see 15 U.S.C. § 78m(b)(2)(B).

33. 15 U.S.C. § 78ff(a).

34. Act of Oct. 12, 1984, Pub. L. 98-473, Title 11, 98 Stat. 1976.

35. See 18 U.S.C. § 215, and the Bank Bribery Amendments Act, Pub. L. 99-370 (Aug. 4, 1986).

which requires proof that the officer or recipient of a thing of value acted corruptly and with intent to bribe. Penalties include fines and imprisonment. The law applies to all federally insured institutions, Federal Home Loan Banks, institutions of the Cooperative Farm Credit System, small business investors companies, bank holding companies and savings and loan associations.

§ 8.06. Criminal liability under RICO.

The Racketeer Influenced and Corrupt Organizations Act (RICO) was enacted as Title IX of the Organized Crime Control Act of 1970.[36] Its criminal provisions were largely ignored from 1970 to 1975 and then a considerable growth in its use by federal prosecutors commenced. The "predicate acts" listed in the statutory definition of "racketeering activity" include fraud-related crimes such as mail fraud, wire fraud and fraud in the sale of securities. The breadth of that definition encouraged the application of RICO to cases involving allegations of fraud in common business and securities transactions and other practices not usually associated with organized criminal activity. Bankruptcy fraud and embezzlement from pension, welfare and union funds are other predicate acts that are included in the definition of racketeering activity and are typical "white collar" crimes.[37]

The activities prohibited by RICO[38] are dealt with through a far-reaching enforcement scheme which includes criminal penalties of imprisonment, fines and forfeiture for violation of those provisions.[39] These penalties are severe and may exceed the statutory penalties for the violations of the predicate acts.

The criminal forfeiture sanction in RICO revived a punishment that had not been used in the United States since

---

36. 18 U.S.C. §§ 1961-1968.

37. Webb & Turow, "RICO Forfeitures in Practice: A Prosecutorial Perspective," 52 U. Cin. L. Rev. 404 (1983).

38. See discussion supra in section 4.17, and 18 U.S.C. § 1962.

39. 18 U.S.C. § 1963.

1790.[40] It deprives a guilty defendant of all property or proceeds he acquired through racketeering activities or unlawful debt collection regardless of whether those assets are themselves "tainted" by use in connection with the illicit acts.[41] The RICO statute was amended in 1984[42] and the provisions for forfeiture broadened and strengthened. Even before that, however, the Supreme Court had given the forfeiture provisions an expansive reading.[43] In its more recent RICO decisions, both criminal[44] and civil,[45] the Supreme Court has given an expansive interpretation to the entire act, which portends an ever-increasing use of this weapon, unless Congress acts to reduce its fearsome potentialities. This is unlikely to happen as to criminal RICO.

The criminal provisions of RICO have been used to convict a state governor for conduct involved in the award of state contracts and leases,[46] to convict the mayor of a village for soliciting bribes and extorting money in return for zoning changes,[47] and to convict a county judge of accepting kickbacks.[48] It has been employed against commissioners,[49] bondsmen,[50] police officers,[51] prison officials,[52] businessmen,[53]

---

40. United States v. L'Hoste, 609 F.2d 790, 813 n.15 (5th Cir.), cert. denied, 449 U.S. 833 (1980).

41. United States v. Ginsberg, 773 F.2d 798, 801 (7th Cir. 1985).

42. Pub. L. 98-473, Title II, 98 Stat. 2192, Comprehensive Crime Control Act of 1984.

43. Russello v. United States, 464 U.S. 16, 78 L.Ed.2d 17, 104 S.Ct. 296 (1983).

44. United States v. Turkette, 452 U.S. 576, 69 L.Ed.2d 246, 101 S.Ct. 2524 (1981).

45. Sedima, S.P.R.L. v. Imrex Co., 473 U.S. 749, 87 L.Ed.2d 346, 104 S.Ct. 3275 (1985).

46. United States v. Mandel, 602 F.2d 653 (4th Cir.) (en banc), reh'g denied, 609 F.2d 1706 (1979), cert. denied, 445 U.S. 961 (1980).

47. United States v. McNary, 620 F.2d 621 (7th Cir. 1980).

48. United States v. Clark, 646 F.2d 1259 (8th Cir. 1981).

49. United States v. Barber, 476 F. Supp. 182 (S.D. W.Va. 1979).

50. United States v. Forsythe, 560 F.2d 1127 (3d Cir. 1977).

51. United States v. Brown, 555 F.2d 407 (5th Cir. 1977), cert. denied, 435 U.S. 904 (1978).

52. United States v. Davis, 576 F.2d 1065 (3d Cir.), cert. denied, 439 U.S. 836 (1978).

53. United States v. Huber, 603 F.2d 387 (2d Cir. 1979), cert. denied, 445 U.S. 927 (1980).

union officers,[54] oil companies,[55] and others, including professional criminals. Fraudulent markups on a cost-plus hospital supply contract were the basis for the conviction in one case,[56] and in another a supplier defrauded the government by supplying substandard shrimp and scheming to evade inspections.[57] Mail fraud, wire fraud and bribery have served as the basis of RICO prosecutions of corporations and their representatives.[58]

Some examples of the types of "enterprises" that have been involved in RICO criminal prosecutions are (a) a theater operated through a pattern of securities and bankruptcy fraud,[59] (b) a law partnership operated through a pattern of payment of bribes,[60] (c) an individual's personal real estate business operated by fraud,[61] (d) a labor union operated through a pattern of unlawful payments,[62] (e) a cooperative engaged in a scheme of securities fraud,[63] and (f) a state governmental agency, the Louisiana Department of Agriculture.[64]

---

54. United States v. Stofsky, 409 F. Supp. 609 (S.D.N.Y. 1973), aff'd, 527 F.2d 237 (2d Cir. 1975), cert. denied, 429 U.S. 819 (1976).

55. United States v. Union Oil Co., No. H-79-31 (S.D. Tex. 1979).

56. United States v. Huber, supra note 53.

57. United States v. Hartley, 678 F.2d 961 (11th Cir.), reh'g denied, 688 F.2d 852 (1982), cert. denied, 459 U.S. 1178 (1983).

58. E.g., United States v. Marubeni America Corp., 611 F.2d 763 (9th Cir. 1980); United States v. Tamura, 694 F.2d 591 (9th Cir. 1982).

59. United States v. Weisman, 624 F.2d 1118 (2d Cir.), cert. denied, 449 U.S. 871 (1980).

60. United States v. Jannotti, 501 F. Supp. 1182 (E.D. Pa. 1980), aff'd, 729 F.2d 213 (3d Cir. 1984).

61. United States v. Benny, 559 F. Supp. 254 (N.D. Cal. 1983).

62. United States v. Provenzano, 688 F.2d 194 (3d Cir.), cert. denied, 103 S.Ct. 492 (1982).

63. United States v. Bledsoe, 674 F.2d 647 (8th Cir.), cert. denied, 459 U.S. 1040 (1982).

64. United States v. Dozier, 672 F.2d 531 (5th Cir.), cert. denied, 459 U.S. 943 (1982).

§ 8.07. Criminal liability under environmental laws.

Environmental law and its impact on corporate officers and directors generally is discussed in Chapter 10. In this section the criminal liability aspect of environmental law is highlighted because it has already begun to present problems for those in corporate leadership.

Statutory prohibitions of environmental pollution are usually accompanied by criminal penalties. Statutes such as the Rivers and Harbors Appropriation Act of 1899,[65] the Clean Air Act,[66] the Federal Water Pollution Control Act,[67] the Toxic Substances Control Act,[68] and numerous other federal and state statutes impose requirements which are supplemented by enforcement agencies. Their violation may result in criminal charges, fines and in some cases imprisonment.

Examples of criminal charges made against corporate officials and their companies include the following:

- Violations of the Clean Water Act and other federal laws.
- Illegally dumping and conspiring to discharge abrasive blasting grit containing arsenic.[69]
- Illegal storage of hazardous waste.
- Conspiracy and failure to notify of release of hazardous waste.
- Burying several hundred barrels filled with sodium hydroxide, hydrochloric acid, and formaldehyde on company property.
- Disposing of hazardous waste without government authorization and making false statements to environmental authorities.[70]

---

65. 33 U.S.C. § 401 et seq.
66. 42 U.S.C. § 7401 et seq.
67. 33 U.S.C. § 1251 et seq.
68. 15 U.S.C. § 2601 et seq.
69. 17 Env't Rep. (BNA) 971 (1986).
70. 16 Env't Rep. (BNA) 1797-98 (1986).

In the Second Circuit,[71] the court imposed civil liability upon an industrial waste disposal service, its president and its vice-president, under the criminal provision of the Rivers and Harbors Appropriation Act of 1899.[72]

All three of the bases of criminal liability discussed in section 8.02 supra may apply in environmental cases. That involving the "responsible share" concept is particularly applicable in cases where intent or guilty knowledge is not a prerequisite to a finding of guilt. Technically, the lack of knowledge is no defense to a charge of pollution violations.[73]

§ 8.08. Criminal liability under securities laws.

Securities law violations may involve directors and officers as principals or as aiders and abettors. Actually the liability is the same, because the complicity statute makes an accomplice liable as if he had committed the crime himself.[74] However an aider and abettor must share the criminal purpose of the principal and must intend to assist the principal in accomplishing it.[75]

With one exception,[76] the federal securities statutes impose criminal penalties for violations, define some separate criminal offenses and establish the violations as felonies. In particular, Section 24 of the Securities Act of 1933[77] and Sections 21 and 32 of the Securities Exchange Act of 1934[78] impose criminal liability with a breadth not equaled in other regulatory statutes. What these statutes do is to convert what would otherwise be a civil violation into a felony, if the offender

---

71. United States v. Pollution Abatement Servs., 763 F.2d 133 (2d Cir.), cert. denied, 106 S.Ct. 605 (1985).

72. 33 U.S.C. § 401 et. seq.

73. CPC Int'l, Inc. v. Illinois Pollution Control Bd., 24 Ill. App. 3d 203, 321 N.E.2d 58 (1975).

74. 18 U.S.C. § 2.

75. See discussion supra in section 8.02.

76. Securities Investor Protection Act of 1970, 15 U.S.C. §§ 80a-1 to 80a-52, has limited criminal provisions.

77. 15 U.S.C. § 77x.

78. Id. §§ 78u and 78ff.

willfully or knowingly violates the act or any rule or regulation thereunder. Professor Brickey has well said that, "The only element that differentiates criminal from civil liability is the actor's state of mind."[79]

If two or more persons conspire to commit an offense against the United States or to defraud the United States, the general federal conspiracy statute[80] applies. When the object of the conspiracy, as in the case of most violations of the securities laws, is a felony, the violation of the conspiracy statute itself is a felony punishable by a fine, prison term or both. The typical penalty for violation of the securities laws is imprisonment of up to five years or a $10,000 fine or both.

In this context a conspiracy to defraud the United States means to interfere with or obstruct a lawful governmental function by deceit, craft or trickery, by means which are dishonest.[81] Such a conspiracy may arise out of a concerted effort to violate the securities laws, even though no pecuniary harm to the government results.[82]

Substantial impetus has been given to "white collar" prosecutions by the surge of insider trading in which corporate executives used confidential information to help themselves or their associates make large profits in the stock market. The arbitrage scandals of the middle 1980's, involving revelations by Ivan Boesky, Martin Siegel and others, devolved from the rash of mergers and acquisitions which made major companies merger or buyout targets. Before the legal proceedings they spawned come to an end, it is predicted that there will be a review of the whole system and probably new and more stringent regulatory laws to prevent a recurrence of such activities.

---

79. Brickey, "Corporate Criminal Liability: A Primer for Corporate Counsel," 40 Bus. Law. 129, 149 (1984).

80. 18 U.S.C. § 371. See also infra section 8.13.

81. Hammerschmidt v. United States, 265 U.S. 182, 188, 68 L.Ed. 968, 44 S.Ct. 511, 512 (1924).

82. United States v. Peltz, 433 F.2d 48 (2d Cir. 1970), cert. denied, 401 U.S. 965 (1971).

§ 8.09. Mail and wire fraud.

The mail fraud statute[83] and the wire fraud statute[84] provide that "(w)hoever having devised or intending to devise any scheme or artifice to defraud, or for obtaining money or property by means of false or fraudulent pretenses, representations or promises" uses the mails or wire, radio or television communication in interstate or foreign commerce "for the purpose of executing such scheme or artifice" shall be fined not more than $1000 or imprisoned not more than five years or both. The use of the mail or wire facilities need not be a major part of the scheme as long as it is "incident to an essential part" of it.[85]

A national standard of fiduciary liability, developed by the federal courts in mail and wire fraud cases, has been held to govern the duties of corporate officers and directors to the shareholders of their corporations.[86] Thus, it was held that there was a statutory violation when the shareholders were defrauded by being deprived of the faithful services of the corporate officials. The courts have construed the word "defraud" broadly.[87] One commentator has said, "The conduct prohibited by these statutes is, therefore, nothing more than an undisclosed breach of duty by anyone labeled a fiduciary."[88] Support for that view is found in a Second Circuit decision wherein the court said that "a mere breach of fiduciary duty, standing alone, may not necessarily constitute mail fraud," but "we have held that the statute is violated when a fiduciary fails to disclose material information 'which

---

83. 18 U.S.C. § 1341.

84. Id. § 1343.

85. Pereira v. United States, 347 U.S. 1, 8, 98 L.Ed. 435, 74 S.Ct. 358 (1954).

86. United States v. Seigel, 717 F.2d 9 (2d Cir. 1983); United States v. Weiss, 752 F.2d 777 (2d Cir. 1985).

87. Weiss v. United States, 122 F.2d 675, 681 (5th Cir. 1941): "The law does not define fraud; it needs no definition; it is as old as falsehood and as versatile as human ingenuity."

88. Note, "Intra-Corporate Mail and Wire Fraud: Criminal Liability for Fiduciary Breach," 94 Yale L.J. 1427, 1431 (1985).

he is under a duty to disclose to another under circumstances where the nondisclosure could or does result in harm to the other.'"[89]

Such decisions ease the way for federal prosecutors to use the mail and wire fraud statutes to attack wrongful conduct of directors and officers in corporate governance, and give impetus to the development of a federal law of corporate fiduciary responsibility.

Violations of the mail and wire fraud statutes may be based on artifices which do not deprive anyone of money or tangible property, and it is not necessary to prove that the wrongdoers benefited from their fraudulent activities.[90]

§ 8.10. False statements.

Making false statements is a basis for criminal liability in various situations and under numerous statutes. Many such statutes are found in the codes of the states. Some examples have been mentioned above.[91] Other such laws are found in the federal statutes. Professor Brickey has summarized most of them in her treatise.[92] Probably one of the most important is that which punishes the making of sworn or unsworn false statements within the jurisdiction of any federal department or agency by a fine of up to $10,000 or imprisonment of not more than five years, or both.[93] Because all business corporations have numerous communications with the federal government and its agencies, this statute has frequent application. False statements in corporate tax returns,[94] or to the Environmental Protection Agency,[95] or before the SEC,[96] or in

89. United States v. Siegel, supra note 86, at 14.

90. United States v. Weiss, supra note 86, at 784.

91. See supra section 8.03.

92. 1 K. Brickey, Corporate Criminal Liability § 13.21 (1984).

93. 18 U.S.C. § 1001.

94. United States v. Beacon Brass Co., 344 U.S. 43, 97 L.Ed. 61, 73 S.Ct. 77 (1952).

95. United States v. Olin Corp., 465 F. Supp. 1120 (W.D.N.Y. 1979).

96. United States v. Mahler, 363 F.2d 673 (2d Cir. 1966).

records subject to inspection by a federal agency[97] are examples of such application.

Among the other federal statutes likely to be invoked when corporate officials falsify reports, statements, testimony or communications in court, before regulatory agencies and otherwise, are the general perjury statute,[98] the subornation of perjury statute,[99] and the false declarations statute.[100]

§ 8.11. Criminal liability under tax laws.

Substantial revisions of the federal tax laws and court decisions such as *United States v. Arthur Young & Company*,[101] have enlarged the exposure of corporate officers and directors to criminal prosecution for tax offenses. Well before the enactment of the Internal Revenue Code of 1986, the Tax Equity and Fiscal Responsibility Act of 1982[102] provided increased penalties for tax evasion[103] and tax perjury,[104] among other tax crimes, and established a separate structure of much larger fines for institutional violators. Those statutes are among the principal enforcement measures employed by the Internal Revenue Service in its continuing effort to punish tax law violations produced by such practices as bribes, kickbacks and payoffs, unlawful deferring of income, expense and payroll padding, and illegal political contributions.

The Supreme Court's unanimous decision in the *Arthur Young* case facilitated the work of the IRS in obtaining corporate information for use in scrutinizing corporate finances. The Court denied any work-product privilege that would permit withholding tax accrual work papers prepared by public accountants for their corporate client. The Court pointed out

---

97. United States v. Diaz, 690 F.2d 1352 (11th Cir. 1982).

98. 18 U.S.C. § 1621.

99. Id. § 1622.

100. 28 U.S.C. § 1746, and see also United States v. Gross, 511 F.2d 910 (3d Cir.), cert. denied, 423 U.S. 924 (1975).

101. 465 U.S. 805, 79 L.Ed.2d 826, 104 S.Ct. 1495 (1984).

102. Pub. L. 97-248, § 329.

103. 26 U.S.C. § 7201, amended by Pub. L. 97-248, § 329(a).

104. 26 U.S.C. § 7206(1), amended by Pub. L. 97-248, § 329(a).

that the statute reflected "a congressional policy choice *in favor of disclosure* of all [relevant] information."[105]

Emphasizing the public interest in a broad disclosure policy as to the findings of independent auditors, the Court stated:

> To insulate from disclosure a certified public accountant's interpretations of the client's financial statements would be to ignore the significance of the accountant's role as a disinterested analyst charged with public obligations.

§8.12. Obstruction of justice.

The Victim and Witness Protection Act of 1982[106] amended and restricted the scope of the federal obstruction of justice statute[107] but left a substantial proscription against altering or destroying corporate documents,[108] endeavoring to obstruct administrative proceedings[109] and most of the other corrupt conduct that was punishable under the former statute. Also, the act created two new offenses prohibiting tampering with witnesses and retaliating against persons because of their participation in an investigation or proceeding.[110]

The amended statutes punish the knowing use or attempted use of intimidation, physical force, threats or use of misleading conduct toward another person with intent to (a) influence any person's testimony in an official proceeding, (b) cause or influence a person to withhold testimony, records, documents or other objects from an official proceeding, (c) alter, destroy or conceal an object for the purpose of impairing its integrity or availability for use in an official proceeding, (d) evade legal process such as a subpoena or subpoena duces tecum (to produce), (e) to cause a person to be absent from a proceeding to which he has been subpoenaed, or (f) to hinder,

---

105. Emphasis by the Court.
106. 18 U.S.C. § 1503 (1976).
107. United States v. Faudman, 640 F.2d 20 (6th Cir. 1981).
108. United States v. McKnight, 799 F.2d 443 (8th Cir. 1986).
109. Roberts v. United States, 239 F.2d 467 (9th Cir. 1956).
110. 18 U.S.C. §§ 1512, 1513.

delay or prevent communication relating to the commission of a federal offense to a law enforcement official or a federal judge.[111]

Harassing or attempting to harass anyone for the purpose of preventing, delaying or dissuading such person from participating in an official proceeding, reporting the commission of a federal offense or causing or assisting in a prosecution is also prohibited. Another section punishes conduct that causes or threatens to cause bodily injury or injury to tangible property on account of a person's participation in an official proceeding.[112]

Emphasizing the breadth of the proscriptions in this phase of the law, the amended statute specifies that punishment may be imposed for the prohibited conduct even if the affected testimony, documentary evidence or other object may not be admissible or may not be free from privilege.[113] And the amended statute provides for penalties of a $250,000 fine and ten years imprisonment.[114]

§ 8.13. Conspiracy.

Conspiracy is an agreement between two or more persons or entities to commit an unlawful act[115] or to employ unlawful means to commit an act that may be lawful or unlawful.[116] The agreement may be inferred from evidence indicating that the alleged conspirators acted in concert with a common purpose to accomplish their objective.[117] When the action is brought under the federal conspiracy statute,[118] at least one member of the conspiracy must commit at least one overt act

---

111. Id. § 1512.
112. Id. § 1513.
113. Id. § 1512(d)(2).
114. Id. § 1512(a).
115. Pettibone v. United States, 148 U.S. 197, 203, 37 L.Ed. 419, 13 S.Ct. 542 (1893).
116. Hammerschmidt v. United States, 265 U.S. 182, 188, 68 L.Ed. 968, 44 S.Ct. 511, 512 (1924).
117. United States v. Mendex, 496 F.2d 128, 130 (5th Cir. 1924).
118. 18 U.S.C. § 371.

248

in furtherance of the conspiracy.[119] Overt acts committed by any members of the conspiracy are chargeable to all members.[120] In cases under the conspiracy provision of RICO[121] there is some authority that proof of overt acts, as such, is not required.[122]

Except in corporate conspiracy prosecutions under the Sherman Act,[123] conspiracies between a corporation and its officers, directors or agents may be a basis of liability.[124] A conspiracy among an active manager of six family-owned corporations and the corporations has been sustained.[125] But the general rule is that a conspiracy cannot be based upon an agreement of a corporation with its officer unless the officer is acting beyond his authority or for his own benefit.[126] In actions involving conspiracies among corporations with the same parent or between parent and subsidiary or among corporations controlled by the same individual, the conspiracies have been sustained.[127]

Conspiracy is a crime frequently charged against corporate officers and directors. Thus another corporate officer was convicted of conspiring to fix prices when he knew his company was involved in price-fixing and took no action to prevent his subordinates from carrying it on.[128]

---

119. United States v. Beskin, 527 F.2d 71, 75 (7th Cir. 1975), cert. denied, 429 U.S. 818 (1976).

120. United States v. Beecroft, 608 F.2d 753, 757 (9th Cir. 1979).

121. 18 U.S.C. § 1962(d). See also supra section 8.06.

122. United States v. Alonso, 740 F.2d 862, 870-72 (11th Cir. 1984); United States v. Coia, 719 F.2d 1120, 1123-24 (11th Cir. 1982).

123. 15 U.S.C. § 1.

124. See Brickey, "Corporate Criminal Liability: A Primer for Corporate Counsel," 40 Bus. Law. 129, 144-45 (1984).

125. United States v. Lowder, 492 F.2d 953 (4th Cir. 1974), cert. denied, 419 U.S. 1092 (1975).

126. See, e.g., United States v. Hartley, 678 F.2d 961 (11th Cir.), reh'g denied, 688 F.2d 852 (1982), cert. denied, 459 U.S. 1178 (1983).

127. Brickey, supra note 124, at 144 n.66.

128. United States v. Gillen, 599 F.2d 541 (3d Cir. 1979).

§ 8.14. Murder.

The title of this section looks out of place in this volume, but the crime of murder became a potential hazard for corporate officials in 1985 in Illinois. Although the case involved outrageous facts, the result has ominous possibilities for future prosecutions.

A former president and part owner of Film Recovery Systems, Inc. and its plant manager and plant foreman were convicted in a non-jury trial of the murder of a workman who died of cyanide poisoning while leaching silver from used X-rays. The trial judge held that the death occurred in "totally unsafe" workplace conditions.[129] He also found the defendants guilty of fourteen counts of reckless conduct stemming from injuries suffered by workers in the plant. They were sentenced to twenty-five years in prison and fined $10,000 each[130] on the murder charges.

Illinois has only one degree of murder. The facts in this case point more toward manslaughter or involuntary homicide than to murder, but the court had no such choice under Illinois law.

Professor Alan Dershowitz, of Harvard Law School, has been quoted as to this case:

> It obviously sends an important message to corporate executives that when they put the lives of their employees at risk they're going to be held responsible, just as when bank robbers put their victims at risk.[131]

Regardless of the outcome of the appeals in the Film Recovery Systems case, it is to be expected that there will be more prosecutions of corporate officers and directors in situations where their neglect or misconduct results in loss of life. However, it seems probable that manslaughter instead of murder

---

129. Richards & Kotlowitz, "Judge Finds 3 Corporate Officials Guilty of Murder in Cyanide Death of Worker," Wall St. Journal June 17, 1985, p. 2 col. 3, from which the other quotations in this section were also taken.

130. The convictions were appealed.

131. See supra note 129.

may be the likely charge. As Professor Norval Morris, of University of Chicago law school, has said:

> The common conception of murder is intent to kill, while the common view of manslaughter is willingness to risk killing.[132]

§ 8.15. Criminal antitrust liability.

Corporate officers and directors who are knowing participants in conduct in violation of the Sherman Act,[133] the Clayton Act[134] or the Robinson Patman Price Discrimination Act[135] may incur personal criminal liability and be subject to heavy fines or imprisonment, or both. Some examples will illustrate.

In *United States v. Wise*,[136] an indictment charging the defendant with violation of Section 1 of the Sherman Act was dismissed on the ground that the Sherman Act did not apply to corporate officers acting in a representative capacity. The district court held that the prosecution should have been under Section 14 of the Clayton Act, noting that Congress had increased the fine under the Sherman Act without disturbing the fine prescribed in the Clayton Act. In a case of first impression in the Supreme Court, the Chief Justice discussed the responsibility of such corporate officers and concluded that the decision should be reversed. It was held that a corporate officer is subject to prosecution under the Sherman Act whenever he knowingly participates in effecting an illegal contract, combination or conspiracy, whether he authorizes, orders or helps perpetrate the offense, and regardless of whether he is acting in a representative capacity.

The Sixth Circuit has held it to be a violation of the Robinson Patman Price Discrimination Act for a president of a

---

132. Id.

133. 15 U.S.C. § 1.

134. Id. § 24.

135. 13 U.S.C. § 13.

136. 370 U.S. 405, 8 L.Ed.2d 590, 82 S.Ct. 1354 (1962), rev'd, 373 U.S. 29, 9 L.Ed.2d 561, 83 S.Ct. 594 (1963).

company to receive and retain for himself a commission paid
by one to whom the company made a sale. Such a transaction
is an unfair trade practice because of its tendency to lessen
competition and create monopoly.[137]

Following the general rule applicable to corporate officials
who engage in criminal acts in the course of their employment,[138] a district court in Missouri has held corporate directors, officers and agents personally liable for acts of their
corporation that violate the antitrust laws when they participate in the activities or authorize them.[139]

§ 8.16. Liability to indemnify for loss resulting from criminal acts.

When the criminal act of a corporate director, officer or
employee constitutes violation of the individual's fiduciary
duty to a corporation, the corporation is entitled to be indemnified by the individual for its loss.[140] Under familiar rules
relating to primary and secondary liability, such a right will
also exist if the corporation itself is blameless and its obligation is solely vicarious.[141]

Corporate officers or employees may be required to indemnify their corporation for losses resulting from violations by
them of the antitrust laws.[142] Such rights to indemnification
may be asserted either directly by the corporation or derivatively by its stockholders on behalf of or for the benefit of the
corporation. Because the wrongdoing employees usually also
possess a control over the corporation that allows them to

---

137. Fitch v. Kentucky-Tennessee Light & Power Co., 136 F.2d 12, 15
(6th Cir. 1943).

138. See supra section 2.11.

139. Bergjans Farm Dairy Co. v. Sanitary Milk Producers, 241 F. Supp.
476, 482 (C.D. Mo. 1965).

140. Clayton v. Farish, 191 Misc. 136, 73 N.Y.S.2d 727 (1947).

141. See Briggs v. Spaulding, 141 U.S. 132, 35 L.Ed. 662, 11 S.Ct. 924
(1891); Builders Supply Co. v. McCabe, 366 Pa. 322, 77 A.2d 368 (1951).
See also supra section 1.14.

142. Wilshire Oil Co. v. Riffe, 409 F.2d 1277 (10th Cir. 1969), following
J.I. Case Co. v. Borak, 377 U.S. 426, 12 L.Ed.2d 423, 84 S.Ct. 1555 (1964).

suppress attempts to rectify their wrong,[143] the corporate loss is traditionally remedied through a derivative action. But the right belongs to the corporation and may be asserted by it.

For example, in Kansas, an oil company was held liable for criminal and civil penalties for violations of the Sherman and Clayton Antitrust Acts. Employees of a newly acquired division had conspired to fix prices in the sale of asphalt to the states of Kansas and Missouri. After the criminal liability of the parent company had been established, it sued one of the division's salesmen for indemnification, alleging that his knowing and unauthorized violation of the antitrust law was a breach of his fiduciary duty to his employer. The Tenth Circuit held that the parent organization was entitled to seek indemnification for criminal fines, civil damages and reasonable attorneys' fees.[144]

Such rights of indemnification have been recognized in other cases in which corporations have suffered losses because of criminal violations by employees, directors or officers. In New York, for example, bank directors were held liable to indemnify their bank for fines imposed upon it as the result of their violation of a law forbidding loans in excess of ten percent of equity, despite the acknowledged intention of the directors to make a profit for the bank in the transaction. The liability was based on negligence.[145]

---

143. Koster v. American Lumbermen's Mut. Cas. Co., 330 U.S. 518, 522, 91 L.Ed. 1067, 1072, 67 S.Ct. 828 (1947). See also infra Chapter 18.

144. Wilshire Oil Co. v. Riffe, supra note 142. See also Wilshire Oil Co. v. Riffe, 381 F.2d 6456 (10th Cir.), cert. denied, 389 U.S. 822 (1967), cert. denied, 396 U.S. 843 (1969).

145. Broderick v. Marcus, 152 Misc. 413, 272 N.Y.S. 455 (1934).

COROLLARY REFERENCES

Abrams, "Criminal Liability of Corporate Officers for Strict Liability Offenses — A Comment on Dotterweich and Park," 28 UCLA L. Rev. 463 (1981).

Brickey, "Criminal Liability of Corporate Officers for Strict Liability Offenses — Another View," 35 Vand. L. Rev. 1337 (1983).

Brickey, "Corporate Criminal Liability: A Primer for Corporate Counsel," 40 Bus. Law. 129 (1984).

"Developments in the Law — Corporate Crime: Regulating Corporate Behavior Through Criminal Sanctions," 92 Harv. L. Rev. 1227 (1979).

Marcus, "Conspiracy: The Criminal Agreement in Theory and Practice," 65 Geo. L. Rev. 925 (1977).

Weiss-Malik, "Imposing Penal Sanctions on the Unwary Corporate Executive: The Unveiled Corporate Criminal," 17 Toledo L. Rev. 383 (1986).

Comment, "Toward a Rational Theory of Criminal Liability for the Corporate Executive," 69 J. Crim. L. & Criminology 75 (1978).

Chapter 9

LIABILITY UNDER ERISA

§ 9.01. The nature of ERISA.

The Employment Retirement Security Act of 1974 (ERISA)[1] regulates all employee benefit plans regardless of whether any purchase of insurance is involved. Such regulation includes any plan or program established or maintained by an employer for the purpose of providing participants or their beneficiaries with medical, surgical, or hospital care or benefits, or benefits in the event of sickness, accident, disability, death or unemployment as well as employer-established plans or programs which provide retirement income to employees. It covers those benefit programs described in Section 302(c) of the Labor Management Relations Act of 1947, other than pensions on retirement or death, and insurance to provide such pensions. Although the primary purpose of ERISA is to protect employees' rights to receive their benefits, it was also drafted to continue "the basic governmental policy of encouraging the growth and development of voluntary private pension plans."[2]

ERISA made amendments and additions to the Internal Revenue Code as well as changes in the labor laws and provided for its administration by the Treasury Department in

---

1. Act of Sept. 2, 1974, Pub. L. 93-406, 88 Stat. 829, 29 U.S.C. § 1001 et seq.

2. Alternose Constr. Co. v. Building & Constr. Trades Council, 443 F. Supp. 492, 505-07 (E.D. Pa. 1977).

255

some instances, the Labor Department in some instances, and by both departments in others.[3] The labor law changes include provisions:

(1) requiring the disclosure and reporting to participants and beneficiaries of financial and other information with respect thereto;

(2) establishing standards of conduct, responsibility, and obligations for fiduciaries of employee benefit plans, and

(3) providing appropriate remedies, sanctions and ready access to the federal courts.[4]

ERISA imposes uniform standards for the operation of pension plans to assure that employees will receive the benefits intended and anticipated as of the time an employee covered by the plan retires or when the plan is terminated. Section 502 of the Act (29 U.S.C. § 1132) provides for the bringing of civil actions by the Secretary of Labor, participants, beneficiaries and fiduciaries for various kinds of relief. A fund may sue or be sued as an entity.

The Act provides for criminal proceedings and penalties,[5] in addition to the civil enforcement of parties' rights.

§ 9.02. Preemption provisions.

There are three provisions of ERISA relating to its preemptive effect:

Section 514(a). Except as provided in subsection (b) of this section [the saving clause], the provisions of this subchapter and subchapter III of this chapter shall supersede any and all state laws insofar as they may now or hereafter relate to any employee benefit plan....[6]

Section 514(b)(2)(A). Except as provided in subparagraph (B) [the deemer clause], nothing in this subchapter shall

---

3. E.g., see 29 U.S.C. § 1202.
4. Id. § 1001(b).
5. E.g., id. §§ 1111, 1131 and 1141.
6. Id. § 1144(a) [preemption clause].

be construed to exempt or relieve any person from any law of any state which regulates insurance, banking, or securities.[7]

Section 514(b)(2)(B). Neither an employee benefit plan ... nor any trust established under such a plan, shall be deemed to be an insurance company or other insurer, bank, trust company, or investment company or to be engaged in the business of insurance or banking for purposes of any law of any state purporting to regulate insurance companies, insurance contracts, banks, trust companies, or investment companies.[8]

Thus, if a state law relates to employee benefit plans it is preempted. The saving clause excepts from preemption laws that regulate insurance, banking or securities. The deemer clause makes clear that a state law that purports to regulate insurance, banking or securities cannot deem an employee benefit plan to be an insurer, bank, trust company or investment company.[9] The phrase "relates to" is given its broad, common-sense meaning such that a state law relates to a benefit plan "in the normal sense of the phrase, if it has any connection with a reference to such a plan."[10]

§ 9.03. Fiduciaries under ERISA.

From the viewpoint of corporate officers and directors some of the most significant portions of the Act are those which deal with fiduciaries, their duties and their liabilities. Because the Act provides for dual jurisdiction by the Department of Labor (Title I) and the Internal Revenue Service (Title II), there is an overlap of authority as to fiduciaries and their transactions, which is provocative of litigation.

---

7. Id. § 1144(b) [saving clause].

8. Id. § 1144(b)(2)(B) [deemer clause].

9. Pilot Life Ins. Co. v. Dedeaux, 481 U.S. —, 95 L.Ed.2d 39, 46, 107 S.Ct. 1549, 1552 (1987).

10. Id., 95 L.Ed.2d at 48, citing Metropolitan Life Ins. Co. v. Massachusetts, 471 U.S. 724, 739, 85 L.Ed.2d 728, 740, 105 S.Ct. 2300 (1985), quoting Shaw v. Delta Air Lines, 463 U.S. 85, 96-97, 77 L.Ed.2d 490, 501, 103 S.Ct. 2890 (1983).

Actions against fiduciaries for breaches of their duties may be brought by a participant, a beneficiary, another fiduciary or the Department of Labor and may result in personal liability and removal from office.[11] The statutory provision permitting the Secretary of Labor to seek "other appropriate equitable relief" is broad enough to authorize the appointment of a receiver after a breach of fiduciary duty of a trustee.[12]

The definition of a fiduciary under ERISA is found in subparagraphs (A) and (B) of Section 3(21) of the Act[13] with a similar definition in Section 4975(e)(3) of the Internal Revenue Code. It states:

(21)(A) Except as otherwise provided in subparagraph (B), a person is a fiduciary with respect to a plan to the extent (i) he exercises any discretionary authority or discretionary control respecting management of such plan or exercises any authority or control respecting management or disposition of its assets, (ii) he renders investment advice for a fee or other compensation, direct or indirect, with respect to any moneys or other property of such plan, or has any authority or responsibility to do so, or (iii) he has any discretionary authority or discretionary responsibility in the administration of such plan. Such term includes any person designated under section 1105(c)(1)(B) of this title.

(B) If any money or other property of an employee benefit plan is invested in securities issued by an investment company registered under the Investment Company Act of 1940, such investment shall not by itself cause such investment company or such investment company's investment adviser or principal underwriter to be deemed to be a fiduciary or a party in interest as those terms are defined in this subchapter, except insofar as such investment company or its investment adviser or principal underwriter acts in connection with an employee benefit plan covering employees of the investment company, the investment adviser, or its principal underwriter. Nothing

---

11. 29 U.S.C. §§ 1109 and 1132(a)(2).

12. Donovan v. Bierwirth, 680 F.2d 263 (2d Cir.), cert. denied, 459 U.S. 1069 (1982).

13. 29 U.S.C. § 1002(21).

contained in this subparagraph shall limit the duties imposed on such investment company, investment adviser,
or principal underwriter by any other law.

Under Section 404 of the Act,[14] a fiduciary must discharge
his duties with respect to a plan solely in the interest of the
plan participants and beneficiaries and

    (A) for the exclusive purpose of:
        (i) providing benefits to participants and their bene-
            ficiaries; and
        (ii) defraying reasonable expenses of administering
            the plan;
    (B) with the care, skill, prudence, and diligence under
       the circumstances then prevailing that a prudent
       man acting in a like capacity and familiar with such
       matters would use in the conduct of an enterprise of
       a like character and with like aims;
    (C) by diversifying the investments of the plan so as to
       minimize the risk of large losses, unless under the
       circumstances it is clearly prudent not to do so; and
    (D) in accordance with the documents and instruments
       governing the plan insofar as such documents and
       instruments are consistent with ERISA.

The courts have held that this statute creates two distinct
duties:

> First, the fiduciary must discharge his duties solely in
> the interest of the plan's participants and for the exclu-
> sive purpose of providing benefits and defraying the cost
> of administering the plan. Second, the fiduciary must
> perform his duties with reasonable care.[15]

The requirement that a fiduciary's duties be discharged
"solely in the interest of the plan's participants" does not
prevent corporate officers who are also trustees of the plan

----

14. Id. § 1104.
15. Ogden v. Michigan Bell Tel. Co., 571 F. Supp. 520, 522 (E.D. Mich.
1983).

from acting in such dual capacities,[16] but their primary loyalty to the plan participants is the only loyalty which may affect their judgment. They owe a duty as trustees to avoid putting themselves in a position where their acts as officers or directors of the corporation will prevent them from functioning with complete loyalty to the plan participants.[17] One court has said:

> This charge imposes an unwavering duty on an ERISA trustee to make decisions with a single-minded devotion to the plan's participants and beneficiaries and, in so doing, to act as a prudent person would act in a similar situation.[18]

While the "prudent man" rule, as applied by numerous courts, was concerned primarily with the investment of trust funds, the ERISA rule is applicable to all duties of a fiduciary with respect to an employee benefit plan. Moreover, under Section 405 of the Act,[19] if a fiduciary's failure to comply with his duties enables some other fiduciary to commit a breach, the derelict fiduciary will be liable for the breach of the co-fiduciary.

§ 9.04. Parties in interest.

The Act defines "party in interest" to include "an employee, officer, director (or an individual having powers or responsibilities similar to those of officers and directors)." Numerous additional "parties in interest" are included in the definition of the term.[20] The labor provisions of ERISA prohibit certain transactions between an employee benefit plan and a party in interest, including those discussed in section 9.05. Lack of harm to the plan or good faith of the party in interest are

---

16. 29 U.S.C. § 1108(e)(3).

17. Donovan v. Bierwirth, 538 F. Supp. 463, 468 (E.D.N.Y. 1981), modified on other grounds, 680 F.2d 263, 271 (2d Cir.), cert. denied, 459 U.S. 1069 (1982).

18. Morse v. Stanley, 732 F.2d 1139, 1145 (2d Cir. 1984).

19. 29 U.S.C. § 1105.

20. Id. § 1002(14)(H).

unavailing as defenses where a transaction is subject to the prohibition and the statutory exemption procedures are not followed.[21]

§ 9.05. Prohibited transactions.

In addition to the general fiduciary standards, Congress has prohibited fiduciaries from engaging in certain specified conduct. These provisions were designed to prevent a trustee "from being put into a position where he has dual loyalties, and, therefore, he cannot act exclusively for the benefit of a plan's participants and beneficiaries."[22]

Subject to certain exemptions which may be granted by the Secretary of Labor,[23] the prohibitions are set out in ERISA as follows:[24]

> (1) A fiduciary with respect to a plan shall not cause the plan to engage in a transaction, if he knows that such transaction constitutes a direct or indirect—
>
> (a) sale or exchange, or leasing, of any property between the plan and a party in interest;
>
> (b) lending of money or other extension of credit between the plan and a party in interest;
>
> (c) furnishing of goods, services, or facilities between the plan and a party in interest;
>
> (d) transfer to, or use by or for the benefit of, a party in interest, of any assets of the plan; or
>
> (e) acquisition, on behalf of the plan, of any employer security or employer real property in violation of section 1107(a) of this title.
>
> (2) No fiduciary who has authority or discretion to control or manage the assets of a plan shall permit the plan to hold any employer security or employer real

---

21. M & R Inv. Co. v. Fitzsimmons, 484 F. Supp. 1041, 1055 (D. Nev. 1980).

22. NRLB v. Amax Coal Co., 453 U.S. 322, 332-34, 69 L.Ed.2d 672, 683, 101 S.Ct. 2789, 2795-97 (1981).

23. 29 U.S.C. § 1108.

24. Id. § 1106(a).

property if he knows or should know that holding such security or real property would constitute an acquisition or holding prohibited by the Act.[25]

In addition, the Act provides:

A fiduciary with respect to a plan shall not —
(1) deal with the assets of the plan in his own interest or for his own account,
(2) in his individual or in any other capacity act in any transaction involving the plan on behalf of a party (or represent a party) whose interests are adverse to the interests of the plan or the interests of its participants or beneficiaries, or
(3) receive any consideration for his own personal account from any party dealing with such plan in connection with a transaction involving the assets of the plan.[26]

The prohibited transactions are such as offer a high potential for loss of plan assets or for insider abuse. The statute is virtually a per se prohibition against the enumerated transactions and the fact that whether a provision has been violated does not depend on whether any harm resulted.[27]

§ 9.06. Officers and directors as fiduciaries.

The Department of Labor, which is responsible for administering ERISA in conjunction with the Internal Revenue Service, periodically issues Interpretive Bulletins. In one such bulletin[28] it was pointed out that directors will be plan fiduciaries only to the extent that they have responsibility for the functions described in Section 3(21)(A) of the Act, which provides, in pertinent part:

---

25. Id. § 1107.
26. Id. § 1106(b).
27. McDougall v. Donovan, 552 F. Supp. 1206, 1215 (N.D. Ill. 1982). See also Leigh v. Engle, 727 F.2d 113, 126 (7th Cir. 1984); Lowen v. Tower Asset Mgt., Inc., 653 F. Supp. 1542, 1553-54 (S.D.N.Y. 1987).
28. 29 C.F.R. § 2509.75-8, at D-4 (1984).

[A] person is a fiduciary with respect to a plan to the extent that (i) he exercises any discretionary authority or control respecting management of such plan or exercises any authority or control respecting management or disposition of its assets, (ii) he renders investment advice for a fee or other compensation, direct or indirect, with respect to any moneys or other property of such plan, or has authority or responsibility to do so, or (iii) he has any discretionary authority or discretionary responsibility in the administration of such a plan.[29]

The same applies to executive officers of the corporation, whose positions, in and of themselves, will not render the officers fiduciaries of the plan.[30]

To the extent that directors or officers become fiduciaries under these rules, their potential liability is limited to the functions which they perform with respect to the plan.[31] Thus ERISA recognizes that directors may be fiduciaries for some purposes and not for others.[32] Officers and directors of the plan sponsor are fiduciaries if they exercise control through the selection of the investment committee, administrative committee or plan officers or directors. Also, in recommending, designing and implementing the conversion of a profit-sharing plan into an employee stock ownership plan a director acted in a fiduciary capacity under the Act and became liable to comply with its standards.[33]

§ 9.07. Liability of officers and directors for delinquent contributions.

Section 515 of ERISA[34] imposes a duty on "employers" to make all necessary contributions to multiemployer pension plans in accordance with the terms of the plan or under the terms of a collectively bargained agreement. Section 502 al-

---

29. 29 U.S.C. § 1002(21)(A).
30. Fulk v. Bagley, 99 F.R.D. 153, 162 (M.D.N.C. 1980).
31. 29 C.F.R. § 2509.75-8, at FR-16 (1984).
32. Leigh v. Engle, supra note 27.
33. See Eaves v. Penn, 587 F.2d 453, 458-59 (10th Cir. 1978).
34. 29 U.S.C. § 1145.

lows a participant, beneficiary or fiduciary of the plan to bring civil enforcement actions against the plan or the employer.[35] Section 3(5) defines "employer" as "any person acting directly as an employer, or indirectly in the interest of an employer, in relation to an employee benefit plan."[36] However, the weight of authority and the better reasoned cases hold that corporate officers and directors are not included in the statutory definition of "person"[37] and are not exposed to liability for their corporation's failure to make such contributions.[38] An exception is made to that rule if the individual officers or directors were acting as "alter egos" of the corporation.[39]

The same result has been reached in actions by participants in single employer plans into which contributions were not paid when due.[40]

In such cases, there are usually state law claims. In cases arising in Pennsylvania, for example, the Pennsylvania Wage Payment and Collection Law[41] is the vehicle upon which plaintiffs attempt to rely. However, under the ERISA broad preemption provision,[42] the courts have uniformly upheld the exclusivity of the Act.[43] Moreover, when actions are brought in the state courts which allege causes of action within the scope of the civil enforcement provision of ERISA

---

35. Id. § 1132.

36. Id. § 1002(5).

37. Id. § 1002(9).

38. Comb v. Indyk, 554 F. Supp. 573, 575 (W.D. Pa. 1982), cited with approval and followed, Solomon v. Klein, 770 F.2d 352, 354 (3d Cir. 1985); Amalgamated Cotton Garment & Allied Indus. Fund v. J.B.C. Co., 608 F. Supp. 158, 166-67 (W.D. Pa. 1984). Cf. Connors v. P & M Coal Co., 801 F.2d 1373, 1376 (D.C. Cir. 1986).

39. Comb v. Indyk, supra note 38. See also Carpenters Health & Welfare Fund v. Kenneth R. Ambrose, Inc., 727 F.2d 279, 283-85 (3d Cir. 1983).

40. E.g., McMahon v. McDowell, 794 F.2d 100 (3d Cir. 1986).

41. 43 Pa. Cons. St. § 260.1 et seq.

42. See supra section 9.02.

43. See also cases cited supra note 10.

Section 502(a),[44] they are removable to the federal courts as claims arising under federal law.[45]

§ 9.08. Employee stock ownership plans.

An employee stock ownership plan (ESOP) is an individual account plan which is a stock bonus plan that is qualified, or a stock bonus plan and money purchase plan, both of which are qualified under 26 U.S.C. § 401, and which is designed to invest primarily in qualifying employer securities.[46] An early case, decided before the enactment of ERISA, upheld purchases of the employer's stock by such a plan as beneficial to the plan, the corporation and the employees.[47]

A leading case involving ERISA and an ESOP, decided by the Fifth Circuit, involved a suit by the Secretary of Labor, under various provisions of ERISA, against several fiduciaries of an ESOP.[48] A contract trucking firm (MCS) established the ESOP. The directors of MCS served as the administrative committee of the ESOP and designated a bank as trustee. Two transactions were called into question. In the first, the directors voted to contribute $288,000 to the ESOP for the purpose of buying stock from Cunningham, one of their number and the chairman, CEO and sole shareholder of MCS. Next, as members of the ESOP administrative committee, they bought fourteen percent of Cunningham's stock. Six months later, in their dual capacities as directors and administrative committee members, they purchased for the ESOP an additional twenty percent of the MCS stock from Cunningham, borrowed money from the trustee bank to make the purchase, and provided sufficient yearly contributions from MCS to the ESOP to amortize the loan. Cunningham participated in the actions to carry out all of the transactions.

---

44. 29 U.S.C. § 1132(a).

45. Metropolitan Life Ins. Co. v. Taylor, 481 U.S. —, 95 L.Ed.2d 55, 107 S.Ct. 1542 (1987).

46. 29 U.S.C. § 1107(6).

47. Herald Co. v. Seawell, 472 F.2d 1081 (10th Cir. 1972).

48. Donovan v. Cunningham, 716 F.2d 1455 (5th Cir. 1983), cert. denied, 467 U.S. 1251 (1984).

The court decided that the directors/administrators breached their duties of prudence under Section 404 of ERISA by failing to make adequate investigation of the value of the stock, and thus they were unable to establish that the ESOP paid adequate consideration for it.[49]

The proliferation of corporate takeovers in recent years[50] has put some ESOPs in a different light than when they originated. When an ESOP is set up in the context of a contest for corporate control, an inference of improper motive arises.[51] It then devolves upon the directors to show that the plan was created to benefit the employees, and not simply to further the aim of management entrenchment. The Second Circuit says that in applying that distinction "courts have looked to factors such as the timing of the ESOP's establishment, the financial impact on the company, the identity of the trustees, and the voting control of the ESOP shares."[52]

§ 9.09. ERISA in the corporate control context.

It is noted in section 9.08 that in the corporate control context some particular problems arise as to ESOPs. Although an ESOP is designed to invest principally in the employer's securities, the issuance of such shares shortly after a challenge to corporate control invokes particular judicial inquiry. In the Rooney, Pace contest with Norlin Corporation, the Second Circuit considered defensive actions taken by a company in fear of being a target of a takeover attempt. It concluded that the ESOP "was created solely as a tool of management self-perpetuation." Judge Irving R. Kaufman wrote:

---

49. Cf. Eaves v. Penn, 587 F.2d 453 (10th Cir. 1978).

50. See infra Chapter 15.

51. E.g., Klaus v. Hi-Shear Corp., 528 F.2d 225, 231-33 (9th Cir. 1975); Podesta v. Calumet Indus., Inc., Fed. Sec. L. Rep. (CCH) ¶96,433 (N.D. Ill. 1978).

52. Norlin Corp. v. Rooney, Pace, Inc., 744 F.2d 255, 266 (2d Cir. 1984). Cf. Terrydale Liquidating Trust v. Barness, 611 F. Supp. 1006, 1018 (S.D.N.Y. 1984). See also Treco, Inc. v. Land of Lincoln Sav. & Loan, 749 F.2d 374, 379 n.8 (7th Cir. 1984).

It was created a mere five days after the district court refused to enjoin further stock purchases by Piezo, and at a time when Norlin's officers were clearly casting about for strategies to deter a challenge to their control. No real consideration was received from the ESOP for the shares. The three trustees appointed to oversee the ESOP were all members of Norlin's board, and voting control of the ESOP shares was retained by the directors.[53]

ERISA impacts corporate actions other than ESOPs. When corporate officers or directors occupy the dual capacities of those positions and fiduciaries of an employee benefit plan, their interests must necessarily be in conflict if a tender offer or other corporate control contest is presented. When the LTV Corporation announced a tender offer for up to seventy percent of the Grumman Corporation's outstanding stock, the officers who were also fiduciaries of the Grumman Corporation Pension Plan which then held 525,000 shares of Grumman stock,[54] were permitted under ERISA to function in both capacities despite their conflicts of interest.[55]

The Grumman directors, including those who were plan fiduciaries, unanimously passed a resolution to fight the takeover. The trustees in a special meeting decided to refuse to tender the plan's stock. At the same meeting they elected to purchase 1,275,000 additional shares of Grumman stock in the plan and did purchase 1,158,000 shares.[56]

The district court found that the plan fiduciaries acted imprudently in purchasing the additional stock. It continued:

> We ... find that their conduct evince (sic) an inability to make independent decisions on behalf of the Pension Plan solely in the interest of its participants and beneficiaries. We reach these conclusions because the trustees' decisions were made without sufficient inquiry into the facts upon which they based their decisions. We find that

---

53. Norlin Corp. v. Rooney, Pace, Inc., supra note 52, at 258.
54. Donovan v. Bierwirth, 538 F. Supp. 463, 465 (E.D.N.Y. 1981), aff'd as modified, 680 F.2d 263 (2d Cir.), cert. denied, 459 U.S. 1069 (1982).
55. Id. at 468.
56. Id. at 465-67.

their conduct was solely motivated by their all-consuming desire to defeat the tender offer.[57]

In the Second Circuit, Judge Henry J. Friendly, writing for the unanimous panel, pointed out that the trustees should have been immediately aware of the difficult position which they occupied as a result of having decided as directors some of the same questions they would have to decide as trustees, and should have explored where their duty lay.[58] He further noted that they failed to measure up to the standard required of them in failing to do a more thorough job in ascertaining the facts.[59] He continued:

> An even more telling point against the trustees is their swift movement from a decision not to tender or sell the shares already in the fund to a decision to invest more than $44,000,000 in the purchase of additional Grumman shares....[60]

In essence, the principle of the greatest significance in this decision is that the directors who were also fiduciaries had a duty to avoid placing themselves in a position where their acts as officers or directors would prevent their functioning with the complete loyalty to participants demanded of them as fiduciaries of the pension plan.[61]

---

57. Id. at 471.
58. 680 F.2d at 272.
59. Id. at 273.
60. Id. at 274.
61. Id. at 271.

COROLLARY REFERENCES

Blan, "ERISA — A Primer for the Insurance Trial Counsel," 53 Ins. Couns. J. 52 (1986).

Little & Thrailkill, "Fiduciaries Under ERISA: A Narrow Path to Tread," 30 Vand. L. Rev. 1 (1977).

Note, "Civil Litigation Under the Employee Retirement Income Security Act of 1974," 49 Miss. L.J. 241 (1978).

Note, "Employee Stock Ownership Plans and Corporate Takeovers: Restraints on the Use of ESOPs by Corporate Officers and Directors to Divert Hostile Takeovers," 10 Pepperdine L. Rev. 731 (1983).

Note, "Interpretive ERISA: Corporate Officer Liability for Delinquent Contributions," 1986 Duke L.J. 710.

Note, "Preemption of State Laws Relating to Employee Benefit Plans: An Analysis of ERISA, Section 514," 62 Tex. L. Rev. 1313 (1984).

Note, "The Duties of Employee Benefit Plan Trustees Under ERISA in Hostile Tender Offers," 82 Colum. L. Rev. 1692 (1982).

Note, "The Right to Jury Trial in Enforcement Actions, Under Section 502(a)(1)(B) of ERISA," 96 Harv. L. Rev. 737 (1983).

Chapter 10

ENVIRONMENTAL, SAFETY, AND EMPLOYMENT-RELATED LIABILITY

§ 10.01. Basis of individual environmental liability.

Coincident with the trend to impose increased personal liability upon corporate directors and officers has been the somewhat sudden appearance and stupendous growth of the environmental movement. A torrent of environmental legislation at both state and federal levels has exposed corporations and those who govern them to new and significant liabilities. Federal environmental legislation is based on a deterrence concept, as a consequence of which individual directors and officers have become viable targets.

Corporate officers and directors, in the performance of their duties, may become subject to civil as well as criminal liability as individuals. Civil liability may be imposed when the director or officer participates in the wrongdoing, directs it, or knowingly permits it to occur.[1] Criminal liability may be imposed on directors or officers who personally commit crimes, aid or abet them, or fail to prevent them, as responsible parties.[2] Those rules apply to the subject matter of this chapter.

---

1. See supra section 2.11.
2. See supra section 8.02.

271

Individual liability frequently results from specific statutory language imposing it. For example, the Superfund Act[3] imposes liability in its Section 107(a)(3) upon any person who arranged for the disposal and transport of hazardous waste. A corporation's vice president who had direct supervision and knowledge of the disposal of drums containing toxic substances was held liable under that section. The court said he "had the power to control" and "the power to direct the negotiations concerning the disposal of wastes."[4]

An "owning stockholder who manage[d] a corporation" was held personally liable under the Superfund Act in a Second Circuit case. The court found it unnecessary to "pierce the corporate veil" because under New York law "a corporate officer who controls corporate conduct and thus is an active participant in that conduct is liable for the torts of the corporation."[5]

Similar reasoning was used as a basis to impose personal liability upon a corporation's president and chemical engineer in another hazardous waste site case in Missouri.[6]

§ 10.02. What law applies.

As late as 1972, the Supreme Court recognized a federal common law that could give rise to a claim for abatement of a nuisance caused by interstate water pollution.[7] But after Congress enacted the Federal Water Pollution Control Act

---

3. Comprehensive Environmental Response, Compensation and Liability Act of 1980 (CERCLA), Pub. L. 96-510, 94 Stat. 2767, 42 U.S.C. § 9601 et seq., amended by the Superfund Amendments and Reauthorization Act of 1986 (SARA), Pub. L. 99-499, 100 Stat. 1615, 1652, 1692, 1774, Oct. 17, 1986.

4. United States v. Northeastern Pharmacy & Chem. Co., 579 F. Supp. 823, 847-49 (W.D. Mo. 1984).

5. New York v. Shore Realty Corp., 759 F.2d 1032, 1052 (2d Cir. 1985).

6. United States v. Conservation Chem. Co., 628 F. Supp. 391, 416-620 (W.D. Mo. 1985).

7. Illinois v. Milwaukee, 406 U.S. 91, 31 L.Ed.2d 712, 92 S.Ct. 1385 (1972).

Amendments of 1972,[8] the Court held that the comprehensive regulatory programs in the statute preempted the common-law right of action.[9]

The federal statute books contain several major environmental acts. For illustrative purposes, five of such acts are outlined in the next five sections. In each instance the statutes are supplemented by numerous regulations having the force of law promulgated by the agencies charged with carrying out the regulatory programs.

Most states have enacted legislation similar to that in the federal domain and the statutes of a particular jurisdiction must be consulted in each instance.[10] State common-law causes of action such as nuisance, negligence, trespass and strict liability may be the source of serious and costly litigation for corporate officers and directors.

Many environmental statutes make some provision for "citizen suits" or the presentation of claims by individuals who suffer damages, but private rights of action are not usually implied from the statutory enactments. For example, the Supreme Court has ruled that Congress did not intend for private remedies to be implied under the Federal Water Pollution Control Act[11] or the Marine Protection, Research, and Sanctuaries Act.[12] Nonetheless, heavy civil penalties and severe criminal punishment are available within the procedures specified in most of the environmental legislation.

---

8. 33 U.S.C. § 1251 et seq.

9. Milwaukee v. Illinois, 451 U.S. 304, 68 L.Ed.2d 114, 101 S.Ct. 1784 (1981).

10. Representative state environmental statutes include Conn. Gen. Stat. Ann. tit. 22a; Del. Code Ann. tit. 7, §§ 6001 to 6030; Mich. Comp. Laws Ann. §§ 299.501 to 299.551; N.J. Stat. Ann. §§ 58:10-23.11 to 58:10-23.34; Chapters 3706 and 6111, Ohio Rev. Code Ann. See also 41 O. Jur. 3d Environmental Protection §§ 1-223.

11. 33 U.S.C. § 1251 et seq.

12. Id. § 1401 et seq.

§ 10.03. CERCLA and SARA.

The Comprehensive Environmental Response Compensation and Liability Act of 1980 (CERCLA)[13] is commonly known as the "Superfund Act." It established a program authorizing the federal government to recover cleanup and response costs from persons responsible for releasing hazardous substances into the environment. It provides for strict civil liability. As shown in section 10.01, it has been applied to officers of a corporation which generated hazardous wastes.[14]

Congress created the Hazardous Substance Response Trust Fund, commonly called the "Superfund," to finance the clean up of the worst hazardous waste sites and provided for actions to recover the amounts disbursed from the Superfund for that purpose.[15] Following the rule that corporate officials who actively participate in the management of a disposal facility can be held personally liable under CERCLA,[16] the courts have not hesitated to impose such liability.[17]

CERCLA provides a means of financing both governmental and private responses and gives a private party the right to recover its response costs from responsible third parties which it may choose to pursue rather than claiming against the Superfund.[18] It imposes a standard of "strict liability," subject only to three affirmative defenses, (1) an act of God, (2) an act of war, or (3) an act or omission of an unrelated third party, i.e., an efficient, intervening cause, if the defendant proves he exercised due care and took precautions

---

13. 42 U.S.C. § 9601 et seq.

14. Supra note 4 and accompanying text.

15. 42 U.S.C. § 9607.

16. United States v. Wade, 577 F. Supp. 1326, 1341 (E.D. Pa. 1983).

17. E.g., United States v. Conservation Chem. Co., 628 F. Supp. 391, 420 (W.D. Mo. 1985); United States v. Carolawn Co., 14 Envtl. L. Rep. (Envtl. L. Inst.) 20699 (D.S.C. June 15, 1984); United States v. Mottolo, 14 Envtl. L. Rep. (Envtl. L. Inst.) 20497 (D.N.H. March 27, 1984).

18. Philadelphia v. Stepan Chem. Co., 544 F. Supp. 1135, 1143 (E.D. Pa. 1982).

against foreseeable acts or omissions of the third party.[19] Thus the liability, although strict, is not absolute.[20]

Joint and several liability may be imposed, but is not mandated,[21] if defendants establish a reasonable basis for apportioning it among them.[22]

The statute expressly provides that no indemnification, hold harmless, or similar agreement or conveyance may transfer liability to anyone else, but does permit agreements to insure or indemnify such liability.[23]

Superfund Amendments and Reauthorization Act of 1986 (SARA)[24] is an extension of the program to clean up hazardous releases at uncontrolled or abandoned hazardous waste sites funded at five times the amount of the original CERCLA program. It prescribes more stringent remedial standards which are expected to increase costs of cleanups. It codifies Environmental Protection Agency (EPA) policies and some court decisions interpreting the old law and includes a potential for citizen suits for violation of Superfund requirements. Enforcement activities will probably be accelerated under the new law.

§ 10.04. Clean Air Act.

The Clean Air Act[25] was enacted to regulate, through controls and guidelines, the complexities of restraining and curtailing modern day air pollution. Its amendments[26] were intended to bring about additional efforts to extend the Act to areas that were not yet in compliance.[27] The Act provides for

---

19. United States v. Price, 577 F. Supp. 1103, 1114 (D.N.J. 1983); 42 U.S.C. § 9607(b).

20. New York v. Shore Realty Corp., 759 F.2d 1032, 1042 (2d Cir. 1985).

21. Colorado v. Asarco, 608 F. Supp. 1484 (D. Colo. 1985).

22. United States v. Wade, supra note 16.

23. 42 U.S.C. § 9607(e)(1).

24. Pub. L. 99-499, 100 Stat. 1615, 1652, 1692, 1774, Oct. 17, 1986.

25. 42 U.S.C. § 7401 et seq.

26. Clean Air Act Amendments of 1977, Pub. L. 95-95.

27. Ohio v. Ruckelshaus, 776 F.2d 1333 (6th Cir.), cert. denied, 106 S.Ct. 2889 (1985).

civil penalties of up to $25,000 per day and injunctive relief[28] and fines of up to $25,000 per day of violation and imprisonment. It expressly includes "any responsible corporate officer" in those subject to such penalties.[29] Subsequent violations are subject to increased penalties. Noncompliance penalties, enforceable in administrative proceedings, must reflect the economic value of the noncompliance.[30]

Citizen suits are provided for under this Act for its enforcement, but not to recover damages.[31] However, it has been held that the omission of "responsible corporate officers" from the definition of the "persons" against whom such citizen suits are maintainable evinces the intent of Congress not to allow corporate officers to be named defendants in such suits.[32]

The Act contains a savings clause[33] under which common-law remedies are preserved. Accordingly, common-law rights of action against corporate officers and directors were not preempted by the statute.[34]

§ 10.05. Clean Water Act.

The objective of the Federal Water Pollution Control Act (FWPCA),[35] frequently called the Clean Water Act, is "to restore and maintain the chemical, physical, and biological integrity of the Nation's waters." It imposes strict permit requirements on persons who discharge pollution into surface water and strict civil liability for discharges into navigable waters. The Environmental Protection Agency (EPA) may sue for civil penalties of up to $10,000 per day. However, it has no authority to assess civil penalties administratively.

---

28. 42 U.S.C. § 7413(b).

29. Id. § 7413(c).

30. Id. § 7420.

31. Id. § 7604.

32. Illinois v. Commonwealth Edison Co., 490 F. Supp. 1145, 1147 (N.D. Ill. 1980).

33. 42 U.S.C. § 7604(e).

34. See United States v. Atlantic-Richfield Co., 478 F. Supp. 1215, 1219-20 (D. Mont. 1979).

35. 33 U.S.C. §§ 1251-1376.

Fault is not required to support a penalty.[36] The liability is a form of strict liability and neither fault nor intent are relevant except in connection with the amount of the penalty.[37]

This Act has a "citizen suit" provision[38] but it relates only to enforcement of the law and does not authorize claims for money damages. However, costs of litigation, including reasonable attorney and expert witness fees, may be awarded. In such suits there must be a "good faith allegation of continuous or intermittent violation." Past violations that are not recurring will not support such actions.[38a]

Criminal penalties of up to $25,000 per day of violation and imprisonment may be imposed upon any person who willfully or negligently violates provisions of the Act, and the word "person" expressly includes "any responsible corporate officer."[39]

For example, in the Third Circuit,[40] the court affirmed a conviction of a corporation engaged in mushroom farming and two of its officers on four counts of willfully, and two counts of negligently, discharging pollutants into navigable waters of the United States without a permit. Rejecting the contention that there was insufficient evidence to convict on the charges in the indictment, the court pointed out that to establish the claim that the discharges giving rise to the first four counts were willful, the government relied on samples collected on four occasions, the absence of rain on the dates in question and the elimination of other possible causes for the pollution. The court concluded that the jury was entitled to infer from the totality of the circumstances surrounding the

---

36. United States v. Texas Pipe Line Co., 611 F.2d 345 (10th Cir. 1979).

37. United States v. Amoco Oil Co., 580 F. Supp. 1042 (W.D. Mo. 1984).

38. 33 U.S.C. § 1365.

38a. Gwaltney of Smithfield, Ltd. v. Chesapeake Bay Foundation, — U.S. —, 98 L.Ed.2d 306, 108 S.Ct. 376 (1987); Pawtuxet Cove Marina, Inc. v. Ciba-Geigy Corp., 807 F.2d 1089 (1st Cir. 1986), cert. denied, 98 L.Ed.2d 483 (1987).

39. Id. § 1319(c).

40. United States v. Frezzo Bros., 602 F.2d 1123 (3d Cir.), cert. denied, 444 U.S. 1074 (1979).

discharges that a willful act precipitated them. The government did not have to present evidence of someone turning on a valve or diverting wastes in order to establish a willful violation of the Act, the court said.

With respect to the two counts of negligent discharges, caused by the inadequate capacity of the holding tank, the court pointed out that there was eyewitness testimony, samples of the pollutants, evidence of rainfall and expert hydrologic evidence of the holding tank's capacity. From such evidence the jury could properly have concluded that the water pollution abatement facilities were negligently maintained by the defendants and were insufficient to prevent discharges of the wastes. Rejecting also the defendants' contention that the administrator of the EPA must either give them some notice of alleged violations of the Act, or institute a civil action before pursuing criminal remedies under the Act, the court pointed out that there was nothing in the text or legislative history of the statute to compel such a conclusion. Rejecting also the contention that the indictment should have been dismissed because the EPA had not promulgated any effluent standards applicable to the compost manufacturing business, the court pointed out that when no effluent limitations have been established for a particular business, the proper procedure is for the business to apply for a permit to discharge pollutants. It held that the defendants, under their interpretation of the statute, could conceivably have continued polluting until EPA promulgated effluent limitations for the compost operation.

In the Sixth Circuit[41] a defendant's conviction of willfully discharging gasoline onto a lake, apparently without a permit, was affirmed. The court concluded that the evidence, while circumstantial, was fully sufficient to justify submission of the issues of identity and scienter to the jury. The defendant was positively identified by two witnesses, fishermen who discovered the gasoline on the ice around a pier and whose concern about the gasoline ultimately resulted in noti-

---

41. United States v. Hamel, 551 F.2d 107 (6th Cir. 1977).

fication of the Coast Guard which sent investigators in response to the call. Furthermore, said the court, the defendant's deceptive responses to the investigators, and his observed journeys to and from a dispenser from which the witnesses noticed gasoline gushing, supported the jury conclusion that the defendant intentionally activated the necessary levers to discharge the gasoline onto the lake.

A district court in Pennsylvania[42] denied defendants' motions to dismiss an indictment charging them with willfully and negligently discharging pollutants apparently without a permit on three separate occasions. With respect to a motion to dismiss the indictment or force the government to elect the particular offense as to each count of the indictment, the court rejected the defendants' contention that the indictment was rendered "duplicitous" by virtue of charging them with what amounted to two separate crimes in the same count, that is, negligent discharge, as well as willful discharge. The court concluded that the terms "willful" and "negligent" merely connoted methods of committing but a single offense, that is, discharge of pollutants into navigable waters, and thus the counts were not duplicitous; in essence, the indictment in each count, merely alleged that the defendants discharged pollutants illegally and the addition of the words "negligently" and "willfully" merely specified the mode or method by which the proscribed conduct was accomplished. Furthermore, said the court, the statute provides but a single penalty for both negligent and willful discharges, a clear indication that the crimes are not separate and distinct.

The court also concluded that the fact that the statute reads "negligently or willfully", whereas the indictment read "negligently and willfully", afforded the defendants no comfort; the court reasoned that once it is determined that the statute defines but a single offense it becomes proper to charge the different means, stated disjunctively in the statute, conjunctively in each count of the indictment and proof of any one of the allegations will sustain a conviction.

---

42. United States v. Hudson, 12 Env't Rep. Cas. (BNA) 1444 (D.C. Pa. 1978).

Similarly, in another Pennsylvania district court decision,[43] the court denied defendants' motions to dismiss on grounds of multiplicity and duplicity, and an omnibus motion to dismiss, indictments charging them with willfully and negligently discharging pollutants without a permit on numerous occasions. The court rejected the defendants' argument that the discharge from the waste water treatment system was not discharged from a "point source" as defined in the Act. The court said that uncollected surface runoff may, but not necessarily, constitute discharge from a point source; that the discharges forming the basis of the indictment in the instant case resulted from spraying an overabundance of waste water onto the surface of irrigation fields, which in turn ran off into a nearby stream through a break in the berm around those fields. The court also rejected the contention that the indictment should be dismissed because the water into which the discharge flowed was not navigable in fact.

The court disagreed with the defendants' contention that the terms "navigable waters" and "waters of the United States" were void for vagueness. The court also rejected the contention that the terms "willfully" and "negligently" were unconstitutionally vague, stating that those terms were clear to a person of average intelligence.

§ 10.06. Toxic Substances Control Act.

The Toxic Substances Control Act of 1976 (TSCA)[44] was enacted to regulate the production and distribution of chemical substances, especially those which present an unreasonable risk of injury to health or to the environment. It provides for civil penalties of up to $25,000 for each violation, including the failure or refusal to establish and maintain records, against "any person." The term is not defined to include re-

---

43. United States v. Oxford Royal Mushroom Prods., 487 F. Supp. 852 (E.D. Pa. 1980).

44. Pub. L. 94-469, 90 Stat. 2003, 15 U.S.C. § 2601 et seq.

sponsible corporate officers as in the Clean Air Act[45] and Clean Water Act,[46] but there is no language excluding them from liability for such penalties.[47]

Citizen suits are provided for under this Act for its enforcement but not to recover damages.[48]

It is worthy of note that TSCA functions and responsibilities and those of the Occupational Safety and Health Administration (OSHA), discussed in section 10.08, may overlap, with resulting pressure upon corporate managers. Probably the highest level of exposure to a toxic substance would be in the work-place setting. Although employee protection is traditionally the domain of OSHA, the larger staff and resources of the Environmental Protection Agency may be able to ban or restrict the use or production of toxic substances of unreasonable risk with greater speed than OSHA can carry out its proceedings leading to regulations. In such an event, civil liability of corporate managers may be exacerbated.

§ 10.07. Resource Conservation and Recovery Act.

The Resource Conservation and Recovery Act of 1976 (RCRA)[49] governs discharge of pollutants onto land and involves a congressional finding that disposal of solid waste and hazardous waste in or on land without careful planning and management can present danger to human health and the environment. The Act provides criminal penalties for persons who knowingly endanger life while violating the Act. In the latter case, persons may be fined up to $250,000 and imprisoned up to fifteen years or both.[50]

---

45. See supra section 10.04.
46. See supra section 10.05.
47. See text infra section 10.07, note 54.
48. 15 U.S.C. § 2619.
49. Pub. L. 95-609, 92 Stat. 3081, 42 U.S.C. § 6901 et seq.
50. 42 U.S.C. § 6928(d).

Civil penalties up to $25,000 per day for noncompliance with orders of the Administrator[51] or for violating any requirement of the Act may be assessed.[52]

Citizen suits are provided for under this Act for its enforcement but not to recover damages.[53]

The circumstance that this statute, like the Toxic Substances Control Act, does not add to its definition of "person" the words "any responsible corporate officer" was afforded no significance in a Third Circuit case.[54] That criminal prosecution involved a corporation and two of its employees, a foreman and the service manager of the trucking department. The district court held that the Act did not apply to the individuals. The Third Circuit reversed quoting the Supreme Court to the effect that an exercise of draftmanship intended to broaden the scope of a criminal provision "can hardly be found ground for relieving from such liability the individual agent of a corporation."[55] It concluded that the two individuals were "persons" under the Act.

§ 10.08. OSHA.

The Occupational Safety and Health Act[56] imposes liability on "employers" but the term does not include corporate officers and directors. The OSHA Review Commission has refused to include a corporate president in the term,[57] although a federal district court in Kansas ruled that a jury should decide whether a corporate vice president was an "employer" within the meaning of OSHA.[58]

---

51. Id. § 6928(a) and (c).

52. Id. § 6928(g).

53. Id. § 6972.

54. United States v. Johnson & Towers, 741 F.2d 662 (3d Cir. 1984).

55. Id. at 665 n.3, citing United States v. Dotterweich, 320 U.S. 277, 282, 88 L.Ed. 48, 64 S.Ct. 134 (1943).

56. 29 U.S.C. § 651 et seq.

57. Vincent Rizzo d.b.a. Vincent Rizzo Const. Co. v. Masoncraft, Inc., Rev. Com. 1975, 1975-76 OSHD (CCH) ¶20,236.

58. United States v. Pinkston Hollar, 1976-77 OSHD (CCH) ¶21,202 (D.C. Kan. 1976).

A Fourth Circuit decision sheds some light on this subject.[59] In proceedings against a corporation and its directors individually, the court held the individuals were employers because they operated the corporation's manufacturing plant during a period when it was dissolved by operation of law for failure to pay franchise taxes. Although the corporation was later reinstated, the West Virginia statute did not relieve the individuals of liability during the period of dissolution.

In this connection, it seems well established that OSHA does not provide an implied cause of action for an employee of an independent contractor against the owner for violations of the Act. The rationale of the Fifth Circuit's decision[60] is that Congress did not intend to create a new private action for damages in favor of employees. The Fourth Circuit reached the same result for the reason that the North Carolina Workmen's Compensation Act precluded such a private remedy.[61]

Charges against five corporate officials and their corporation were dismissed in Cook County, Illinois when the court ruled that OSHA preempted the state from applying its criminal law to conduct involving federally regulated safety and health issues in the workplace.[62] The court held that the conduct the state was attempting to regulate was conduct related to working conditions and that such conduct was exclusively regulated by OSHA. The decision followed an earlier decision of the Illinois Supreme Court that "the only method by which a state may assume responsibility for development and enforcement of safety and health standards with respect to which federal standards have been adopted" is through an approved plan under OSHA.[63]

---

59. Moore v. Occupational Safety & Health Rev. Comm., 591 F.2d 991 (4th Cir. 1979).

60. Jeter v. St. Regis Paper Co., 507 F.2d 973, 976-77 (5th Cir. 1975).

61. Byrd v. Fieldcrest Mills, 496 F.2d 1323 (4th Cir. 1974).

62. Illinois v. Chicago Magnet Wire Corp., 157 Ill. App. 3d 794, 510 N.E.2d 173, 110 Ill. Dec. 142 (1987).

63. Stanislawski v. Indus. Comm., 99 Ill. 2d 36, 75 Ill. Dec. 405, 457 N.E.2d 399, 401 (1983).

§ 10.09. Basis of individual liability for employment practices.

Title VII of the Civil Rights Act of 1964 makes it "an unlawful employment practice for an employer ... to discriminate against any individual with respect to his compensation, terms, conditions, or privileges of employment because of such individual's race, color, religion, sex or national origin."[64] The term "employer" includes any "agent" of an employer.[65]

In the Fair Labor Standards Act "employer" includes any person acting directly or indirectly in the interest of an employer in relation to an employee.[66] The Age Discrimination in Employment Act of 1967 includes in the term "employer" any "agent" of such employer.[67]

In similar statutes enacted by state legislatures there is less uniformity. The Ohio law includes in the term "employer" any person acting in the interest of an employer, directly or indirectly.[68] But the Indiana[69] and Illinois[70] statutes contain no such provisions. There are similar variances in other state statutory provisions.

A corporate employer can act only through individual supervisors and employees, which includes officers. "[D]iscrimination is rarely carried out pursuant to a formal vote of a corporation's board of directors."[71] Thus a bank vice president who supervised the work of a female employee was held individually liable for her sexual harassment.[72] A plant manager who made personnel decisions came within the defi-

---

64. 42 U.S.C. § 2000e-2(a)(1).

65. Id. § 2000e(b).

66. 29 U.S.C. § 203(d).

67. Id. § 630(b).

68. Ohio Rev. Code Ann. § 4112.01(A)(2).

69. Ind. Code § 22-9-1-3(h).

70. Ill. Rev. Stat. Ann. ch. 68, § 2.101(B).

71. Meritor Sav. Bank v. Vinson, 477 U.S. 57, 75, 91 L.Ed.2d 49, 64, 106 S.Ct. 2399, 2410 (1986), Justice Marshall concurring.

72. Id.

nition of employer in a race and sex discrimination case.[73] But a nonsupervisory employee who was merely a co-worker of the complainant would not be liable for sexual harassment under Title VII.[74]

In the District of Columbia the court ruled that four individual officers of an unincorporated labor union could be held subject to liability as employers where termination of employment resulted from a discriminatory conspiracy.[75]

An age discrimination action in Nevada involved ten individuals sued in their individual capacities and as officers or officials of the corporate employer. Pending development of the facts, the court held they were properly joined as defendants.[76]

In such cases, the Sixth Circuit has pointed out that the essential question in applying the agency principle is whether the discriminatory act took place in the scope of the agent's employment. Also, where the agent is both an agent and a supervisor, his knowledge will be imputed to the corporation's management.[77]

§ 10.10. Actions for wrongful discharge.

Especially in situations where the employment is at will, there has been a spate of litigation in various forms. Long ago the Supreme Court recognized that an employee has a significant interest in his continued employment.[78] That principle was recognized in a Michigan case where a secretary sued the president of a labor union for discharging her as an employee of the union because she spurned his sexual advances.[79] A summary judgment for the defendant was reversed. The court

---

73. Jeter v. Boswell, 554 F. Supp. 946 (N.D. W.Va. 1983).

74. Guyette v. Stauffer Chem. Co., 518 F. Supp. 521 (D.N.J. 1981).

75. Thompson v. International Ass'n of Machinists & Aerospace Workers, 580 F. Supp. 662, 668-69 (D.D.C. 1984).

76. Wasilchuk v. Harvey's Wagon Wheel, 610 F. Supp. 206 (D. Nev. 1985).

77. Yates & Mathis v. AVCO Corp., 819 F.2d 630 (6th Cir. 1987).

78. Truax v. Raich, 239 U.S. 33, 60 L.Ed. 131, 36 S.Ct. 7 (1915).

79. Tash v. Houston, 74 Mich. App. 566, 254 N.W.2d 579 (1977).

held that the union president, like a corporate director, could not interfere with the plaintiff's employment relationship with the union unless he acted in good faith and in the belief that his actions would benefit the union.

It is reasonably well established that employment is presumed to be at will unless the facts and circumstances indicate otherwise.[80] Unless otherwise agreed, either party to an employment at will may terminate it for any reason that is not contrary to law.[81] As the above Michigan case shows, the unlawful termination may result from common-law proscriptions as well as from statutory prohibitions.[82] The Ohio court has held that among the factors to be considered in determining the right to terminate employment are the character of the employment, custom, the course of dealing between the parties, company policy, employee handbooks and oral representations.[83]

§ 10.11. Race discrimination: Section 1981 claims.

Title 42, Section 1981, United States Code, guarantees to all persons the same rights as are enjoyed by white citizens. It affords a federal remedy against discrimination in private employment on the basis of race, which may include both equitable and legal relief, and compensatory and punitive damages.[84] When corporate directors voluntarily and intentionally participate in the infringement of civil rights, they

---

80. E.g., Henkel v. Educational Research Council, 45 Ohio St. 2d 249, 344 N.E.2d 118 (1976); Martin v. New York Life Ins. Co., 148 N.Y. 117, 42 N.E. 416 (1895); Forrer v. Sears, Roebuck & Co., 36 Wis. 388, 153 N.W. 287 (1967).

81. Mers v. Dispatch Printing Co., 19 Ohio St. 3d 100, 483 N.E.2d 150 (1985).

82. E.g., Ill. Rev. Stat. Ann., ch. 68, § 2.102; Ind. Code §§ 22-9-1-1 to 22-9-1-13; ch. 4112, Ohio Rev. Code Ann.; 42 U.S.C. § 2000(e); 29 U.S.C. §§ 623(a) and 794; 29 U.S.C. § 158(a).

83. Mers v. Dispatch Printing Co., supra note 81, at 104.

84. Johnson v. Railway Express Agency, 421 U.S. 454, 460, 44 L.Ed.2d 295, 95 S.Ct. 1716, 1720 (1975).

are personally liable.[85] Proof of bad intent and evil motive is not required and ignorance of the law "though engendered by lawyers' advice, and corroborated by lower federal courts is no defense."[86]

In applying such rules to a Section 1981 action by a college professor of Arab origin and Muslim religion, the Third Circuit considered the position of defendants who were members of the college's tenure committee and ruled:

> If individuals are personally involved in the discrimination ... and if they intentionally caused the college to infringe on Appellant's Section 1981 rights, or if they authorized, directed or participated in the alleged discrimination, they may be held liable.[87]

§ 10.12. Discriminatory work environment.

The Title VII proscription of discrimination with respect to an individual's employment[88] prohibits conduct which has the purpose or effect of creating an intimidating, hostile, or offensive working environment.[89] Because Title VII includes any "agent" in the definition of "employer",[90] management-level employees, corporate officers and directors may be held individually liable where they carry on the proscribed activities[91] or fail to take reasonable steps to prevent them.[92]

The Supreme Court has held that the language of Title VII is not limited to "economic" or "tangible" discrimination but is intended "to strike at the entire spectrum of disparate

---

85. Tillman v. Wheaton-Haven Recreation Ass'n, 517 F.2d 1141, 1146 (4th Cir. 1975); Columbia Briargate Co. v. First Nat'l Bank, 713 F.2d 1052, 1055 (4th Cir. 1983); Weaver v. Gross, 605 F. Supp. 210, 213 (D.D.C. 1985).

86. Tillman v. Wheaton-Haven Recreation Ass'n, supra note 85, at 1146.

87. Al-Khazraji v. St. Francis College, 784 F.2d 505, 518 (3d Cir. 1986), aff'd on other grounds, 481 U.S. —, 95 L.Ed.2d 582, 107 S.Ct. 2022 (1987).

88. See supra section 10.09.

89. EEOC Guidelines, 29 C.F.R. § 1604.11(a)(3).

90. 42 U.S.C. § 2000e(b).

91. Meritor Sav. Bank v. Vinson, 477 U.S. 57, 91 L.Ed.2d 49, 106 S.Ct. 2399 (1986).

92. Hunter v. Allis-Chalmers Corp., 797 F.2d 1417, 1421 (7th Cir. 1986).

treatment" of men and women or blacks and whites in employment.[93] The "hostile environment" principle has been used to identify unconstitutional racial, religious, national origin and sexual discrimination.[94]

---

93. Meritor Sav. Bank v. Vinson, supra note 91. Cf. Hunter v. Allis-Chalmers Corp., supra note 92, at 1422.

94. Scott v. Sears, Roebuck & Co., 798 F.2d 210, 213 (7th Cir. 1986).

COROLLARY REFERENCES

"Corporate Officer Liability for Hazardous Waste Disposal: What Are the Consequences?," 38 Mercer L. Rev. 677 (1987).

Dore, "The Standard of Civil Liability for Hazardous Waste Disposal Activity: Some Quirks of Superfund," 57 Notre Dame Law. 260 (1981).

Emerson, "The Director as Corporate Legal Monitor: Environmental Legislation and Pandora's Box," 15 Seton Hall L. Rev. 593 (1985).

Giblin & Kelly, "Judicial Development of Standard of Liability in Government Enforcement Actions Under the Comprehensive Environmental Response, Compensation and Liability Act," 33 Cleve. St. L. Rev. 1 (1984).

Moore & Kowalski, "When is One Generator Liable for Another's Waste," 33 Cleve. St. L. Rev. 93 (1984).

Newell, "Discrimination and Employment Law," 136 New L.J. 699 (1986).

Wipf, "In Search of Liability for Hazardous Waste Dumping," 29 S.D.L. Rev. 493 (1984).

Comment, "Putting Polluters in Jail: The Imposition of Criminal Sanctions on Corporate Defendants Under Environmental Statutes," 20 Land & Water L. Rev. 93 (1985).

Note, "Generator Liability Under Superfund for Clean-up of Abandoned Hazardous Waste Dumpsites," 130 U. Pa. L. Rev. 1229 (1983).

Chapter 11

ACCOUNTANTS, ATTORNEYS, BROKERS AND DEALERS

§ 11.01. The accountant's role.

The accountant plays a critical role in the modern corporation. Especially since the enactment of the Foreign Corrupt Practices Act of 1977 (FCPA), the keeping of accurate books and records has become a heavier burden on corporate management. The FCPA[1] imposes bookkeeping and internal accounting control responsibilities on public companies, in addition to prohibiting payment of bribes by all companies. In addition, it imposes civil liabilities and criminal penalties for violation of its requirements.

Directors cannot function effectively without an adequate and continuing flow of information to them about their corpo-

---

1. Pub. L. 95-213, tit. I, 91 Stat. 1494 (1977), codified at 15 U.S.C. §§ 78m, 78dd-1, 78dd-2, 78ff.

ration, its goals, programs and activities. Outside directors, in particular, are substantially dependent upon the audit function to reflect the true state of corporate affairs.[2]

The audit function is concerned with the financial audit as well as the audit of management, both of which involve the corporation's independent accountants. They provide a capability enabling directors to audit management's performance not only in the area of net profits, but in such other fields as market penetration, comparative costs, capital and operating budget processes, cash and sales forecasting techniques, and conflict-of-interest procedures.[3] Moreover, one commentator suggests that "truly independent accountants [can provide a capability that] would enable [the directors] to audit management's results in meeting relevant nonfinancial objectives, such as compliance with law, due respect for the environment, provision of safe working conditions, nondiscrimination, and fair treatment of the consumer."[4]

In addition to the audit function, however comprehensive it may be, accountants customarily render tax services and management advisory services of all types, such as recruiting executives, developing data systems, searching out and recommending merger candidates, and promoting tax shelter opportunities for corporate employees as part of compensation planning.[5]

Bound by high standards of ethics, usually independent of the client's economic fate, and guided by generally accepted accounting principles, independent accountants are in a strategic position to influence management because, without their cooperation, many transactions would not be feasible.[6]

---

2. Leech and Mundheim, "The Outside Director of the Public Held Corporation," 31 Bus. Law. 1799, 1814 (1976).

3. Eisenberg, "Legal Models of Management Structure in the Modern Corporation: Officers, Directors and Accountants," 63 Calif. L. Rev. 375, 436, 437 (1975).

4. Id. at 437.

5. Fiflis, "Current Problems of Accountants' Responsibilities to Third Parties," 28 Vand. L. Rev. 31, 34-35 (1975).

6. Id. at 33 n.7.

§ 11.02. Auditing and accounting practices and standards.

The main determinant of accounting practices is the Financial Accounting Standards Board (FASB) which succeeded the Accounting Principles Board in 1973. It is the primary principle-making body of the accounting profession. It is composed of seven members, appointed for staggered, five-year terms by the trustees of the Financial Accounting Foundation (FAF), an independent corporation.[7] It is aided in its pronouncements by the Financial Accounting Advisory Council (FAAC), consisting of twenty-seven members who meet at least annually to prepare advisory opinions as to the effectiveness of the FASB's efforts.[8]

Generally accepted accounting principles, reasonably applied, are intended to produce fair financial statements.[9] The phrase "generally accepted accounting principles" is a technical accounting term which encompasses the conventions, rules and procedures necessary to define accepted accounting practice at a particular time. Those conventions, rules and procedures provide a standard by which to measure financial presentations.

The auditing standards executive committee of the auditing standards division of the American Institute of Certified Public Accountants (AICPA) is responsible for the development and interpretation of auditing standards. It wields near-absolute power in the area of auditing control,[10] although the Securities and Exchange Commission has not been hesitant to establish its views as to auditing standards.[11]

---

7. Id. at 50.

8. Adams, "Lessening the Legal Liability of Auditors," 32 Bus. Law. 1037, 1056 (1977).

9. Hill, "Responsibilities and Liabilities of Auditors and Accountants — An Accountant's View," 30 Bus. Law. 169, 176 (1975).

10. Id.; Adams, supra note 8, at 1057.

11. Fiflis, supra note 5, at 45-49. See also SEC Regulations S-X, Rule 2-02, 17 C.F.R. § 210.2-02 (1974).

A Ninth Circuit decision has pointed out the difference between the Generally Accepted Auditing Standards (GAAS) and the Generally Accepted Accounting Principles (GAAP):

> "Generally Accepted Accounting Principles" (GAAP) establish guidelines relating to the process by which the transactions and events of a business entity are measured, recorded, and classified in accordance with a conventional format. GAAS thus differs from GAAP; the former involves how an auditor goes about obtaining information, while the latter involves the format in which to present the information.[12]

In a subsequent decision the same court "assumed" that generally accepted accounting standards do not provide protection from liability when an accountant "fails to reveal material facts which he knows or which, but for a deliberate refusal to become informed, he should have known" should be revealed.[13]

§ 11.03. Audit committees of corporate boards.

Audit committees have become almost universal.[14] The New York Stock Exchange requires that they be comprised of outside directors. Also, the SEC, in agreeing to consent decrees in enforcement actions against various issuer corporations, frequently requires the establishment and maintenance of an audit committee composed of nonmanagement directors.[15] Some such decrees specify specific functions which the audit committee shall perform, such as the review of the corporation's financial controls and accounting practices and of all future financial reports filed with the SEC.[16]

---

12. SEC v. Arthur Young & Co., 590 F.2d 785, 789 n.4 (9th Cir. 1979).

13. Admiralty Fund v. Hugh Johnson & Co., 677 F.2d 1301, 1313 n.15 (9th Cir. 1982).

14. See supra section 1.11.

15. See, e.g., SEC v. Gulf & Western Indus., Inc., Fed. Sec. L. Rep. (CCH) ¶98,324 (D.D.C. 1981); SEC v. Killearn Props., Inc., Fed. Sec. L. Rep. (CCH) ¶96,256 (N.D. Fla. 1977).

16. SEC v. McLouth Steel Corp., Fed. Sec. L. Rep. (CCH) ¶98,032 (D.D.C. 1981).

In 1978, the SEC adopted rules which require reporting corporations to disclose to shareholders whether they have audit committees, and if so, to state what functions they perform. However, a report by a special AICPA committee on audit committees concluded that there is no reasonable basis for the accounting profession to require that corporations establish audit committees as a condition to an accountant's accepting an audit engagement.[17]

§ 11.04. Detection of fraud.

Auditors are not detectives hired to ferret out fraud, but if they chance on signs of fraud they may not avert their eyes—they must investigate.[18] When an auditor has reason to doubt that the corporate affairs are being honestly conducted, he must extend his audit procedures to learn whether his suspicions are justified.[19]

An auditor's duty "does not permit him to wait for an alarm bell to arouse him to investigation."[20] This is borne out by the AICPA's Statement on Accounting Standards No. 16, "The Independent Auditor's Responsibility for Detection of Errors and Irregularities." It provides that

> [U]nder generally accepted auditing standards, the independent auditor has the responsibility, within the inherent limitations of the auditing process, to search for errors or irregularities that would have a material effect on the financial statements, and to exercise due skill and care in the conduct of that examination.[21]

By reason of this standard, it appears that the independent auditor has a mandate to be sensitive to transactions that are

---

17. SEC Rel. No. 34-15384, Fed. Sec. L. Rep. (CCH) ¶81,766 (Dec. 6, 1978). 484 Sec. Reg. & L. Rep. (BNA) 0-1 (Jan. 3, 1979).

18. Cenco, Inc. v. Seidman & Seidman, 686 F.2d 449, 454 (7th Cir.), cert. denied, 459 U.S. 880 (1982).

19. United States v. Simon, 425 F.2d 796, 806, 807 (2d Cir. 1969), cert. denied, 397 U.S. 1006 (1970).

20. Fiflis, "Current Problems of Accountants' Responsibilities to Third Parties," 28 Vand. L. Rev. 31, 97 (1975).

21. Quotation from AICPA Professional Standards, Vol. 1, AU § 327 (1977).

prone to fraud. Hence, the courts will expect him to perform extended auditing procedures if his examination indicates that material errors or irregularities may exist.[22]

§ 11.05. Auditor's duty of disclosure.

Public disclosure of corporate financial irregularities is constantly sought by regulators as well as plaintiffs in class action and derivative suits, especially under the antifraud provisions of the Securities Acts. Accountants and auditors must face up to charges, as principals and as aiders and abettors, of failing to disclose or concealing corporate financial information of which they had or should have had knowledge. An accounting firm, whose only financial interest was an auditing fee, may have the same exposure as personnel of the audited corporation who actually committed irregular or illegal acts.

When public accountants know that their reports will be relied on by investors, they have a special duty to issue a truthful report and to disclose information to which they had access and which was not available to the investors. In a Second Circuit case[23] dealing with such a situation, the district court held that the accountant's professional duty of full disclosure to investors could not "be fulfilled merely by following generally accepted accounting principles." The court went on to state that "if application of accounting principles alone will not adequately inform investors, accountants, as well as insiders, must take pains to lay bare all the facts needed by investors to interpret the financial statements accurately."[24]

---

22. Coopers & Lybrand Comment 5, in Newsletter, Vol. 19, No. 14, April, 1977, at 6. Cf. National Surety Corp. v. Lybrand, 256 A.D. 226, 9 N.Y.S.2d 554, 563 (1939); Pacific Acceptance Corp., Ltd. v. Forsyth, 92 N.S.W. 29, 65-66 (1970), an Australian case which expresses an explicit disapproval of generally accepted auditing standards as a limitation on the scope of an auditor's duty.

23. Herzfeld v. Laventhol, Krekstein, Horwath & Horwath, 540 F.2d 27 (2d Cir. 1976).

24. Herzfeld v. Laventhol, Krekstein, Horwath & Horwath, 378 F. Supp. 112, 122 (S.D.N.Y. 1974), aff'd in part, rev'd in part, 540 F.2d 27, 34 (2d Cir. 1976).

In affirming on this ground, the Second Circuit stated:

> The function of an accountant is not merely to verify the correctness of the addition and subtraction of the company's bookkeepers. Nor does it take a fiscal wizard to appreciate the elemental and universal accounting principle that revenue should not be recognized until the "earning process is complete or virtually complete," and "an exchange has taken place."

Because the accountants violated those principles and disregarded Statements on Accounting Procedure No. 33 of the AICPA, the court found their audit "materially and knowingly misleading."

Cases arising in the Ninth Circuit involve that circuit's "flexible duty standard" which states that:

> [These] factors are relevant in determining the scope of the duty to disclose material facts under Rule 10b-5: (1) the relationship of defendant to plaintiff; (2) defendant's access to the information as compared to that of plaintiff; (3) defendant's benefit derived from the relationship; (4) defendant's awareness of whether plaintiff was relying on their relationship in making his or her investment decisions; and (5) defendant's activity in initiating the transaction in question.[25]

When the Ninth Circuit applied those factors in determining an accountant's duty in auditing the financial statements of three mutual funds, it ruled that "the relationship of an auditor to the firm it audits creates a narrow duty of disclosure."[26] The court continued:

> The relationship itself is occasional. The auditor's access to information about the firm depends to a greater or lesser degree on the firm's producing documents under its control. The auditor's benefit from the relationship consists in a fee for professional services. While the auditor may know that persons dealing with the firm and the firm's own directors will rely in some ways on the audit opinion, rarely if ever can the firm itself be expected to base investments decisions on what an audit reveals. [Ci-

---

25. Zweig v. Hearst Corp., 594 F.2d 1261, 1268 (9th Cir. 1979).
26. Pegasus Fund, Inc. v. Laraneta, 617 F.2d 1335, 1340 (9th Cir. 1980).

tation omitted.] Reckless disregard of this narrow duty is conduct of an extreme sort and should be found sparingly. To do otherwise would be to impose a more far-reaching duty than the facts of this case justify.

§ 11.06. Common-law liability.

The leading case on the common-law liability of accountants for improper performance of their professional duties is *Ultramares Corporation v. Touche*.[27] In that case Judge Benjamin Cardozo was confronted by a trend to eliminate privity as an element of recovery in physical tort actions, but feared exposing accountants "to a liability in an indeterminate amount for an indeterminate time to an indeterminate class."[28] Accordingly, he opted for the position that liability should extend not only to their clients but also to persons who are recipients of the defendant's report as the "end and aim of the transaction," which was somewhat broader than privity.[29] If the accountant's report had been "primarily for the benefit of the [client] ... and only incidentally or collaterally for the use of those to whom [the client] might exhibit it thereafter," the accountant would not have been held liable to such third parties.

A significant 1977 case, *White v. Guarente*,[30] decided by the same New York court that had decided *Ultramares* forty-six years earlier, involved an action by a limited partner against an accounting firm employed to audit and prepare tax returns for the limited partnership. Its reports, inter alia, failed to comment on substantial withdrawals of capital by the general partners. The court held that the accounting firm "must have been aware that a limited partner would necessarily rely on or make use of the audit and tax returns of the

---

27. 255 N.Y. 170, 174 N.E. 441 (1931).

28. Id., 174 N.E. at 444. Cf. Landell v. Lybrand, 264 Pa. 406, 107 A. 783 (1919).

29. See Rusch Factors, Inc. v. Levin, 284 F. Supp. 85 (D.R.I. 1968).

30. 43 N.Y.2d 356, 401 N.Y.S.2d 474, 372 N.E.2d 315, 319 (1977). Cf. Bolger v. Laventhol, Krekstein, Horwath & Horwath, 381 F. Supp. 260 (S.D.N.Y. 1974).

partnership." It ruled that the limited partners constituted a "fixed, definable and contemplated group" for whose benefit the audit was made and the tax returns prepared. The court quoted from the decision of the Seventh Circuit in *Hochfelder v. Ernst & Ernst*[31] to the effect that the courts have extended accountants' liability to the members of such a limited class and thus have diminished the impact of *Ultramares*.

Subsequently, there has been a trend to require accountants to respond to persons who foreseeably relied on their reports. It is led by an Ohio decision[32] holding that limited partners had standing to sue accountants who audited the books of their limited partnership. The court found that the limited partners were members of a limited class whose reliance upon the accountants' certified audits for purpose of investment strategy was specifically foreseen. The Ohio court adopted the interpretation of the 1931 *Ultramares* case made in the 1977 New York decision of *White v. Guarente*.

However, a 1985 New York decision decried the trend to permit recovery "by any foreseeable plaintiff'" and stated its intent "to preserve the wisdom and policy set forth in" *Ultramares* and *White*. The court wrote:

> Before accountants may be held liable in negligence to noncontractual parties who rely to their detriment on inaccurate financial reports, certain prerequisites must be satisfied: (1) the accountants must have been aware that the financial reports were to be used for a particular purpose or purposes; (2) in the furtherance of which a known party or parties was intended to rely; and (3) there must have been some conduct on the part of the accountants linking them to that party or parties, which evinces the accountants' understanding of that party or parties' reliance.[33]

---

31. 503 F.2d 1100, 1107 (7th Cir. 1974), rev'd on other grounds, 425 U.S. 185, 47 L.Ed.2d 668, 96 S.Ct. 1375, reh'g denied, 425 U.S. 985 (1976).

32. Haddon View Inv. Co. v. Coopers & Lybrand, 70 Ohio St. 2d 154, 436 N.E.2d 212 (1982). See also Touche, Ross & Co. v. Commercial Union Ins. Co., 514 So. 2d 315 (Miss. 1987).

33. Credit Alliance Corp. v. Arthur Andersen & Co., 65 N.Y.2d 536, 483 N.E.2d 110, 118, modified, 66 N.Y.2d 812, 489 N.E.2d 249 (1985). See also Toro Co. v. Krouse Kern & Co., 827 F.2d 155 (7th Cir. 1987).

In Massachusetts a corporation (Giant) filed audited financial statements with the Securities and Exchange Commission in connection with annual reports to shareholders. Giant then negotiated with plaintiffs to buy their businesses in New Jersey and entered into a merger agreement with them. During the negotiations, Giant made a public stock offering and included in the prospectus financial statements audited by a Big Eight accounting firm. The firm also audited Giant's 1972 statements upon which plaintiffs claimed they relied in making the merger agreement. Some of the information certified by the accountants was incorrect.[34]

Giant filed for bankruptcy and the Giant stock acquired by plaintiffs in the merger became worthless. In their suit against the accountants, plaintiffs charged fraudulent misrepresentation, gross negligence, negligence and breach of warranty. The accountants asserted lack of privity among their defenses.

In upholding the claim of negligent misrepresentation against the accountants, the New Jersey court drew a parallel between such a claim and one arising out of a defective product. Justice Schreiber wrote, "If recovery for defective products may include economic loss, why should such loss not be compensable if caused by negligent misrepresentation?"

The opinion appears to extend the potential liability of the accountants "to all those whom that auditor should reasonably foresee as recipients from the company of the statements for its proper business purposes, provided that the recipients rely on the statements pursuant to those business purposes."[35]

A Wisconsin case involved a bank which reviewed financial statements prepared by an accountant before making loans to the accountant's client.[36] The statements contained substan-

---

34. H. Rosenblum, Inc. v. Adler, 93 N.J. 324, 461 A.2d 138, 141, 35 A.L.R.4th 199 (1983).

35. Id., 461 A.2d at 153.

36. Citizens State Bank v. Timm, Schmidt & Co., 113 Wis. 2d 376, 335 N.W.2d 361 (1983).

tial and material errors. The client went into receivership and was liquidated. The bank sued the accountant to recoup its loss.

The court reversed a summary judgment for the accountant and remanded the case for trial. Citing the New Jersey case, Justice Day wrote that liability would be imposed upon the accountant for the foreseeable injuries resulting from his negligent acts unless, on the facts as determined at trial, recovery should be denied on grounds of public policy.

In both the New Jersey and Wisconsin cases, the court referred to the availability of liability insurance for accountants to spread the loss.

The rejection of the privity requirement gained at least implicit support from the Supreme Court in the *Arthur Young* case[37] where the court stated, in dicta:

> By certifying the public reports that collectively depict a corporation's financial status, the independent auditor assumes a public responsibility transcending any employment relationship with the client. The independent public accountant performing this special function owes ultimate allegiance to the corporation's creditors and stockholders, as well as the investing public. This "public watchdog" function demands that the accountant maintain total independence from the client at all times and requires complete fidelity to the public trust.

In order to avoid liability to unreasonably remote plaintiffs, jurisdictions which have rejected the privity rule generally apply the common-law tort concept of reasonable foreseeability. A New York district court has held that accountants who certified the financial statements of a private investment partnership were not liable to a mutual fund which relied on those financial statements to hire the partnership's investment advisor.[38] The court reasoned that the financial statements were for the use of the general and limited partners,

---

37. United States v. Arthur Young & Co., 465 U.S. 805, 79 L.Ed.2d 826, 104 S.Ct. 1495 (1984).

38. Competitive Assocs., Inc. v. Laventhol, Krekstein, Horwath & Horwath, 478 F. Supp. 1328 (S.D.N.Y. 1979).

potential new investors, and other persons who might do business with the partnership, and that it was not reasonably foreseeable that they would have some indirect influence on plaintiffs in hiring the partnership's investment advisor.

A few courts, however, continue to require privity in negligence actions by third parties against accountants.[39] Those decisions recognize that if the accountants are found to be grossly negligent or to have made intentional misrepresentations, the privity requirement would not be applicable.

A New York district court in applying the privity requirement, has held that officers and directors of a corporation who were sued for fraud and breach of fiduciary duty had no standing to assert a third-party claim against the corporation's accountants.[40] Because the accountants contracted to perform only accounting functions, the court ruled that their duties ran only to the corporation, not to its directors and officers.

§ 11.07. Statutory liability.

Statutory liability of accountants is most apt to involve the federal securities acts, under which such liability has been imposed in several instances. As in the cases of attorneys and underwriters, one of the more important court decisions is the *BarChris* case.[41] Although this decision was handed down in 1968, it has an important place in the literature dealing with this subject. *BarChris* involved liability under Section 11 of the Securities Act.[42] The accounting firm asserted a "due diligence" defense under the statute, which the court denied. It summarized its conclusions by stating:

> [The accountant in charge] did not spend an adequate amount of time in a task of this magnitude. Most impor-

---

39. Investors Tax Sheltered Real Estate, Ltd. v. Laventhol, Krekstein, Horwath & Horwath, 370 So.2d 815 (Fla. App. 1979); Shofstall v. Allied Van Lines, Inc., 455 F. Supp. 351 (N.D. Ill. 1978).

40. Stratton Group, Ltd. v. Sprayregen, 466 F. Supp. 1180 (S.D.N.Y. 1979). See also Strong v. France, 474 F.2d 747, 752 (9th Cir. 1973).

41. Escott v. BarChris Const. Corp., 283 F. Supp. 643 (S.D.N.Y. 1968).

42. 15 U.S.C. § 77k.

tant of all, he was too easily satisfied with glib answers to his inquiries.... [T]here were enough danger signals in the materials which he did examine to require further investigation on his part.... It is not always sufficient merely to ask questions.[43]

Liability may be imposed upon accountants under Section 12(2) of the 1933 Act[44] in a proper case. Privity or scienter have been required[45] and the Northern District of Ohio has called for proof of causation.[46] Aiding or abetting is a basis for such liability under that section,[47] and in an action under Section 14(a) of the 1934 Act.[48] Section 10(b) of the Securities Exchange Act of 1934 and SEC Rule 10b-5 thereunder have imposed liability upon accountants.

The Yale Express Systems, Inc. litigation[49] raises questions as to the legal responsibility of an accountant to make disclosure when he comes into possession of information which renders a prior report inaccurate.

In a Ninth Circuit case from Idaho decided in 1971, that court laid the foundation for its less than expansive view of Section 10(b) liability.[50] It refused to impose liability upon an independent accountant where there had been affirmative disclosure of his findings to prospective investors. The accountant had been retained on three separate occasions to prepare financial statements for a corporation. He found the corporation's books and records seriously deficient and made several recommendations to the board of directors for im-

---

43. Escott v. BarChris Const. Corp., supra note 41, at 703. Cf. Ahern v. Gaussoin, 611 F. Supp. 1465, 1482-85 (D. Or. 1985).

44. E.g., Sandusky Land, Ltd. v. Uniplan Groups, Inc., 400 F. Supp. 440 (N.D. Ohio 1975).

45. See Lanza v. Drexel & Co., 479 F.2d 1277 (2d Cir. 1973) (en banc).

46. Sandusky Land, Ltd. v. Uniplan Groups, Inc., supra note 44, at 443.

47. See In re Caesar's Palace Sec. Litig., 360 F. Supp. 366 (S.D.N.Y. 1973).

48. In re Clinton Oil Co. Sec. Litig., Fed. Sec. L. Rep. (CCH) ¶96,015, at p. 91,576 (D. Kan. 1977).

49. See Fischer v. Kletz, 266 F. Supp. 180 (S.D.N.Y. 1967).

50. Wessel v. Buhler, 437 F.2d 279 (9th Cir. 1971). Cf. Hudson v. Capital Mgt. Int'l, Inc., 565 F. Supp. 615, 623 (N.D. Cal. 1983).

provement. While he questioned certain entries on the corporation's books, he nevertheless prepared, over a period of seventeen months, two unaudited statements and one audited
statement for it. In bringing the suit against him and certain
officers and directors, the shareholders alleged that the financial statements were misleading and were made "in connection with the purchase or sale of any security" within the
meaning of Rule 10b-5.

Although, arguendo, all three of the accountant's financial
statements were misleading, the court nonetheless exonerated him with a ruling that none of the three financial statements was made "in a manner reasonably calculated to influence the investing public."[51] In so holding, the court pointed
out that no information was disseminated publicly in any
way; that there was no evidence that any investor ever saw
the statements until after the litigation began; that the accountant had delivered the statements to the board of directors for uses unconnected with stock issuance; and that no
one before suit ever saw them, except the officers and directors of the corporation and the agencies to which they were
directed. The court declined to "stretch Rule 10b-5 to cover
[the accountant's] financial statements."

In *Sharp v. Coopers & Lybrand*,[52] the Third Circuit reaffirmed its established view that respondeat superior is not
generally a basis to impose secondary liability under Rule
10b-5.[53] In so doing, however, it carved out an exception for
such entities as accounting firms which made reports or representations to influence the investing public.

In the *Sharp* case, an accounting firm which drafted an
opinion letter on the tax consequences of an oil and gas investment, knowing the letter would be used to influence in-

---

51. See SEC v. Texas Gulf Sulphur Co., 401 F.2d 833, 862 (2d Cir. 1968),
cert. denied sub nom. Coates v. SEC, 394 U.S. 976 (1969) and 404 U.S. 1005
(1971), reh'g denied, 404 U.S. 1064 (1972).

52. 649 F.2d 175 (3d Cir. 1981).

53. See Rochez Bros., Inc. v. Rhoades, 527 F.2d 880 (3d Cir. 1975), cert.
denied, 425 U.S. 993 (1976); Gould v. American-Hawaiian S.S. Co., 535
F.2d 761 (3d Cir. 1976).

vestor decisions, was found liable to the investors under Rule 10b-5 for the fraudulent acts of one of its employees in connection with the letter. Although the jury in the trial court found that no partner of the accounting firm possessed the necessary scienter to violate Rule 10b-5, the appellate court held that the firm had placed itself in a position where the investing public would place their trust and confidence in it. The court said that: "[t]he expectation that investment decisions would be made on the basis of the opinion letter required the firm to exercise a 'stringent duty to supervise' its employees in drafting and issuing the letter." Thus, the doctrine of respondeat superior was invoked to hold the firm liable under Rule 10b-5 for the fraudulent acts of its employees.

The Ninth Circuit has held, pursuant to Section 11(f) of the Securities Act, that an accountant who is charged with misconduct in the issuance of securities may recover contribution from controlling persons and others who, if sued separately, would have also been liable.[54] However, the accountants were not permitted to seek indemnity from controlling persons of the issuer because such indemnity would undermine the statutory purposes of assuring the diligent performance of their duty and deterring negligence.

§ 11.08. The effect of "Hochfelder."

For the accounting profession (and perhaps for all professionals engaged in any aspect of securities law) the most significant court decision in recent years is *Ernst & Ernst v. Hochfelder,*[55] in which the Supreme Court held that a private action for damages will not lie under Section 10(b) of the Exchange Act and Rule 10b-5 thereunder in the absence of any allegation of scienter—intent to deceive, manipulate, or defraud. In commenting upon this decision, Ernst & Ernst's general counsel stated:

---

54. Laventhol, Krekstein, Horwath & Horwath v. Horwitch, 637 F.2d 672 (9th Cir. 1980).

55. 425 U.S. 185, 47 L.Ed.2d 668, 96 S.Ct. 1375, reh'g denied, 425 U.S. 985 (1976).

The establishment of this rule will have a substantial impact on future litigation against accountants and others under Section 10(b), which is the most common basis of suits against professionals in the securities area. While it is easy to allege negligence, we feel that plaintiffs will have to hesitate before alleging that Ernst & Ernst in any situation ever "intended to deceive."[56]

While endorsing this decision as "substantial aid to [accountants'] litigation problems but not a panacea," the chairman of the board of another "Big Eight" accounting firm suggested that "future cases are more likely now to arise under common law in the states, in which the test of legal misconduct of accountants continues to be one of mere negligence."[57]

Since *Hochfelder,* ordinary negligence is insufficient to support liability of accountants under Rule 10b-5. Scienter is required.

Although the Supreme Court left open the question whether recklessness would suffice as scienter, most of the courts to address this question after *Hochfelder* have concluded that recklessness satisfies the scienter requirement.[58] The Sixth Circuit has written that the recklessness standard falls somewhere between intent and negligence.[59]

The Third Circuit has ruled that accountants act with the requisite scienter if they lack a reasonable basis for believing

---

56. Ernst & Ernst Nat'l Office Information Release, Retrieval No. 34125, 4/7/76.

57. Griffin, "The Beleaguered Accountants: A Defendant's Viewpoint," 62 A.B.A. J. 759, 763 (1976).

58. E.g., IIT, An Int'l Inv. Trust v. Cornfeld, 619 F.2d 909, 923 (2d Cir. 1980); Coleco Indus., Inc. v. Berman, 567 F.2d 569, 574 (3d Cir 1977); SEC v. Southwest Coal & Energy Co., 624 F.2d 1312, 1321 (5th Cir. 1980); Mansbach v. Prescott, Ball & Turben, 598 F.2d 1017, 1023 (6th Cir. 1979); Sunstrand Corp. v. Sun Chem. Corp., 553 F.2d 1033, 1040 (7th Cir. 1977); Keirnan v. Homeland, Inc., 611 F.2d 785, 787 (9th Cir. 1980); Wertheim Co. v. Codding Embryological Sciences, Inc., 620 F.2d 764, 766-67 (10th Cir. 1980); SEC v. Carriba Air, Inc., 681 F.2d 1318, 1324 (11th Cir. 1982). See also Mullis v. Merrill Lynch, Pierce, Fenner & Smith, Inc., 492 F. Supp. 1345, 1353 (D. Nev. 1980); Frankel v. Wyllie & Thornhill, Inc., 537 F. Supp. 730, 740 (W.D. Va. 1982).

59. Mansbach v. Prescott, Ball & Turben, 598 F.2d 1017, 1025 n.36 (6th Cir. 1979).

that their report or audit is accurate.[60] In that case the accountants had been engaged to perform certain accounting services, including the review of financial statements and issuance of an audit report. The court concluded that the accountants' failure to detect misleading information in the balance sheet was due to their negligence in preparing their audit report. However, such negligence did not satisfy the scienter requirement because the accountants did not lack a genuine and reasonable belief that the information in the audit report was accurate in all material respects. The court further held that the plaintiff had the burden to affirmatively show that the accountants acted with scienter. In addition to actions against accountants under Rule 10b-5, the Sixth Circuit has concluded that scienter must be shown in a private action against outside accountants under Section 14(a) of the Exchange Act in connection with incorrect statements in proxy materials.[61]

§ 11.09. SEC proceedings against accountants and attorneys.

The SEC has continued to maintain its control over the competency and integrity of accountants and attorneys by using its power under its Rule 2(e),[62] which pertains to professionals generally.

Following a long line of authority in which the courts have recognized the power of an administrative agency to discipline professionals who practice before it,[63] the Second Circuit in 1979 expressly held that Rule 2(e) is "reasonably related" to the purposes of the securities laws and "does not violate, nor is it inconsistent with, any other provision of the securi-

---

60. McLean v. Alexander, 599 F.2d 1190 (3d Cir. 1979).

61. Adams v. Standard Knitting Mills, Inc., 623 F.2d 422 (6th Cir. 1980).

62. 17 C.F.R. § 201.2(e) (1982).

63. E.g., Goldsmith v. United States Bd. of Tax Appeals, 270 U.S. 117, 70 L.Ed. 494, 46 S.Ct. 215 (1926); Herman v. Dulles, 92 App. D.C. 303, 205 F.2d 715 (1953); Fields v. SEC, 495 F.2d 1075 (D.C. 1974); Kivitz v. SEC, 154 App. D.C. 372, 475 F.2d 956 (1973); Koden v. United States Dept. of Justice, 564 F.2d 228 (7th Cir. 1977).

ties laws."[64] The court went on to state that the Rule is "a necessary element adjunct to the Commission's power to protect the integrity of its administrative procedures and the public in general."

In Chief Judge Kaufman's concurrence he declared: "Our opinion today affirms the ability of the SEC to ensure that the professionals who practice before it — on whose probity the viability of the regulatory process depends — meet the highest ethical standards."

Seven years later, the Ninth Circuit upheld the SEC in barring an accountant from practicing before it, followed the 1979 decisions and pointed out that "no court ha[d] since disagreed with that ruling."[65]

The SEC has consistently stated that it may enjoin or otherwise sanction an entire accounting firm for alleged misconduct of certain of the firm's members or employees,[66] but the Second Circuit has raised a question whether the SEC could hold an entire firm vicariously liable under Rule 2(e).[67] The question was left unresolved by the court, thereby creating uncertainty as to the scope of the SEC's authority under the Rule.

Examples of sanctions adopted by the SEC against accountants under Rule 2(e) and the consent process include censuring of accounting firms,[68] peer review of accounting firms,[69] suspending client development and solicitation,[70] temporar-

64. Touche Ross & Co. v. SEC, 609 F.2d 570, 582 (2d Cir. 1979).

65. Davy v. SEC, 792 F.2d 1418, 1421 (9th Cir. 1986).

66. E.g., ASR No. 248, In Matter of Ernst & Ernst, Fed. Sec. L. Rep (CCH) ¶72,270 (1978); ASR No. 285, In Matter of Lester Witte & Co., Fed Sec. L. Rep. (CCH) ¶72,307 (1980).

67. Touche Ross & Co. v. SEC, supra note 64, at 582 n.21.

68. E.g., ASR No. 153A, In re Touche Ross & Co., Fed. Sec. L. Rep. (CCH) ¶72,175A (1979).

69. E.g., ASR No. 173, In re Peat, Marwick, Mitchell & Co., Fed. Sec. L. Rep. (CCH) ¶72,195 (1979).

70. Id.

71. E.g., ASR No. 153A, In re Ernst & Ernst, Fed. Sec. L. Rep. (CCH) ¶72,175A (1979).

ily[71] and permanently[72] suspending partners from practice, and requiring continuing education.[73]

The SEC has always insisted that attorneys are also subject to disqualification proceedings on grounds similar to those applicable to accountants. Moreover it has ruled that a law firm acting as general counsel of a reporting corporation has a collective responsibility for the adequacy of filed reports.[74]

A decision of an administrative law judge in a Rule 2(e) proceeding points out some of the hazards that must be faced by lawyers in SEC practice.[75] He held that two attorneys representing National Telephone Company "(a) assisted management in its efforts to conceal material facts concerning its financial condition and (b) failed to inform the board of directors concerning management's unwillingness to make such disclosures." The decision included findings that the attorneys had willfully violated and aided and abetted violations of Sections 10(b) and 13(a) of the Exchange Act and several Commission rules.

A petition seeking review was granted by the Commission which permitted the public and the bar to file amicus curiae briefs on the legal and policy issues involved in the matter. In 1981 the Commission reversed the findings of the administrative law judge.

In an extended opinion, the Commission ruled that the attorneys did not have sufficient involvement in their client's affairs to be direct, primary violators. It examined their lia-

---

72. E.g., ASR No. 275, In re D. Darrel L. Nielson, Fed. Sec. L. Rep. (CCH) ¶72,297 (1980).

73. E.g., ASR No. 168, In re Benjamin Botwinick & Co., Fed. Sec. L. Rep. (CCH) ¶72,190 (1975).

74. Keating, Meuthing & Klekamp, Sec. Exch. Act Release No. 15982 (July 2, 1979), Fed. Sec. L. Rep. (CCH) ¶82,124.

75. In re Carter, Fed. Sec. L. Rep. (CCH) ¶82,175 (1979).

bility as aiders and abettors and found an absence of wrongful intent.[76]

As its test the Commission required a showing that the attorneys intended "to foster the illegal activity."[77]

An important part of the decision is the Commission's definition of "unethical or improper professional conduct," as the term is used in Rule 2(e)(1)(ii), to be "applicable only to conduct occurring after the date of this opinion," as follows:

> When a lawyer with significant responsibilities in the effectuation of a company's compliance with the disclosure requirements of the federal securities laws becomes aware that his client is engaged in a substantial and continuing failure to satisfy those disclosure requirements, his continued participation violates professional standards unless he takes prompt steps to end the client's noncompliance.

The Commission opined that "counseling adequate disclosure" is initially sufficient, even if the lawyer's advice is not accepted. But, said the Commission:

> [T]here comes a point at which a reasonable lawyer must conclude that his advice is not being followed or even sought in good faith, and that his client is involved in a continuing course of violating the securities laws. At this critical juncture, the lawyer must take further, more affirmative steps in order to avoid the inference that he has been co-opted, willingly or unwillingly, into the scheme of non-disclosure.

The Commission did not spell out what it believed the lawyer should do at that juncture. It mentioned resignation, a direct approach to one or more directors, and an attempt to enlist the aid of other members of the firm's management, as options. But it declared:

> What is required, in short, is some prompt action that leads to the conclusion that the lawyer is engaged in efforts to correct the underlying problem, rather than having capitulated to the desires of a strong-willed, but misguided client.

---

76. In re Carter & Johnson, Fed. Sec. L. Rep. (CCH) ¶82,847, 22 SEC Docket 292, Sec. Exch. Act Release No. 17597 (1981).

77. Id., 22 SEC Docket at 318.

The Commission's use of Rule 2(e) against attorneys who are corporate officers presents some hazards because the Commission has consistently ruled that proof of scienter is not required in Rule 2(e) proceedings.[78] Even after *Hochfelder*,[79] the Commission's General Counsel has pointed out the advantages of using Rule 2(e) where absence of scienter might prevent Rule 10b-5 proceedings.[80] It has been suggested that corporate officers "charged on the basis of activities undertaken in good faith should challenge the Commission's failure to apply the scienter requirement to Rule 2(e) proceedings."[81]

§ 11.10. Aiding and abetting.

In addition to their exposure as potential primary wrongdoers, accountants, attorneys, brokers and dealers are liable to find themselves joined as defendants in actions under the federal securities laws as well as in actions against corporate officers and directors for breaches of their fiduciary responsibilities. However, it is important to bear in mind Judge Richard A. Posner's statement:

> There is no tort of aiding and abetting under Illinois law or, so far as we know, the law of any other state.... Anyone who would be guilty in a criminal proceeding of aiding and abetting a fraud would be liable under tort law as a participant in the fraud, since aider-abettor liability requires participation in the criminal venture.[82]

A Seventh Circuit decision relating to the liability of a law firm and an accounting firm for violation of the Securities

---

78. In re Haskins & Sells and Stewart, Accounting Series Release No. 73 (Oct. 30, 1952), Fed. Sec. L. Rep. (CCH) ¶72,092, at p. 62,197 (1982).

79. Ernst & Ernst v. Hochfelder, 425 U.S. 185, 47 L.Ed.2d 668, 96 S.Ct. 1375, reh'g denied, 425 U.S. 985 (1976).

80. Siedel, "Rule 2(e) and Corporate Officers," 39 Bus. Law. 455, 471 (1984).

81. Id. at 472-73.

82. Cenco, Inc. v. Seidman & Seidman, 686 F.2d 449, 453 (7th Cir.), cert. denied, 459 U.S. 880 (1982).

Acts holds that aiders, abettors, conspirators, and the like may be held liable "only if they have the same mental state required for primary liability."[83] Scienter is necessary.

Accountants

The *Equity Funding* litigation involved numerous charges against several accounting firms. In fact, in the settlement of that litigation accounting firms and their partners, employees and agents paid $42 million out of the total settlement sum of $60 million. When the district court ruled on motions filed by defendants in that litigation, it dealt extensively with the subject of aiding and abetting by accountants.[84]

The elements of aider and abettor liability of accountants defined in that decision are substantially the same as those detailed by the Sixth Circuit in *Securities and Exchange Commission v. Coffey,*[85] by the Second Circuit in *Hirsch v. duPont,*[86] and by the Third Circuit in *Landy v. Federal Deposit Insurance Corporation.*[87] The Sixth Circuit's requirement that the accused aider-abettor must have knowingly and substantially assisted the violation by the primary wrongdoer is a requirement that the plaintiff must "show some causal connection between the conduct of the aider and abettor and the harm done plaintiffs by the principals before liability can attach to the conduct of the aider and abettor."[88] In that context, the *Equity Funding* court ruled that no defendant could be held liable for aiding and abetting "the con-

---

83. Barker v. Henderson, Franklin, Starnes & Holt, 797 F.2d 490 (7th Cir. 1986).

84. In re Equity Funding Corp. of Am. Sec. Litig., 416 F. Supp. 161 (C.D. Cal. 1976).

85. 493 F.2d 1304, 1317 (6th Cir. 1974), cert. denied, 420 U.S. 908 (1975).

86. 553 F.2d 750, 759 (2d Cir. 1977).

87. 486 F.2d 139, 164-167 (3d Cir. 1973), cert. denied, 416 U.S. 960 (1974).

88. See In re Equity Funding Corp. of Am. Sec. Litig., supra note 84, at 180.

duct of any primary defendant that occurred prior to the time
... the secondary defendant became an aider and abettor."[89]

When applying the "substantial assistance" element of an
aiding and abetting claim to suits by investors against accountants, courts have generally concluded that the element
is satisfied if the accountant participated in the preparation
of public documents which contained the allegedly material
omissions or misrepresentations.[90]

However, where the accountant accurately records a series
of fraudulent transactions in the corporate books, but does
not knowingly participate in the preparation of any prospectus or offering for the company, he has not substantially assisted the fraud and is not subject to aiding and abetting
liability, according to a California district court.[91] The court
noted that the accountant's services were not a substantial
factor in causing the underlying securities law violations because he had no authority to influence the company's affairs
and because the accountant's accurate reporting actually
made exposure of the fraud more likely.

In the case of accountants charged with aiding and abetting the primary wrongdoer, the subject of knowledge is also
of consequence. It appears to be established in the Second
Circuit that "knowledge of the fraud, and not merely the
undisclosed material facts, is indispensable."[92] The Third Circuit has cited "the alleged aiders' and abettors' knowledge" of
"the doing of a wrongful act."[93] The Sixth Circuit required

---

89. Id. at 181. See also Morgan v. Prudential Funds, Inc., 446 F. Supp.
628, 633 (S.D.N.Y. 1978).

90. E.g., Clark v. Cameron-Brown Co., Fed. Sec. L. Rep. (CCH) ¶97,539
(M.D.N.C. 1980); In re Investors Funding Corp. of New York Sec. Litig.,
523 F. Supp. 550 (S.D.N.Y. 1980).

91. Mendelsohn v. Capital Underwriters, Inc., 490 F. Supp. 1069 (N.D.
Cal. 1979).

92. Hirsch v. duPont, supra note 86, at 759; Faturik v. Woodmere Sec.,
Inc., 431 F. Supp. 894, 896 (S.D.N.Y. 1977).

93. Gould v. American-Hawaiian S.S. Co., 535 F.2d 761, 779 (3d Cir.
1976).

"some showing that [the alleged aiders-abettors] were aware of the [primary wrongdoer's] alleged misrepresentations."[94]

This matter of knowledge, sometimes called a "state of mind requirement," is related to the "scienter" requirement of *Ernst & Ernst v. Hochfelder*. It was a factor in the Second Circuit's specification of "knowledge of the fraud, and not merely the undisclosed material facts."[95] Knowledge is, of course, something less than intent. This raises the question of whether recklessness would meet the knowledge requirement.[96]

Another factor of consequence in cases charging accountants with aiding and abetting is the question of reliance. In a misrepresentation action, the Second Circuit held that reliance was shown by proving that the misrepresentation was "a significant contributing cause" of the plaintiff's damages.[97] The same circuit has also written:

> This Court has also expressed the view that a plaintiff need not prove that nondisclosure of material facts induced its purchases, but need only allege that it would not have acted as it did had it known of the information withheld by defendants.[98]

That is, in essence, the tort law test of "causation in fact."[99] At least that much of a showing appears to be an essential element of such a claim.[100]

---

94. SEC v. Coffey, 493 F.2d 1304, 1316 n.30 (6th Cir. 1974), cert. denied, 420 U.S. 908 (1975).

95. Hirsch v. duPont, 553 F.2d 750, 759 (2d Cir. 1977).

96. Cf. Herzfeld v. Laventhol, Krekstein, Horwath & Horwath, 540 F.2d 27, 34 (2d Cir. 1976).

97. Id. at 33, 34.

98. Competitive Assocs., Inc. v. Laventhol, Krekstein, Horwath & Horwath, 516 F.2d 811, 814 (2d Cir. 1975); McLean v. Alexander, 420 F. Supp. 1057, 1077 (D. Del. 1976).

99. Chasins v. Smith, Barney & Co., 438 F.2d 1167, 1172 (2d Cir. 1970).

100. Cf. Brennan v. Midwestern United Life Ins. Co., 259 F. Supp. 673 (N.D. Ind. 1966), 286 F. Supp. 702 (N.D. Ind. 1968), aff'd, 417 F.2d 147 (7th Cir. 1969), cert. denied, 397 U.S. 989 (1970).

Attorneys

The Southern District of New York has reiterated the general rule that inaction does not constitute "substantial assistance" and will not create aider and abettor liability except when it was designed intentionally to aid and abet the primary wrongdoing.[101] In that case an attorney was absolved of liability as an aider and abettor when the complaint against him merely alleged that he "intended to aid the ... fraudulent scheme by remaining silent" and not disclosing material information of which he was aware.

The Securities and Exchange Commission, in its *Carter & Johnson* proceedings,[102] sought to identify the legal principles applicable to all aiding and abetting decisions under the securities laws. It found that generally the following three elements would be present:

(1) There exists an independent securities law violation committed by some other party;

(2) The aider and abettor knowingly and substantially assisted the conduct that constitutes the violation; and

(3) The aider and abettor was aware or knew that his role was part of an activity that was improper or illegal.

In the context of that proceeding the first element was self-evident. The Commission viewed the second element as generally satisfied in the context of a securities lawyer performing professional duties:

> [H]e is inevitably deeply involved in his client's disclosure activities and often participates in the drafting of instruments.... And he does so knowing that he is participating in the preparation of disclosure documents — that is his job.

---

101. Quintel Corp., N.V. v. Citibank, N.A., 589 F. Supp. 1235 (S.D.N.Y. 1984).

102. In re Carter & Johnson, Fed. Sec. L. Rep. (CCH) ¶82,847, 22 SEC Docket 292, Sec. Exch. Act Release No. 17597 (1981).

As to the third element, the Commission found that in an SEC Rule 2(e) proceeding against a lawyer, "the crucial inquiry inevitably tends to focus on the awareness or the intent element of the offense of aiding and abetting."

In the course of its discussion, the Commission accepted the Fifth Circuit concept that "an aider and abettor should be found liable only if scienter of the high 'conscious intent' variety can be found" unless "some special duty of disclosure exists."[103] That level of intent, in this proceeding, required a showing that the respondent intended "to foster the illegal activity."

The effect of *Hochfelder*[104] on claims of aiding and abetting by accountants is probably about the same with respect to such claims against attorneys. Thus there must be proof that an attorney knew or should have known what his client's conduct was or was about to be, and also knew that such conduct was violative of law.[105] Because of his fiduciary relationship, it may be that recklessness will satisfy this requirement. However, the conduct must have been "highly unreasonable."[106]

Brokers and dealers

The subject of aiding and abetting is becoming significant in broker-dealer cases, as it has become in other actions under the federal securities laws. In the *Shearson, Hammill* litigation, for example, the broker-dealer filed third-party complaints charging that the National Bank of North America aided and abetted the issuer, Tidal Marine International

---

103. See Woodward v. Metro Bank of Dallas, 522 F.2d 84, 97 (5th Cir. 1975).

104. Ernst & Ernst v. Hochfelder, 425 U.S. 185, 47 L.Ed.2d 668, 96 S.Ct. 1375, reh'g denied, 425 U.S. 985 (1976).

105. Brennan v. Midwestern United Life Ins. Co., supra note 100, 259 F. Supp. at 680; see Hirsch v. duPont, 553 F.2d 750, 759 (2d Cir. 1977); Gould v. American-Hawaiian S.S. Co., 535 F.2d 761, 779 (3d Cir. 1976).

106. Rolf v. Blythe, Eastman Dillon & Co., 570 F.2d 38, 47 (2d Cir. 1978); Ross v. Bolton, Fed. Sec. L. Rep. (CCH) ¶92,879 at 94,264 (S.D.N.Y. 1986).

Corporation, in giving false information to the broker-dealer and the public with the intention of raising the price of Tidal's stock and assisting the sale of its securities.[107] It was alleged, inter alia, that the bank falsified its books to conceal the violation of its legal lending limit and "to assist officers of Tidal in concealing a certain amount of its secured debt."

The court cited *Brennan v. Midwestern United Life Insurance Company*[108] in support of the view that the falsification of the bank's books constituted "substantial assistance or encouragement" of the fraud.[109] It distinguished *Wessel v. Buhler*[110] and *Landy v. Federal Deposit Insurance Corporation*[111] and required trial of the aiding and abetting charges.

Aiding and abetting claims provide an alternative to indemnification or contribution to enable broker-dealers to pass on the burden of loss in such cases.

§ 11.11. The business lawyer's role.

Because of the increasing complexity of the law, businessmen must be in almost continual contact with their attorneys instead of engaging in sporadic and infrequent consultations. The practice of calling upon counsel only in time of trouble has given way to a practice of depending upon lawyers for intelligence or early warning, so that adequate plans can be made and appropriate action taken before positions have been established. Regulatory statutes and agency rules require business action of specified kinds. Thus business activity is not merely limited by law; it is dictated precisely by law.

The business lawyer who interprets the requirements of such statutes and regulations has become more essential in the day-by-day work of corporate management, which has

---

107. Odette v. Shearson, Hammill & Co., 394 F. Supp. 946, 960 (S.D.N.Y. 1975).

108. Supra note 100.

109. Odette v. Shearson, Hammill & Co., supra note 107, at 961.

110. 437 F.2d 279 (9th Cir. 1971).

111. 486 F.2d 139 (3d Cir. 1973), cert. denied, 416 U.S. 960 (1974).

resulted in greater use of both in-house legal staffs and out-side counsel. This growth of corporate law practice has caused legal costs to soar. As a result corporate managements have become more attentive to the efficiency and productivity of their lawyers.

Legal work, whether conducted by an in-house staff or by outside counsel, is a necessary operating expense. Consequently its control is essential if the "bottom line" is to show a profit for today's business corporations. This need has given impetus to a trend toward greater use of the in-house legal staff, but outside counsel continue to serve in essential roles.

A business lawyer does not shed the cloak of his profession when he functions as an officer or director of his client corporation. In a Second Circuit case,[112] for example, the defendant was an officer and director of the plaintiff corporation and was also its attorney. When charged with defrauding the corporation, he claimed he had acted as corporate secretary but not as attorney. The court declined to make any such distinction.

§ 11.12. Conflicts of interest.

In Rule 1.13 of the Model Rules of Professional Conduct[113] it is provided, in part:

> (a) A lawyer employed or retained by an organization represents the organization acting through its duly organized constituents.
>
> * * *
>
> (e) A lawyer representing an organization may also represent any of its directors, officers, employees, members, shareholders or other constituents, subject to the provisions of Rule 1.7....[114]

---

112. Commonwealth Fin. Corp. v. McHarg, 282 F. 560 (2d Cir. 1922).

113. Adopted by the House of Delegates of the American Bar Association on August 2, 1983. The Rules do not have legal effect unless adopted in a state, but may have some persuasive significance.

114. Rule 1.7, among other things, requires consent of clients when conflicting interests are involved.

Aside from problems presented by other provisions of Model Rule 1.13, the corporation's lawyer, especially if he is also a director, owes fiduciary duties to all shareholders for the violation of which liability will be imposed. For example, in a Kansas case,[115] a lawyer-director, who was not a shareholder, negotiated the sale of all the corporation's stock at an attractive price, but exacted a three percent "finder's fee" for himself from the purchaser. In an action by minority shareholders, the lawyer-director was held liable to disgorge his "finder's fee" for violation of his fiduciary duty by accepting compensation from the purchaser without the express approval of his "principal," the minority shareholders.

It is not unusual, in today's complex business climate, for conflicts of interest to occur between such groups as controlling majority shareholders and public minority shareholders, the active promoters of a new business and the passive suppliers of its capital, incumbent management and shareholders who seek to replace such management, holders of different classes of stock, and different factions of shareholders each seeking to enhance its own position.

Such situations create difficulties for corporate counsel who has a natural tendency to be loyal to management and to consider management as his client. His failure to do so may affect his personal stake in the matter, yet his overriding concern for the corporate entity must remain uppermost if there are conflicts with its interests.

It is not always easy to define the entity's interest in contrast to that of directors, officers, employees, or groups or classes of shareholders. For securities lawyers the difficulty is increased because of the trend to impose upon them substantial liabilities and responsibilities to the investing public.[116]

In any area of intracorporate conflict a law firm acting as principal outside counsel for a corporation will be well ad-

---

115. Delano v. Kitch, 663 F.2d 990 (10th Cir. 1981), cert. denied, 456 U.S. 946 (1982).

116. See Marsh, "Relations with Management and Individual Financial Interests," 33 Bus. Law. (Special Issue) 1227 (1978).

vised to define and limit its role at the earliest sign of such conflict. In a real crisis, the different levels of the corporation may all need separate legal counsel. However, it would be irresponsible to recommend the employment of separate counsel unless the risk of conflict is both real and imminent.[117]

As complex corporate litigation has increased in scope and intensity a new advocate's tool has been created and developed: the motion to disqualify the adverse party's lawyers.[118] Among the claims asserted as grounds for disqualification of counsel are:

(1) because he or his firm formerly represented the party seeking disqualification with the risk that client confidences may be disclosed;[119]

(2) because of the current representation of differing or conflicting interests, thereby preventing the lawyer from exercising independent professional judgment;[120]

(3) because the lawyer or his firm has undertaken employment in a matter in which he had substantial

---

117. See Cutler, "The Role of the Private Law Firm," 33 Bus. Law. (Special Issue) 1549, 1556 (1978).

118. Ruder, "Disqualification of Counsel: Disclosures of Client Confidences, Conflicts of Interest, and Prior Government Service," 35 Bus. Law. 963 (1980).

119. See, e.g., Novo Terapeutisk Laboratorium v. Baxter Travenol Labs, Inc., 607 F.2d 186 (7th Cir. 1979) (en banc); Westinghouse Elec. Corp. v. Gulf Oil Corp., 588 F.2d 221 (7th Cir. 1978); Westinghouse Elec. Corp. v. Kerr-McGee Corp., 580 F.2d 1311 (7th Cir.), cert. denied, 439 U.S. 955, rev'd, 588 F.2d 221 (7th Cir. 1978); Schloetter v. Railoc of Indiana, Inc., 546 F.2d 706 (7th Cir. 1976); Laskey Bros. of W. Va., Inc. v. Warner Bros. Pictures, Inc., 224 F.2d 824 (2d Cir. 1955). See also Silver Chrysler Plymouth, Inc. v. Chrysler Motors Corp., 518 F.2d 751 (2d Cir. 1975). But cf. Unified Sewerage Agency of Washington County, Ore. v. Jelco, Inc., 646 F.2d 1339 (9th Cir. 1981).

120. See, e.g., International Bus. Mach. Corp. v. Levin, 579 F.2d 271 (3d Cir. 1978); cf. Westinghouse Elec. Corp. v. Gulf Oil Corp., supra note 119.

responsibility when he was a government employee.[121]

Such motions pose sensitive and difficult problems under the ABA Code of Professional Responsibility, and also raise the question whether such a procedure is the appropriate remedy to deal with the problem in the context of complex litigation, usually involving large multi-city law firms.[122]

The Second Circuit has adopted what it terms "a restrained approach," conceding that it will not "correct all possible ethical conflicts." However, the court believes that to invite the wholesale filing of motions for tactical reasons would result in "needless disruption and delay of litigation, thereby impairing the efficient administration of justice."[123]

Collateral to these principal questions but of major significance is the subject of the disqualification of an entire law firm once one member of the firm has been disqualified from representing a particular client in federal court. In these days of multi-state, multi-section and very large law firms, this question is arising with frequency.

The Northern District of Ohio has taken the position that without an affirmative showing of exchange of confidential information, an attorney in one section of a multi-section law firm (bond counsel section) will not automatically be presumed to have imparted confidential information to an attorney in another section (litigation) of the same firm.[124]

---

121. Armstrong v. McAlpin, 625 F.2d 433 (2d Cir. 1980) (en banc), cert. granted, judgment vacated and case remanded to Second Circuit with instructions that appeal be dismissed, 449 U.S. 1106 (1981). Board of Educ. of City of N.Y. v. Nyquist, 590 F.2d 1241 (2d Cir. 1979); Woods v. Covington County Bank, 537 F.2d 804 (5th Cir. 1976).

122. Westinghouse Elec. Corp. v. Rio Algom, Ltd., 448 F. Supp. 1284, 1287 (N.D. Ill.), aff'd in part and rev'd in part, 580 F.2d 1311 (7th Cir.), cert. denied, 439 U.S. 955, rev'd, 588 F.2d 221 (7th Cir. 1978).

123. Bottaro v. Hatton Assocs., 680 F.2d 895, 896 (2d Cir. 1982).

124. City of Cleveland v. Cleveland Elec. Illuminating Co., 440 F. Supp. 193 (N.D. Ohio 1976), aff'd without opinion, 573 F.2d 1310 (6th Cir. 1977), cert. denied, 435 U.S. 996 (1978); cf. General Elec. Co. v. Valeron Corp., 428 F. Supp. 68 (E.D. Mich. 1977).

It is necessary that each such case be analyzed in the light of its particular facts, but there are numerous decisions disqualifying an entire law firm where one member thereof was disqualified because of conflict of interest.[125]

§ 11.13. The attorney as an adviser to management.

The corporate manager has many advisers. Accountants, actuaries, compensation specialists, investment advisers, risk managers and others are available to assist him, but the corporate lawyer has a special place in this structure.

Although the duties and responsibilities of a corporate attorney are similar to those of attorneys representing individuals, a few distinctions deserve comment. First, the corporate attorney should realize that he serves two clients simultaneously: the corporate official or employee with whom he deals personally and his ultimate client, the corporation itself. Only rarely will the attorney have a conflict of interest as the duties to the client and the corporation usually coincide.

Second, it is sometimes appropriate for corporate counsel to concern himself with such business problems as may be intertwined with the corporation's purely legal affairs. As a general rule he should restrict his function to legal problems or at least express his opinion on business matters only when asked to do so. The corporate executive may seek the judgment, knowledge and expertise of the lawyer, but the executive has the responsibility for the overall operation and must assume the obligation of making policy decisions. When corporate counsel takes a position on the legality of corporate action, and feels strongly enough to be insistent, his views are likely to be accepted. However, counsel is not the keeper of the corporate conscience and should not pass upon the

---

125. See, e.g., International Bus. Mach. Corp. v. Levin, supra note 120; Cinema 5, Ltd. v. Cinerama, Inc., 528 F.2d 1384 (2d Cir. 1976); United States v. Kitchin, 592 F.2d 900 (5th Cir.), cert. denied, 444 U.S. 843 (1979); Schloetter v. Railoc of Indiana, Inc., supra note 119. See also Price v. Admiral Ins. Co., 481 F. Supp. 374 (E.D. Pa. 1979).

moral and ethical standards to be met by the corporation. Where the legal position is not certain, and a judgment as to risk must be made, the decision is for management, not counsel. If counsel's position on a legal matter is not accepted by management, he simply faces the same problems as any other lawyer whose client refuses to take his advice.

A significant part of the work of legal counsel in advising corporate management falls in the area of preventive advice to anticipate problems and recommend actions to prevent them from arising. The ability of a lawyer to provide such advice must come from (1) an intimate knowledge of the business with particular sensitivity to changes in policy and operating procedures, and (2) intimate knowledge of all changes in law and regulations which might possibly have an impact on the business.[126] Obviously, a close relationship between legal counsel and top management is essential for those purposes. That relationship involves a sort of interdependence, which marks an important difference between the lawyer as an adviser and the accountant as an auditor whose independence of his client is indispensable.

§ 11.14. The attorney as a director.

The topic of the lawyer as a director is not new. Lawyers serve as directors of many corporations of all sizes and types. In-house general counsel are frequently named directors and it is not unusual for a lawyer whose firm serves a corporation as its principal outside counsel to sit on the board. That problems may arise from such an arrangement is all too true.

It is likely that the lawyer-director whose firm serves as counsel for the corporation will be identified as a management director rather than as an outside director.[127] Moreover, his regular participation in a business atmosphere involving nonlegal considerations may cause his fellow directors to be

---

126. Rast, "What the Chief Executive Looks for in his Corporate Law Department," 33 Bus. Law. 811, 814 (1978).

127. See, e.g., Feit v. Leasco Data Processing Equip. Corp., 332 F. Supp. 544, 575-76 (E.D.N.Y. 1971).

less responsive to his legal advice, when the occasion for a strong position occurs.[128] As a director, the lawyer is charged with adherence to the standards of obedience, diligence and loyalty that are the three basic duties of the corporate director.

Professor David S. Ruder declares that the fiduciary duty of a director has particular significance when that director is also a lawyer. He observes:

> Certainly the lawyer is aware of familiar principles preventing him from seizing corporate opportunities, competing with his corporation, dealing with the corporation on advantageous terms, selling his corporate office, transferring control of the corporation without adequate investigation and otherwise engaging in practices which enrich himself at the corporation's expense. In view of the fiduciary relationship owed by the lawyer-director, the fees charged by his firm to the corporation should be carefully scrutinized for fairness.... Even the selection of the lawyer-director's [law] firm to perform services for the corporation may be subject to challenge.[129]

In the light of the special expertise, experience and knowledge of the lawyer-director, it is to be expected that the standard of care to be imposed upon him would be "such care as the ordinarily prudent lawyer-director would use under similar circumstances in a like position."[130]

Among the more important complications that a lawyer faces when he puts on the second hat of a corporate director are (1) the difficulty of identifying his corporate client; (2) the decision whether to be an "inside" or "outside" director and the resulting effect on his individual legal liability; (3) problems relating to responses by his law firm or by him to auditors' requests for information; (4) his compounded liability under the securities laws; (5) the loss of his independence; (6)

---

128. See Ruder, Panel Discussion, "The Case Against the Lawyer-Director," 30 Bus. Law. (Special Issue) 51, 52 (1975).

129. Id. at 54.

130. Id. at 58. See also Harris, "The Case For the Lawyer-Director," 30 Bus. Law. (Special Issue) 58 (1975).

the probable loss of his attorney-client privilege; (7) his status as a deputy for his law firm; (8) significant conflicts of interest; and (9) questions of liability insurance coverage for the multiple risks he undertakes.[131]

In its active pursuit of liability claims resulting from bank failures, The Federal Deposit Insurance Corporation has studied whether lawyer-directors can be sued as legal advisers, as well as directors, and whether the culpability of such an individual can be extended to his law firm.[132]

§ 11.15. The attorney's role in disclosure.

When the SEC filed its complaint in the *National Student Marketing* case[133] it gave clear notice that it intended to hold lawyers who represent clients in securities transactions to standards of conduct which would reflect and protect the interests of the investing public.[134]

The chief accountant of the Securities and Exchange Commission pointed out that the Commission seeks "to focus its enforcement efforts at key points where maximum impact can be achieved." To this end, he observed:

[E]nforcement efforts involving professionals, such as accountants and lawyers, have been important even though the numbers of cases in which professionals were involved has not been great. The reasoning of the Commission is simple: these professionals are an essential element in providing access to the market place, since the sale of securities cannot take place without their involvement. Professional responsibility at these points of access can prevent many questionable activities before they occur.[135]

---

131. See Knepper, "Liability of Lawyer-Directors," 40 Ohio St. L.J. 341 (1979).

132. Graham, "Lawyers' Liability Eyed in Failed Bank Scenario," Vol. VI, No. 1 Legal Times of Washington 1, June 6, 1983.

133. SEC v. National Student Mktg. Corp., Fed. Sec. L. Rep. (CCH) ¶93,360 (D.D.C. 1972).

134. Cheek, "Professional Responsibility and Self-Regulation of the Securities Lawyers," 32 Wash. & Lee L. Rev. 597 (1975).

135. Burton, "SEC Enforcement and Professional Accountants: Philosophy, Objectives and Approach," 28 Vand. L. Rev. 19 (1975).

In this light it has been held that lawyers may have participating liability[136] in the securities process as "experts" and "underwriters"[137] as being liable for aiding and abetting a transaction unless they prevent misstatements.[138] Although it has been argued that *Ernst & Ernst v. Hochfelder*[139] destroys or delimits such liability, the Second Circuit has stated:

> We do not believe the Supreme Court intended that those who play an indispensable role in the sale ... should not be subject to SEC initiated, injunctive restraint.[140]

As a general rule an attorney will not be held liable for failing to disclose information unless the circumstances impart a duty to disclose.[141] No such duty arises from the mere possession of information.[142]

In California it was contended that in certain circumstances "securities lawyers must act as 'independent public attorneys' whose standard of conduct must reflect and protect the interest of the investing public."[143]

The court noted that the lawyer in question was not a securities lawyer and then stated:

> [T]o apply plaintiff's proposition under the facts of this case would create a duty of disclosure for attorneys that is far broader than that proposed in the draft of the

---

136. Black & Co. v. Nova-Tech. Inc., 333 F. Supp. 468 (D. Or. 1971).

137. Andrews v. Blue, 489 F.2d 367 (10th Cir. 1973).

138. E.g., SEC v. Spectrum, Inc., 489 F.2d 535, 541 (2d Cir. 1973); SEC v. Universal Major Indus. Corp., 546 F.2d 1044, 1046 (2d Cir. 1976). See also SEC v. National Student Mktg. Corp., Fed. Sec. L. Rep. (CCH) ¶96,540 (D.D.C. 1978).

139. 425 U.S. 185, 47 L.Ed.2d 668, 96 S.Ct. 1375, reh'g denied, 425 U.S. 985 (1976).

140. SEC v. Universal Major Indus. Corp., supra note 138, at 1046.

141. Barker v. Henderson, Franklin, Starnes & Holt, 797 F.2d 490, 495 (7th Cir. 1986); Von Boeckel v. Weiss, Fed. Sec. L. Rep. (CCH) ¶99,648 at 97,589 (N.D. Cal. 1983).

142. Barker v. Henderson, Franklin, Starnes & Holt, supra note 141, citing Chiarella v. United States, 445 U.S. 222, 236, 63 L.Ed.2d 348, 100 S.Ct. 1108 (1980).

143. Von Boeckel v. Weiss, supra note 141, at 97, 590.

Model Rules of Professional Conduct and rejected by the organized bar. This court is not disposed to [impose] such a rule on the profession.[144]

Chiarella v. United States held that "[w]hen an allegation of fraud is based on nondisclosure, there can be no fraud absent a duty to speak."[145] The opinion, delivered by Justice Powell, went further to state that such a duty to speak arises when one party has information "that the other [party] is entitled to know because of a fiduciary or other similar relation of trust and confidence between them."[146] It is necessary to identify a relationship between the parties that gives rise to a duty to speak before liability may be imposed for nondisclosure. Inferentially, it follows that unless a claimant first proves that he had placed trust and confidence in an attorney, the latter will not be held liable to the claimant for nondisclosure.[147]

The uniformly accepted duties of lawyers under the securities laws focus on opinion letters and the preparation of prospectuses. However, recent case law demonstrates some tendency toward imposing liability upon lawyers, as aiders and abettors of a client's fraud, where they knowingly provide substantial assistance.[148] In this area the term "substantial assistance" is controversial.

---

144. Id.

145. 445 U.S. 222, 63 L.Ed.2d 348, 110 S.Ct. 1108 (1980).

146. Id. at 228, citing Restatement (Second) of Torts § 551(2)(a) (1976) and referring to James and Gray, "Misrepresentation," 37 Md. L. Rev. 488, 523-527 (1978).

147. But cf. SEC v. Coffey, 493 F.2d 1304, 1315 n.24 (6th Cir. 1974), cert. denied, 420 U.S. 908 (1975).

148. See, e.g., SEC v. National Student Mktg. Corp., 457 F. Supp. 682 (D.D.C. 1978); but cf. Wachovia Bank & Trust Co. v. National Student Mktg. Corp., 650 F.2d 342 (D.C. Cir. 1980); Kidwell ex rel. Penfold v. Meikle, 597 F.2d 1273 (9th Cir. 1979); Felts v. National Account Sys. Ass'n, 469 F. Supp. 54 (N.D. Miss. 1978); SEC v. Century Mtg. Co., Fed. Sec. L. Rep. (CCH) ¶96,777 (D. Utah 1979); SEC v. Coven, 581 F.2d 1020 (2d Cir. 1978), cert. denied, 440 U.S. 950 (1979).

§ 11.16. Attorneys' responses to auditors' inquiries.

Although the American Bar Association (ABA) and the American Institute of Certified Public Accountants (AICPA) reached an agreement in 1976 as to responses by attorneys to audit letters, some hard issues were not faced by the compromise and others were not resolved. Both disclosure and privilege are relevant to such responses.

When independent certified public accountants audit corporate financial statements prepared by management, they are required to undertake an independent investigation to verify the information provided by management.

> Sufficient competent evidential matter is to be obtained through inspection, observation, inquiries and confirmations to affirm a reasonable basis for an opinion regarding the financial statements under examination.[149]

In addition, the Financial Accounting Standards Board (FASB), in its Statements of Accounting Standards has stated some rules intended to guide such investigations.

One of the conflicts between attorneys and auditors has always related to the disclosure of "loss contingencies" arising from pending or threatened litigation and from unasserted possible claims. The statements issued by ABA and AICPA in their settlement differ as to the treatment of those subjects and the attorney's professional responsibility to advise his client concerning the disclosure of such loss contingencies.[150] The SEC has pressed for full disclosure of "contingent liabilities," which is the term it uses instead of "loss contingencies."[151] However, the SEC has not furnished specific guidelines for such disclosure, although it has sub-

---

149. Herzfeld v. Laventhol, Krekstein, Horwath & Horwath, 540 F.2d 27, 35 (2d Cir. 1976).

150. "Attorney Responses to Audit Letters: The Problem of Disclosing Loss Contingencies Arising from Litigation and Unasserted Claims," 51 N.Y.U. L. Rev. 838, 873-84 (1976), reprinted in 1977 Securities L. Rev. 755, 790-801.

151. See SEC Securities Act Release No. 5386, Fed. Sec. L. Rep. (CCH) ¶79,342 at 83,030 (Apr. 20, 1973).

stantial powers to penalize for inadequate audits and to influence auditing procedures.[152]

In responding to auditors' inquiries, attorneys may violate the confidences of their clients in analyzing the merits of pending or threatened litigation and the nature and extent of a client's probable liability. Moreover, disclosure of unasserted possible claims may trigger the assertion of such claims with resulting increased legal expenses.

The confidentiality of the attorney-client relationship may also be invaded by the audit letter and the attorney's response. Accountants are entitled to a privilege with respect to client-accountant disclosures in less than half of the states,[153] and such a privilege is not recognized by federal rules of evidence and practice.[154] Consequently, a corporate lawyer (in-house or outside) must be aware that upon disclosure of a privileged matter to auditors, the privilege may, as a practical matter, be lost.[155]

§ 11.17. Private actions against broker-dealers.

A broker-dealer is a person or firm regularly engaged in the purchase or sale of securities to the general public. The "broker" aspect of this business consists of buying or selling securities for the account of another for a commission; the "dealer" aspect consists of trading for one's own account or making a market in a particular security. Both aspects are usually combined in the same firm, although the persons operating it are commonly called stock "brokers."

An SEC Special Study points out that many firms perform two or more of the broker-dealer, investment banker, underwriter, marketmaker, investment adviser and investment manager functions. Because each such function involves its

---

152. E.g., see SEC Accounting Series Release No. 153, Fed. Sec. L. Rep. (CCH) ¶72,175 (Feb. 25, 1974).

153. See Katsoris, "Confidential Communications — The Accountants' Dilemma," 35 Fordham L. Rev. 51, 55-64 (1966).

154. Baylor v. Mading-Dugan Drug Co., 57 F.R.D. 509 (N.D. Ill. 1972).

155. Driver, "The Inside General Counsel's Response to Auditors' Inquiries," 30 Bus. Law. (Special Issue) 217, 219 (1975).

own set of obligations to particular persons or groups, and because the self-interest of the broker-dealer may be involved in any or all such functions, "there are multifarious possibilities of conflict of obligation or interest in matters large and small."[156]

Most state Blue Sky laws require the licensing of broker-dealers as to their intrastate activities. The Securities Exchange Act of 1934[157] and the Maloney Act of 1938[158] require licensing or "registration" as to interstate activities. The federal regulation is the more significant since it regulates nearly every transaction affecting interstate commerce. Few broker-dealers find it expedient to limit their activities to purely intrastate sales with the result that nearly all are regulated by the federal law.

A broker-dealer is commonly a member of one of the major stock exchanges. These exchanges subject him to further regulation under a set of rules with which he must comply. The counterpart of the exchanges as to over-the-counter trading is the National Association of Security Dealers (NASD). It too has a set of rules with which the broker-dealer must comply.[159] The SEC is empowered to regulate broker-dealers in over-the-counter transactions as well as those conducted through an exchange.[160]

There is some authority that the violation by a broker-dealer of a securities statute or SEC rule promulgated thereunder may be the basis for a private civil action.[161] Additionally, there are still-developing actions at common law which may be available. Such actions may include those for negligence,[162] rescission,[163] breach of warranty of fitness for a par-

---

156. SEC, Special Study of Securities Markets, H.R. Doc. No. 95, 88th Cong., 1st Sess., pt. 5, at 65-66 (1963).

157. 15 U.S.C. § 78 et seq.

158. Id. § 78o-3 as amended 1975.

159. NASD Manual (CCH) ¶¶2151-2178.

160. 15 U.S.C. § 78o(b)(7).

161. See infra section 11.19.

162. Merrill Lynch, Pierce, Fenner & Smith, Inc. v. Bocock, 247 F. Supp. 373 (S.D. Tex. 1965); Mercury Inv. Co. v. A.G. Edwards & Sons, 295 F. Supp. 1160 (S.D. Tex. 1969).

163. 3 Loss, Securities Regulation 1626, 1627 (2d ed. 1988).

ticular purpose,[164] breach of a fiduciary obligation in failing to act in the customer's interest,[165] or common-law deceit.[166] However, the broad venue and service provisions of the securities acts and the increasingly liberal interpretations of those acts by the federal courts seem to offer more promising avenues of success against broker-dealers.[167]

In a series of actions against a broker-dealer in the Southern District of New York,[168] the plaintiffs asserted two claims of fraud: one was based on nondisclosure of inside information which deprived plaintiffs of as favorable a selling opportunity as was available to those who traded on inside information tipped to them, and the other was based on misrepresentations of fact by the broker-dealer and its representatives which caused plaintiffs to purchase certain shares or to continue to hold such shares already owned.

District Judge Inzer B. Wyatt, in two 1971 decisions, epitomized the first of those claims to mean that "defendant tipped off certain favored customers about poor Douglas earnings; the favored customers were able to sell their Douglas shares at higher prices because the public did not have the inside information of poor Douglas earnings; and plaintiff, not having been favored, lost the opportunity to sell on the basis of

---

164. Mundheim, "Professional Responsibilities of Broker-Dealers: The Suitability Doctrine," 1965 Duke L.J. 445.

165. Twomey v. Mitchum, Jones & Templeton, Inc., 262 Cal. App. 2d 690, 69 Cal. Rptr. 222 (1968).

166. Loss, supra note 163, at 1628.

167. See J.I. Case Co. v. Borak, 377 U.S. 426, 12 L.Ed.2d 423, 84 S.Ct. 1555 (1964). See also Colonial Realty Corp. v. Bache & Co., 358 F.2d 178 (2d Cir.), cert. denied, 385 U.S. 817 (1966).

168. Hirsh v. Merrill Lynch, Pierce, Fenner & Smith, Inc., 311 F. Supp. 1283 (S.D.N.Y. 1970); Baehr v. Merrill Lynch, Pierce, Fenner & Smith, Inc., Fed. Sec. L. Rep. (CCH) ¶93,227 (S.D.N.Y. 1970); Sanders v. Merrill Lynch, Pierce, Fenner & Smith, Inc., Fed. Sec. L. Rep. (CCH) ¶93,226 (S.D.N.Y. 1970); Smachlo v. Merrill Lynch, Pierce, Fenner & Smith, Inc., Fed. Sec. L. Rep. (CCH) ¶93,148 (S.D.N.Y. 1971); Shulof v. Merrill Lynch, Pierce, Fenner & Smith, Inc., Fed. Sec. L. Rep. (CCH) ¶93,147 (S.D.N.Y. 1971).

the inside information."[169] As to the second claim, Judge Wyatt pointed out that the plaintiffs had "requested advice about whether to sell or hold their Douglas shares and were told by an employee of defendant that they should hold them on account of good earning prospects for Douglas, even though defendant had information, not then public, that the prospects were poor."[170]

The first claim was rejected as related to the situation described in *Levine v. Seilon, Inc.*[171] claiming "compensation for the premium [they] might have extracted from some innocent victim if [they] had known of the fraud and the buyer did not." The second claim was rejected because the plaintiffs did not allege reliance on defendant's misrepresentation.[172]

Following the land-mark decision of the SEC in *In re Cady, Roberts and Company*,[173] and the increasing recognition of problems under SEC Rule 10b-5, which it inspired, the activities of broker-dealers have undergone close scrutiny by the courts and by regulatory authorities.

§ 11.18. Broker-dealer who is also a director.

Complex problems are presented when litigation results from transactions in which a corporation director is also a partner in a broker-dealer firm. In this situation the fiduciary obligation of such person as a director to keep inside information confidential, does not relieve him of his concomitant fiduciary obligation to his customer in making recommendations concerning his corporation's securities.[174] In

---

169. Shulof v. Merrill Lynch, Pierce, Fenner & Smith, Inc., supra note 168, at 91,134.

170. Smachlo v. Merrill Lynch, Pierce, Fenner & Smith, Inc., supra note 168, at 91,137.

171. 439 F.2d 328 (2d Cir. 1971).

172. See List v. Fashion Park, Inc., 340 F.2d 457, 462, 463 (2d Cir.), cert. denied sub nom. List v. Lerner, 382 U.S. 811, reh'g denied, 382 U.S. 933 (1965).

173. 40 SEC 907 (1961).

174. Black v. Shearson, Hammill & Co., 266 Cal. App. 2d 362, 72 Cal. Rptr. 157 (1968).

other words, a person may not escape from one fiduciary obligation by accepting another fiduciary obligation that conflicts with it.

Like other broker-dealers, a broker-dealer who is also a corporate director may be liable for the violation of securities statutes and rules as well as the rules of the stock exchanges and of the National Association of Securities Dealers.[175] Like any other director, a broker-dealer-director warrants that statements in a prospectus signed by him are accurate.[176]

The president and principal shareholder of a registered broker-dealer also served as a director and principal officer of a manufacturing company. He was convicted of fraud in the sale of the manufacturing company's securities when he failed to disclose its deteriorating financial condition and his own inside relationship to it.[177]

The disclosure requirements and restrictions on the use of inside information have particular significance as to such persons. In *Cady, Roberts*,[178] the SEC censured a brokerage firm for trading on inside information obtained from a corporate director. The director had notified the broker of a dividend decrease just voted by the directors of the corporation and not yet known publicly. The broker then sold shares for discretionary accounts before the news was disclosed on the Dow Jones broad tape. The broker's conduct was treated as an abuse of exchange trading.

When a partner in a broker-dealer firm is also a corporate director, his exposure for passing on inside information to his firm is serious. Where his firm is acting in any respect as an investment analyst, the conflict of interest may ripen into

---

175. E.g., Buttrey v. Merrill Lynch, Pierce, Fenner & Smith, Inc., 410 F.2d 135 (7th Cir.), cert. denied, 396 U.S. 838 (1969); Avern Trust v. Clarke, 415 F.2d 1238 (7th Cir. 1969), cert. denied, 397 U.S. 963 (1970). See also South Side Bank & Trust Co. v. Walston & Co., 425 F.2d 40 (7th Cir. 1970).

176. Gould v. Tricon, Inc., 272 F. Supp. 385, 392 (S.D.N.Y. 1967).

177. United States v. Benson, 487 F.2d 978 (3d Cir. 1973).

178. In re Cady, Roberts & Co., 40 SEC 907 (1961).

strict liability if trading results without public disclosure of the inside information.[179]

In the over-the-counter markets, broker-dealers have been held to a standard that approaches a duty to investigate. The Second Circuit takes the position that a broker-dealer, because of his title and position, implicitly represents that he has an adequate and reasonable basis for his recommendations of such securities.[180] The central role of the broker-dealer in the securities process is one factor in that court's imposition upon him of a duty of inquiry.[181]

§ 11.19. Actions based on NYSE or NASD rules.

There is a division of authority as to whether private causes of action exist against broker-dealers under the federal securities laws, for violation of the New York Stock Exchange "know your customer" rule[182] and the "suitability" rule of the National Association of Securities Dealers.[183]

Since the decision of the Supreme Court in *Touche Ross & Company v. Redington*[184] and *Transamerica Mortgage Advisers, Incorporated v. Lewis*,[185] the decisions of the lower courts have reflected a restrictive approach to implying such private rights of action. Thus the Ninth Circuit has noted that neither Section 6(b)[186] nor Section 27[187] of the Exchange Act may provide a foundation for such actions.[188] And in the Southern District of New York the court applied the four

---

179. See also In re Invs. Mgt. Co., Fed. Sec. L. Rep. (CCH) ¶77,832 (1970).

180. Hanly v. SEC, 415 F.2d 589, 597 (2d Cir. 1969); see also "Distribution by Broker-Dealers of Unregistered Securities," SEC Securities Act Release No. 4445, at 3 (Feb. 2, 1962).

181. E.g., Levine v. SEC, 436 F.2d 88, 90, 91 (2d Cir. 1971).

182. Rule 405, New York Stock Exchange.

183. Sec. 2, Art. III, Rules of Fair Practice, NASD.

184. 442 U.S. 560, 61 L.Ed.2d 82, 99 S.Ct. 2479 (1979).

185. 444 U.S. 11, 62 L.Ed.2d 146, 100 S.Ct. 242 (1979).

186. 15 U.S.C. § 78f(b).

187. Id. § 78aa.

188. Jablon v. Dean Witter & Co., 614 F.2d 677, 686-81 (9th Cir. 1980).

factor test of *Cort v. Ash*[189] in reaching the same conclusion.[190]

In the Eighth Circuit a district court decision in Missouri has ruled that for violation of such rules to be actionable they must operate as a fraud upon the plaintiff and there must be proof that the defendant acted with scienter.[191]

§ 11.20. Arbitration of antifraud disputes.

Since at least 1953 the law has been considered settled that claims under the federal securities acts were not arbitrable and that the jurisdiction of the federal courts to hear such claims could not be waived.[192] However, the Supreme Court's decision in *Shearson/American Express, Inc. v. McMahon*[193] changed all that, although four justices dissented on this point.

After the Court's decision in *Wilko v. Swan*,[194] which related to the Securities Act of 1933, each of the eight circuits that addressed the issue concluded that holding of *Wilko* was fully applicable to claims arising under the Securities Exchange Act of 1934.[195] Only after Justice White's concurrence

---

189. 422 U.S. 66, 45 L.Ed.2d 26, 95 S.Ct. 2080 (1975).

190. Jaksich v. Thomson McKinnon Sec., Inc., 582 F. Supp. 485, 499-501 (S.D.N.Y. 1984). See also Zemaitis v. Merrill Lynch, Pierce, Fenner & Smith, 583 F. Supp. 1552, 1553 (W.D.N.Y. 1984) and Klock v. Lehmann Bros. Kuhn Loeb, Inc., 584 F. Supp. 210, 216-18 (S.D.N.Y. 1984). Cf. Thompson v. Smith Barney, Harris & Upham, 539 F. Supp. 859, 864-65 (N.D. Ga. 1982), aff'd, 709 F.2d 1413, 1419 (11th Cir. 1983).

191. Smith v. Smith Barney, Harris & Upham, 505 F. Supp. 1380, 1384-86 (W.D. Mo. 1981), citing among other authorities Buttrey v. Merrill Lynch, Pierce, Fenner & Smith, Inc., 410 F.2d 135 (7th Cir.), cert. denied, 396 U.S. 838 (1969).

192. See, e.g., Zemaitis v. Merrill Lynch, Pierce, Fenner & Smith, supra note 190, at 1554.

193. 482 U.S. —, 96 L.Ed.2d 185, 107 S.Ct. 107, Fed. Sec. L. Rep. (CCH) ¶93,265 (1987).

194. 346 U.S. 427, 98 L.Ed. 168, 74 S.Ct. 182 (1953).

195. Shearson/American Express, Inc. v. McMahon, supra note 193, dissenting opinion of Justice Blackmun, 96 L.Ed.2d 207 at n.6.

in *Dean Reynolds, Incorporated v. Byrd,*[196] about doubting *Wilko's* inapplicability to the 1934 Act, two circuits held it to be inapplicable.[197] Certiorari was granted in *McMahon* to resolve the conflict among the circuits.

Justice O'Connor, delivering the Court's opinion, recognized "the mistrust of arbitration that formed the basis for the *Wilko* opinion in 1954," and found it difficult to square with the favorable assessment of arbitration "that has prevailed" since that time. Although Justice Blackmun cited the enactment of both securities acts "to protect investors from predatory behavior of securities industry personnel," Justice O'Connor rejected the contention that arbitration would "weaken [the McMahons'] ability to recover under the [Exchange] Act," going so far as to note that "most of the reasons given in *Wilko* have been rejected subsequently by the Court as a basis for holding claims to be nonarbitrable."

Accordingly, claims under Section 10(b) and other provisions of the 1934 Act are subject to arbitration under the Federal Arbitration Act.[198]

§ 11.21. Tipping by broker-dealers.

In *Shapiro v. Merrill Lynch, Pierce, Fenner and Smith, Incorporated,*[199] the broker-dealer learned of the McDonnell Douglas (Douglas Aircraft) changed earnings position (which had not been publicly disclosed) and divulged this information to certain institutional investors who sold their Douglas common stock without disclosing the inside information to the public. In the district court, Judge Charles H. Tenney wrote:

> Had Merrill Lynch and the individual defendants refrained from divulging the earnings information to the selling defendants, or had the selling defendants decided

---

196. 470 U.S. 213, 224, 84 L.Ed.2d 158, 167-68, 105 S.Ct. 1238 (1985).

197. Shearson/American Express, Inc. v. McMahon, supra note 193, dissenting opinion of Justice Stevens, 96 L.Ed.2d 220 at n.1.

198. 9 U.S.C. §§ 1-4.

199. 353 F. Supp. 264 (S.D.N.Y. 1972), aff'd, 495 F.2d 228 (2d Cir. 1974).

not to trade, there would have been no liability for plaintiffs' injury due to the eventual public disclosure of Douglas' poor financial position.... [B]y trading in Douglas stock on a national securities exchange they assumed the duty to disclose the information to all potential buyers. It is the breach of this duty that gives rise to defendants' liability.[200]

Among the tippees who sold the Douglas stock were four unregistered investment advisors. One of them, Investors Management Company, was the subject of an action by the SEC,[201] which is a landmark in the area of the liability of "tippees," and even "remote tippees," who made sales and short sales on the basis of the tipped information. While the result was merely censure of the respondents, the impact of the decision has been substantial.

When Douglas told its broker-dealer's vice-president of substantially reduced earnings and profit estimates, he informed the broker-dealer's employees and decision-making personnel who then made sales and short sales in obvious reliance thereon. The SEC's view was that such actions "came within the ambit and were violative of the antifraud prohibitions of the securities laws." The "requisite elements for the imposition of responsibility" found to be present were that:

(1) The information was material and nonpublic;
(2) The tippee knew or had reason to know that the information was nonpublic and had been obtained improperly by selective revelation, or otherwise; and
(3) The information was a factor in the tippee's decision to trade.

The SEC decision rejected the contentions of the respondents that no violation could be found without a showing that

---

200. Id., 353 F. Supp. at 278. But compare the Sixth Circuit's view in Fridrich v. Bradford, 542 F.2d 307, 318 (6th Cir. 1976), cert. denied, 429 U.S. 1053 (1977).

201. In the Matter of Invs. Mgt. Co., Fed. Sec. L. Rep. (CCH) ¶78,163 (1971); Securities Exch. Act Rel. No. 9267 (1971); Investors Advisors Act Release No. 289 (July 29, 1971). Cf. Shulof v. Merrill Lynch, Pierce, Fenner & Smith, Inc., Fed. Sec. L. Rep. (CCH) ¶93,147 (S.D.N.Y. 1971).

the recipient of the tip occupied a special relationship with the insider corporate source, giving him access to nonpublic information, or that he knew the information was disclosed in breach of a fiduciary duty not to reveal it.

Establishment of a tipper-tippee relationship may expose the broker-dealer to additional liability for damages to the tippee. Such was the basis of an important Supreme Court decision which held that the participation of the tippee in the wrongdoing was no defense to his action.[202]

The case was decided on a motion to dismiss the investor's complaint which alleged that Lazzaro, a representative of the broker-dealer, and Neadeau, president of an oil and gas exploration company, had conspired to manipulate the market value of the company's stock for their financial benefit. In the course of the scheme, Lazzaro "tipped" false information to the investor, which Neadeau refused to verify, on the ground that it was "not public knowledge." However, he insisted that Lazzaro was "very trustworthy and a good man." The investor lost substantial sums when the market price of the stock fell below $1.00 per share.[203]

In sustaining the investor's position, the Supreme Court held that such a claim could be barred by the plaintiff's own culpability only where (1) as a direct result of his own actions the plaintiff was at least substantially equally responsible for the violations of law, and (2) preclusion of the suit would not significantly interfere with the effective enforcement of the securities laws and protection of the investing public.[204] Even in a situation where an investor is not free from blame, such a private damage action serves not only to compensate the injured investor, but also to deter fraud and manipulation by exposing those considering unlawful conduct to the threat of private damage liability.

---

202. Bateman Eichler, Hill Richards, Inc. v. Berner, 472 U.S. 299, 86 L.Ed.2d 215, 105 S.Ct. 2622 (1985).

203. See Berner v. Lazzaro, 730 F.2d 1319, 1320 (9th Cir. 1984).

204. 472 U.S. at 310-11.

COROLLARY REFERENCES

Briloff, "The Corporate Governance and Accountability Malaise: An Accountant's Perspective," 9 J. Corp. L. 473 (1984).

Brodsky & Swanson, "The Expanded Liability of Accountants for Negligence," 12 Sec. Reg. L.J. 252 (1984).

Fleischer, Mundheim & Murphy, "An Initial Inquiry Into the Responsibility to Disclose Market Information," 121 U. Pa. L. Rev. 798 (1973), reprinted and updated in 1973 Sec. L. Rev. 3.

Glickman, "'Tippee' Liability Under Section 10(b) and Rule 10b-5 of the Securities Exchange Act of 1934," 20 Kan. L. Rev. 47 (1971).

Gruenbaum & Steinberg, "Accountants' Liability and Responsibility: Securities, Criminal and Common Law," 13 Loyola U.L. Rev. (L.A.) 247 (1980).

Hooker, "Lawyers' Responses to Audit Inquiries and the Attorney-Client Privilege," 35 Bus. Law. 1021 (1980).

Isbell, "An Overview of Accountants' Duties and Liabilities Under the Federal Securities Laws and a Closer Look at Whistle-Blowing," 35 Ohio St. L.J. 261 (1974).

Isbell, "The Continental Vending Case: Lessons for the Profession," 130 Journal of Accountancy 33 (August, 1970).

Kinsey, "Communications Among Attorneys, Management and Auditors," 36 Bus. Law. 727 (1981).

Kirk, "Corporate Accounting and Accountability in Turbulent Times," 9 J. Corp. L. 559 (1984).

Knepper, "Liability of Lawyer-Directors," 40 Ohio St. L.J. 341 (1979).

Leibensperger, "The Erosion of Ultramares: Expansion of Accountants' Liability to Third Parties for Negligence," 69 Mass. L. Rev. 54 (1984).

Lewis, "The Availability of the Attorney-Client and Work-Product Privileges in Shareholder Litigation," 32 Clev. St. L. Rev. 189 (1984).

"Liability of Attorneys for Legal Opinions Under the Federal Securities Laws," 27 B.C. L. Rev. 325 (1986).

Lipton and Mazur, "The Chinese Wall Solution to the Conflict Problems of Securities Firms," 50 N.Y.U. L. Rev. 459 (1975), reprinted in 1976 Sec. L. Rev. 565.

Lowenfels, "Implied Liabilities Based upon Stock Exchange Rules," 66 Colum. L. Rev. 12 (1966).

Marsh, "Rule 2(e) Proceedings," 35 Bus. Law. 987 (1980).

Rediker, "Civil Liability of Broker-Dealers Under SEC and NASD Suitability Rules," 22 Ala. L. Rev. 15 (1969).

Rogoff, "Legal Regulation of Over-The-Counter Market Manipulation: Critique and Proposal," 28 Maine L. Rev. 149 (1976), reprinted in 1977 Sec. L. Rev. 123.

Vernava & Hepp, "Responsibility of the Accountant Under the Federal Securities Exchange Act of 1934," 6 J. Corp. L. 317 (1981).

Walker, "Accountants' Liability — The Scienter Standard Under Section 10(b) and Rule 10b-5 of the Securities Exchange Act of 1934," 63 Marq. L. Rev. 243 (1979).

Whitney, "Rule 10b-6: The Special Study's Rediscovered Rule," 62 Mich. L. Rev. 567 (1964).

Wiener, "Common Law Liability of the Certified Public Accountant for Negligent Misrepresentation," 20 San Diego L. Rev. 233 (1983).

Note, "Globus: A Prolific Generator of Nice Questions," 33 Ohio St. L.J. 898 (1972).

Note, "SEC Disciplinary Hearings — Touche Ross v. SEC — Rule 2(e) Validated in First Public Proceeding: Uncertainty Ahead for Securities Practitioners," 5 J. Corp. L. 433 (1980).

Chapter 12

FINANCIAL INSTITUTIONS AND THEIR MANAGEMENT

§ 12.01. Duties of directors and officers, generally.

In general, directors and officers of financial institutions have the same duties and owe the same fiduciary obligations as do persons holding similar positions in other types of corporations. To some extent there is a trend to hold directors of financial institutions more strictly than those of business corporations.[1] Thus in a 1981 New Jersey case the court noted a "distinguishing circumstance" in that depositors or beneficiaries of banks or other corporations holding trust funds "can reasonably expect the director to act with ordinary prudence concerning the funds held in a fiduciary capacity."[2] In that case the court equated a reinsurance broker with a bank and

---

1. See, e.g., recital of bank directors' responsibilities, infra section 12.03, text at note 32.

2. Francis v. United Jersey Bank, 87 N.J. 15, 37, 432 A.2d 814, 825 (1981).

found that the trust and confidence inherent in the reinsurance business required a degree of care commensurate with that of banking.[3]

The general rule is that directors and officers of a bank owe it the utmost good faith in the performance of their duties; they are required to discharge those duties with that degree of care which reasonably attaches to such official positions.[4] Directors and officers of savings and loan associations[5] and life insurance companies[6] undertake similar responsibilities. All such directors and officers owe to their corporations the three basic duties: obedience, diligence and loyalty.[7] These obligations are owed to the financial institution itself, to its stockholders as individuals[8] and in some cases to its depositors and creditors.

§ 12.02. Statutory liability.

Directors of financial institutions have duties imposed by statute as well as those imposed by common law. These statutes furnish the exclusive rules for determining whether their provisions have been violated, but this does not prevent application of common-law rules to measure violations of common-law duties.[9] Knowledge of the law is charged to directors of financial institutions and they are held responsible for knowing what they ought to know.[10]

---

3. See also Litwin v. Allen, 25 N.Y.S.2d 667 (S.Ct. 1940); Broderick v. Marcus, 152 Misc. 413, 418, 272 N.Y.S. 455, 461 (1934); Medford Trust Co. v. McKnight, 292 Mass. 1, 197 N.E. 649 (1935).

4. Briggs v. Spaulding, 141 U.S. 132, 35 L.Ed. 662, 11 S.Ct. 924 (1891).

5. Prairie State Bldg. & Loan Ass'n v. Nubling, 170 Ill. 240, 48 N.E. 1016 (1897).

6. See, generally, Hershman, "Liabilities and Responsibilities of Corporate Officers and Directors," 33 Bus. Law. 263, 268-74 (1977).

7. See First State Bank of Temple v. Metropolitan Cas. Ins. Co. of N.Y., 125 Tex. 113, 79 S.W.2d 835 (1935).

8. Peoples Sav. Bank v. Stoddard, 359 Mich. 297, 102 N.W.2d 777 (1960).

9. Bowerman v. Hamner, 250 U.S. 504, 63 L.Ed. 1113, 39 S.Ct. 549 (1919). See supra section 12.01.

10. E.g., Yates v. Jones Nat'l Bank, 206 U.S. 158, 168, 51 L.Ed. 1002, 27 S.Ct. 638 (1907).

Bank directors may be held liable for losses resulting from their willful and knowing violation of the National Bank Act, Section 93(a),[11] and the Federal Reserve Act, Section 22(f).[12] This use of "willful and knowing" is something less than a strict scienter standard but, in this context, it is more than negligence. For example, a director will be held liable for damages under Section 93(a) if he knew or should have known that a loan which he approved exceeded the bank's statutory lending limit.[13]

Additional statutory liability arises under the sanctions provided by the Financial Institutions Regulatory and Control Act of 1978[14] and other federal statutes.[15] In some instances a director need not have known his conduct was unlawful as long as he knew the facts.[16] The Sixth Circuit has held a bank director liable for statutory violations resulting from simple negligence, which is the failure to exercise ordinary care.[17] Insured banks[18] are subject to termination, cease and desist orders, and other sanctions, which may be issued against their directors, officers, employees, agents or other persons participating in the conduct of the banks' affairs.[19]

Federal savings and loan associations[20] are regulated by statute and by the regulations of the Federal Home Loan Bank Board (FHLBB)[21] which may impose sanctions, including cease and desist orders, upon them and their directors, officers, employees, agents and others.[22]

---

11. 12 U.S.C. § 93(a).

12. Id. § 530.

13. Corsicana Nat'l Bank v. Johnson, 251 U.S. 68, 71, 64 L.Ed. 141, 40 S.Ct. 82 (1919).

14. Pub. L. 95-630, 92 Stat. 3641 (1978).

15. See infra section 12.06.

16. See del Junco v. Conover, 682 F.2d 1338, 1342 (9th Cir. 1982), cert. denied, 459 U.S. 1146 (1983).

17. Fitzpatrick v. FDIC, 765 F.2d 569, 576 (6th Cir. 1985).

18. For definition, see 12 U.S.C. § 1814.

19. Others are also included. See id. § 1818.

20. Defined in id. § 1462(d).

21. See id. § 1464(c) et seq.

22. Id. § 1464(d).

State banks and savings associations, organized under particular state statutes, are subject to regulation by the states, as well as by the federal agencies if they are insured by the Federal Deposit Insurance Corporation (FDIC) or Federal Deposit Insurance Corporation Federal Savings and Loan Insurance Corporation (FSLIC).[23]

Liabilities of directors of state banks are frequently imposed by state statutes for knowingly violating or knowingly permitting violations by any of the officers, agents or employees of the bank.[24] Similar liabilities are imposed on savings and loan directors.[25]

§ 12.03. Bank directors, generally.

In determining the standards of care and diligence required of bank directors and officers, statutory restrictions and standards and uses of the banking business must be taken into consideration.[26] Federal statutes impose personal liability upon directors who "knowingly violate, or knowingly permit" any of the bank's officers or agents to violate any provisions of the National Bank Act.[27] However, a director will not be shielded from liability because of lack of knowledge of wrongdoing, if his ignorance "was the result of gross inattention in the discharge of his voluntarily assumed and sworn duty.[28]

In a case involving a Connecticut bank holding company it was contended that outside directors were not liable because

---

23. See, generally, 10 Am. Jur. 2d Banks § 17.

24. E.g., Ohio Rev. Code Ann. § 1115.06; Tenn. Code Ann. §§ 45-2-1702, 45-2-1704 to 45-2-1706, 45-2-1715, 45-2-1716.

25. E.g., Ch. 1153, Ohio Rev. Code Ann.

26. The leading cases on the liability of bank directors are Briggs v. Spaulding, 141 U.S. 132, 35 L.Ed. 662, 11 S.Ct. 924 (1891); Bowerman v. Hamner, 250 U.S. 504, 63 L.Ed. 1113, 39 S.Ct. 549 (1919); Corsicana Nat'l Bank v. Johnson, 251 U.S. 68, 64 L.Ed. 141, 40 S.Ct. 82 (1919); Anderson v. Atherton, 302 U.S. 643, 82 L.Ed. 500, 58 S.Ct. 53 (1937); Gamble v. Brown, 29 F.2d 366 (4th Cir. 1928); FDIC v. Mason, 115 F.2d 548 (3d Cir. 1940); Michelson v. Penney, 135 F.2d 409 (2d Cir. 1943).

27. 12 U.S.C. § 93.

28. Bowerman v. Hamner, supra note 26.

they had neither information nor reasonable notice of certain transactions. The Second Circuit said:

> [L]ack of knowledge is not necessarily a defense, if it is the result of an abdication of directorial responsibility... Directors who willingly allow others to make major decisions affecting the future of the corporation wholly without supervision or oversight may not defend on their lack of knowledge, for that ignorance itself is a breach of fiduciary duty.[29]

The court believed that the issue turned on how and why the outside directors were left in the dark, and required an analysis of the role of each.

The Third Circuit has held it to be "a general principle of banking law" that:

> If, through recklessness and inattention to the duties confided to [a director], frauds and misconduct are perpetrated by other officers and agents or codirectors, which ordinary care on his part would have prevented, [a director of a bank] is personally liable for the loss resulting.[30]

Outlining some of the specific duties of bank directors, imposed by common law, the Michigan court has stated:

> [T]he director must have a general knowledge of the financial condition of the institution, its system of management and daily workings, and exercise a reasonable degree of oversight and supervision of the bank's affairs.

In so doing, the director must exercise "care in the selection of officers, providing for audits and examinations and reports as reasonably seem necessary."

With respect to day-by-day attention to responsibility, the decision stated:

> The director cannot disregard matters presented to the board of directors nor a failure to present what should be

---

29. Joy v. North, 692 F.2d 880, 896 (2d Cir. 1982), cert. denied, 460 U.S. 1051 (1983).

30. First State Bank of Hudson County v. United States, 599 F.2d 558, 562 (3d Cir. 1979), cert. denied, 444 U.S. 1013 (1980), citing 1 Michie on Banks and Banking ch. 3, § 63 (1973).

shown nor close his eyes to suspicious conduct of officers or employees nor conduct which could put an ordinarily careful person on guard and cause him to inquire.[31]

A description of the duties of bank directors as defined at common law is found in a Massachusetts case:

Directors are bound to exercise ordinary prudence and skill to care for and invest the money entrusted to the bank, in accordance with its charter and the governing statutes.

They must be animated by the utmost good faith.

They hold themselves out as having the superintendence and management of all the concerns of the bank. They thereby engage to conduct its business as men of reasonable ability, necessary intelligence and sound judgment ought to conduct it. They must be diligent in ascertaining and in keeping informed as to the condition of its affairs; they must to a reasonable extent control and supervise its executive officers and agents; they must display understanding and insight proportionate to the particular circumstances under which they act.

They need not exhibit greater wisdom and foresight than may be fairly expected of the ordinary man in similar conditions. They invite the confidence of the depositing public and must afford the protection thereby implied....

They are not required to be expert accountants or familiar with the details of bookkeeping or to know everything disclosed by the books of the bank. Having regard to the nature and extent of the affairs of the bank and the customs of banking, directors are justified in committing the conduct of the main business to officers and subordinates and, in the absence of grounds for distrust, to assume that such persons will be upright in the performance of their duties. They are entitled to rely upon the information and advice given them by executive officers whose probity and competency are not under just suspicion but they cannot surrender to them the responsibilities resting on directors. They are liable for negligence in the performance of those responsibilities even though they have acted in good faith.

---

31. Trembert v. Mott, 271 Mich. 683, 261 N.W. 109, 114 (1935).

Impracticable obligations are not imposed on them. But they must direct and not be led. They must heed warnings from responsible sources. They must do something to see that statutes established for the protection of depositors are observed and followed.

For errors of judgment while acting with integrity, "skill and prudence, measured according to the demands of the duties or business which they have taken upon themselves, they are not to be held liable; but they cannot excuse themselves from the consequences of their misconduct or of their ignorance or negligence by averring that they have failed merely to exercise ordinary skill, care and vigilance."[32]

The trend of the court decisions lends support to the concept that directors of banks and savings and loan institutions will probably be held to a higher degree of care than their counterparts in business corporations. Banking is regulated to a far greater extent than is a routine business, and banking is enmeshed in a vast web of legal restraints. To illustrate, when the national banking laws are placed alongside such statutes as the Delaware Corporation Law or the Model Business Corporation Act, some plain differences appear:

1. Bank directors take an oath of office, nonbank directors do not.
2. Bank directors have residence and citizenship requirements, nonbank directors do not.
3. Occupations involving successful and honorable persons — investment bankers, for example — are barred from bank boards. In fact, the same person cannot be employed as janitor by a bank and a securities firm across the street. There is no general parallel in other businesses.
4. A bank director must own some stock. Again, this parallel condition does not generally exist in nonbanking firms.
5. A bank director's conduct of that office may result in his being subject to a cease-and-desist order, or quite

---

32. Prudential Trust Co. v. Brown, 271 Mass. 132, 171 N.E. 42, 44-45 (1930).

possibly even being suspended or removed from that office. This is a sword of Damocles without analogy in general business.[33]

§ 12.04. Insured bank directors.

Directors of national banks and those of state banks which are members of the Federal Reserve System are governed by most of the same federal statutes and regulations,[34] although directors of state banks must also conform to the requirements of state statutes.[35] Because the civil liability of directors of national banks arises exclusively from the national banking laws to the extent that such laws deal with that subject,[36] the case law defining the civil liability of corporate officers and directors generally is not fully applicable here.[37]

The oath required of directors of national banks calls for them to "diligently and honestly administer the affairs of such [national banking] association, and ... not knowingly violate or willingly permit to be violated any of the provisions of" the national banking laws.[38] That formidable obligation establishes two bases of liability, one at common law for failure to exercise due care and diligence, the other under the national banking laws. But when a bank director completely neglects his duty to the extent that he literally abandons his directorial duties, the statutes will not extend any area of protection to him.[39]

Perhaps the earliest reported decision holding bank directors liable for common-law negligence was handed down in New York more than a century ago. The directors had con-

---

33. Dunne, "The Liability of Bank Directors Under the New Federal Common Law or Swift v. Tyson Resurgent," 8 Forum 286, 295 (1972).

34. E.g., 12 U.S.C. § 93.

35. E.g., Ohio Rev. Code Ann. § 1115.06. See also Squire v. Guardian Trust Co., 79 Ohio App. 371, 382, 72 N.E.2d 137, 145 (1947).

36. Yates v. Jones Nat'l Bank, 206 U.S. 158, 51 L.Ed. 1002, 27 S.Ct. 638 (1907); Thomas v. Taylor, 224 U.S. 73, 56 L.Ed. 673, 32 S.Ct. 403 (1912); Jones Nat'l Bank v. Yates, 240 U.S. 541, 60 L.Ed. 788, 36 S.Ct. 429 (1916).

37. See also 12 U.S.C. § 1818(e)(7).

38. Id. § 73. Also, state laws may require a similar oath of directors and officers of state institutions. E.g., Ohio Rev. Code Ann. § 1115.04.

39. Michelsen v. Penney, 135 F.2d 409, 419 (2d Cir. 1943).

structed a new bank building while their institution was in a precarious financial condition. They were held personally liable to repay their bank's loss.[40]

A decade later, the Supreme Court decided the much criticized but still leading case of *Briggs v. Spaulding*.[41] It stated some pragmatic rules for the liability of bank directors, but exonerated one whose abdication of his responsibilities would probably have brought disaster upon him in today's legal climate.[42]

During the first twenty years of the century, a series of decisions by the Supreme Court established the statutory basis of liability of national bank directors under the national banking laws.[43] Then the Sixth Circuit, believing itself limited to enforcing statutory liability,[44] was reversed by the Supreme Court and ordered to consider the common-law grounds as well.[45] On rehearing, the Sixth Circuit found common-law negligence in cases specifically covered by statute, and in cases not so covered. It held that a "national bank is not a private corporation in which stockholders alone are interested. It is a quasi governmental agency..., and one of its principal purposes among others is to hold and safekeep the money of its depositors."[46]

Today, bonding companies that assert subrogation rights under bankers' blanket bonds[47] and fidelity bonds,[48] and the

---

40. Hun v. Cary, 82 N.Y. 65, 59 How. Prac. 439 (1880).

41. 141 U.S. 132, 35 L.Ed. 662, 11 S.Ct. 924 (1891).

42. See Barnes v. Andrews, 298 F. 614, 616 (S.D. N.Y. 1924); and cf. Michelsen v. Penney, supra note 39, at 418-19.

43. Yates v. Jones Nat'l Bank, supra note 36; Thomas v. Taylor, supra note 36; Jones Nat'l Bank v. Yates, supra note 36. And cf. Chesbrough v. Woodworth, 244 U.S. 72, 61 L.Ed. 1000, 37 S.Ct. 579 (1917).

44. Atherton v. Anderson, 86 F.2d 518 (6th Cir. 1936).

45. See Anderson v. Atherton, 302 U.S. 643, 82 L.Ed. 500, 58 S.Ct. 53 (1937).

46. Atherton v. Anderson, 99 F.2d 883 (6th Cir. 1938).

47. See Kenney, "Bank Directors' and Officers' Liability," 38 Ins. Couns. J. 575 (1971).

48. American Sur. Co. v. Bank of Cal., 133 F.2d 160 (9th Cir. 1943). See also Knox, "The Financial Institution Bond — Traditional Fidelity Coverage or Coverage for Corporate 'Goofs'?," 8 Forum 301 (1972).

Federal Deposit Insurance Corporation[49] are leading complainants in actions against errant national bank directors to recoup losses resulting from both common-law negligence and statutory misconduct. Individual actions by parties damaged due to conversion of assets,[50] suits by purchasers of a bank's stock to recover for fraudulent acts of the bank's directors and officers,[51] derivative suits,[52] and class actions in behalf of stockholders or depositors[53] are common and frequent, especially under the antifraud provisions of the federal securities acts.[54]

The Ninth Circuit has determined[55] that state law causes of action against national bank directors are not allowable if the allegedly unlawful conduct comes within the scope of the National Bank Act.[56] However, shareholders were not precluded from bringing pendent state claims against a director where it was shown that he had engaged in fraudulent activity that went far beyond the narrow range of conduct prohibited by the Act.[57]

Moreover, the provision of the Act was held not exclusive in that it did not restrict the ability of the court to consider

---

49. 12 U.S.C. § 1811 et seq.; FDIC v. Mason, 115 F.2d 548 (3d Cir. 1940); FDIC v. Aetna Cas. & Sur. Co., 426 F.2d 729 (5th Cir. 1970).

50. E.g., Bank of the Orient v. Superior Court, 67 Cal. App. 3d 588, 136 Cal. Rptr. 741 (1977).

51. E.g., Imperial Supply Co., Profit Sharing Trust v. Northern Ohio Bank, 430 F. Supp. 339 (N.D. Ohio 1976).

52. E.g., Mueller v. MacBan, 62 Cal. App. 3d 258, 132 Cal. Rptr. 222 (1976).

53. E.g., Fowler v. Elm Creek State Bank, 198 Neb. 631, 254 N.W.2d 415 (1977).

54. See also Ruder, "Increasing Danger of Loss for Financial Institutions Under the Federal Securities Laws," 8 Forum 323 (1972).

55. Harmsen v. Smith, 693 F.2d 932, 939 (9th Cir. 1982), cert. denied, 464 U.S. 822 (1983). But cf. Warren v. Manufacturers Nat'l Bank, 759 F.2d 542 (6th Cir. 1985).

56. 12 U.S.C. § 93.

57. 693 F.2d at 939.

claims under Section 10(b) of the Securities Exchange Act of 1934.[58] The court said:

> The application of section 10(b) to bank directors burdens them with no duties or responsibilities that conflict with the directives of the Bank Act. It does impose additional duties or responsibilities, but we must construe the two potentially overlapping statutes in the manner that gives effect to each.[59]

A variation of that situation produced a different result in the Sixth Circuit. Bank holding company shareholders were not allowed to maintain a private cause of action against corporate directors and officers for violation of the "rule of prudence" set forth in 12 C.F.R. 1.4 issued pursuant to 12 U.S.C. § 93(b).[60]

The court found that the shareholders did have direct and derivative causes of action for violations of 12 U.S.C. § 24 (limitation on investments), § 82 (limitations on indebtedness) and § 84 (limitation on extending unsecured credit), but concluded that the defendants had not violated those statutes.[61] As to the regulation, the court concluded that Congress, in enacting 12 U.S.C. § 93(b) did not intend to create a remedy by way of a private suit for violations of the regulation.[62]

The court found that the shareholders had a cause of action under 12 U.S.C. § 375b by virtue of 12 U.S.C. § 503, but again concluded that no violation had occurred.[63]

Although plaintiff also attempted to assert claims under the Bank Holding Company Act and some other sections,[64] they were also dismissed.

---

58. 15 U.S.C. § 78j(b).

59. 693 F.2d at 940.

60. Marx v Centran Corp., 747 F.2d 1536 (6th Cir. 1984), cert. denied, 471 U.S. 1255 (1985).

61. Id. at 1540-43.

62. Id. at 1543-47.

63. Id. at 1547-48.

64. Id. at 1548-52.

§ 12.05. FDIC litigation.

One of the primary duties of the Federal Deposit Insurance Corporation is to pay depositors of a failed bank. To do so, it may liquidate the bank's assets and pay the depositors, covering any shortfall with insurance funds, or it may arrange for another bank to purchase the failed bank and reopen it without interrupting banking operations and with no loss to depositors. The latter procedure is usually preferred for a variety of reasons.[65] It is commonly known as a purchase and assumption (P&A) transaction.

State bank agencies have authority to close state banks. The Comptroller of the Currency has broad discretion to determine when a national bank is insolvent.[66] In most cases the FDIC is appointed receiver by the appropriate authority and thus functions in a dual capacity: as receiver and as corporate insurer simultaneously.[67]

Because the P&A must be accomplished speedily, the purchasing bank need take only those assets of the highest banking quality. Other assets are returned to the FDIC, as receiver, which sells them to FDIC, as insurer, in its corporate capacity. It then attempts to minimize the loss to the insurance fund.

As a general rule, the FDIC will bring suit against the directors of a failed bank, seeking recovery for damages to the bank resulting from the directors' negligence and violations of banking law and regulations. It sues as receiver of the bank, or in its corporate capacity asserting claims which it acquired from the receiver in a P&A transaction. The right to maintain and control lawsuits against the officers and directors of a failed bank belongs exclusively to FDIC except as to

---

65. See Gunter v. Hutcheson, 674 F.2d 862, 865 (11th Cir.), cert. denied, 459 U.S. 826 (1982); Norcross, "The Bank Insolvency Game: FDIC Superpowers, The D'Oench Doctrine, and Federal Common Law," 103 Banking L.J. 316, 318 n.12, 319 n.14 (1986).

66. Liberty Nat'l Bank v. McIntosh, 16 F.2d 906, 908 (4th Cir.), cert. denied, 273 U.S. 783 (1917).

67. Gunter v. Hutcheson, supra note 65, at 865.

certain claims in which the alleged wrongful conduct does not come within the scope of the National Bank Act.[68]

In such actions FDIC makes use of whatever tools are available. Thus, in Colorado, FDIC sued a former vice-president of the failed Aurora Mountain Bank and twenty-one other defendants accusing them of a scheme to defraud the bank and violations of the Racketeer Influenced and Corrupt Organizations Act (RICO) and the Colorado Organized Crime Control Act (COCCA). Treble damages were sought. Pending trial, the district court granted injunctive relief to FDIC under COCCA to prevent defendants from disposing of their assets.[69]

A typical action by FDIC, as assignee, against directors and officers and their D & O insurer alleged their breach of fiduciary duties by permitting the bank president to make numerous improvident loans. The court applied Wisconsin's direct action statute permitting joinder of the insurer and held that (1) a breach of fiduciary duty was a negligence claim, and (2) the financial losses suffered by the bank constituted "injury to property."[70]

Another "deep pocket" from which funds may be recovered is the bankers' blanket bond. The FDIC, as assignee of the bank, may maintain an action against the surety on the bond without joining the bank directors and officers as defendants. At least one court has denied the surety's motion to implead the directors and officers as third party defendants.[71] The weight of authority, however, appears to permit such im-

---

68. FDIC v. American Bank Trust Shares, Inc., 558 F.2d 711 (4th Cir. 1977); FDIC v. American Bank Trust Shares, Inc., 629 F.2d 951, 953 (4th Cir. 1980); Harmsen v. Smith, 693 F.2d 932, 939 (9th Cir. 1982), cert. denied, 464 U.S. 822 (1983). See also Warren v. Manufacturers National Bank, 759 F.2d 542 (6th Cir. 1985), and Gaff v. FDIC, 814 F.2d 311 (6th Cir. 1987).

69. FDIC v. John Antonio, et al., No. 85-C-1298, U.S.D.Ct., D. Colo. (filed Nov. 10, 1986).

70. FDIC v. MGIC Indem. Corp., 462 F. Supp. 759 (E.D. Wis. 1978).

71. FDIC v. National Sur. Corp., 13 F.R.D. 201 (E.D. Wis. 1950). See also Murray & Nocera, "Surety's Remedies to Recover Fidelity Loss," 51 Ins. Couns. J. 566, 582-83 (1984).

pleader, although the claims of the surety are based on its subrogation to the rights of the bank and not on any independent duty of the directors and officers to the surety.[72]

While the subrogated surety may assert the rights of the bank against its directors and officers, there is authority that the balance of equities will not permit the surety to recover over from directors and officers for mere negligence.[73] This rule is based on the principle that a fidelity insurer, in exchange for a paid premium, assumes the risk of the negligence of the bank's management.

In such actions the respective terms of the bond and of the D & O insurance policy covering the directors will come into play. The Fifth Circuit has held that a finding of liability under the bond, which covers "dishonest or fraudulent acts", results in exclusion of the loss from coverage of the D & O policy which does not insure "active and deliberate dishonesty."[74]

The FDIC, either as receiver or in its corporate capacity, stands in the position of a good faith purchaser for value and is immune to any personal defense to any instrument unless it had actual knowledge of the defense when it acquired the instrument.[75] There is a presumption that FDIC had no knowledge of any defenses.[76] And FDIC has no duty, in either

---

72. FDIC v. National Sur. Corp., 434 F. Supp. 61 (E.D.N.Y. 1977); Community Fed. Sav. & Loan Ass'n v. Transamerica Ins. Co., 559 F. Supp. 536 (E.D. Mo. 1983).

73. First Nat'l Bank of Columbus v. Hansen, 84 Wis. 2d 422, 267 N.W.2d 367 (1978); Dixie Nat'l Bank of Dade County v. Employers Com. Union Ins. Co. of Am., 463 So. 2d 1147 (Fla. 1985). Contra: FDIC v. National Sur. Corp., supra note 72; Manufacturers Bank & Trust Co. v. Transamerica Ins. Co., 568 F. Supp. 790 (E.D. Mo. 1981); Community Fed. Sav. & Loan Ass'n v. Transamerica Ins. Co., supra note 72; Fidelity Nat'l Bank v. Aetna Cas. & Sur. Co., 584 F. Supp. 1019 (M.D. La. 1984).

74. Elgin Nat'l Bank v. Home Indem. Co., 583 F.2d 1281 (5th Cir. 1978).

75. Gunter v. Hutcheson, 674 F.2d 862 (11th Cir.), cert. denied, 459 U.S. 826 (1982); Gilman v. FDIC, 660 F.2d 688 (6th Cir. 1981); FDIC v. Chaney, 19 Ohio App. 3d 277, 280, 484 N.E.2d 174 (1984); FDIC v. Hatmaker, 756 F.2d 34, 37 (6th Cir. 1985).

76. FDIC v. Armstrong, 784 F.2d 741, 745 (6th Cir. 1986).

of its capacities, to examine the assets of a failed bank before it enters into a P&A transaction.[77] In actions by FDIC against a bank's directors and officers it may be entitled to immunity from such defenses even though they would have been available against the bank.[78]

Moreover, FDIC is not required to warn the directors and officers of a bank about wrongdoing of bank officials discovered by FDIC. The Third Circuit holds that the "duty to discover fraud in their institutions is upon the bank directors."[79]

Especially in actions by FDIC and FSLIC the accrual of statutes of limitations may be critical. If the statutes began to run when the offending transaction occurs, many claims would be barred. Accordingly, the better rule is that the cause of action does not accrue while the culpable directors remain in control.[80] It accrues when the governmental agency takes over and a receiver is appointed.

§ 12.06. Sanctions by supervisory agencies.

In addition to the traditional civil actions against bank directors, they are subject to civil penalties, cease and desist orders, suspension or removal from office and may be prohibited from participating in the affairs of a bank insured by FDIC.[81] Directors of federally chartered thrift institutions and FSLIC-insured state-chartered thrifts are subject to simi-

---

77. FDIC v. Wood, 758 F.2d 156, 162 (6th Cir. 1985).

78. FDIC v. National Union Fire Ins. Co., 630 F. Supp. 1149 (W.D. La. 1986).

79. First State Bank of Hudson County v. United States, 599 F.2d 558, 563 (3d Cir. 1979), cert. denied, 444 U.S. 1013 (1980).

80. FDIC v. Bird, 516 F. Supp. 647, 650-52 (D.P.R. 1981); FSLIC v. Williams, 599 F. Supp. 1184 (D. Md. 1984).

81. The Federal Reserve Act, 12 U.S.C. §§ 371c, 375, 375a, 375b and 376, and the Bank Holding Company Act, id. § 1972, provide for civil penalties up to $1000 per day. Cease and desist orders may be issued under the Federal Deposit Insurance Act, id. § 1818(b), and the National Banking Act, see id. §§ 93, 504, 1818(i)(2) and 1818(i)(3). And id. 1817(j)(5) provides a penalty up to $10,000 per day for willful violation of the Change of Bank Control Act of 1978.

lar cease and desist orders and suspension orders.[82] Sanctions of these types are probably not subject to indemnification and may not be insurable.

Such sanctions, including cease and desist orders and civil money penalties, may be imposed upon banks and their directors under the Federal Deposit Insurance Act[83] and the Financial Institutions Regulatory and Interest Rate Control Act of 1978.[84] Although bank directors and officers may be liable to private parties and to FDIC and FSLIC for any damages resulting from violations of their duties under the Federal Reserve Act[85] and the Federal Deposit Insurance Act,[86] they may also be required to pay civil money penalties, whether or not damages result.[87]

The Sixth Circuit has held that Congress intended the Financial Institutions Regulatory Act to be a re-emphasis, if not an extension, of bank directors' fiduciary duties, and that the American Law Institute's Principles of Corporate Governance provides appropriate guidance to effectuate the congressional interest. Willfulness is not an essential element of such violations.[88]

Under 12 U.S.C. § 1818, the FDIC may terminate the status of a bank as an insured bank, may remove a director, officer or other person from office or prohibit his participation in the conduct of the affairs of an insured bank. Such sanctions are proper remedies for engaging in unsound banking practices.[89] The 1978 amendment of 12 U.S.C. § 1818(b)(1) gave the Comptroller of the Currency authority to issue an order of removal or to cease and desist against a particular director, officer or employee without taking action against

---

82. See 12 U.S.C. §§ 1464(d) and 1730(e).

83. See id. § 1818.

84. Pub. L. 95-630, 92 Stat. 3641 (1978).

85. 12 U.S.C. § 503.

86. Id. § 1828(j)(2).

87. Fitzpatrick v. FDIC, 765 F.2d 569, 575 (6th Cir. 1985).

88. Id. at 576, citing ALI §§ 4.01, 4.02 (Tent. Draft No. 4, 1985).

89. Bank of Dixie v. FDIC, 766 F.2d 175 (5th Cir. 1985); Sunshine State Bank v. FDIC, 783 F.2d 1580 (11th Cir. 1986).

the bank itself.[90] The Supreme Court will accord "considerable weight" to an executive department's construction of a statutory scheme it is entrusted to administer.[90a]

Directors of a national bank operate in an area closely regulated by federal law, and cannot maintain ignorance of the law as a defense. In so holding,[91] the Ninth Circuit affirmed a decision of the Comptroller of the Currency requiring directors to indemnify their bank for loans exceeding the statutory limit. This indemnification included collection fees and attorneys' fees the bank had paid for the directors.[92] The court cited a Supreme Court decision which stated that if a director "deliberately refrained from investigating that which it was his duty to investigate, any resulting violation of the statute must be regarded as 'in effect intentional'...."[93]

However, neither the Ninth Circuit nor the Eighth Circuit,[94] in a similar case, addressed the initial issue of whether the Comptroller had the authority to order directors to indemnify their bank without instituting an action to seek damages from the directors pursuant to 12 U.S.C. § 93. When that question came before the Seventh Circuit, en banc, it held that the Comptroller lacked such authority under 12 U.S.C. § 1818(b)(1) and was relegated to bringing a proper court action to impose personal liability upon the directors.[95]

Nonetheless, the Comptroller has wide discretion and the exercise of his discretion will not be disturbed except when the action taken is contrary to law.[96]

---

90. Larimore v. Comptroller of Currency, 789 F.2d 1244, 1251 (7th Cir. 1986) (en banc).

90a. Chevron U.S.A. v. Natural Resources Defense Council, 469 U.S. 837, 844, 81 L.Ed.2d 694, 704, 104 S.Ct. 2778 (1984).

91. del Junco v. Conover, 682 F.2d 1338, 1342 (9th Cir. 1982), cert. denied, 459 U.S. 1146 (1983).

92. Id. at 1339-40.

93. Id. at 1342, citing Corsicana Nat'l Bank v. Johnson, 251 U.S. 68, 71-72, 64 L.Ed. 141, 40 S.Ct. 82, 84 (1919).

94. See First Nat'l Bank of Eden v. Department of Treasury, 568 F.2d 610 (8th Cir. 1978).

95. Larimore v. Comptroller of Currency, supra note 90.

96. First Nat'l Bank of LaMarque v. Smith, 610 F.2d 1258, 1264 (5th Cir. 1980).

In the supervision of thrift institutions similar powers are vested in the Federal Home Loan Bank Board (FHLBB) and its insurance arm, the Federal Savings and Loan Insurance Corporation, although their powers are somewhat limited as to imposing civil money penalties.[97]

The Federal Financial Institutions Examination Council, consisting of representatives of the Comptroller, FDIC, Federal Reserve Board, FHLBB and the National Credit Union Association,[98] is charged with establishing uniform principles and standards for examining financial institutions and making recommendations for uniformity in supervisory matters.[99] In 1980 it issued a policy statement which enumerated thirteen factors to be considered in determining whether a violation warrants application of the civil money penalty procedure,[100] as follows:

    (1) Evidence that the violation or pattern of violations was intentional or committed with a disregard of the law or the consequences to the institution;

    (2) The frequency or recurrence of violations and the length of time the violation has been outstanding;

    (3) Continuation of the violation after the respondent becomes aware of it, or its immediate cessation and correction;

    (4) Failure to cooperate with the agency in effecting early resolution of the problem;

    (5) Evidence of concealment of the violation, or its voluntary disclosure;

    (6) Any threat of or actual loss or other harm to the institution, including harm to public confidence in the institution, and the degree of any such harm;

    (7) Evidence that participants or their associates received financial or other gain or benefit or preferential treatment as a result of the violation;

---

97. 12 U.S.C. §§ 1464(d)(12), 1720(p)(1), 1818(j).
98. Id. § 3303.
99. Id. § 3305.
100. 45 Fed. Reg. 59, 423 (1980).

(8) Evidence of any restitution by the participants in the violation;

(9) History of prior violations, particularly where similarities exist between those and the violation under consideration;

(10) Previous criticism of the institution for similar violations;

(11) Presence or absence of a compliance program and its effectiveness;

(12) Tendency to create unsafe or unsound banking practices or breach of fiduciary duty; and

(13) The existence of agreements, commitments, or orders intended to prevent the violation.[101]

§ 12.07. Economic benefits belong to bank.

It is a fiduciary duty of an officer, director or controlling owner of any business entity to make certain that the economic rewards accruing from corporate opportunity inure to all owners of the enterprise. This obligation is even stronger in the case of a bank, both because of the fiduciary nature of banking and because of the duty to depositors. Officers and directors of banks generally owe a greater duty to depositors than other corporate officers and directors owe to shareholders.[102]

Thus a bank officer who receives a bonus or other consideration for procuring a loan of the bank's funds commits a breach of trust, and the benefit belongs to the bank and may be recovered by it.[103] On this premise the Fifth Circuit upheld a directive of the Comptroller of the Currency that all commissions and other economic benefits derived from the place-

---

101. See also Nichols, "FIRA: Emerging Patterns of Director Liability," 103 Banking L.J. 151, 162-63 and 179-80 (1986), which discusses the policy statement.

102. Gadd v. Pearson, 351 F. Supp. 895, 903 (M.D. Fla. 1972).

103. Fleishhacker v. Blum, 109 F.2d 543, 545-46 (9th Cir.), cert. denied, 311 U.S. 665 (1940).

ment of credit life and disability insurance should be credited to the bank for the benefit of all shareholders.[104]

§ 12.08. Insured savings and loan directors.

Officers and directors of federal savings and loan associations and other insured institutions are charged with fiduciary obligations to their associations and their savings account holders.[105] Also, in management of their institutions they are required to obey the regulations of the Federal Home Loan Bank Board (FHLBB) governing the internal management of such institutions. Those regulations have the force of law [106]

Because the federal common law governing federal savings and loan associations includes the usual common-law fiduciary duties of officers and directors, claims for waste, appropriation of business opportunities, fraud, conversion, unjust enrichment, breach of contract and the like are deemed to arise under federal common law.[107]

When the Supreme Court of Illinois decided *Kerrigan v. Unity Savings Association,*[108] it set off a wave of lawsuits against directors and officers of savings and loan associations.[109] In *Kerrigan,* the court held that directors of a state savings and loan association had improperly diverted a corporate opportunity from the association and had breached their fiduciary duties by causing individual borrowers to be re-

---

104. First Nat'l Bank of LaMarque v. Smith, 436 F. Supp. 824 (S.D. Tex. 1977), aff'd in part, vacated in part, 610 F.2d 1258 (5th Cir. 1980).

105. 12 U.S.C. § 1464(d)(4)(A) and 1724; City Fed. Sav. & Loan Ass'n v. Crowley, 393 F. Supp. 644 (E.D. Wis. 1975). Some state laws require an oath to "diligently and honestly administer the affairs of the association, and ... not knowingly violate, or willingly permit to be violated, any law applicable to such association." E.g., Ohio Rev. Code Ann. § 1151.17.

106. City Fed. Sav. & Loan Ass'n v. Crowley, supra note 105, at 651.

107. Beverly Hills Fed. Sav. & Loan Ass'n v. FHLBB, 371 F. Supp. 306, 314 (C.D. Cal. 1973).

108. 58 Ill. 2d 20, 317 N.E.2d 39 (1974).

109. E.g., Rettig v. Arlington Heights Fed. Sav. & Loan Ass'n, 405 F. Supp. 819 (N.D. Ill. 1975).

ferred to a director-controlled insurance agency to purchase insurance needed in connection with their loans. The court started with "the basic proposition that a director of a corporation owes a fiduciary duty to it."[110] It went on to hold that if directors fail to disclose and tender a business opportunity to their corporation, "the prophylactic purpose of the rule imposing a fiduciary obligation requires that the directors be foreclosed from exploiting that opportunity on their own behalf."[111] The judgment in this derivative action imposed liability upon the directors and remanded the case to the trial court to fix the damages.[112]

In similar actions involving federal savings and loan associations chartered by the FHLBB,[113] the board's rules and regulations and the federal common law were held to have pre-empted the field, so that any alleged violation of directors' fiduciary duties will be determined thereunder.[114] When directors' conduct is not specifically defined by any specific regulation of the board, the court may rely upon the federal common law to fill out the board's regulatory scheme.[115]

An important decision of the Kansas Supreme Court demonstrates that state statutes may place higher standards of duty on savings and loan institution officers than on officers

---

110. Kerrigan v. Unity Sav. Ass'n, supra note 108, 317 N.E.2d at 43, citing Shlensky v. South Parkway Bldg. Corp., 19 Ill. 2d 268, 166 N.E.2d 793 (1960).

111. Id. See also Vendo Co. v. Stoner, 58 Ill. 2d 289, 321 N.E.2d 1 (1974); Patient Care Servs., S.C. v. Segal, 32 Ill. App. 3d 1021, 337 N.E.2d 471, 478, 480 (1975); Zokoych v. Spalding, 36 Ill. App. 3d 654, 344 N.E.2d 805, 814 (1976). The same rule was applied to prevent a governmental officer from misappropriating a business opportunity belonging to a municipality in Chicago ex rel. Cohen v. Keane, 64 Ill. 2d 559, 2 Ill. Dec. 285, 357 N.E.2d 452 (1976).

112. Kerrigan v. Unity Sav. Ass'n, supra note 108, 317 N.E.2d at 45.

113. See 12 U.S.C. § 1461 et seq.

114. Rettig v. Arlington Heights Fed. Sav. & Loan Ass'n, supra note 109, at 823.

115. Id. at 826. See also Beverly Hills Fed. Sav. & Loan Ass'n v. FHLBB, supra note 107, at 314; City Fed. Sav. & Loan Ass'n v. Crowley, supra note 106, at 656.

of ordinary for profit corporations. In denying to savings and loan directors defenses available to other corporate directors, the court stated, as a matter of public policy:

> The potentiality for harm to Kansas citizens from mismanagement of savings and loan associations is enormous. A large percentage of their investors place their life savings in such institutions, relying upon the officers of such institutions to discharge their duties properly. When a savings and loan association fails, the domino effect can be staggering. Public confidence in all savings and loans is shaken. Declining deposits in savings and loan associations have a direct effect on the construction, sale and resale of homes, which in turn affects many other areas of our economy.[116]

In 1987 the FHLBB, as operating head of the Federal Savings and Loan Insurance Corporation (FSLIC), adopted and published a Statement of Policy concerning the standards under which FSLIC determines when to file lawsuits and pursue claims against officers and directors of insured savings and loan institutions that have failed.[117] The Statement of Policy pointed out that claims brought against such persons "have been based on egregious conduct by those pursued, not simple errors of judgment." It incorporated an earlier memorandum which included the following guidelines, among others:

- The duty of care includes the responsibility of the directors to select and retain competent management; to oversee the activities of the institution by attending directors' meetings; to require that adequate and reliable information is provided upon which they can make decisions; to carefully review the documentation which is provided; to make the necessary policy decisions upon which management is to operate the institution; to monitor the activities that are delegated to the officers of the

---

116. FSLIC v. Huff, 237 Kan. 873, 704 P.2d 372 (1985).

117. FHLBB Accountability of Directors and Officers, Policy Statement, 52 Fed. Reg. 22682 (June 15, 1987).

institution to insure that the board of directors' policies are being carried out; and to establish controls to assure themselves that the institution is being operated in a safe and sound manner and in compliance with law and regulations.

- There must be an adequate system of checks and balances between management and the outside directors of a thrift institution to insure that the outside directors, who constitute a majority of the board, are promptly and fully informed of serious problems in the institution.
- While the outside directors cannot normally be expected to directly establish an adequate system of internal controls, they are responsible to ensure that one is put in place and that it is operating satisfactorily. This responsibility can be adequately met [by] properly structuring the board of directors into appropriate committees and by the use of outside experts and a compliance officer reporting directly to the board.
- Each director's meeting should include a review of financial reports. Figures used in the reports should be verified if they appear at all questionable and not simply accepted at face value. Federal and/or state examination report recommendations should be promptly followed.
- Directors are responsible for operating results. As such, adherence to the following procedures should assist the board of directors in obtaining adequate and accurate information upon which to make informed decisions.
  (1) Thorough documentation evidencing the details of all business transactions should be an integral part of an institution's books and records. The records should reflect regulatory compliance and adherence to safe and sound procedures. The directors should have full access to such records and should utilize them in decisionmaking relative to loan approvals, investment transactions, etc. The board of directors' meeting minutes should indicate that the directors are cognizant of and have studied documentation upon which their decisionmaking is based. Each director should

363

have the opportunity to review, and modify if necessary, the minutes before they are approved.

(2) An audit committee, composed totally of outside directors, should be appointed to select the outside auditing firm and discuss the scope and results of the audit. It is recommended that the audit committee also select and employ a compliance officer who should be under the direction and control of the audit committee. Membership on the audit committee should not be considered a mere titular honor but a demanding responsibility requiring an active role.

(3) The employment of a compliance officer is also recommended as part of a sound checks and balances system. It is the duty of this officer to monitor all institution business transactions to ensure their compliance with regulatory provisions and their safety and soundness. The officer should be selected by and report to the audit committee.

(4) Compliance audits may be made annually by the internal compliance officer, or in the absence of such an employee, by the board of directors' audit committee or its outside auditor. An audit of this nature will give the institution an opportunity to resolve or remedy any internal problems which might later be the subject of an adverse Bank Board or state examination report.

- The actions (or inactions) of an institution's board of directors will be scrutinized by examiners at each examination. Examiners should report as deficiencies those instances where boards are not adequately involved in or informed of institution affairs; where the system of checks and balances between management and the board is deficient; where minutes do not reflect a clear record of their deliberations or where actions do not reflect safety and soundness. Supervisory Agents should require whatever corrective action is deemed appropriate.

§ 12.09. FSLIC litigation.

The Federal Savings and Loan Insurance Corporation was created by the National Housing Act. It operates under the direction of the Federal Home Loan Bank Board (FHLBB). The statutory scheme prescribing the procedure for federal savings and loan associations authorizes FSLIC to be appointed as conservator or receiver of any federal savings and loan association[118] or other insured association[119] in default. It further authorizes FSLIC, once the receivership has been established, "to take such action as may be necessary to put (the institution) in a sound and solvent condition."[120] When Congress amended the statutory provisions governing FSLIC's receivership functions, it meant to give FSLIC and FOIC parallel authority over their respective institutions.[120a] Accordingly, there is authority that the federal common law supporting FOIC's powers applies with equal force to FSLIC.[120b]

The statute permits an association placed in receivership to bring a federal court action to remove FSLIC as receiver, but the sole question before the court is whether a statutory ground authorizing the appointment of FSLIC exists.[121] When the receiver is appointed by a state official acting pursuant to state law, a challenge to the receivership can be made in state court.[122]

Actions against directors and officers of an insured institution which arise from violations of the Home Owners Loan Act come within FHLBB's enforcement powers. No private

---

118. 12 U.S.C. § 1729(b).

119. Id. § 1729(c).

120. Biscayne Fed. Sav. & Loan Ass'n v. FHLBB, 720 F.2d 1499 (11th Cir. 1983), cert. denied, 467 U.S. 1215 (1984).

120a. Morrison-Knudsen Co. v. CHG Int'l, Inc., 811 F.2d 1209, 1221 (9th Cir. 1987).

120b. Federal Sav. & Loan Ins. Corp. v. Hsi, 657 F. Supp. 1333, 1338 (E.D. La. 1986). And see supra section 12.05.

121. Id. at 1503.

122. Telegraph Sav. & Loan Ass'n v. Schilling, 703 F.2d 1019, 1023 (7th Cir. 1983) (en banc).

right of action is provided in the statutes. The federal interest in uniform regulation of insured institutions, supports recognition of a federal common-law cause of action for breach of the fiduciary duties of directors and officers. To the extent that such a claim does not involve violation of the Home Owners Loan Act a private cause of action may exist.[123]

FSLIC, as the designee of FHLBB, seeks to recoup losses of defaulting insured associations. It takes assignments of their claims and pursues officers, directors and employees of insured associations for such misconduct as "intentional and negligent breach of fiduciary duty, fraud, waste, violation of various federal statutes and regulations, and diversion of corporate opportunities."[124]

FSLIC has a dual nature. It may assert a claim standing in the shoes of an association pursuant to assignment and it may exercise its discretion while performing in its capacity as a federal regulatory agency. In the first capacity, it may be susceptible to counterclaims for recoupment under appropriate circumstances. In its other capacity, it has a separate and distinct nature from the United States and counterclaims against the United States are inappropriate.[125] Punitive damages may be recoverable from such directors and officers in a FSLIC action for breach of fiduciary duty upon a showing of "gross neglect of duty indicating reckless indifference to the rights of others."[126]

It appears to be established that FSLIC should be able to act quickly in reorganizing, operating or dissolving a failed institution without interference by other judicial or regulatory authorities.[127]

---

123. First Hawaiian Bank v. Alexander, 558 F. Supp. 1128 (D. Haw. 1983). Cf. Harmsen v. Smith, 693 F.2d 932 (9th Cir. 1982), cert. denied, 464 U.S. 822 (1983).

124. FSLIC v. Williams, 599 F. Supp. 1184, 1190 (D. Md. 1984).

125. Id. at 1202.

126. Id. at 1215.

127. North Miss. Sav. & Loan Ass'n v. Hudspeth, 756 F.2d 1096, 1101 (5th Cir. 1985); Keller v. Antioch Sav. & Loan Ass'n, 143 Ill. App. 3d 278, 492 N.E.2d 937 (1986).

§ 12.10. Credit union officials.

After seventy-eight years that credit unions have been functioning, more than fifty-two million people now belong to them. Thus credit unions are financial institutions that must be ranked with banks, savings and loans, and insurance companies for purposes of regulation.

The first credit union organized in the United States received its charter in 1909 from the State of New Hampshire. Massachusetts enacted the first credit union statute that same year.[128] By 1934 when the first federal credit union statute was enacted,[129] thirty-eight states and the District of Columbia had credit union laws. The federal act[130] did not eliminate state credit unions, but it did provide for conversions from state to federal charter and vice versa.[131] In 1970 the National Credit Union Administration (NCUA) was required to insure federal credit unions and was permitted to insure other credit unions.[132]

Federal insurance was accompanied by greater supervision of the affairs of insured credit unions, including sanctions similar to those applicable to insured banks and savings and loan associations. They include termination of insurance, issuance of cease and desist orders, suspension and removal of credit union officers, and imposition of monetary penalties for unsafe or unsound practices in conducting a credit union's business. It has been held that NCUA's powers are analogous to those of the Federal Home Loan Bank Board and the Comptroller of the Currency.[133]

The Seventh Circuit has held that persons removed from a credit committee of a federal credit union have no private

---

128. La Caisse Populaire Ste-Marie v. United States, 425 F. Supp. 512, 515 (D.N.H. 1975), aff'd, 563 F.2d 3505 (1st Cir. 1977).

129. Pub. L. 73-467, 48 Stat. 1216 (1934).

130. 12 U.S.C. § 1781 et seq.

131. Typical state credit union statutes will be found in Fla. Stat. Ann. ch. 657; Ill. Rev. Stat. ch. 17, § 4451; N.Y. Banking Law § 450 et seq.; Ch. 1733, Ohio Rev. Code Ann.

132. 12 U.S.C. § 1786.

133. National Alliance of Postal & Fed. Employees v. Nickerson, 424 F. Supp. 323, 325 (D.D.C. 1976).

right of action under the Federal Credit Union Act against those who removed them, but may bring an action for monetary, declaratory and injunctive relief under the federal common law.[134] In so holding, the court followed a district court decision under the Home Owners Loan Act[135] which also applied the federal common law.[136] In view of the similarity of the statutes and of the regulatory schemes, it appears that claims against credit union officials may be prosecuted like claims against directors of savings and loan associations.

§ 12.11. Insurance company directors and officers.

The insurance laws of the various states apply the common-law standards and the corporation law statutory standards to directors and officers of insurance companies.[137] Hence, the common-law and statutory duties and liabilities of corporations generally will be applied to insurance company management, unless a specific statute provides otherwise.[138] There are statutes in many states which deal with particular subjects relating to directors and officers of insurance companies and impose specific requirements. Such subjects include directors and management generally,[139] directors' and officers' conflicts of interest,[140] approval of investments,[141] dividends and reserves,[142] compensation of directors,[143] interlock-

---

134. Barany v. Buller, 670 F.2d 726, 729 (7th Cir. 1982).

135. 12 U.S.C. § 1461 et seq.

136. Rettig v. Arlington Hts. Fed. Sav. & Loan Ass'n, 405 F. Supp. 819 (N.D. Ill. 1975).

137. E.g., N.Y. Ins. Law § 1202(c) makes N.Y. Bus. Corp. Law § 717 (duties of directors) applicable to insurance companies.

138. Wever, "Liabilities of Officers and Directors of Insurance Companies," 1973 Ins. L.J. 392.

139. E.g., N.Y. Ins. Law §§ 1202, 1209.

140. E.g., Ill. Rev. Stat. ch. 73, § 736.2.

141. E.g., N.Y. Ins. Law § 1411; Mass. Gen. Laws Ann. ch. 175, § 193I.

142. E.g., N.Y. Ins. Law § 1211(a).

143. E.g., 40 Pa. C.S.A. § 437.

ing directorates,[144] and personal liability of directors and officers.[145]

Investment criteria are explicit in most life insurance legislation. Quality of investments is frequently spelled out, and there are usually express limitations on the percentages of a company's assets that may be placed in particular types of investments.[146] Directors' liability may result from failure to conform to statutory criteria,[147] or from failure to meet the "business judgment" or "prudent man" rules of the common law.[148]

While such specific provisions in state insurance laws identify some particular problems which confront insurance company directors and officers, there are other problems as well. The enactments of insurance holding company acts have permitted investments in other business ventures which, in some instances, have subjected insurance companies to regulation by laws of other agencies such as the Federal Trade Commission, Federal Communications Commission, and the Federal Reserve Board.

In cases involving the sale of insurance company products which constitute securities, the Securities and Exchange Commission and the federal securities laws have dealt with insurance companies, thus involving their directors and officers. An early case in this area, *Securities and Exchange Commission v. Variable Annuity Life Insurance Company,*[149] applied the securities laws to an investment contract.[150] Cases such as this, and a trend toward erosion of the

---

144. E.g., Cal. Ins. Code '§ 725.

145. 40 Pa. C.S.A. § 506.1(r).

146. E.g., N.Y. Ins. Law §§ 1401 to 1414.

147. E.g., Mass. Gen. Laws Ann. ch. 175, § 193I.

148. Cf. Medford Trust Co. v. McKnight, 292 Mass. 1, 197 N.E. 649 (1935).

149. 359 U.S. 65, 3 L.Ed.2d 640, 79 S.Ct. 618 (1959).

150. See also SEC v. National Sec., Inc., 393 U.S. 453, 21 L.Ed.2d 668, 89 S.Ct. 564 (1969); and Prudential Ins. Co. of Am. v. SEC, 326 F.2d 383 (3d Cir. 1964). For subsequent developments in this area, see Blank, Keen, Payne and Miller, "Variable Life Insurance and the Federal Securities Laws," 60 Va. L. Rev. 71 (1974).

McCarran-Ferguson Act and its replacement with federal regulation of the insurance industry, have opened the door to numerous new concerns for insurance company directors. Existing products of the insurance industry, heretofore considered exempt from federal securities regulation, must be reevaluated. New products must be reviewed and the desirability or necessity of registration considered.[151]

The 1969 decision in *Securities and Exchange Commission v. National Securities, Incorporated,* sought to undo the merger of two stock life insurance companies on the ground that the proxy solicitation materials mailed to the stockholders (1) contained positive misrepresentations of material facts, and (2) failed to state material facts necessary to make the statements in the proxies not misleading in the light of the circumstances under which they were made. The lower courts had held that the McCarran-Ferguson Act[152] precluded the granting of injunctive relief for the alleged violations because Arizona law controlled.[153] The Supreme Court reversed and remanded.[154]

In the Supreme Court, Justice Marshall delivered the opinion. He pointed out that the McCarran-Ferguson Act did not purport to make the states supreme in regulating the activities of insurance companies. Its language, he said, referred not to the persons or companies subject to state regulation, but rather to laws "regulating the business of insurance." Accordingly, he ruled that the State of Arizona, in enacting laws relating to the solicitation of proxies, was not engaged in insurance regulation but rather in securities regulation, which was not within the scope of the McCarran-Ferguson Act.

---

151. Consideration should also be given to the potential effect of such cases as Daniel v. International Bhd. of Teamsters, 561 F.2d 1223 (7th Cir. 1977), holding an employee's interest in an involuntary, noncontributory pension plan to be a security.

152. 15 U.S.C. § 1012(b).

153. SEC v. National Sec., Inc., 252 F. Supp. 623 (D. Ariz. 1966), aff'd, 387 F.2d 25 (9th Cir. 1967).

154. SEC v. National Sec., Inc., supra note 150.

In 1971 the Supreme Court decided *Superintendent of Insurance of New York v. Bankers Life and Casualty Company,*[155] which eliminated all doubt about the application of the federal securities laws to all insurance companies, including mutual insurance companies. The implication of that decision is that any fraudulent transaction or any wrongdoing that involves false statements or omissions of material facts, and which also touches on the purchase and sale of securities, can be remedied under SEC Rule 10b-5.[156] Accordingly, directors and officers of insurance companies must expect to be dealt with in the same manner and to the same extent as officers of other corporations, especially financial institutions, with respect to their fiduciary obligations and their liabilities under applicable state and federal laws.

Mutual insurance companies, which have no stockholders, are not excluded. The effect of the *Bankers Life and Casualty* case is to apply the "purchase and sale of securities" language of Rule 10b-5 to dealings of an insurance company in any securities in its portfolio. Thus, directors, officers and controlling persons of insurance companies may be the targets of suits resulting from the purchase or sale of securities in their companies' portfolios, if material information is misstated or concealed, or if other fraudulent, manipulative or deceptive dealings are involved.

Actually, the impact of the federal securities laws goes beyond litigation arising directly under Rule 10b-5, or even under the federal securities acts. These laws have served as the basis for a whole new body of corporation law which also is beginning to involve common-law fraud and breaches of fiduciary responsibilities. The Supreme Court ruled that the fraud provisions of the federal securities acts should be con-

---

155. 404 U.S. 6, 30 L.Ed.2d 128, 92 S.Ct. 165 (1971), and see Rule 10b-5, 17 C.F.R. § 240.10b-5, quoted in n.4 therein. See also Miller and Subak, "Lessons for Future Counseling of Insurers Involving Ethics, Liabilities and Securities Regulation," 10 Forum 1155, 1158 (1975).

156. See also Affiliated Ute Citizens of Utah v. United States, 406 U.S. 128, 31 L.Ed.2d 741, 92 S.Ct. 1456 (1971), reh'g denied, 407 U.S. 916 and 408 U.S. 931 (1972).

strued flexibly to effectuate their remedial purposes, although later decisions suggest that Rule 10b-5 itself will not be made a catchall for any and every type of corporate mismanagement or directorial impropriety.[157] The Sixth Circuit has held, for example, that fraud by directors is usually a breach of fiduciary duty. However, that court refused to apply Rule 10b-5 to a breach of fiduciary duty in formulating the terms of a merger.[158]

In the *Equity Funding* litigation,[159] the federal securities laws were used as the principal vehicles to seek redress for directorial and official fraud and mismanagement. The procedure is another indication of the anticipated increase in impact of the federal securities laws on insurance companies.

The Employment Retirement Security Act of 1974 (ERISA)[160] contains serious consequences for directors and officers of insurance companies. They may be especially affected by the effect of ERISA upon (1) employee benefit plans for their own company's employees, and (2) accounts by which employee benefit plans of other employers are funded and vested by their insurance company. Not only the statutes themselves, but also the regulations and interpretive bulletins of the Labor Department and the Internal Revenue Service bear on these subjects.

§ 12.12. Liability to depositors and creditors.

The fiduciary duty of bank officers and directors is owed to the depositors and shareholders of the bank.[161] Persons who are in control of a bank, regardless of their titles, if any, have the same fiduciary responsibility.[162]

---

157. E.g., Blue Chip Stamps v. Manor Drug Stores, 421 U.S. 723, 44 L.Ed.2d 539, 95 S.Ct. 1917 (1975); Ernst & Ernst v. Hochfelder, 425 U.S. 185, 47 L.Ed.2d 668, 96 S.Ct. 1375, reh'g denied, 425 U.S. 985 (1976).

158. Marsh v. Armada Corp., 533 F.2d 978, 984 (6th Cir. 1976).

159. E.g., In re Equity Funding Corp. of Am. Sec. Litig., 416 F. Supp. 161 (C.D. Cal. 1976).

160. 28 U.S.C. § 1001 et seq. See supra Chapter 9.

161. Lane v. Chowning, 610 F.2d 1385, 1388-89 (8th Cir. 1979).

162. Garner v. Pearson, 545 F. Supp. 549, 557 (M.D. Fla. 1982).

As a rule, wrongdoing by bank officers or directors that adversely affects all depositors creates a liability which is an asset of the bank, and only it or its receiver may sue for its recovery. Individual depositors may sue in their own right, if they suffer a wrong that is distinctly theirs and not common to all.[163]

Depositors of a bank stand in the position of creditors.[164] In that capacity, under the common-law rule, they may not maintain an action against the bank's directors and officers for breaches of duty which resulted in damage to the creditors. Again, the right of action is an asset of the bank.[165] But when state [166] or federal[167] statutes impose liability for losses suffered by creditors, they may recover their actual losses.[168]

Of course, they may also recover from directors and officers for losses due to fraud,[169] as well as for active participation in any intentionally wrongful act which directly operates to the prejudice of a depositor or creditor.[170]

In a landmark case in which recovery from a dominant director was upheld, the Second Circuit stated that where the director "substantially abdicated the responsibilities of his office, then the common-law principle — which is in addition

---

163. Adato v. Kagan, 599 F.2d 1111, 1117 (2d Cir. 1979).

164. Crocker-Citizens Nat'l Bank v. Control Metals Corp., 566 F.2d 631 (9th Cir. 1971); Miller v. Wells Fargo Bank Int'l Corp., 540 F.2d 548 (2d Cir. 1976); United States v. Bank of Celina, 721 F.2d 163 (6th Cir. 1983).

165. Annotation, "Right of creditor of corporation to maintain a personal action against directors or officers for mismanagement," 50 A.L.R. 462, 463 (1927); Hi-Pro Fish Prod., Inc. v. McClure, 224 F. Supp. 485, 489-90 (E.D. Ark. 1963).

166. E.g., Ohio Rev. Code Ann. § 1115.06; Mass. Gen. L. ch. 156, § 37.

167. E.g., 12 U.S.C. § 93.

168. Hart v. Guardian Trust Co., 48 Ohio L. Abs. 545, 75 N.E.2d 570 (1945); National Refracteries Co. v. Bay State Builders Supply Co., 137 N.E.2d 221 (Mass. 1956).

169. Society Milion Athena v. National Bank of Greece, 169 Misc. 882, 9 N.Y.S.2d 177 (1938), aff'd, 256 A.D. 804, 9 N.Y.S.2d 895, modified on other grounds, 281 N.Y. 282, 22 N.E.2d 374 (1939).

170. E.g., United States Fid. & Guar. Co. v. Corning State Sav. Bank, 154 Iowa 588, 134 N.W. 857 (1912); Daniels v. Berry, 148 S.C. 446, 146 S.E. 420 (1929).

to the statutory rules — operates to make him liable for losses improperly incurred by his co-officers to whom he has abandoned the operation of the bank." The court ruled that a legislative enactment of a standard of due care should be considered as the controlling test of negligence.[171]

Officers and directors of savings and loan associations,[172] and of banks [173] are not liable for mistakes in judgment if their acts are fairly within the scope of responsibility confided to them. Thus the fact that an investment is hazardous will not subject savings and loan association directors to personal liability for making a loan, if the loan was not prohibited by statute and they acted with the ordinary care and prudence of business men.[174] Under the common-law rules, bank directors are not personally liable because they assent to the receipt of deposits with knowledge that their bank is insolvent.[175]

§ 12.13. Liability for false statement or report.

Criminal liability may be imposed on corporate officers and directors under 18 U.S.C. § 1014, for knowingly making a false statement of material facts for the purpose of influencing the action of a federal or federal-affiliated institution or agency. The requirement of "materiality" means that all statements supplied to such institutions or agencies, which have the capacity to influence their decisions, must be accurate or at least not knowingly false. Reliance by the institution or agency is not an element of the offense.[176]

---

171. Michelsen v. Penney, 135 F.2d 409, 419 (2d Cir. 1943). Cf. Bowerman v. Hamner, 250 U.S. 504, 63 L.Ed. 1113, 39 S.Ct. 549 (1919).

172. Citizens Bldg., Loan & Sav. Ass'n of Plainfield v. Coriell, 34 N.J. Eq. 383 (1881).

173. 9 Ohio Jur. 3d Banks § 79.

174. E.g., Sheffield & South Yorkshire Permanent Bldg. Soc. v. Aizlewood, L.R. 44 Ch. D. 412 (1890).

175. Oleson v. Retzlaff, 184 Minn. 624, 238 N.W. 12, aff'd, 184 Minn. 624, 239 N.W. 672 (1931). Cf. Solomon v. Bates, 118 N.C. 311, 24 S.E. 378 (1896).

176. United States v. Goberman, 458 F.2d 226 (3d Cir. 1972); United States v. Glassey, 715 F.2d 352 (7th Cir.), cert. dismissed, 464 U.S. 1032 (1983).

This statute applies to directors and officers of financial institutions. For example, a false written statement by the manager of the mortgage loan department of a national bank to the Home Owners' Loan Corporation for the purpose of influencing its action upon a loan application was held a violation of a predecessor of 18 U.S.C. § 1014.[177]

A private right of action to recover damages resulting from a violation of this statute is not maintainable.[178] In rendering a decision to that effect, the court held (1) that a private right would not be implied from a purely penal statute as distinguished from a regulatory statute, and (2) effective state remedies were readily available.[179]

Civil liability is imposed upon directors of national banks by the national banking laws. The subjects covered by those laws are pre-empted and may not be the basis of actions to enforce common-law claims. Thus, there is no common-law liability for fraud imposed upon bank directors based upon false reports made by them.[180]

Directors of state banks may be held personally liable to those injured by false statements or reports.[181]

§ 12.14. Liability arising out of loans.

Transactions involving loans have been the basis for more actions against bank officers and directors than any other item. Frequently such matters involve 12 U.S.C. § 84, which places restrictions on the extension of unsecured credit by national banks. Under 12 U.S.C. § 93, a bank director who participates in or assents to an excessive loan is personally

---

177. United States v. Kreidler, 11 F. Supp. 402 (S.D. Iowa 1935).

178. Olympic Capital Corp. v. Newman, 276 F. Supp. 646 (C.D. Cal. 1967), distinguishing Reass v. United States, 99 F.2d 752 (4th Cir. 1938).

179. Id. at 657. See also Note, "Implying Civil Remedies From Federal Regulatory Statutes," 77 Harv. L. Rev. 285 (1963).

180. Yates v. Jones Nat'l Bank, 206 U.S. 158, 51 L.Ed. 1002, 27 S.Ct. 638 (1907); Thomas v. Taylor, 224 U.S. 73, 56 L.Ed. 673, 32 S.Ct. 403 (1912); Jones Nat'l Bank v. Yates, 240 U.S. 541, 60 L.Ed. 788, 36 S.Ct. 429 (1916).

181. See 10 Am. Jur. 2d Banks § 200.

liable for the resulting loss.[182] Deliberately refraining from investigating what a director should investigate may be enough to impose liability.[183]

In such a case, if the excessive loan is the result of a single transaction, the directors who participated in or assented to it are liable for the entire sum loaned plus interest and less salvage.[184] If the excessive loan is the result of a series of transactions, the damages may consist of only the excess over the loan limit.[185]

State statutes may impose personal liability upon officers and directors who participate in the making of loans to or guaranteed by bank directors or officers in violation of statutory restrictions.[186]

Under 12 U.S.C. § 375b, national banks are prohibited from making loans to certain insiders, such as their own officers or individuals or companies owning more than a certain percentage of the bank's stock. A private cause of action for violation of that statute is provided by 12 U.S.C. § 503, and personal liability for damages may be imposed on directors and officers of member banks of the Federal Reserve System.[187]

The mere fact that a loan is hazardous will not, of itself, impose personal liability upon directors who assented to it, if it does not violate statutory restrictions.[188] And savings and loan association directors have not been held liable for losses

---

182. Corsicana Nat'l Bank v. Johnson, 251 U.S. 68, 64 L.Ed. 141, 40 S.Ct. 82 (1919).

183. Payne v. Ostrus, 50 F.2d 1039 (8th Cir. 1931). But cf. Holman v. Cross, 75 F.2d 909 (6th Cir. 1935).

184. McQueen v. First Nat'l Bank, 36 Ariz. 74, 283 P. 273 (1929); Holman v. Cross, supra note 183.

185. First Nat'l Bank of Lincolnwood v. Keller, 318 F. Supp. 339 (N.D. Ill. 1970), aff'd by 7th Cir., January 5, 1972 (unreported).

186. E.g., Ohio Rev. Code Ann. § 1107.22; Mass. Ann. Laws ch. 168, § 29. See also Nutt v. State ex rel. Fulton, 53 Ohio App. 492, 5 N.E.2d 708 (1936).

187. Marx v. Centran Corp., 747 F.2d 1536, 1547-48 (6th Cir. 1984), cert. denied, 471 U.S. 1255 (1985).

188. Olesen v. Retzlaff, 184 Minn. 624, 238 N.W. 12, aff'd, 184 Minn. 624, 239 N.W. 672 (1931).

resulting from an honest mistake in the value of land upon which they loaned money for their association.[189] However, the common law requires directors of financial institutions to use the reasonable care of prudent business men in loaning their institutions' funds.[190] They may be held personally liable when, by the exercise of due diligence, they could have prevented losses resulting from the making of a bad loan.[191]

When directors delegate their duty of supervising loans to a committee[192] or to an officer,[193] they cannot escape personal liability for bad loans if, by the exercise of reasonable care and due diligence, they could have prevented the bad loans and resulting losses.

§ 12.15. Liability for loan participations.

Banks usually do not plan loan participations with a view toward the possible impact of the antifraud provisions of the federal securities laws and particularly Rule 10b-5 under the Securities Exchange Act of 1934.[194] However, under the *Howey* test,[195] as modified by *United Housing Foundation, Incorporated v. Forman*,[196] it is likely that a loan participation will be treated as a security.[197] In that event, participating banks will be able to require disclosure by the lead bank,

---

189. Citizens Bldg., Loan & Sav. Ass'n v. Coriell, 34 N.J.Eq. 383 (1881).

190. E.g., Ellis v. H.P. Gates Mercantile Co., 103 Miss. 560, 60 So. 649 (1913). See also Bowerman v. Hamner, 250 U.S. 504, 63 L.Ed. 1113, 39 S.Ct. 549 (1919).

191. Union Nat'l Bank v. Hill, 148 Mo. 380, 49 S.W. 1012 (1899).

192. Wilkinson v. Dodd, 40 N.J. Eq. 123, 2 A. 360 (1885), aff'd, 41 N.J. Eq. 566, 7 A. 337 (1886), aff'd, 42 N.J. Eq. 647, 9 A. 685 (1887).

193. Warner v. Penoyer, 91 F. 587 (2d Cir. 1898); Wallace v. Lincoln Sav. Bank, 89 Tenn. 630, 15 S.W. 448 (1891). Cf. Wallach v. Billings, 277 Ill. 218, 115 N.E. 382, cert. denied, 244 U.S. 659 (1917).

194. See Isaac, "Loan Participations and the Securities Laws," 59 J. Com. Bank Lending 50 (Oct. 1975).

195. SEC v. W.J. Howey Co., 328 U.S. 293, 299, 90 L.Ed. 1244, 66 S.Ct. 1100 (1946).

196. 421 U.S. 837, 44 L.Ed.2d 621, 95 S.Ct. 2051 (1975).

197. Cf. Lehigh Valley Trust Co. v. Central Nat'l Bank, 409 F.2d 989, 992 (5th Cir. 1969).

and may rely upon Rule 10b-5 to extend the lead bank's liability to co-conspirators,[198] aiders and abettors, and controlling persons.

In a loan participation, the lead bank attracts the capital needed to support the loan and handles the lending arrangements with the borrower. It has been described as "the focal point in the entire lending structure" so that other participants "invest in the judgment and skill of the lead bank in making the enterprise a success."[199]

When, as is generally the case, the participating banks have no independent relationship with the borrower,[200] the federal securities laws may impose a duty upon the lead bank to disclose all material information to the participants prior to the time they make their investment decisions. One commentator suggests that there are three categories of information that may be considered material to the loan participant. They are (1) the creditworthiness of the borrower, (2) conflicts of interest indicating the absence of arms-length dealing between the management of the lead bank and the borrower, and (3) information relating to the managerial ability and integrity of the lead bank.[201]

It may be possible to structure loan participations so that all the elements of the *Howey-Forman* definition of a security are satisfied. Generally, however, such structuring may be impracticable. Also, the customary disclaimer in a participation certificate of all warranties as to the collectibility of the loan and the financial condition of the borrower will be unavailing because of the anti-waiver provision in the Securities Exchange Act.[202]

§ 12.16. Liability for neglect of duties.

The failure of bank directors to perform the duties imposed upon them by statutes, regulations and court decisions will

---

198. See Ferguson v. Omnimedia, Inc., 469 F.2d 194 (1st Cir. 1972).

199. Note, "Bank Loan Participations: The Affirmative Duty to Disclose Under SEC Rule 10b-5," 27 Syracuse L. Rev. 807, 819 (1976).

200. Id. at 825.

201. Id. at 825-29.

202. See 15 U.S.C. § 78cc(a).

impose liability upon them for losses suffered by the derelictions of bank officers or subordinates. For example, a significant decision of the Tenth Circuit under Oklahoma law held a bank's chairman and director liable for $1.4 million for losses to the bank resulting from improper investments made by his son, the bank president.[203]

Meek, the chairman, delegated the day-to-day operations of the bank to Maxwell, his son, and spent considerable time vacationing in Vermont and traveling. Semi-retired, he kept some contact with his son and occasionally attended board meetings. Beginning in 1977 the son initiated some highly-leveraged investments in Government National Mortgage Association (GNMA) certifications which were subject to repurchase contracts. The market price of the GNMAs fluctuated as interest rates rose or fell. The bank also had to pay interest to the broker and cover price differentials on the GNMA investment, all of which produced a series of losses to the bank. Within two years the losses totalled $1.4 million.

In affirming the judgment of the district court, the Tenth Circuit pointed out:

> There is no separate standard for an ordinarily prudent non-resident director or an ordinarily prudent semi-retired director. The standard does not vary depending on one's residence or retirement status. The obligation to the corporation, and ultimately to the creditors and depositors, is the same. After all, we are applying a standard of care which the legislature intended to govern those who are charged with responsibility for other people's money.[204]

In summary, the court ruled that Meek failed to monitor the investment decisions of his son, delegated too much authority to him, and failed to respond to the bank's increasing exposure to risk.

§ 12.17. Liability arising from personal dealings.

Personal dealings of bank officers and directors may be the basis of claims against them by administrative officials and

---

203. Hoye v. Meek, 795 F.2d 893 (10th Cir. 1986).
204. Id. at 896.

agencies which, in turn, may lead to litigation by bank stock-holders as a class or derivatively in behalf of the bank. For example, the civil action by the Securities and Exchange Commission and the Comptroller of the Currency filed in the United States District Court in Georgia, April 26, 1978, charged a former bank president, T. Bertram Lance, with extensive family financial dealings.[205]

The ninety-page complaint alleged that The National Bank of Georgia (NBG), The Calhoun First National Bank (CFNB), and Lance engaged in financial irregularities and unsound banking practices, including:

(a) substantial and prolonged overdrafting in checking accounts at CFNB of Lance, his wife, certain relatives, friends, business associates, and entities controlled by them;

(b) questionable loans to bank officers and directors and persons and entities related to them;

(c) misleading entries on the bank's books and records;

(d) loans by NBG, arranged by Lance, to his relatives, business associates and friends, some of which loans he guaranteed, but his personal financial statements did not reflect certain of his liabilities;

(e) loans by NBG to Lance's relatives and associates on preferential terms and without adequate regard to the creditworthiness of the borrowers;

(f) proceeds of loans at NBG used to pay overdrafts and loans at CFNB which had been criticized by the Comptroller;

(g) proceeds of loans at NBG used for purposes other than as represented by the borrowers;

(h) financial statements provided by NBG understated borrowers liabilities and overstated their net worth;

(i) no meaningful monitoring by NBG's board of directors of the NBG management in carrying out its responsibilities.

---

205. SEC v. Nat'l Bank of Ga., Fed. Sec. L. Rep. (CCH) ¶96,402 (N.D. Ga. 1978).

Simultaneously with the filing of the complaint, the court entered its judgment enjoining Lance and the banks from violations of the antifraud, reporting and proxy provisions of the federal securities laws. The judgment also contained various specific requirements, including orders that Lance should refrain from providing certain personal guaranties, update and amend his personal financial statements, submit accurate personal financial statements when obtaining loans or other extensions of credit, refrain from overdrafts other than such as are generally available to other bank customers, and refrain from obtaining loans for use by him in any campaign for elective office, except as permitted by law.

In Oklahoma the fact that a bank president engaged in extensive personal dealings and thereby caused substantial damage to the bank was held not to impose liability on the other directors and officers in the absence of evidence that they knew of the wrongdoing or had learned of something to excite their suspicions.[206] Despite that decision in 1972, it may be questioned whether the same result would occur today in a similar case, in light of recent rulings as to the responsibilities of directors.[207]

§ 12.18. Illustrations of grounds for personal liability.

In illustrating possible grounds for imposing personal liability upon directors and officers of financial institutions, it must be borne in mind that each case must be evaluated on its particular facts and the applicable law of its jurisdiction. Also, many of the potential liabilities of directors of corporations generally will apply to directors and officers of financial institutions. Subject to those qualifications, the following list is illustrative:

    (1)   Assenting in or failure to prevent loans to executive officers, directors or shareholders in excessive

---

206. FDIC v. Boone, 361 F. Supp. 133, 165-66 (W.D. Okla. 1972).

207. E.g., Preston-Thomas Constr., Inc. v. Central Leasing Corp., 518 P.2d 1125, 1125 (Okla. App. 1974); Hoye v. Meek, supra note 203, at 896 ("directors and officers are charged with knowledge of those things which it is their duty to know and ignorance is not a basis for escaping liability").

amounts, on an unsound basis, or at preferential rates;

(2) Assenting in or failure to prevent improvident loans with inadequate security;

(3) Assenting in or failure to prevent loans upon false or fraudulent financial statements;

(4) Assenting in or failure to prevent imprudent overdrafts;

(5) Assenting in or failure to prevent publication or filing of a false statement or report;

(6) Assenting in or failing to prevent waste, theft or squandering of the institution's assets;

(7) Assenting in or failure to prevent payment of excessive salaries;

(8) Assenting in or failing to prevent antitrust violations resulting in the imposition of civil or criminal penalties upon the institution;

(9) Declaring and paying, or assenting in the declaration and payment of excessive, unlawful or unreasonable dividends;

(10) Dereliction of director's duties by inattention, ignorance or negligence;

(11) Disclosure of private information with resulting damage to customer, depositor or shareholders;

(12) Discriminatory disclosure or nondisclosure of non-public information gained by virtue of official position;

(13) Discrimination against customers, depositors, employees or shareholders;

(14) Disregarding provisions of the institution's charter or bylaws;

(15) Disregarding regulations of state or federal regulatory agencies;

(16) Failure to bond personnel;

(17) Failure to establish and maintain a sound investment policy;

(18) Failure to establish good internal controls and audit procedures;

382

(19) Failing to exercise due diligence to prevent defalcations by officers or employees;

(20) Failure to install and secure a sound, supervised loan program;

(21) Failure to keep informed of their institution's solvency;

(22) Failure to know, understand and comply with statutes that govern their duties and obligations;

(23) Fiduciary derelictions resulting in damage to the institution or losses to shareholders, depositors or creditors;

(24) Fiduciary derelictions under ERISA;

(25) Fraudulent or deceitful conduct;

(26) Improper private disclosure of inside information before public announcement;

(27) Inadequate supervision of officers, employees or committees to whom directors have delegated some of their responsibilities;

(28) Inadequate supervision of trust department activities;

(29) Invasion of privacy of depositors, employees or shareholders;

(30) Misuse of the institution's funds to pay expenses of or reward directors, officers or management employees;

(31) Participating in any intentionally wrongful act which directly operates to the prejudice of depositors or creditors;

(32) Trading in or recommending the institution's securities without adequate disclosure of material inside information;

(33) Violation of state or federal criminal statutes with resulting damage to the institution.[208]

---

208. See also pamphlet, "Duties and Liabilities of Directors of National Banks," published by the Office of Comptroller of the Currency.

COROLLARY REFERENCES

Baker, "Outside Directors of Failing Banks: When Are They Personally Liable?," 101 Banking L.J. 292 (1984).

Burgee, "Purchase and Assumption Transactions Under Federal Deposit Insurance Act," 14 Forum 1146 (1977).

Deal, "Bank Regulatory Enforcement — 1985 Developments," 42 Bus. Law. 145 (1986).

Deal, "Liability of Bank Officers," 39 Bus. Law. 1083 (1984).

Dunne, "The Liability of Bank Directors Under the New Federal Common Law or Swift v. Tyson Resurgent," 8 Forum 286 (1972).

Foley, "The Federal Deposit Insurance Corporation v. Wood: The FDIC and the Failed Bank, and the Seemingly Insurmountable Presumption," 17 U. of Tol. L. Rev. 693 (1986).

Glidden, "National Bank Directors' Liability: The Case for Private Rights of Action," 102 Banking L.J. 142 (1985).

Grunewald & Golden, "Bank Director Liability Post-FIRA: How to Avoid It," 98 Banking L.J. 412 (1981).

Hershman, "Liabilities and Responsibilities of Corporate Officers and Directors," 33 Bus. Law. 263 (1977).

Kenney, "Bank Directors' and Officers' Liability," 38 Ins. Couns. J. 575 (1971).

Knepper, "A Primer on Bank Directors' and Officers' Indemnification and Liability Insurance," 156 The Bankers Magazine 88 (Summer, 1973).

Knepper, "An Overview of D & O Liability for Insurance Company Directors and Officers," 45 Ins. Couns. J. 63 (1978).

Nichols, "FIRA: Emerging Patterns of Director Liability," 103 Banking L.J. 151 (1986).

Norcross, "The Bank Insolvency Game: FDIC Superpowers, The D'Oench Doctrine, and Federal Common Law," 103 Banking L.J. 316 (1986).

Schroeder, "Handling the Complex Fidelity or Financial Institution Bond Claim: The Liablity of the Insured's Officers and Directors and Their D & O Carrier," 21 Tort & Ins. L.J. 269 (1986).

Shockey, "Discovery in Bank Regulatory Enforcement Actions," 42 Bus. Law. 91 (1986).

Skillern, "Closing and Liquidation of Banks in Texas," 26 Sw. L.J. 830 (1972).

Skillern, "Federal Deposit Insurance Corporation and the Failed Bank: The Past Decade," 99 Banking L.J. 233-257, 292-325 (1982).

Vartanian & Schley, "Bank Officer and Director Liability — Regulatory Actions," 39 Bus. Law. 1021 (1984).

Note, "Public Creditors of Financial Institutions: The Case for a Derivative Right of Action," 86 Yale L.J. 1422 (1977).

Annotation, "Liability of national bank directors for excessive loans under National Bank Act," 11 A.L.R. Fed. 606 (1972).

Comment, "A Realistic Duty of Care for Outside Bank Directors," 51 Tenn. L. Rev. 569 (1984).

Chapter 13

NONPROFIT AND CHARITABLE ORGANIZATIONS

§ 13.01. Nonprofit organizations: generally.

The term "nonprofit" used in this chapter is intended to be synonymous with "not-for-profit," regardless of distinctions suggested by some commentators.[1] The most commonly accepted criterion of this type of corporation is whether any income or profit resulting from its operations is distributable to its members, directors or officers.[2] The phrase "income or profit" means "net income or profit" because the payment of reasonable compensation to members, directors or officers for services rendered is proper.[3]

The term "organizations" in the chapter title indicates that the matters discussed relate not only to directors and officers of nonprofit corporations, but also to like officials of associations, leagues, churches, educational institutions and other such groups.

---

1. E.g., Weeks, "The Not-For-Profit Business Corporation," 19 Clev. St. L. Rev. 303 (1970). But see Oleck, Non-profit Corporations, Organizations and Associations 9 (3d ed. 1974).

2. E.g., Model Non-Profit Corp. Act § 2.01(c) (1964). Mich. Comp. Laws § 450.117; Ohio Rev. Code Ann. § 1702.01(C).

3. Model Non-Profit Corp. Act § 26.

387

Professor Howard L. Oleck,[4] a recognized authority in this field, has defined a nonprofit organization as follows:

> ... one that is not used for personal financial enrichment of any of its members or managers, and no portion of the money or property of which is permitted to inure to the benefit of any private individual, except as a proper grant according to its state-approved purpose, or as salaries paid for employee-type services rendered to the organization.[5]

In case of uncertainty as to whether a particular corporation is organized and operated for profit or nonprofit, the general rule is that its character will be determined by the authority it actually possesses and may exercise under its charter.[6] Another oft-stated rule is that what the corporation actually does is of more importance in determining its status than what it professes to be.[7]

On the other hand, the fact that a corporation is organized and operated not for profit does not mean that it may not have gain or profit or net income; rather, it means that all "profit" must be used for the purposes set forth in the articles and cannot be distributed as income to the members.[8] Intangible or nonpecuniary benefits to the members, however, from improved facilities or improved business conditions, and the like, will not usually change the corporation's nonprofit status.[9]

In certain instances particular corporate activities may be of such a nature as to deprive a nonprofit corporation of its tax exemption.[10] In that event, unless such activities were

---

4. Professor of Law, Wake Forest University.

5. Oleck, "Nature of American Non-Profit Organizations," 17 N.Y.L.F. 1066, 1074, 1075 (1971).

6. State ex rel. Russell v. Sweeney, 153 Ohio St. 66, 91 N.E.2d 13 (1951).

7. Central Credit Union v. Comptroller, 243 Md. 175, 220 A.2d 568, 570 (1966); Shaker Med. Center Hosp. v. Blue Cross, 115 Ohio App. 497, 183 N.E.2d 628 (1962).

8. American Jersey Cattle Club v. Glander, 152 Ohio St. 506, 90 N.E.2d 433 (1950).

9. State v. Lally, 59 Wash. 2d 849, 270 P.2d 971 (1962).

10. Supra note 8.

authorized by the charter or bylaws, or were expressly approved by the members, the corporate officers and directors may be held liable for the loss.[11]

§ 13.02. Duties of nonprofit corporation directors and officers.

Directors and officers of a nonprofit corporation are fiduciaries who are required to exercise their powers in accordance with the duties imposed by the applicable state statutes.[12] They are usually required to exercise due care and undivided loyalty to the corporation's interests in the same manner as are persons holding similar positions in business corporations.[13]

Several state legislatures have adopted substantially identical language in their business corporation statutes and nonprofit corporation acts.[14]

In Delaware, the general corporation law applies to all corporations, stock and nonstock as well as business and nonprofit (including charitable and religious).[15] Aside from the statutes, there has been some confusion and conflict under case law as to whether the duties of directors and officers of nonprofit organizations should be governed by trust standards, business or corporate standards, or some combination thereof.

One commentator suggests that nonprofit organizations may be classified in three categories: donative nonprofits, to serve donors; mutual benefit nonprofits, to serve customers; and cooperative corporations to serve producers.[16] That being

---

11. See Diedrick v. Helm, 217 Minn. 483, 14 N.W.2d 913 (1944); Neese v. Brown, 218 Tenn. 686, 405 S.W.2d 577 (1964).

12. Raven's Cove Townhouses, Inc. v. Knuppe Dev. Co., 113 Cal. App. 2d 783, 799, 171 Cal. Rptr. 334 (1981).

13. E.g., Mile-O-Mo Fishing Club, Inc. v. Noble, 62 Ill. App. 2d 50, 210 N.E.2d 12 (1965).

14. E.g., Cal. Corp. Code §§ 5000-9927; N.Y. Not-for-Profit Corp. Law § 701 et seq.; Ch. 1702, Ohio Rev. Code Ann.

15. Del. Code Ann. tit. 8, § 101 et seq.

16. Ellman, "Another Theory of Nonprofit Corporations," 80 Mich. L. Rev. 999, 1050 (1982).

the case, it is understandable that a single nonprofit statute to govern all three categories may not be a realistic objective.

Of course a nonprofit corporation code provides only part of the law applicable to such organizations. Tax laws, in particular, and other statutes conferring benefits are also significant. And many questions untreated by legislation must be answered by court decisions under the common law. All of the above will be noted in the discussions which follow.

§ 13.03. Charitable organizations: characteristics.

Charitable or eleemosynary organizations are such as are created, not for private gain or profit, but for charitable purposes. They are private corporations endowed by private benefactions, even though incorporated for the administration of a public charity. Their directors are sometimes called trustees, but their legal position is the same, no matter by what name they are called. They stand in a fiduciary relation as far as corporate business is concerned.[17]

Educational institutions,[18] hospitals open to anyone,[19] religious organizations,[20] art galleries and student loan foundations[21] are examples of charitable organizations.

§ 13.04. Duties of charitable corporation directors and officers.

The modern trend is to apply corporate rather than trust principles in defining the duties of directors of charitable corporations. Thus a New Jersey court ruled that the trustees of a charitable corporation could properly enter into a contract with a bank executor for custodial and investment service. The court concluded that the responsibilities of members of a

---

17. Gilbert v. McLeod Infirmary, 219 S.C. 174, 64 S.E.2d 524 (1951).

18. E.g., Trustees of Dartmouth College v. Woodward, 17 U.S. 518, 4 L.Ed. 629 (1819).

19. Holden Hosp. Corp. v. Southern Ill. Hosp. Corp., 22 Ill. 2d 150, 174 N.E.2d 793, 795 (1961).

20. In re Estate of Freshour, 185 Kan. 434, 345 P.2d 689 (1959).

21. Sessions v. Skelton, 163 Ohio St. 409, 127 N.E.2d 378 (1955).

charitable corporation's governing board should be considered more under the developed law of corporations than of trustees.[22] But the law is unsettled on this point.[23] In considering whether a charitable corporation's directors were bound by the same standards as trustees of a charitable trust, California held that all "property held by a benevolent corporation is impressed with the charitable trust [and] the presumption follows that it will be so used."[24] West Virginia has ruled that bequest of a fund to the Bluefield State College as a permanent endowment should be applied in accordance with the testator's wish.[25] There is substantial additional authority to like effect.[26]

The trend to recognize that trustees of charitable trusts and directors of charitable corporations may be appropriately governed by principles derived from the law of business corporations is evidenced by the widespread adoption of the Uniform Management of Institutional Funds Act (UMIFA), now in effect in twenty-eight states and the District of Columbia.[27] That statute applies a "business judgment" rule to such directors and trustees instead of the "prudent man" rule usually applied to private trustees. Under the common law, and especially in states where the UMIFA has not been enacted, different standards may apply to corporate boards and trust boards.

In the District of Columbia, before the adoption of UMIFA, a federal court wrote:

---

22. Midlantic Nat'l Bank v. Frank G. Thompson Found., 170 N.J. Super. 125, 405 A.2d 866 (1979).

23. Stern v. Lucy Webb Hayes Nat'l Training School for Deaconesses & Missionaries, 381 F. Supp. 1003 (D.D.C. 1974).

24. Smarkand of Santa Barbara, Inc. v. County of Santa Barbara, 216 Cal. App. 2d 341, 31 Cal. Rptr. 151, 159 (1963).

25. State ex rel. West Virginia Bd. of Educ. v. Sims, 113 W. Va. 269, 101 S.E.2d 190 (1957).

26. See, e.g., Blackwell, "The Charitable Corporation and the Charitable Trust," 24 Wash. U.L.Q. 1 (1938); Lincoln, "A Question on Gifts to Charitable Corporations," 25 Va. L. Rev. 764 (1929); Note, "The Charitable Corporation," 64 Harv. L. Rev. 1168 (1951).

27. E.g., Ohio Rev. Code Ann. § 1715.51 et seq. See also infra section 13.14.

> Both trustees and corporate directors are liable for losses
> occasioned by their negligent mismanagement of invest-
> ments. However, the degree of care required appears to
> differ in many jurisdictions. A trustee is uniformly held
> to a high standard of care and will be liable for simple
> negligence, while a director must often have committed
> "gross negligence" or otherwise be guilty of more than
> mere mistakes of judgment.[28]

That decision dealt with claims of mismanagement, nonmanagement and self-dealing by trustees of a nonprofit, charitable hospital. Noting that board members of most large
charitable institutions fall in the same class as corporate directors, as distinguished from traditional trustees, the court
required of them the exercise of ordinary and reasonable care
in the performance of their duties, exhibiting honesty and
good faith.[29]

In an order issued contemporaneously with his Memorandum Opinion, Judge Gesell held that each director or trustee
of a charitable hospital organized under the Non-Profit Corporation Act of the District of Columbia[30] has a continuing
duty of loyalty and care in the management of the hospital's
fiscal and investment affairs and acts in violation of that duty
if:

(1) he fails, while assigned to a particular committee of
the Board having stated financial or investment responsibilities under the bylaws of the corporation, to
use diligence in supervising and periodically inquiring into the acts of those officers, employees and outside experts to whom any duty to make day-to-day
financial or investment decisions within such committee's responsibility has been assigned or delegated,[31] or

---

28. Stern v. Lucy Webb Hayes, etc., supra note 23, at 1013.

29. See also Beard v. Achenbach Mem. Hosp. Ass'n, 170 F.2d 859, 862
(10th Cir. 1948). Cf. Blankenship v. Boyle, 329 F. Supp. 1089 (D.D.C. 1971).

30. D.C. Code Ann. § 29-501 et seq.

31. See Cary & Bright, The Law and Lore of Endowment Funds: Report
to the Ford Foundation 58-61 (1969); Restatement (Second) of Trusts, § 379,

(2) he knowingly permits the hospital to enter into business transactions with himself or with any corporation, partnership or association in which he holds a position as trustee, director, partner, general manager, principal officer or substantial shareholder without previously having informed all persons charged with approving that transaction of his interest or position and of any significant facts known to him indicating that the transaction might not be in the best interests of the hospital,[32] or

(3) he actively participates in, except as required by the preceding paragraph, or votes in favor of a decision by the board or any committee or subcommittee thereof to transact business with himself or with any corporation partnership or association in which he holds a position as trustee, director, partner, general manager, principal officer, or substantial shareholder; or

(4) he fails to perform his duties honestly in good faith, and with reasonable diligence and care. Notwithstanding directors of a charitable corporation may serve without compensation, and that they fill part-time offices for which many of them have no special competency, they may not abstain from discharging their fiduciary duties which require their participation actively and fully in management of the corporate affairs. The law does not permit the creation of a sterilized board of directors.

---

comment b (1959); Heit v. Bixby, 276 F. Supp. 217, 231 (E.D. Mo. 1967); cf. DePinto v. Provident Sec. Life Ins. Co., 374 F.2d 37 (9th Cir.), cert. denied, 389 U.S. 822 (1967).

32. Mayflower Hotel Stockholders Protective Comm. v. Mayflower Hotel Corp., 89 U.S. App. D.C. 171, 193 F.2d 666 (1951); Fowle Mem. Hosp. Co. v. Nicholson, 189 N.C. 44, 126 S.E. 94 (1925).

§ 13.05. Financial management.

In all categories of nonprofit organizations[33] financial management is a heavy responsibility of directors or trustees. Their task is sometimes more difficult than that of their counterparts in the business corporation field for several reasons. Service is the criterion of success for the nonprofit organization, not profitability. Measurement of service has few guidelines.

Money-making is, of course, not the objective of nonprofit organizations and state laws vary as to the treatment of permissible business activities of such entities. Some state laws prohibit any business activity that does not directly promote the declared corporate purposes.[34] The Model Nonprofit Corporation Act and the New York Not-For-Profit Corporation Law, to the contrary, permit nonprofit corporations to realize profits from unrelated business activities. But prudent investment of funds and providing adequate safeguards for them involve internal controls not only of funds but also of securities, equipment, buildings and land. Controlling, administering and planning the use of resources are of major importance in financial management of nonprofit organizations.

Such entities need to keep their administrative costs under control so that the charity dollar may be spent for charitable purposes. But the contributor expects an accounting and may be apt to hold the director or trustee legally and morally accountable for the successes or failures of his organization. Violations of duty in financial management procedures may impose liability upon directors to restore losses caused by breaches of duty,[35] to provide detailed accounting of their

---

33. See supra section 13.02, at note 16.

34. Oleck, Non-profit Corporations, Organizations, and Associations 184 (3d ed. 1974).

35. Schroeder v. American Nat'l Red Cross, 215 Wis. 54, 254 N.W. 371 (1934).

activities,[36] and they are subject to being enjoined from further wrongdoing.[37]

In the area of financial management, the director's duty of loyalty is of particular significance. Most violations of that duty involve self-dealing or conflict of interest. Variance among state laws in this respect makes it necessary to be familiar with the applicable provisions. Moreover, whenever private foundations are concerned, the federal tax statutes and regulations relating to such entities must be consulted.

§ 13.06. Associations: characteristics.

Generally, the term "association"[38] is employed to indicate a collection of persons who have joined together for a specified objective. The term signifies a confederation or union of persons for particular purposes. At common law an association was not a legal entity and had no separate status distinct from its members.[39] However, in several states such organizations have been accorded entity status and are permitted by statute to contract and sue or be sued in their own names.[40] And some courts have held that the "legal fiction of the entity for all purposes of law of corporations is equally applicable to unincorporated labor unions."[41]

---

36. Woodside Presbyterian Church v. Burden, 240 A.D. 43, 269 N.Y.S. 682 (1923), appeal dismissed, 267 N.Y. 690, 191 N.E. 629 (1934).

37. Healy v. Loomis Inst., 102 Conn. 410, 128 A. 774 (1925).

38. Also referred to as a "voluntary association" or an "unincorporated association."

39. Martin v. Curran, 303 N.Y. 276, 101 N.E.2d 683 (1951). Cf. Lyons v. American Legion Post No. 650 Realty Co., 172 Ohio St. 331, 175 N.E.2d 733 (1961).

40. E.g., ch. 1745, Ohio Rev. Code Ann. See also State ex rel. Ohio High School Athletic Ass'n v. Judges of Court of Common Pleas, 173 Ohio St. 239, 181 N.E.2d 261 (1962); Curtis v. Albion-Brown's Post 590 Am. Legion, 74 Ill. App. 2d 144, 219 N.E.2d 386 (1966). See also, e.g., Cal. Civ. Proc. Code § 388; Del. Code Ann. tit. 10, § 3904; Mich. Comp. Laws § 600.2051; Va. Code Ann. § 8.01-15.

41. E.g., Maizga v. International Union of Operating Eng'rs, 2 Ohio App. 2d 153, 165, 196 N.E.2d 324, 331 (1964), aff'd, 2 Ohio St. 2d 49, 205 N.E.2d 884 (1965).

Whether the members of an association are bound by a judgment against it depends (1) upon particular statutes relating to that subject[42] or (2) whether individual members were required to be joined[43] or have been served with process.[44]

The individual members of an association are, of course, personally liable for torts which they themselves commit or in which they participate or ratify.[45] Where a statute permits suit against an association as an entity, it is merely cumulative unless it expressly abolishes the liability of the members individually.[46]

Associations are found in most areas of society where people join together in a common interest. Churches, unions, fraternal societies, trade and political organizations, medical societies and lawyers organizations are a few. There is a relative dearth of legislation relating to associations because legislatures seem to prefer the corporate form.

The management of an association has only the powers granted by its charter and bylaws, absent express statutory provisions. Thus, members of an association may have more control over management than in the case of a nonprofit corporation.[47]

§ 13.07. Duties of association directors and officers.

During the directors' and officers' liability crisis in the middle 1980's, some states enacted special statutes to confer qualified immunities from liability upon directors of various

---

42. E.g., Del. Code Ann. tit. 10, § 3904.

43. See Brunson, "Some Problems Presented by Unincorporated Associations in Civil Procedure," 7 S.C.L.Q. 394, 419 (1955).

44. E.g., Md. Code Ann., Cts. & Jud. Proc. §§ 6-408, 11-105; N.C. Gen. Stat. § 1-69.1.

45. E.g., Montgomery Ward & Co. v. Langer, 168 F.2d 182 (8th Cir. 1948).

46. Lyons v. American Legion Post No. 650 Realty Co., supra note 39.

47. E.g., Dillard Univ. v. Local Union 1419, 169 So. 2d 221 (La. App. 1964).

charitable organizations.[48] Some of the statutes afforded such protection to directors and trustees of associations, societies and other organizations.[49] Subject to such special immunities, the officers and directors of associations have the same powers, duties and liabilities as their counterparts in business corporations.

Association directors may not take secret profits from dealings with or for the association and may be required to account to the association for such profits,[50] the same as corporate officers.[51] They are personally liable for fraud or breach of their fiduciary duty in the conduct of the association's affairs.[52] They have a duty to promote the common interest of the association members and must perform their duties in accordance with the association's constitution and bylaws.[53] If they incur indebtedness in excess of the amount limited in the bylaws or other regulations, they may be held personally liable and cannot seek indemnity or contribution from other association members who did not assent to their actions.[54]

There is also authority that personal liability may arise if an association's officer acts without authority or in excess of his authority.[55]

Generally association directors or officers may be subject to criminal liability for acts performed in their official capacities.[56] The rule may be to the contrary if the statute imposes no duty on the officer but puts it on the association.[57] Such

---

48. See infra section 13.14.

49. E.g., N.Y. Not-for-Profit Corp. Law § 720a; Ohio Rev. Code Ann. § 2305.38.

50. Ferguson v. Crawford, 151 Ark. 503, 236 S.W. 837 (1922).

51. Cf. Diamond v. Oreamuno, 24 N.Y.2d 494, 301 N.Y.S.2d 78, 248 N.E.2d 910 (1969).

52. Ferguson v. Crawford, supra note 50.

53. Rachford v. Indemnity Ins. Co. of North Am., 183 F. Supp. 875 (S.D. Cal. 1960).

54. McFadden v. Leeka, 48 Ohio St. 513, 28 N.E. 874 (1891).

55. Pacific Freight Lines v. Valley Motor Lines, 72 Cal. App. 2d 505, 164 P.2d 901 (1946).

56. See People v. Gilmore, 273 Ill. 143, 112 N.E. 458 (1916).

57. Day v. State, 341 N.E.2d 209 (Ind. App. 1976).

officers may be held in contempt for disobedience, with knowledge, of an injunction against their association.[58]

§ 13.08. Duties of directors of condominium associations.

Statutes regulating condominium ownership are in effect in all states.[59] While there are similarities among the statutory provisions, there are also substantial differences. Accordingly, generalized observations as to questions of tort liability are not possible. Because many areas of legal conflict are not dealt with in the statutes, there are open questions as to the liabilities of the various condominium entities, such as the manager, the board of directors or managers, the developer, the association or the members.

In instances where condominium statutes do not cover the subject, nonprofit corporation statutes or the law relating to voluntary associations may be applicable. The common-law rules may furnish answers in some instances.[60]

Directors and officers of a condominium association owe fiduciary duties to the association and may be held liable for their breach. In a Florida case, such liability was imposed for failure to collect maintenance payments from the developer.[61] In another Florida action, suit was brought against condominium directors and officers for secretly including an escalation clause in a long-term recreational lease. The court held the action proper against the directors and officers but not against a corporate lessor who allegedly controlled the directors.[62]

---

58. W.B. Conkey Co. v. Russell, 111 F. 417 (D. Ind. 1901), appeal dismissed sub nom. Bessette v. W.B. Conkey Co., 133 F. 165 (7th Cir. 1904), cert. denied, 196 U.S. 638 (1905).

59. E.g., Cal. Civ. Code § 1350 et seq.; Fla. Stat. Ann. § 714.101 et seq.; Ill. Ann. Stat. ch. 30, § 301 et seq.; Mich. Comp. Laws § 559.101 et seq.; N.Y. Real Prop. Law § 339-d et seq.; Ohio Rev. Code Ann. § 5311.01.

60. E.g., Schoondyke v. Heil, Heil, Smart & Golee, Inc., 89 Ill. App. 3d 640, 44 Ill. Dec. 802, 411 N.E.2d 1168 (1980).

61. B & J Holding Co. v. Weiss, 353 So. 2d 141 (Fla. App. 1977).

62. Fairways Royale Ass'n v. Hasam Realty Corp., 419 So. 2d 667 (Fla. App. 1982).

Actions arising out of the condition of the condominium premises are common. Although some such actions are against the association alone, experience suggests that sooner or later the directors and officers will be named as defendants.[63] Also actions have been brought by unit owners,[64] lessees and guests for bodily injuries arising from muggings and assault and robbery on the premises, involving third persons.[65]

A California decision held that condominium directors would be personally liable to a unit owner who was molested, raped and robbed by a third party. Inadequate lighting of the premises was known to the directors who failed to act to correct the condition and, in fact, took other action which may have exacerbated the risk.[66]

The opinion in that case also makes the point that directors cannot be held vicariously liable for a corporation's torts in which they do not participate. Their liability stems from their own wrongdoing, not from their status as directors or officers and not from the fiduciary duty they owe to the corporation and its members.[67]

§ 13.09. Cooperatives: characteristics.

Cooperatives fall within the category of mutual benefit organizations which are formed to serve their members. Although the Model Non-Profit Corporation Act[68] excludes cooperatives from its provisions, many state acts do not do so.[69] Cooperatives may be formed for a variety of purposes[70] but

---

63. Frances T. v. Village Green Owners Ass'n, 229 Cal. Rptr. 456 (1986).

64. See White v. Cox, 17 Cal. App. 3d 824, 95 Cal. Rptr. 259 (1971).

65. Admiral's Port Condominium Ass'n v. Feldman, 426 So. 2d 1054 (Fla. App. 1983); King v. Ilikai Properties, Inc., 632 P.2d 657 (Haw. App. 1981).

66. Frances T. v. Village Green Owners Ass'n, supra note 63.

67. See also Bowes v. Cincinnati Riverfront Coliseum, Inc., 12 Ohio App. 3d 12, 465 N.E.2d 905 (1983).

68. Model Non-Profit Corp. Act § 1 et seq. (1973).

69. Ill. Rev. Stat. ch. 32, § 163a3.

70. E.g., electrification, telephone service, water supply facilities, ownership of residential or business real property.

the most common is the agricultural cooperative. There are numerous state statutes regulating such organizations,[71] to which reference must be made in particular cases.

Cooperatives are usually incorporated under state law and are frequently viewed by the courts as business corporations. But they differ, in particular, from business corporations in their purpose of achieving economies for their members and patrons through collective efforts. In many respects directors and officers of cooperatives will be subjected to the same liabilities as their counterparts in business corporations.

As a natural result of the types of activity engaged in by cooperatives, considerable litigation involving them has related to the antitrust laws. Cooperatives are not immune from antitrust prosecution and civil proceedings, although Section 6 of the Clayton Act[72] and the Capper-Volstead Act[73] permit farmers to act together in cooperatives not having capital stock and extend exemption from antitrust laws to agricultural producers in associations with or without capital stock when they act together to collectively handle, market and process agricultural products. In fact, an agricultural cooperative may be formed for the sole purpose of fixing the prices at which its members' products will be sold.

Two or more cooperatives may voluntarily join together for the sole purpose of setting uniform prices for their members.[74] But such powers do not permit cooperatives to engage in anti-competitive practices in order to monopolize trade or restrain competition.[75] A cooperative may not acquire or exercise monopoly power in a predatory fashion by the use of such tactics as picketing and harrassment.[76]

---

71. See Baarda, U.S. Dep't of Agriculture, State Incorporation Statutes for Farmer Cooperatives (Oct., 1982).

72. 15 U.S.C. § 17.

73. 7 U.S.C. § 291 et seq.

74. United States v. Dairymen, Inc., 660 F.2d 192, 194 (6th Cir. 1981).

75. Maryland & Va. Milk Producers Ass'n v. United States, 362 U.S. 458, 467, 4 L.Ed.2d 880, 80 S.Ct. 847, 854 (1960).

76. Fairdale Farms, Inc. v. Yankee Milk, Inc., 635 F.2d 1037, 1044 (2d Cir. 1980).

Most states have statutes providing that cooperatives do not violate the state's antitrust laws either by operations or by agreements with members. Most such statutes allow intercooperative agreements.[77]

Cooperatives customarily use patronage refunds to return savings or net margins to their patrons. The timing, amount and manner of payment of patronage refunds is usually specified in the bylaws and is subject to the discretion of the directors. Because the demands of members for such refunds frequently conflict with the needs of the cooperative to use the money to finance its activities, these matters are often sources of litigation.[78]

As cooperatives have increased the scope of their activities, governmental regulation has correspondingly expanded. It follows that more litigation has resulted and is to be anticipated in the future.

§ 13.10. Duties of directors and officers of cooperatives.

Directors of cooperatives, elected by the members, constitute the governing body of the organization. They function as do directors of business corporations and have comparable responsibilities. They owe fiduciary obligations to the members, to their fellow directors and, in some instances, to creditors. Their duties include loyalty, diligence and obedience.[79]

Even more than in business corporations, directors of cooperatives are likely to be inexperienced in corporate business and affairs and not cognizant of the time requirements and legal burdens that accompany their offices. In the past, there was scant litigation against directors of cooperatives, but current economic conditions and the litigious temper of people

---

77. See, e.g., Stark County Milk Producers Ass'n v. Tabeling, 129 Ohio St. 159, 194 N.E. 16, 19 (1934); Kansas Wheat Growers Ass'n v. Schulte, 113 Kan. 672, 216 P. 311 (1932).

78. Berde, "Overview of Legal Problems Affecting Cooperatives," 2 Agric. L.J. 40, 47 (1980).

79. E.g., Lake Region Packing Ass'n v. Furze, 327 So. 2d 212, 217 (Fla. 1976); First Nat'l Bank v. Baron County Coop. Dairy, 252 N.W.2d 57, 59-60 (Wis. 1977).

generally is changing that situation. Moreover, personal liability for dereliction of their duties is an ever-present prospect.

The duties of directors and officers of cooperatives are imposed by the state statutes which govern them,[80] federal laws which control them and court decisions interpreting such statutes and declaring the common law.[81] They are entitled to rely on representations of officials and committees, as are directors of business corporations, but may be held liable if such reliance is misplaced.[82]

In dealing with members, directors may not prefer one group of members over another[83] or take any special advantage not available to members who are not directors.[84] They may not operate a competing business or use their positions to blunt the cooperative's competitive effort for the benefit of another enterprise.[85]

As in the case of business corporations, directors of cooperatives who engage in unauthorized and ultra vires activity will be held liable for losses so caused.[86] When such directors fail to properly supervise officers of their cooperative, they may be held liable for resulting losses, if the harm could have been prevented by the directors' diligence.[87]

When statutes, articles or bylaws of cooperatives limit the amount of interest payable on capital stock or patronage-based equity, exceeding those limits may impose liability upon directors who participate in the act. A proper balance

---

80. See Baarda, supra note 71.

81. See supra Chapters 1 through 5.

82. E.g., Parish v. Maryland & Va. Milk Producers Ass'n, 250 Md. 24, 242 A.2d 512 (1968).

83. Box v. Northrup Corp., 459 F. Supp. 540 (S.D.N.Y. 1978).

84. E.g., Wisconsin Ave. Assocs. v. 2720 Wis. Ave. Coop. Ass'n, 441 A.2d 956 (D.C. App. 1982).

85. Torea Land and Cattle Co. v. Linsenmeyer, 100 Ariz. 107, 412 P.2d 47 (1966).

86. Faberberg v. Phoenix Flour Mills Co., 50 Ariz. 227, 71 P.2d 1022 (1927).

87. Parish v. Maryland & Va. Milk Producers Ass'n, supra note 82.

should be developed and maintained between amounts paid to preferred stockholders and active members.[88]

Numerous criminal statutes, state and federal, may impose criminal liability on directors of cooperatives, and new areas of such vulnerability result from the growing diversity of cooperative businesses and ventures. Their directors should regularly seek appropriate legal advice to keep in touch with ever-changing rules, regulations and procedures.

In some instances both criminal and civil liability may be imposed upon a director on account of particular acts. For example, in a Second Circuit case the defendants were farmers who served the cooperative as directors without compensation. They authorized an installment purchase of farm machinery under a conditional sales agreement by which title to the machinery would remain in the manufacturer until full payment. Disregarding that provision, the directors authorized a chattel mortgage to a bank for additional security for the cooperative's debts. The participating directors were held liable for conversion of the machinery. Because the conditional sales agreement had not been recorded, the bank was not charged with constructive knowledge of it.[89] In such cases it must be proved that the directors either participated in the wrongdoing or had knowledge of it.[90]

§ 13.11. Liability for dealing with the organization.

Transactions between trustees of a charitable corporation and the organization may be held invalid if they are in any way unfair to the corporation. Thus a sale of an infirmary's real property to one of its trustees was nullified when the court found it was not "the result of the untrammeled reason and judgment" of the board of trustees.[91] Such transactions are subjected to close scrutiny and the courts apply a strin-

---

88. Collie v. Little River Coop., Inc., 236 Ark. 725, 370 S.W.2d 62 (1963).

89. Aeroglade Corp. v. Zeh, 301 F.2d 420 (2d Cir. 1962).

90. See also Lowell Hoit & Co. v. Detig, 320 Ill. App. 179, 50 N.E.2d 602 (1943).

91. Gilbert v. McLeod Infirmary, 219 S.C. 174, 64 S.E.2d 524 (1951).

gent test of fairness to the institution.[92] The burden of proof of fairness and of the good faith of the transaction is on the director or officer who purchases corporate assets.[93]

§ 13.12. Duty to invest: the prudent man rule.

While directors of charitable corporations are exempt from personal liability for the debts, liabilities or obligations of the corporation, they are not immune from personal liability for their own fraud, bad faith, negligent acts or other breaches of their duties.[94]

In a California action, there was a dispute among the directors of a charitable corporation as a result of which they kept it in a state of suspended animation for a five-year period. They allowed trust income to accumulate in a noninterest-bearing account and took no steps to invest it. The attorney general sued to remove the directors and surcharge them for the earnings that should have been obtained from the uninvested money.[95]

Sustaining the attorney general's position, the court held that taking an unreasonable time to invest the money was a breach of the duty to use diligence to make a trust productive.[96] This duty was applied to accumulated income as well as principal.

Because the directors did not act as men of prudence, discretion, and intelligence would have acted in the management of their own affairs, they violated the prudent man investment rule. The court distinguished executors and administrators whose "primary obligation is to safeguard assets," and held that good faith was no defense to an action

---

92. Columbus Outdoor Adv. Co. v. Harris, 127 F.2d 38, 42 (6th Cir. 1942).

93. McDermott v. O'Neil Oil Co., 200 Wis. 423, 228 N.W. 481 (1920).

94. Holt v. College of Osteopathic Physicians & Surgeons, 61 Cal. 2d 750, 757, 40 Cal. Rptr. 244, 394 P.2d 932 (1964).

95. Lynch v. John M. Redfield Found., 9 Cal. App. 3d 298, 88 Cal. Rptr. 86 (1970).

96. Higgins v. City of Santa Monica, 62 Cal. 2d 24, 29, 41 Cal. Rptr. 9, 396 P.2d 41 (1964).

against trustees based on negligence.[97] The surcharge was imposed and the defendant-directors were removed from office.

§ 13.13. Liability of school and college officials.

Public universities,[98] private colleges,[99] and public school boards of education, have some of the attributes of charitable corporations and in some instances, private colleges are organized as nonprofit corporations. As a consequence, the law relating to the liability of managers of nonprofit organizations has some application to the members of the governing boards and administrators of such institutions of learning.

A leading case, involving the right of the managers of a state supported college to expel students for misconduct[100] named the president of the college and the members of the state board of education, which governed the college, as defendants. A demonstration in a lunch grill, when the six black plaintiffs demanded to be served, and other mass public demonstrations were cited as reasons for the expulsions. The court held that the "private interest involved in this case [was] the right to remain at a public institution of higher learning in which the plaintiffs were students in good standing."[101] It ruled that a notice containing specific charges and an adequate hearing were required for due process. In addition, the students were entitled to information regarding the evidence to be presented against them, and an opportunity to offer evidence in their own behalf.[102]

Another college president was named as defendant in an action under 42 U.S.C. §§ 1981 and 1983, and other statutes, in which the Supreme Court held it was an abridgement of

---

97. Id.

98. See Chambers, The Colleges and the Courts 1962-1966, at 127-33 (1967).

99. Id. at 153-70.

100. Dixon v. Alabama State Bd. of Educ., 294 F.2d 150 (5th Cir.), cert. denied, 368 U.S. 930 (1961).

101. Id. at 157.

102. Id. at 159. Cf. Woody v. Burns, 188 So. 3d 56 (Fla. App. 1966).

individual rights under the First Amendment for the college administration to deny official recognition, without justification, to a college group such as a branch of Students for a Democratic Society.[103]

"State action," in a case based on 42 U.S.C. § 1983, was determined favorably to the plaintiffs in a class action alleging employment discrimination against women faculty members at the University of Pittsburgh.[104] The university's chancellor was named as a defendant. However, the United States Supreme Court subsequently ruled that for purposes of a claim under 42 U.S.C. § 1983 a private school does not act under color of state law in discharging employees, if the decision to discharge the employees was not compelled or influenced by any state regulation and if the school's fiscal relationship with the state was not different from that of contractors generally performing services for the government.[105] In so holding, the court affirmed the dismissal of a Section 1983 claim against the private school and its directors. The court reasoned that acts of private corporations do not become acts of the government by reason of the corporation's significant or even total engagement in performing public contracts or dependence upon the receipt of public funds.

Public school officials, in the context of imposing disciplinary penalties, are not liable in damages so long as they cannot reasonably know that their action violates clearly established constitutional rights for students, and provided they do not act with malicious intention to cause constitutional, or other, injury.[106] School board members function both as legislators and adjudicators in the disciplinary process. To impose

---

103. Healy v. James, 408 U.S. 169, 33 L.Ed.2d 266, 92 S.Ct. 2338 (1972). Cf. Papish v. Board of Curators of Univ. of Mo., 410 U.S. 667, 35 L.Ed.2d 618, 93 S.Ct. 1197 (1973).

104. Bradshaw v. University of Pittsburgh, 552 F.2d 948 (3d Cir. 1977).

105. Rendell-Baker v. Kohn, 457 U.S. 830, 73 L.Ed.2d 418, 102 S.Ct. 2764 (1982).

106. Wood v. Strickland, 420 U.S. 308, 43 L.Ed.2d 214, 95 S.Ct. 992 (1975), cited in Imbler v. Pachtman, 424 U.S. 409, 419, 47 L.Ed.2d 128, 137, 96 S.Ct. 984, 990 (1976).

liability for damages for every action which is subsequently found to have been violative of a student's constitutional rights, and which caused compensable injury, would unfairly impose the burden of mistakes made in good faith in the course of exercising discretion within the scope of official duties.[107]

However, for a school board member to be entitled to special exemption from the categorical language of the Civil Rights Act of 1871,[108] the member must conform to a standard of conduct based not only on permissible intentions, but also on knowledge of the basic, unquestioned constitutional rights of his charges. Hence, if he knew or reasonably should have known that his action would violate a student's constitutional rights, or if he acted with malicious intent to cause a deprivation of constitutional rights or other injury to the student, the school board member would not be immune from liability.[109]

The foregoing rule would appear to impose liability upon a school official who acted sincerely and in good faith, but who was found, after the fact, to have acted in ignorance of "settled, indisputable law." That seems to be a higher standard of care than the court imposed upon state officials in the Kent State University cases, wherein Chief Justice Burger wrote:

> It is the existence of reasonable grounds for the belief formed at the time and in light of all the circumstances, coupled with good-faith belief, that affords a basis for qualified immunity of executive officers for acts performed in the course of official conduct.[110]

Despite the apparent severity of the rule of *Wood v. Strickland,* members of a public school board of education were not held liable under 42 U.S.C. § 1983 to respond in damages to a teacher discharged because of pregnancy. The Sixth Circuit

---

107. Wood v. Strickland, supra note 106, 420 U.S. at 319, 43 L.Ed.2d at 223, 95 S.Ct. at 999.

108. 42 U.S.C. § 1983.

109. Wood v. Strickland, supra note 106, 420 U.S. at 322, 43 L.Ed.2d at 225, 95 S.Ct. at 1000, 1001.

110. Scheuer v. Rhodes, 416 U.S. 232, 247, 40 L.Ed.2d 90, 103, 94 S.Ct. 1683, 1692 (1974).

recognized the duty of the board members under *Strickland* to act in good faith, but held that at the time the board acted there was no adjudication then in effect, and binding on the board, deciding that its pregnancy policy was unconstitutional.[111]

§ 13.14. Statutes affecting liability.

The Uniform Management of Institutional Funds Act applies to the governing boards of charitable organizations, whether or not incorporated. It is in effect in twenty-eight states and the District of Columbia.[112] Its established standard of care follows the business judgment principle, directing that members of a governing board of an institution shall exercise ordinary business care and prudence under the facts and circumstances prevailing at the time of the action or decision.[113]

In the case of private foundations, the Internal Revenue Code imposes penalty taxes on a specified list of prohibited transactions, which include the sale, transfer or use for the benefit of "a disqualified person" of income or assets of the foundation. The term "disqualified person" includes foundation managers, who are directors, officers, trustees and certain employees.[114]

Beginning in 1986, several states have enacted legislation limiting the liability of organization directors and trustees in actions alleging violations of fiduciary responsibility. Some of the more significant are the following:

Connecticut

Any director, officer or trustee of an organization that qualifies under I.R.C. § 501(c), who is not compensated for ser-

---

111. Shirley v. Chagrin Falls Exempted Village School Bd. of Educ., 521 F.2d 1329 (6th Cir. 1975).

112. E.g., Cal. Educ. Code § 94600; Ky. Rev. Stat. Ann. § 273.510; Mich. Comp. Laws § 451.1201; Ohio Rev. Code Ann. § 1715.51.

113. Sec. 6 of UMIFA, codified in Ohio Rev. Code Ann. § 1715.56.

114. See 26 U.S.C. §§ 4941-4946.

vices, is immune for any civil liability for any act within the scope of official functions unless it constitutes willful, or wanton misconduct.[115]

Delaware

The amendments to the Delaware General Corporation Law[116] are equally applicable to nonprofit corporations.

Hawaii

Hawaiian law now provides that any person who serves as an officer or director of a nonprofit corporation without remuneration or expectation of remuneration is not liable for damage, injury or loss caused by such person's breach of duties in the absence of gross negligence.[117]

Minnesota

Effective in March, 1986, Minnesota eliminated the liability of directors and trustees of Minnesota nonprofit corporations or associations for damages occasioned solely by reason of membership in or participation in board activities, provided the director or trustee is not compensated for services.

Minnesota also authorizes creation of "indemnification trust funds," funded by contributions from their beneficiaries, to indemnify such organizations and their officers, directors and agents from financial loss due to legal liabilities other than for employee benefits, property loss, or workers compensation.[118]

New York

The New York Not-for-Profit Corporation Law was amended to eliminate liability to third parties of uncompensated directors, officers or trustees of organizations that qual-

---

115. Pub. Act 86-338, § 10.
116. See discussion supra section 7.04.
117. S.B. 1550-86, amending ch. 416, Haw. Rev. Stat.
118. Minn. Stat. § 60A.29. See also §§ 317.201 and 300.83.

ify under I.R.C. § 501(c)(3), in the absence of gross negligence or conduct which "was intended to cause the resulting harm to the person asserting such liability."[119]

Ohio

Two separate enactments have recently been adopted by the Ohio General Assembly in an attempt to ease the liability concerns of trustees, officers and volunteers of Ohio nonprofit corporations. The first, which became effective October 14, 1986, conferred qualified immunity from civil liability in tort upon uncompensated volunteers, including trustees and officers, of nonprofit charitable organizations except hospitals.[120] The immunity is granted in civil actions which allege injury, death or loss to persons or property provided various ill-defined standards apply. Although the enactment was subsequently amended to apply equally to charitable hospital volunteers, its vague and confusing language created uncertainty as to what extent it provided meaningful protection to its intended beneficiaries.

The second enactment became effective March 29, 1988.[120a] Developed by the Corporation Law Committee of the Ohio State Bar Association, this enactment amended the Ohio Nonprofit Corporation Law in a manner substantially similar to the amendments to the Ohio General Corporation Law in November, 1986.[120b] Among other things, the legislation:

(a) clarifies that a nonprofit corporation may indemnify an uncompensated volunteer to the same extent as a trustee, officer, employee or agent of the corporation ("compensation" does not include expense reimbursement, modest perquisites, or the payment of insurance premiums for the benefit of the volunteer);

(b) requires the corporation to advance defense expenses for its trustees and uncompensated volunteers, unless certain exceptions apply;

---

119. N.Y. Not-for-Profit Corp. Law § 720a.
120. Ohio Rev. Code Ann. § 2305.38.
120a. Am. Sub. H.B. No. 533, amending ch. 1702, Ohio Rev. Code.
120b. See supra section 7.08.

    (c) permits a corporation to furnish protection similar to insurance, including trust funds, letters of credit or self-insurance and to purchase such insurance from a person in which the corporation has a financial interest;

    (d) eliminates the liability of a trustee unless it is proved by clear and convincing evidence that the act or omission of the trustee was undertaken with a deliberate intent to cause injury to the corporation or with a reckless disregard for the best interests of the corporation, unless certain exceptions apply.

Pennsylvania

The Pennsylvania Directors' Liability Act, effective January 1, 1987,[121] applies to nonprofit corporations as well as business corporations. Other legislation, enacted earlier in 1986, substantially limits the liability of officers, directors and trustees of nonprofit corporations who serve without compensation.[122]

---

121. See discussion supra in section 7.11.
122. See H.B. No. 2072, session of 1986, §§ 8362, 8363.

COROLLARY REFERENCES

Brown, "The Not-For-Profit Corporation Director: Legal Liabilities and Protection," 28 Fed'n Ins. Couns. Q. 57 (Fall, 1977).

Fee and Hoberg, "Potential Liability of Directors of Agricultural Cooperatives," 37 Ark. L. Rev. 60 (1983).

Harvey, "The Public-Spirited Defendant and Others: Liability of Directors and Officers of Not-For-Profit Corporations," 17 J. Marshall L. Rev. 665 (1984).

Karst, "The Efficiency of the Charitable Dollar: An Unfulfilled State Responsibility," 73 Harv. L. Rev. 433 (1960).

Marsh, "Governance of Non-Profit Organizations: An Appropriate Standard of Conduct for Trustees and Directors of Museums and Other Cultural Institutions," 85 Dick. L. Rev. 607 (1981).

Oleck, Non-profit Corporations, Organizations and Associations (3d ed. 1974).

Oleck, "Non-Profit Types, Uses, and Abuses," 19 Clev. St. L. Rev. 207 (1970).

Pasley, "Exclusion and Expulsion from Non-Profit Organizations — The Civil Rights Aspect," 14 Clev. Mar. L. Rev. 203 (1965).

Pasley, "Non-Profit Corporations — Accountability of Directors and Officers," 21 Bus. Law. 621 (1966).

Silard, "A Constitutional Forecast: Demise of the 'State Action' Limit on the Equal Protection Guarantee," 66 Colum. L. Rev. 855 (1966).

Weeks, "The Not-for-Profit Corporation Law," 47 N.Y.U. L. Rev. 761 (1972).

Wilkinston & Frye, "Assessing Your Personal Liability," Trustee 13 (Dec., 1986).

Note, "State Action: Theories for Applying Constitutional Restrictions to Private Activity," 74 Colum. L. Rev. 656 (1974).

Chapter 14

FEDERAL SECURITIES LAWS

§ 14.01. Origin and nature of federal securities laws.

Originally, the rules governing the organization and operation of corporations were regarded as matters of state law. Although this is still largely the case, there have developed several important exceptions, the most prominent of which involves the myriad of federal rules and regulations now applicable to the issuance and sale of corporate stocks, bonds and other securities.

These federal requirements are generally supplemental to any applicable state securities laws. As a result of the many railroad and mining stock frauds beginning around the turn of the century, most states enacted securities antifraud statutes, popularly known as "Blue Sky" laws. Generally, these laws set up state securities commissions charged with the duty to investigate the soundness of new issues of securities and to approve or disapprove them. They also provided for the licensing of brokers and the general supervision by the appropriate commission or board of all securities sales within the state.

Unfortunately, the redactors of the Blue Sky laws could not foresee the great advances in communications and transportation which were to occur after World War I. They could not

413

divine the creation of great country-wide stock exchanges which would make intrastate sales (over which they had jurisdiction) the exception and interstate sales (which they could not effectively regulate) the rule.

After 1929 it became apparent that no single state could deal effectively with the excesses which caused the stock market crash. Country-wide regulation was necessary, and this could be accomplished only at the federal level. The Securities Act of 1933[1] was thus conceived and enacted. This Act focused on the initial offering and sale of securities of companies and provided generally for compulsory registration and full, honest disclosure as a prerequisite to such an offer or sale. Violations created civil liability and were punishable as criminal offenses. The Securities Exchange Act of 1934[2] focused on the secondary trading market by, among other things, creating the Securities and Exchange Commission (SEC), giving it broad investigative and regulatory powers to prevent fraud in the securities business, and setting up a system of minimum standards governing transactions in corporate securities. Again, civil liability and criminal penalties were provided for violations.

A fundamental distinction between most state securities law systems and the federal regulatory framework is that the state laws typically require the securities transaction to be "fair" to the investing public whereas the federal laws merely require full and truthful disclosure of all material information. In referring to the state securities law systems which are "overlaid with [the] rigorous, duplicative, technical and burdensome federal securities law," Professor Alfred F. Conard has written that:

> The combined system of corporation and securities laws is probably the strictest in the world, and certainly the most cumbersome.[3]

---

1. 15 U.S.C. § 77a et seq.

2. Id. § 78a et seq.

3. Conard, "An Overview of the Laws of Corporations," 71 Mich. L. Rev. 623, 667 (1973).

The passing years have seen additional federal statutes relating to particular aspects of the securities business, but the Acts of 1933 and 1934 remain the statutory backbone for most modern federal securities regulation. Being federal statutes, they pre-empt state law in the areas with which they deal to the extent of a conflict between the federal and state law. Where no such conflict exists, the remedies provided by the federal securities laws are cumulative with other remedies under state and common law.[4] Having been passed pursuant to the power of Congress to regulate interstate commerce, federal laws are not applicable to transactions of a purely intrastate character which are still governed by the state Blue Sky laws. Because of the broad reach and interpretation of the term "interstate commerce," this limitation has proven to be of little import.

Although neither the 1933 Act nor the 1934 Act purports to affect the basic corporation laws of the states as they relate to the organization and general powers of state-created corporations, their broad scope has profoundly affected how corporations are operated and governed.

§ 14.02. A federal law of corporations.

The 1933 Act and the 1934 Act were destined to become the backbone for what is now variously referred to as the "federal law of corporations,"[5] the "federal law of corporate responsibility,"[6] or the "new law of corporate fiduciary relations."[7] It has been said that while this law depends upon relationships

---

4. Herman & MacLean v. Huddleston, 459 U.S. 375, 383, 74 L.Ed.2d 548, 103 S.Ct. 683 (1983).

5. E.g., Friendly, "In Praise of Erie — and of the New Federal Common Law," 39 N.Y.U. L. Rev. 385 (1964); Ruder, "Pitfalls in the Development of a Federal Law of Corporations by Implication Through Rule 10b-5," 59 Nw. U.L. Rev. 185 (1964).

6. In re Cady, Roberts & Co., 40 SEC 907, 910 (1961).

7. Ruder, "Current Developments in the Federal Law of Corporate Fiduciary Relations — Standing to Sue Under Rule 10b-5," 26 Bus. Law. 1289, 1300 (1971).

arising from state law, it is in fact the "creation of a new federal law of management-stockholder relations."[8]

Section 10(b)[9] and Rule 10b-5[10] of the 1934 Act have proven to be the most productive in spawning a federal law of corporations. The statute and rule are vague and ill-defined in scope. Thus, through court construction, law has been created which is as much judge-made as is the classic common law of the states. Rule 10b-5 afforded an effective tool for the SEC in conducting extensive internal corporate investigations and regulatory activities[11] and was quickly accepted as the basis of private actions for damages.[12]

Rule 10b-5 has been used as a means of dealing with such matters as an issue of stock in exchange for spurious assets,[13] a short-form merger to eliminate minority shareholders,[14] misleading statements to obtain votes for approval of a corporate transaction,[15] nondisclosure of reasons for "going private,"[16] and misappropriation of the proceeds of a sale of government bonds.[17] In Rule 10b-5 actions, the federal courts have written extensively about the fiduciary doctrine and have laid down detailed and comprehensive rules defining the fiduciary duties of corporate officers and directors.[18]

---

8. McClure v. Borne Chem. Co., 292 F.2d 824, 834 (3d Cir.), cert. denied, 368 U.S. 939 (1961).

9. 15 U.S.C. § 78j(b).

10. 17 C.F.R. § 240.10b-5.

11. E.g., In re Ward La France Truck Corp., 13 SEC 373 (1943); In re Cady, Roberts & Co., supra note 6.

12. Kardon v. National Gypsum Co., 73 F. Supp. 798 (E.D. Pa.), modified, 83 F. Supp. 613 (E.D. Pa. 1947).

13. Hooper v. Mountain States Sec. Corp., 282 F.2d 195 (5th Cir. 1960).

14. Marshel v. AFW Fabrics Corp., 533 F.2d 1277 (2d Cir.), vacated and remanded for a determination of mootness, 429 U.S. 881, 50 L.Ed.2d 162, 97 S.Ct. 228 (1976), remanded to district court to stay proceedings, 552 F.2d 471 (2d Cir. 1977).

15. Schlick v. Penn-Dixie Cement Corp., 507 F.2d 374 (2d Cir. 1974).

16. SEC v. Parklane Hosiery Co., 558 F.2d 1083 (2d Cir. 1977).

17. Superintendent of Ins. of N.Y. v. Bankers Life & Cas. Co., 404 U.S. 6, 30 L.Ed.2d 128, 92 S.Ct. 165 (1971).

18. E.g., Lanza v. Drexel & Co., 479 F.2d 1277 (2d Cir. 1973) (en banc); Harman v. Willbern, 374 F. Supp. 1149 (D. Kan. 1974), aff'd, 520 F.2d 1333 (10th Cir. 1975).

Several decisions of the Supreme Court in 1975 and 1976 began to indicate a disposition to reduce the volume of federal litigation in this area and to show deference to the priority of state corporation law.[19] But it was the decision in *Santa Fe Industries, Incorporated v. Green*[20] in March, 1977, that took a giant step to interrupt the trend, and to establish a new basis for dealing with securities and corporate law matters in a more restrictive fashion.

In *Green,* the Second Circuit had followed the federal corporation law trend by deciding that Rule 10b-5 reached "breaches of fiduciary duty by a majority against minority shareholders without any charge of misrepresentation or lack of disclosure."[21] The duty was "to deal fairly with minority shareholders," and the breach was brought about "by effecting the merger without any justifiable business purpose."[22] However, no appellate decision before this one and the Second Circuit's decision in *Marshel v. AFW Fabric Corporation*[23] "had permitted a 10b-5 claim without some element of misrepresentation or nondisclosure."[24]

Justice White turned first to the language of the statute, Section 10(b), to control his interpretation of the rule. He

---

19. Blue Chip Stamps v. Manor Drug Stores, 421 U.S. 723, 44 L.Ed.2d 539, 95 S.Ct. 1917 (1975); Rondeau v. Mosinee Paper Corp., 422 U.S. 49, 45 L.Ed.2d 12, 95 S.Ct. 2069 (1975); United Hous. Found., Inc. v. Forman, 421 U.S. 837, 44 L.Ed.2d 621, 95 S.Ct. 2051 (1975); Securities Inv. Protection Corp. v. Barbour, 421 U.S. 412, 44 L.Ed.2d 263, 95 S.Ct. 1733 (1975); Ernst & Ernst v. Hochfelder, 425 U.S. 185, 47 L.Ed.2d 668, 96 S.Ct. 1375, reh'g denied, 425 U.S. 985 (1976).

20. 430 U.S. 462, 51 L.Ed.2d 480, 97 S.Ct. 1292 (1977).

21. See Green v. Santa Fe Indus., Inc., 533 F.2d 1283, 1287 (2d Cir. 1976).

22. Id. at 1291. Cf. Popkin v. Bishop, 464 F.2d 714 (2d Cir. 1972); Marshel v. AFW Fabric Corp., 533 F.2d 1277 (2d Cir.), vacated and remanded for a determination of mootness, 429 U.S. 881, 50 L.Ed.2d 162, 97 S.Ct. 228 (1976), remanded to district court to stay proceedings, 552 F.2d 471 (2d Cir. 1977).

23. Marshel v. AFW Fabric Corp., supra note 22.

24. Note, 89 Harv. L. Rev. 1917, 1926 (1976), cited in Santa Fe Indus., Inc. v. Green, 430 U.S. 462, 51 L.Ed.2d 480, 493, 97 S.Ct. 1292, 1302 n.15 (1977).

found in it "no indication that Congress meant to prohibit any conduct not involving manipulation or deception."[25] Accepting the view that manipulation was "virtually a term of art when used in connection with securities markets," he opined that Congress would not have chosen this term "if it had meant to bring within the scope of § 10(b) instances of corporate mismanagement such as this, in which the essence of the complaint is that shareholders were treated unfairly by a fiduciary."[26] He also suggested that such a claim is "one traditionally relegated to state law."[27]

The *Green* opinion expressed concern about bringing within Rule 10b-5, a "wide variety of corporate conduct traditionally left to state regulation." In addition to posing a "danger of vexatious litigation," such an extension of the federal securities laws "would overlap and quite possibly interfere with state corporate law."[28]

Justice White appeared anxious to contain the spread of federal corporate law development. He wrote, "[a]bsent a clear indication of congressional intent, we are reluctant to federalize the substantial portion of the law of corporations that deals with transactions in securities, particularly where established state policies of corporate regulation would be overridden."[29]

This antagonism towards an expansive federal law of corporations was reiterated by the Supreme Court in several subsequent decisions. In *Burks v. Lasker*,[30] the Court held that the federal securities laws should be approached by recognizing that they were generally "enacted against the background of existing state law; Congress has never indicated that the entire corpus of state corporation law is to be replaced simply because a plaintiff's cause of action is based

---

25. Santa Fe Indus., Inc. v. Green, supra note 24, 51 L.Ed.2d at 492, 97 S.Ct. at 1300.
26. Id., 51 L.Ed.2d at 493-94, 97 S.Ct. at 1302.
27. Id., 51 L.Ed.2d at 495, 97 S.Ct. at 1303.
28. Id., 51 L.Ed.2d at 495, 97 S.Ct. at 1303.
29. Id., 97 S.Ct. at 1304.
30. 441 U.S. 471, 60 L.Ed.2d 404, 99 S.Ct. 1831 (1979).

upon a federal statute."[31] Likewise, in *Marine Bank v. Weaver*,[32] the Court indicated that the securities laws generally and the antifraud provisions particularly were not intended to provide a "broad federal remedy for all fraud."

The Supreme Court has recently suggested that this tendency to restrain the expansion of a federal law of corporations may not be as certain as many believed. In *Herman & MacLean v. Huddleston*,[33] the Court rendered its most expansive securities law decision since 1975 in upholding a private right of action under Section 10(b) and Rule 10b-5 notwithstanding the availability of an express remedy under Section 11 of the Securities Act. Section 10(b) was referred to by the Court as a "catchall" antifraud provision. In addition, the Court recently liberally construed the RICO[34] federal statute and recognized its applicability to "garden variety fraud" claims against legitimate businesses. In a dissenting opinion, Justice Marshall stated that the majority opinion "simply revolutionizes private litigation; it validates the federalization of broad areas of state common law frauds."[35] The use of the RICO statute as a basis for expanding federal corporate law may be of limited duration if the statute is amended to reduce its scope, at least in civil actions, as many predict will occur.

Numerous lower courts and the SEC have persisted in their attempts to expand federal corporate law. Subject to a few limited exceptions, lower courts have successfully circumvented the *Santa Fe* decision and have continued to assert that a breach of a fiduciary duty may be a basis for a federal law claim when the breach is coupled with either nondisclosure or misleading disclosure as to the material facts relating

---

31. Id., 441 U.S. at 478.

32. 455 U.S. 551, 71 L.Ed.2d 409, 102 S.Ct. 1220 (1982).

33. 459 U.S. 375, 74 L.Ed.2d 548, 103 S.Ct. 683 (1983).

34. The Racketeer Influenced and Corrupt Organizations Act, 18 U.S.C. § 1961 et seq.

35. Sedima, S.P.R.L. v. Imrex Co., Inc., 473 U.S. 479, 87 L.Ed.2d 346, 105 S.Ct. 3275, 3293 (1985).

to that breach.[36] These cases, in effect, hold that "deception" is present and thus a federal cause of action exists whenever a corporate fiduciary does not disclose facts which could be used to enjoin that fiduciary. Judge Aldisert, in his dissent in *Healey v. Catalyst Recovery of Pennsylvania, Incorporated,* declared that this very expansive definition of "deception" overruled the Supreme Court in *Santa Fe* and "federalized" a substantial portion of the law of corporations that deals with transactions in securities.[37] A few lower courts have recognized the impropriety of such a result and have refused to expand the federal securities laws to include mere breaches of a director's fiduciary duties.[38]

The SEC has likewise refused to halt its march towards an expanding federal corporate law. It issued a staff report on corporate accountability which recommends a wide variety of actions in such areas as political activities, environmental compliance, and constituency of a board of directors and board committees.[39] The report stated that absent meaningful progress by corporations, additional rule making by the SEC and perhaps legislative proposals would be necessary. In addition, in various enforcement proceedings, the SEC has required fundamental corporate changes, including the creation of audit committees and the requirement that a designated percentage of the directors be outsiders.[40]

---

36. Mayer v. Oil Field Sys. Corp., 721 F.2d 59 (2d Cir. 1983); Goldberg v. Meridor, 567 F.2d 209 (2d Cir. 1977), cert. denied, 434 U.S. 1069 (1978); IIT, An Int'l Inv. Trust v. Cornfeld, 619 F.2d 909 (2d Cir. 1980); Wright v. Heizer Corp., 560 F.2d 236 (7th Cir. 1977), cert. denied, 434 U.S. 1066 (1978); Alabama Farm Bur. Mut. Cas. Co. v. American Fid. Life Ins. Co., 606 F.2d 602 (5th Cir. 1979), cert. denied, 449 U.S. 820 (1980); Healey v. Catalyst Recovery of Pa., Inc., 616 F.2d 641 (3d Cir. 1980).

37. Supra note 36, 616 F.2d at 661, quoting Santa Fe Indus., Inc. v. Green, 430 U.S. at 479.

38. Panter v. Marshall Field & Co., 646 F.2d 271 (7th Cir.), cert. denied, 454 U.S. 1092 (1981); Data Probe Acquisition Corp. v. Datatab, Inc., 722 F.2d 1 (2d Cir. 1983), cert. denied, 104 S.Ct. 1326 (1984).

39. SEC Staff Report on Corporate Accountability, Fed. Sec. L. Rep. (CCH) ¶82,674 (Sept. 4, 1980).

40. See SEC v. Catain, Sec. Reg. & L. Rep. (BNA) No. 562, A-7 (C.D. Cal. 1980), where a company and its chief executive officer settled SEC charges

It seems likely that since the lower federal courts and the SEC have continued their philosophy of federal corporate law expansion and since certain factions of the private sector are suggesting the need for a uniform law of corporate governance, the Supreme Court, and perhaps Congress, may be required either to reestablish firmly or to abandon antagonism toward an expanding federal corporate law.

§ 14.03. Definition of security.

As indicated by their titles, the 1933 Act and the 1934 Act are applicable only to transactions involving "securities." With slight differences, both Acts define a "security" with great detail and breadth.[41] For example, the 1933 Act defines "security" as:

> Any note, stock, treasury stock, bond, debenture, evidence of indebtedness, certificate of interest or participation in any profit-sharing agreement, collateral-trust certificate, preorganization certificate or subscription, transferable share, investment contract, voting-trust certificate, certificate of deposit for a security, fractional undivided interest in oil, gas, or other mineral rights, or, in general, any interest or instrument commonly known as a "security," or any certificate of interest or participation in, temporary or interim certificate for, receipt for, guarantee of, or warrant or right to subscribe to or purchase, any of the foregoing.

While most securities litigation involves publicly traded securities of corporations, these definitions encompass other types of financial arrangements. The complexity and ingenuity of the financial industry are such that after more than fifty years of experience there is still considerable doubt in many instances as to whether a particular transaction involves a "security."

---

by agreeing to restructure the board of directors so that a majority would be outside directors, and to establish an audit committee of entirely outside directors, and SEC v. Tesoro Petroleum Corp., Fed. Sec. L. Rep. (CCH) ¶97,699 (D.D.C. 1980), where a company settled SEC charges by agreeing to appoint a new director approved by the SEC to oversee the audit committee and company disclosure procedures.

41. 15 U.S.C. § 77b(b); id. § 78c(a)(10).

Items for which "securities" status has been recognized to varying degrees include notes, certificates of deposit, loan participations, annuity contracts, pension and employee benefit plans, insurance policies, partnership interests, leases, franchises, commodity trading accounts, and precious metals.[42] Although not specifically included within the statutory definitions, many financial transactions are treated as securities because they constitute an "investment contract," which is included within the definition. The Supreme Court has defined an investment contract broadly as an investment in a common venture with a reasonable expectation of profits to be derived from the entrepreneurial or managerial efforts of others.[43]

The technical characterization of an arrangement may be as important as the substantive terms in determining if the federal securities laws apply. For example, the Supreme Court recently rejected the sale-of-business doctrine and held that a sale of a "security" exists where the stock of a business is sold to a purchaser who will have managerial control of the business.[44] Although the purchaser in the transaction is actually purchasing a commercial venture, not a passive investment anticipating profits derived from the efforts of others and although the same economic result could be obtained by purchasing the assets rather than the stock of the business, the transaction is subject to the federal securities laws.

§ 14.04. False or misleading registration statements.

Section 11 of the 1933 Act[45] imposes a high standard of care upon the issuer of securities and other designated persons by

---

42. See, generally, Orbe, "A Security: The Quest for a Definition," 12 Sec. Reg. L.J. 220 (Fall 1984); Schneider, Definition of a "Security" — 1983/1984 Update, 17 The Review of Securities Regulation 851 (Standard & Poor's, Sept. 12, 1984).

43. SEC v. W.J. Howey Co., 328 U.S. 293, 90 L.Ed. 1244, 66 S.Ct. 1100 (1946).

44. Landreth Timber Co. v. Landreth, 471 U.S. 681, 85 L.Ed.2d 692, 105 S.Ct. 2297 (1985).

45. 15 U.S.C. § 77k.

imposing civil liability when an effective registration statement contains an untrue statement of a material fact or an omission to state a material fact required to be set forth. The designated persons who may be personally liable are:

(1) every person who signed the registration statement;

(2) every person who was a director of (or person performing similar functions) or partner in the issuer at the time of the filing of the part of the registration statement with respect to which his liability is asserted;

(3) every person who, with his consent, is named in the registration statement as being or about to become a director, person performing similar functions, or partner;

(4) every accountant, engineer, or appraiser, or any person whose profession gives authority to a statement made by him, who has with his consent been named as having prepared or certified any part of the registration statement, or as having prepared or certified any report or valuation which is used in connection with the registration statement, with respect to the statement in such registration statement, report, or valuation, which purports to have been prepared or certified by him;

(5) every underwriter with respect to such security.

As indicated, although all directors may be liable under Section 11 without regard to whether they signed the registration statement, officers may be liable only if they sign the statement. Section 6[46] of the 1933 Act requires the principal executive officer or officers, the principal financial officer and the principal accounting officer to sign. This limitation on officer liability has been strictly interpreted. For example, a chief financial officer who did not sign the registration state-

---

46. Id. § 77f.

423

ment despite being required to do so by Section 6 escaped liability under Section 11.[47]

A "material fact" is defined by the SEC as a matter "as to which an average prudent investor ought reasonably to be informed before purchasing the security registered."[48] In defining "material" under Rule 14a-9 of the 1934 Act, the Supreme Court has stated that "an omitted fact is material if there is substantial likelihood that a reasonable shareholder would consider it important in deciding how to vote."[49] As to Section 11, some cases suggest a fact is material if it is a fact which in reasonable and objective contemplation might affect the value of the corporation's securities.[50]

Any person acquiring any security registered under the subject registration statement has standing as a plaintiff to bring suit under Section 11. This includes not only purchasers in the offering, but also persons who purchased in the aftermarket.[51]

A plaintiff in a Section 11 action is not required to show that he relied upon the untrue statement or omission unless he acquired the security after the issuer had made generally available to its security holders an earnings statement covering a period of at least twelve months beginning after the effective date of the registration statement.[52] In addition, a plaintiff need not prove causation, scienter or privity.[53]

The principal defenses to an action under Section 11 are (1) that the purchaser knew of the untruth or omission at the

---

47. Ahern v. Gaussoin, 1985-86 Fed. Sec. L. Rep. (CCH) ¶92,332 (D.C. Or. 1985).

48. 17 C.F.R. 230.405(1).

49. TSC Indus., Inc. v. Northway, Inc., 426 U.S. 438, 448-49, 48 L.Ed.2d 757, 96 S.Ct. 2126 (1976).

50. Feit v. Leasco Data Processing Equip. Corp., 332 F. Supp. 544, 569 (E.D.N.Y. 1971); Kohler v. Kohler Co., 319 F.2d 634, 642 (7th Cir. 1963).

51. McFarland v. Memorex, 493 F. Supp. 631, 641-42 (N.D. Cal. 1980); In re Equity Funding Corp. of Am. Sec. Litig., 416 F. Supp. 161, 187 (C.D. Cal. 1976).

52. 15 U.S.C. § 77k(a).

53. In re Gap Stores Sec. Litig., 79 F.R.D. 283, 297 (N.D. Cal. 1978); see also Unicorn Field, Inc. v. Cannon Group, Inc., 60 F.R.D. 217, 227 (S.D.N.Y. 1973).

time he acquired the security,[54] or (2) that the defendant exercised due diligence.[55] The due diligence defense is not available to the issuer, whose liability is absolute except for the statute of limitations or proof that the purchaser knew of the untruth or omission.[56]

The statute applies a different due diligence standard depending upon whether the part of the registration statement at issue was made on the authority of an expert. The "non-expertised" part is that part (1) not purporting to be made on authority of an expert, (2) not purporting to be a copy of or extract from a report or valuation of an expert, and (3) not purporting to be made on the authority of a public official document or statement. As to that part, a defendant must prove that he made a "reasonable investigation" after which he had "reasonable ground to believe and did believe, at the time such part of the registration statement became effective, that the statements therein were true and that there was no omission to state a material fact required to be stated therein or necessary to make the statements therein not misleading."[57]

In determining what constitutes "reasonable investigation" and "reasonable ground for belief," the standard will be that required of a prudent man in the management of his own property.[58]

As to the "expertised" part of the registration statement, a "non-expert" defendant need prove only that "he had no reasonable ground to believe and did not believe, at the time such part of the registration statement became effective," that there was an untrue statement or an omission of any material fact therein. He is not required to prove that he

---

54. 15 U.S.C. § 77k(a).

55. Id. § 77k(b)(3) and (c).

56. Alton Box Bd. Co. v. Goldman, Sachs & Co., 418 F. Supp. 1149 (E.D. Mo. 1976).

57. 15 U.S.C. § 77k(b)(3)(A).

58. Id. § 77k(c).

believed the statements were true or that he made a "reasonable investigation."[59]

An "expert" defendant, as to any part of the registration statement made upon his authority as an expert or purporting to be a copy of or extract from a report or valuation by him as an expert, must prove that he made a "reasonable investigation" after which he had "reasonable ground to believe and did believe, at the time such part of the registration statement became effective," that the statements were true and that no material facts were omitted.[60]

Inside directors and directors with specialized knowledge about the issuer and the offering are expected to make a more complete investigation than outside directors. Each must undertake an investigation that a reasonably prudent person in a similar position would conduct. In *Escott v. BarChris Construction Corporation,*[61] which is the leading case applying these standards under Section 11, the court imposed such stringent requirements of knowledge of corporate affairs on inside directors that it is reasonable to conclude that liability will probably lie in practically all cases of misrepresentation. Indeed, the liability of inside directors approaches the absolute liability of the issuer.

In the *BarChris* case, the court also addressed the liability of a lawyer-director and a newly appointed outside director. With respect to the lawyer-director, the court treated him as an outside director despite the fact that the lawyer was the issuer's outside general counsel, had devoted more than 780 hours (97-1/2 eight-hour days) on *BarChris* affairs in the two-year period preceding the registration and had prepared the subject registration statement. However, he was then held to a very high standard of independent investigation of the registration statement because of his peculiar expertise and access to information. In a related case, an attorney-director was found to be so intimately involved in the registration

---

59. Id. § 77k(b)(3)(C) and (D).

60. Id. § 77k(b)(3)(B).

61. 283 F. Supp. 643 (S.D.N.Y. 1968).

426

process that it would have been a "gross distortion of reality" to treat him as anything but an inside director.[62]

The *BarChris* court also discussed the liability of an outside director who was appointed within weeks prior to the effective date of the registration statement and who relied entirely upon the assurances of the issuer's managing directors that the prospectus and registration statement were accurate. The court stated that Section 11 responsibilities and liabilities are imposed on a director "no matter how new he is" and that he is presumed to know his responsibility when he becomes a director. In holding the director liable, the court noted that a prudent man would not act on an important matter without any personal knowledge of the relevant facts and in sole reliance on the representations of comparative strangers.

Any suit under Section 11 must be brought within one year after discovery of the untrue statement or omission was or should have been made.[63] For this purpose, sophisticated investors are not held to a higher standard than nonsophisticated investors.[64] In no event may suit be brought later than three years after the public offering.[65]

Compensatory damages recoverable for a Section 11 violation equal the amount paid (not exceeding the initial offering price of the securities) less (1) the value at the date suit was brought, (2) the price at which the security was sold prior to suit, or (3) the price at which the security was sold after suit was filed, if the resulting damages are less than as calculated at the date of suit.[66] The damages do not include any price declines proven by the defendant to be due to factors other than the misleading nature of the registration statement. The maximum recovery is the price at which the securities

---

62. Feit v. Leasco Data Processing Equip. Corp., supra note 50.

63. 15 U.S.C. § 77m.

64. In re Commonwealth Oil/Tesoro Petroleum Sec. Litig., 484 F. Supp. 253, 257-58 (W.D. Tex. 1979).

65. 15 U.S.C. § 77m.

66. Id. § 77k(e).

were offered to the public.[67] Although a defendant may obtain contribution (i.e., sharing the burden of paying the damages) from a co-violator of Section 11,[68] indemnification (i.e., removing the burden of paying damages) has generally been prohibited as undermining the statutory purpose of assuring diligent performance of duties.[69]

The Supreme Court has ruled that the availability of an express remedy under Section 11 does not prevent an investor from also bringing suit under the antifraud rule of the 1934 Act.[70]

§ 14.05. False or misleading prospectuses or communications.

Section 12(1)[71] of the 1933 Act imposes civil liability for rescission or damages upon any person who offers or sells a security in violation of Section 5,[72] which is the registration provision. This subsection essentially creates absolute liability upon a showing of the jurisdictional use of interstate commerce or the mails, the lack of the required registration, and the sale of a security by the defendant. The seller's awareness of the violation and the purchaser's reliance on the seller's conduct or disclosure are irrelevant.

Section 12(2),[73] on the other hand, is the general remedy under the 1933 Act for defrauded purchasers of securities, whether or not the sale was required to be registered. Under this subsection, a plaintiff must prove (a) an offer or sale of a security, (b) by use of any means of interstate commerce or the mails, (c) through a prospectus or oral communication, (d) which includes an untrue statement of a material fact or

---

67. Id. § 77k(g).

68. Id. § 77k(f).

69. See Laventhol, Krekstein, Horwath & Horwath v. Horwitch, 637 F.2d 672 (9th Cir. 1980).

70. Herman & MacLean v. Huddleston, 459 U.S. 375, 74 L.Ed.2d 548, 103 S.Ct. 683 (1983). See infra section 14.13.

71. 15 U.S.C. § 77l(1).

72. Id. § 77e.

73. Id. § 77l(2).

omits to state a material fact, and (e) the plaintiff did not know and in the exercise of reasonable care could not have known of the untrue statements or omissions when he purchased the securities.[74] Once these elements are shown, a plaintiff need not prove that he received or relied upon the untruthful communication[75] or that the purchase would not have occurred absent the material misrepresentation or omission.[76] Similarly, courts have held that no proof of fraud or deceit, nor any showing of knowing misrepresentation or reckless disregard of the truth is required.[77]

Liability under Section 12 is limited by its terms to persons who offer or sell a security. Courts, though, have generally not limited the reach of Section 12 liability to only the actual seller. How far this liability expands beyond the actual seller is a developing and unsettled area of the law.

A few federal courts permit recovery under Section 12 only from the actual seller of the securities or one in privity with the seller.[78] These courts reason that any broader definition would frustrate the statutory scheme since Section 11 of the 1933 Act gives a purchaser a cause of action for misrepresentation against persons other than the immediate seller (i.e., persons who signed the registration statement, directors of the issuer, accountants and underwriters). In the words of one court, these statutes are not "commissions to the federal courts to ride abroad on a great white horse like the Lone Ranger righting all wrongs."[79]

Most courts, though, have expanded the class of persons potentially liable under Section 12 by broadly defining the

---

74. In re Itel Sec. Litig., 89 F.R.D. 104, 115 (N.D. Col. 1981).

75. DeMarco v. Edens, 390 F.2d 836, 841 (2d Cir. 1968); Saunders v. John Nuveen & Co., 619 F.2d 1222, 1225-26 (7th Cir. 1980), cert. denied, 450 U.S. 1005 (1981).

76. Hill York v. American Int'l Franchises, 448 F.2d 696 (5th Cir. 1971).

77. Cf. Franklin Sav. Bank of N.Y. v. Levy, 551 F.2d 521, 526-27 (2d Cir. 1977).

78. E.g., Collins v. Signetics Corp., 605 F.2d 110 (3d Cir. 1979); Benoay v. Decker, 517 F. Supp. 490 (E.D. Mich. 1981), aff'd without opinion, 735 F.2d 1363 (6th Cir. 1984).

79. Davis v. Avco Fin. Serv., Inc., 739 F.2d 1057 (6th Cir. 1984).

term "seller" to include those whose participation in the buy-sell transaction is a substantial factor in causing the transaction to take place.[80]

Examples of application of this "causation" approach include the following: an attorney who was an active negotiator in merger talks was found to be a "seller" of securities in a corporate merger because his actions were a "substantial factor" in causing the sale;[81] a company's manager, who negligently misrepresented that sale of the company's securities was a "good quality investment," was a "seller" because his actions directly and proximately caused the purchaser's loss;[82] a corporate president, who was a "necessary participant" and "substantial factor" in the sale by his corporation of unregistered securities, was a "seller" even though he had no actual contact with offerees.[83]

Since this type of "causation" analysis is highly factual, it is difficult to predict with certainty how far the liability extends. For example, at least one court has permitted a securities purchaser to pursue a Section 12(2) claim against directors by charging that they substantially participated in the preparation of the misleading prospectus.[84] Other courts, though, have ruled that participation only in the preparation of the registration statement is not the type of "substantial participation" on which Section 12(2) liability may be based.[85]

Once the elements of a Section 12(2) claim are shown, a defendant may escape liability only if it can be shown that

---

80. Pharo v. Smith, 621 F.2d 656 (5th Cir.), reh'g granted and case remanded on different grounds, 625 F.2d 1226 (5th Cir. 1980); Junker v. Crory, 650 F.2d 1349 (5th Cir. 1981); Croy v. Campbell, 624 F.2d 709 (5th Cir. 1980); SEC v. Holschuh, 694 F.2d 130 (7th Cir. 1982); Stokes v. Lokken, 644 F.2d 779 (8th Cir. 1981); SEC v. Murphy, 626 F.2d 633 (9th Cir. 1980).

81. Junker v. Crory, supra note 80.

82. Davis v. Avco Fin. Serv., Inc., supra note 79.

83. SEC v. Holschuh, supra note 80. Cf. Simkins v. National Executive Planners, Ltd., Fed. Sec. L. Rep. (CCH) ¶98,304 (M.D.N.C. 1981).

84. Klein v. Computer Devices, Inc., 591 F. Supp. 270 (S.D.N.Y. 1984).

85. See cases cited in Diasonics Sec. Litig., 599 F. Supp. 447 (N.D. Cal. 1984).

the defendant did not know, and could not have known through the exercise of reasonable care, of the untruth or omission[86] or that the suit was not brought within one year after discovery was or should have been made and in any event within three years after the offer or sale.[87] In determining whether a defendant exercised reasonable care, the following factors have been considered by at least one court:

- The amount of planning and promotional participation, such as designing the deal and contacting and attempting to persuade potential purchasers.
- Access to source data against which the truth or falsity of representations can be tested.
- Relative skill in ferreting out the truth.
- Pecuniary interest in the transaction's completion.
- The existence of a relationship of trust and confidence between the plaintiff and the alleged "seller."[88]

If the purchaser still owns the securities, they must be tendered to the seller. Once liability is established, the purchaser is entitled to recover the consideration paid for the securities, plus interest, and minus any amount of income received on the securities.[89] The Supreme Court has held that in calculating this rescissionary recovery, the amount of tax benefits received as a result of investment in the securities is not "income" on the securities and, therefore, the recoverable amount need not be reduced by those tax benefits.[90] A purchaser who no longer owns the securities may recover damages. The purchaser does not have a choice of remedies between rescission or damages.[91]

---

86. 15 U.S.C. § 77l(2).

87. Id. § 77m.

88. Davis v. Avco Fin. Serv., Inc., supra note 79.

89. 15 U.S.C. § 77l.

90. Randall v. Loftsgaarden, 478 U.S. 106, 92 L.Ed.2d 525, 106 S.Ct. 3143 (1986).

91. Wigand v. Flo-Tek, Inc., 609 F.2d 1028 (2d Cir. 1979).

Like Section 11, indemnification is generally not permitted for Section 12 liability, although contribution between code-fendants is available.[92]

§ 14.06. Antifraud provisions.

The primary goal of the federal securities laws is to ensure that persons involved in a securities transaction have reasonably equal access to material information about the transaction and the securities. Although certain provisions of the securities laws require specific types of disclosures under specific circumstances, the backbone of the entire federal securities law disclosure structure is the antifraud provisions of the 1933 and 1934 Acts; i.e. Section 17(a)[93] of the 1933 Act and Section 10(b)[94] of the 1934 Act. Both provisions are substantially broader in scope than Sections 11 or 12 of the 1933 Act. Their applicability is not limited to securities issuances, filing requirements, or issuer transactions. Rather, these provisions are potentially applicable to any transaction involving securities, regardless of the size of the corporation or nature of the transaction.

Section 17(a). The antifraud provision of the 1933 Act is the lesser used of the two provisions. The reasons are that there has been a split of authority as to whether a private right of action may be implied under the section[95] and that in some respects Section 17 is narrower in scope than Section 10(b). In recent years, Section 17 has been used against directors and officers with increased frequency. This is, in part, due to the fact that a Section 17 claim may be brought in either a state or federal court whereas a Section 10(b) claim may be brought only in a federal court.[96]

Section 17(a) prohibits any person in the offer or sale of securities to use any means or instruments of transportation

---

92. Kennedy v. Josephthal & Co., Inc., Fed. Sec. L. Rep. (CCH) ¶99,204 (D.C. Mass. 1983).

93. 15 U.S.C. § 77g(a).

94. Id. § 78j(a).

95. See infra section 14.13.

96. 15 U.S.C. § 77v; id. § 78aa.

or communication in interstate commerce or by use of the mails, directly or indirectly:

    (1) to employ any device, scheme, or artifice to defraud, or

    (2) to obtain money or property by means of any untrue statement of a material fact or any omission to state a material fact necessary in order to make the statements made, in the light of the circumstances under which they were made, not misleading, or

    (3) to engage in any transaction, practice, or course of business which operates or would operate as a fraud or deceit upon the purchaser.

Unlike Section 10(b),[97] Section 17 requires the fraud or misrepresentation to occur "in an offer or sale of securities." The Supreme Court has broadly applied that phrase in two respects. First, in *United States v. Naftalin*,[98] the Court ruled that Section 17(a) regulates not only the initial offering and sale of securities by the issuer, but also secondary trading. Secondly, in *Rubin v. United States*,[99] the Court ruled that "sale" for purposes of Section 17(a) includes the pledge of stock to secure a loan. As a result, a corporate vice president, seeking a corporate loan from a commercial bank, who assisted other corporate officers in preparing a false and misleading financial statement, was properly indicted for violation of Section 17(a).

Although the Supreme Court has decided that scienter must be proven in a private action under Rule 10b-5,[100] the standard of culpability under Section 17(a) remains unsettled. The Supreme Court held in *Aaron v. Securities & Exchange Commission*[101] that in an SEC enforcement proceed-

---

97. Section 10(b) prohibits fraud or misrepresentations "in connection with the purchase or sale."

98. 441 U.S. 768, 60 L.Ed.2d 624, 99 S.Ct. 2077 (1979).

99. 449 U.S. 424, 66 L.Ed.2d 633, 101 S.Ct. 698 (1981).

100. Ernst & Ernst v. Hochfelder, 425 U.S. 185, 47 L.Ed.2d 668, 96 S.Ct. 1375, reh'g denied, 425 U.S. 985 (1976).

101. 446 U.S. 680, 64 L.Ed.2d 611, 100 S.Ct. 1945 (1980).

ing scienter must be pleaded in order to state a claim for violation of Section 17(a)(1), but not for Section 17(a)(2) or (3). The Court reasoned that subsection (1) of Section 17(a) proscribes only knowing or intentional misconduct, whereas subsections (2) and (3) do not focus on the degree of culpability of the person responsible for the conduct. Although the Court analyzed Section 17(a) only as to an SEC civil injunction suit, it is at least arguable that its holding is equally applicable to private civil damage suits. Even though a few courts have ruled after *Aaron* that mere negligence is sufficient to state a claim for relief under Section 17(a),[102] the majority rule appears to require the pleading of scienter.[103]

Unlike Sections 11 and 12, Section 17(a) does not limit a plaintiff's remedy to rescission or recovery of the purchase price, but actual damages may be covered.[104] At the election of the plaintiff, rescission is also available.[105] Punitive damages may not be recoverable for violation of Section 17(a).[106]

Section 10(b). As early as 1969, the Supreme Court recognized that Section 10(b) of the 1934 Act and SEC Rule 10b-5[107] promulgated thereunder might "well be the most litigated provisions in the federal securities laws."[108] Since 1969, that frequency has increased substantially. In most suits under Sections 11, 12(2) and 17 of the 1933 Act and Sections 9, 14 and 18 of the 1934 Act, Section 10(b) and Rule 10b-5 have also been cited as bases for the alleged liability.

So far as is here pertinent, Section 10(b) provides:

---

102. E.g., Hudson v. Capital Mgt. Int'l, Inc., Fed. Sec. L. Rep. (CCH) ¶99,222 (N.D. Cal. 1982).

103. E.g., Zatkin v. Primuth, 551 F. Supp. 39, 45 (S.D. Cal. 1982); In re Nucorp Energy Sec. Litig., Fed. Sec. L. Rep. (CCH) ¶99,157 (S.D. Cal. 1983).

104. Pfeffer v. Cressaty, 223 F. Supp. 756-57 (S.D.N.Y. 1963).

105. The Value Line Fund, Inc. v. Marcus, Fed. Sec. L. Rep. (CCH) ¶91,523 (S.D.N.Y. 1965).

106. See Flaks v. Koegel, 504 F.2d 702, 706 (2d Cir. 1974).

107. 17 C.F.R. § 240.10b-5.

108. SEC v. National Sec., Inc., 393 U.S. 453, 465, 21 L.Ed.2d 668, 89 S.Ct. 564, 571 (1969).

It shall be unlawful for any person, directly or indirectly, by the use of any means or instrumentality of interstate commerce or of the mails, or of any facility of any national securities exchange —

* * *

(b) To use or employ, in connection with the purchase or sale of any security registered on a national securities exchange or any security not so registered, any manipulative or deceptive device or contrivance in contravention of such rules and regulations as the Commission may prescribe as necessary or appropriate in the public interest or for the protection of investors.

In 1942, acting under the authority granted to it by the 1934 Act, the SEC promulgated Rule 10b-5, which provides:

It shall be unlawful for any person, directly or indirectly, by the use of any means or instrumentality of interstate commerce, or of the mails or of any facility of any national securities exchange,

(a) To employ any device, scheme, or artifice to defraud,

(b) To make any untrue statement of a material fact or to omit to state a material fact necessary in order to make the statements made, in the light of the circumstances under which they were made, not misleading, or

(c) To engage in any act, practice, or course of business which operates or would operate as a fraud or deceit upon any person, in connection with the purchase or sale of any security.

These provisions have been referred to by the Supreme Court as "catchall" antifraud provisions[109] and have served as the foundation for the creation of a federal law of corporations.[110] Unlike Section 17(a), the fraudulent conduct or misrepresentation need only be "in connection with" the subject transaction, not "in" the transaction. Similarly, the statute and rule apply to both purchases and sales, not just sales.

---

109. Ernst & Ernst v. Hochfelder, supra note 100, 425 U.S. at 203.
110. See supra section 14.02.

Like Section 17(a), neither Section 10(b) nor Rule 10b-5 expressly provides a private civil right of action. However, unlike Section 17(a), it is now universally accepted that such a private action exists. Although the Supreme Court has expressed some disfavor for implying private rights of actions under the federal securities laws generally,[111] it has recently held that the existence of a Rule 10b-5 implied private right of action is "simply beyond peradventure," noting such a remedy has been consistently recognized since 1946.[112]

Beginning in 1975, the Supreme Court took steps to limit the expanding application of this statute and rule. In *Blue Chip Stamps v. Manor Drug Stores*,[113] the Court limited the class of plaintiffs by ruling that only an actual purchaser or seller of the securities in question has standing to sue. In its decision, the Court observed the existence of policy considerations which support the barring of three principal classes of potential plaintiffs from access to private action relief under Rule 10b-5:

(1) Potential purchasers of shares, either in a new offering or on the nation's post-distribution trading markets, who allege they decided not to purchase because of an unduly gloomy representation or the omission of favorable material which made the issues appear to be a less favorable investment than it actually was;

(2) Actual shareholders in the issuer who alleged they decided not to sell their shares because of an unduly rosy representation or a failure to disclose unfavorable material; and

111. Touche Ross & Co. v. Redington, 442 U.S. 560, 61 L.Ed.2d 82, 99 S.Ct. 2479 (1979); Transamerica Mtg. Advisors, Inc. v. Lewis, 444 U.S. 11, 62 L.Ed.2d 146, 100 S.Ct. 242 (1979). See Cannon v. University of Chicago, 441 U.S. 677, 60 L.Ed.2d 560, 99 S.Ct. 1946 (1979); Great American Fed. Sav. & Loan Ass'n v. Novotny, 442 U.S. 366, 60 L.Ed.2d 957, 99 S.Ct. 2345 (1979); Universities Research Ass'n v. Contu, 450 U.S. 754, 67 L.Ed.2d 662, 101 S.Ct. 1451 (1981).

112. Herman & MacLean v. Huddleston, 459 U.S. 375, 74 L.Ed.2d 548, 555, 103 S.Ct. 683 (1983).

113. 421 U.S. 723, 44 L.Ed.2d 539, 95 S.Ct. 1917 (1975).

(3) Shareholders, creditors, and perhaps others related to an issuer who suffered loss due to corporate or insider activities in connection with the purchase or sale of securities which violate Rule 10b-5.

Failure to so limit Rule 10b-5 suits could, in the opinion of the Court, result in vexatious litigation caused by a widely expanded class of plaintiffs bringing nuisance or "strike" suits and opening litigation to factual issues the proof of which would largely depend on uncorroborated oral testimony of persons who never acted, but claimed that illegal activities deterred them from purchasing or selling securities.

There have been two primary issues since *Blue Chip* with respect to the standing of a plaintiff to enforce Rule 10b-5: what is a "sale" of securities, and who is a purchaser or seller of securities?

With respect to the definition of "sale," the Supreme Court has rendered an expansive definition, holding that a pledge of stock is an "offer" or "sale" of securities for purposes of Section 17(a) of the 1933 Act.[114] The term "sale" was defined in Section 2(3) of the 1933 Act to include every "disposition" of an "interest in a security for value." Hence, the Court concluded that the pledge was a sale for purposes of Section 17(a), stating: "Although pledges transfer less than absolute title, the interest thus transferred nonetheless is an 'interest in a security'."[115] Although the definitional provisions of the 1933 Act differ from those of the 1934 Act, the Supreme Court has recently indicated the *Rubin* holding should be expanded to the 1934 Act and Rule 10b-5 by stating that a pledge is the equivalent of a sale for purposes of each of the antifraud provisions of the federal securities laws.[116]

A change in the terms of a security may also invoke the protections of Rule 10b-5. It has been held that changes in the

114. Rubin v. United States, 449 U.S. 424, 66 L.Ed.2d 633, 101 S.Ct. 698 (1981).

115. Id., 101 S.Ct. at 701.

116. Marine Bank v. Weaver, 455 U.S. 551, 71 L.Ed.2d 409, 102 S.Ct. 1220 (1982).

rights of a security holder can qualify as the "purchase" of a new security under Rule 10b-5 if there is such a significant change in the nature of the investment or in the investment risks as to amount to a new investment.[117]

In addition to defining a sale, courts have also attempted to define who is a purchaser or seller for purposes of standing. A forced seller (i.e., one who does not voluntarily sell his securities) is now generally recognized to have standing under Rule 10b-5.[118] However, a person who merely lost an opportunity to purchase stock because of allegedly fraudulent activity has no standing.[119]

Within a year after the *Blue Chip* decision, the Supreme Court again limited the applicability of Rule 10b-5 by ruling that a plaintiff must prove by a preponderance of the evidence that the defendant acted with "scienter," a mental state embracing intent to deceive, manipulate or defraud.[120] The Court noted that mere negligence is not actionable under the antifraud provisions.

The Court in *Hochfelder* did not define the term "scienter" and in subsequent cases has not clearly defined the term other than in general terms.[121]

Since *Hochfelder,* the overwhelming majority of lower federal courts has held that a showing of recklessness is sufficient to satisfy the scienter requirement,[122] although those

---

117. Keys v. Wolfe, 709 F.2d 413 (5th Cir. 1983); Rathborne v. Rathborne, 683 F.2d 914 (5th Cir. 1982).

118. Falls v. Fickling, 621 F.2d 1362 (5th Cir. 1980); Alley v. Miramon, 614 F.2d 1372 (5th Cir. 1980); Broad v. Rockwell Int'l Corp., 614 F.2d 418 (5th Cir. 1980), aff'd on other grounds en banc, 642 F.2d 929 (5th Cir. 1981).

119. Collins v. Signetics Corp., 605 F.2d 110 (3d Cir. 1979).

120. Ernst & Ernst v. Hochfelder, supra note 100.

121. In Aaron v. SEC, 446 U.S. 680, 64 L.Ed.2d 611, 100 S.Ct. 1945 (1980), the court ruled that "scienter" was a requisite element of a civil enforcement action by the SEC to enjoin violations of Rule 10b-5 but defined "scienter" only as a "mental state embracing intent to deceive, manipulate or defraud."

122. E.g., J.H. Cohn & Co. v. American Appraisal Assocs., 628 F.2d 994 (7th Cir. 1980); Mihara v. Dean Witter & Co., 619 F.2d 814 (9th Cir. 1980);

courts disagree as to what "recklessness" means in this context. Simple references to tort doctrines will not be adequate to resolve this controversy.[123]

Some courts have adopted a liberal definition to the effect that a primary wrongdoer acts recklessly if he fails or refuses, after being put on notice of a possible material misstatement or nondisclosure, to apprise himself of the facts when he can do so without any extraordinary effort.[124] Most courts, though, have adopted a more strict definition of recklessness, i.e., an extreme departure from the standards of ordinary care to the extent that the fraudulent activity was either known to the defendant or so obvious that the defendant must have been aware of it.[125]

An example of this more strict standard, as it applies to outside directors, is found in a recent Eastern District of Virginia case in which four "outside" directors of a corporation and others were sued for securities fraud under Rule 10b-5 in connection with a "going private" tender offer. In dismissing the claims against the outside directors for lack of scienter, the court found that the outside directors did not have knowledge of any misstatements or omissions in the tender offer material and did not draft the material. Because the court ruled that outside directors had no duty to ensure that all material adverse information is disclosed, it found no scienter

Mansbach v. Prescott, Ball & Turben, 598 F.2d 1017 (8th Cir. 1979); Healey v. Catalyst Recovery of Pa., Inc., 616 F.2d 641 (3d Cir. 1980); Oleck v. Fischer, 623 F.2d 791 (2d Cir. 1980).

123. Pegasus Fund, Inc. v. Laraneta, 617 F.2d 1335, 1340 (9th Cir. 1980). For a discussion of the various definitions which have been adopted, see Steinberg and Gruenbaum, "Variations of 'Recklessness' after Hochfelder and Aaron," 8 Sec. Reg. L.J. 179 (1980).

124. Lanza v. Drexel & Co., 479 F.2d 1277 (2d Cir. 1973); IIT, An Int'l Inv. Trust v. Cornfeld, 619 F.2d 909 (2d Cir. 1980); Greene v. Emersons, Ltd., Fed. Sec. L. Rep. (CCH) ¶97,266 (S.D.N.Y. 1980), aff'd on other grounds sub nom. Kenneth Leventhal & Co. v. Joyner Wholesale Co., 736 F.2d 29 (2d Cir. 1984).

125. E.g., Healey v. Catalyst Recovery of Pa., Inc., 616 F.2d 641 (3d Cir. 1980); McLean v. Alexander, 599 F.2d 1190 (3d Cir. 1979); Mansbach v. Prescott, Ball & Turben, 598 F.2d 1017 (6th Cir. 1979).

in failing to disclose certain information.[126] However, where corporate officers are involved in the preparation and publication of false financial statements with the knowledge that material inventory overvaluations resulted in inflated corporate profits, a jury may properly find those officers acted with the requisite scienter.[127]

Under either the liberal or the more strict definition, direct evidence of a defendant's actual state of mind is not necessary. Circumstantial evidence, including motivation,[128] is often the principal, if not the only means of proving recklessness and bad faith.[129]

Although unresolved in *Hochfelder,* the Supreme Court subsequently ruled that the SEC must also prove scienter as an element of a civil enforcement action to enjoin violations of Section 10(b) and Rule 10b-5.[130]

Following *Blue Chip* and *Hochfelder,* the Supreme Court continued its restrictive interpretation of Rule 10b-5 in *Santa Fe Industries, Incorporated v. Green,*[131] in which it was held that a breach of fiduciary duty by corporate officers, directors and others does not violate the antifraud rules of the federal securities laws without a showing of deception, misrepresentation or nondisclosure. Redress for corporate mismanagement whereby shareholders were treated unfairly by a fiduciary was left to state regulation.

Notwithstanding this restrictive opinion, lower courts have kept Rule 10b-5 alive with respect to corporate mismanagement. Although the basic holding in the *Green* opinion (i.e., absent manipulative or deceptive activity, a Rule 10b-5 action will not lie for corporate mismanagement) is still recognized as the applicable law by lower federal courts, those

---

126. In re Action Indus. Tender Offer, 572 F. Supp. 846 (E.D. Va. 1983).

127. Sirota v. Solitron Devices, Inc., 673 F.2d 566 (2d Cir.), cert. denied, 459 U.S. 838 (1982).

128. Dirks v. SEC, 463 U.S. 646, 77 L.Ed.2d 911, 927 n.23, 103 S.Ct. 3255 (1983).

129. McLean v. Alexander, 599 F.2d 1190, 1198 (3d Cir. 1979).

130. Aaron v. SEC, supra note 121.

131. 430 U.S. 462, 51 L.Ed.2d 480, 97 S.Ct. 1292 (1977).

courts have interpreted "deception" broadly, thereby eliminating many of the restrictions imposed by *Green.*

Such implicit overruling of *Green* by the lower courts began shortly after it was decided. In *Goldberg v. Meridor,*[132] the Second Circuit, speaking through Judge Henry J. Friendly, held that a Rule 10b-5 action existed in a derivative suit on behalf of a subsidiary corporation alleging that a sale to the subsidiary of all of the parent corporation's assets and liabilities in exchange for the subsidiary's stock was grossly unfair. The court held:

> [T]here is deception of the corporation (in effect, of its minority shareholders) when the corporation is influenced by its controlling shareholder to engage in a transaction adverse to the corporation's interests (in effect, the minority shareholders' interests) and there is nondisclosure or misleading disclosure as to the material facts of the transaction.[133]

In essence, the court decided that if a fiduciary does not disclose facts which could be used by minority shareholders to enjoin the fiduciary under state law, the fiduciary has deceived the minority, thereby giving rise to a Rule 10b-5 action. The effect of this holding was noted by a dissenting opinion in *Goldberg:*

> [U]nder the majority's reasoning the failure to inform stockholders of a proposed defalcation gives rise to a cause of action under 10b-5. Thus, the majority has neatly undone the holdings of *Green, Piper,* and *Cort* by creating a federal cause of action for a breach of fiduciary duty that will apply in all cases, save for those rare instances where the fiduciary denounces himself in advance.[134]

The *Goldberg* rationale has been adopted by other circuits.[135] Examples of Rule 10b-5 actions under this rationale,

---

132. 567 F.2d 209 (2d Cir. 1977), cert. denied, 434 U.S. 1069 (1978).
133. Id. at 217.
134. Id. at 225, dissenting opinion of Judge Meskill.
135. IIT, An Int'l Inv. Trust v. Cornfeld, 619 F.2d 909 (2d Cir. 1980); Kidwell ex rel. Penfold v. Meikle, 597 F.2d 1273 (9th Cir. 1979); Alabama

in which courts have found the requisite deception, include a derivative suit on behalf of a corporation against its directors alleging that the directors failed to disclose the inflationary effect of the corporation's stock repurchase plan on the market price of the corporation's stock;[136] a minority shareholder action against the corporation's officers and directors alleging nondisclosure of information regarding a merger, which information could have been the basis of enjoining the merger in state court;[137] and an action by members and directors of a nonprofit corporation against fellow directors and others alleging nondisclosure of information relating to the sale of corporate assets, which information could have been the basis for a state law injunction even though the plaintiffs were not entitled to vote on the transaction in question.[138]

This circumvention of *Green* has not been unanimous or without its limitations. Several cases have denied a shareholder's attempt to "bootstrap" a breach of fiduciary duty claim into a federal securities law action by alleging that the disclosure philosophy of the statute obligates a corporate manager to reveal either the culpability of his activities or the impure motives for entering into an allegedly improper transaction.[139] Also, in order to prove that nondisclosure was material and caused the suffered loss, most courts have required a showing that the plaintiff would have succeeded or had a reasonable probability of succeeding in a state court

Farm Bur. Mut. Cas. Co. v. American Fid. Life Ins. Co., 606 F.2d 602 (5th Cir. 1979), cert. denied, 449 U.S. 820 (1980); Healey v. Catalyst Recovery of Pa., Inc., 616 F.2d 641 (3d Cir. 1980). Cf. Biesenbach v. Guenther, 588 F.2d 400 (3d Cir. 1978); Kaplan v. Bennett, 465 F. Supp. 555 (S.D.N.Y. 1979).

136. Alabama Farm Bur. Mut. Cas. Co. v. American Fid. Life Ins. Co., supra note 135.

137. Healey v. Catalyst Recovery of Pa., Inc., supra note 135.

138. Kidwell ex rel. Penfold v. Meikle, supra note 135.

139. Panter v. Marshall Field & Co., 646 F.2d 271 (7th Cir.), cert. denied, 454 U.S. 1092 (1981); Bucher v. Shumway, Fed. Sec. L. Rep. (CCH) ¶97,142, aff'd, 622 F.2d 572 (2d Cir. 1980); In re Sunshine Mining Co. Sec. Litig., 496 F. Supp. 9 (S.D.N.Y. 1979).

action if the undisclosed information concerning the mismanagement had been disclosed.[140]

These cases suggest that where the directors of a corporation have a conflict of interest or are otherwise not truly
independent and disinterested, full disclosure to shareholders
of matters relating to corporate management must be made
even as to matters which do not require shareholder approval. Where, however, shareholder approval is not required, full disclosure to a disinterested board of directors
may be equivalent to full disclosure to the shareholders, since
knowledge of the disinterested majority of the board may be
attributed to the corporation and its shareholders, thereby
precluding a finding of "deception."[141]

Only misrepresentations or omissions of material facts are
actionable under Section 10(b) and Rule 10b-5. The Supreme
Court has ruled that a fact is material if "there is a substantial likelihood that a reasonable shareholder would consider
it important" in making an investment decision.[142]

In addition to being material, the misrepresentation or
omission must also result in or cause the plaintiff's damage.
The type of proof necessary to satisfy this requirement varies
depending upon whether the alleged conduct involves a misrepresentation or an omission. In either event, it is generally
easier for a plaintiff to prove reliance and causation under
Section 10(b) and Rule 10b-5 than under common-law fraud.

---

140. Mayer v. Oil Field Sys. Corp., 721 F.2d 59 (2d Cir. 1983); Madison
Consultants v. FDIC, 710 F.2d 57 (2d Cir. 1983); Kidwell ex rel. Penfold v.
Meikle, supra note 135; Healey v. Catalyst Recovery of Pa., Inc., supra note
135; Alabama Farm Bur. Mut. Cas. Ins. Co. v. American Fid. Life Ins. Co.,
supra note 135. Cf. United States v. Margala, 662 F.2d 622 (9th Cir. 1981).

141. Maldonado v. Flynn, 597 F.2d 789, 793 (2d Cir.), on remand, 477 F.
Supp. 1007 (S.D.N.Y. 1979) and 485 F. Supp. 274 (S.D.N.Y. 1980), rev'd on
other grounds, 671 F.2d 729 (2d Cir. 1982). See also Kaplan v. Bennett, 465
F. Supp. 555, 565-66 (S.D.N.Y. 1979); Goldberger v. Baker, 442 F. Supp.
659, 665 (S.D.N.Y. 1977); Tyco Labs., Inc. v. Kimball, 444 F. Supp. 292,
297-98 (E.D. Pa. 1977); Falkenberg v. Baldwin, Fed. Sec. L. Rep. (CCH)
¶96,086 (S.D.N.Y. 1977).

142. TSC Indus., Inc. v. Northway, Inc., 426 U.S. 438, 48 L.Ed.2d 757, 96
S.Ct. 2126 (1976).

In cases involving a misrepresentation, the Supreme Court has recognized a rebuttable presumption of reliance with respect to transactions in an open and developed securities market. In *Basic Incorporated v. Levinson*, [143] the Court supported the "fraud-on-the-market" theory, which assumes that the price in an open and developed market for a company's securities reflects all available material information about that company, including materially false or misleading statements by the company. [144] Under this theory, shareholders rely on the integrity of the market price in deciding whether to buy or sell a security. Accordingly, such shareholders are presumed to rely on false or misleading statements by the company even if they never actually hear or read those statements themselves. [145] The Court stated such a presumption relieves the Rule 10b-5 plaintiff of an unrealistic evidentiary burden and is consistent with and supportive of the 1934 Act's policy of requiring full disclosure and fostering reliance on market integrity. The presumption may be rebutted by a showing that the market price was not affected by the misrepresentation or that the plaintiff did not trade in reliance on the integrity of the market price. In Rule 10b-5 proceedings not involving an open and developed securities market, affirmative proof of reliance is required. [146]

In cases involving an omission, the Supreme Court has ruled that affirmative proof of reliance may not be a prerequi-

---

143. — U.S. —, 108 S.Ct. 978, 56 U.S.L.W. 4232 (March 7, 1988).

144. Peil v. Speiser, 806 F.2d 1154, 1160-61 (3d Cir. 1986).

145. Blackie v. Barrack, 524 F.2d 891 (9th Cir. 1975), cert. denied, 429 U.S. 816 (1976); Panzirer v. Wolf, 663 F.2d 365 (2d Cir. 1981), cert. granted on reliance issue, 458 U.S. 1105, vacated as moot, 459 U.S. 1027 (1982); Ross v. A.H. Robins Co., Inc., 607 F.2d 545, 553 (2d Cir. 1979), cert. denied, 446 U.S. 946 (1980); Shores v. Sklar, 647 F.2d 462 (5th Cir. 1981), cert. denied, 455 U.S. 936 (1983); T.J. Raney & Sons v. Fort Cobb, Okla. Irrigation Fuel Auth., 717 F.2d 1330, 1332-33 (10th Cir. 1983); Kennedy v. Tallant, 710 F.2d 711, 713 (11th Cir. 1983); Lipton v. Documation, Inc., 734 F.2d 740 (11th Cir. 1984).

146. Huddleston v. Herman & MacLean, 640 F.2d 534, 548 (5th Cir.), modified on other grounds, 650 F.2d 815 (5th Cir. 1981), aff'd in part, rev'd in part, 459 U.S. 375 (1983).

site to recovery. In *Affiliated Ute Citizens of Utah v. United States*,[147] the Court held that where a fiduciary in a face-to-face transaction elected to "stand mute" and failed to disclose material facts, "positive proof of reliance is not necessary to recovery. All that is necessary is that the facts withheld be material in the sense that a reasonable investor might have considered them important in the making of this [investment] decision."[148] Most courts have interpreted the *Ute* decision to create a rebuttable presumption of reliance when a defendant allegedly fails to disclose material information.[149]

Distinguishing omissions from misrepresentations for purposes of applying the applicable reliance test has proved difficult in some instances.

In the circuit court decision in *Huddleston v. Herman & MacLean*,[150] omissions of material fact in a prospectus were treated as misrepresentations and, therefore, no presumption of reliance arose. The court found that the defendants did not "stand mute" in the face of a duty to disclose as did the defendants in *Affiliated Ute* and that the difficulties of proving reliance which justify the presumption in omission cases was not present.

In another case,[151] a corporate officer stated in a quarterly report that the corporation's new business "gives us confidence for the future." However, the next issued quarterly report indicated significant declines in both sales and earnings. An investor, who purchased shares in the corporation after issuance of the first report but before issuance of the second, sued the corporation and the officer, alleging he had purchased the shares in reliance on misleading information.

---

147. 406 U.S. 128, 31 L.Ed.2d 741, 92 S.Ct. 1456, reh'g denied, 407 U.S. 916, 32 L.Ed.2d 692, 92 S.Ct. 2430 and 408 U.S. 931, 33 L.Ed.2d 345, 92 S.Ct. 2478 (1972).

148. Id., 406 U.S. at 153-54.

149. See, e.g., Rifkin v. Crow, 474 F.2d 256, 262 (5th Cir. 1978); Blackie v. Barrack, supra note 144.

150. Supra note 143.

151. Wilson v. Comtech Telecommunications Corp., 648 F.2d 88 (2d Cir. 1981).

The court found these facts to be a misrepresentation, rather than an omission, and held that in such a case, reliance will not be presumed since such a presumption is applicable only to situations in which no positive statement exists. The omission to update the report was treated as a misrepresentation rather than an omission because it related back to an earlier statement and it was reasonable to believe the earlier statement stood.

In situations involving both omissions and misrepresentations, some courts have applied the presumption of reliance[152] while others have not.[153]

A plaintiff must prove not only the existence or presumption of reliance, but also that the reliance was justified. This has been referred to as a requirement of due diligence by the plaintiff. Since *Hochfelder*, courts generally have ruled that the standard of care for plaintiffs should not be greater than the standard for defendants and, therefore, recklessness, not negligence, is the applicable standard.[154] This recklessness standard has been described as requiring proof that the plaintiff refused to investigate in disregard of a known risk or a risk so obvious that it must be presumed to be known, which risk was so great that it was highly probable harm would follow.[155]

Damages for violation of Section 10(b) are typically measured by the difference between what the plaintiff paid for the securities and what the securities were actually worth on the date of purchase (i.e., out-of-pocket loss).[156] Rescission of

---

152. Sharp v. Coopers & Lybrand, 649 F.2d 175, 188 (3d Cir. 1981), cert. denied, 455 U.S. 938 (1982); Austin v. Loftsgaarden, 675 F.2d 168, 178 (8th Cir. 1982); Feldman v. Pioneer Petroleum, Inc., Fed. Sec. L. Rep. (CCH) ¶99,173 (W.D. Okla. 1983).

153. Sundstrand Corp. v. Sun Chem. Corp., 553 F.2d 1033, 1040 (7th Cir.), cert. denied, 434 U.S. 875 (1977); Holdsworth v. Strong, 545 F.2d 687, 693 (10th Cir. 1976).

154. See, e.g., Nelson v. Serwold, 576 F.2d 1332, 1338 (9th Cir. 1977); Bell v. Cameron Meadows Land Co., 669 F.2d 1278, 1283 (9th Cir. 1982).

155. Dupuy v. Dupuy, 551 F.2d 1005, 1020 (5th Cir. 1977).

156. Janigan v. Taylor, 344 F.2d 781, 786 (1st Cir. 1965); Estate Counseling Serv., Inc. v. Merrill Lynch, Pierce, Fenner & Smith, Inc., 303 F.2d 527, 533 (10th Cir. 1962).

the transaction has been a recognized remedy also.[157] Punitive damages are not recoverable,[158] although prejudgment interest may be awarded in the court's discretion.[159]

There is no express statute of limitations period under either Sections 17(a) or 10(b). Therefore, courts apply the state statute of limitations most analogous. Although the "Blue Sky" statute of limitations contained within the state securities statutes is sometimes applied, the longer limitations period for fraud actions is most often chosen for equitable reasons.[160] However, when determining when the statute of limitations period begins to run, the courts must look to federal law, not the state law.[161]

§ 14.07. Proxy statements.

In recent years, substantially more companies are finding themselves engaged in proxy solicitations involving an array of ordinary and extraordinary business decisions. Among other reasons, this dramatic increase can be attributed to attempts by outsiders to examine more closely corporate governance, to obtain control of the corporation through a cheaper procedure than a hostile tender offer and to cause management sufficient problems to induce them to purchase the dissident's shares at a premium (frequently called "greenmail"[162]). With this increased frequency of proxy solicitations, directors and officers are being subjected to increased liability exposure for the preparation of proxy statements.

---

157. Garnaty v. Stifel, Nicolaus & Co., Inc., 559 F.2d 1357, 1360 (8th Cir. 1977).

158. Byrnes v. Faulkner, Dawkins & Sullivan, 550 F.2d 1303, 1313 (2d Cir. 1977).

159. Sundstrand Corp. v. Sun Chem. Corp., 553 F.2d 1033, 1051 (7th Cir.), cert. denied, 434 U.S. 875 (1977).

160. United Cal. Bank v. Salik, 481 F.2d 1012, 1015 (9th Cir. 1973) ("[T]he broad remedial policies of the federal securities laws are best served by a longer, not a shorter, statute of limitation").

161. Clute v. Davenport Co., 584 F. Supp. 1562 (D. Conn. 1984); Engl v. Berg, 514 F. Supp. 1146 (E.D. Pa. 1981).

162. See infra section 15.06.

A major objective of the disclosure provisions of the 1934 Act was the regulation of proxy solicitations. Section 14(a)[163] makes it unlawful for any person, including directors and officers, to solicit or to permit the use of his name to solicit any proxy or consent or authorization in respect of a registered security in contravention of the SEC's rules and regulations. This provision "was intended to promote the free exercise of the voting rights of stockholders by ensuring that proxies would be solicited with explanation to the stockholder of the real nature of the questions for which authority to cast his vote is sought."[164]

Rule 14a-9[165] bars the use of any proxy or communication containing any statement which is false or misleading with respect to any material fact, or which omits to state any material fact necessary to make the statements therein not false or misleading. It also prohibits omissions necessary to correct earlier communications on the same subject which have become false or misleading. Corporate officers and directors are covered by those provisions.

Since 1964, it has been clear that stockholders who have been injured as a result of false or misleading proxy solicitations can bring a direct or derivative private action for damages or other appropriate relief.[166] However, that unchallenged premise was placed in some doubt in 1979 by the Supreme Court in the *Redington*[167] case, which refused to imply a private right of action under Section 17 of the 1934 Act:

> We do not now question the actual holding of [the *Borak* case], ... To the extent our analysis in today's decision

---

163. 15 U.S.C. § 78n(a).

164. TSC Indus., Inc. v. Northway, Inc., 426 U.S. 438, 444, 48 L.Ed.2d 757, 763, 96 S.Ct. 2126, 2130 (1976), citing Mills v. Electric Auto-Lite Co., 396 U.S. 375, 381, 24 L.Ed.2d 593, 90 S.Ct. 616, 620 (1970), quoting H.R. Rep. No. 1383, 73rd Cong., 2d Sess., 14 (1934); S. Rep. No. 792, 73rd Cong., 2d Sess., 12 (1934).

165. 17 C.F.R. § 240.14a-9.

166. J.I. Case Co. v. Borak, 377 U.S. 426, 12 L.Ed. 423, 84 S.Ct. 155 (1964).

167. Touche Ross & Co. v. Redington, 442 U.S. 560, 61 L.Ed.2d 82, 99 S.Ct. 2479 (1979).

differs from that of the Court in *Borak,* it suffices to say that in a series of cases since *Borak* we have adhered to a stricter standard for the implication of private causes of action, and we follow that stricter standard today.[168]

Whether this language is mere idle dictum or a foretelling of decisions to come will be determined only with the passage of time. Subsequent Supreme Court decisions, though, suggest the Section 14(a) private action will continue to be implied from legislative intent.[169]

Although similar in intent to the antifraud rules of Section 17(a) of the 1933 Act and Section 10(b) of the 1934 Act, Section 14(a) contains some important differences for private suits. Unlike the antifraud rules, negligence alone can result in liability for those involved with the issuance of proxy statements.[170] Thus, a director, even an outside non-management director, may be held liable if he or she knew, or in the exercise of due diligence should have known, that the proxy statement contained false or misleading statements or omissions. When determining a particular director's due diligence, courts are permitted to consider the individual's position with the corporation and his relationship to the pertinent information found to be erroneously and incompletely disclosed.[171]

The concepts of materiality and causation as applied to actions under Section 14(a) have been the subject of considerable litigation. The Supreme Court has ruled that a misstatement or omission is "material" for purposes of Section 14(a) if there is a "substantial likelihood that a reasonable shareholder would consider it important in deciding how to vote."[172] This definition, if applied broadly, could permit shareholders to use Section 14(a) as a vehicle to seek redress

---

168. Id., 442 U.S. at 578.

169. Cannon v. University of Chicago, 441 U.S. 667, 60 L.Ed.2d 560, 99 S.Ct. 1946 (1979). See also Rauchman v. Mobil Corp., 739 F.2d 205 (6th Cir. 1984).

170. Gould v. American-Hawaiian S.S. Co., 535 F.2d 761 (3d Cir. 1976).

171. Id.

172. TSC Indus., Inc. v. Northway, Inc., supra note 164.

for alleged mismanagement or breach of fiduciary duty, which are state law issues.

Most courts have refused to adopt such a broad application of this definition, at least with respect to "qualitative" information (i.e., information that does not have a direct economic impact on the company, but may put the company or the director nominee in a bad light). Instead, those courts have held that unless there are allegations of self-dealing, dishonesty or deceit by the directors which inures to their personal benefit, director misconduct of the type traditionally relegated to state corporate law need not be disclosed in proxy solicitation materials for the election of directors.[173] Under those rules, the nondisclosure of alleged breaches of fiduciary duty and waste of corporate assets, unadorned by self-dealing allegations, are not material and thus not actionable under Section 14(a).

With respect to proxies relating to the submission of management proposals to shareholders, directors have been found not to be liable for omitting from a proxy statement information relating to the directors' motive for the proposals, possible alternatives to the proposals or alleged breaches of the directors' fiduciary duties in connection with the proposals.[174]

In contrast, misstatements or omissions involving self-dealing are deemed material in proxy solicitations for the election of directors since self-dealing presents opportunities for abuse of a corporate position of trust. As the Second Circuit has stated, shareholders are entitled to truthful presentation of factual information "impugning the honesty, loyalty or competency of directors" in their dealings with the corporation.[175] However, information concerning uncharged criminal con-

---

173. Gaines v. Haughton, 645 F.2d 761 (9th Cir. 1981); Bertoglio v. Texas Int'l Co., 488 F. Supp. 630, 650 (D. Del. 1980); Lewis v. Valley, 476 F. Supp. 62, 65-66 (S.D.N.Y. 1979); Amalgamated Clothing & Textile Workers Union, AFL-CIO v. J.P. Stevens & Co., 475 F. Supp. 328, 330-332 (S.D.N.Y. 1979).

174. District 65, U.A.W. v. Harper & Row Publishers, Inc., 576 F. Supp. 1468, 1486 (S.D.N.Y. 1983).

175. Maldondo v. Flynn, 597 F.2d 789 (2d Cir. 1979).

duct or unadjudicated allegations of a "breach of trust" by a
director nominee is not material and need not be disclosed.[176]

Thus, the materiality of the undisclosed information depends upon the nature of the misconduct involved. Allegations of director misconduct involving breach of trust or self-
dealing are presumptively material, while allegations of simple breach of fiduciary duty and waste of corporate assets are
not material.

Likewise, the causation element is dependent upon
whether shareholder approval was necessary for the challenged transaction. Where shareholder approval is necessary,
the Supreme Court has ruled that if the misstatement or
omission was material, a sufficient causal relationship between violation and injury is established; proof that the violation actually had a decisive effect on the voting is not required.[177] This conclusive presumption of causation has been
applied even where the defective proxy solicitation was directed to only the minority shareholders who could not have
blocked the proposed transaction through the exercise of
proxy votes.[178]

This causation presumption has not been applied, though,
in suits under Section 14(a) which attempt to recover from
directors and others illegal or improper payments which were
not properly disclosed in proxies. Courts there have tended to
require a showing of a "transactional causation"; i.e., the authorization of the questioned payments must be the subject
matter of the proxies.[179] Those cases conclude that if the im-

---

176. United States v. Matthews, 737 F.2d 38 (2d Cir. 1986); GAF Corp. v.
Heyman, 724 F.2d 727 (2d Cir. 1983).

177. Mills v. Electric Auto-Lite Co., 396 U.S. 375, 24 L.Ed.2d 593, 90
S.Ct. 616 (1970). See also Gaines v. Haughton, supra note 173; Weisberg v.
Coastal States Gas Corp., 609 F.2d 650 (2d Cir. 1979), cert. denied, 445 U.S.
951 (1980).

178. Schlick v. Penn-Dixie Cement Corp., 507 F.2d 374 (2d Cir. 1974).

179. Gaines v. Haughton, supra note 173; Rosengarten v. International
Tel. & Tel. Corp., 466 F. Supp. 817 (S.D.N.Y. 1979); Herman v. Beretta,
Fed. Sec. L. Rep. (CCH) ¶96,574 (S.D.N.Y. 1978); Zilker v. Klein, 519 F.
Supp. 1070 (N.D. Ill. 1981).

proper payments are merely an incident to the reelection of the directors, no Section 14(a) action lies for recovery of the payments because there is no direct nexus between the misleading proxy and the flawed transaction.

Either monetary damages or injunctive relief have been awarded for Section 14(a) violations. However, the remedy must relate only to the transaction for which approval was specifically solicited by the flawed proxy materials.[180] The actions of directors elected by tainted proxies cannot be voided.

§ 14.08. Tender offers.

Few areas have caused as much liability exposure for directors in recent years as hostile takeovers. Although state law claims for breach of fiduciary duty are frequently alleged in lawsuits against directors in this context,[181] the primary basis for liability under the federal securities law is the Williams Act[182] and Section 14(e)[183] thereof.

The Williams Act, enacted in 1968, added Sections 13(d), 13(e), 14(d), 14(e) and 14(f) to the Securities Exchange Act of 1934 for the purpose of regulating tender offers in the national marketplace. Courts have recognized that participants in tender offers, as in proxy contests, act "under the stresses of the market place. They act quickly, sometimes impulsively, often in angry response to what they consider, whether rightly or wrongly, to be low blows by the other side."[184] Therefore, the primary objective of the Williams Act is to protect investors by requiring certain minimum disclosures to and by providing specific benefits for shareholders of the target corporation. In so doing, the statutes seek not to tip

---

180. Zilker v. Klein, supra note 179.

181. See infra Chapter 15.

182. Act of July 29, 1968, P.L. 90-439, 82 Stat. 454 (1968), amending 15 U.S.C. §§ 78m and 78n.

183. 15 U.S.C. § 78n(e).

184. Electronic Specialty Co. v. International Controls Corp., 409 F.2d 937, 948 (2d Cir. 1969).

the balance either in favor of the bidder seeking control of the company or the target's management which is trying to defeat the bid.

A key provision in this statutory framework is Section 14(e), which is a broad antifraud provision aimed at the conduct of any person making or opposing a tender offer, requesting tenders, or otherwise seeking to influence the outcome of the tender offer. The statute prohibits any fraudulent, deceptive or manipulative act or practice with language similar to Section 10(b). Although potentially broad in its application, Section 14(e) has been interpreted by the Supreme Court rather narrowly, thereby forcing persons seeking recourse in tender offers to turn to state law claims more frequently.

The first significant restriction of Section 14(e) occurred in the *Piper v. Chris-Craft Industries* case.[185] The Supreme Court there ruled that a tender offeror, suing in that capacity, has no standing to sue under Section 14(e) for allegedly fraudulent activity by the successful bidder, its investment advisor and the directors of the target company. The Court concluded that the purpose of the legislation was the protection of investors confronted by a tender offer. Tender offerors were not intended beneficiaries of the statute, and therefore only shareholders of the target have standing to sue under Section 14(e).

The second significant restriction in the scope of Section 14(e) occurred in 1985 and dealt with the application of the statute to various defensive tactics undertaken by the directors and officers of the target company. Prior to that time, some courts had ruled that certain defensive tactics used by the target's management constituted manipulative acts prohibited by Section 14(e) even though no deception occurred. For example, in *Mobil Corporation v. Marathon Oil Company,*[186] the court ruled that the issuance by a target corporation of lock-up options which were intended to thwart a pend-

---

185. Piper v. Chris-Craft Indus., Inc., 430 U.S. 1, 51 L.Ed.2d 124, 97 S.Ct. 926, reh'g denied, 430 U.S. 976 (1977).
186. 669 F.2d 366 (6th Cir. 1981).

ing tender offer was a manipulative act under Section 14(e). Using a broader definition than applied in Section 10(b) cases, the court defined "manipulation" as an "affecting of the market for, or price of, securities by artificial means, i.e., means unrelated to the natural forces of supply and demand"[187] and thus found the issuance of the options was manipulative since they had the effect of circumventing the natural forces of market demand by choking off a potential auction for control of the target.

The Supreme Court rejected this broad interpretation of "manipulation." In *Schreiber v. Burlington Northern, Incorporated*,[188] the Court ruled that defensive tactics affecting the market price of a company's stock, restraining bidders or affecting the possibility of a tender offer may be manipulative or fraudulent under Section 14(e) only if such acts were not fully disclosed. "Manipulation" was interpreted to connote conduct designed to deceive or defraud investors by controlling or artificially affecting the price of securities. Fully disclosed acts may not be found to be manipulative even if they artificially affect the price of stock.

In another restrictive interpretation of Section 14(e), several appellate courts[189] have ruled that shareholders may not recover under Section 14(e) from the target's directors and officers for fraudulent or manipulative conduct which caused a proposed tender offer to be withdrawn before it became effective. Because the shareholders never had the chance to tender their shares, the shareholders cannot establish the requisite reliance on the manipulative conduct.

Although Section 14(e) refers to manipulation or fraud "in connection with any tender offer," neither the 1934 Act nor SEC rules define a "tender offer." Despite numerous judicial attempts at defining the phrase, an exact definition is still

---

187. Id. at 374.

188. 472 U.S. 1, 86 L.Ed.2d 1, 105 S.Ct. 2458 (1985).

189. See, e.g., Panter v. Marshall Field & Co., 646 F.2d 271 (7th Cir.), cert. denied, 454 U.S. 1092 (1981); Lewis v. McGraw, 619 F.2d 192 (2d Cir.), cert. denied, 449 U.S. 951 (1980).

lacking. Open market purchases[190] and privately negotiated purchases[191] have not been considered a "tender offer" for purposes of the Williams Act unless the pressure and the likelihood of hasty, uninformed selling that is present in traditional tender offers is shown.

§ 14.09. Short-swing profits.

Among the many hazards awaiting corporate officers and directors under the federal securities laws, one of the most important is that embodied in Section 16(b)[192] of the 1934 Act. Unlike other provisions of the Act, this statute is not concerned with obligations of the issuer corporation, but rather with the potential misuse of inside information by officers, directors and substantial shareholders.

Because the detection of inside trading is typically quite difficult, Congress adopted a prophylactic rule which imposes liability on a director, officer or beneficial owner of ten percent or more of the company's securities if such insider purchased and sold, or sold and purchased, the company's securities within a six-month period. It is immaterial whether the insider actually made the transactions based on inside information. The mere possibility that such misuse of inside information might occur was of sufficient concern to Congress that this per se liability statute was enacted. The Supreme Court has said: "[T]he only method Congress deemed effective to curb the evils of insider trading was a flat rule taking the profits out of a class of transactions in which the possibility of abuse was believed to be intolerably great."[193]

---

190. Kennecott Copper Corp. v. Curtiss-Wright Corp., 584 F.2d 1195 (2d Cir. 1978); Chromalloy Am. Corp. v. Sun Chem. Corp., 474 F. Supp. 1341 (E.D. Mo.), aff'd, 611 F.2d 240 (8th Cir. 1979); Calumet Indus., Inc. v. MacClure, Fed. Sec. L. Rep. (CCH) ¶96,434 (N.D. Ill. 1978).

191. Financial Gen. Bankshares, Inc. v. Lance, 80 F.R.D. 22 (D.D.C. 1978); S-G Sec. Inc. v. Fuqua Inv. Co., 466 F. Supp. 1114 (D. Mass. 1978); Brascan Ltd. v. Edper Equities, Ltd., Fed. Sec. L. Rep. (CCH) ¶96,882 (S.D.N.Y. 1979); Wellman v. Dickinson, 475 F. Supp. 783 (S.D.N.Y. 1979).

192. 15 U.S.C. § 78p(b).

193. Reliance Elec. Co. v. Emerson Elec. Co., 404 U.S. 418, 422, 30 L.Ed.2d 575, 92 S.Ct. 596 (1972).

If short-swing profit is realized, the statute requires the insider to disgorge the profit to the corporation. The only means for enforcing Section 16(b) liability is an action by the corporation or a derivative action initiated by any shareholder.

Unlike Section 10(b) and other 1934 Act provisions, Section 16(b) does not apply to all corporations with equity securities. Rather, a company must have a class of equity securities registered under Section 12 of the 1934 Act in order for the provision to apply.

Despite its seemingly simple, all-encompassing prohibition against short-swing profits, a number of issues have arisen and continue to arise. First, who is an officer or director for purposes of the statute? Rule 3b-2[194] of the SEC provides that an "officer" is any person who is the president, vice-president, secretary, treasurer (or principal financial officer), comptroller (or principal accounting officer) and any person routinely performing corresponding functions with respect to the corporation. Assistant officers[195] and officers of subsidiaries[196] are not typically considered officers for this purpose unless they independently perform important executive duties.

For purposes of Section 16(b), a "director" includes not only a duly elected director but also any person performing similar functions with respect to the corporation.[197] However, at least with respect to the beneficial ownership reporting requirements in Section 16(a), an honorary director who takes no part in formulating or in deciding policy issues and who has no access to inside information is not treated as a director.[198] A person who designates another to serve as his representative on the board of directors is himself also considered a

---

194. 17 C.F.R. § 240.3b-2.

195. Lockheed Aircraft Corp. v. Rathman, 106 F. Supp. 810 (S.D. Cal. 1952); Lockheed Aircraft Corp. v. Campbell, 110 F. Supp. 282 (S.D. Cal. 1953).

196. Lee Nat'l Corp. v. Segur, 281 F. Supp. 851 (E.D. Pa. 1968).

197. Section 3(a)(7), 1934 Act, 15 U.S.C. § 78c(a)(7).

198. 17 C.F.R. § 241.18114, Question 2.

director by deputization.[199] This situation most frequently occurs when a corporation appoints a representative to serve on the board of another corporation in which it owns a substantial block of stock. The appointing corporation will be required to disgorge any short-swing profit from trading in the other corporation's stock. The statute may also apply if the director or officer enters into short-swing transactions as trustee of a trust or if the director or officer is the beneficial owner of securities held in the name of another person.[200]

Another important issue under Section 16(b) is what constitutes a purchase and sale. The 1934 Act broadly defines "purchase" and "sale" to include contracts to buy or sell.[201] Each of the following has been held to be a sale: an option,[202] the exercise of an option,[203] the conversion of debentures into common stock,[204] and a pledge of stock to a bank to secure a loan which was sold by the bank with the pledgor's knowledge.[205] It is unclear, though, whether a purchase or sale occurs if the transaction is involuntary. The Supreme Court has held that Section 16(b) does not apply to an involuntary transaction pursuant to a merger where there was an absence of the possibility of speculative abuse of inside information.[206] Lower courts have reached conflicting results with respect to

---

199. Feder v. Martin Marietta Corp., 406 F.2d 260 (2d Cir. 1969); Blau v. Lehman, 368 U.S. 403, 7 L.Ed.2d 403, 82 S.Ct. 451 (1962); 17 C.F.R. § 241.18114, Question 3 and n.16.

200. See, e.g., 17 C.F.R. §§ 241.7793 and 241.18114, Question 4; Rule 16a-8, 17 C.F.R. § 240.16a-8.

201. Section 3(a)(13), (14), 1934 Act, 15 U.S.C. § 78c(a)(13), (14).

202. Bershad v. McDonough, 428 F.2d 693, 697 (7th Cir. 1970), cert. denied, 400 U.S. 992 (1971).

203. Booth v. Varian Assocs., 334 F.2d 1 (1st Cir. 1964), cert. denied, 379 U.S. 961 (1965).

204. Park & Tilford, Inc. v. Schulte, 160 F.2d 984 (2d Cir.), cert. denied, 332 U.S. 761 (1947) (opportunity for misuse of inside information existed); but see Blau v. Lamb, 363 F.2d 507 (2d Cir. 1966), cert. denied, 385 U.S. 1002 (1967) (no such opportunity).

205. Alloys Unlimited, Inc. v. Gilbert, 319 F. Supp. 617 (S.D.N.Y. 1970).

206. Kern County Land Co. v. Occidental Petroleum Corp., 411 U.S. 582, 36 L.Ed.2d 503, 93 S.Ct. 1736 (1973).

the applicability of Section 16(b) to involuntary transactions.[207] Other unorthodox transactions present potential Section 16(b) liability as well. For example, the "greenmail" situation in which the target company buys out the unwanted suitor frequently raises the specter of Section 16(b) liability if the seller made purchases after becoming a ten-percent shareholder.

In order for Section 16(b) to apply, the officer or director must have that status only at the time of the purchase or sale, but not both.[208] This is to be contrasted with ten-percent beneficial owners, who must have that status at the time of both the purchase and sale. With respect to a ten-percent beneficial owner, there has been substantial uncertainty as to the meaning of "at the time of". The question has been whether the purchase by which an outsider first achieves ten-percent beneficial owner status may be treated as the "purchase" in the "purchase and sale". The Supreme Court has ruled that a beneficial owner is accountable under Section 16(b) only if he was a ten-percent beneficial owner prior to the purchase in question.[209]

Under Section 16(b), the general theory for measuring any profit realized from the transaction is one that forecloses any possibility of profit, viz., the lowest priced stock bought versus the highest priced stock sold.[210] In mergers, however, the problem of determining profits is more complex. To decide the purchase and selling prices in mergers, some courts look at the value to the purchaser of the consideration given to deter-

---

207. Cf. Super Stores, Inc. v. Reiner, 737 F.2d 962 (11th Cir. 1984) (involuntary sale of shares by an unsuccessful bidder in a tender offer within scope of Section 16(b)); Portnoy v. Revlon, 650 F.2d 895 (7th Cir. 1981) (involuntary exchange of shares in a merger not within scope of Section 16(b) where there is no likelihood of access to material inside information).

208. Arrow Distrib. Corp. v. Baumgartner, 783 F.2d 1274 (5th Cir. 1986).

209. Foremost-McKesson, Inc. v. Provident Sec. Corp., 423 U.S. 232, 46 L.Ed.2d 464, 96 S.Ct. 508 (1976).

210. Smolowe v. Delendo Corp., 136 F.2d 231, (2d Cir.), cert. denied, 320 U.S. 751 (1943). See also Reliance Elec. Co. v. Emerson Elec. Co., 404 U.S. 418, 30 L.Ed.2d 575, 92 S.Ct. 596 (1972), aff'g 434 F.2d 918 (8th Cir. 1970).

mine the purchase price.[211] Others look to the value to the seller of the consideration received to determine the sales price.[212]

§ 14.10. Corporate reports and records.

Any corporation whose securities are registered on a trading exchange or in the over-the-counter market or whose securities are otherwise registered under Section 12(g) of the 1934 Act is required to file periodic reports with the SEC and maintain certain minimum records. Directors and officers of the corporation may be personally liable if the corporation fails to comply with these reporting and record requirements.

These "registered" or "reporting" companies are required, among other things, to file quarterly financial reports on Form 10-Q, annual reports on Form 10-K and monthly reports on Form 8-K to the extent certain significant events occurred. Other reports must be filed, for example, in connection with shareholder meetings, material changes in the amount of outstanding securities and changes in the company's name.

Directors and officers are prohibited from hindering, delaying or obstructing the filing of any such report without just cause.[213] In addition, Section 18[214] of the 1934 Act expressly creates a private right of action for "false or misleading" statements contained in any application, report or document filed with the SEC.

In order for there to be a recovery under Section 18, there must be a showing of (1) a false and misleading statement of a material fact in an application, report or document filed pursuant to the 1934 Act or any rule or regulation thereun-

---

211. E.g., Stella v. Graham-Paige Motors Corp., 259 F.2d 476, 479 (2d Cir. 1958), cert. denied, 359 U.S. 914 (1959); Marquette Cement Mfg. Co. v. Andreas, 239 F. Supp. 962, 967, 968 (S.D.N.Y. 1965).

212. E.g., Park & Tilford, Inc. v. Schulte, 160 F.2d 984, 986 (2d Cir.), cert. denied, 332 U.S. 761 (1947); Blau v. Mission Corp., 212 F.2d 77, 81 (2d Cir.), cert. denied, 347 U.S. 1016 (1954).

213. 15 U.S.C. § 78t(c).

214. Id. § 78r.

der, or in any undertaking in a registration statement, (2) a purchase or sale of a security which was affected by the statement, (3) lack of knowledge by the buyer or seller, as the case may be, that the statement was false or misleading, and (4) reliance by such person upon the statement. A director or officer may escape liability by showing he or she acted in good faith and had no knowledge that the statement was false or misleading.

A court may require a bond, court costs may be assessed, and there is a short statute of limitations.[215] Contrary to Section 10(b), the plaintiff need not prove scienter;[216] the burden is upon the defendant to show his good faith and lack of knowledge. But "something more than negligence on the part of the defendant is required for recovery."[217]

Because of the "good faith" defense, the short statute of limitations and the reliance requirement applicable to a Section 18 action, plaintiffs have tended to use the more expansive Rule 10b-5 rather than Section 18 to allege misstatements in documents filed with the SEC. In light of the Supreme Court's recently expansive recognition of the Rule 10b-5 private right of action for conduct which also constitutes a violation of an express civil remedy provision of the federal securities laws,[218] it appears likely this practice will continue and Section 18(a) will remain an infrequently used section by private litigants. There is some authority, though, which suggests Section 18(a) should be the exclusive remedy for violations thereof.[219]

---

215. Any action under Section 18 must be brought within one year after the discovery of the facts constituting the cause of action and within three years after such cause of action accrued.

216. See supra section 14.06.

217. Ernst & Ernst v. Hochfelder, 425 U.S. 185, 211, 47 L.Ed.2d 668, 687, 96 S.Ct. 1375, 1390 n.31, reh'g denied, 425 U.S. 985 (1976).

218. Herman & MacLean v. Huddleston, 459 U.S. 375, 74 L.Ed.2d 548, 103 S.Ct. 683 (1983).

219. Berman v. Richford Indus., Inc., Fed. Sec. L. Rep. (CCH) ¶96,518 (S.D.N.Y. 1978); Pearlstein v. Justice Mtg. Invs., Fed. Sec. L. Rep. (CCH) ¶96,760 (N.D. Tex. 1978); McKee v. Federal's, Inc., Fed. Sec. L. Rep. (CCH)

The failure of directors and officers to maintain proper internal books and records may also give rise to personal liability. Section 13(b)(2) and (3)[220] of the 1934 Act, which embodies the accounting provisions of the Foreign Corrupt Practices Act of 1977, requires an SEC reporting issuer to keep books, records, and accounts which, in reasonable detail, accurately and fairly reflect the transactions and asset dispositions of the issuer. Perhaps more importantly, the statute also requires the company to maintain an adequate system of internal accounting controls.

SEC promulgated regulations[221] prohibit the falsification of corporate books, records or accounts by any person, including directors and officers. In addition, those regulations prohibit directors and officers from making false, misleading or incomplete statements to an accountant in connection with an audit of a company's financial statements or the preparation of required reports.

§ 14.11. Investment company directors.

An investment company invests in the securities of other companies and issues securities of its own. Because these companies are typically incorporated pursuant to state law, and issue securities like other corporations, many of the general state and federal securities law standards applicable to directors and officers of other types of corporations are equally applicable to directors and officers of investment companies. However, because of the unique nature of investment companies and the special conflicts of interest created by the typical investment company, the Investment Company Act of 1940[222] ("1940 Act") was enacted to provide an additional layer of regulation and protection with respect to these companies.

¶96,958 (E.D. Mich. 1979); Kulchok v. Government Employees Ins. Co., Fed. Sec. L. Rep. (CCH) ¶96,002 (D.D.C. 1977).
  220. 15 U.S.C. § 78m(b)(2) and (3).
  221. 17 C.F.R. § 240.13b2.
  222. 15 U.S.C. § 80a-1, et seq.

Typically, an investment company is organized and operated by an investment adviser. Although the shareholders and investment adviser both have a common interest in improving the investment performance and increasing the assets of the company, important conflicts exist, for example, with respect to the level of management fees and sales charges and the termination of the investment advisor relationship.

The 1940 Act sought to minimize the possibilities of abuse by investment advisers and investment company managers. In addition to broadening the disclosure requirements otherwise applicable under the 1933 and 1934 Acts, the 1940 Act prescribes numerous operational requirements for investment companies. A fundamental element of this regulatory framework is the independent, disinterested director, to whom the 1940 Act assigns a host of special duties involving supervision of management and financial auditing. For example, disinterested directors are required to review and approve the contracts of the investment adviser and principal underwriter, to appoint other independent directors to fill vacancies and to select independent accountants.

At least forty percent of an investment company's board must be composed of independent outside directors, who may not have a close family or substantial financial relationship with the investment company and its advisers and officers. In addition, no person who has, within ten years, been convicted of a felony or misdemeanor involving securities trading in the industry may serve as a director or officer of the company.

The SEC has adopted a rule providing minimum standards of conduct for persons actively involved in the management, portfolio selection, or underwriting functions of investment companies.[223] Among other things, this rule contains general antifraud and antimanipulation provisions and requires each investment company to prescribe standards and procedures reasonably designed to prevent the fraudulent and manipulative activities prohibited by the rule.

---

223. 17 C.F.R. § 270.17j-1.

§ 14.12. Secondary liability.

Liability for violations of the federal securities laws can arise not only if the director or officer directly violated the statute, but also if a person whom the director or officer controlled or assisted directly violated the statute. This theory of secondary or vicarious liability arises under the doctrines of "controlling person," "aiding and abetting," "respondeat superior," and "conspiracy."

Controlling Person

Both the 1933[224] and the 1934[225] Acts contain provisions holding a party secondarily liable where a person under their control has committed a primary violation of that Act. Although the two statutes vary to some degree, they have been largely interpreted the same.[226] In order to be liable as a controlling person it must be shown that a primary violation has occurred and that the defendant controls the person responsible for the primary violation.

Congress intentionally refused to define the term control, in order that it might receive its broadest possible meaning:

> When reference is made to "control", the term is intended to include actual control as well as what has been called legally enforceable control. (See *Handy & Harmon v. Burnet* (1931) 284 U.S. 136.) It was thought undesirable to attempt to define the term. It would be difficult if not impossible to enumerate or to anticipate the many ways in which actual control may be exerted. A few examples of these methods used are stock ownership, lease, contract, and agency. It is well known that actual control sometimes may be exerted through ownership of much less than a majority of the stock of a corporation either by the ownership of such stock alone or though such ownership in combination with other factors.[227]

---

224. Section 15; 15 U.S.C. § 77o.
225. Section 20(a); 15 U.S.C. § 78t(a).
226. Pharo v. Smith, 621 F.2d 656, 673 (5th Cir. 1980).
227. H.R. Rep. No. 1383, 73rd Cong., 2d Sess. 26 (1934).

The courts have observed this congressional directive in construing who was intended to be a controlling person:

> The statute is remedial and is to be construed liberally. It has been interpreted as requiring only some indirect means of discipline or influence short of actual direction to hold a "controlling person" liable.[228]

The SEC has defined "control" in similarly broad terms:

> The term "control" (including the terms "controlling", "controlled by" and "under common control with") means the possession, direct or indirect, of the power to direct or cause the direction of the management and policies of a person, whether through the ownership of voting securities, by contracts, or otherwise.[229]

Although many factors are involved in determining if one is a controlling person, courts have given heavy consideration to the potential power to influence and control the activities of a person, as opposed to the actual exercise of such power.[230] A director of a corporation, though, is not automatically liable as a controlling person. There must be some showing of actual participation in the corporation's operation or some influence before the consequences of control may be imposed.[231]

Courts are in conflict as to whether the plaintiff must prove that the defendant "culpably participated" in the underlying securities violation. Although some courts have ruled that the plaintiff need not prove the defendant participated in the wrongful transactions,[232] most courts require such a showing.[233]

---

228. Myzel v. Fields, 386 F.2d 718, 738 (8th Cir. 1967), cert. denied, 390 U.S. 951 (1968). See also Gould v. American-Hawaiian S.S. Co., 535 F.2d 761, 779 (3d Cir. 1976); SEC v. Management Dyn, Inc., 515 F.2d 801, 812 (2d Cir. 1975); Strong v. France, 474 F.2d 747, 752 (9th Cir. 1973); Klapmeier v. Telecheck Int'l, Inc., 482 F.2d 247, 256 (8th Cir. 1973).

229. 17 C.F.R. § 230.405(f).

230. Rockey Bros. Inc. v. Rhoades, 527 F.2d 880, 890-91 (3d Cir. 1975).

231. Herm v. Stafford, 663 F.2d 669 (6th Cir. 1981).

232. G.A. Thompson & Co., Inc. v. Partridge, 636 F.2d 945 (5th Cir. 1981); Metge v. Baehler, 577 F. Supp. 810 (S.D. Iowa 1984).

233. Rockey Bros. Inc. v. Rhoades, supra note 230; Carpenter v. Harris,

The statutes provide that a defendant can escape liability as a controlling person if it can be shown that he had no knowledge of or reasonable ground to believe in the existence of the facts giving rise to the liability of the controlled person, or with respect to 1934 Act violations, acted in good faith and did not directly or indirectly induce the action constituting the violation.

Aiding and Abetting

Aiding and abetting is a judicially created doctrine of secondary liability which is not explicitly found in the federal securities laws. Although the Supreme Court has repeatedly declined to express an opinion on the validity of this doctrine under the 1934 Act,[234] lower courts clearly recognize aiding and abetting liability under the securities laws.[235]

The elements of a cause of action for aiding and abetting liability are:

(1) The existence of an independent primary violation of the federal securities law;

(2) Actual knowledge by the alleged aider and abettor of (i) the primary violation and of (ii) his or her role in furthering it; and

(3) Substantial assistance in the wrong.[236]

There are two fundamental issues under this doctrine which are particularly important to directors and officers. First, what type of scienter is required under the second ele-

Upham & Co., Inc., 594 F.2d 388 (4th Cir. 1979); Christoffel v. E.F. Hutton & Co., Inc., 588 F.2d 665 (9th Cir. 1978).

234. See Herman & MacLean v. Huddleston, 459 U.S. 375, 74 L.Ed.2d 548, 103 S.Ct. 683 (1983); Ernst & Ernst v. Hochfelder, 425 U.S. 185, 47 L.Ed.2d 668, 96 S.Ct. 1375, reh'g denied, 425 U.S. 985 (1976).

235. See, e.g., Armstrong v. McAlpin, 699 F.2d 79 (2d Cir. 1983); IIT, An Int'l Inv. Trust v. Cornfeld, 619 F.2d 909 (2d Cir. 1980).

236. See Harmsen v. Smith, 693 F.2d 932, 943 (9th Cir. 1982), cert. denied, 464 U.S. 822 (1983); Investors Research Corp. v. SEC, 628 F.2d 168, 178 (D.C. Cir.), cert. denied, 449 U.S. 919 (1980); IIT, An Int'l Inv. Trust v. Cornfeld, supra note 235, at 922.

ment of the three-prong test? Recklessness has been held by some courts to satisfy this scienter requirement.[237] However, a greater number of courts have held that the standard is a variable one, scaling upward as the assistance becomes more remote. Under this theory, recklessness is a proper standard only when the alleged aider and abettor is in a fiduciary relationship with the plaintiff, and that "something closer to an actual intent to aid in a fraud" must be shown in other cases.[238] If the transaction involved is extraordinary in nature, less evidence of scienter may be required than with respect to transactions in the ordinary course of business.[239]

When the aiding and abetting allegation is premised on passive assistance, reckless conduct will satisfy the scienter requirement only where there is an independent duty to act.[240] Absent such a duty, aiding and abetting liability requires proof of "scienter of the high 'conscious intent' variety."[241] Some courts, though, have applied the recklessness standard where the alleged aider and abettor had reason to foresee his conduct being relied upon by third parties, even though no fiduciary relationship existed.[242]

The second significant issue under the aiding and abetting doctrine is what liability exists for passive assistance? According to some courts, inaction may be a form of assistance if it is shown that the silence was consciously intended to aid the securities law violation.[243]

---

237. Herm v. Stafford, 663 F.2d 669 (6th Cir. 1981).

238. Edwards & Hanly v. Wells Fargo Sec. Clearance Corp., 602 F.2d 478, 485 (2d Cir. 1979), cert. denied, 444 U.S. 1045 (1980); Sirota v. Solitron Devices, Inc., 673 F.2d 566 (2d Cir.), cert. denied, 459 U.S. 838 (1982); Armstrong v. McAlpin, supra note 235. See also Frankel v. Wyllie & Thornhill, Inc., 537 F. Supp. 730 (W.D. Va. 1982).

239. SEC v. Washington County Util. Dist., 676 F.2d 218 (6th Cir. 1982).

240. IIT, An Int'l Inv. Trust v. Cornfeld, supra note 235.

241. Id. at 925.

242. Oleck v. Fischer, Fed. Sec. L. Rep. (CCH) ¶96,898 (S.D.N.Y. 1979), aff'd on other grounds, 623 F.2d 791 (2d Cir. 1980); McLean v. Alexander, 420 F. Supp. 1057, 1082 (D. Del. 1976), rev'd on other grounds, 599 F.2d 1190 (3d Cir. 1979).

243. SEC v. Coffey, 493 F.2d 1304 (6th Cir. 1974), cert. denied, 420 U.S. 908 (1975).

Courts have held that silence or inaction may be the basis for aiding and abetting liability only if (1) there is an independent duty to act which the alleged aider and abettor breaches, or (2) the alleged aider and abettor consciously intends by his inaction to bring about the securities law violation.[244] Those cases suggest that when there is no independent duty to act and the alleged assistance is only by inaction, neither reckless behavior nor knowledge of the primary misconduct is a sufficient basis alone for imposing aiding and abetting liability. In such situations, liability will be established only where intent to assist the primary violation is shown.

As these principles are applied to directors, it has been held that since outside directors owe no fiduciary duty to purchasers of company securities, the failure of such directors to discover the improprieties of company officers did not constitute aiding and abetting liability under Rule 10b-5.[245] Similarly, persons named as directors in an offering memorandum without their knowledge did not have aider and abettor liability with respect to omissions in that offering where such persons did not knowingly assist any primary violations of securities laws and where their inaction was not consciously intended to further the promoter's allegedly fraudulent activity.[246]

There is some authority that aiding and abetting standards are less rigorous in SEC injunction suits than in private damage actions. In *Wellman v. Dickinson*,[247] the district court states: "Scienter is clearly not necessary in an enforcement action brought by the Commission."

With respect to SEC administrative actions, the Commission has articulated some rather restrictive standards. In a

---

244. IIT, An Int'l Inv. Trust v. Cornfeld, supra note 235, at 925-27; Harmsen v. Smith, supra note 236; Monsen v. Consolidated Dressed Beef Co., 579 F.2d 793, 799-803 (3d Cir.), cert. denied, 439 U.S. 930 (1978).

245. Greene v. Emersons, Ltd., Fed. Sec. L. Rep. (CCH) ¶97,226 (S.D.N.Y. 1980), aff'd on other grounds sub nom. Kenneth Leventhal & Co. v. Joyner Whsle. Co., 736 F.2d 29 (2d Cir. 1984).

246. Cleary v. Perfectune, Inc., 700 F.2d 774 (1st Cir. 1983).

247. 475 F. Supp. 783, 831 (S.D.N.Y. 1979).

1981 decision,[248] the Commission stated that there must be proof that the aider and abettor actually "was aware or knew that his role was part of an activity that was improper or illegal." Thus, the SEC found that an attorney lacked the requisite scienter even though he actively assisted in the preparation of misleading disclosure documents and knew of the undisclosed material facts. The Commission also concluded that, with respect to passive assistance, there must be proof that the respondents "either consciously intended to assist [the] violation, or that they breached a duty to disclose or act and had some degree of scienter."[249]

Respondeat Superior

Under common-law agency or respondeat superior principles, a principal or employer is liable for the wrongful acts committed by his subordinate or employee if the acts occurred within the scope of the agency or employment. Because this doctrine imposes liability even though no principal or controlling person is completely without fault, there is some question whether the doctrine should apply to claims for violations of the federal securities laws.

Some courts feel that imposing liability without fault under this doctrine contravenes the Congressional intent of the controlling person sections of the 1933 and 1934 Acts in that a defendant should not be held liable without providing him the statutory defense of good faith.[250] These courts find that Section 15 of the 1933 Act and Section 20(a) of the 1934 Act are the exclusive remedy for federal securities law violations against a controlling person.

---

248. In re Carter & Johnson, Fed. Sec. L. Rep. (CCH) ¶82, 847, 22 SEC Docket 292, Securities Exch. Act Rel. No. 17597 (1981).

249. Cf. In re Merrill Lynch, Pierce, Fenner & Smith, Inc., 26 SEC Docket 254 (Oct. 5, 1982) (continuation of activities with knowledge of activities' improprieties sufficient scienter for aiding and abetting).

250. Carpenter v. Harris, Upham & Co., 594 F.2d 388 (4th Cir. 1979); Myzel v. Fields, 386 F.2d 718 (8th Cir. 1967), cert. denied, 390 U.S. 951 (1968); Christoffel v. E.F. Hutton & Co., 588 F.2d 665 (9th Cir. 1978).

The present trend in the majority of courts, though, is to find that the doctrine of respondeat superior can be applied in private damage actions under the securities laws concurrently with Section 20(a) of the 1934 Act.[251] Those decisions generally rely on Section 28(a) of the 1934 Act which specifically provides that the rights and remedies provided by that Act are in addition to any and all rights and remedies that may exist at law or in equity. Courts have also noted that the control liability provisions of the securities laws were designed to prevent directors from evading their responsibilities under the securities laws through the use of "dummy" directors to act in their stead[252] and that there is no evidence that Congress intended those provisions to be a limitation on liability.[253]

One of the different effects which result from being found liable under the vicarious or secondary liability doctrine rather than as a direct participant is the possible limitation of recoupment from co-defendants. For example, in a situation where the company sold unregistered oil and gas leases to investors, a state court held the company directors jointly and severally liable to the innocent investors under a respondeat superior theory. The directors then filed a federal securities fraud claim under Section 10(b) of the 1934 Act against certain lead investors who were intimately involved in the sales transactions. In the securities law case, the court ruled

251. Marbury Mgt., Inc. v. Kohn, 629 F.2d 705 (2d Cir.), cert. denied, 449 U.S. 1011 (1980); Sharp v. Coopers & Lybrand, 649 F.2d 175 (3d Cir. 1981); Paul F. Newton & Co. v. Texas Commerce Bank, 630 F.2d 1111 (5th Cir. 1980); Holloway v. Howerdd, 536 F.2d 690 (6th Cir. 1976); Henricksen v. Henricksen, 640 F.2d 880 (7th Cir. 1981).

252. See S. Rep. No. 47, 73rd Cong., 1st Sess. 5 (1983); H.R. Conf. Rep. No. 152, 73rd Cong., 1st Sess. 27 (1933); Hearings Before the Senate Committee on Banking and Currency on S. Res. 84 (72d Cong.) and S. Res. 56 and 97, 73rd Cong., 1st Sess. pt. 15, at 6571 (1934).

253. Paul F. Newton & Co. v. Texas Commerce Bank, supra note 251, at 1118; Marbury Mgt., Inc. v. Kohn, supra note 251, at 716; Holloway v. Howerdd, supra note 251, at 695; Fey v. Walston & Co., 493 F.2d 1036, 1052 (7th Cir. 1974); Johns Hopkins Univ. v. Hutton, 422 F.2d 1124, 1130 (4th Cir. 1970).

the directors were not sellers of the securities and, therefore, could not satisfy the "purchaser-seller" requirement of Section 10(b). As a result, the claims by the directors were dismissed.[254]

Conspiracy

Though similar to aiding and abetting, civil conspiracy contains as a key element an agreement between co-conspirators. The elements of a civil conspiracy cause of action are:

(1) an agreement between two or more persons;
(2) to participate in an unlawful act or a lawful act in an unlawful manner;
(3) an injury caused by an unlawful overt act performed by one of the parties to the agreement; and
(4) which overt act was done pursuant to and in furtherance of the common scheme.[255]

The requisite agreement need not be expressed and is often inferred from the facts. For example, officers of a corporation whose conduct violated Section 17(a) of the 1933 Act have been found to have a tacit agreement between them concerning the activity giving rise to the securities law violations.[256] Co-conspirators are typically jointly and severally liable for the full amount of damages suffered by the plaintiff since the participation of each defendant is typically important to the success of the scheme and there is no way to apportion guilt.[257] A co-conspirator may also be liable for acts occurring and damages accruing prior to the time he joined or assisted in the conspiracy.[258]

---

254. Brannan v. Eisenstein, 804 F.2d 1041 (8th Cir. 1986).

255. Halberstarn v. Welch, 705 F.2d 472 (D.C. Cir. 1983).

256. United States v. Fishbein, 446 F.2d 1201 (9th Cir. 1971).

257. Ross v. Licht, 263 F. Supp. 395 (S.D.N.Y. 1967).

258. In re Cenco Inc. Sec. Litig., 529 F. Supp. 411 (N.D. Ill. 1982); In re Home-Stake Prod. Co. Sec., 76 F.R.D. 351 (N.D. Okla. 1977).

§ 14.13. Implied rights of action.

Some of the federal securities law statutes defining the duties and responsibilities of the issuer of securities and, among others, its directors and officers expressly recognize that a violation of that statute may be remedied by the injured person bringing a private cause of action against the violator. Many other federal securities law statutes, though, are silent as to whether a private cause of action for violation of that statute is proper. In recent years, few other issues under the federal securities laws have received more Supreme Court analysis. By the Court's own admission, its approach to this issue has "changed significantly".[259]

The Court first established definitive guidelines in this area during 1975. In *Cort v. Ash*,[260] the Supreme Court identified four factors as relevant in determining whether a private remedy is implicit in a statute not expressly providing one. They are:

(1) Whether the plaintiff is one of the class for whose especial benefit the statute was enacted;

(2) Whether there is any indication of legislative intent, explicit or implicit, either to create such a remedy or to deny one;

(3) Whether it is consistent with the underlying purposes of the legislative scheme to imply such a remedy for the plaintiff; and

(4) Whether the cause of action is one traditionally relegated to state law.

Although the Court continues occasionally to cite *Cort v. Ash* as articulating the approach to be used in determining whether a federal statute implies a private right of action[261]

---

259. Merrill Lynch, Pierce, Fenner & Smith, Inc. v. Curran, 465 U.S. 353, 374, 72 L.Ed.2d 182, 102 S.Ct. 1825 (1982).

260. 422 U.S. 66, 45 L.Ed.2d 26, 95 S.Ct. 2080 (1975).

261. E.g., Merrill Lynch, Pierce, Fenner & Smith, Inc. v. Curran, supra note 259, 456 U.S. at 374; Universities Research Ass'n v. Contu, 450 U.S. 754, 67 L.Ed.2d 662, 101 S.Ct. 1451 (1981).

the only one of the four *Cort* tests which is now applied by the Court is whether Congress intended to permit a private right of action.[262] When determining congressional intent for this purpose, the Court, prior to 1982, looked principally at the express language of the statute and the legislative history of the statute at the time of its adoption. Under that analysis, the Court rarely concluded a private right of action should be implied,[263] since typically neither the statute nor the legislative history contemplated or addressed the issue. The Court's philosophy was summarized in its statement: "[W]hen Congress wished to provide a private damage remedy, it knew how to do so and did so expressly."[264]

This analysis was changed slightly but significantly beginning in 1982, when the Supreme Court began to examine the legislative intent behind a statute not only at the time the statute was adopted, but also at the time of any subsequent amendments. In the *Curran*[265] case, the first to adopt this more liberal analysis, the Court ruled that an investor may bring an implied private action under the Commodities Ex-

---

262. Merrill Lynch, Pierce, Fenner & Smith, Inc. v. Curran, supra note 259; Touche Ross & Co. v. Redington, 442 U.S. 560, 61 L.Ed.2d 82, 99 S.Ct. 2479 (1979); Transamerica Mtg. Advisors, Inc. v. Lewis, 444 U.S. 11, 62 L.Ed.2d 146, 100 S.Ct. 242 (1979).

263. Touche Ross & Co. v. Redington, supra note 262 (no private action implied under Section 17(a) of the 1934 Act); Transamerica Mtg. Advisors, Inc. v. Lewis, supra note 262 (no private action implied under Section 215 of the Investment Advisers Act); Great Am. Fed. Sav. & Loan Ass'n v. Novotny, 442 U.S. 336, 60 L.Ed.2d 957, 99 S.Ct. 2345 (1979) (no private action implied under 42 U.S.C. § 1985(3) for alleged violations of Title VII of the Civil Rights Act of 1964); Kissinger v. Reporters Committee for Freedom of the Press, 445 U.S. 136, 63 L.Ed.2d 267, 100 S.Ct. 960 (1979) (no private action implied for violations of the Federal Records Act or the Federal Records Disposal Act); Universities Research Ass'n v. Contu, supra note 261 (no private action implied for back wages under the so-called Davis-Bacon Act); California v. Sierra Club, 451 U.S. 287, 68 L.Ed.2d 101, 101 S.Ct. 1775 (1981) (no private action implied for violation of § 10 of the Rivers and Harbors Act of 1899).

264. Touche Ross & Co. v. Redington, supra note 262, 442 U.S. at 572.

265. Merrill Lynch, Pierce, Fenner & Smith, Inc. v. Curran, supra note 259.

change Act (CEA) seeking damages against a broker for fraudulent and deceptive conduct. The Court noted that prior to 1974, when the CEA was comprehensively amended, federal courts routinely and consistently recognized an implied private cause of action for violation of that Act. Because the 1974 amendments left intact the statutory provisions under which the federal court has implied a private action, the Court held that Congress affirmatively intended to preserve that remedy and, therefore, a private action should continue to be implied.

The Supreme Court then applied this more liberal analysis to Section 10(b) and Rule 10b-5. In the *Huddleston*[266] case, the Court ruled that an investor may maintain an implied right of action under Rule 10b-5 for misrepresentations in a registration statement despite the availability of a more limited but express remedy under Section 11 of the Securities Act of 1933. The Court recognized that a Section 10(b) implied private action has been consistently recognized for more than thirty-five years and its existence is "simply beyond peradventure." The real issue was whether federal securities statutes which provide express private remedies for certain violations should be the exclusive remedy for such violations or whether the securities law should be given a cumulative construction, thereby permitting a Rule 10b-5 private action in addition to the express remedy. The Court noted that in 1975, Congress enacted substantial amendments to the securities laws but left Section 10(b) intact, thereby suggesting that Congress intended to ratify the "consistent and routine" implication by federal courts of a Section 10(b) implied private action despite the existence of a more limited express remedy. Such a cumulative construction was found to further the broad remedial purposes of the securities laws. The Supreme Court concluded: "We therefore reject an interpreta-

---

266. Hermann & MacLean v. Huddleston, 459 U.S. 375, 74 L.Ed.2d 548, 103 S.Ct. 683 (1983).

tion of the securities laws that displaces an action under Section 10(b)."[267]

The state of the law in this area as interpreted by the lower federal courts is currently confusing, at best. Most of the decisions which pre-date the *Curran* and *Huddleston* Supreme Court decisions tend to deny the existence of implied remedies under a variety of federal securities law provisions. For example, courts denied an implied cause of action under Section 17(a) of the 1933 Securities Act,[268] although some courts permitted such an action under subsection (3) thereof[269] or implied such an action but read into the section some of the limitations and restrictions of Sections 11 and 12 of the Act.[270] Other provisions for which courts refused to imply a private remedy include Section 13(d)[271] and Schedule 13D thereunder,[272] and Section 7[273] and Regulation T thereunder[274] (the margin rule), Sections 16(a)[275] and 11(d)[276] of the 1934 Act and stock exchange and N.A.S.D. rules.[277]

However, more recent cases have tended to be more lenient in implying a private cause of action, particularly when the

---

267. Id., 459 U.S. at 387.

268. E.g., Landry v. All Am. Assurance Co., 688 F.2d 381 (5th Cir. 1982); Basile v. Merrill Lynch, Pierce, Fenner & Smith, Inc., 551 F. Supp. 580 (S.D. Ohio 1982); In re New York City Mun. Sec. Litig., 507 F. Supp. 169 (S.D.N.Y. 1980); Marbury Mgt., Inc. v. Kohn, 470 F. Supp. 509 (S.D.N.Y. 1979); McFarland v. Memorex Corp., 493 F. Supp. 631 (N.D. Cal. 1980).

269. Demoe v. Dean Witter & Co., 476 F. Supp. 275 (D. Alaska 1979).

270. In re Gap Stores Sec. Litig., 457 F. Supp. 1135 (N.D. Cal. 1978).

271. Berman v. Metzger, Fed. Sec. L. Rep. (CCH) ¶97,857 (D.D.C. 1981).

272. Dan River, Inc. v. Unitex, Ltd., 624 F.2d 1216 (4th Cir. 1980), cert. denied, 449 U.S. 1101 (1981).

273. Gilman v. FDIC, 660 F.2d 688 (6th Cir. 1981).

274. Martin v. Howard, Weil, Labouisse, Fredericks, Inc., Fed. Sec. L. Rep. (CCH) ¶97,586 (E.D. La. 1980); Furer v. Paine Webber, Jackson & Curtis, Inc., Fed. Sec. L. Rep. (CCH) ¶98,367 (C.D. Cal. 1981).

275. Scientex Corp. v. Kay, 689 F.2d 879 (9th Cir. 1982).

276. Sennett v. Oppenheimer & Co., 502 F. Supp. 939 (N.D. Ill. 1980).

277. E.g., Jablon v. Dean Witter & Co., 614 F.2d 677 (9th Cir. 1980); Wellman v. Dickinson, 475 F. Supp. 783 (S.D.N.Y. 1979), aff'd, 682 F.2d 355 (2d Cir. 1982); Siedman v. Merrill Lynch, Pierce, Fenner & Smith, Inc., 465 F. Supp. 1233 (S.D.N.Y. 1979).

court's analysis is based on the analysis articulated in these recent Supreme Court decisions rather than on the prior lower court precedent. For example, recent decisions recognize implied actions under the anti-fraud rules of Section 17(a) of the 1933 Act,[278] although courts remain split on this issue,[279] and the tender offer rules of Sections 13(d)[280] and the "going private" rules of Section 13(e)[281] of the 1934 Act.

---

278. Bennett v. United States Trust Co. of N.Y., 770 F.2d 308 (2d Cir. 1985); Mosher v. Kane, 784 F.2d 1385 (9th Cir. 1986); Levine v. Futransky, 636 F. Supp. 899 (N.D. Ill. 1986).

279. E.g., Puchall v. Houghton, Cluck, Coughlin & Riley, 823 F.2d 1349 (9th Cir. 1987).

280. Jacobs v. Pabst Brewing Co., 549 F. Supp. 1050 (D. Del. 1982).

281. Howing Co. v. Nationwide Corp., 826 F.2d 1470 (6th Cir. 1987).

COROLLARY REFERENCES

Banoff, "Regulatory Subsidies, Efficient Markets, and Shelf Registration: An Analysis of Rule 415," 70 Va. L. Rev. 135 (1984).

Beatty, "Exchange-Traded Options and Section 16(b): Panacea or Plague for Insider's Short-Swing Profits?," 38 Bus. Law. 515 (1983).

Black, "Fraud on the Market: A Criticism of Dispensing With Reliance Requirements in Certain Open Market Transactions," 62 N.C.L. Rev. 435 (1984).

Block & Schwarzfeld, "Corporate Mismanagement and Breach of Fiduciary Duty After Santa Fe v. Green," 2 Corp. L. Rev. 91 (1979).

Brunelle, "A 'Contemporary Legal Context' Analysis of Aiding and Abetting," 11 Sec. Reg. L.J. 182 (1983).

Conard, "Securities Regulation in the Burger Court," 56 U. Colo. L. Rev. 193 (1985), reprinted in 18 Sec. L. Rev. 3 (1986).

Conard, "Tender Offer Fraud: The Secret Meaning of Subsection 14(e)," 40 Bus. Law. 87 (1984).

Fitzpatrick & Carman, "Respondeat Superior and the Federal Securities Laws: A Round Peg in a Square Hole," 12 Hofstra L. Rev. 1 (1983).

Good, "An Examination of Investment Analyst Liability Under Rule 10b-5," 1984 Ariz. St. L.J. 129 (1984).

Hacker & Rotunda, "Officers, Directors, and Their Professional Advisers: Rights, Duties and Liabilities," 3 Corp. L. Rev. 252 (1980).

Hazen, "Implied Private Remedies Under Federal Statutes: Neither a Death Knell Nor a Moratorium — Civil Rights, Securities Regulation, and Beyond," 33 Vand. L. Rev. 1333 (1980).

Jacobs, "Rule 10b-5 and Self-Dealing by Corporate Fiduciaries: An Analysis," 48 U. Cin. L. Rev. 643 (1979).

Jorden & Grief, "Federal Securities Fraud and State Law Fiduciary," 19 Idaho L. Rev. 21 (1983).

Langevoort, "The Insider Trading Sanctions Act of 1984 and its Effect on Existing Law," 37 Vand. L. Rev. 1273 (1984).

Macey, "Special Interest Groups Legislation and the Judicial Function," "The Dilemma of Glass-Steagall," 33 Emory L.J. 1 (1984).

Mathews, "Litigation and Settlement of SEC Administrative Enforcement Proceedings," 29 Cath. U.L. Rev. 215 (1980).

Orbe, "A Security: The Quest for a Definition," 12 Sec. Reg. L.J. 220 (Fall, 1984).

Pitt & Israel, "Implied Rights: While ALI Debates, Court Eviscerates," Legal Times of Washington, 1979.

Ruder, "Multiple Defendants in Securities Law Fraud Cases: Aiding and Abetting, Conspiracy, In Pari Delicto, Indemnification and Contribution," 120 U. Pa. L. Rev. 597 (1972).

Schneider, "Definition of a 'Security' — 1983/1984 Update," 17 Rev. of Sec. Reg. 851 (1984).

Seemann, "Brokers Blanket Bonds: Proof Requirements in Rule 10b-5 Case," 20 Forum 498 (1985).

Silberberg & Pollack, "Are the Courts Expanding the Meaning of 'Manipulation' under the Federal Securities Law?," 11 Sec. Reg. L.J. 265-81 (1983).

Smaltz, "Tactical Considerations for Effective Representation During a Government Investigation," 16 Am. Crim. L. Rev. 383 (1979).

Steinberg, "Aaron's Unanswered Questions," 4 Corp. L. Rev. 166 (1981).

Steinberg, "Section 17(a) of the Securities Act of 1933 After Naftalin and Redington," 68 Geo. L.J. 163 (1979).

Steinberg & Gruenbaum, "Variations of 'Recklessness' After Hochfelder and Aaron," 8 Sec. Reg. L.J. 179 (1980).

Thompson, "The Measure of Recovery Under Rule 10b-5: A Restitution Alternative to Tort Damages," 37 Vand. L. Rev. 349 (1984).

Wang, "Recent Developments in the Federal Law Regulating Stock Market Inside Trading," 16 Sec. L. Rev. 219 (1984).

Note, "Implied Private Rights of Action: The Courts Search for Limitations in a Confused Area of the Law," 13 Cumb. L. Rev. 569 (1983).

Note, "The Burden of Control: Derivative Liability Under Section 20(a) of the Securities Exchange Act of 1934," 48 N.Y.U. L. Rev. 1019 (1973).

Note, "The Fraud on the Market Theory," 95 Harv. L. Rev. (1982).

Comment, "Securities Fraud: The Tax Benefit Offset Rule of Damages in Securities Fraud," 70 Minn. L. Rev. 1185 (1986).

Annotation, "Controlling Person's Liability Under § 20(a) of Securities Act of 1934, (15 U.S.C.S. § 78t(a))," 38 A.L.R. Fed. 725 (1980).

Annotation, "Misrepresentation in Proxy Solicitation—State Cases," 20 A.L.R.4th 1287 (1983).

Annotation, "Who Is 'Issuer' or 'Owner of any Security of the Issuer' for Purposes of Enforcing Short-Swing Profits Provisions of § 16(b) of the Securities Exchange Act of 1934 (15 U.S.C.S. § 78p(b))," 51 A.L.R. Fed. 785 (1981).

Chapter 15

LIABILITY IN TAKEOVERS, MERGERS AND BUYOUTS

§ 15.01. Nature of problem.

The frequency and magnitude of contests for corporate control have virtually exploded in recent years. Judge Irving R. Kaufman succinctly described the situation as follows:

> Contests for corporate control have become ever more frequent phenomena on the American business scene. Waged with the intensity of military campaigns and the weaponry of seemingly bottomless bankrolls, these battles determine the destinies of large and small corporations alike. Elaborate strategies and ingenious tactics have been developed both to facilitate takeover attempts and to defend against them ... The efforts of targeted management to resist acquisitive moves, and the means they employ, have been alternatively praised and damned.[1]

By definition, directors of the target company are intimately involved in any takeover. They analyze and respond to the bid on behalf of the corporation and its shareholders. Accordingly, they frequently become the targets of litigation when someone becomes dissatisfied with the director's response to the bid. Depending on the nature of the bid and the board's response to it, these potential plaintiffs may

---

1. Norlin Corp. v. Rooney, Pace, Inc., 744 F.2d 255, 258 (2d Cir. 1984).

479

include shareholders of the corporation, the persons or entity making the bid, creditors and regulatory agencies.

Historically, the predominant judicial view has been to defer to the business judgment of a target's directors as they analyze, accept or defend the corporation against takeover bids, unless the directors' "sole or primary motive" was to retain control. Cases suggested that once the board of directors reached a good-faith conclusion that a takeover was not in the best interests of the corporation and its shareholders, the board could do virtually anything to oppose control bids even if the shareholders clearly wanted the control premium.[2] Refusal by the target's board to accept a takeover bid containing a premium or to negotiate with the raider was found not to constitute a prima facie breach of fiduciary duty.[3] Some cases stated that directors have a duty to oppose takeover attempts which they determine to be detrimental to the interests of the corporation and its shareholders.[4]

With the increased judicial analysis in the 1980's of director conduct in the takeover context, greater concern was expressed as to the appropriateness of applying traditional business judgment rule principles to this situation. The inherent conflict of interest which all directors face in a takeover bid context raised questions about whether the directors' decisions were made in good faith and whether the directors were disinterested and independent. It was suggested that the self-interest of directors to remain in office and to prevent an outsider from obtaining control of "their" corporation tainted the objectivity of the directors.

---

2. See, e.g., Crouse-Hinds Co. v. InterNorth, Inc., 634 F.2d 690 (2d Cir. 1980); Treadway Cos., Inc. v. Care Corp., 638 F.2d 357 (2d Cir. 1980); Buffalo Forge Co. v. Ogden Corp., 717 F.2d 757 (2d Cir. 1983).

3. Pogostin v. Rice, 480 A.2d 619, 627 (Del. 1984).

4. See, e.g., MacAndrews & Forbes Holding, Inc. v. Revlon, Inc., 501 A.2d 1239 (Del. Ch. 1985), aff'd sub nom. Revlon, Inc. v. MacAndrews & Forbes Holdings, 506 A.2d 173 (Del. 1986); Panter v. Marshall Field & Co., 486 F. Supp. 1168, 1195 (N.D. Ill. 1980), aff'd, 646 F.2d 271 (7th Cir.), cert. denied, 454 U.S. 1091 (1981) (under Delaware law).

This criticism originally surfaced in strong dissenting opinions in several cases. For example, Judge Cudahy stated in a dissenting opinion:

> [The] majority here has moved one giant step closer to shredding whatever constraints still remain upon the ability of corporate directors to place self interest before shareholder interests in resisting a hostile tender offer for control of the corporation. I emphatically disagree that the business judgment rule should clothe directors, battling blindly to fend off a threat to their control, with an almost irrebuttable presumption of sound business judgment, prevailing over everything but the elusive hobgoblins of fraud, bad faith or abuse of discretion.[5]

This inherent conflict of interest is not necessarily eliminated by nonmanagement, "independent" directors deciding whether a takeover bid should be accepted or rejected. Several courts have noted the likely allegiance and empathy which outside directors feel toward their fellow management directors.[6]

These concerns culminated in a series of landmark decisions by the Delaware Supreme Court during 1985. Although a few isolated cases[7] before then attempted to redefine the standards of directors in the takeover context, it was not until these 1985 decisions that guidelines were established which recognized the unique role of directors in the takeover context.

As discussed in the succeeding sections of this chapter, several fundamental principles now clearly apply to directors who respond to a takeover proposal:

1. The board of directors must make a thorough, well-documented investigation before acting;

---

5. Panter v. Marshall Field & Co., 646 F.2d 271, 299 (7th Cir.), cert. denied, 454 U.S. 1091 (1981). See also dissenting opinion in Johnson v. Trueblood, 629 F.2d 287, 301 (3d Cir. 1980).

6. See, e.g., Zapata Corp. v. Maldonado, 430 A.2d 779, 787 (Del. 1981); Norlin Corp. v. Rooney, Pace, Inc., supra note 1.

7. See, e.g., Norlin Corp. v. Rooney, Pace, Inc., supra note 1.

2. Any defensive measure adopted by the board must be reasonable in relation to the reasonably perceived threat posed by the takeover bid; and

3. If control of the corporation is to be sold, the board must not interfere with the open, unrestrained bidding process.

§ 15.02. Informed decision.

The first and most highly publicized of the 1985 Delaware Supreme Court cases involved a situation where directors approved a merger of their corporation into another corporation. In *Smith v. Van Gorkom*,[8] the court found the directors of Trans Union Corporation personally liable for approving an inadequate merger proposal.

In that case, Van Gorkom, president of Trans Union, commenced merger negotiations without the prior approval of the Trans Union Board. Van Gorkom reached an agreement with the Marmon Group to sell Trans Union to Marmon for $55 per share. That price, which represented a premium of approximately 50% over the market value of the stock, was based solely on calculations by Trans Union's chief financial officer. Van Gorkom then hastily called a meeting of the Trans Union directors to approve the transaction. The directors were not given the merger agreement before or during the meeting and only three of the ten directors reportedly knew the purpose of the meeting in advance. After a twenty-minute oral report on the terms of the merger by Van Gorkom and a two-hour discussion by the directors, the transaction was approved, and the merger agreement was executed later that day without having been read by any director. Thereafter, an investment banking firm was retained to see if competing offers might bring a better deal. The Trans Union shareholders overwhelmingly approved the transaction several months later.

The Delaware Supreme Court ruled that the directors were grossly negligent in approving the transaction and were,

---

8. 488 A.2d 858 (Del. 1985).

therefore, personally liable to the extent the "intrinsic value" of the shares exceeded the $55 per share merger price. The court cited a number of facts to support its decision, including the facts that the directors relied entirely upon an oral presentation and had no written documentation with respect to the proposal; that the board acted hastily, without prior consideration of the proposal; that the premium over market price was accepted without sufficient valuation information (the market price of the stock was found to be an insufficient basis from which to measure the appropriateness of the offering price); that the directors did not sufficiently provide for competing offers to be obtained; that the directors did not make sufficient inquiry of management concerning the transaction; and that subsequent director action did not cure the initial inappropriate action in approving the acquisition. The court further held that the shareholders' overwhelming approval of the transaction did not preclude liability because the shareholders had not been appropriately informed of material information.

Following the court's ruling as to liability, the case was remanded to the trial court for a determination of damages. The case was ultimately settled for a reported $23.5 million.

Contrary to some views, the *Van Gorkom* decision can and probably should be read as consistent with prior decisions interpreting the business judgment rule. It has been widely accepted that directors, pursuant to their duty of care, have an obligation to adequately inform themselves of all material facts prior to any decision.[9] There was no question the directors subjectively believed the merger was in the best interest of the Trans Union shareholders. However, the court determined that this subjective belief was irrelevant where there was an absence of objective evidence to demonstrate that the directors had critically assessed the information relevant to the valuation of the company.

The significance of the *Van Gorkom* decision is the importance which the court placed upon the appearance of proper

---

9. Aronson v. Lewis, 473 A.2d 805, 812 (Del. 1984); Kaplan v. Centrex Corp., 284 A.2d 119, 124 (Del. Ch. 1971).

conduct. Although the directors may well have possessed all the necessary information concerning the transaction to make an informed decision, they failed to create an appearance or evidence of such knowledge and informed consideration.

Directors should not, however, create a mere "paper trail" at the expense of honestly analyzing and evaluating the decision. For example, in *EAC Industries, Incorporated v. Frantz Manufacturing Company*,[10] the Delaware Chancery Court issued an injunction against a scheme to entrench management. The court ignored the board's ratification of management's defensive actions, characterizing them as "mere window dressing" and held that where directors acted at a hastily called meeting from a "script" prepared by counsel, without knowledge or discussion of the subject, and where the meeting had the "aura of inevitability," neither the prepared script nor an "improvised" fairness opinion would save the directors' actions from a challenge pursuant to *Smith v. Van Gorkom.*

From these cases a number of procedural safeguards can be recommended. When analyzing takeover bids, directors must adopt procedures and methods which allow for the identification and examination of all relevant factors. Use of independent experts, such as investment bankers, accountants, attorneys and special independent committees of the board, is essential and their conclusions and recommendations should be reviewed closely. Copies of all proposed agreements, or at least accurate summaries thereof, should be available for review prior to the board meeting if at all possible. Reasonable inquiry must be made into the bases of the price or values assigned to the transaction and the extent of negotiating with respect to the terms of the transaction.

Full disclosure of all material information must be made. Care is required to avoid misleading statements or half-truths in press releases and proxy statements. This may also include disclosures concerning the existence or lack of any

---

10. Case No. 8003 (Del. Ch.), aff'd, 501 A.2d 401 (Del. 1985).

internal valuation studies, the extent of negotiations, and even the thoroughness with which the transaction was discussed and analyzed.

Finally, thorough documentation must be created and maintained of all activity taken in connection with the analysis of and response to the takeover bid. Not only the board minutes, but other reports, memoranda and documents should reflect what was considered, how it was considered, and why certain conclusions were reached.

§ 15.03. Modified business judgment rule.

In addition to addressing the duties of directors when approving a takeover, the Delaware Supreme Court in 1985 also established the basic contours within which a board must act in order to justifiably rely on the protection of the business judgment rule when opposing a hostile takeover bid.

In *Unocal Corporation v. Mesa Petroleum Company,*[11] the Delaware Supreme Court upheld a defensive action taken by the Unocal board in response to an effort by Mesa to acquire the company. In an attempt to thwart the Mesa bid, directors of Unocal approved an exchange offer pursuant to which Unocal stock held by the public would be exchanged for valuable debt securities. However, the shares held by the hostile offeror were precluded from participating in that exchange offer.

The court analyzed the propriety of the directors' discriminating defensive tactic in the context of the business judgment rule and stated that a board has the "fundamental duty and obligation to protect the corporate enterprise, which included stockholders, from harm reasonably perceived, irrespective of its source."[12] The court made it clear that the board's duty extends to takeovers:

> When a board addresses a pending takeover bid, it has an obligation to determine whether the offer is in the best interest of the corporation and its shareholders. In that

---

11. 493 A.2d 946 (Del. 1985).
12. Id. at 955.

485

respect, a board's duty is no different from any other responsibility it shoulders, and its decisions should be no less entitled to the respect they otherwise would be accorded in the realm of the business judgment.[13]

The court, though, did not render an unbridled endorsement of the traditional business judgment rule to takeover contests. For the first time, the court explicitly recognized that the business judgment rule in the takeover context should be different from the business judgment rule as applied in the context of an ordinary business transaction. Because of the "omnipresent specter that a board may be acting primarily in its own interests, rather than those of the corporation and its shareholders," the court concluded the board's duties are "enhanced" in the takeover context.[14]

In light of this inherent conflict of interest, the court held that unlike a traditional application of the rule, the initial burden of proof is upon the directors to show:

(1) they had reasonable grounds to believe that a danger or threat to "corporate policy and effectiveness existed"; and

(2) the defensive measure was reasonable in relation to the threat posed.

According to the court, these "threats" may include inadequacy of price, inappropriate nature and timing of the offer, question of illegality, risk of nonconsummation, quality of securities offered, and the impact on corporate constituents other than shareholders (i.e., creditors, customers, employees and perhaps even the community generally). As a result, directors now appear to have the duty to analyze thoroughly these and other elements of any takeover bid.

This modified business judgment rule in the takeover context has generally been adopted in other jurisdictions as

---

13. Id. at 954.
14. Id. See also discussion supra section 6.14.

well.[15] However, unlike *Unocal,* at least some courts have refused to place the initial burden of proof on the directors.[16]

Since the *Unocal* case, courts have attempted to apply this modified business judgment rule to various situations. An important application occurred in *Moran v. Household International, Incorporated,*[17] where the Delaware Supreme Court considered the propriety of the board adopting a "poison pill" shareholder rights plan as a defensive mechanism to ward off possible future tender offers. Although the action taken was not in response to a specific takeover bid, the court found that the board adopted the defensive mechanism in the good faith belief that it was necessary to protect the corporation from coercive acquisition techniques, that the board was informed as to the details of the plan, and that the plan was reasonable in relation to the threat posed. Accordingly, the directors were protected by the business judgment rule.

§ 15.04. Directors as auctioneers.

In yet another ruling by the Delaware Supreme Court in 1985 (although the formal opinion was not released until 1986), the court held that directors breached their fiduciary duty by issuing a "lock-up" option to a "white knight."[18] The court affirmed a Chancery Court decision which found that during the course of competing tender offers for Revlon, the Revlon directors concluded there would be a sale of their company. At that point, in the Supreme Court's view, the directors' role changed from that of a board fending off a hostile acquiror to that of an "auctioneer" endeavoring to secure the "highest price for the pieces" of the enterprise. In essence, the

---

15. See, e.g., Hanson Trust PLC v. ML SCM Acquisition, Inc., 781 F.2d 264 (2d Cir. 1986); Dynamics Corp. of Am. v. CTS Corp., 805 F.2d 705 (7th Cir. 1986), rev'd on other grounds sub nom. CTS Corp. v. Dynamics Corp. of Am., 481 U.S. —, 95 L.Ed.2d 67, 107 S.Ct. 1637 (1987).

16. See, e.g., Hanson Trust PLC v. ML SCM Acquisition, Inc., supra note 15.

17. 500 A.2d 1346 (Del. 1985).

18. Revlon, Inc. v. MacAndrews & Forbes Holdings, Inc., 506 A.2d 173 (Del. 1986).

directors' duties to the corporate entity largely terminated, leaving only the duty to the shareholders to maximize their return.

According to the court, once the board members became auctioneers, price became the paramount consideration. The primary duty of the directors was to sell the company to the highest bidder. Moreover, the court expressed great doubt whether during the auctioning process the board could consider the interests of any constituency group other than the shareholders.

Because the court found that the intent of the Revlon directors in granting the lock-up option was effectively to put an end to the auction for the company at the expense of other bidders and Revlon shareholders, personal liability for the directors existed. The case was ultimately settled for a reported $20 million.

Other jurisdictions subsequently adopted this same analysis.[19] Among other things, these decisions emphasize the fluid nature of the duties of directors in the takeover context. Each board decision must be scrutinized in light of the facts and circumstances which then exist. Although the rejection of and defense against a hostile takeover bid may be appropriate at an early stage, subsequent developments may remove the justifications for opposition. Hence, a permissible defensive technique at one time in the contest may be impermissible and create personal liability if used at another time.

§ 15.05. Takeover defenses.

One result of the "merger mania" of the 1980's has been the dramatic increase in the complexity and creativity of bidding strategies and defensive responses. Defensive tactics with exotic names and complicated terms have been used with increasing frequency to thwart hostile takeover attempts. These defensive techniques are designed primarily to increase the bargaining position of the board of the target cor-

---

19. See, e.g., Edelman v. Fruehauf Corp., 798 F.2d 882 (6th Cir. 1986); Hastings-Murtach v. Texas Air Corp., 649 F. Supp. 479 (S.D. Fla. 1986).

poration. No takeover defense (with the possible exception of concentrating the voting securities in friendly hands) can make a corporation acquisition proof, but some can increase the leverage of the board in finding a better deal.

Listed below are summaries of some of the more widely used defensive techniques:

Poison pill. This defense is designed to make a takeover prohibitively expensive by issuing a special class of stock (the "poison pill") which is activated only on the occurrence of specified triggering events (e.g., merger or other business combination) and which the successful acquiror will have to then "swallow." The pill typically can be redeemed for a nominal price by the company if the board approves the triggering transaction.

For example, a common "poison pill" is a shareholder rights plan pursuant to which a special class of preferred stock is authorized and distributed to shareholders as a dividend. In the event of a hostile takeover, this preferred stock becomes convertible into stock requiring high dividend payments. An acquiror is then forced either to purchase the shares at a high price or to pay the expensive dividends.

Because of the judicial acceptance of this technique,[20] it has been one of the most frequently used defenses. However, adoption of a "poison pill" may not be done blindly. Directors must reasonably identify a danger to corporate policy and effectiveness and must conclude that the pill is reasonable in relation to the threat posed. Frequently, directors are presented with a dilemma: whether to adopt a poison pill in advance of a takeover bid, thereby creating some general protections, or to defer the decision concerning adoption until an actual takeover bid occurs, thereby retaining flexibility to adopt a poison pill tailored to a specific bidder, circumstances and objectives.

Shark repellants. This defensive technique involves amending the charter or bylaws of the target company to

---

20. Unocal Corp. v. Mesa Petroleum Co., supra note 11; Moran v. Household Int'l, Inc., supra note 17.

489

render the company less vulnerable to takeover by increasing the difficulty of obtaining control of the corporation. Because they make a company less attractive as a target, they "repel" takeover "sharks."

Examples of "shark repellants" include amendments to (i) restrict changes in the board of directors (for example, staggering terms for directors, limiting the power to remove directors, limiting the power of shareholders to fill vacancies on the board, and limiting the size of the board), (ii) require a supermajority or minority group vote of shareholders to approve specified business combinations, and (iii) require similar consideration be paid at all stages of a takeover, thereby protecting against coercive two-tier tender offers.

Courts have generally permitted the adoption of shark repellants, although state corporate law restrictions as well as director fiduciary duty issues must both be examined.[21]

Lock-up. This technique involves an arrangement whereby the target company gives one bidder an advantage in acquiring the target company over other bidders. For example, the target may issue to one bidder options to purchase treasury or unissued shares or certain key assets of the target ("crown jewels").

Courts have variously reacted to the use by directors of a lock-up defense. Some lock-up options are beneficial to shareholders because they induce a bidder to compete for control of the company, thereby creating an auction that maximizes shareholder profits. In those instances, the "white knight" bidder will enter the takeover contest only if it receives some compensation for the risks and costs involved. Under such conditions, courts have approved the issuance of lock-up options.[22]

---

21. Seibert v. Gulton Indus., Inc., 5 Del. J. Corp. L. 514 (Del. Ch. 1979), aff'd without opinion, 414 A.2d 822 (Del. 1980); Martin Marietta Corp. v. Bendix, 549 F. Supp. 623 (D. Md. 1982). But see Joseph E. Seagram & Sons, Inc. v. Conoco, Inc., 519 F. Supp. 506 (D. Del. 1981).

22. See, e.g., Whittaker Corp. v. Edgar, 535 F. Supp. 933 (E.D. Ill. 1982); Buffalo Forge Co. v. Ogden Corp., 555 F. Supp. 892 (W.D.N.Y.), aff'd, 717 F.2d 757 (2d Cir.), cert. denied, 464 U.S. 1018 (1983).

However, in other situations lock-up options merely prefer one bidder over another. By precluding bidders to compete in an open, unrestrained auction, the lock-up is detrimental to the shareholders' goal of maximizing their profits. In that situation, courts have not approved of this defensive technique and have held the directors who approved the issuance of the options personally liable.[23]

Issuance of new shares. This defensive technique involves the target company selectively issuing new shares, thereby diluting the interest of outstanding shares (including shares owned by the hostile bidder) and making it more expensive for the bidder to acquire a controlling interest. The newly issued shares are typically sold to a friendly "white squire" who is likely to vote the shares with management.

These types of selective sales have been upheld as within the directors' business judgment where the directors properly determine that the takeover is not in the best interests of shareholders and where the issuance is not for the sole or primary purpose of entrenching management.[24] However, this technique has been enjoined where there is no independent legitimate business purpose for the transaction,[25] where the issuance of new shares occurred after control has already passed to a hostile bidder,[26] or where the issuance effectively assured that the incumbent directors would maintain voting control of the company.[27]

Reacquisition of shares. This defensive technique involves the purchase by the target company of some of its outstanding stock, thereby lessening the bidder's opportunity to obtain a majority of the shares by removing shares from the trading market and making the target less attractive to the

---

23. Revlon, Inc. v. MacAndrews & Forbes Holdings, Inc., supra note 18; Hanson Trust PLC v. ML SCM Acquisition, Inc., supra note 15.

24. See, e.g., Chris-Craft Indus., Inc. v. Piper Aircraft Corp., 480 F.2d 341, 365 (2d Cir. 1973).

25. Consolidated Amusement Co. v. Rugoff, Fed. Sec. L. Rep. (CCH) ¶96,584 (S.D.N.Y. 1978).

26. EAC Indus., Inc. v. Frantz Mfg. Co., 501 A.2d 401 (Del. 1985).

27. Norlin Corp. v. Rooney, Pace, Inc., 744 F.2d 255 (2d Cir. 1984).

bidder by increasing the target company's liabilities (assuming the company borrows money to finance the reacquisition).

This repurchase program can take the form of selective repurchases or a general tender offer by the target for its own shares ("self-tender"). A selective repurchase program or exclusionary tender offer was upheld by the Delaware Supreme Court as within the business judgment of directors where the directors reasonably perceived the hostile bid represented a threat to corporate policy and effectiveness and the repurchase program adopted was reasonable in relation to the threat posed.[28] However, shortly after that decision, the SEC amended the tender offer rules to prohibit exclusionary tender offers and to require the same price be made available in a tender offer to all holders of the same class of stock.[29]

Self-tenders which are open to all shareholders have generally been upheld by the courts,[30] subject to the *Unocal* modified business judgment rule analysis.

§ 15.06. Greenmail and golden parachutes.

Two defensive techniques which have caused great controversy and concern among directors, shareholders, commentators and legislators are greenmail and golden parachutes. Limited authority now exists to guide directors in whether and how these techniques may be implemented. Accordingly, a board may be proceeding in many cases at its own peril if it adopts these techniques.

Greenmail payments are generally defined as the buy-back or targeted repurchase by a corporation of its shares, often at a substantial premium over market value, from a bidder or other dissident shareholder who is perceived as a threat to the best interest of the corporation. Historically, such repurchases have been tested under business judgment rule princi-

---

28. Unocal Corp. v. Mesa Petroleum Co., 493 A.2d 946 (Del. 1985).

29. 17 C.F.R. § 240.14d-10.

30. See, e.g., GAF Corp. v. Union Carbide Corp., 624 F. Supp. 1016 (S.D.N.Y. 1985); Revlon, Inc. v. MacAndrews & Forbes Holdings, Inc., 506 A.2d 173 (Del. 1986).

ples and have generally been upheld.[31] Those cases recognize that a corporation may serve legitimate business purposes through green mail payments, for example, by maintaining control over the corporation's destiny, preventing a takeover at a time that is disadvantageous to its shareholders and avoiding time consuming, disruptive and expensive dissension with a shareholder.

In *Polk v. Good*,[32] the Delaware Supreme Court broadly reaffirmed the right of a board of directors to authorize the repurchase of the stock of a dissident shareholder at a premium if, after reasonable investigation, the board has a justifiable belief that the dissident poses a reasonable threat to the corporation. The court, in analyzing the actions of Texaco's board of directors in approving the repurchase of 9.9% of its shares from the Bass family, noted that ten outside directors approved the transaction consistent with the advice rendered by the investment banker and legal counsel for the corporation, thereby making a prima facie showing of good faith and reasonable investigation. The court explicitly rejected the plaintiffs' contention that because of increased greenmail activity, traditional Delaware doctrine should be amended and new restraints should be imposed upon directors' judgments concerning stock repurchases.

Not all court decisions, though, have supported the payment by directors of greenmail. The increased use and publicity of this technique have resulted in increased criticism and judicial scrutiny. For example, in *Heckman v. Ahmanson*,[33] a California court of appeals affirmed the issuance of a preliminary injunction imposing a constructive trust on the $60 million profit earned by Saul Steinberg and his associates from their resale of Disney stock to the corporation in exchange for dismissal of certain litigation. The court found that the plaintiff shareholders were likely to succeed on the merits of their

---

31. See, e.g., Cheff v. Mathes, 199 A.2d 548 (Del. 1964); Heine v. Signal Cos., Fed. Sec. L. Rep. (CCH) ¶95,898 (S.D.N.Y. 1977).
32. 507 A.2d 531 (Del. 1986).
33. 168 Cal. App. 3d 119, 214 Cal. Rptr. 177 (1985).

claim against the Disney directors for breach of fiduciary duty in approving the payment. The court effectively found the business judgment rule inapplicable since the greenmail payments were merely defensive strategies against a hostile takeover and, therefore, bestowed personal benefit on the directors. As a result, the directors were required to demonstrate not only that the transaction was entered into in good faith, but also that the transaction was inherently fair.

Other cases have viewed directors approving a stock repurchase in the context of a tender offer as subject to an inherent conflict of interest, thus requiring the board to prove the repurchase was primarily in the interest of the corporation.[34]

Current federal securities law does not restrict greenmail transactions, although at least one court which so held nonetheless stated that greenmail may be "an extremely serious wrong looking for a remedy."[35] The SEC requires full disclosure of such payments or the adoption in the corporation's charter of anti-greenmail provisions.[36] In addition, if the repurchases were from directors for a price over the prevailing market price, stock exchange rules may require shareholder approval.[37]

Congress has indirectly attempted to discourage golden parachute payments by amending the Internal Revenue Code to impose a 20% nondeductible excise tax to the employee on "excess parachute payments," which are payments to top executives or key personnel in the event of a change in control in amounts exceeding three times the employee's average annual compensation for the five years preceding its change in corporate control.[37a] Such payments are also nondeductible to the corporation.

The term "golden parachute" refers generally to "an agreement between a corporation and its top officers which guar-

---

34. Petty v. Penntech Papers, Inc., 347 A.2d 140, 143 (Del. Ch. 1975); Condec Corp. v. Lunkenheimer Co., 43 Del. Ch. 353, 230 A.2d 769, 773-74 (1967).

35. Pin v. Texaco, Inc., 793 F.2d 1448 (5th Cir. 1986).

36. Exchange Act Rel. No. 34-15230 (Oct. 13, 1978).

37. See, e.g., NYSE Listed Company Manual § 312.

37a. Section 4999, Internal Revenue Code of 1986.

antee those officers continued employment, payment of a lump-sum or other benefits in the event of a change of corporate ownership."[38] Among other things, golden parachute arrangements allegedly serve a valid corporate purpose by providing the following benefits:

(a) Compensate employees who face a high risk that their employment will be arbitrarily terminated following a change in control;

(b) Enable the corporation to attract and retain competent executives who might otherwise be attracted by an employment opportunity offering greater security;

(c) Encourage objective evaluations of takeover bids by executives subject to possible dismissal or reduction of responsibility following a change in corporate control; and

(d) Discourage the successful bidders from arbitrarily eliminating good existing management.

However, it can be argued that golden parachute arrangements do not serve any valid business purpose for the following reasons, among others:

(a) Executives should not receive special benefits to encourage action which they are already obligated to perform pursuant to their fiduciary obligations to shareholders; and

(b) Such arrangements encourage qualified executives to resign, often without real cause, in order to collect the parachute benefits.

The limited authority which currently exists variously condemns or upholds golden parachute arrangements, depending upon the perceived purpose behind the arrangement, the specific provisions of the arrangement and the manner and circumstances in which the arrangement was adopted.[39]

---

38. Schrieber v. Burlington Northern, Inc., 472 U.S. 1, 86 L.Ed.2d 1, 105 S.Ct. 2458 (1985).

39. See, e.g., Koenigs v. Joseph Schlitz Brewing Co., 126 Wis. 2d 349, 377 N.W.2d 593 (1985) (golden parachute arrangement treated as provision

In an apparent response to strong public criticism of these arrangements, Congress, as part of the Tax Reform Act of 1984, devised a complex formula to limit the size of any golden parachute awarded after June 14, 1984.[40] Pursuant to the enactment, no parachute subject to the restrictions may be more than three times an executive's base pay, averaged over the previous five years. Any payments in excess of this restriction are nondeductible to the corporation and subject the recipient to a 20% excise tax in addition to the basic income tax.

Because golden parachute arrangements typically injure all shareholders only indirectly by reducing the general value of the corporation, litigation challenging their use generally takes the form of shareholder derivative suits. However, if the complaining shareholder ceases to be a shareholder as a result of a business combination which triggers the parachute, the shareholder will likely lose standing to prosecute the suit.[41] Accordingly, the circumstances under which the arrangements may be challenged are limited, thus explaining the relatively few cases analyzing such arrangements.

§ 15.07. Director constituents.

When analyzing director conduct in the change-of-control context, a fundamental element of the analysis is whose interests the directors should be protecting. Although it is generally accepted that a corporation should be managed primarily in the interest of its shareholders, some courts have recog-

---

for liquidated damages and upheld as consistent with the corporation's right to assure executives of their job security during "rough times"); Federal Sav. & Loan Ins. Corp. v. Bass, 576 F. Supp. 848 (N.D. Del. 1983) (employment agreements entered into when a savings and loan was in a precarious financial position and which provided for termination payments in the event of insolvency, merger or consolidation constituted an "unsafe or unsound practice" under FHLBB regulations); Buckhorn, Inc. v. Ropak Corp., 656 F. Supp. 209 (S.D. Ohio 1987) (severance payment agreements which are triggered only upon a change in control constituted a reasonable method of insuring the retention of key employees).

40. Sections 280G and 4999, Internal Revenue Code of 1986.

41. Lewis v. Anderson, 477 A.2d 1040 (Del. 1984).

nized that in the takeover context constituents beyond share-holders are a proper concern of directors.[42]

Two recent Delaware Supreme Court decisions shed considerable light on this question. In the *Unocal* case,[43] the court stated that directors may properly consider a takeover bid's effect on constituents other than the stockholders, including creditors, customers, employees, and perhaps even the community generally. Such a broad classification of constituents suggests broad deference to the directors' analysis and response to a takeover bid.

However, the Delaware Supreme Court just months later further explained its statement in *Unocal*, thereby significantly limiting its effect. In the *Revlon* case,[44] the court stated that non-shareholder interests may be considered if "there are rationally related benefits accruing to the stockholders." In that case, it was held that the directors should be mere "auctioneers" under the circumstances and were required to sell the company to the highest bidder.[45] Therefore, the court expressed great doubt whether the directors could consider the interests of any constituents other than the shareholders.

In order to at least partially avoid the narrow constituent base recognized in the *Revlon* case, a number of states have subsequently amended their corporation statutes to permit directors when responding to a takeover bid to consider the

---

42. See, e.g., Herald Co. v. Seawell, 472 F.2d 1081 (10th Cir. 1972) (upholding defensive maneuvers by a newspaper against a raider with a history of labor difficulties); GAF Corp. v. Union Carbide Corp., 624 F. Supp. 1016, 1018-19 (S.D.N.Y. 1985) ("The protection of loyal employees, including managers, of the organization is not anathema in the Court-house"); Gelco Corp. v. Coniston Partners, 652 F. Supp. 829, 850 (D. Minn. 1986), aff'd in part and vacated in part, 811 F.2d 414 (8th Cir. 1987) (board may consider factors other than price, including interests of non-share-holder constituencies in determining adequacy of takeover bid).

43. Unocal Corp. v. Mesa Petroleum Co., 493 A.2d 946, 954-55 (Del. 1985).

44. Revlon, Inc. v. MacAndrews & Forbes Holdings Inc., 506 A.2d 173 (Del. 1986).

45. See supra section 15.04.

interests of numerous constituents and other factors, including the long-term and short-term interests of the corporation and its shareholders, the interests of employees, suppliers, creditors and customers, the national and state economy and community and societal considerations.[46]

§ 15.08. Responsibilities under ERISA.

The use of employee benefit plans which hold stock of the target company to defend against a takeover bid poses a significant potential for liability. Such a defensive strategy inevitably engenders a variety of ERISA issues, particularly where an officer or director of the company sponsoring the plan is a plan fiduciary with control of the plan's investments. The insider is placed in an inherently conflicting position in that a corporate official's duty of loyalty to the corporation may conflict with his fiduciary obligations to the plan and its participants.

The leading case in analyzing the fiduciary responsibilities under ERISA in corporate takeovers is *Donovan v. Bierwirth*[47] which involved an unfriendly tender offer by LTV Corporation for the stock of Grumman Corporation. The Grumman board determined the tender offer was inadequate and not in the best interests of the corporation, its shareholders or employees. As a defensive measure, among other things, the trustees for the Grumman pension plan purchased shares of stock in Grumman in the open market at prices reflecting the market's anticipation of a successful tender offer. The defenses were successful, the bid failed and the stock price immediately fell, resulting in an unrealized loss to the pension plan of approximately $20 million.

In litigation brought by the Department of Labor, the court ruled that the trustees breached their fiduciary duty under ERISA by failing to investigate and analyze properly the fac-

---

46. See, e.g., Ohio Rev. Code Ann. § 1701.59(E).

47. 538 F. Supp. 463 (E.D.N.Y. 1981), aff'd as modified, 680 F.2d 263 (2d Cir.), cert. denied, 459 U.S. 1069 (1982). See also discussion supra in section 9.09.

tors relevant to their investment options. Although rejecting the assertion that a corporate insider acting as a plan trustee during a control contest represents a per se violation of ERISA, the court did rule that resignation by the trustees would have been the appropriate course of action under the circumstances.

From a purely financial standpoint, it would appear that plan trustees should typically tender shares of the target-sponsor company which it owns since the tender price is invariably higher than the then market price. However, courts recognize that other factors may be considered, including the effect of the proposed takeover on the long-term viability of the plan.[48]

A particularly effective use of employee benefit plans to thwart a takeover bid is the establishment of an employee stock ownership plan (ESOP) which acquires a significant percentage of company stock. This defensive technique presents particularly sensitive liability issues. For example, in *Norlin Corporation v. Rooney, Pace, Incorporated*[49] the court ruled that if directors of a target corporation establish or use an ESOP in a hostile takeover setting, the directors must show that the plan was in fact created to benefit the employees and not simply to further the aim of managerial entrenchment. In applying that distinction, courts have looked to factors such as the timing of the ESOP's establishment, the financial impact on the company, and identity of the trustees, and the voting control of the ESOP shares.[50] Funding of an ESOP by the target company directors after the company was acquired has been found to be an attempt

---

48. See, e.g., Withers v. Teachers' Retirement Sys. of N.Y., 447 F. Supp. 1248 (S.D.N.Y. 1978); Donovan v. Bierwirth, supra note 47, 680 F.2d at 273.

49. 744 F.2d 255 (2d Cir. 1984).

50. See, e.g., Buckhorn, Inc. v. Ropak Corp., 656 F. Supp. 209 (S.D. Ohio 1987). See also discussion supra in section 9.08; Klaus v. Hi-Shear Corp., 528 F.2d 225 (9th Cir. 1975) (issuance of shares to an ESOP shortly after a challenge to corporate control may create an inference of improper motive).

by the directors to perpetuate their control and thus the business judgment rule did not apply.[51]

Plan trustees should consider the following precautionary guidelines when responding to a hostile tender offer:

(a) The trustees should retain independent, qualified experts, including attorneys, accountants and investment advisors, to evaluate alternatives and advise the trustees. The experts generally used by the company should not be used by the trustees because of their likely conflict of interest.

(b) The trustees should make a thorough, well documented investigation and analysis of all investment alternatives and the likely results of each. Among other things, the risk of loss, the opportunity for gain, the impact on the fulfillment of the plan's purposes, the resulting diversity and liquidity of plan assets, and the accuracy and reasonableness of assumptions made by experts should carefully be examined for each alternative.

(c) The trustees should document all meetings, discussions, alternatives, investigations, analysis, expert opinions and recommendations, relevant factors considered, and reasons for selecting certain options. Absent this documentation, the trustees will have difficulty proving in court at a later date the prudence and propriety of their actions.

(d) The trustees should not participate or appear to participate in any decisions by the company with respect to responding to the hostile tender offer. Any plan trustee who is an active officer of the company should consider resigning as trustee or disqualifying himself from consideration of plan alternatives.

(e) The trustees should request indemnification from the company to the fullest extent permitted by law.

The Department of Labor has also issued extensive guidelines that may assist management in determining whether,

---

51. Frantz Mfg. Co. v. EAC Indus., 501 A.2d 401 (Del. 1985).

and to what extent, management of the target company lawfully may use its benefit plans as a defensive device.[52]

§ 15.09. State takeover legislation.

Since 1982, it has been widely believed that state statutes attempting to regulate takeovers of publicly held corporations were unconstitutional and ineffective. This belief was based upon the United States Supreme Court decision in *Edgar v. MITE*,[53] where the court held that the Illinois anti-takeover statute impermissibly interfered with interstate commerce and was preempted by the federal securities law regulation of tender offers. The ruling effectively invalidated takeover laws of thirty-seven states.

After the *MITE* case, several of the states adopted various forms of new anti-takeover statutes ("second generation" takeover statutes) designed to protect companies from hostile takeovers in a way which the states hoped would satisfy the constitutional questions raised in *MITE*. However, lower federal courts[54] consistently ruled that these new types of statutes were unconstitutional because they either interfered with interstate commerce or conflicted with the federal securities law regulation of tender offers as contained in the Williams Act.

As a result, hostile takeovers proceeded in a relatively unregulated legal environment, except for certain minimum disclosure and timing requirements under the federal securities laws. In attempts to provide more effective defense barriers, many corporations chose to enact their own takeover defenses, such as anti-takeover charter amendments and poison pill shareholders' rights plans. The adoption of most of

---

52. Department of Labor Advisory Opinion on Fiduciary Responsibility in Connection with Attempted Corporate Takeovers (Apr. 30, 1984).

53. 457 U.S. 624, 73 L.Ed.2d 269, 102 S.Ct. 2629 (1982).

54. See, e.g., Mesa Petroleum Co. v. Cities Serv. Co., 715 F.2d 1425 (10th Cir. 1983); Telvest v. Bradshaw, 697 F.2d 576 (4th Cir. 1983); Martin-Marietta Corp. v. Bendix Corp., 690 F.2d 558 (6th Cir. 1982); National City Lines, Inc. v. LLC Corp., 687 F.2d 1122 (8th Cir. 1982).

these defensive devices were either approved or recommended by the company's directors, thereby giving rise to claims of managerial entrenchment against the directors.

In a surprising decision rendered April 21, 1987, the Supreme Court in *CTS Corporation v. Dynamics Corporation of America*[55] ruled that one of these second generation anti-takeover state statutes, the Indiana Control Share Acquisition Act of 1986, was constitutional. That Act provides that an acquiror of 20%, 33 1/3% or 50% of shares in an Indiana corporation must obtain approval of a majority of the outstanding shares and a majority of the disinterested outstanding shares before it can exercise the voting rights of the purchased shares. The Court found it was possible to comply with both the federal Williams Act and the Indiana Act and concluded that the Indiana law does not discriminate against interstate commerce or inconsistently regulates activities in interstate commerce:

> No principle of corporate law and practice is more firmly established than a state's authority to regulate domestic corporations, including the authority to define the voting rights of shareholders.[56]

It is currently uncertain what effect the *CTS* decision will have on the validity of the numerous other second-generation state anti-takeover statutes adopted both before and after the decision. Although the Supreme Court seemed to issue a sweeping affirmation of the states' rights to regulate corporate governance, many second-generation statutes differ significantly from the Indiana statute upheld in *CTS*. These statutes generally take one of five different forms. Some states have enacted more than one of the indicated forms.

Control share acquisition statutes. This form of takeover regulation requires the approval of a designated percentage of disinterested shares before the bidder can vote, or in some states, can purchase the targeted shares. This approach recognizes that an acquisition of a controlling block of stock is a

---

55. 481 U.S. —, 95 L.Ed.2d 67, 107 S.Ct. 1637 (1987).
56. Id., 109 S.Ct. at 1642.

fundamental change in the corporation's existence and operation and therefore should require the same shareholder approval as a corporate merger, consolidation or other type of fundamental change. Because this is the type of statute approved by the Supreme Court in *CTS,* many states adopting new anti-takeover legislation since April, 1987 have selected this form of regulation.

Fair-price statutes. This form of statute requires a raider to pay all shareholders the same price for their stock, thereby effectively eliminating coercive two-tier tender offers in which the raider acquires a controlling block of stock by offering an attractive premium, and then forces the remaining stockholders to sell at a much lower price. A variation of this approach which has been enacted in a few states is to require a raider to purchase at the same price all shares tendered if the raider acquires a designated percentage ownership. Although control share acquisition statutes are gaining in popularity, the fair-price type of statute remains the most popular type of takeover law.

Moratorium statutes. This form of takeover legislation is also aimed at eliminating coercive two-tier tenders offers by prohibiting the acquiror from engaging in specified business combinations with the company for a specified period (typically three or five years) following the acquiror's stock acquisition unless the transaction is approved by the disinterested directors prior to the acquiror's acquisition.

Heightened disclosure statutes. This form of statute requires an offeror to file with the state securities department or other state agency specified information concerning the proposed offer. The offeror may not commence a takeover bid during a proscribed waiting period following that information filing. These statutes are similar in approach to the pre-*MITE* disclosure statutes but reflect an effort to minimize constitutional objections raised in *MITE.*

Expanded constituency statutes. This type of statute permits the board of directors of the target company to consider the interests of constituents other than the corporation's shareholders. For example, the statutes variously permit the

503

board, in considering the best interests of the corporation, to consider the effects of any action upon employees, suppliers, customers, creditors, communities in which the corporation is located, the state or national economy, and the long term interests of the corporation and its shareholders. Unlike the other forms of state statutes, this type of statute is principally intended to protect directors of the target corporation against personal liability rather than protect the shareholders against corrosive or deceptive takeover tactics.

The *CTS* decision may have significant impact on director liability in the takeover setting. Some of the "second generation" state takeover statutes require or permit the directors of the target company to make determinations which directly impact the applicability and effect of the statutes. For example, some states provide that the restrictions contained in the statute do not apply if a majority of disinterested directors approve the transaction.[57] Under those statutes, a key issue which is likely to be litigated will be the reasonableness and propriety of the decision by the board to either approve or disapprove the transaction. Thus, D & O litigation may continue to be a central focus of many takeovers.

In addition, assuming some of these second generation state anti-takeover statutes are found constitutional in light of the *CTS* case, it appears likely that raiders will be discouraged, at least to some extent, in proceeding with certain hostile tender offers. An alternative takeover mechanism which may become more attractive and more prevalent is acquisition of control through a proxy contest. Again, D & O litigation may become a central focus of such a takeover attempt since the adequacy and accuracy of disclosures by the directors in their attempt to obtain proxies may become a factor in the contest.

Although the *CTS* decision may result in a legal environment more favorable to the target company than to the raider, it should not be presumed that the decision and the

---

57. See, e.g., Del. Code Ann. tit. 8, § 203; N.Y. Bus. Corp. Law § 912; N.J. Bus. Corp. Act, § 14A:10A; Mich. Comp. Laws Ann. § 450.1775 et seq.

numerous anti-takeover statutes which may be validated thereby will necessarily relieve directors and officers of liability exposure in the change of control context. As long as there are economic incentives for raiders to acquire target companies, it is reasonable to assume that mechanisms will be found to accomplish those hostile takeovers. Because of the intimate involvement and inherent conflicts of target directors in that process, it is also reasonably likely that their involvement will continue to be the subject of judicial analysis and the basis for potential personal liability.

§ 15.10. Minority shareholder squeeze-outs.

Not infrequently, persons in control of a company seek to eliminate the interest in the company owned by minority shareholders. Because holders of a majority of the voting shares in a corporation have the ability to elect and control a majority of the directors and to determine the outcome of many shareholder votes, such controlling shareholders have tremendous power to "squeeze out" the minority holders.

The techniques available are seemingly endless. For example, the majority shareholders may refuse to declare dividends; drain the company's earnings through exorbitant salaries and bonuses, high rental or other contractual arrangements; sell or transfer assets; loan money; and merge or consolidate the company into a corporation not owned by the minority shareholders.

Director liability under these situations may be acute. To the extent the directors personally benefit from their decisions, they are not disinterested and lose the protection of the business judgment rule. In that situation, they are forced to prove the "entire fairness" of the transaction to the corporation and the minority shareholders if personal liability is to be avoided.

Typically, courts will apply the more protective business judgment standard to review directors' decisions in fixing salaries, declaring or withholding dividends, authorizing contracts or otherwise fixing business policies unless particu-

505

larly egregious circumstances exist which indicate a motive to squeeze out minority shareholders.[58]

However, with respect to mergers with entities owned by the majority shareholders (i.e. parent-subsidiary mergers) a more obvious conflict of interest exists and therefore courts typically do not apply the business judgment rule.[59] A series of Delaware Supreme Court decisions are particularly instructive of the analysis used for director conduct in these types of mergers.

In a trilogy of decisions in 1977 through 1979, the Delaware court ruled that cash-out mergers which forced minority shareholders to receive cash for their interest in the corporation must have a valid business purpose and must be "entirely fair" to the minority shareholders.[60] These decisions recognized the unique vulnerability of minority shareholders in this type of transaction and suggested that the standard of care becomes greater as the size of the minority interest becomes smaller.[61]

In 1983, the Delaware Supreme Court modified this analysis by expanding the concept of "fairness" and eliminating the necessity to show a valid business purpose for the merger.[62] Fairness for these purposes was described by the court as follows:

> The concept of fairness has two basic aspects: fair dealing and fair price. The former embraces questions of when the transaction was timed, how it was initiated, structured, negotiated, disclosed to the directors, and how the

58. See, e.g., Iwasaki v. Iwasaki Bros., Inc., 58 Or. App. 543, 649 P.2d 598 (1982) ("[C]ourts will not interfere in legitimate business decisions of private corporations just to resolve disputes between majority and minority stockholders"); Sinclair Oil Corp. v. Levien, 280 A.2d 717 (Del. 1971) (business judgment rule applies when minority shareholders receive appropriate share of dividend).

59. Sterling v. Mayflower Hotel Corp., 93 A.2d 107 (Del. 1952).

60. Singer v. Magnavox Co., 380 A.2d 969 (Del. 1977); Tanzer v. International Gen. Indus., Inc., 379 A.2d 1121 (Del. 1977); Roland Int'l Corp. v. Najjar, 407 A.2d 1032 (Del. 1979).

61. See Roland Int'l Corp. v. Najjar, supra note 60, at 1036.

62. Weinberger v. UOP, Inc., 457 A.2d 701 (Del. 1983).

approvals of the directors and the stockholders were obtained. The latter aspect of fairness relates to the economic and financial considerations of the proposed merger, including all relevant factors: assets, market value, earnings, future prospects, and any other elements that affect the intrinsic or inherent value of a company's stock.[63]

This broad definition of fairness represented an expansion of analysis because, among other things, the court required consideration of all relevant factors involving the value of a company to determine the fairness of the price. Prior cases had limited the price analysis to the very structured and mechanistic procedures set forth in the appraisal rights statute.[64]

With respect to the business purpose requirement, the court found such a showing to be unnecessary since the interests of minority shareholders are adequately protected by the expanded concept of "entire fairness" and the broad appraisal remedy available. Even without the business purpose requirement, the court ruled that trial courts have "broad discretion ... to fashion such relief as the facts of a given case may dictate."[65]

---

63. Id. at 713.

64. See Jacques Coe & Co. v. Minneapolis-Moline Co., 75 A.2d 244, 247 (Del. Ch. 1950); Tri-Continental Corp. v. Battye, 66 A.2d 910, 917-18 (Del. Ch. 1949).

65. Weinberger v. UOP, Inc., supra note 62, at 715.

COROLLARY REFERENCES

Booth, "Is There Any Valid Reason Why Target Managers Oppose Tender Offers?," 14 Sec. Reg. L.J. 43 (1986).

Booth, "Management Buyouts, Shareholder Welfare, and the Limits of Fiduciary Duty," 60 N.Y.U. L. Rev. 630 (1985).

Burgman & Cox, "Corporate Directors, Corporate Realities and Deliberative Process: An Analysis of the Trans Union Case," 11 J. Corp. L. 311 (1986).

Coffee, "Regulating the Market for Corporate Control: A Critical Assessment of Tender Offer's Role in Corporate Governance," 84 Colum. L. Rev. 1145 (1984).

Easterbrook & Fischel, "The Proper Role of a Target's Management in Responding to a Tender Offer," 94 Harv. L. Rev. 1161, 1162 (1981).

Gordon, "Corporate Disclosure of Merger Negotiations — When Does the Investor Have a Right to Know?," 36 Syracuse L. Rev. 1155 (1985).

Gutman, "Tender Offer Defensive Tactics and the Business Judgment Rule," 58 N.Y.U. L. Rev. 621 (1983).

Helman & Junewicz, "A Fresh Look at Poison Pills," 42 Bus. Law. 771 (1987).

Lipton & Brownstein, "Takeover Responses and Directors' Responsibilities — An Update," 40 Bus. Law. 1403 (1985).

Lipton, "Takeover Bids in the Target's Boardroom," 35 Bus. Law. 101 (1979).

Lipton, "Takeover Bids in the Target's Boardroom, An Update After One Year," 36 Bus. Law. 1017 (1981).

Manning, "Life in the Boardroom After Van Gorkom," 41 Bus. Law. 1 (1985).

Maxa, "The Legality of Lock-ups Under Section 14(e) of the Williams Act: Balancing the Scales," 26 Wm. & Mary L. Rev. 115 (1984).

Palmieri, "Fiduciary Responsibilities Under ERISA in Corporate Takeovers," 13 J. of Corp. Tax 127 (1986).

Poser, "Misuse of Confidential Information Concerning a Tender Offer as a Securities Fraud," 49 Brooklyn L. Rev. 1265 (1983).

Rosenzweig & Orens, "Tipping the Scales — The Business Judgment Rule in the Anti-takeover Context," 14 Sec. Reg. L.J. 23 (1986).

Siegel, "Tender Offer Defensive Tactics: A Proposal for Reform," 36 Hastings L.J. 377 (1985), reprinted in 18 Sec. L. Rev. 401 (1986).

Subak, "A Snapshot of the Law Being Carved in Stone," 42 Bus. Law. 761 (1987).

Zalecki, "The Duties of Corporate Directors in Takeover Context: A Rationale for Judicial Focus Upon the Deliberative Process," 17 Toledo L. Rev. 313 (1986).

Note, "Achieving Waivers in Corporate Cash Mergers: Weinberger v. UOP, Inc.," 16 Conn. L. Rev. 95 (1983).

Note, "Delaware's Attempt to Swallow a New Takeover Defense: The Poison Pill Preferred Stock," 10 Del. J. Corp. L. 569 (1985).

Note, "Golden Parachutes and Draconian Measures Aimed at Control: Is Internal Revenue Code Section 280g the Proper Regulatory Mode of Shareholder Protection?," 54 U. Cin. L. Rev. 1293 (1986).

Note, "Golden Parachutes: Untangling the Ripcords," 39 Stan. L. Rev. 955 (1987).

Note, "Greenmail: Targeted Stock Repurchase and the Management Entrenchment Hypothesis," 98 Harv. L. Rev. 1045 (1985).

Note, "Mining the Safe Harbor? The Business Judgment Rule After Trans Union," 10 Del. J. Corp. L. 545 (1985).

Note, "Minority Shareholders and Cashout Mergers: The Delaware Court Offers Plaintiffs Greater Protection and a Procedural Dilemma — Weinberger v. UOP, Inc., 457 A.2d 701 (Del. 1983)," 59 Wash. L. Rev. 119 (1983).

Note, "Protecting Shareholders Against Partial and Two-Tiered Takeovers: The 'Poison Pill' Preferred," 97 Harv. L. Rev. 1964 (1984).

Note, "Tender Offer Defensive Tactics and the Business Judgment Rule," 58 N.Y.U. L. Rev. 621, 629-39 (1983).

Note, "The Presumptions and Burdens of the Duty of Loyalty Regarding Target Company Defensive Tactics," 48 Ohio St. L.J. 273 (1987).

Chapter 16

DISCLOSURE AND MISUSE OF BUSINESS INFORMATION

§ 16.01. Disclosure philosophy.

When Congress was working on the Securities Act of 1933 it had before it the recommendation of President Franklin D. Roosevelt, who said:

> I recommend to Congress legislation for Federal supervision of traffic in investment securities in interstate commerce....
>
> There is ... an obligation upon us to insist that every issue of new securities to be sold in interstate commerce shall be accompanied by full publicity and information, and that no essentially important element attending the issue shall be concealed from the buying public.
>
> This proposal adds to the ancient rule of caveat emptor, the further doctrine "let the seller also beware." It puts the burden of telling the whole truth on the seller. It should give impetus to honest dealing in securities and thereby bring back public confidence.
>
> The purpose of the legislation I suggest is to protect the public with the least possible interference to honest business.[1]

Following that recommendation, the 1933 Act embraced the philosophy of disclosure and put aside the conflicting phi-

---

1. H.R. Rep. No. 85, at 1-2, 73rd Cong., 1st Sess. (1933).

511

losophy that the federal government should determine, on the merits of individual securities, whether securities should be issued or sold.[2] Such activities were left to the states under their respective Blue Sky laws.

The same philosophy of disclosure was carried over into the Securities Exchange Act of 1934. In providing for the regulation of securities, it relies primarily on disclosure in connection with the distribution of and trading in securities. Such disclosure is intended to ensure that securities markets will operate in a free and open fashion and that "the price of a security will more nearly correspond with its actual value."[3]

The issue of corporate disclosure of information poses difficult and recurring problems. Timely disclosure enhances investor confidence in the securities markets by providing the market with valuable information. Issuers who fail to disclose material information on a timely basis may become subject to liability under the express disclosure provisions of the federal and state securities laws as well as the anti-fraud provisions of the federal securities laws, particularly Rule 10b-5 promulgated under the Securities Exchange Act of 1934. Yet, an issuer who prematurely discloses inherently fluid and uncertain business developments, such as preliminary merger negotiations, may harm its business position and also risks Rule 10b-5 liability for misleading or incomplete disclosure in the event that negotiations collapse. Thus, issuers may face a perplexing disclosure dilemma ... damned if they do and damned if they don't.

Whether information must be disclosed by a corporation requires resolution of two distinct issues: there must exist a duty to disclose and the information must be material. Those issues are discussed in the next succeeding sections.

---

2. See H.R. 5480, 73rd Cong., 1st Sess., section 6 (1933), the "Thompson Bill."

3. Schoenbaum, "The Relationship Between Corporate Disclosure and Corporate Responsibility," 40 Fordham L. Rev. 565, 576, 577 (1972).

§ 16.02. Duty to disclose.

Although disclosure is the fundamental philosophy of the federal securities laws, it is not without limitations. In the absence of the issuer selling or buying its own stock, insider trading, previous inaccurate disclosures or mandatory SEC filings, there is neither a judicial nor statutory requirement to make disclosure.[4] This general rule has been criticized by commentators[5] who contend that all material nonpublic information should be promptly disclosed. There is presently no judicial or SEC support for this position, although cases suggest that companies should act reasonably and be able to justify the timing of the disclosure.

In the seminal case of *SEC v. Texas Gulf Sulphur*,[6] the Second Circuit Court of Appeals held that the withholding by the company of the disclosure of a large mineral discovery while the company bought up additional acreage surrounding the exploration site was justified because it served a valid corporate purpose. In a footnote the court specifically dispelled the notion of an absolute, immediate duty to disclose:

> We do not suggest that material facts must be disclosed immediately, the timing of disclosure is a matter for the business judgment of the corporate officers entrusted with the management of the corporation within the affirmative disclosure requirements promulgated by the exchanges and by the SEC.[7]

In essence, the court recognized that full, absolute and immediate disclosure concerning crucial corporate develop-

---

4. Staffin v. Greenberg, 672 F.2d 1196 (3d Cir. 1982); SEC v. Texas Gulf Sulphur, 401 F.2d 833 (2d Cir. 1968), cert. denied, 394 U.S. 976 (1969); Starkman v. Marathon Oil Co., 772 F.2d 231 (6th Cir. 1985). But see Financial Indus. Fund, Inc. v. McDonnell Douglas Corp., 474 F.2d 514 (10th Cir.), cert. denied, 414 U.S. 874 (1973).

5. Bauman, "Rule 10b-5 and the Corporation's Affirmative Duty to Disclose," 67 Geo. L.J. 935, 937 (1979); Talesnick, "Corporate Silence and Rule 10b-5: Does a Publicly-Held Corporation Have an Affirmative Obligation to Disclose?," 49 Den. L.J. 369, 412 (1973).

6. Supra note 4.

7. SEC v. Texas Gulf Sulphur, supra note 4, 401 F.2d at 850, n.12.

ments may often impede corporate success and therefore the decision as to when to disclose should be protected by the business judgment rule.[8]

The *Texas Gulf* decision, though, did hold that a corporation which nevertheless voluntarily chooses to make a public statement concerning material corporate events does have a duty to disclose sufficient information so that the statement is not "false or misleading or ... so incomplete as to mislead."[9]

In addition, a duty exists to correct prior issuer statements. In *Ross v. A.H. Robins, Incorporated*,[10] Robins, the manufacturer of the "Dalkon Shield" IUD contraceptive device had issued statements in its annual report about the effectiveness and safety of its product. Subsequently, an undisclosed report indicated that the device was not effective and that several product liability suits had been filed against the company. The court ruled that the company's failure to correct its prior statements when the company became aware of subsequent events that rendered those prior statements misleading gave rise to a claim under Rule 10b-5 of the 1934 Act. SEC releases[11] and stock exchange rules[12] similarly recognize a duty to correct.

This obligation to correct prior inaccurate statements exists so long as the prior statements remain "alive," i.e., "so long as traders in the market can reasonably be expected to rely on the statement."[13] After enough time has passed and sufficient other information becomes public so that reliance

---

8. See State Teachers' Retirement Bd. v. Fluor Corp., 654 F.2d 843 (2d Cir. 1981).

9. SEC v. Texas Gulf Sulphur, supra note 4, 401 F.2d at 862. See also First Va. Bank Shares v. Benson, 559 F.2d 1307 (5th Cir. 1977), cert. denied, 435 U.S. 952 (1978).

10. 465 F. Supp. 904 (S.D.N.Y.), rev'd on other grounds, 607 F.2d 545 (2d Cir. 1979), cert. denied, 446 U.S. 946, reh'g denied, 448 U.S. 911 (1980).

11. See, e.g., General Introduction to Regulation S-K; Securities Act Rel. No. 5447 (Dec. 20, 1973); Securities Act Rel. No. 6001 (Nov. 29, 1978).

12. Intercontinental Indus. v. American Stock Exch., 452 F.2d 935 (5th Cir. 1971), cert. denied, 409 U.S. 482 (1972).

13. Ross v. A.H. Robins, Inc., 465 F. Supp. at 908.

on previously disclosed information is unreasonable, the duty to correct ceases.[14]

The duty to correct generally does not extend to statements by third parties or rumors in the marketplace so long as the company is not involved in the publication of and is not attributed with having made or endorsed the statement or rumor.[15]

Another situation where the duty to disclose arises is when a company or its directors or officers trade in the company's stock. The SEC and courts have adopted a "disclose or abstain" rule which requires the company or insider to disclose all material, nonpublic information or abstain from trading in the stock.[16]

§ 16.03. Disclosure of material information.

When a duty to disclose exists, a corporation and its directors and officers are obligated to disclose all material information. The test of materiality under the federal securities laws is equated with the fundamental purpose of the disclosure philosophy, i.e., the protection of investors. Thus the test depends upon the impact on the investor. It does not speak to the subjective preferences of an actual, individual investor, but rather to the objective preferences of an "average prudent investor," who is obviously a close relative to the "ordinarily prudent person" of negligence law significance.[17]

---

14. Warner Communications, Inc. v. Murdock, 581 F. Supp. 1482, 1489-90, n.13 (D. Del. 1984).

15. Elkind v. Liggett & Myers, 635 F.2d 156 (2d Cir. 1980); Electronic Specialty Co. v. International Controls Corp., 409 F.2d 937 (2d Cir. 1969); Zuckerman v. Harnischfeger Corp., 591 F. Supp. 112 (S.D.N.Y. 1984). But see NYSE Company Manual § 202.05 (issuer required "promptly to dispel unfounded rumors which result in unusual market activity or price variations").

16. In re Cady, Roberts & Co., 40 S.E.C. 907, 911 (1961); Gert v. Elgin Nat'l Indus., Inc., 773 F.2d 154, 158-59 (7th Cir. 1985).

17. See, e.g., Smallwood v. Pearl Brewing Co., 489 F.2d 579 (5th Cir.), cert. denied, 419 U.S. 873 (1974); Kohler v. Kohler Co., 319 F.2d 634 (7th Cir. 1963).

The leading authority defining what information is material is the Supreme Court decision in *TSC Industries, Incorporated v. Northway, Incorporated*,[18] where the Court described materiality for purposes of the federal securities law proxy rules as follows:

> An omitted fact is material if there is a substantial likelihood that a reasonable shareholder would consider it important in deciding how to vote. This standard ... does not require proof of a substantial likelihood that disclosure of the omitted fact would have caused the reasonable shareholder to change his vote. What the standard does contemplate is a showing of a substantial likelihood that, under all the circumstances, the omitted fact would have assumed actual significance in the deliberations of the reasonable shareholder. Put another way, there must be a substantial likelihood that the disclosure of the omitted fact would have been viewed by the reasonable investor as having significantly altered the "total mix" of information made available.[19]

Although the *TSC* definition of materiality was articulated in the context of the SEC proxy rules, it has since been applied to Rule 10b-5,[20] Section 17(a) of the 1933 Act,[21] the tender offer antifraud provisions in Section 14(e) of the 1934 Act[22] and Section 206 of the Investment Advisers Act.[23]

Court decisions have recognized that this materiality standard should be flexible and is dependent, in part, upon the setting in which the issue arises. For example, the standard may be relaxed somewhat in the context either of a disputed proxy contest or a takeover bid since there is an adverse party to correct any overstatement or even some omissions.[24]

---

18. 426 U.S. 438, 48 L.Ed.2d 757, 96 S.Ct. 2126 (1976).

19. Id., 426 U.S. at 449, 48 L.Ed.2d at 766, 96 S.Ct. at 2132.

20. Healey v. Catalyst Recovery of Pa., Inc., 616 F.2d 641 (3d Cir. 1980).

21. Steadman v. SEC, 603 F.2d 1126 (5th Cir. 1979), aff'd on other grounds, 450 U.S. 91, 67 L.Ed.2d 69, 101 S.Ct. 999 (1981).

22. Prudent Real Estate Trust v. Johncamp Realty, Inc., 599 F.2d 1140 (2d Cir. 1979).

23. Steadman v. SEC, supra note 21.

24. SEC v. Falstaff Brewing Corp., 629 F.2d 62 (D.C. Cir. 1980); Seaboard World Airlines, Inc. v. Tiger Int'l, Inc., 600 F.2d 355 (2d Cir. 1979).

However, the standard may be increased after there has been one misrepresentation of a material fact. In holding a corporate president and chairman of the board liable to a stock purchaser for misrepresentation of material facts, a Florida district court has pointed out that "given one set of very material misrepresentations, the threshold of materiality will likely drop for a second or third set of misrepresentations."[25]

Materiality for information disclosure purposes must be distinguished from materiality for financial accounting purposes. The latter is a much broader concept. For example, the Foreign Corrupt Practices Act of 1977 requires, among other things, that a SEC reporting company maintain books, records and accounts that "in reasonable detail, accurately and fairly reflect the transactions and dispositions of the assets" of the company.[26] As one court recognized, this broad concept of materiality for financial accounting reflects a congressional determination that the scope of the federal securities laws should be expanded beyond the traditional ambit of disclosure requirements and will "significantly augment the degree of federal involvement in the internal management of public corporations."[27]

§ 16.04. Disclosure of soft information.

Particularly difficult disclosure issues arise with respect to "soft" information, i.e., information that is not factual, such as reflections on managerial quality, projections and forecasts, plans and future intentions, legal uncertainties, proposals, negotiations, motives and purposes. Soft information is to be contrasted with "factual" information which typically is objectively verifiable historical data.

Conflicting concerns complicate the disclosure analysis for soft information. Because this information usually cannot be

---

25. Alna Capital Assocs. v. Wagner, 532 F. Supp. 591, 599 (S.D. Fla. 1982).

26. Securities Exchange Act, Section 13(b)(2)(A), 15 U.S.C. § 78j(b)(2)(A).

27. SEC v. World-Wide Coin Invs., Ltd., 567 F. Supp. 724 (N.D. Ga. 1983).

verified, concern exists about its reliability and the potential for investors giving greater credence to the information than is warranted. However, the information frequently is viewed as important by investors and therefore is considered material under the traditional materiality concept. Accordingly, courts tend to weigh these conflicting considerations in light of the nature of the particular soft information at issue. The following summarizes judicial treatment of different types of soft information:

Managerial quality. The SEC has held a long-standing belief that information directly relating to the quality and integrity of management is material and should be disclosed because it "is an essential ingredient of an informed investment decision."[28] Then SEC Chairman William L. Cary explained:

> Of cardinal importance in any business is the quality of its management.... Managerial talent consists of personal attributes, essentially subjective in nature, that frequently defy meaningful analysis through the impersonal medium of a prospectus.... The integrity of management — its willingness to place its duty to public shareholders over personal interest — is an equally elusive factor for the application of disclosure standards.[29]

An example of the SEC's adherence to those comments is found in the requirement that where a corporate director or executive officer is the subject of a securities-related injunction, the subject matter of which being material to an evaluation of the integrity and ability of the director or officer, the injunctive order must be disclosed in a registration statement.[30]

Courts have followed the SEC lead and have frequently held that facts relating to management's quality and integrity should be disclosed. For example, the failure to disclose the chief executive officer's prior conviction and prison sen-

---

28. In re Franchard Corp., 42 S.E.C. 163, 170 (1964).
29. Id. at 169, 170.
30. Louis J. Lefkowitz, Fed. Sec. L. Rep. CCH ¶80,760 (Aug. 6, 1976).

tence for insurance fraud was found to be a material nondisclosure.[31]

Facts relating to management self-dealing,[32] payments of bribes and kickbacks,[33] and falsification by directors of corporate books and records[34] have also been considered material. Courts view such information as "directly relevant to a determination of whether they are qualified to exercise stewardship of the company."[35]

This materiality standard, though, does not require a company and its management to predict and disclose its potential misconduct before the existence of misconduct is properly determined by a court.[36] The general rule is that "federal securities laws do not impose a duty upon parties to publicly admit the culpability of their actions."[37]

Projections and forecasts. The issue of materiality and thus the necessity to disclose projections and forecasts typically arises when a shareholder first sells his securities in a transaction involving conflicts of interest with the purchaser (e.g. going private or leveraged buyout transactions), hostile tenders or white knight transactions and then claims he was defrauded in the sale because favorable projections or forecasts about the company were not disclosed.

Most courts addressing the issue have ruled that such disclosure is not required.[38] For example, in *Starkman v. Mara-*

---

31. SEC v. Scott, 565 F. Supp. 1513 (S.D.N.Y. 1983), aff'd, 734 F.2d 118 (2d Cir. 1984).

32. Maldonado v. Flynn, 597 F.2d 789 (2d Cir. 1979); Halpern v. Armstrong, 491 F. Supp. 365 (S.D.N.Y. 1980).

33. SEC v. Washington County Util. Dist., 676 F.2d 218 (6th Cir. 1982); United States v. Fields, 592 F.2d 638 (2d Cir. 1978), cert. denied, 442 U.S. 917 (1979).

34. SEC v. Joseph Schlitz Brewing Co., 452 F. Supp. 824 (E.D. Wis. 1978).

35. Maldonado v. Flynn, supra note 32, at 796.

36. Warner Communications, Inc. v. Murdock, 581 F. Supp. 1482 (D. Del. 1984).

37. Id. at 1490.

38. See, e.g., Radol v. Thomas, 772 F.2d 244 (6th Cir. 1985).

thon Oil Company,[39] the Sixth Circuit Court of Appeals ruled that:

> [A] tender offer target must disclose projections and asset appraisals based upon predictions regarding future economic and corporate events only if the predictions underlying the appraisal or projection are substantially certain to hold and are virtually as certain as hard facts.[40]

A few courts, though, require such disclosure, weighing on a case-by-case basis "the potential aid such information will give a shareholder against the potential harm, such as undue reliance, if the information is received with a proper cautionary note."[41]

The SEC has declined to require disclosure of projections in filings.[42] However, the SEC has adopted several safe-harbor rules applicable to an issuer which voluntarily discloses projections made in good faith and on a reasonable basis.[43] Absent these safe-harbor rules, which are intended to encourage issuers to disclose projections, voluntary disclosure ran the risk of being labeled misleading and deceptive.

Plans and future intentions. Most cases hold that on the particular facts presented there was no obligation to disclose a plan or intended future act.[44] The typical justification for non-disclosure is that the plan was too contingent or the action was not sufficiently committed or determined.

When the company voluntarily discloses certain plans or future intentions, the disclosure must, of course, be accurate. Thus, a statement that a company "may" undertake negotia-

---

39. 772 F.2d 231 (6th Cir. 1985), cert. denied, 106 S.Ct. 1195 (1986).

40. Id. at 241.

41. Flynn v. Bass Bros. Enters., Inc., 744 F.2d 978 (3d Cir. 1984).

42. See Exchange Act Rel. No. 6084 (June 25, 1979); Mendell v. Greenberg, Fed. Sec. L. Rep. CCH ¶92,218 (S.D.N.Y. July 11, 1985).

43. See Rule 175, 17 CFR § 230.175 (1985); Rule 3b-6, 17 CFR § 230.3b-6 (1985).

44. See, e.g., TransWorld Airlines, Inc. v. Icahn, 609 F. Supp. 825 (S.D.N.Y. 1985); Pantry Pride, Inc. v. Rooney, 598 F. Supp. 891 (S.D.N.Y. 1984).

tions was misleading when substantive discussions had already begun.[45]

Disclosure of plans, purposes and similar intentions is required in various Williams Act filings relating to tender offers.[46]

Legal uncertainties. When a bona fide contest about legal matters exists, it is generally adequate to disclose the dispute and possible consequences without predicting the outcome. However, it may be misleading to imply that a valid defense or genuine dispute exists when there is none. For example, *Gearhart Industries, Incorporated v. Smith International, Incorporated,*[47] held that where the company admitted liability in a lawsuit and thus the only issue remaining was the amount of damages, it was misleading to state that the company and its counsel believe that meritorious defenses exist. The court did state, though, that the company was not obligated to predict the amount of damages.

Motive and purpose. It is generally recognized that the antifraud rules of the federal securities laws do not compel disclosure of motive, purpose or reasons for actions taken, even if they are impure. Similarly, disclosure is typically not required that a transaction has no proper corporate purpose.[48]

However, the SEC has occasionally alleged successfully that disclosure was inadequate because, in part, motives were not disclosed. For example, the SEC has prevailed in arguing improper lack of disclosure that the purpose of a transaction was to enable the principal shareholder to discharge his per-

---

45. Revlon, Inc., SEC Rel. No. 34-23, 320, Fed. Sec. L. Rep. CCH ¶84,006 (June 25, 1986).

46. E.g., Schedule 13D, Item 4; Schedule 13E-3, Item 5; and Schedule 14D, Item 5.

47. 592 F. Supp. 203 (N.D. Tex.), aff'd in part and modified in part, vacated in part on other grounds, 741 F.2d 707 (5th Cir. 1984).

48. Panter v. Marshall Fields & Co., 646 F.2d 271 (7th Cir.), cert. denied, 454 U.S. 1092 (1981); Warner Communications, Inc. v. Murdock, 581 F. Supp. 1482 (D. Del. 1984).

521

sonal debts[49] or to interpose antitrust obstacles to a takeover bid.[50]

Where a motive or purpose is voluntarily disclosed, plaintiffs have been unsuccessful in alleging that the disclosure was improper because the real or true motive was not disclosed. It is generally not necessary to rank or quantify the significance of multiple reasons.[51]

Social goals. Over the last twenty years, the SEC has maintained a continuing program intended to require sufficient disclosures to permit public interest groups and others to make socially responsible investment decisions. For example, all environmental proceedings brought by governmental authorities must be disclosed in various SEC disclosure documents.[52] Likewise, if a corporation has an environmental policy which is reasonably likely to result in fines, penalties or significant effects on the corporation, a disclosure regarding the possibility of such fines, penalties or effects may be necessary in order to prevent misleading disclosures.[53]

The SEC, though, has declined to adopt broader proposals which would require interim disclosure of activity or events which may have an impact upon the environment.[54] Likewise, the SEC has not required disclosure under the proxy rules of a company's general health and safety program.[55]

With respect to labor matters, a New York District Court has held that the failure expressly to disclose in proxy materials that director nominees participated in a concerted effort to thwart the labor laws and failed to perform their responsi-

---

49. SEC v. Parklane Hosiery Co., 558 F.2d 1083 (2d Cir. 1977).

50. SEC v. Royal Indus., Inc., Fed. Sec. L. Rep. CCH ¶95,773 (D.D.C. Nov. 16, 1976).

51. Kademian v. Ladish Co., 792 F.2d 614 (7th Cir. 1986); Panter v. Marshall Fields & Co., supra note 48.

52. Securities Act Rel. No. 33-6130; Exchange Act Rel. No. 34-16224, Fed. Sec. L. Rep. CCH ¶23,507B (Sept. 27, 1979).

53. Id.

54. Securities Act Rel. No. 33-5704 (May 6, 1976).

55. General Dynamics Corp., Fed. Sec. L. Rep. CCH ¶76,372 (Feb. 25, 1980).

bility to ensure that the company management did not engage in such conduct did not violate the proxy rules.[56] In so holding, the court found such information related to management's business judgment and that "the proxy rules simply do not require management to accuse itself of antisocial or illegal policies."

§ 16.05. Disclosure of merger negotiations.

One of the most important and confusing issues of disclosure involves when and how a publicly held company must disclose to investors that discussions are under way that may lead to a corporate merger. Premature disclosure may jeopardize the negotiation of the transaction; delinquent disclosure may subject the company and its directors and officers to enormous liability exposure. This dilemma has been recognized by courts:

> Such [merger] negotiations are inherently fluid and the eventual outcome is shrouded in uncertainty. Disclosure may in fact be more misleading than secrecy so far as investment decisions are concerned. We are not confronted here with a failure to disclose hard facts which definitely affect a company's financial prospects. Rather, we deal with complex bargaining between two (and often more) parties which may fail as well as succeed, or may succeed on terms which vary greatly from those under consideration at the suggested time of disclosure. We have no doubt that had Pan Am disclosed the existence of negotiations on August 15 and had those negotiations failed, we would have been asked to decide a section [sic] 10b-5 action challenging that disclosure.[57]

In 1988, the Supreme Court added some clarity to the applicable guidelines in the area. In *Basic, Inc. v. Levison,*[58] the Court reviewed and remanded a Sixth Circuit ruling that

---

56. Amalgamated Clothing & Textile Workers Union, AFL-CIO v. J.P. Stevens & Co., 475 F. Supp. 328 (S.D.N.Y. 1979), vacated and remanded on other grounds, 638 F.2d 7 (2d Cir. 1980).

57. Reiss v. Pan Am. World Airways, 711 F.2d 11, 14 (2d Cir. 1983).

58. 108 S.Ct. 978 (1988).

Basic, Inc. had violated Rule 10b-5 by making public statements that Basic was unaware of any present or pending developments that would account for the high volume of trading and price fluctuations of its stock on the New York Stock Exchange (NYSE).

At the time of these announcements, executives of Basic and Combustion Engineering, Inc. were engaged in a series of meetings, telephone calls, and exchanges of information about the possible acquisition of Basic by Combustion.

Contacts between a Combustion vice president and the chairman of Basic had begun as early as September, 1976, and in January, 1977, the Basic chairman informed the company's board of directors of the discussions. In October, 1977, Basic retained an investment banker to prepare an evaluation of the company for use in merger negotiations.

Shortly thereafter, the price and trading volume of Basic stock ran up, and Basic issued a press release denying that merger negotiations were under way. The company rumored to be acquiring Basic at that time was, however, a company other than Combustion.

In negotiations in June, 1978, Combustion suggested a price of $28 per share, which Basic rejected as too low. In September, a representative of Basic, responding to NYSE inquiries about the possible cause of the unusual trading activity in its stock, said that the company was unaware of any development that would spur such active trading. In early November, Basic included a similar statement in its nine-month report to shareholders.

On November 27, 1978, Combustion proposed a price of $35, which Basic again rejected as too low. On December 18, Basic requested a halt to trading in its shares and, on December 19, announced it had agreed with Combustion to be acquired at a price of $46 per share.

The Sixth Circuit held that even if these preliminary merger negotiations were in themselves immaterial under the securities laws, they became material by virtue of Basic's statement denying their existence and of the company's knowing what caused the unusual market activity.

The court emphasized the disclosure duty as being one of speaking truthfully once the company chooses to speak. Although the company had the discretion of speaking or not speaking with regard to preliminary merger discussions, once it spoke it was required to speak truthfully.

Other courts had reached the opposite result. For example, the Third Circuit under virtually the same fact pattern ruled that the company acted properly by announcing during merger negotiations that it knew of no reason for unusual market activity in its stock.[59] The court held that as a matter of law merger discussions are not material until the companies have agreed on the price and structure of the proposed transaction.

The SEC indicated that in appropriate circumstances a company may give a "no comment" response to press inquiries concerning preliminary merger discussions, though a "no developments" response at a time when the company is engaged in preliminary negotiations may be misleading.[60]

These conflicting standards of materiality were reviewed by the Supreme Court in the *Basic* case, where the Court declined to adopt a bright-line rule concerning the disclosure of preliminary merger negotiations. Instead, the Court adopted a case-by-case analysis which requires a company and its management to weigh the probability that a merger will occur and the magnitude of the effects of such a merger on the companies involved. According to the court, when assessing the probability that the merger will occur, it is appropriate to examine the interest in the transaction "at the highest corporate levels," as evidenced by board resolutions, instructions to investment bankers, actual negotiations, and the like. To assess the magnitude of the effects of the merger, the Court cited the need to consider such facts as the size of the companies involved and the potential premium over mar-

---

59. Greenfield v. Heublein, 742 F.2d 751 (3d Cir. 1984), cert. denied, 469 U.S. 1215 (1985).

60. In re Carnation Co., SEC Rel. No. 34-22214, Fed. Sec. L. Rep. CCH ¶83,810 (July 8, 1985).

ket value, although no particular event or factor short of closing the transaction necessarily renders the merger discussions material.

The *Basic* decision is consistent with classic materiality analysis and is intended to fulfill the federal securities law's fundamental purpose of full disclosure. However, more so than in many other areas of disclosure, the decision may place directors and officers in a difficult disclosure dilemma of either premature or delinquent disclosure of merger negotiations. As the Court noted, though, "the comfort of corporate managers" was an insufficient reason for it to adopt bright-line rules concerning what is and is not material.

The Court did recognize the possibility that a "no comment" statement may be an appropriate response to questions. Under some circumstances, though, a company may not be permitted simply to provide the neutral "no comment" response. For example, if a company has a policy of truthfully denying merger rumors when no discussions are underway, the issuance of a "no comment" statement when it is in the midst of negotiations may be tantamount to an admission that merger discussions are underway and thus further disclosure may be necessary. Also stock exchange rules[61] require a listed company to explain unusual market activities if it appears that information on pending developments has leaked out. A response of "no comment" to the likely inquiry from an exchange concerning unusual market activity will not satisfy the exchange's requirements. Thus, the company may be under considerable pressure either to say inaccurately that there has been no development that explains the market activity or to announce prematurely the existence of negotiations.

§ 16.06. Insider trading — Background.

The misuse by corporate insiders and others of material, undisclosed information has been the source of growing con-

---

61. New York Stock Exchange Rules 202.03 and 401.

cern and attention in recent years. Few other areas of D&O liability have received as much collective attention from courts, regulators, Congress, and the public media as "insider trading." Fueled at least in part by the explosion in the frequency and size of tender offers, a widespread perception has been created that stock trading based upon nonpublic information is common.

In response to this perceived threat to the integrity of the stock market system, the SEC has made insider trading an enforcement priority. The number and sophistication of SEC investigations and proceedings in this area have increased dramatically. The highly publicized cases involving Ivan Boesky and others demonstrate the vigor of the SEC and the United States Attorney's Office in this area.

The state of the law involving insider trading is currently in flux. Case law is continuing to refine and question the definition of insider trading and the scope of prohibited transactions, Congress is evaluating the sufficiency of and considering modifications to existing statutes in the area and some commentators[62] are questioning what, if any, harm is caused by insider trading.

No statutory definition of "insider trading" currently exists. Instead, Congress has allowed the SEC and the judicial system to oversee the evolution of a definition.[63] However, sentiment appears to be shifting in favor of adopting a statutory definition.[64] Even absent such a definition, it is clear that "trading while in possession of material nonpublic information" is a minimum prerequisite for an insider trading case.[65] The concept of materiality is discussed in

---

62. Carlton & Fischel, "The Regulation of Insider Trading," 35 Stan. L. Rev. 857, 879 (1983).

63. See "The Insider Trading Sanctions Act of 1984: Hearing Before the Subcomm. on Securities of the Comm. on Banking, Housing and Urban Affairs," 98th Cong., 2d Sess. 35-37 (Apr. 3, 1984).

64. See, e.g., S. 1380, 100th Cong., 1st Sess.

65. 130 Cong. Rec. S. 8912 (daily ed. June 29, 1984) (remarks of Sen. D'Amato).

other portions of this text.[66] "Nonpublic" information is information not generally available to ordinary investors in the marketplace.[67]

The following list of information is exemplary of the types of information that could be material and thus if not disclosed to the trading public could give rise to an insider trading allegation if directors or officers trade in securities while in possession of this information:

- stock splits or stock dividends;
- changes in management or control;
- financial results for the company or a major division;
- bankruptcy proceedings;
- increase or decrease in dividends;
- public offerings or private sales of debt or equity securities;
- significant merger or acquisition proposals or agreements;
- significant new products or discoveries;
- significant litigation or disputes with customers, suppliers or contractors;
- governmental investigations;
- joint ventures; and any other event requiring the filing of a current report under the Securities Exchange Act.

Prior to the enactment of the federal securities laws, there generally existed no prohibition against directors, officers and other insiders trading in the stock of their corporation. As a result of the federal securities laws and the many cases interpreting those laws, there now exists six theories under which corporate insiders may be liable for insider trading:

    (1) Corporate insiders who trade in securities of the corporation while in possession of material nonpublic

---

66. See supra section 16.03.

67. Investors Mgt. Co., Inc., 44 S.E.C. 633, 643 (1971). See also Dirks v. SEC, 463 U.S. 646, 653 n.12 (1983).

information may be liable pursuant to the antifraud provisions of the federal securities laws.[68]

(2) Corporate directors, officers and 10% beneficial owners who purchase and sell stock within a six-month period must disgorge all profits under Section 16(b) of the 1934 Act whether or not they knew of material nonpublic information.[69]

(3) Corporate insiders who trade in securities of other corporations while in possession of inside information which relates to a tender offer and the insider knew or should have known that the information came from the target, the offeror or agents of either the target or the offeror may be liable under Rule 14e-3.[70]

(4) Corporate insiders may be liable under the misappropriation theory because they violated a duty to their corporation by using information obtained in the course of their employment for personal gain.[71]

(5) Corporate insiders may be liable under the mail and wire fraud statutes as depriving another of money or property by means of false or fraudulent pretenses, representations or promises.[71a]

(6) Corporate insiders may be liable under the tipper/tippee theory of liability.[72]

Regardless of the legal theory used, the fundamental objection to insider trading arises from the insider's access and conversion to personal benefit of information intended to be available only for a corporate purpose and from the perceived unfairness of allowing an insider to take advantage of that information knowing it is unavailable to the investing public. The SEC has recognized that "a significant purpose of the Exchange Act was to eliminate the idea that the use of in-

---

68. See infra section 16.07.
69. See supra section 14.09.
70. 17 C.F.R. 240.14e-3. See infra section 16.07.
71. See infra section 16.07.
71a. See infra section 16.07.
72. See infra section 16.08.

sider information for personal advantage was a normal emolument of corporate office."[73]

§ 16.07. Insider trading — Theories of liability.

Liability for insider trading under Rule 10b-5 and other antifraud provisions of the federal securities laws is premised on two principal theories: the "disclose or abstain" and the "misappropriation" theories. Originally recognized in *In re Cady, Roberts & Company*,[74] the disclose or abstain rule was adopted by the Supreme Court in *Chiarella v. United States*,[75] where the court quoted with approval from *Cady, Roberts & Company*:

> An affirmative duty to disclose material information has been traditionally imposed on corporate "insiders," particularly officers, directors, or controlling stockholders. [The SEC] and the courts have consistently held that insiders must disclose material facts which are known to ... persons with whom they deal and which, if known, would affect their investment judgment.[76]

If disclosure would be "improper or unrealistic," the "alternative is to forego the transaction."[77]

However, the SEC did not prevail in the *Chiarella* case. The Court held that the person misusing the inside information owed no duty to disclose the information.

Mr. Chiarella was a printer's employee. He deciphered the identity of five public companies that were to be the targets of acquisition efforts by other companies. He gleaned his knowledge from confidential financial documents entrusted to his employer for printing. By using the nonpublic inside information, Chiarella entered into seventeen pre-announcement stock transactions, realizing a $30,000 profit. He did not induce any trades, make any affirmative statements or have

---

73. In re Cady, Roberts & Co., 40 S.E.C. 907 (1961).
74. Id.
75. 445 U.S. 222, 63 L.Ed.2d 348, 100 S.Ct. 1108 (1980).
76. Id., 445 U.S. at 227.
77. In re Cady, Roberts & Co., supra note 73, at 911.

any contact with the target company shareholders from whom he purchased the stock. After being discovered, Chiarella disgorged all his profits and was subsequently convicted of securities fraud.

The Supreme Court reversed the conviction and held that an outsider who fails to disclose material nonpublic information prior to the consummation of a securities transaction violates Rule 10b-5 only if he is under an independent duty to disclose such information. Such a duty to disclose arises, according to the Court, only if the person is an insider, a fiduciary or a person having "a relationship of trust and confidence" with the parties to the transaction.[78] The Court refused to endorse a generic duty under Rule 10b-5 to the securities marketplace or to conclude that all instances of unequal access to, or all unfair or undisclosed uses of material nonpublic information are necessarily unlawful. Rather, the Court adopted the common-law principle that a special relationship must exist before a duty to disclose inside information arises.

In cases dealing with misuse of inside information by outsiders since *Chiarella,* the requisite special relationship has been asserted in transactions involving attorneys for the corporation,[79] broker-dealers who were acting as managers of the corporation's tender offer,[80] and employees (and their co-conspirators) of an investment banking firm which obtained confidential, nonpublic information concerning possible

---

78. Chiarella v. United States, supra note 75, 445 U.S. at 230.

79. United States v. Hall, No. 80 Cr. 692 (S.D.N.Y. 1980) (attorney, who purchased stock of certain of his clients prior to the public announcements of acquisitions and material corporate transactions, entered a guilty plea to a securities fraud criminal action, thereby apparently becoming the first person ever convicted (other than Chiarella whose conviction was reversed) for using inside information to trade in securities).

80. SEC v. Roussel, Fed. Sec. L. Rep. CCH ¶97,531 (D. Kan. 1980) (broker-dealer violated Rule 10b-5 when it purchased target company stockholder's shares in open market while acting at the same time as manager of the tender offer and failing to inform sellers that shares purchased would be immediately resold to the bidder at premium).

mergers, acquisitions and tender offers.[81] With regard to attorneys, the SEC, in a litigation release concerning partners and associates of a patent law firm who consented to disgorging all the profits which they had realized from transactions entered into while in possession of material nonpublic information relating to the allowance of a patent claim by the United States Patent Office, emphasized "its concern with respect to the use of material nonpublic information by partners, associates and employees of law firms."[82]

The *Chiarella* decision represented a significant erosion of the "disclose or abstain" rule for many outsiders, although the rule remained clearly applicable to directors, officers and other insiders trading in the securities of their corporation. Accordingly, the SEC began pursuing a refined theory of liability for those outsiders who under the *Chiarella* decision escaped the prohibitions against insider trading — the "misappropriation" theory. This theory is based on the legal premise that one who misappropriates someone else's information, converts it to his or her own personal use and trades on that information violates Rule 10b-5.

The misappropriation theory was first successfully utilized in *United States v. Newman*.[83] The Second Circuit held that a charge of criminal liability under Section 10(b) could be maintained against a trader for misuse of confidential information in connection with trading in the stock of various companies involved in takeovers and mergers. The court reasoned that under the federal securities laws, as "[i]n other areas of the law, deceitful misappropriation of confidential information by a fiduciary, whether described as theft, conversion, or breach of trust, has consistently been held to be

---

81. Moss v. Morgan Stanley, Inc., 719 F.2d 5 (2d Cir.) cert. denied, 104 S.Ct. 1280 (1983). The court addressed a question left unresolved in Chiarella and held that the trader who obtained the insider information owed no duty to the acquiring companies which would support a conviction under Rule 10b-5.

82. SEC v. Lerner, David, Littenberg & Samuel, Litig. Rel. No. 9049 (D.D.C. 1980), 19 SEC Docket 1153 (Apr. 15, 1980).

83. 664 F.2d 12 (2d Cir. 1981), cert. denied, 464 U.S. 863 (1983).

unlawful."[84] Accordingly, the court approved the maintenance of a criminal action under Section 10(b) where the indictment showed a breach of an employee's duty of trust to his employer and the employer's clients, even though there was no duty owed to the persons with whom the person traded.

The Supreme Court recently considered a case which tested the viability and contours of the misappropriation theory.[85] In this case, the lower court decisions applied the misappropriation theory to corporate outsiders. Mr. Winans, a writer for the Wall Street Journal, wrote a column entitled "Heard on the Street," which reported on current corporate developments. The lower courts found that these reports often had an effect on the price of the securities of the corporations discussed in the column. The Journal did not use any confidential information directly obtained from the companies, but had a policy not to reveal the identity of the companies to be discussed in the column prior to publication and not to trade on the basis of pending stories. The lower courts found that Winans knew of this policy, yet violated it by disclosing the identities of corporations to be discussed to a stockbroker, who traded on this information a number of times.

The Second Circuit upheld Winans' conviction and ruled that the antifraud provisions of the federal securities laws:

> proscribe an employee's unlawful misappropriation from his employer, a financial newspaper, of material nonpublic information ... in connection with a scheme to purchase and sell securities to be analyzed or otherwise discussed in future columns in that newspaper.[86]

The Supreme Court was evenly divided four-to-four with respect to whether Winans' conviction under the securities laws based upon the misappropriation theory was proper. Ac-

---

84. Id. at 18.

85. United States v. Winans, 612 F. Supp. 827 (S.D.N.Y. 1985), aff'd in part and rev'd in part sub nom. United States v. Carpenter, 791 F.2d 1024 (2d Cir. 1986), aff'd, 108 S.Ct. 316 (1987).

86. Id., 791 F.2d 1024, 1026.

cordingly, lower courts may continue to adopt that theory in future insider trading cases.

More importantly, the Supreme Court unanimously affirmed Winans' conviction based upon violations of the mail and wire fraud statutes. The Court found those statutes applicable to any scheme to deprive another of money or property by means of false or fraudulent pretenses, representations or promises, including injuring another's property rights by dishonest methods, trick, deceit, chicane or overreaching. The Court rejected an argument that the mail and wire fraud statutes require a monetary loss, noting instead that "it is sufficient that the Journal has been deprived of its right to exclusive use of the information, for exclusivity is an important aspect of confidential business information and most private property for that matter."

The Court delivered a clear and unequivocal message to directors, officers and others who seek to misappropriate material nonpublic information for their own benefit by quoting with approval from the New York Supreme Court:

> It is well established, as a general proposition, that a person who acquires special knowledge or information by virtue of a confidential or fiduciary relationship with another is not free to exploit that knowledge or information for his own personal benefit but must account to his principal for any profits derived therefrom.[87]

In addition to endorsing the SEC efforts to curb insider trading, the Supreme Court decision also appears to have indirectly endorsed the imposition of treble damages upon an insider trader. It appears likely that most insider trading cases will now be based primarily upon violations of the mail and wire fraud statutes, which are also indictable offenses under RICO. Accordingly, the treble damage award under the RICO statute may be sought with increasing frequency against insider traders.

---

87. Id., 108 S.Ct. at 321, quoting from Diamond v. Oreamuno, 24 N.Y.2d 494, 497, 248 N.E.2d 910, 912 (1969).

Although liability of corporate insiders for trading in their own corporation's securities while in possession of material inside information clearly exists without reliance on the broader "misappropriation" theory or the mail and wire fraud statutes, these more expansive theories will create additional potential liability for directors and officers. For example, corporate executives in the ordinary course of business frequently learn of material nonpublic information about another corporation. Depending on the circumstances, those corporate executives may be liable if they trade in the other corporation's stock while in possession of that information.

Insider trading liability in the tender offer context has been a particularly acute concern of the SEC. As a result, the SEC has adopted Rule 14e-3 under Section 14(e) of the 1934 Act. Generally, the rule establishes a "disclose or abstain from trading" duty for any person or his tippee who possesses material information relating to a tender offer if the person or his tippee knows or has reason to know that the information is nonpublic and was received directly or indirectly from the offeror, the subject corporation, any of their affiliated persons, or any person acting on behalf of either company. In its release adopting the rule, the Commission asserted that trading by persons "who unlawfully obtain or misappropriate material, nonpublic information violates Rule 10b-5 when they trade on such information" and that "no inference" should be drawn concerning the application of Rule 10b-5 to situations covered by Rule 14e-3.[88]

§ 16.08. Insider trading — Liability of tipper.

Not only are insiders and others forbidden to use undisclosed corporate information to their own advantage, but they may not give such information to an outsider for the purpose of exploiting the information for personal gain. A "tipper" is a person who divulges such information; a "tippee" is one who receives such information.

---

88. Securities and Exchange Act Rel. No. 17120 (Sept. 4, 1980), 20 SEC Docket 1242 (Sept. 16, 1980).

The Supreme Court has clearly recognized that a corporate insider may be personally liable as a tipper even if the insider does not personally trade in the securities.[89] To be so liable, the insider must breach a fiduciary duty to shareholders by personally benefiting, either directly or indirectly, from his disclosure. Such a test promises to yield unpredictable, case-by-case results, although the Supreme Court in *Dirks* attempted to illustrate situations where objective facts and circumstances justify an inference of personal gain:

> For example, there may be a relationship between the insider and the recipient that suggests a quid pro quo from the latter, or an intention to benefit the particular recipient. The elements of fiduciary duty and exploitation of nonpublic information also exist when an insider makes a gift of confidential information to a trading relative or friend. The tip and trade resemble trading by the insider himself followed by a gift of the profits to the recipient.[90]

The requisite personal benefit realized by the tipper need not be limited to financial profit. For example, it has been held that the revealing of inside information to a friend and professional colleague bestowed a "reputational benefit" on the tipper and, therefore, the requisite personal gain was present.[91]

Though the tipping of material information is a violation of the insider's fiduciary duty, no injury occurs until the information is used by the tippee. A tippee's entry into the market with superior knowledge poses the threat that the tippee may profit at the expense of investors who are disadvantaged by not having the inside information. In the case of such a violation, both the tipper and the tippee are liable. If, on the other hand, the insider and the tippee choose not to trade, no injury

---

89. Chiarella v. United States, 445 U.S. 222, 63 L.Ed.2d 348, 100 S.Ct. 1108 (1980); Dirks v. SEC, 463 U.S. 646, 77 L.Ed.2d 911, 103 S.Ct. 3255 (1983).

90. Dirks v. SEC, supra note 89, 103 S.Ct. at 3266.

91. SEC v. Gaspar, Fed. Sec. L. Rep. CCH ¶92,004 (S.D.N.Y. 1985).

may be claimed by outside investors since the public has no right to the undisclosed information.

§ 16.09. Insider trading — Civil liability.

Due to the impersonal nature of stock transactions through an organized stock exchange, shareholders rarely allege or successfully recover damages from an insider who traded while in possession of material, nonpublic information. Instead, the SEC traditionally has been the primary party to sue for insider trading violations. However, in response to the increased publicity and detection of improper insider trading activity, there has been an increase in the number of civil lawsuits filed against insiders by shareholders, the corporation and other injured parties. The law in this area is currently unsettled, although initial case authority suggests this area could become a source of significant personal liability exposure for those who misuse business information.

Shareholders are frequently denied the right to recover directly from directors and officers of the corporation for insider trading because the standing and causation elements of a Section 10(b) cause of action cannot be satisfied.[92] For example, the plaintiff shareholder must be an actual purchaser or seller of the securities[93] and must prove some connection between the plaintiff's loss and the defendant's actions.[94] This requisite connection is established if the plaintiff shareholder traded contemporaneously with the insider,[95] although separation of the plaintiff's and defendant's trades by as little as seven days has been found to be an insufficient nexus to support causation.[96]

---

92. See generally supra section 14.06.

93. Blue Chip Stamps v. Manor Drug Stores, 421 U.S. 723, 44 L.Ed.2d 539, 95 S.Ct. 1917 (1975).

94. Superintendent of Ins. of N.Y. v. Bankers Life & Cas. Co., 404 U.S. 6, 30 L.Ed.2d 128, 92 S.Ct. 165 (1971).

95. See, e.g., Wilson v. Comtech Telecommunications Corp., 648 F.2d 88, 94-5 (2d Cir. 1981).

96. Kreindler v. Sambo's Restaurants, Inc., Fed. Sec. L. Rep. CCH ¶98,312 (S.D.N.Y. 1981).

A further difficulty arises if the person who misuses the inside information is not an insider to the corporation and therefore may not have a duty to the trading shareholders. The Second Circuit has ruled in *Moss v. Morgan Stanley, Incorporated*[97] that shareholders of a target corporation in a takeover bid may not sue for insider trading violations persons who were involved in representing the acquiring company and persons who obtained confidential information from the acquiring company's financial advisor. The court found the defendants had no special or direct relationship of trust or confidentiality with the target or its shareholders and therefore had no duty of disclosure to the shareholders of the target. However, where the corporate insiders were the source of the material inside information, private standing may exist.[98]

In addition to injured shareholders, others are now bringing suits against insider traders alleging different types of injury. For example, corporations, either directly or derivatively, are now suing their officers, directors and other insiders for trading on material nonpublic information. Several courts have permitted such claims, noting that insider trading causes two distinct harms, one to the trading shareholders and one to the corporation.[99]

One of the primary issues in these cases is what, if any, damages were suffered by the corporation. Courts have suggested the insider trading may cause harm to the corporation's goodwill[100] or reputation.[101] Some of these suits are brought by or on behalf of a corporation which has acquired another corporation and allege that they paid a higher price for the target because the insider trading escalated the mar-

---

97. 719 F.2d 5 (2d Cir. 1983), cert. denied, 465 U.S. 1025 (1984).

98. See, e.g., O'Connor and Assocs. v. Dean Witter Reynolds, 600 F. Supp. 702 (S.D.N.Y. 1985).

99. In re ORFA Sec. Litig., 654 F. Supp. 1449 (D.N.J. 1987). See also Diamond v. Oreamuno, 24 N.Y.2d 494, 248 N.E.2d 910 (1969); Brophy v. Cities Serv. Co., 70 A.2d 5 (Del. 1949).

100. In re ORFA Sec. Litig., supra note 99.

101. Diamond v. Oreamuno, supra note 99.

ket price of the target's stock.[102] If successful, such theories of recovery may result in enormous liability exposure to insider traders.

Another potential plaintiff is a tippee who alleges that insider information disclosed to him or her by the tipper-defendant was false, causing substantial trading losses. An important defense in any such lawsuit is the in pari delicto (of equal fault) defense. Under that doctrine, an action for damages under the federal securities laws may be barred on grounds of the tippee's own culpability where (1) as a direct result of his own actions, the tippee bears at least substantially equal responsibility for the violations he seeks to redress, and (2) preclusion of suit would not significantly interfere with the effective enforcement of the securities laws and protection of the investing public.[103]

The Supreme Court has considered that defense in a suit by a tippee against the tipper and has ruled the defense inapplicable.[104] The Court rejected the contention that an investor who trades on a tip of inside information is necessarily as blameworthy as a corporate insider who discloses the information for personal gain. Absent other culpable actions by a tippee outweighing the tipper's breach of duty, the tippee cannot be characterized as being of substantially equal culpability as his tipper and thus is permitted to sue the tipper for false disclosure.

In a unanimous decision, the Court stated:

> The public interest will most frequently be advanced if defrauded tippees are permitted to bring suit and to expose illegal practices by corporate insiders and broker-dealers to full public view.[105]

Although this case limits the application of the in pari delicto defense, it does not eliminate it totally. The Court did

---

102. See, e.g., FMC Corp. v. Boesky, No. 86-9879, slip op. (N.D. Ill. Apr. 16, 1985).

103. Bateman Eichler, Hill Richards, Inc. v. Berner, 472 U.S. 299, 86 L.Ed.2d 215, 105 S.Ct. 2622 (1985).

104. Id.

105. Id., 105 S.Ct. at 2632.

recognize that situations might arise in which the relative culpabilities of the tippee and his insider source merit application of the defense. For example, in a subsequent district court decision, the defense of in pari delicto was allowed to prevent a powerful financier who instigated a trading scheme from suing a corporate insider for tipping information which led to trading losses.[106] The culpability of the tippee outweighed that of the weak "insider tout" who gave him the information. Barring the tippee from suing also enhanced the purposes of the federal securities laws by "cutting off the transaction at its root."

An area of current uncertainty is the question of when and whether an employer is liable for the insider trading activities of its employee. This issue partially overlaps with issues raised by the misappropriation theory discussed above. Questions concerning scope of employment and adequacy of supervision will touch, ultimately, questions concerning the existence and scope of one's duties as an employee.

§ 16.10. Insider Trading Sanctions Act of 1984.

On August 10, 1984, Congress enacted the Insider Trading Sanctions Act,[107] in response to congressional perception that insider trading activity was increasing, that existing remedies did not have sufficient deterrent effect, and that the SEC's remedial powers should be supplemented. The express purpose of the Sanctions Act is "to increase the sanctions against trading in securities while in the possession of material nonpublic information."[108]

The Sanctions Act amended Section 21(d) of the 1934 Act to provide the SEC with the authority to seek a penalty against (1) any person who purchases or sells securities while in pos-

---

106. Rothberg v. Rosenbloom, 628 F. Supp. 746 (E.D. Pa. 1986).

107. Pub. L. 98-376, 98 Stat. 1264 (1984).

108. Preamble to the Sanctions Act, Pub. L. 98-376, 98 Stat. 1264 (1984) (codified as amended in scattered sections of 15 U.S.C. § 78); see also H.R. Rep. No. 355, 98th Cong., 2d Sess., reprinted in U.S. Code Cong. & Admin. News 2274, 2275.

session of material nonpublic information in violation of the 1934 Act or the rules promulgated thereunder; and (2) any person who, by communicating material nonpublic information to such other person, aids and abets another in the purchase or sale of securities while in possession of material nonpublic information (i.e. tippers).

The authorized penalty may be up to "three times the profit gained or loss avoided" as a result of insider trading, measured by "the difference between the purchase or sale price of the security and the value of that security as measured by the trading price of the security a reasonable period after public dissemination of the nonpublic information."[109] The penalty is to be determined "in light of the facts and circumstances ... and shall be payable into the Treasury of the United States."[110]

Before the Sanctions Act was passed, the SEC could only seek disgorgement of the profits gained by insider trading — a wholly unsatisfactory remedy, because it put the trader in the same position as he would have been had he not violated the insider trading laws. The new penalty, which in contrast to disgorgement is a real penalty, was intended to increase significantly the deterrent effect of the insider trading prohibitions.

The Sanctions Act also increases the potential penalty for a criminal violation of the 1934 Act, including insider trading, from $10,000 to $100,000.

To come within the penalty provisions, a transaction must: (1) be on or through the facilities of a national securities exchange or from or through a broker or dealer; and (2) not be part of a public offering by an issuer of securities other than standardized options. A person is not subject to this penalty solely because of having aided and abetted an insider trading violation, unless the person communicated nonpublic information. The penalty cannot be imposed on a person solely for employing or controlling another person who violated the law.

---

109. 15 U.S.C. § 78u(d)(2).
110. Id.

541

The penalty may be used in addition to existing remedies available to the SEC. Thus, the Commission may seek (1) a court order enjoining the violator from breaking the law again; (2) disgorgement of ill-gotten gains which may, if appropriate, be paid into an escrow fund so that traders or other private parties damaged by the insider trading can obtain compensation for their losses; and (3) the imposition of the civil money penalty payable to the United States Treasury.

Although the SEC seeks to invoke these penalty provisions in almost every insider trading case it brings, there is a growing perception in light of the large insider trading scandals reported during 1987 that these penalties still do not create sufficient deterrence. Accordingly, several stricter insider trading bills have been introduced in Congress which, among other things, will increase the maximum penalty significantly. It appears likely some new legislation in this area is imminent.

§ 16.11. Compliance programs.

The need for comprehensive procedures to prevent leaks of confidential information and trading on the basis of material nonpublic information is of paramount importance. The installation of preventive measures will not stop determined wrongdoers from abusing inside information. The procedures will, however, educate and guide the vast majority of employees on avoiding illegal conduct.

If problems occur notwithstanding a corporation's reasonable efforts to prevent them, the fact that the corporation had in place well-designed policies and procedures and enforced them with appropriate vigor may prevent the corporation and its management from being charged with wrongdoing or at least mitigate the severity of sanctions imposed.[111] If no compliance program is in place and problems occur, the corporation may have to adopt procedures and restrictions in settling an enforcement action that would be much more onerous and

---

111. See, e.g., SEC v. Lum's Inc., 365 F. Supp. 1046 (S.D.N.Y. 1973); SEC v. Geon Indus., Inc., 531 F.2d 39 (2d Cir. 1976).

unwieldy than the procedures the corporation might have devised for itself in advance as a preventive measure, without the SEC's assistance.

The SEC has stated that education is "at the heart of an effective compliance program." All corporations should have strong and explicit policies and guidelines to (1) restrict access to and disclosure of material nonpublic information, and (2) restrict trading. Punishment for an employee who violates these policies and guidelines should be swift and certain.

These policies and guidelines may, among other things:

(1) Describe the legal liabilities, ethical obligations and appearance of impropriety affecting the corporation and its employees.

(2) Define "nonpublic" and "material" information.

(3) Prohibit employees from trading in the company's securities while in possession of material nonpublic information.

(4) Prohibit employees from trading in the company's securities except during specified periods such as following the mailing of the annual report or except through an established program administered by a broker pursuant to which the timing of purchases is outside the control of the officer or director.

(5) Prohibit employees from trading in securities of corporations with which the company is negotiating.

(6) Prohibit employees from trading in puts and calls and other short term trading in the company's securities.

(7) Adopt approval and reporting procedures for all trading.

(8) Prohibit employees from disclosing in any manner any nonpublic information concerning the company, including disclosure to personal or social friends.

(9) Limit the access of material nonpublic information by physically labeling it as "confidential" and by using sign-out sheets, lock-up procedures and restricted access areas.

543

(10) Prohibit employees from recommending or express-
ing any opinion as to trading in the company's securities.

(11) Designate an individual or department with the
company to handle all inquiries from analysts,
stockbrokers, investment advisors, the public media
or others.

The policies and guidelines should be clearly set forth in a
written statement or manual which is circulated to all personnel. Each employee, including all new employees, should
sign a statement acknowledging their understanding of the
corporate policy and agreeing to abide by it. The company
should periodically review and update this statement or manual in view of new legal developments. Any updated material
should be redistributed to and recertified by each employee.

§ 16.12. Directors as policemen of business information.

Director and officer liability for nondisclosure of material
information has been significantly altered in recent years.
Based upon growing pressure from both the public and private sector, the SEC has at least started to divest itself in
certain areas of the role as chief "policeman" for securities
law compliance and has placed much of the burden of that
role on a company's officers and directors. This role shifting
will undoubtedly result in directors and officers spending
more time in the courtroom, since not only have their legal
responsibilities increased, but shareholder expectations have
also been increased.

Perhaps the most significant development in this context is
the new requirement that a majority of directors sign a company's Form 10-K, the annual report of the company's activities which is filed with the SEC.[112] Previously, only a top
officer of the company needed to sign the report. This new
signature requirement could have a substantial impact on

---

112. Securities Exchange Act Rel. No. 17114, Securities Act Rel. No.
6231, Fed. Sec. L. Rep. CCH ¶72,301 (Sept. 2, 1980).

director liability not only to the SEC, but also to share-holders. A director who signs the Form 10-K should make a meaningful effort to understand, verify and approve the contents of the report, because if the report contains material misstatements or omissions, the director signing it may incur personal liability. Whether the SEC, shareholders, or the courts will actively pursue this new offensive weapon against directors is yet to be seen.

The SEC has also shifted its focus from Form 10-K to the shareholder's annual report as the major disclosure document under the Securities Exchange Act.[113] As a result of this shift, increased disclosures, primarily in the areas of financial information and management's prospective discussion of the company's financial condition, are required in the annual report to shareholders.[114] In addition, as part of its comprehensive proxy review program, the SEC has adopted numerous additional disclosure requirements for proxy statements, including requirements for disclosure of certain relationships and transactions involving management and of compensation for executive officers and directors.[115] The SEC is also actively promoting the integration of Form 10-K with the annual report to shareholders, thereby permitting companies to prepare only one document to be used for both purposes.[116] Although intended to reduce the burden of disclosure, these changes may result in increased liabilities for officers and directors to shareholders, because the form of the shareholder's annual report and proxy statements may be more technical, boilerplate and "unreadable," thereby causing more confusion and less meaningful disclosure to the shareholders.

In 1982, the SEC implemented the "final stage" of its ongoing project to integrate the disclosure provisions of the 1933

---

113. Id.

114. Id.

115. Securities Act Rel. Nos. 33-6441 and 33-6486, Fed. Sec. L. Rep. CCH ¶¶83,281 (Dec. 2, 1982) and 83,425 (Sept. 23, 1983).

116. Supra note 112.

Act with those of the 1934 Act by adopting new registration statement forms which rely heavily on the issuer's period reports required by the 1934 Act.[117] Previously, as part of that project, the SEC had issued numerous releases which, among other things, created an optional short form registration in certain business combination transactions, proposed a new three-tier registration system based on the size and history of the issuer and the extent of trading in the subject securities, and integrated the registration of securities offered through employee plans with reports filed under the 1934 Act.[118]

The SEC further reduced the disclosure requirements for certain issues of securities by adopting Regulation D, which provides for an exemption from registration for the issuance of securities in certain small or limited issuances.[119]

A procedure has been adopted by the SEC to permit persons disclosing information to it to protect the confidentiality of certain sensitive information.[120] Pursuant to this procedure, a person submitting information to the SEC may request that such information not be disclosed in response to a Freedom of Information Act request.

These developments indicate that the SEC has recognized the onerous, if not abusive nature of many federal securities law disclosure requirements and evidence an intent by the SEC at least partially to relieve companies and their management of some of the disclosure burdens without decreasing the information provided to shareholders.

A major approach taken by the SEC to accomplish this is to recognize and encourage incorporating by reference materials

---

117. Forms S-2 and S-3, Rel. No. 33-6383, Fed. Sec. L. Rep. (CCH) ¶72,328 (May 24, 1982).

118. SEC Rel. Nos. 33-6231, 33-6233, 33-6234, Fed. Sec. L. Rep. (CCH) ¶¶72,301, 72,302 and 72,303, respectively (Sept. 2, 1980); SEC Rel. Nos. 33-6232, 33-6235, 33-6236, Fed. Sec. L. Rep. (CCH) ¶¶82,648, 82,649 and 82,650, respectively (Sept. 2, 1980); SEC Rel. No. 33-6202, Fed. Sec. L. Rep. (CCH) ¶82,486 (Apr. 2, 1980).

119. 17 C.F.R. §§ 230.501-230.506.

120. SEC Rel. No. 33-6241, Fed. Sec. L. Rep. (CCH) ¶82,652 (Sept. 12, 1980).

from one disclosure document to another disclosure document. Use of incorporation by reference creates several new liability issues for directors and officers.

    (1) What obligation is there to reiterate or summarize in an incorporating document matters which were disclosed in the incorporated document?

    (2) What obligation is there to update matters previously disclosed in the incorporated document?

    (3) What obligation is there to disclose matters not disclosed in that incorporated document, but which, as a result of subsequent events, should not be disclosed?

    (4) Is the person who actively prepared the incorporated document considered to be an active preparer of the incorporating document?

    (5) Does Section 11 of the Securities Act, which establishes a reasonably precise delineation of the duties of various classes of corporate participants in the preparation of disclosure documents under the Act, apply to the preparation of documents under the Exchange Act which are incorporated into a Securities Act document?

If incorporation by reference is to serve a meaningful role in reducing the burden of information disclosure, the classic materiality test and other traditional securities law principles may not be totally appropriate in resolving these issues.

COROLLARY REFERENCES

Bagby, "The Evolving Controversy Over Insider Trading," 24 Am. Bus. L.J. 571 (1987).

Bagby & Ruhnka, "The Obligation to Disclose Business Plans Under Extraordinary and Adverse Conditions," 15 Sec. Reg. L.J. 69 (1987).

Bainbridge, "The Insider Trading Prohibition: A Legal and Economic Enigma," 38 U. Fla. L. Rev. 35 (1986).

Bough, "Directors' Accounting Duties," 447 J. Bus. L. (1985).

Cottrell, "Insider Dealing in the United States: The Law, The Cases, The De-Regulation Issue," 136 New L.J. 88-90, 112-14, 150-2 (1986).

Cox, "Insider Trading and Contracting: A Critical Response to the 'Chicago School,'" 1986 Duke L.J. 628.

Fulton, "Barricades to Insider Trading," 7 Cal. Law. 28 (1987).

Janvey, "SEC Investigation of Insider Trading," 13 Sec. Reg. L.J. 299 (1986).

Kripke, "The SEC and Corporate Disclosure," Law and Business, Inc., New York, 1979, reviewed in 35 Bus. Law. 655 (1980).

Longstreth, "SEC Disclosure Policy Regarding Management Integrity," 38 Bus. Law. 1413 (1983).

Olson & Wheat, "Disclosure Problems of Troubled Companies," 14 Inst. on Sec. Reg. 135 (1983).

Seligman, "The Reformulation of Federal Securities Law Concerning Non-public Information," 73 Geo. L.J. 1083 (1985).

Silver, "Penalizing Insider Trading: A Critical Assessment of the Insider Trading Sanctions Act of 1984," 1985 Duke L.J. 960.

"Symposium on Insider Trading," 13 Hofstra L. Rev. (1984).

Note, "In Pari Delicto and Insider Trading: Dead or Alive?," 52 Brooklyn L. Rev. 1169 (1987).

Note, "Insider Trading: Circumventing the Restrictive Contours of the Chiarella and Dirks Decisions," U. Ill. L. Rev. 503 (1985).

Note, "The Insider Trading Sanctions Act of 1984: Did Congress and the SEC Go Home Too Early?," 19 U.C. Davis L. Rev. 497 (1986).

Note, "The SEC and Corporate Disclosure: A Program," 36 Bus. Law. 119 (1980).

Chapter 17
LEGAL REPRESENTATION; CONDUCTING THE DEFENSE

Section

§ 17.01. Selection of defense counsel.

There are various situations involved in the liability of corporate officers and directors where the potential for an attorney's representation of multiple clients may exist. In any such situation, an attorney may not engage in or continue multiple employment unless two conditions are satisfied:

> (1) Each client must consent to the multiple representation after full disclosure of the risks;
> (2) It must be "obvious" that the attorney can adequately represent the interests of each client.[1]

An example of a situation in which the conditions could not be satisfied appeared in a class action against a realtor in which willful wrongdoing was alleged, punitive damages were sought, and the liability insurer offered to defend but told the realtor that the policy's $5,000 deductible clause applied to each member of the class. The Ninth Circuit held:

> This case presents a plain conflict of interest. It is against [realtor's] interest to have the class certified. It is

---

1. Unified Sewerage Agency, Inc. v. Jelco Inc., 640 F.2d 1339, 1345 (9th Cir. 1981); Messing v. FDI, Inc., 439 F. Supp. 776, 781-84 (D.N.J. 1977).

> in [insurer's] best interest to have the class certified be-
> cause [insurer] is claiming a $5,000 deductible for each
> member of the class. Moreover, [insurer's] best interests
> are served by a finding of willful conduct because it thus
> may not be deemed liable. [Realtor] on the other hand,
> could suffer a greater loss by a finding of willful conduct
> because [realtor] would then be liable for punitive dam-
> ages [which were not insurable under California law].[2]

In that case, the insurance company's policy contained a
specific obligation to defend the action, but the court permitted the insured realtor to select his own legal counsel to handle the defense and required the insurer to pay the legal fees
and defense costs.[3]

The D & O policy rarely, if ever, contains any "duty to
defend" provisions, unlike casualty policies generally which
provide for the insurer to select defense counsel, direct the
defense, and pay the legal fees and expenses as they are incurred. Under the D & O policy the insured controls the defense of the action, retains counsel of his choice and directs
the defense. The insurer must be consulted about the selection of counsel and any proposed settlement, but its consent
may not be unreasonably withheld. The D & O policy customarily includes in its definition of the "Loss" to be paid by the
insurer "costs, charges and expenses (excluding salaries of
officers or employees of the [insured]) incurred in the defense
of actions, suits or proceedings and appeals therefrom."[4] That
language has been interpreted as follows:

> By defining litigation expenses as a loss they are subject
> to the exclusions set forth elsewhere in the policy the
> same as any other loss. The policy ... contemplates pay-

---

2. Previews, Inc. v. California Union Ins. Co., 640 F.2d 1026, 1028 (9th
Cir. 1981); Nandorf, Inc. v. CNA Ins. Co., 479 N.E.2d 988 (Ill. App. 1985).

3. Cf. San Diego Navy Fed. Credit Union v. Cumis Ins. Soc'y, Inc., 162
Cal. App. 3d 358, 208 Cal. Rptr. 494 (1984) holding that when an insurer
sends out a reservation of rights letter, the insured has the right to select
defense counsel to be paid by the insurer.

4. See discussion infra Chapter 21.

ment of defense costs as a loss if indemnification is required.[5]

§ 17.02. Separate or joint defense.

The D & O policy will contain a provision, substantially as follows:

> No defense costs shall be incurred or settlements made without the [Insurer's] consent, which shall not be unreasonably withheld. The [Insurer] shall not be liable for any settlements or defense costs to which it has not consented.

In most actions against corporate officers and directors there will be several defendants, including individual directors and officers and the corporation. The individual directors may include "inside" and "outside" directors, the former usually officers who are involved in the corporation's management. Such an alignment may produce additional conflicts of interest, or at least claims of conflicts, such as

corporation vs. outside directors
insiders vs. outsiders
individuals vs. individuals
officers vs. outside directors.

The D & O policy does not insure the corporation except as to reimbursement for indemnification by it of officers and directors. This coverage does not apply to the corporation's liability for its own wrongdoing, even though accomplished through agents. Subject to the policy's conditions and exclusions, it also extends coverage to the officers and directors individually for loss resulting from their wrongful acts.

All insureds are entitled to select and retain legal counsel, subject to the above defense clause. Typically, the corporation will want its regular outside counsel to represent it and the

---

5. Okada v. MGIC Indem. Corp., 795 F.2d 1450, 1459 (9th Cir. 1986), Hall, J. dissenting. See also Continental Cas. Co. v. Board of Educ., 302 Md. 516, 489 A.2d 536, 538-43 (1985), and cases cited infra section 21.09 note 99.

defendants who are its directors and officers. When conflicts among the defendants appear, as they frequently do, some different alignment of clients and attorneys may be necessary. But it is the concern of the insurer as well as those insured to conserve defense costs. The policy is a wasting asset. As defense costs accrue, they reduce the policy limits available for settlements or the payment of judgments.[6]

A reasonably common result of these factors has the corporation and the insiders jointly represented by one counsel, sometimes the corporation's regular counsel, and one or more separate counsel representing the outside directors. Of course, all clients involved in any joint representation must consent to it and the insurer will expect defense counsel to obtain such consents.

The insurer is also concerned with the quality, ability and experience of proposed defense counsel, potential conflict among joint clients, and the possibility that any of the attorneys may become involved as witnesses in the litigation. Where attorneys have participated in the planning or execution of the transaction which is the subject of the action, they may be key witnesses and thus disqualified from conducting the litigation. To ascertain such a situation at the outset will ordinarily avoid the expense of disqualification proceedings, or the substitution and reorientation of defense counsel at a later date.

§ 17.03. The duty-to-defend concept.

Liability insurance policies generally involve two duties, to defend the insured and to pay a judgment rendered against the insured or reimburse him if he has been compelled to pay one. Under such policies the duty to defend is measured by the allegations of the complaint. While the two duties are somewhat coextensive, the duty to defend is broader than the

---

6. Cf. In re THC Fin. Corp., 86 F.R.D. 721, 734-35 (D. Haw. 1980). See also Tillman v. Wheaton-Hayes Rec. Ass'n, 580 F.2d 1222, 1229 (4th Cir. 1978).

duty to pay a judgment.[7] When the complaint contains allegations which give rise to any potential liability under the policy the duty to defend is triggered.[8]

As is discussed in more depth in Chapter 21, directors' and officers' liability policies were originally designed and have always been intended as indemnity or reimbursement policies.[9] They require only that the insurer indemnify its insured for losses incurred, with the definition of loss including defense costs.[10] The D & O policy does not contain an express commitment to defend. In fact some such policies state:

> The Insurer does not, under the terms of this policy, assume any duty to defend, nor are the costs, charges and expenses of defense payable by the Insurer in addition to the limit of liability. Costs, charges and expenses of defense are subject to the provisions of Clause 5 [relating to limit and retention].[11]

However, in the case of defense costs the dispute as to the insurer's obligations may be more than a matter of wording; it appears to involve fundamental insurance concepts, not the least of which is whether a D & O policy is a "liability" policy or an "indemnity" policy.[12]

§ 17.04. Funding the defense.

Some D & O policies contain an "option" clause providing that the insurer may, at its option and upon request advance, on behalf of the directors and officers, expenses, which they

---

7. Donnelly v. Transportation Ins. Co., 589 F.2d 761, 765 (4th Cir. 1978).

8. Previews, Inc. v. California Union Ins. Co., supra note 2, at 1027; Maneikis v. St. Paul Ins. Co., 655 F.2d 818, 811 (7th Cir. 1981).

9. See infra section 21.08.

10. Zaborac v. American Cas. Co., 663 F. Supp. 330 (C.D. Ill. 1987); Continental Cas. Co. v. Board of Educ., 302 Md. 516, 489 A.2d 536, 543 (1985). Contra, Okada v. MGIC Indem. Co., 608 F. Supp. 383 (D. Haw. 1985), aff'd in part, rev'd in part, 795 F.2d 1450 (9th Cir. 1986), amended 823 F.2d 276 (9th Cir. 1987).

11. E.g., National Union Fire Ins. Co. of Pittsburgh, Pa. Corp. Reimbursement Policy Form 8749 (6/85), Clause 6(a). See Appendix C.

12. See discussion infra section 21.08.

have incurred in connection with claims made against them, prior to disposition of such claims.[13] Probably the right to make such advances exists with or without the option clause. In at least one of the court decisions rendered to date, substantial sums had been advanced as defense costs by the insurer before it ceased to make advancements and the litigation resulted.[14]

Most actions against corporate directors and officers involve several claims of alleged wrongdoing, some of which usually fall outside the coverage of the D & O policy. Because defense costs are part of "Loss" (a defined term), the insurer has no obligation to pay such costs for the defense of claims not covered or excluded by the policy provisions.[15] Accordingly, the insurer usually proceeds under a full reservation of its rights[16] until the progress of the litigation and perhaps a final judgment have resolved any coverage questions.

Because no defense costs may be incurred without the insurer's consent, the manner of giving consent may have a bearing on the time of the funding of the defense. For example, one policy form states:

> No Defense Costs shall be incurred or settlements made without the Company's consent, which shall not be unreasonably withheld. The Company shall not be liable for any settlements or Defense Costs to which it has not consented. If the Insured Organization is a defendant in a legal action along with any Insured Person and the Company shall unconditionally consent to the incurring of Defense Costs, then the Company may, at its sole option, advance such Defense Costs on behalf of all Insureds until an appropriate allocation of Defense Costs among the Insured Person(s) and the Insured Organization is agreed to by the Company and the Insured. If the Company shall unconditionally consent to the incurring of Defense Costs, the Company shall advance Defense Costs periodically during the course of legal proceedings.

---

13. E.g., the MGIC Indem. Co. policy construed in Okada v. MGIC Indem. Co., supra note 10.

14. Id. More than $1 million had been advanced.

15. See discussion infra section 21.09.

16. See infra section 17.05.

That language appears to presume the insurer's options, but does impose a duty to advance defense costs periodically, if the consent to incur such costs is unconditional.

Another policy, which limits the coverage to independent directors,[16a] clearly provides for advancement of defense expenses on a current basis, except such as are being paid on a current basis by the corporation or another insurer.

The duty-to-defend concept requires an insurer to defend the entire action, if any claims come within the coverage of the policy.[17] Even then, there may be allocation of legal expenses between covered and noncovered claims in a proper case.[18] When a D & O policy is involved, there is authority that an insurer has no obligation to reimburse insureds for their defense costs until such an allocation has been made. Until then "the question of whether [the insurer] is to pay losses on an 'as incurred' basis is moot."[19] When defense costs are part of the "Loss," there is an Illinois rule holding that an insurer's duty to pay indemnification will not be defined until the adjudication of the underlying action, even under a comprehensive general liability policy requiring current payment of defense costs as part of a duty to defend.[20]

A simple solution to the problems that arise as to funding the defense is an interim funding agreement entered into among the defendants and the insurer. When undertaken in good faith such an agreement may deal with most of the troublesome matters, including:

16a. Aetna Cas. & Sur. Co. Independent Directors Liability Policy Form (F-1842) ED. 3-38. See Appendix C.

17. See supra section 17.03.

18. E.g., Gray v. Zurich Ins. Co., 65 Cal. 2d 263, 54 Cal. Rptr. 104, 419 P.2d 168 (1966).

19. E.g., Bank of Commerce & Trust Co. v. National Union Fire Ins. Co. of Pittsburgh, Pa., 651 F. Supp. 474, 476-77 (N.D. Okla. 1986). Contra, Pepsico Inc. v. Continental Cas. Co., 640 F. Supp. 656, 659 (S.D.N.Y. 1986). See also cases cited in section 21.09 note 99.

20. Maryland Cas. Co. v. Chicago & N.W. Transp. Co., 126 Ill. App. 3d 150, 81 Ill. Dec. 289, 466 N.E.2d 1091 (1st Dist. 1984), cited with approval in Zaborac v. American Cas. Co., supra note 10.

(1) agreements as to what claims are covered, or must
be held in abeyance for coverage purposes until termination of the underlying action;

(2) allocation of defense costs among such claims;[21]

(3) allocation of defense costs among insured and uninsured defendants, especially when the corporation
and some of the individual defendants are represented by the same counsel;[22]

(4) recognition that any self-insured retentions and any
co-insurance payments will be made and proof furnished before calling upon the insurer for interim
funding;[23]

(5) contents and timing of billing statements;[24]

(6) status reports and other reports to insurer;[25]

(7) timing of payments to defense counsel;[26]

(8) procedure as to discovery, consultants and experts,
computers and other matters involved in control of
costs;[27]

(9) cooperation among defense counsel;[28]

(10) reservations of rights;

(11) provision for termination of interim funding agreement upon notice.

§ 17.05. Insurer's coverage counsel.

It is common practice of D & O insurers to employ coverage
counsel to advise them and represent their interests in the
handling of D & O claims and litigation. In general, coverage
counsel speaks for the insurer and acts in its behalf in controversies relating to coverage, prepares reservations of rights,
communications and interim funding agreements, advises

---

21. See discussion infra section 17.06.
22. Id.
23. See discussion infra section 17.07.
24. See discussion infra section 17.08.
25. See discussion infra section 17.09.
26. See discussion infra section 17.08.
27. See discussion infra section 17.09.
28. See discussion infra section 17.10.

the insurer as to its rights and obligations under the D & O policy, and works closely with defense counsel to enhance the quality and cost effectiveness of the defense provided for the insureds. Coverage counsel customarily monitors the litigation in the underlying actions and counsels with the insurer as to liability, procedure, settlement, and all other related matters.

The policies and practices of a particular insurer and the attitudes and experience of coverage counsel will determine the manner of handling particular accounts. There may be considerable variations in methods, and in some cases the involvement of coverage counsel will be more extensive than in others. Because of experience in the area, coverage counsel should be a worthwhile resource for defense counsel and usually will be able to supply research materials, briefs, court decisions, and other relevant information to make it less necessary for defense counsel "to reinvent the wheel" in every new case.

At the outset, the insurer will furnish to coverage counsel the initial claim or suit notice, copies of initial pleadings, and complete coverage information including copies of all policies and endorsements. Following a thorough and prompt analysis, coverage counsel will draft a reservation of rights letter (sometimes called a "position letter") or an acknowledgment of claims letter, whichever is appropriate, to be sent by the insurer to the insureds.

It frequently happens that the complaint in the action will assert claims which may not be within the coverage of the policy, or will raise questions as to coverage which may not be possible of determination until the case has been decided. In such a situation, the insurer is not required to forfeit any defenses it may have to its liability under the policy, but may preserve them by means of a reservation of rights.[29] If an

---

29. Motorists Mut. Ins. Co. v. Trainer, 33 Ohio St. 2d 41, 294 N.E.2d 874 (1973); 7C Appleman, Insurance Law & Practice § 4682 (Berdal ed. 1979).

insurer proceeds in that manner, it will not be estopped to assert any policy defenses that may be available to it.[30]

Concurrently with the above activity, coverage counsel will establish a line of communication with the insured corporation and its corporate legal counsel in preparation for identification and approval of defense counsel and dealing with questions relating to the competency and experience of such counsel and any possible conflicts of interest.

The D & O policy requires the insured to obtain the consent of the insurer before incurring any costs, charges or expenses that would be recoverable as "Loss" (a defined term) under the policy. Under that provision, the insured will be expected to submit adequate information as to defense counsel, their competency, and their experience in D & O litigation. When sufficient information is available as to possible conflicts of interest, consideration may be given to the question of joint or separate defenses.[31] During this period, coverage counsel will also deal with the subjects of cost containment and litigation control.

Insurers will have their own preferences as to reporting by coverage counsel. The first report, within thirty to sixty days of the assignment, will (1) summarize the facts and the issues, (2) evaluate liability on a preliminary basis, (3) review applicable statutes and any controlling court decisions, (4) estimate settlement possibilities and costs, (5) estimate the potential exposures to damages, defense costs and monitoring costs, and (6) outline the general plan of defense and discovery. In this report it should be possible to state whether the matter will be handled under the corporate reimbursement part of the policy or under the direct or D & O part.[32]

Subsequent reports of coverage counsel (again, as directed by the involved insurer) will ordinarily be made at least every sixty days, although any significant developments should be reported immediately. In such subsequent reports,

---

30. Appleman, supra note 29, at § 4694.
31. See discussion supra section 17.02.
32. See discussion infra section 21.05.

the following, at least, should be covered as and when appropriate:

(1) Copies of relevant and material papers, including all court decisions;

(2) The progress of discovery and summaries of depositions (which should be furnished to coverage counsel by defense counsel unless an actual review of critical testimony is necessary);

(3) Subsequent events and information, especially relating to liability and any changes in prior estimates of damages, defense costs and monitoring;

(4) Transmittal of the bills of defense counsel, with appropriate comment;[33]

(5) Any developments reflecting upon any conflicts of interest of any parties or counsel.

The insurer will expect coverage counsel to provide regular, timely and sufficiently complete reports that the insurer may establish and update adequate reserves, anticipate the need for any substantial expenditures and their timing, be in a position to consent to or recommend a settlement, and keep its reinsurers adequately informed.

§ 17.06. Allocation of costs.

As noted in section 17.04 it is frequently necessary to allocate defense costs between covered and noncovered claims. Also allocations may be necessary between insured and uninsured parties to the litigation. A problem that is ever-challenging is the allocation of such costs, especially attorneys' fees, between the corporation and the individual directors and officers, when the underlying action involves all of them. The D & O policy does not insure the corporation for anything except reimbursement for indemnification provided to its directors and officers.[34] When the corporation is named a defendant its defense costs will not be paid by the insurer. If the

---

33. See discussion supra section 17.08.
34. See supra section 17.02 and infra section 21.05.

same counsel represent the corporation and some or all of the individual defendants, the problem is compounded because it is difficult to segregate the services performed for the corporation from those performed for the individuals.

The insurer and the individuals share a common interest in allocating as much of the defense costs as possible to the corporation so as to conserve the funds provided by the policy. The more that is paid out for defense costs, the less remains for settlement, payment of judgments against the individuals or reimbursement of the corporation for indemnification of the individuals.

Of course, the corporation may employ separate counsel to represent it but, in the absence of a conflict of interest among the defendants, this may involve duplication of the legal effort with a resulting increase in total defense costs as well as in the costs allocable to the directors and officers.

A Sixth Circuit case states the rules applicable to allocating defense costs. An insurer must bear the entire cost of defense when "there is no reasonable means of prorating the costs of defense between the covered and the not-covered items." However, an insurer contracts to pay only the costs of defending claims covered by the policy. Where a distinction can be made between claims covered and those not covered, "the insured must pay its fair share for the defense of the noncovered risk."[35]

The Maryland court applied these principles to a policy which included defense costs in the definition of "Loss" and stated:

> Legal services and expenses are reasonably related to a covered count if they would have been rendered by reasonably competent counsel engaged to defend a suit ... arising out of the same factual background ... but which

---

35. Insurance Co. of N. Am. v. Forty-Eight Insulations, Inc., 633 F.2d 1212, 1224-25 (6th Cir. 1980), cert. denied, 454 U.S. 1109 (1981). See also Starkville Mun. Sep. School Dist. v. Continental Cas. Co., 772 F.2d 168 (5th Cir. 1985); Crest v. Insurance Co. of N. Am., 520 F. Supp. 601, 604-05 (D. Utah 1982).

alleged only the matters complained of in [the covered counts].[36]

In the Southern District of New York the court held that the insurer had no contemporaneous duty to pay all defense costs, where a portion of the costs was attributable not to the directors and officers but to the defense of the corporation itself. It stated that "[o]nly defense costs incurred on behalf of the directors and officers are within the 'Loss' definition of the policy." However, the court went on to hold that to avoid total liability, the insurer had the burden to show the amount that the uninsured defendants were equitably entitled to share.[37]

§ 17.07. Retentions and co-insurance.

All D & O policies provide for "retentions" or "deductibles." The retention is self-insured, in most cases, and the insurer's duty to pay begins when the retention is exhausted. But a deductible clause is not the same as self-insurance.[38]

When there is a retention or a retained limit, the insurer's liability is limited to the loss in excess of that amount.[39] In that respect the policy is treated like an excess policy which pays toward the insured's liability only if it exceeds the limit of the primary policy.[40]

An example of a "deductible" is found in a Ninth Circuit case in which the policy provided "$5,000 for each claim shall be deducted from the total amount of all sums that the Company agrees to pay."[41] However, it has been held that the

---

36. Continental Cas. Co. v. Board of Educ., 302 Md. 516, 489 A.2d 536 (1985).

37. Pepsico, Inc. v. Continental Cas. Co., 640 F. Supp. 656, 666 (S.D.N.Y. 1986). Cf. Shapiro v. American Home Assur. Co., 616 F. Supp. 906, 913 (D. Mass. 1985).

38. 8A Appleman, Insurance Law & Practice § 4912 (1981).

39. Molina v. United States Fire Ins. Co., 574 F.2d 1176 (4th Cir. 1978).

40. Aviles v. Burgos, 783 F.2d 270, 278 (1st Cir. 1986).

41. Combined Communications Corp. v. Seaboard Sur. Co., 641 F.2d 743, 744 n.2 (9th Cir. 1981).

functional purpose of a "deductible" is to alter the point at which an insurance company's obligation to pay will ripen.[42]

Under most D & O policies the retention or deductible applies to the "Loss," which means that it also applies to the payment of defense costs. There will usually be a deductible or retention as to each individual for each loss up to an aggregate for all individuals against whom claims are made. There will be a specified deductible for the corporation as to the corporate reimbursement coverage. Between 1984 and 1986 all deductibles in D & O policies increased, the personal deductibles by an average of 44%, the aggregates by 196% and the corporate reimbursement deductibles by 1,326%.[43] However, the trend appeared to be reversing itself in 1987.

Traditionally D & O policies have contained co-insurance provisions under which the insureds must bear 5% of each loss in excess of the retention or deductible. This amount may not be reinsured, because it is intended as a claim deterrent. Since the early 1980's most insurers have been receptive to waiving the co-insurance requirement at least for payments in excess of $1 million over the retention or deductible.

The insured is expected to spend the retention or deductible before the insurer is called upon to make any payments, even on an interim basis. After the retention or deductible, payments by the insurer will take cognizance of the co-insurance provision, if it is in effect.

§ 17.08. Billing and payment of defense counsel.

The billing statements of defense counsel must disclose what work was performed and by whom, the time devoted to it, and the identity of the parties in whose behalf it was done. When insured and uninsured parties are represented by the same counsel or work is performed on covered and noncovered claims, the allocation of the charges among them should be made in the billing statements. The date of each time

---

42. American Nurses Ass'n v. Passaic Gen. Hosp., 98 N.J. 83, 484 A.2d 670, 673 (1985). See discussion infra section 21.11.

43. See infra section 22.06, Wyatt Survey 75.

entry should be stated together with what was done and the charge for that entry, based on the agreed rate multiplied by the time. Bills should be submitted monthly, which will enable coverage counsel and the insurer to keep informed of the progress of the litigation. As a general rule, a law firm's computerized billing statement should suffice for this purpose, but if it is not in sufficient detail, defense counsel will be expected to furnish any necessary additional information.

All costs and expense items should be set forth in detail in the billing statements, with sufficient identification that the items charged can be reconciled with the receipts obtained by coverage counsel for the payment of each item.

As in the case of fees, there should be allocations of such costs among covered and noncovered claims and insured and noninsured parties. The customary practice is for defense counsel to advance payment of such costs during the discovery and the litigation and include the items in their monthly statements. Occasionally, by special arrangement in advance, provisions may be made to submit cost invoices to the insurer for direct payment.

Billing statements will be reviewed by coverage counsel and transmitted to the insurer with appropriate comments. It is a common practice for insurers to pay such statements quarterly or semiannually to allow time for adequate review and to control the administrative costs of processing the payments. When several defense counsel are involved in the litigation, their billing statements should be scheduled for payments at the same times so that comparisons of their contents may be made efficiently. Attention to such programming will contribute to prompt payments of statements and help control litigation costs.

§ 17.09. Control of costs.

Coverage counsel usually represents the insurer in establishing procedures with defense counsel so that the litigation is handled in a competent and cost-effective manner. At the outset coverage counsel will obtain descriptions of the defense lawyers and paralegals who will be working on the litigation, information as to their experience and their billing rates. Such rates should be in line with the prevailing rates for similar work in the area. It may be well to include such information in any interim funding agreement.[44]

As early as possible, defense counsel should be asked to outline their overall plan for the handling of the litigation, and to provide an estimate of the time and expense to conduct adequate discovery, including a projected deposition schedule. An effort should be made to establish a realistic budget for defense costs, including attorneys' fees. At this time procedures should be set for dealing with retentions and deductibles and for handling items of substantial expense such as those relating to consultants, expert witnesses and activities in which defense counsel may want to involve several attorneys at the same time. Such items should be dealt with in a manner that will permit coverage counsel to approve and make recommendations to the insurer before the expense is incurred. When several defense counsel are engaged in representing various insured defendants, it is essential to minimize duplications of activities.

It will be necessary for defense counsel to provide status reports with reasonable frequency to supplement the information provided in their billing statements. Summaries of depositions should be furnished to coverage counsel except, in rare instances, when actual transcripts should be examined, and care should be taken to eliminate excess costs by avoiding purchase of unnecessary copies of transcripts and exhibits.

Defense counsel should report all significant events immediately and should give continuing attention to settlement prospects.

§ 17.10. Cooperation among counsel.

The inclusion of defense costs in the policy limit, and the resulting reduction in coverage as such costs are incurred

---

44. See supra section 17.04.

make it essential for defense counsel among themselves and with coverage counsel to cooperate as fully as is realistic to conserve the policy fund. The defense effort must be coordinated if it is to be efficient. This entails utilizing the available expertise of various defense personnel with maximum effectiveness and eliminating unnecessary duplication of services in all instances.

In cases where large numbers of documents are involved, a common document repository may result in substantial savings, for example. Coordination with respect to the selection and utilization of expert witnesses and consultants is of particular importance, because such experts, in cases of this type, are usually quite expensive.

Keeping coverage counsel adequately informed of all developments will help ensure that the insurance company is kept abreast of the risks and exposures of the litigation and that it will be prepared to do its part as the occasion arises. It is essential that the insurer have adequate warning of the need to provide a substantial sum for settlement or payment of a judgment, and that it be able to evaluate settlement demands as they are presented. It owes obligations to its reinsurers as well as to carriers of excess insurance and needs to be kept informed in order to meet them.

There are reciprocal duties of full and fair disclosure between a casualty insurance company and its insured.[45] This applies to D & O insurance. Cooperation among counsel will encourage the performance of such duties.

§ 17.11. Privileged communications.

A report or other communication from an insured to an insurer concerning a casualty covered by its policy of insurance, which is transmitted to counsel for the purpose of preparing a defense to a possible law suit growing out of such casualty, is generally held to be a privileged communication both as to the insurer and its insured.[46] In proceedings involv-

---

45. Geng v. American Liberty Ins. Co., 423 F.2d 115, 120 (5th Cir. 1976).
46. People v. Ryan, 30 Ill. 2d 456, 460, 197 N.E.2d 15 (1964); In re Klemann, 132 Ohio St. 187, 194, 5 N.E.2d 492 (1936).

ing a D & O insurance policy, even if the policy does not impose a duty to defend upon the insurer,[47] its obligation to pay defense costs would seem to lead to the same result. The insurer and the insured have a common interest in making a successful defense and the work of both defense counsel and coverage counsel in that respect is to that end.[48]

There is a dearth of reported cases applying the privileged communication principle to D & O litigation, but some of the cases in other areas have advocated an insurer-insured privilege which ı ıy be broad enough to apply here.[49] And a New York court has said that communication between an insured and his insurer should be "accorded substantially the same immunity from disclosure to an adversary as that given communication by a client to his attorney."[50]

If the insured and insurer come into conflict over the coverage question, the same authorities hold that the privileged communication rule will not then apply.[51] Because such conflicts are fairly common in D & O matters, reasonable caution should be exercised by all parties and counsel in the communication of information that may have prejudicial characteristics.

§ 17.12. Some points as to settlements.

Litigation in the D & O area is expensive.[52] Thus early settlement negotiations are advantageous, especially if costly discovery procedures can be diminished or eliminated. Also it

---

47. See supra section 17.03.

48. See Travelers Ins. Co. v. Superior Court, 143 Cal. App. 3d 436, 191 Cal. Rptr. 871 (1983).

49. E.g., Cain v. Barker, 540 S.W.2d 50, 53 (Mo. 1976); Puckett v. Broome, 53 Tenn. App. 663, 679, 385 S.W.2d 762, 770 (1964).

50. Cataldo v. Monroe, 38 Misc. 768, 771, 238 N.Y.S.2d 855, 858, aff'd, 19 A.D.2d 852, 243 N.Y.S.2d 986 (1963). Contra Jacobi v. Podevels, 23 Wis. 2d 152, 127 N.W.2d 73, 76 (1964); Gottleib v. Bresler, 24 F.R.D. 371, 372 (D.D.C. 1959).

51. See also Simpson v. Motorists Mut. Ins. Co., 494 F.2d 850, 855 (7th Cir.), cert. denied, 419 U.S. 901 (1974).

52. See infra section 22.04.

may be possible to obtain voluntary dismissals of some individual defendants whose presence is not really necessary for the litigation. As soon as the parties can familiarize themselves with the facts and evaluate the potential liability on a preliminary basis, settlement negotiations will usually prove beneficial. If the trial judge or a settlement judge or magistrate is active in this process, so much the better.

Usually it is desirable to work toward what is sometimes termed a "global settlement" in which all claims of all parties are extinguished. Otherwise, defendants who do not settle may bring the settling defendants back into the litigation under third-party or similar practices. Coverage counsel, in behalf of the D & O insurer will want to head off any potential future claims as well as making sure that all pending claims are extinguished. If the litigation is a class action, an expanded settlement class may help to accomplish these objectives.[53]

Where multiple defendants are involved as is usually the case in D & O litigation, it may require some serious negotiating among counsel for the defendants and the carriers of those who are insured to put together a settlement fund. The uninsured exposure of the corporation in most cases, and of individuals as to claims not covered by insurance, will be in direct conflict with the exposure of D & O insurers and any other insurers who may be involved, as far as contributions to the settlement fund are concerned.

The involvement of coverage counsel in the settlement proceedings will usually depend on the attitudes of the D & O insurer and of defense counsel in that respect. Each case should be considered separately to determine how the negotiations can best be handled, although, generally, defense counsel will conduct the proceedings keeping coverage counsel informed and obtaining settlement authority from them.

---

53. See infra section 18.06.

COROLLARY REFERENCES

Berg, "After Cumis: Regaining Control of the Defense," 27 For the Defense 13 (1985).

Bisceglia, "Practical Aspects of Directors' and Officers' Liability Insurance — Allocating and Advancing Legal Fees and the Duty to Defend," 32 UCLA L. Rev. 690 (1985).

Oettle & Howard, "D & O Insurance: Judicially Transforming a 'Duty to Pay' Policy into a 'Duty to Defend' Policy," 22 Tort & Ins. Prac. J. 337 (1987).

Annotation, "Insured-Insurer Communications as Privileged," 55 A.L.R.4th 336 (1987).

Chapter 18

CLASS, DERIVATIVE AND DIRECT ACTIONS

§ 18.01. Definition of terms; distinctions.

The legal tools to enforce the liability of corporate officers and directors are class actions, derivative actions and direct actions. Each performs a particular function and there are important distinctions among them.

Class actions. The class action has acquired special significance in proceedings under the federal securities laws and in actions based on common-law fraud, price-fixing and violations of civil rights, because it may be effectively employed in the interests of small investors and other claimants whose individual claims would be of insufficient size to justify litigation of separate actions.

One or more plaintiffs may sue for the benefit of those who have a similar interest in the outcome. Thus, an entire class may be given relief for multiple wrongs committed by a defendant. Such actions are especially useful in the corporate context where, regardless of the amounts of individual claims, it would be practically, if not literally, impossible to join all the numerous shareholders of a widely held public corporation.

Class actions may be distinguished from derivative actions by determining who was harmed. When the loss is to the shareholders of a group or class and affects all similarly situated in the same manner, a class action is appropriate.

569

Derivative actions. A derivative action is a suit brought by one or more shareholders to enforce a cause of action belonging to the corporation.[1] Justice Robert H. Jackson described it as "an invention of equity to supply the want of an adequate remedy to redress breaches of fiduciary duty by corporate managers."[2] The relief to be granted to the corporation through the named plaintiff, its representative, must be the same as if the corporation, itself, had brought the action.[3]

The nature of the action controls in determining whether it is a derivative action or a class action. In a Delaware case, for example, plaintiff brought a class action asserting improper vote buying by management. He alleged that sanctions would be imposed indirectly on the shareholders by payment of severance benefits if the incumbent directors were to be ousted. The court dismissed the action because its nature was for waste which was damaging to the corporation and only indirectly caused loss to the shareholders.[4] In another Delaware action, where the injury was to a shareholder, individually, the court ruled that a direct action rather than a derivative action was appropriate.[5]

There are gray areas between derivative actions and suits brought by shareholders for their own benefit. Thus, diminution in the value of stock resulting from a wrong to the corporation is ordinarily a derivative claim and not a direct or class claim.[6]

Derivative actions are not limited to those seeking to compel directors to pay or restore money to a corporation. They

---

1. Ross v. Bernhard, 396 U.S. 531, 534, 24 L.Ed.2d 729, 734, 90 S.Ct. 733, 736 (1970).

2. Koster v. (American) Lumbermens Mut. Cas. Co., 330 U.S. 518, 522, 91 L.Ed.2d 1067, 67 S.Ct. 828, 830 (1947).

3. Liken v. Shaffer, 64 F. Supp. 432 (N.D. Iowa 1946).

4. Colonial Secs. Corp. v. Allen, Civil Action No. 6778 (Del. Ch. April 18, 1983). See also Twohy v. First Nat'l Bank, 758 F.2d 1185, 1194 (7th Cir. 1985).

5. Reeves v. Transport Data Communications, Inc., 318 A.2d 147 (Del. Ch. 1974).

6. Wright v. Heizer Corp., 411 F. Supp. 23 (N.D. Ill. 1975), modified, 560 F.2d 236 (7th Cir. 1977).

may be concerned with other duties to be performed by directors. An action is brought in the right of the corporation whenever it involves a court's power to direct the management of the corporation's affairs.[7]

Direct actions. A direct action is one brought by a shareholder to recover from corporate officers, directors or others for a loss sustained by him which is separate and distinct from that of other shareholders generally.[8] Although any injury may affect numerous shareholders, it may be the subject of a direct action if it is not an injury to the corporation, itself.[9] When an injury affects numerous shareholders and the other criteria are present, the direct action may be prosecuted as a class action.

§ 18.02. Class actions: certification of class.

Identification of the class is essential for the court to protect absentee interests, to be aware of any differences of interest within the class and to take steps to accommodate those interests. When only injunctive or declaratory relief is sought, a class may be defined as consisting of all persons who have been or will be affected by the conduct of the defendants.[10] But such a definition would be unsatisfactory where the class members were asserting damage claims. Then greater precision is needed, in order that individual class members can be identified.[11]

The requirement of some concreteness of a class has been held satisfied by members who relied on the same prospectus;[12] minority shareholders of a savings and loan association who were damaged by controlling shareholders' breach of

---

7. Gordon v. Elliman, 306 N.Y. 456, 119 N.E.2d 331, 335 (1954).

8. 19 Am. Jur. 2d 147, Corporations § 2245; Simcox v. San Juan Shipyards, Inc., 754 F.2d 430, 438 (1st Cir. 1985).

9. Jones v. H.F. Ahmanson & Co., 1 Cal. 3d 93, 81 Cal. Rptr. 592, 460 P.2d 464 (1969).

10. Rice v. Philadelphia, 66 F.R.D. 17, 20 (E.D. Pa. 1974).

11. Id. at 19.

12. Sultan v. Bessemer-Birmingham Motel Ass'n, Fed. Sec. L. Rep. (CCH) ¶93,012 (S.D.N.Y. 1970).

their fiduciary duties;[13] parties who concurred in wrongfully causing a company's stock to fluctuate;[14] class members who tendered under the same written tender offer;[15] plaintiffs who relied on "a complete failure to disclose any material facts — which default was necessarily common to all shareholders" and established a common course of conduct;[16] and individuals or entities who owned stock in a corporation at the time of its merger with another company.[17]

As soon as possible after the commencement of an action brought as a class action, the court must determine by order whether it is to be so maintained. The order may be conditional and may be altered or amended before any decision on the merits.[18] The determination depends on satisfaction of the mandatory provisions of Rule 23(a) and a requisite number of the discretionary provisions of Rule 23(b). If there is a negative determination, the case will proceed as a nonclass action, although the court may still be receptive to interventions before the decision on the merits so that the litigation may cover as many interests as can conveniently be handled.

Whether there is a proper class does not depend on whether there is a claim for which relief may be granted. No showing of probable success on the merits is required to achieve certification. The question is whether the criteria of Rule 23 have been satisfied.[19]

---

13. Jones v. H.F. Ahmanson & Co., supra note 9.

14. Carpenter v. Hall, 311 F. Supp. 1099, 1111 (S.D. Tex. 1970).

15. Epstein v. Weiss, 50 F.R.D. 387 (E.D. La. 1970).

16. Esplin v. Hirschi, 402 F.2d 94, 100 (10th Cir. 1968), cert. denied, 394 U.S. 928 (1969).

17. Mader v. Armel, 402 F.2d 158 (6th Cir. 1968), cert. denied sub nom. Young v. Mader, 394 U.S. 930 (1969), cert. denied, 409 U.S. 1023 (1972). See also later decision in Fed. Sec. L. Rep. (CCH) ¶93,027 (S.D. Ohio 1971), aff'd, ¶93,530 (6th Cir. 1972).

18. Rule 23, Fed. R. Civ. P., governs all federal court class actions and is the pattern for applicable rules or statutes in most states. However, some local rules require a motion for certification within a specified time after commencement of the action. See, e.g., S.D.N.Y. Rule 11; S.D. Ohio Rule 3.9.3; E.D. Pa. Rule 45(c).

19. Miller v. Mackey Int'l, 452 F.2d 424, 427 (5th Cir. 1971).

Because the judge who rules on class certification must be informed about the nature and scope of the class, some discovery may be appropriate before the decision. If so, such discovery should be overseen by the court to prevent abuses by a plaintiff or intimidation of absentees or withholding of information by a defendant.[20]

§ 18.03. Class actions: prerequisites.

Under Federal Rule of Civil Procedure 23 and comparable state rules and statutes, there are four mandatory prerequisites for maintaining class actions.

First, the aggregate of potential claimants similarly situated must be so numerous that their joinder would be impracticable. The term "impracticable" refers to the difficulty of joining all members of the class as parties to the action.[21] A class action has been sustained in cases involving as few as eighteen claimants[22] and as many as 6,000,000.[23] Certification was denied, however as to a class of thirty-nine, which was held to be too small.[24]

Second, there must be questions of law or fact common to the class. Neither the rule nor the Advisory Committee's Note defines "common question" and the courts have had some difficulty with it. The First Circuit has suggested that the appropriate inquiry is whether the named plaintiffs have the same case to prove as the other class members.[25] The Ninth Circuit has asked if the class members were "united by a common interest."[26]

---

20. Burns v. Thiokol Chem. Corp., 483 F.2d 300, 305-307, (5th Cir. 1973).

21. Harris v. Palm Springs Alpine Estates, 329 F.2d 909, 913, 914 (9th Cir. 1964).

22. Cypress v. Newport News Gen. & Nonsectarian Hosp. Ass'n, 375 F.2d 648 (4th Cir. 1967).

23. Eisen v. Carlisle & Jacquelin, 479 F.2d 1005, 1008 (2d Cir. 1973), vacated on other grounds, 417 U.S. 156 (1974).

24. Atwood v. National Bank of Lima, 115 F.2d 861 (6th Cir. 1940).

25. Castro v. Beecher, 459 F.2d 725, 729-731 (1st Cir. 1972).

26. Blackie v. Barrack, 524 F.2d 891 (9th Cir. 1975), cert. denied, 429 U.S. 816 (1976).

Third, the claims of the named plaintiffs as representatives of the class must be typical of the claims of those being represented. This requirement is somewhat related to the definition of the class. The first test to be applied under this requirement is whether the representative has interests which conflict with interests of others in the class. Any such conflict must be genuine, must go to the heart of the controversy, and must relate directly to the subject matter of the action.[27] An example of such a conflict would be when the relief sought by the named plaintiff "is different from what the rest of the class would want."[28]

Fourth, the named plaintiff must be a member of the class he represents and must "be able to show injury to himself in order to entitle him to seek judicial relief."[29] The Ninth Circuit has said that adequacy of representation depends on the qualifications of counsel for the named plaintiff, an absence of antagonism, a sharing of interests between the representative and the absentees, and the unlikelihood that the suit is collusive.[30] The courts are not in agreement as to whether disagreement within the class is a valid reason for refusing class certification.[31] Generally courts have adequate facilities to protect particular interests of class members when there are differences in factual matters underlying their claims or if class members differ as to theories of liability. Of course, all-pervasive antagonism among class members would be judicially irreconcilable.[32]

---

27. Redmond v. Commerce Trust Co., 114 F.2d 140, 151 (8th Cir.), cert. denied, 323 U.S. 776 (1944), reh'g denied, 323 U.S. 819 (1945).

28. Madonick v. Denison Mines Ltd., 63 F.R.D. 657, 659 (S.D.N.Y. 1974).

29. Kansas City v. Williams, 205 F.2d 47, 51 (8th Cir.), cert. denied, 346 U.S. 826 (1953).

30. In re Northern Dist. of Cal., Dalkon Shield (IUD) Prods. Liab. Litig., 693 F.2d 847, 855 (9th Cir. 1982), cert. denied, 459 U.S. 1171 (1983).

31. Compare, e.g., Schy v. Susquehanna Corp., 419 F.2d 1112, 1116-17 (7th Cir.), cert. denied, 400 U.S. 826 (1970), with Knuth v. Erie-Crawford Dairy Coop. Ass'n, 395 F.2d 420, 428 (3d Cir. 1968), cert. denied, 410 U.S. 913 (1973), and Gates v. Dalton, 67 F.R.D. 621, 630-32 (E.D.N.Y. 1975).

32. "Developments in the Law: Class Actions," 89 Harv. L. Rev. 1318, 1490-98 (1976).

§ 18.04. Class actions: discretionary provisions.

In addition to meeting all four of the mandatory prerequisites, a class action must meet at least one of the additional tests identified in Rule 23(b). The tests relate to the type or effect of the relief sought.

Subdivision (b)(1) of the Rule provides for maintaining a class action when the prosecution of separate actions by or against individual members of the class would be likely to create difficulties. Under Clause (A), a class action may be used to avoid a risk of inconsistent or varying adjudications with respect to individual class members which would establish incompatible standards of conduct for the party opposing the class. Illustrations are separate actions by individuals against a municipality to invalidate a bond issue; or separate actions by landowners respecting a claimed nuisance.[33]

Under Clause (B) of subdivision (b)(1), the rule deals with situations where a judgment in a nonclass action, while not technically binding upon others similarly situated, might have that effect. Illustrations are actions by shareholders to compel the declaration of a dividend; or an action by or against persons having claims against a fund insufficient to satisfy all of them.[34]

Subdivision (b)(2) of the Rule is intended to reach situations where a party has taken action or refused to take action with respect to a class and final relief of an injunctive nature or of a corresponding declarative nature, settling the legality of the behavior with respect to the class as a whole, is appropriate.[35] Illustrations are civil rights actions challenging a pattern of practice,[36] or such a practice discriminating unlaw-

---

33. See Advisory Committee Note, 39 F.R.D. 73, 100 (1966). See also Technograph Printed Circuits, Ltd. v. Methode Elec., Inc., 285 F. Supp. 714 (N.D. Ill. 1968); Maricopa County Mun. Water Conservation Dist. No. One v. Looney, 219 F.2d 529 (9th Cir. 1955).

34. See Advisory Committee Note, 39 F.R.D. 73, 101 (1966). See also Dann v. Studebaker-Packard Corp., 288 F.2d 201 (6th Cir. 1961).

35. Advisory Committee Note, 39 F.R.D. 73, 103 (1966).

36. Rice v. City of Philadelphia, 66 F.R.D. 17 (E.D. Pa. 1974).

fully against a class whose members may not be specifically identifiable.[37]

Subdivision (b)(3) of the Rule is intended to encompass cases "in which a class action would achieve economies of time, effort and expense, and promote uniformity of decision as to persons similarly situated, without sacrificing procedural fairness or bringing about other undesirable results."[38]

The two aspects of Rule 23(b)(3) which require consideration are that the court must find (1) that the questions of law or fact common to the members of the class predominate over any questions affecting only individual members, and (2) that a class action is superior to other available methods for the fair and efficient adjudication of the controversy.

Here the court's task is to inquire whether the requirements of Rule 23 have been met, not whether the plaintiff is likely to prevail on the merits of the action.[39] The procedure followed in some cases of a preliminary hearing (or "mini" hearing) on the merits to ascertain which party was most likely to prevail was repudiated by the Supreme Court in *Eisen IV*.[40]

Superiority

The Third Circuit has suggested that in order to make a superiority finding the court must undertake (1) an informed consideration of alternative available methods of adjudication of each issue, (2) a comparison as to all whose interests may be involved between such alternative methods and a class action, and (3) a comparison of the efficiency of adjudication by each method.[41] The question of the manageability of the suit as a class action has been discussed in most reported

---

37. E.g., Breen v. School Bd., 304 F.2d 118 (4th Cir. 1962).

38. Advisory Committee Note, 39 F.R.D. 73, 102-03.

39. Weathers v. Peters Realty Corp., 499 F.2d 1197, 1201 (6th Cir. 1974).

40. Eisen v. Carlisle & Jacquelin, 417 U.S. 156, 40 L.Ed.2d 732, 94 S.Ct. 2140 (1974).

41. Katz v. Carte Blanche Corp., 496 F.2d 747, 757 (3d Cir.), cert. denied, 419 U.S. 885 (1974).

cases in the massive class action area and has been one of the difficult hurdles for the courts to overcome in resolving the superiority problem. Professor Wright has written that "maintenance of class actions in controversies that are unmanageable ... brought the rule into disrepute even for the cases to which it is well suited."[42] His previous warning that this might happen was timely but has been ignored. Another commentator has suggested that Rule 23 has been utilized "to bring into the federal courts literally millions of claims which otherwise would never have been litigated."[43]

Among the separate but interrelated variables involved in a court's analysis of the management question may be:

(1) The size of the class, which may vary from a few persons who dealt with a small institution to millions of defrauded customers of a countrywide chain;

(2) Class members who may be identifiable with ease, or only after the expenditure of considerable time, effort, and money;

(3) Actual damages suffered by individual class members of a few cents to hundreds of dollars, or no actual damages, limiting the recovery to the statutory civil penalties;[44]

(4) The presence of counterclaims against individual members of the class, which may result in excluding them from the action, or separate trials;[45]

(5) Miniscule benefits to individual class members, even from a very large dollar recovery in which the only benefits of consequence would inure to the attorneys by reason of fees awarded to them.[46]

---

42. Wright, Law of Federal Courts § 72 at 346 (3d ed. 1976).

43. Pollock, "Class Actions Reconsidered: Theory and Practice Under Amended Rule 23," 28 Bus. Law. 741, 742 (1973).

44. Travers & Landers, "The Consumer Class Action," 18 Kan. L. Rev. 812, 826 (1970).

45. See Albert v. United States Indus., 59 F.R.D. 491, 499 (C.D. Cal. 1973).

46. E.g., Eisen v. Carlisle & Jacquelin (Eisen II), 391 F.2d 555, 571 (2d Cir. 1968).

Because a satisfactory answer to the management question may be determinative of the superiority requirement, all such questions have a direct bearing on the matter of superiority.

Common questions

The ideal class action probably would be a suit in which each class member had a claim identical in all factual and legal issues with those of his fellow class members. Recognizing that no such situation is likely to exist, the question in a particular case must be whether the court will acknowledge the existence of individual differences between class members, yet declare that the common questions predominate.

The Advisory Committee's Note points out that "only where this predominance exists [can] economies ... be achieved by means of the class action device."[47] Because any real economy in such cases is probably impossible of attainment, the courts have looked for standards to weigh the relative importance of issues which may be tried in common or must be judged separately.[48]

Under this provision, class actions in securities cases have been held proper "where there has been a standardized misrepresentation to a group through a prospectus, proxy statement, financial statements or form letter."[49] Pomerantz and Haudek[50] have stated that "the class questions are deemed to predominate if at least some of the false representations were in writing and reached all members of the class." Thus, even if individual issues exist, the class issues will predominate whenever the complaint alleges a common course of conduct in violation of common statutory provisions over a period of time directed against the members of a class who have relied thereon to their detriment. In numerous instances, the pre-

---

47. Advisory Committee Note, 39 F.R.D. 73, 103 (1966).
48. "Developments in the Law: Class Actions," 89 Harv. L. Rev. 1318, 1506 (1976).
49. Moscarelli v. Stamm, 288 F. Supp. 453, 462 (E.D.N.Y. 1968).
50. Pomerantz & Haudek, "Class Actions," 2 Rev. Sec. Reg. 939 (1969).

dominance of the class issue results from defendants' failure to disclose material information; this has been referred to as a sin of omission "necessarily common to all shareholders."[51]

In cases involving a "common course of conduct" it has been held that individual questions of reliance and damages will not defeat class action treatment.[52] Positive proof of reliance is not a prerequisite to recovery in such cases.

The predominance inquiry can best be made after the manageability inquiry has been taken up. As a result, the predominance question seems to have taken second place to the subject of superiority as a method of adjudication. Nonetheless, both elements must exist to validate a claim under subdivision (b)(3) of the rule.

§ 18.05. Class actions: notices.

In *Hansberry v. Lee*[53] the Supreme Court held that nonlitigating members of a class may be bound by a judgment in a class action if the procedure in the action "fairly insures the protection of the interests of absent parties who are to be bound by it." Judge Harold R. Medina has stated that "notice is required as a matter of due process in all representative actions."[54] Accordingly, subdivision (c)(2) of Rule 23 makes special provisions for notice to the nonlitigating members of the class, as well as those taking an active part in the case, when the action is maintained under subdivision (b)(3). Since the Supreme Court's decision in *Eisen* IV,[55] compliance with

---

51. Epstein v. Weiss, 50 F.R.D. 387, 394 (E.D. La. 1970) and Mader v. Armel, 402 F.2d 158 (6th Cir. 1968), cert. denied sub nom. Young v. Mader, 394 U.S. 930 (1969), cert. denied, 409 U.S. 1023 (1972). See also later decision in Fed. Sec. L. Rep. (CCH) ¶93,027 (S.D. Ohio 1971), aff'd, ¶93,530 (6th Cir. 1972).

52. See, e.g., Blackie v. Barrack, 524 F.2d 891 (9th Cir. 1975), cert. denied, 429 U.S. 816 (1976). As to damages, see United States Fin. Sec. Litig., 64 F.R.D. 443, 448 n.5 (S.D. Cal. 1974).

53. 311 U.S. 32, 42, 85 L.Ed. 22, 61 S.Ct. 115 (1940).

54. Eisen v. Carlisle & Jacquelin (Eisen II), 391 F.2d 555, 564 (2d Cir. 1968).

55. Eisen v. Carlisle & Jacquelin, 417 U.S. 156, 40 L.Ed.2d 732, 94 S.Ct. 2140 (1974).

those requirements is mandatory. The notice must be sent to all class members whose names and addresses may be ascertained with reasonable effort.

The absent class members must be notified (1) that the court will exclude them from the class, if they so request by a specified time, (2) that the judgment, whether favorable or not, will include all class members who do not request exclusion, and (3) that any class member who does not request exclusion may enter an appearance through personal legal counsel. In *Eisen* IV, Justice Powell declared that only individual notices mailed to class members identifiable with reasonable effort would comply with the mandate of the rule. He brushed aside the contention that the prohibitive cost of 2,250,000 such mailings could end the case as a class action and frustrate the petitioner's attempt to vindicate policies underlying the antitrust and securities laws, stating, "There is nothing in Rule 23 to suggest that the notice requirements can be tailored to fit the pocketbooks of particular plaintiffs."

Under other provisions of Rule 23, and state rules and statutes which resemble it, courts may notify the named and absentee parties of a variety of matters. The trend is in favor of sufficient notice to make reasonably certain that nonlitigant members of the class will be sufficiently informed to be able to protect their rights. The decisions place the responsibility for such notices and for adequate representation upon the trial judge through the use of subclasses, issuance of orders to protect absentees, and notices inviting intervention or opting out.[56]

§ 18.06. Class actions: settlement and dismissal.

Subdivision (e) of Rule 23 expressly provides that a class action may not be dismissed or compromised without approval of the court after notice to all members of the class. The manner of giving such notice is left to the court's discretion. Courts have recognized that the trial judge must act as a

---

56. See also Mullane v. Central Hanover Bank & Trust Co., 339 U.S. 306, 94 L.Ed. 865, 70 S.Ct. 652 (1950).

"guardian" for the interests of nonlitigating class members to make sure that they have had adequate representation during settlement proceedings.[57] The wisdom of this requirement has been demonstrated by decisions in cases in which plaintiffs, having attained their personal objectives, have sought dismissal of class actions.[58] It has been well said that "an allegation of class representation is attended by serious consequences" and that "no litigant should be permitted to enhance his own bargaining power by merely suggesting that he is acting for a class of litigants."[59]

When a settlement is proposed to be made on behalf of an entire plaintiff-class, various categories of antagonism may appear such as (1) conflict between the named plaintiff's attorney and the class,[60] (2) conflict between the named plaintiff and the class,[61] or conflict among competing interests within the class.[62] Sometimes the parties negotiate the definition of the settlement class as well as the nature of the relief to be granted.[63] In such a case the court may give preliminary

---

57. E.g., Girsh v. Jepson, 521 F.2d 153, 157 (3d Cir. 1975); Grunin v. International House of Pancakes, 513 F.2d 114, 123 (8th Cir.), cert. denied, 423 U.S. 864 (1975); Norman v. McKee, 431 F.2d 769, 774 (9th Cir. 1970), cert. denied sub nom. ISI Corp. v. Myers, 401 U.S. 912 (1971).

58. E.g., Saltzman v. Technicolor, Inc., 51 F.R.D. 178 (S.D.N.Y. 1970).

59. Philadelphia Elec. Co. v. Anaconda Am. Brass Co., 42 F.R.D. 324, 328 (E.D. Pa. 1967).

60. In re Coordinated Pretrial Proceedings in Antibiotics Antitrust Actions, 410 F. Supp. 680 (D. Minn. 1975), one group of class members recovered some $364 each, but class attorneys shared $10 million in fees. Wolfram, "The Antibiotic Class Actions," 1976 Research J. 251, 327-37, 359.

61. E.g., West Virginia v. Chas. Pfizer & Co., 314 F. Supp. 710 (S.D.N.Y. 1970), aff'd, 440 F.2d 1079 (2d Cir.), cert. denied sub nom. Cotler Drugs, Inc. v. Chas. Pfizer & Co., 404 U.S. 871 (1971). Cf. Gonzales v. Cassidy, 474 F.2d 67 (5th Cir. 1973).

62. E.g., Purcell v. Keane, 54 F.R.D. 455 (E.D. Pa. 1972). See also "Developments in the Law: Class Actions," 89 Harv. L. Rev. 1318, 1552, 1553 (1976).

63. See, e.g., Detroit v. Grinnell Corp., 495 F.2d 448 (2d Cir. 1974), 560 F.2d 1093 (2d Cir. 1977); Girsh v. Jepson, 521 F.2d 153 (3d Cir. 1975).

approval to a tentative settlement class[64] and authorize notice to class members telling them the terms of the settlement and giving them options as to their procedure.[65] Thereafter, the court may hold a final hearing and rule on the class definition and the adequacy of the proposed settlement.[66]

When a class action settlement is presented to the court for approval, certain reasonably well-recognized tests are applied. Of course, the court cannot fully try the case at the settlement hearing because one of the purposes of settlement is to avoid the time and expense of a full trial.[67] The principal tests to be applied are:

(1) Whether there is any fraud or collusion in the compromise;

(2) Whether the interests of all members of the class are adequately protected;[68]

(3) The likelihood of success in the action;[69]

(4) A comparison of results obtained by settlement and results to be anticipated in the event of trial;[70] and

(5) The absence of objections.[71]

Although trial courts are not expected to convert settlement hearings into trials on the merits, they are expected to

64. E.g., see Esplin v. Hirschi, 402 F.2d 94, 99 (10th Cir. 1968), cert. denied, 394 U.S. 928 (1969).

65. E.g., Philadelphia Hous. Auth. v. American Radiator & Std. San. Corp., 323 F. Supp. 364 (E.D. Pa. 1970) (tentative approval), 322 F. Supp. 834 (E.D. Pa.) (final approval), modified on other grounds sub nom. Ace Heating & Plumbing Co. v. Crane Co., 453 F.2d 30 (3d Cir. 1971).

66. Manual for Complex Litigation Second § 30.45 (5th ed. 1985) questions the "settlement class" procedure.

67. See Neuwirth v. Allen, Fed. Sec. L. Rep. (CCH) ¶91,324 (S.D.N.Y.), aff'd, 338 F.2d 2 (2d Cir. 1964).

68. Powell v. Pennsylvania R.R., 166 F. Supp. 448 (E.D. Pa. 1958), modified, 267 F.2d 241 (3d Cir. 1959).

69. Neuman v. Electronic Specialty Co., Fed. Sec. L. Rep. (CCH) ¶92,955 (N.D. Ill. 1971).

70. Percodani v. Riker-Maxon Corp., 50 F.R.D. 473 (S.D.N.Y. 1970). Subsequent decision reported in Fed. Sec. L. Rep. (CCH) ¶93,337 (S.D.N.Y. 1972).

71. 980 Fifth Ave. Corp. v. Ring, Fed. Sec. L. Rep. (CCH) ¶92,865 (S.D.N.Y. 1970).

explore the facts sufficiently to make intelligent determinations as to adequacy and fairness. If not satisfied that class members have been adequately represented the court may explore that issue before taking up a proposed settlement and may order that class members be notified and given an opportunity to signify whether they consider the representation fair and adequate.[72]

A good summary of the factors to be considered in such a situation was made by District Judge Thomas F. Croake, in 1970:

> First, it must be remembered that a settlement is the result of a compromise, and in effecting a compromise each of the parties must expect to make some surrender in order to prevent unprofitable litigation...
>
> Second, all concerned must remember that there is no place in a settlement for a plaintiff's pursuing revenge against certain alleged wrongdoers...
>
> [Third,] the court must also keep in mind the fact that recommendation of acceptance by experienced and competent counsel is a fact entitled to great weight.
>
> And lastly it must be remembered that the role of the court is limited to the extent that its business judgment is not to be substituted for that of the parties who worked out the settlement accord unless the settlement, taken as a whole, appears so unfair on its face as to preclude judicial approval.[73]

In the foregoing case Judge Croake did not approve the proposed settlement. His principal reason was that he thought the plaintiffs had greater opportunities for success than those offered by the proposed compromise. In the eight months following his decision, there were developments which proved the correctness of his judgment. A new settlement package was presented to Judge Croake which was approved by him in 1971. Under it, the plaintiffs derived benefits of some three million dollars as compared to the 1.8 million dollars offered previously. Also, voluminous discovery

---

72. Plummer v. Chemical Bank, 668 F.2d 654, 659 (2d Cir. 1982).

73. Percodani v. Riker-Maxon Corp., Fed. Sec. L. Rep. (CCH) ¶92,823 at 90,084 (S.D.N.Y. 1970).

during the intervening period made the court "better able to view the settlement offer within a reasonable context."[74]

A defendant may settle with any or all of the putative class members on an individual basis, and thereby reduce his potential exposure to liability.[75] The named plaintiff cannot prevent negotiations for such settlements between the defendant and putative class members who are of a mind to do this.[76]

If class certification has not been ordered when the named plaintiff moves for dismissal, the court may presume that the class allegation is valid for the purpose of giving notice,[77] or instead of relying upon Rule 23(e), the court may order notice under Rule 23(d)(2).[78] By whatever procedure, notice of dismissal of a class action is intended to fairly ensure the protection of absent class members intended to be bound.[79]

§ 18.07. Derivative actions: standing to sue.

Under the federal rule and the statutes of most states, it is required that the plaintiff have been a shareholder or member of the corporation or association at the time of the transaction of which complaint is made or that the share or membership, if acquired thereafter, devolved by operation of law.[80] In that event, the plaintiff's predecessor must have met the time requirement.[81] There is some authority that a plaintiff

---

74. Percodani v. Riker-Maxon Corp., Fed. Sec. L. Rep. (CCH) ¶93,153 at 91,143 (S.D.N.Y. 1971).

75. E.g., American Fin. Sys. v. Harlow, 65 F.R.D. 572, 574 (D. Md. 1974).

76. Weight Watchers of Philadelphia v. Weight Watchers Int'l, 455 F.2d 770, 773 (2d Cir. 1972).

77. Philadelphia Elec. Co. v. Anaconda Am. Brass Co., 42 F.R.D. 324, 326 (E.D. Pa. 1967); see also Jarblum v. Frigitemp Corp., Fed. Sec. L. Rep. (CCH) ¶94,009 (S.D.N.Y. 1973).

78. E.g., Rothman v. Gould, 52 F.R.D. 494, 499, 500 (S.D.N.Y. 1971).

79. Berse v. Berman, 60 F.R.D. 414 (S.D.N.Y. 1973).

80. Rule 23.1, Fed. R. Civ. P., governs all federal court derivative actions and is the pattern for many state statutes. See, e.g., Del. Code Ann. tit. 8, § 327; Ohio Civil Rule 23.1; N.Y. Bus. Corp. Law § 626.

81. Hirshfeld v. Briskin, 447 F.2d 694 (7th Cir. 1971).

must also be a shareholder when the suit is brought[82] and continue that status during the pendency of the action.[83]

The federal rule is that beneficial ownership of the shares will suffice.[84] California and New York permit suit by either an owner of record or a beneficial owner.[85]

A shareholder in a parent company has been permitted to sue on behalf of a subsidiary, whether of the first tier[86] or second tier.[87] Generally, creditors lack standing to maintain derivative actions, although some recent decisions tend to permit that procedure.[88] To the extent that holders of convertible subordinated debentures are creditors under state law instead of a type of shareholder as provided by the Securities Exchange Act, there is authority pro[89] and con[90] as to their standing to maintain derivative actions.

In Colorado a limited partner was allowed to maintain a derivative action against the general partners for breach of their fiduciary duties. The court compared the status of the limited partner to that of a trust beneficiary or a preferred shareholder.[91]

Directors and officers may not escape liability merely because their corporation has been dissolved. In a New York case a corporation was dissolved and its assets acquired by another company. Subsequently, the shareholders of the dissolved corporation sued its officers and directors, contending

---

82. deHaas v. Empire Petroleum Co., 435 F.2d 1223 (10th Cir. 1970).

83. Rothenberg v. United Brands, Fed. Sec. L. Rep. (CCH) ¶96,045 (S.D.N.Y. 1977); Orenstein v. Compusamp, 19 F.R. Serv. 2d 466 (S.D.N.Y. 1974).

84. E.g., Drachman v. Harvey, 453 F.2d 722 (2d Cir. 1971).

85. Cal. Corp. Code § 800(b)(1); N.Y. Bus. Corp. Law § 626.

86. Goldstein v. Groesbeck, 142 F.2d 422 (2d Cir.), cert. denied, 323 U.S. 737 (1944).

87. Upson v. Otis, 155 F.2d 606 (2d Cir. 1946).

88. See, e.g., supra section 5.07.

89. E.g., Hoff v. Springregan, 52 F.R.D. 243 (S.D.N.Y. 1971); In re United States Fin. Sec. Litig., 69 F.R.D. 24, 35-36 (S.D. Cal. 1975).

90. Harff v. Kerkorian, 324 A.2d 215 (Del. Ch. 1974), aff'd, 347 A.2d 133 (Del. 1975); Brooks v. Weiser, 57 F.R.D. 491 (S.D.N.Y. 1972).

91. Moore v. 1600 Downing Street, Ltd., 668 P.2d 16 (Colo. App. 1983).

that their mismanagement had depressed the value of the assets which enabled the other company to acquire them for less than their actual value. The court held that the plaintiffs had standing to maintain a derivative action, despite the dissolution of the corporation.[92]

Rule 23.1 imposes substantial standards of responsibility, liability and accountability upon a derivative action plaintiff. Justice Robert H. Jackson explained them, as follows:

> He sues, not for himself alone, but as a representative of a class comprising all who are similarly situated. The interests of all in the redress of the wrongs are taken into his hands, dependent upon his diligence, wisdom and integrity. And while the stockholders have chosen the corporate director or manager, they have no such election as to a plaintiff who steps forward to represent them. He is a self-chosen representative and a volunteer champion. The Federal Constitution does not oblige the State to place its litigating and adjudicating processes at the disposal of such a representative, at least without imposing standards of responsibility, liability and accountability which it considers will protect the interest he elects himself to represent.[93]

Among the other requirements of Rule 23.1 and most of the state rules and statutes relating to derivative actions is the important one that the plaintiff and his counsel must fairly and adequately represent the interests of the shareholders or members similarly situated in interest in enforcing the rights of the corporation or association.[94] This is also a constitutional mandate.[95] Generally the question of adequate representation depends on (1) whether the plaintiff's attorney is qualified, experienced and generally able to conduct the litigation, and (2) whether the plaintiff's interests are antago-

---

92. Independent Inv. Protective League v. Time, Inc., 50 N.Y.2d 259, 428 N.Y.S.2d 671, 406 N.E.2d 486 (1980).

93. Cohen v. Beneficial Indus. Loan Corp., 337 U.S. 541, 550, 93 L.Ed. 1528, 69 S.Ct. 1221, 1227 (1949).

94. Barrett v. Southern Conn. Gas Co., 172 Conn. 362, 374 A.2d 1051 (1971).

95. Hansberry v. Lee, 311 U.S. 32, 85 L.Ed. 22, 61 S.Ct. 115 (1949).

nistic to those of the other shareholders or members similarly situated.[96]

The corporation is a necessary party-defendant in the derivative action and this requirement poses a problem as to representation of the corporation and its directors who are usually the actual defendants. A New Jersey district court has said that "the interests of the two groups will almost always be diverse." However, if the directors are accused of fraud, the corporation must always have independent counsel.[97] When inside and outside directors are named as defendants, "joint representation presents a real potential for conflict," but with full disclosure these groups may consent to that arrangement.[98]

§ 18.08. Derivative actions: the demand requirement.

Because a derivative action impinges on the managerial freedom of directors,[99] such an action may not be maintained until a demand has been made upon the directors to bring the action and they have been allowed a reasonable time to do so.[100] An exception to that rule exists if such a demand would be useless or futile. In the leading case of *Aronson v. Lewis*[101] the Delaware court held that the demand could be excused only "where facts are alleged with particularity which create a reasonable doubt that the directors' action was entitled to the protection of the business judgment rule."[102] Such reasonable doubt must relate to (1) whether the directors are disinterested and independent and (2) whether the challenged transaction was otherwise the product of a valid exercise of business judgment. The court emphasized that specific alle-

---

96. E.g., Wetzel v. Liberty Mut. Ins. Co., 508 F.2d 239, 247 (3d Cir.), cert. denied, 421 U.S. 1011 (1975).

97. Messing v. FDI, Inc., 439 F. Supp. 776, 782 (D.N.J. 1977).

98. Id. at 784.

99. Aronson v. Lewis, 473 A.2d 805, 811 (Del. 1984).

100. Rule 23.1, Fed. R. Civ. P.; Cal. Corp. Code § 800(b)(2); N.Y. Bus. Corp. Law § 626(c).

101. Aronson v. Lewis, supra note 99.

102. Id. at 808. See also Pogostin v. Rice, 480 A.2d 619, 624 (Del. 1984).

gations are required and conclusive averments will not suffice.

Declaring that a "cardinal precept of the General Corporation law of the State of Delaware is that directors, rather than shareholders, manage the business and affairs of the corporation," the Delaware court identified the demand requirement as a recognition of that precept. Moreover, the "business judgment rule is an acknowledgment of the managerial prerogatives of Delaware directors."[103]

A plaintiff may establish that a demand is futile under Delaware law by alleging either a breach of the duty of loyalty or a breach of the duty of care. In federal court actions, particularly when the securities laws or other federal statutes are involved, the courts are inclined to apply federal law to the demand requirement of Rule 23.1.[104] That law requires a breach of the duty of loyalty in order for the demand to be excused.[105] In the absence of specific allegations of self-dealing or bias on the part of a majority of the board, mere director approval and acquiescence in the alleged misdeeds are insufficient to render demand futile.[106]

The trend of the decisions since *Aronson v. Lewis* suggests that it will be widely recognized in the state courts as the proper rule applicable to the demand requirement in derivative actions. What extent of directorial involvement must exist to establish futility of demand will probably go on a case-by-case basis. New York has been liberal in excusing the demand;[107] Massachusetts has been conservative.[108] A Mis-

---

103. Id. at 812.

104. E.g., Lewis v. Graves, 701 F.2d 245 (2d Cir. 1983); Heit v. Baird, 567 F.2d 1157 (1st Cir. 1977); Vernars v. Young, 539 F.2d 966 (3d Cir. 1976).

105. E.g., In re Kauffmans Mut. Fund Actions, 479 F.2d 257 (1st Cir.), cert. denied, 414 U.S. 857 (1973).

106. Consumers Power Co. Derivative Litig., Fed. Sec. L. Rep. ¶92,975 (E.D. Mich. 1986).

107. Barr v. Wackman, 36 N.Y.2d 371, 368 N.Y.S.2d 497, 329 N.E.2d 180 (1975).

108. Palley v. Baird, 365 Mass. 737, 254 N.E.2d 894 (1970); Datz v. Keller, 347 Mass. 766, 196 N.E.2d 922 (1964).

souri court required a demand despite the fact that the named defendants constituted a majority of the executive committee, but not of the entire board.[109]

Rule 23.1 provides for a demand on shareholders, if necessary. State laws vary on this subject. Massachusetts is strict.[110] New York and Delaware have no such requirement.[111] In cases where federal jurisdiction is based on diversity of citizenship, it is an open question whether a provision for a demand is substantive or procedural.[112]

§ 18.09. Derivative actions: settlement and dismissal.

A derivative action may not be dismissed or settled without the approval of the court. Notice must be given the shareholders or class members in such a manner as the court directs[113] unless the court rules that the action was not properly brought,[114] that the forum has no jurisdiction over the person[115] or the cause is dismissed after trial on the merits.

A shareholder-plaintiff, bringing a derivative action, stands in a fiduciary capacity with respect to the other shareholders. He will be required to account for any benefit received personally for discontinuing the action, including any premium paid for his shares.[116] Such plaintiff may not voluntarily dismiss the action without court approval. Even if no

---

109. O'Maley v. ISC Indus., 519 S.W.2d 346 (Mo. App. 1975).

110. See cases cited supra note 108.

111. Greenspun v. Lindley, 36 N.Y.2d 473, 369 N.Y.S.2d 123, 330 N.E.2d 79 (1975).

112. Compare Steinberg v. Hardy, 90 F. Supp. 167 (D. Conn. 1950) with Meltzer v. Atlantic Res. Corp., 330 F.2d 946 (4th Cir.), cert. denied sub nom. Scurlock v. Meltzer, 379 U.S. 841 (1964). In Aronson v. Lewis, 473 A.2d 805, 809 (Del. 1984), the trial court called it "substantive," citing Lewis v. Aronson, 466 A.2d 375, 380 (Del. Ch. 1983).

113. Rule 23.1, Fed. R. Civ. P. See also, e.g., N.Y. Bus. Corp. Law § 626(d), and Ohio Civil Rule 23.1.

114. Polakoff v. Delaware Steeplechase & Race Ass'n, 264 F. Supp. 915 (D. Del. 1966).

115. Marcus v. Textile Banking Co., 38 F.R.D. 185 (S.D.N.Y. 1965).

116. See N.Y. Bus. Corp. Law § 626(e); Clark v. Greenburg, 296 N.Y. 146, 71 N.E.2d 443 (1947).

other shareholder, after notice, seeks to intervene or object, a court-approved dismissal should be without prejudice to any new action for the same cause.[117]

Although individual notice of settlement or dismissal is not required, the risks of ineffective notice are substantial. Failure of due process in this respect[118] may destroy the res judicata effect of a judgment, tolling of statutes of limitation, and raise questions as to adequate representation, extra costs and expenses and further litigation.[119]

The court's duty in dealing with a settlement proposal is summarized in a Delaware decision:

> The Court's responsibility at this juncture is to determine whether or not the proposed settlement terms are fair, reasonable and adequate, a settlement hearing not being in any sense a rehearsal of a trial.... [T]he question now for decision is whether or not the terms of the settlement are fair and reasonable when weighed against the probability of recovery at trial on the asserted claims.... In making this evaluation, the function of the Court is merely to determine such probability and to go no further.... Finally, the recovery of monetary damages from director defendants is not a sine qua non to settlement of a derivative action.[120]

That analysis accords with the general rules relating to settlements in derivative as well as class actions.

In a 1972 decision[121] Chief Judge Henry J. Friendly of the Second Circuit emphasized the duty of the court to exercise particular care to afford a full opportunity for hearing where the plaintiff in a derivative action opposes a settlement negotiated and recommended by the plaintiff's attorney. Although

---

117. Tryforos v. Icarian Dev. Co., 518 F.2d 1258 (7th Cir. 1975), cert. denied sub nom. Manta v. Tryforos, 423 U.S. 1091 (1976); Beaver Assocs. v. Cannon, 59 F.R.D. 508 (S.D.N.Y. 1973).

118. See Eisen v. Carlisle & Jacquelin, 417 U.S. 156, 40 L.Ed.2d 732, 94 S.Ct. 2140 (1974).

119. Greenspan v. Bogan, 492 F.2d 251 (1st Cir. 1974); Papilsky v. Berndt, 466 F.2d 251 (2d Cir. 1971), cert. denied, 409 U.S. 1077 (1972).

120. Prince v. Bensinger, 244 A.2d 89, 93 (Del. Ch. 1968).

121. Saylor v. Lindsley, 456 F.2d 896 (2d Cir. 1972).

recognizing that the plaintiff's assent is not essential to a settlement in a derivative action, Judge Friendly said:

> The attorney remains bound to keep his client fully informed of settlement negotiations, to advise the client before signing a stipulation of settlement on his behalf, and, if the client has objected, to inform the court of this when presenting the settlement, so that it may devise procedures whereby the plaintiff, with a new attorney, may himself conduct further inquiry, if so advised.[122]

The court observed further that "the interests of the plaintiff in a stockholder's derivative suit and of his attorney are by no means congruent." Both, said the court, are presumed to be "interested in maximizing the recovery," but the risks of litigation to the lawyer are different and substantially greater than the risks to the shareholder-plaintiff. Also, in case of the attorney, Judge Friendly observed, a "relatively small settlement may well produce an allowance bearing a higher ratio to the cost of the work than a much larger recovery obtained only after extensive discovery, a long trial and an appeal."

It was emphasized that the recognition of the potential conflict of interest between attorney and shareholder-plaintiff should not in itself mandate rejection of a settlement opposed by the plaintiff so long as he is afforded the right to develop the basis for his objection in an adequate hearing.

In this same decision, Judge Friendly inquired into the likelihood of recovery of substantially more than the proposed settlement. Limiting his discussion to what the court considered "plaintiff's most promising theory," he found sufficient unexplored issues of potential merit to conclude that the "plaintiff, through his new counsel, and the other objectors should be allowed to delve somewhat more deeply into the merits of this action."[123]

---

122. Id. at 900.

123. Id. at 904. See also Protective Comm. for Indep. Stockholders of TMT Trailer Ferry v. Anderson, 390 U.S. 414, 424, 20 L.Ed.2d 1, 9, 88 S.Ct. 1157, reh'g denied, 391 U.S. 909 (1968).

§ 18.10. Derivative actions: termination; judicial review.

Beginning with a district court decision in the Second Circuit in 1976,[124] there has been a volume of litigation involving the powers of directors and special litigation committees created by them to bring about the termination of derivative actions. The basis for this litigation is the contention that the directors retain their managerial authority in either (1) the demand-refused case when the board refuses to bring the action, or (2) the demand-excused case when the pleaded facts show that a demand would be futile.[125] Following some confusion in the lower courts, the Supreme Court, in *Burks v. Lasker,*[126] directed a two-step analysis to determine the power of a special litigation committee to obtain dismissal of a derivative action: (1) whether the applicable state law permits the directors to delegate authority to dismiss the action to the committee, and (2) whether such a rule is consistent with the policies underlying the federal securities laws. Because only Minnesota has a statute controlling the termination of derivative actions,[127] the courts were called upon to make this decision.

The first tests, as to the applicable state law, found affirmative answers in New York[128] and Delaware.[129] Both concluded that a special litigation committee of disinterested directors had the power to dismiss a derivative action. The New York court held that the substantive aspects of a special litigation committee's decision to terminate the action fell "squarely within the embrace of the business judgment doctrine"[130] and were not subject to judicial inquiry. It found no triable issues as to the committee's diligence, independence or good faith. The Delaware court held that in either the demand-refused or

124. Gall v. Exxon Corp., 418 F. Supp. 508 (S.D.N.Y. 1976).

125. See supra sections 6.15 and 18.08.

126. 441 U.S. 471, 60 L.Ed.2d 404, 99 S.Ct. 1831 (1979).

127. Minn. Stat. Ann. § 302A.243.

128. Auerbach v. Bennett, 47 N.Y. 619, 419 N.Y.S.2d 929, 393 N.E.2d 994 (1979).

129. Zapata Corp. v. Maldonado, 430 A.2d 779 (Del. 1981), rev'g Maldonado v. Flynn, 413 A.2d 1251 (Del. Ch. 1980).

130. Auerbach v. Bennett, supra note 128, 47 N.Y.2d at 633-34.

the demand-excused case, the board retains its authority to make decisions regarding corporate litigation; that the board may delegate its managerial authority to a committee of independent disinterested directors; and that even in a demand-excused case the board had the power to appoint a committee of one or more disinterested directors to determine whether the derivative action should be pursued or dismissal sought.[131]

The Delaware court, however, significantly expanded the scope of review by requiring the chancery court (1) to inquire into the independence and good faith of the committee and review the reasonableness of the committee's investigation,[132] and (2) to apply its own independent business judgment to decide whether the motion to dismiss should be granted in a demand-excused case.[133] The Delaware court subsequently held that the second step was discretionary and could be waived.[134] Nonetheless, if the second step is taken, the business judgment rule is virtually ignored.

The federal courts have been busy with cases requiring analyses of various state laws to ascertain the powers of special litigation committees to terminate derivative actions. In their interpretations of the laws of California,[135] Connecticut,[136] Minnesota,[137] Ohio,[138] Texas,[139] Massachusetts,[140] and

---

131. Zapata Corp. v. Maldonado, supra note 129, 430 A.2d at 786. See also Aronson v. Lewis, 473 A.2d 805, 813 (Del. 1984).

132. Id. at 788.

133. Id. at 789.

134. Kaplan v. Wyatt, 499 A.2d 5 (Del. 1985).

135. Lewis v. Anderson, 615 F.2d 778 (9th Cir. 1979), cert. denied, 449 U.S. 869 (1980); Gaines v. Haughton, 645 F.2d 761 (9th Cir. 1981), cert. denied, 454 U.S. 1145 (1982).

136. Joy v. North, 692 F.2d 880 (2d Cir. 1982), cert. denied, 460 U.S. 1051 (1983).

137. Abbey v. Control Data Corp., 603 F.2d 724 (8th Cir. 1979), cert. denied, 444 U.S. 1017 (1980).

138. In re General Tire & Rubber Co. Sec. Litig., 726 F.2d 1075 (6th Cir.), cert. denied, 105 S.Ct. 187 (1984).

139. Clark v. Lomas & Nettleton Fin. Corp., 625 F.2d 49 (5th Cir. 1980), cert. denied, 450 U.S. 1029 (1981).

140. Hasan v. Clevetrust Realty Invs., 729 F.2d 372 (6th Cir. 1984).

Michigan,[141] federal courts predicted the rules that states would apply. Under Iowa law a federal court followed the Delaware two-step rule,[142] but the state supreme court required resort to a court to appoint a special panel when a majority of a corporation's directors had been named as defendants in a derivative action.[143]

A 1986 decision of the Supreme Court of North Carolina adopted a modified version of the New York approach. It imposed on the defendants the burden of proving that the directors were disinterested and independent and conducted a thorough investigation. If so, the good faith of the directors would be presumed.[144]

The second test of *Burks v. Lasker,* whether the state's business judgment rule is inconsistent with the policies underlying the federal securities laws, has presented no problems of consequence. The *Burks* court found no such inconsistency in the dismissal of a suit under the Investment Company Act and Investment Advisors Act. It differentiated actions under Section 16(b) of the Securities Exchange Act relating to short-swing profits.[145]

The Ninth Circuit found no such inconsistency as to claims under Section 10(b) of the Securities Exchange Act and Rule 10b-5.[146] As to proxy statements and Sections 13(a) and 14(a) of the Securities Exchange Act, the Ninth Circuit reached a similar conclusion.[147] The Sixth Circuit found no conflict between the policies of Section 14(a) and the business judgment rule "where a connection between the underlying allegations

---

141. Genzer v. Cunningham, 498 F. Supp. 682 (E.D. Mich. 1980).

142. Watts v. Des Moines Register & Tribune, 525 F. Supp. 1311 (S.D. Iowa 1981).

143. Miller v. Register & Tribune Syndicate, Inc., 336 N.W.2d 709 (Iowa 1983).

144. Alford v. Shaw, 318 N.C. 284, 349 S.E.2d 41 (1986).

145. Burks v. Lasker, supra note 126, 441 U.S. at 482-84 n.13.

146. Lewis v. Anderson, supra note 135, at 783-84.

147. Gaines v. Haughton, supra note 135, at 774.

and the *proxy process* is absent," namely the absence of a causal link.[148]

Construing Massachusetts law, the Sixth Circuit declined to apply a presumption of good faith to a special litigation committee in a derivative action involving a Massachusetts real estate investment trust with its principal office in Ohio. The one-man committee consisted of the only trustee not named as a defendant in the action.[149]

Judge Nathaniel R. Jones, who also wrote the opinion in the earlier Ohio case, noted "the realities of corporate collegiality" and declared that "a reviewing court must scrutinize the record to determine whether a genuine issue of material fact exists as to the committee's independence, good faith and procedural fairness".

In this case, the committee's report raised "serious questions about the integrity of [its] findings," and demonstrated several "significant business relationships between [the committee] and the defendants." Compared to the investigation in *Auerbach v. Bennett,* there was a lack of "the thoroughness which is necessary for a truly objective and meaningful recommendation." The district court's summary judgment sustaining the committee's investigation was vacated and the case remanded for trial on its merits.

§ 18.11. Derivative actions: termination; business judgment rule.

The Delaware court has held:

> The function of the business judgment rule is of paramount significance in the context of a derivative action. It comes into play in several ways — in addressing a demand, in the determination of demand futility, in efforts by independent disinterested directors to dismiss the action as inimical to the corporation's best interests, and generally as a defense to the merits of the suit.[150]

---

148. In re General Tire & Rubber Co. Sec. Litig., supra note 138, at 1082.
149. Hasan v. Clevetrust Realty Invs., supra note 140.
150. Aronson v. Lewis, 473 A.2d 805, 812 (Del. 1984).

In determining demand futility, the court examines the facts alleged in the complaint to determine whether they create a reasonable doubt as to the disinterestedness and independence of the directors at the time the complaint was filed. Directorial interest exists whenever divided loyalties are present, or a director has received, or is entitled to receive, a personal financial benefit from the challenged transaction which is not available equally to the shareholders.[151] Directors can neither appear on both sides of a transaction nor expect to derive any personal financial benefit from it in the sense of self-dealing, unless it is a benefit devolving upon the corporation or all shareholders generally.[152] The question of independence flows from an analysis of the factual allegations pertaining to the influences upon the directors' performance of their duties generally, and more specifically in respect to the challenged transaction.[153]

In this analysis, the directors' duty of loyalty is of high importance.[154] When violations of that duty are alleged as facts with particularity, and support a reasonable doubt that the directors are disinterested and independent, the court's inquiry ends.[155]

The second part of the court's analysis focuses on the substantive nature of the challenged transaction and the board's approval of it. Here the court reviews the transaction against the factual background of the complaint to determine whether a reasonable doubt exists that the transaction was a valid exercise of business judgment.[156] Where demand is excused, a shareholder possesses the ability to initiate a derivative action, but the right to prosecute it may be terminated by the exercise of applicable standards of the business judgment rule.[157] Where demand is required and is refused, the court

---

151. Pogostin v. Rice, 480 A.2d 619, 624 (Del. 1984).
152. Sinclair Oil Co. v. Levien, 280 A.2d 717, 720 (Del. 1971).
153. Aronson v. Lewis, supra note 150, at 814, 816.
154. See supra Chapters 3 and 6.
155. Pogostin v. Rice, supra note 151, at 624-25.
156. Aronson v. Lewis, supra note 150, at 814.
157. Id. at 813.

may apply the principles of the business judgment rule in assessing the sufficiency of the refusal.[158]

In the context of change-of-control situations arising out of various types of takeovers and defenses against them, what was originally almost a routine application of the business judgment rule to uphold directorial actions is now being re-examined by the courts.[159] Especially where a complaint alleges that the corporate machinery was manipulated by the directors for the sole or primary purpose of perpetuating themselves in office and retaining their perquisites, courts are by-passing the business judgment rule and making their own assessments of the validity of the directors' decisions.[160]

In the reported cases dealing with this subject, there are some recurring principles that appear to be reasonably predictable:

(1) The directors must be adequately informed and must make a thorough, well-documented investigation and obtain sufficient expert advice before acting;

(2) Any defensive measure adopted to resist the threatened takeover must be reasonable in relation to the perceived threat posed by the takeover;

(3) When the directors conclude that a change of control or a breakup of the corporation is inevitable, the directors should not seek to manage the sale, should not interfere with open and unrestrained bidding, and should permit the shareholders to obtain the "highest price for the pieces" of the enterprise.[161]

---

158. Id. See also Abramowitz v. Posner, 672 F.2d 1025 (2d Cir. 1982).

159. See supra Chapter 6.

160. E.g., Smith v. Van Gorkom, 488 A.2d 858 (Del. 1985); Unocal Corp. v. Mesa Petroleum Co., 493 A.2d 946 (Del. 1985); Moran v. Household Int'l, Inc., 500 A.2d 1346 (Del. 1985); Hanson Trust PLC. v. ML SCM Acquisition, Inc., 781 F.2d 264 (2d Cir. 1986); Edelman v. Freuhauf Corp., 798 F.2d 882 (6th Cir. 1986).

161. Revlon, Inc. v. MacAndrews & Forbes Holdings, Inc., 506 A.2d 173 (Del. 1986).

COROLLARY REFERENCES

"Attorney-Client Privilege in Class Actions: Fashioning an Exception to Promote Adequacy of Representation," 97 Harv. L. Rev. 947 (1984).

Bernfeld, "Class Actions and Federal Securities Laws," 55 Cornell L. Rev. 78 (1969).

Block & Prussin, "Termination of Derivative Suits Against Directors on Business Judgment Grounds: From Zapata to Aronson," 39 Bus. Law. 1502 (1984).

Block, Prussin & Wachtel, "Dismissal of Derivative Actions Under the Business Judgment Rule: Zapata One Year Later," 38 Bus. Law. 401 (1983).

Burgman & Cox, "Corporate Directors, Corporate Realities and Deliberative Process: An Analysis of the Trans Union Case," 11 J. Corp. L. 311 (1986).

"Class Actions: Certification and Notice Requirements," 68 Geo. L.J. 1009 (1980).

"Class Actions and Statutes of Limitations," 48 U. Chi. L. Rev. 106 (1981).

"Class Actions: Judicial Control of Defense Communication With Absent Class Members," 59 Ind. L.J. 1343 (1983-84).

Cox, "Searching for the Corporation's Voice in Derivative Suit Litigation: A Critique of Zapata," 1982 Duke L.J. 959.

"Developments in the Law: Class Actions," 89 Harv. L. Rev. 1318 (1976).

"Director Independence and Derivative Suit Settlements," 1983 Duke L.J. 645.

Frankel, "Some Preliminary Observations Concerning Civil Rule 23," 43 F.R.D. 39 (1967).

Comment, "Miller v. Register & Tribune Syndicate: A New Approach to Special Litigation Committees," 9 J. Corp. L. 981 (1984).

Note, "Business Judgment Rule in Derivative Suits Against Directors," 65 Cornell L. Rev. 600 (1980).

Chapter 19

DEFENSES AND PROTECTIVE MEASURES

§ 19.01. Overview of chapter.

Since *Texas Gulf Sulphur*[1] and *BarChris*[2] were decided in 1968, the courts have developed a complex set of rules governing the control and management of corporations. The litigation in which those rules developed has imposed substantial burdens on persons serving as corporate directors and has placed their personal fortunes in jeopardy.

To make matters worse, the "D & O crisis" of the mid-1980's resulted in a dearth of available D & O insurance and caused numerous corporations to lose the services of some outside directors who were unwilling to retain their positions without insurance protection.

The defense of corporate directors and officers in future litigation and the provision of some realistic means to protect them from personal loss is the subject of this chapter. Defense involves preventive measures to avoid such litigation and also relates to relief from liability. Protection includes indem-

---

1. SEC v. Texas Gulf Sulphur Co., 401 F.2d 833 (2d Cir. 1968), cert. denied sub nom. Coates v. SEC, 394 U.S. 976 (1969), cert. denied, 404 U.S. 1005 (1971), reh'g denied, 404 U.S. 1064 (1972).
2. Escott v. BarChris Constr. Corp., 283 F. Supp. 643 (S.D.N.Y. 1968).

nification from loss,[3] liability insurance,[4] and alternatives to such insurance.

§ 19.02. Checklist of potential liabilities.

To identify some of the problem areas deserving special attention of corporate officers and directors, the following list is offered. It is not all-inclusive, because these problems change frequently. The classifications are arbitrary, for ease of reference, and some items may be classified in one or more areas.

Management, business and operations

(1) Acquiescence in conduct of fellow directors engaged in improper activity.
(2) Aiding or abetting misconduct of others.
(3) Attending directors' meetings and committee meetings.
(4) Avoiding unlawful political contributions.
(5) Awareness of internal management controls.
(6) Compensation arrangements and reports of compensation committee.
(7) Continuing a wrongful practice after learning of its impropriety.
(8) Cooperation with regulatory authorities.
(9) Corporate acquisition which would result in loss of corporate assets.
(10) Corporate financial delinquencies.
(11) Counsel's advice as to possible libel or slander.
(12) Dealing responsibly with corporate debts.
(13) Dishonored corporate checks.
(14) Dissent from improper acts of board or committees and recording of dissent.
(15) Executive committee proceedings.
(16) Extending credit only as warranted.

---

3. See infra Chapter 20.
4. See infra Chapter 21.

(17)   Filing annual and periodic reports.

(18)   Guarding against corporate payment of bribes or making other illegal payments.

(19)   Inefficient management resulting in losses.

(20)   Informal dissolution or liquidation of corporation.

(21)   Infringement of patents, copyrights or trademarks.

(22)   Minutes of board and of all committees.

(23)   Misuse or nonuse of electronic data processing.

(24)   Monthly operational reports and financial statements.

(25)   Qualifying corporation in other states where it does business.

(26)   Receiving personal benefit or gain as a consequence of service performed as an officer or director.

(27)   Reports of auditors and of audit committee.

(28)   Recording dissent from wrongful acts at meetings not attended, after reviewing minutes.

(29)   Selling or transferring corporate assets only for adequate consideration.

(30)   Shirking responsibility.

(31)   Statements of corporate policy in areas that frequently generate litigation.

Informed business judgment

(32)   Being inquisitive.

(33)   Consulting legal counsel, auditors, other experts and corporation's officers and managers to obtain information.

(34)   Decisions based on adequate information and intelligent and advised judgment.

(35)   Examining reports and documents before signing.

(36)   Ignorance of corporate books and records.

(37)   Inspecting corporation's books and records when necessary to keep abreast of its activities.

(38)   Making reasonable investigations as necessary.

(39)   Making use of all available information.

(40) Registration statements and other reports and filings.

(41) Using expertise of your own and of others.

(42) Verifying facts in official documents before signing and filing them.

Unauthorized or ultra vires actions

(43) Activities in which the corporation engages as being only those permitted by its corporate powers.

(44) Compensation and benefits paid to directors and officers, verified for reasonableness.

(45) Consulting counsel for advice as to corporate powers under statutes, charter and bylaws.

(46) Declaring and paying dividends only as provided in corporate powers.

(47) Distributing assets with adequate provision to pay or secure corporate debts.

(48) Dividends paid, adequate and not excessive.

(49) Obedience to charter and bylaw provisions.

(50) Political contributions by corporation as being only those authorized by law.

Self-dealing and conflicts of interest

(51) Awareness of conflicts of interest.

(52) Conduct of fellow directors engaged in self-dealing.

(53) Contracts with corporation involving self-dealing.

(54) Corporate contracts as corporate assets.

(55) Corporate opportunities when seized by directors or officers.

(56) Disclosing personal interest in management transactions.

(57) Engaging in a competitive enterprise.

(58) Inside information used to obtain secret profits.

(59) Key employees as corporate assets.

(60) Loans by or to corporate officers, directors, or shareholders as involving self-dealing.

602

(61) Preference at expense of creditors or other share-
      holders.
(62) Transactions between corporations having com-
      mon directors.
(63) Transactions with other entities in which an officer
      or director is interested.

Change of control situations

(64) Analysis of the nature of a takeover as involving
      determination whether an antitakeover measure is
      reasonable in relation to the threat imposed.
(65) Antitakeover measures implemented by a board as
      involving a good faith and reasonable investigation
      to determine the existence of a danger to the corpo-
      ration's policy and effectiveness.
(66) Expenditure of corporate funds in proxy contests as
      subject to directors' duties of loyalty, care and dili-
      gence.
(67) Merger of the corporation as involving directors'
      duties of care and loyalty to the corporation and its
      shareholders.
(68) Offerors of competing acquisition offers as being
      entitled to equal treatment.
(69) Purchase of shares by corporation primarily to re-
      tain management in control.
(70) Rejecting of acquisition offer and refusal to submit
      it to shareholders.
(71) Sale of a controlling interest as involving duty of
      loyalty and requiring awareness of buyer's inten-
      tions as to looting corporation.
(72) Takeover bids and related matters as involving di-
      rectors' duties of care, loyalty and diligence to cor-
      poration and shareholders.
(73) Takeover threats causing reality of a break-up of
      the corporation, resulting duty of directors to ob-
      tain highest stock price for benefit of shareholders.

Other matters involving shares and shareholders

(74) Annual reports.

(75) Beneficial ownership of shares, application of Section 16(b) of Securities Exchange Act.

(76) Control person's vicarious liability.

(77) Deceptive representations.

(78) Delivery of securities promptly after sale.

(79) Disclosures insufficiently or improperly made.

(80) Discrimination against minority shareholders.

(81) Fraudulent conduct in connection with purchase or sale of security.

(82) Fraudulent methods, misstatements or omissions relating to material facts.

(83) Fraudulent reports, financial statements or certificates.

(84) Freezeout mergers without business purpose.

(85) Insider making short sales.

(86) Insider trading without disclosure of nonpublic information.

(87) Interstate use of mails in sale of unregistered securities.

(88) Material misstatements in filings, registration statements or reports to agencies.

(89) Misuse of insider information.

(90) Prospectuses and communications with investors.

(91) Proxy contest filings.

(92) Proxy statements.

(93) Reports to SEC and state agencies.

(94) SEC filings.

(96) Short-swing profits in stock trading.

(97) Tipping by insiders.

Disclosures

(98) Conflicts of interest.

(99) Earnings forecasts or reports.

(100) Extent of board participation in improper actions.

(101) Illegal payments.

(102) Material facts.
(103) Political contributions.
(104) Pre-tax losses.
(105) Publicizing information as to favorable or unfavorable transactions or occurrences.
(106) Sales information.
(107) Sufficiency of disclosures.
(108) Surplus earnings.
(109) Timeliness of disclosures.

Matters involving taxes

(110) Causing corporation to incur unnecessary tax liability or penalty.
(111) Failing to monitor filing of tax returns and payment of taxes.
(112) Failure to obey requirements of tax laws and regulations.
(113) Failure to require withholding in connection with Social Security or income taxes.
(114) Failure to secure funds withheld for Social Security or income taxes.
(115) Unreasonable accumulation of surplus.

Miscellaneous matters

(116) Aiding and abetting actions of others.
(117) Carelessness in concluding business or legal matters.
(118) Commercial bribery not disclosed.
(119) Consenting to improper or illegal actions resulting in losses.
(120) Detecting and preventing embezzlement of corporate funds.
(121) Failing to see what could be seen by merely looking.
(122) Federal Election Campaign Act.
(123) Foreign Corrupt Practices Act of 1977.
(124) Fraudulent interstate transactions.

(125) Inducing corporation to commit breach of contract.

(126) Inducing intentional or careless wrongdoing by corporation.

(127) Ignoring statutory or regulatory requirements.

(128) Insufficient monitoring or supervision of officers or other employees.

(129) Nondisclosure of questionable or unlawful actions.

(130) Racketeering activity.

(131) Treble damages or civil fines for statutory violations.

(132) Use of mails to defraud.

(133) Use of wire services, telephones, radio or television to defraud.

(134) Wasting corporate assets.

(135) Willful wrongdoing.

§ 19.03. Guidelines for directors: generally.

Guidelines to help corporate directors do a better job of performing their duties have been advocated or written by some[5] and abandoned by others, including the SEC. It planned to issue such guidelines under the antifraud provisions of the federal securities laws[6] but did not do so.[7]

Boards of directors make decisions that entail risks consciously assumed. They are not courts and the participating directors are neither researchers seeking truth nor scientists working in narrow fields of specialization.[8] Moreover, boards reach conclusions by discussion, compromise and consensus, engaging in "a continuing flow of supervisory process, punc-

---

5. E.g., Blough, "The Outside Director at Work on the Board," 45 N.Y.S.B.J. 467, 472-74 (1973); Sommer, "Directors and the Federal Securities Laws," Fed. Sec. L. Rep. (CCH) ¶79,669 (1974); "The Role and Composition of the Board of Directors of the Large Publicly Owned Corporation — Statement of the Business Roundtable," 33 Bus. Law. 2099 (1978).

6. Garrett, "The SEC Study of Directors' Guidelines," 11 Conference Board Record 57 (1974).

7. Prentice-Hall Corp., Report Bull., Jan. 2, 1975.

8. See Manning, "The Business Judgment Rule and the Director's Duty of Attention: Time for Reality," 39 Bus. Law. 1477, 1482 (1984).

tuated only occasionally by a discrete transactional decision."[9] In such a climate, guidelines are difficult to prepare with sufficient scope and flexibility to deal with the variety of problems presented.

Nonetheless two sets of directors' guidelines are presented and discussed in sections 19.04 and 19.05 of this chapter.

§ 19.04. Guidelines: the Corporate Director's Guidebook.

Guidelines that give promise of being realistic and are sufficiently comprehensive to be helpful are found in the Corporate Director's Guidebook.[10] It is intended as a reference for analysis and comment by lawyers, their corporate clients, scholars and others, and is reviewed and reappraised on a continuing basis.[11]

Director attributes

The Guidebook defines the principal qualities of an effective corporate director to include "strength of character, an inquiring and independent mind, practical wisdom and mature judgment." He is admonished to "avoid taking an adversary attitude in his relationship with management," but is encouraged to develop a "healthy" skepticism and a bias toward seeking outside advice where "actual or potential conflicts of interest involving management, or those advising management are presented."[12]

Basic duties

Legal obligations of directors fall into two broad categories: a duty of loyalty and a duty of care, which is said to include a

---

9. Id. at 1494.

10. Prepared by the Committee on Corporate Laws, Section of Corporation, Banking and Business Law, American Bar Association, and published in 33 Bus. Law. 1595 (1978).

11. Preface, 33 Bus. Law. 1595, 1596 (1978).

12. 33 Bus. Law. 1595, 1608 (1978).

607

duty to be attentive to the corporation's business.[13] This is "diligence," the third of the three basic duties[14] of corporate directors.

Conflict of interest should be disclosed and a director should abstain from acting on any matter in which he is personally interested. If a transaction involves possible conflict of interest, its fairness to the corporation ought to be of primary concern.[15] A director is expected to deal in confidence with corporate matters unless he knows that particular information is generally known.[16]

A director's duty of care is discussed in Chapter 2. Several of the terms used in that discussion are taken up by the Guidebook which explains their customary meaning. For example:

> "*in good faith*" means honestly or in an honest manner;
>
> "*he reasonably believes*" establishes "the objectivity of the standard governing director conduct";
>
> "*best interests of the corporation*" points to the director's primary allegiance;
>
> "*ordinarily prudent person*" focuses on the basic director attributes of common sense, practical wisdom and informed judgment;
>
> "*in a like position*" recognizes that a director's role will vary with circumstances, limits criticism of his performance to the time of action or nonaction, and recognizes that a director's special qualifications and the duties assigned to him may impose greater responsibilities upon him.[17]

In discussing the director's duty of attention, the Guidebook alludes to attendance at meetings, review of ade-

---

13. Id. at 1599-1600.

14. Supra section 1.05 and Chapter 2.

15. 33 Bus. Law. 1595, 1599. See also "Corporate Director's Guidebook: Comments Submitted by the American Society of Corporate Secretaries," 33 Bus. Law. 321 (1977).

16. 33 Bus. Law. 1595, 1600.

17. 33 Bus. Law. 1595, 1601.

quate information to be supplied to him, reading material distributed to members of the board, and monitoring the activities of those to whom the board delegates responsibilities.[18]

Reliance

Reliance is dealt with by the Guidebook in terms of the reliance provisions of Sections 35 and 42 of the Model Business Corporation Act. The necessity for delegation of responsibilities is recognized.[19]

Business judgment rule

Decision making is dealt with in the Guidebook on the basis of the "business judgment" rule. The Guidebook states that for this rule to apply, a director must have "acted in good faith and with a reasonable basis for believing that the action authorized was in the lawful and legitimate furtherance of the corporation's purposes, and must have exercised his honest business judgment after due consideration of what he reasonably believed to be the relevant factors."[20]

Orientation

The Guidebook's discussion of orientation of the new corporate director is based on a theoretical framework which conceives that the primary role of the board is to "monitor" management's activities rather than actually to "manage" the business. The Guidebook recommends that a new director become familiar with basic corporate records and minutes of recent board and board committee minutes; corporate disclosure documents such as the latest SEC Form 10-K report; recent annual reports to shareholders and the most recent proxy statement; board structure and board committee organization; biographical data of the current board and current

---

18. See supra sections 1.02 to 1.05.
19. Cf. supra sections 2.04 to 2.07.
20. See supra section 1.13 and Chapter 6.

management personnel; planning documents and studies; and the corporation's outlook concerning current prospects and problems, critical issues to be confronted, and long-range objectives.

The Guidebook also recommends that new directors should be made aware of the corporation's conflicts of interest and compliance with law policies and procedures; also that they inquire if regular corporate counsel is in a position to have knowledge of, and to advise with respect to, such conflicts and compliance.

Identification of responsibilities

The Guidebook asserts that "the fundamental responsibility of the individual corporate director is to represent the interests of the shareholders as a group, as the owners of the enterprise, in directing the business and affairs of the corporation within the law."[21] In the discussion it is stated that neither the corporation nor the individual director is directly responsible to other constituencies "except to the extent expressly provided by public law ... or private contract...." It has been questioned whether that statement accurately reflects the increasing exposure to criminal liability and punitive damages based on injuries to employees, customers, or the general public arising from corporate products and operations.[22]

In the discussion of an individual director's duty to manage, the Guidebook interprets the phrase "managed under the direction of" to require directors, among other things, to "review and confirm basic corporate objectives," "select competent senior executives and monitor personnel policies and procedures," and also to "review the performance of the senior managers thus selected and monitor the performance of the enterprise."[23]

---

21. 33 Bus. Law. 1592, 1605-06.

22. Report of the Committee on Corporate Law Departments on Corporate Director's Guidebook, 33 Bus. Law. 1341, 1342 (1977).

23. 33 Bus. Law. 1595, 1607. Cf. discussion supra section 1.03.

Other duties assigned to directors by this part of the Guidebook include:

— adopting or changing bylaws
— approving amendments to the articles (subject to shareholder approval)
— canceling reacquired shares
— allocating to capital surplus consideration received for shares without par value
— changing the registered officer or agent
— approving any plan of merger or consolidation (subject to shareholder approval)
— recommending dissolution
— declaring dividends
— electing corporate officers
— calling special shareholders' meetings
— giving attention to material changes in the corporation's assets resulting from whatever factors
— being concerned that the corporation's disclosure documents are complete and accurate
— voting against proposals with which he disagrees and having his dissent and the reasons for it recorded in the minutes.[24]

Areas of special concern

The Guidebook analyzes twelve areas of special concern to individual directors and worthy of specific mention. They are:

— information flow from management to board members
— informed judgment based on adequate information
— information obtained from outside sources
— opportunities to become familiar with management personnel and corporate facilities
— board organization, composition, and continuity
— frequency and regularity of meeting of board and board committees

---

24. 33 Bus. Law. 1595, 1607-08.

— advance agenda and supporting materials for meetings of board and board committees
— executive development, including sufficient depth of middle management
— awareness and reassessment of management authority, including internal accounting controls
— adequacy of employee benefit and compensation programs, including potential fiduciary liability under ERISA
— protection of the corporation's assets, including insurance, patents, inventions, trade secrets, and conflicts of interest
— policies to ensure compliance with applicable laws both domestic and foreign.[25]

Duties under the federal securities laws are discussed in the Guidebook,[26] as are liabilities under state and federal laws and indemnification and insurance.[27]

The last eight pages of the Guidebook consist of a proposed model for the board of directors of a publicly-owned corporation.[28] It is premised on the principle that directors will not participate in day-to-day management but will act in the role of overseers of the corporation and monitors of its management. This "model" is the most controversial portion of the Guidebook and has prompted the widest comment.[29] Nonetheless it contains numerous suggestions worthy of the careful consideration of corporate counsel.

Supplement on tender offers

In the mid-1980's the Guidebook was supplemented by guidelines for directors in planning for and responding to

---

25. Id. at 1608-10.
26. Id. at 1611-14. See also supra Chapters 14 to 16.
27. 33 Bus. Law. 1595, 1614-18. See also infra Chapters 20 and 21.
28. 33 Bus. Law. 1595, 1619-28.
29. Report of the Committee, supra note 22, at 1842-44 and 1850-54.

unsolicited tender offers. A draft was released for comment.[30] It was then revised and issued in its final form.[31]

Emphasizing the responsibility of the directors to determine whether such a tender offer is in the corporation's best interests and whether it enhances shareholder interests and protects the interests of shareholders, these guidelines are suggested:

In advance of an unsolicited tender offer

Periodically, in advance of any threat of takeover, consider the corporation's present circumstances and future prospects, evaluate defensive measures and determine what to adopt or to recommend to the shareholders. In this review, directors may consider seeking outside professional advice from such as investment bankers, legal counsel, and proxy solicitation organizations.[32]

Recommendations to shareholders

Directors may decide to recommend charter amendments (sometimes called "shark repellents") without determining that the corporation is either vulnerable to, or particularly liable to be the target of, an unsolicited takeover attempt. In doing so directors should consider:

(i)   the particular kinds of takeovers that will be affected by each proposal;

(ii)   the likely short-term and long-term impact on the market value of the corporation's outstanding capital stock;

(iii)   the effect on continuing stock exchange listings, if applicable, and its materiality;

(iv)   the impact on the corporation's ability to effect a friendly business combination or related investment transaction;

---

30. Guidelines for Directors: Planning for and Responding to Unsolicited Tender Offers, 41 Bus. Law. 209 (1985).

31. Amendments, 41 Bus. Law. 1341 (1986).

32. 41 Bus. Law. 209, 213 (1985).

(v)   the legality of the proposal (for example, the impairment of shareholder rights);

(vi)   the duration of the proposal and when and whether it should be reviewed and reconsidered;

(vii)   the extent to which submission of the proposal might itself encourage takeover activity against the corporation;

(viii) whether shareholder approval should be geared to a vote of disinterested shareholders or some super majority provision.[33]

Action without shareholder approval

Bearing in mind that management entrenchment is not a valid reason for antitakeover actions, directors have various options open to them that may affect prospective takeovers and can be and often are justified on their own merits. Examples may include:

— purchase by a corporation of its own stock;
— issuance of shares to ESOP's;
— acquisition of companies in regulated industries in which any change in control requires prior government approval;
— acquisition of companies that could create antitrust problems for potential acquirers;
— the sale of significant assets;
— lockup agreements, in which a third party is given an option on a significant asset or block of stock;
— "poison pills" in the form of issuance of rights to make an unfriendly takeover unattractive.[34]

Director actions in responding to offer

With a caveat that director actions are constantly being tested in the courts, the following are some basic guidelines that may not apply in every case:

---

33. Id. at 214-16.
34. Id. at 216. See also supra section 6.14 and Chapter 15.

— the entire board of directors should participate in evaluating an outside tender offer;

— let the procedures reflect appropriate concern for the personal interest on the part of management directors;

— review the financial aspects of the offer including
  (i) present and historical market value of shares;
  (ii) premiums paid in other relevant transactions;
  (iii) liquidation and breakup values of the corporation's assets and component operations;
  (iv) the prospects of the corporation;
  (v) the estimated prospects of its stock on a going-concern basis over the next several years;

— consider the prospects for obtaining and methods of achieving a better offer, such as seeking other bids, pursuing negotiating strategies (perhaps including defensive tactics), and potential or total liquidation;

— if the offer is partial or two-tier, the impact on the remaining shareholders and on the prospects of the corporation if the offer is successful;

— if the offer is partial or two-tier, its potential including the offeror's reputation and financial condition;

— the value and investment attributes of the noncash consideration, if any;

— legal and regulatory matters or other considerations that could impede or prevent the consummation of the transaction;

— employee, supplier, customer, and local community interests;

— whether the offer is adequate;

— whether remaining independent is a valid alternative to the offer.

The board should determine what, if any, outside experts should be consulted to assist in the evaluation of the offer.[35]

---

35. 41 Bus. Law. 209, 217-18; 41 Bus. Law. 1341, 1342.

Defensive actions by the board

Once a board decides to oppose a takeover, it has some latitude in the actions it deems advisable, but the directors must have reasonable grounds to believe that a danger to corporate policy exists and that the proposed defensive measure is reasonable in relation to the threat posed. Otherwise, the result of the defensive tactics must be a transaction that is objectively and intrinsically fair.[36]

§ 19.05. Guidelines: the Lanza decision.

Lanza v. Drexel and Company[37] was a sequel to the landmark *BarChris* decision,[38] and involved litigation by plaintiffs who had exchanged stock of Victor Billiard Company for BarChris stock. They alleged they were misled by representations and omissions in the BarChris registration statement. Less than a year after the exchange of stock, BarChris filed for bankruptcy.

After commencing a rescission action in an effort to recover their stock from the ruins of BarChris, the plaintiffs were forced to pay the trustee in bankruptcy $100,000 which they had borrowed in order to regain control of Victor Billiard Company. In this action they claimed from various former officers and directors of BarChris compensatory damages of some $250,000 plus punitive damages, costs and attorneys' fees. Plaintiffs invoked Section 10(b) of the 1934 Act, Rule 10b-5 promulgated thereunder, Section 17(a) of the 1933 Act, together with common-law fraud doctrines and an action for a "prima facie tort."

The thrust of the Second Circuit's decision is the ruling of Judge Frankel exonerating the underwriter-director, Cole-

---

36. 41 Bus. Law. 209, 219. But cf. Unocal Corp. v. Mesa Petroleum Co., 493 A.2d 946, 955 (Del. 1985), and A.C. Acquisitions Corp. v. Anderson, Clayton & Co., 519 A.2d 103, 115 (Del. Ch. 1986). See also supra Chapter 15.

37. Fed. Sec. L. Rep. (CCH) ¶92,826 (S.D.N.Y. 1970), aff'd, 479 F.2d 1277 (2d Cir. 1973) (en banc).

38. Escott v. BarChris Constr. Corp., 283 F. Supp. 643 (S.D.N.Y. 1968).

man, and his firm, Drexel and Company. The court's concern was with Coleman's responsibility (if any) for the fraud perpetrated by other officers and directors.

The majority concluded that Coleman did not have an affirmative duty, as a director, to scrutinize the BarChris-Victor negotiations prior to giving his approval of the sale, and that in order to hold him liable the plaintiffs had the burden of establishing that his failure to discover the misrepresentations and omissions amounted to a willful, deliberate or reckless disregard for truth and was the equivalent of knowledge. The majority held that this burden was not sustained and that Coleman "played an active and concerned role in BarChris's affairs" and more than met the "standard of responsibility" imposed upon him.[39]

Two of the dissenting judges believed that Coleman's conduct "constituted reckless disregard for the truth." The other two dissenters would have held Coleman and Drexel and Company liable for Coleman's negligent omission to state material facts to the plaintiffs-purchasers.

Majority guidelines

In the majority decision, the following guidelines for directors are delineated:

- A director is not an insurer of the honesty of individual officers of the corporation in their negotiations which involve the purchase or sale of the corporation's stock.[40]
- A director, who does not conduct negotiations, participate therein or have knowledge thereof, is not under a duty to investigate each transaction or to inquire what representations were made, by whom and to whom, or independently to check on the truth of statements made or documents represented during such negotiations.

---

39. Lanza v. Drexel & Co., supra note 37, 479 F.2d at 1306.
40. Id. at 1281.

- A director in his capacity as a director (nonparticipant in a transaction) owes no duty to ensure that all material, adverse information is conveyed to the prospective purchasers of his corporation's stock.[41]
- At common law there was no obligation upon directors to ensure that all material, adverse information be conveyed to prospective purchasers of the company's stock. Liability should be imposed for the consequences of the director's own misconduct, not vicariously for the misconduct of others.[42]
- A "control" person will not be held liable where he did not exercise that control to bring about the action upon which liability is based.
- Under Section 12(2) of the 1933 Act, liability does not result solely from signing a registration statement or occupying a status such as that of a director.[43]
- A director's obligation to prospective purchasers of his corporation's stock is secondary, not primary, and must be found, if at all, in provisions other than Rule 10b-5 or in the doctrines of aiding and abetting, conspiracy, or substantial participation.[44]
- Certainly not everyone who has knowledge of improper activities in the field of securities transactions is required to report such activities. Yet there are circumstances under which a person may become an aider or abettor by merely failing to take action.[45]
- A director may have an obligation to maintain an awareness of significant corporate developments and to consider any material, adverse developments which come to his attention.
- Outside directors, who are not full-time employees of the corporation, should supervise the performance of

---

41. Id. at 1289.
42. Id. at 1292.
43. Id. at 1298.
44. Id. at 1301.
45. Id. at 1303.

management, which involves balancing (1) a skepticism toward management's assessment of its performance and (2) a trust in the integrity and competence of management.[46]

- State Blue Sky laws universally exempt directors from liability for fraud perpetrated by corporate officers unless the directors are in some meaningful sense culpable participants in the fraud.[47]

Minority guidelines

The dissenting judges spelled out the following propositions, on the basis of which they would have imposed liability upon Coleman and his firm, Drexel and Company:

- Section 10(b) and Rule 10-b-5 impose upon a director of a corporation that is selling its shares the obligation not to defraud the purchaser by either misstating or omitting to state material facts. The director cannot escape that duty by failing to inform himself of the facts and developments relevant to the sale.
- The distinction between an "inside" director and an "outside" director is irrelevant in this case because Coleman did nothing at all. He had no right to close his eyes to the activities of the corporation, including the purchase of the Victor shares.
- Coleman's vote to approve the exchange of shares was a representation to the plaintiffs-purchasers that he had sufficiently inquired as to the facts upon which the BarChris-Victor negotiations were based and that he was satisfied with the correctness of those facts. That representation was false.
- Coleman's failure to do anything to inform himself of the progress and character of the BarChris-Victor negotiations, at least after the "point of crisis" meeting, which was held eight days before the transaction was

---

46. Id. at 1306.
47. Id. at 1308.

closed, was a breach of the duty he owed as a director and a "controlling person" to the Victor shareholders.[48]

- If Coleman's failure to act was negligent as opposed to calculated, that should not insulate him from liability when action on his part might have prevented the fraud perpetrated by the corporation whose activities he was under a duty to supervise.

- Coleman's conduct constituted reckless disregard for the truth. Despite being the most experienced board member with regard to financial and business matters, knowing of his corporation's business reverses and severe internal dissension, and being on notice that the plaintiffs-purchasers might not have been informed thereof, he made no attempt to ascertain whether such information had been disclosed.

- Coleman was placed on the BarChris board at the behest of Drexel and Company to protect its financial stake in the BarChris operations; hence, the relationship between Coleman and Drexel and Company constituted control by Drexel and Company and established that Drexel and Company did in fact induce Coleman to act or not to act.

- In this action, based on Coleman's failure to speak, affirmative reliance is not a necessary element of a claim for relief.

- A director cannot avoid liability by pleading ignorance where his knowledge and experience tell him that certain events or circumstances known to him require that further inquiry be made.[49]

Significance of guidelines

When the *Lanza* decision was handed down it appeared that the suggestions of the minority judges were probably better guidelines than the discussion of scienter, negligence

---

48. Id. at 1317-19.
49. Id. at 1320-21.

and recklessness in the majority opinion.[50] The trend of the court decisions since then confirms that view.[51]

§ 19.06. Orientation of outside directors.

Frequently, outside directors, sometimes called "nonmanagement directors" or "independent directors" will need considerable orientation before undertaking their duties. The Corporate Director's Guidebook spells out a program for directorial orientation.[52] By way of particular concern for the newly-appointed outside director, Professors Leech and Mundheim[53] have suggested an orientation program which they consider "complete but by no means unreasonable even for a fairly small public corporation."[54] They recommend that an outside director appointee should not accept the post until he has received as much of the following as he thinks desirable or as he has been assured will be made available to him when he has taken office:

(1) Acquire information about the board of directors:
  — the organization of the board;
  — the established procedures for carrying out board responsibilities.
(2) Acquire and review information regarding key operating management:
  — biographies (resumes);
  — compensation, including recent history;
  — incentives, how earned and how paid;
  — summary of terms of employment contracts.
(3) Acquire and review information on company structure and history, using:
  — recent disclosure documents filed with the Securities and Exchange Commission, such as registra-

---

50. Sommer, "Directors and the Federal Securities Laws," Fed. Sec. L. Rep. (CCH) ¶79,699, at 83,806 (1974).

51. See discussion supra Chapters 1 and 6.

52. See supra section 19.04.

53. Leech & Mundheim, "The Outside Director of the Publicly Held Corporation," 31 Bus. Law. 1799 (1976).

54. Id. at 1812. See also supra section 1.10.

tion statements, 10K reports and proxy statements;
— corporate minutes for recent years.
(4) Acquire and review:
— reports and manuals describing the business and its problems;
— facilities information (take a tour if possible).
(5) Acquire and review documents relating to financial status:
— budgets for current and past year;
— latest management letter from the company's independent auditor;
— capital: real property, equipment and status of working capital;
— off balance sheet financial information;
— description and current financial status of pension plan;
— leases in effect (real property and major equipment).
(6) Request existing reports in areas of concern based on industry and history of company.
(7) Visit with top management.
(8) Visit with outside independent auditor alone:
— to get a feel for the profit and loss picture;
— to get a feel for balance sheet of the company;
— to get a feel for long-term financial picture if possible;
— to get a view of the company and its management in comparison with other companies in the industry.
(9) Visit with outside counsel alone to get a feel for the major legal problems facing the company.

§ 19.07. Preventive planning; financial institutions.

Generally

In order to develop a practical program to minimize the risks of liability for corporate officers and directors, active cooperation is required among management, the board, corporate counsel, and the corporate accountants and auditors. They should communicate freely and frequently and should devote a substantial amount of time to long-range prevention. This communication and planning is not easy to bring about, either in a large organization or a small one, but the only alternative is a "crash squad" type of activity to put out fires and deal with explosions, as they occur.

Much material is available in the literature which will suggest particular procedures available to corporations of various sizes and types. Two points, however, which should receive special consideration have to do with (1) regular management memoranda, and (2) a pamphlet on directors' and officers' duties and the laws which affect them. Both projects will require the participation of the corporation's legal counsel. Simplicity of expression and avoidance of burdensome details are of some importance.

The corporation's legal counsel should likewise be encouraged to keep abreast of current developments in the pertinent laws and regulations and should be supplied with adequate looseleaf services and reports to enable him to perform this task.

Corporate officers and directors should keep open their lines of communication, and legal counsel should be expected to consult with management about potentially troublesome situations before they ripen into litigation.

Financial institutions: planning

The consent decree in *Securities and Exchange Commission v. Union Planters Corporation*,[55] lists detailed procedures to avoid future violations of the Exchange Act, which were agreed to by a bank holding company and its principal bank. They merit consideration as a means of preventive planning for financial institutions. They include the following:

---

55. Fed. Sec. L. Rep. (CCH) ¶95,003 (W.D. Tenn. 1975).

(1)   The preparation and circulation not less frequently than semiannually to each officer, trader or salesman in the Investment Division of an extract of the applicable current Rules of Fair Practice of the National Association of Security Dealers (NASD);

(2)   The review of the Investment Division, at least annually, under the direction and guidance of the chief administrative officer of the Company, with the advice and assistance of his chief financial officer and legal counsel, to ensure that its policies and procedures with respect to both the Trading Account and Investment Account and the legal, accounting and record-keeping requirements and procedures in the Division and its Operations Department are in compliance with applicable law;

(3)   The preparation of written guidelines to Trading Account and Investment Account policies including: types of securities, general mix of securities, maximum underwriting positions, reporting of losses, valuation procedures, reporting slow-moving inventory, concessions on purchases and sales, forbidden transactions, and approvals and review of transactions;

(4)   The written confirmation by the officers, traders and salesmen in the Investment Division of the trading and investment policies and guidelines;

(5)   The preparation and circulation to all appropriate personnel of a detailed statement of accounting policies and requirements for security transactions within the Investment Division, covering the trading account, investment account, and special situations such as: short sales, arbitrage transactions, commercial paper and money market activity including federal funds, securities sold under agreements to repurchase, securities purchased under agreements to resell, and certificates of deposits sold to New York banks;

(6) The implementation of a continuing training program for the Investment Division's personnel, including a periodic review of previously established policies;

(7) The continuous review by the Manager of the Investment Division, with the advice of counsel, of legal developments relating to applicable securities activities and the dissemination of legal advice defining illegal activities, including free riding, to all personnel in the Investment Division and periodic confirmation to such personnel that any employee is subject to immediate dismissal who (1) engages in any practice or activity which is either illegal or contrary to established Bank policy or procedures or (2) invests personally, whether directly or indirectly, in any security other than with the limitation established by the Division, without the specific approval of the Manager;

(8) The monthly reporting by the Operations Department of the Investment Division, with responsibility for the orderly handling of paperwork, book entries and the implementation in that Division of the Bank's accounting policies and requirements, to both the Manager of the Bond Investment Division and the Bank's Financial Division;

(9) The maintenance as soon as practicable hereafter of the books and records of the Investment Division relating to all securities transactions and positions in accordance with the applicable provisions of Regulation 240.17a-3 under Section 17 of the Exchange Act;

(10) The establishment of a management committee to include at least three outside directors of the Bank to supervise specifically the Investment Division and transactions involving its Investment Account and Trading Account, which Committee should meet at least monthly and should submit to the

Board of Directors regular reports on the status and operations of that Division.

§ 19.08. Defenses: generally.

Performance of a director's three basic duties of diligence, loyalty and obedience[56] should avoid claims of wrongdoing and provide the best possible defenses. If such claims are made, however, evidence to refute them, supported by documentation, will usually be required. This circumstance suggests that proper and adequate records should be maintained, with the anticipation that their disclosure may be compelled.

The business judgment rule[57] is an acknowledgment of the management prerogatives of corporate directors and is a presumption that they acted on an informed basis and in the honest belief that the action taken was in the best interests of the corporation.[58] That rule and its presumption provide strong defensive support for directors accused of wrongdoing. Their decisions are protected by the business judgment rule, but the process by which such decisions are reached must be apparent on the record.

The Delaware case of *Smith v. Van Gorkom*[59] demonstrates that board minutes which do not disclose what the directors knew or did are of little defensive value.[60] The careful, accurate and complete preparation of board and committee minutes may well be corporate directors' best defense against liability.

The corporation laws of most states contain provisions relieving directors of liability if they dissent from improper distribution of the corporation's assets, the making of loans prohibited by statute, or the declaration or payment of dividends contrary to law.[61]

---

56. See supra section 1.05 and Chapters 2, 3, and 4.
57. See supra section 1.13 and Chapter 6.
58. Aronson v. Lewis, 473 A.2d 805, 815 (Del. 1984).
59. 488 A.2d 858 (Del. 1985).
60. Id. at 874, 875 n.16, 878, 883 n.25.
61. See, e.g., Del. Code Ann. tit. 8, § 174; N.Y. Bus. Corp. Law § 719; Ohio Rev. Code Ann. § 1701.95.

Beginning in the 1980's several states enacted statutes delineating the standards to be applied to directorial action and declaring that directors who complied therewith should have "no liability."[62] During the so-called D & O crisis in the mid-1980's several states enacted new statutes further limiting the liability of corporate directors to pay damages.[63] All such statutory provisions may be the bases for defenses of directors charged with violation of their duties.

In most instances defenses depend on questions of fact to which the pertinent law is applied. Thus most of the legal points made in the various chapters may have some involvement in directorial defenses when the facts of particular cases are established. Likewise, following guidelines and conforming to recognized procedures will assist such defenses.

§ 19.09. Defenses: attorney and client privilege; work product.

Attorney-client privilege has a direct relationship to the defenses of directors because of the extensive communication between corporate counsel, in house or outside, and corporate directors, officers and employees. Because some jurisdictions follow the Model Code of Professional Responsibility and others the Model Rules of Professional Responsibility, there is a difference in the attorney-client relationship in some cases.

Under the Model Code,[64] a corporate attorney's allegiance is to the corporation and not to any shareholder, director, officer, employee, or other person connected with it. Under the Model Rules[65] the lawyer retained by an organization "represents the organization, including its directors, officers,

---

62. E.g., § 8.30, Revised Model Bus. Corp. Act, based on state statutes such as: Cal. Corp. Code §§ 309, 316; Fla. Stat. Ann. § 607.111; Wash. Rev. Code §§ 23A.08.343, 23A.08.345.

63. See supra Chapter 7.

64. American Bar Ass'n Model Code of Professional Responsibility, adopted by the House of Delegates 1969.

65. American Bar Ass'n Model Rules of Professional Conduct, Rule 1.13, adopted by the House of Delegates 1983.

627

employees, members, shareholders or other constituents as a group, except where the interest of one or more of the group may be adverse to the organization's interest." In intracorporation disputes as between management and shareholder or between majority and minority shareholders, the obligations may also be different under the Code and the Rules.

Since the Supreme Court's decision in *Upjohn Company v. United States,*[66] the privilege attaching to communications between corporate counsel and corporate directors has been clarified. That decision "breathed new vitality into the attorney-client privilege and the attorney work product doctrine and ... firmly established a new privilege of corporations to engage in critical self-evalution."[67]

In *Upjohn,* the Supreme Court resolved the conflicting views of the federal circuits on the scope of attorney-client privilege particularly as respects lower level corporate employees. It also spoke to the work-product doctrine in the clearest terms since *Hickman v. Taylor.*[68]

In *Upjohn,* the company conducted an internal investigation of alleged "questionable payments" discovered during an audit of one of its foreign subsidiaries. The inquiry involved written responses to questionnaires and personal interviews with "all foreign, general and area managers" and some thirty-three other Upjohn officers or employees. It was conducted by Upjohn's inside vice-president, secretary and general counsel who was assisted by outside counsel and the board chairman. Significant amounts of such "questionable payments" were thus confirmed.

Upjohn voluntarily submitted a preliminary report of its findings to the SEC with a copy to the IRS. When IRS commenced an investigation to determine the tax consequences of the payments, Upjohn gave IRS a list of all employees inter-

---

66. 449 U.S. 925, 66 L.Ed.2d 584, 101 S.Ct. 677 (1981).

67. Pitt, "The 'Upjohn' Decision: 'To Thine Own Self Be True,'" Legal Times (Washington), Jan. 26, 1981, at 20, col. 1.

68. 329 U.S. 495, 91 L.Ed. 451, 67 S.Ct. 385 (1947).

viewed, agreed to permit IRS to interview them and agreed to transport some inaccessible foreign employees to more convenient locations for interviews. That was not enough for IRS which issued a summons pursuant to 28 U.S.C. § 7602, demanding the actual questionnaires and counsel's interview notes and memoranda. Upjohn resisted such disclosure on grounds of attorney-client privilege and because the documents constituted attorneys' work product. The government filed suit to enforce the summons.

Attorney-client privilege

In reversing, the Supreme Court upheld the attorney-client privilege for corporations and declared that it should be construed broadly and not narrowly. It recognized the purpose of the privilege "to encourage full and frank communication between attorneys and their clients and thereby promote broader public interests in the observance of law and administration of justice." It emphasized that the assistance of skilled lawyers "can only be safely and readily availed of when free from the consequences or the apprehension of disclosure."[69]

One perceptive commentator[70] suggests that the court "adopted an eight-pronged test" making the attorney-client privilege applicable to:

(1) a communication,
(2) to corporate counsel "acting as such,"
(3) made by corporate employees who are aware of its legal implications,
(4) concerning "matters within the scope of the employees' corporate duties,"
(5) at the direction of corporate superiors,
(6) in order to obtain legal advice for the company,
(7) the communications being considered "highly confidential" when made, and

---

69. Upjohn Co. v. United States, supra note 66.
70. Pitt, supra note 67.

(8) thereafter kept confidential by the company.[71]

The opinion emphasizes that the privilege only protects disclosure of the underlying facts by those who communicated with the attorney. Moreover, Justice Rehnquist reminded his readers that the court was deciding only the case before it and did "not undertake to draft a set of rules which should govern challenges to investigatory subpoenas."[72]

Work-product doctrine

The Supreme Court also reversed the Sixth Circuit on its holding as to the work-product doctrine. Recognizing the "strong public policy" underlying the work-product doctrine the court quoted from *Hickman v. Taylor*[73] and cited Federal Rule of Civil Procedure 26(b)(3):

> In ordering discovery of such materials ... the court shall protect against disclosure of the mental impressions, conclusions, opinions, or legal theories of an attorney or other representative of a party concerning the litigation.[74]

In *Upjohn* the discovery sought was of the attorney's notes and memoranda of oral statements made by witnesses. The opinion states that such disclosure "is particularly disfavored because it tends to reveal the attorney's mental processes," in particular what he saw fit to write down regarding witnesses' "remarks."

The opinion does not discuss whether the material sought to be discovered was prepared in "anticipation of litigation." A commentator has suggested that the upholding of the work-product doctrine in *Upjohn* presumably reflects the court's view that any attempt by a corporation to ferret out instances of wrongdoing" is a process undertaken in "antici-

---

71. Id.

72. Upjohn Co. v. United States, supra note 66, 449 U.S. at 396.

73. Supra note 68, 329 U.S. at 510-11.

74. 449 U.S. at 400.

pation of litigation."[75] If that suggestion is valid, then *Upjohn* has indeed broadened the "in anticipation of litigation" standard of the work-product doctrine.

The Garner rule

When litigation pits corporate shareholders against management, there is authority that management may not invoke attorney-client privilege to prevent the shareholders from interrogating the corporation's attorneys. The rationale is that since a corporation acts only for its shareholders, they are entitled to see written communications, and they have the right to inquire about oral communications between their corporation and its legal counsel.

In a combined shareholders' class action and derivative action for fraud in the sale of securities, the Fifth Circuit held that the attorney-client privilege had viability for the corporate client but was subject to the right of the shareholders-plaintiffs to show cause why the privilege should not be invoked.[76]

Upjohn recognizes that the "attorney and client must be able to predict with some degree of certainty whether particular discussions will be protected" by the privilege. It has been urged that, under *Garner,* discussions of corporate managers and company attorneys may be invaded by shareholders.[77] But *Garner's* premise that management's duties run ultimately to the benefit of the shareholders[78] supports the contention that *Upjohn* and *Garner* are both viable.[79]

---

75. Pitt, supra note 67.

76. Garner v. Wolfinbarger, 430 F.2d 1093 (5th Cir. 1970), cert. denied, 401 U.S. 974 (1971).

77. See Kirby, "New Life for the Corporate Attorney-Client Privilege in Shareholder Litigation," 69 A.B.A. J. 174 (1983).

78. Garner v. Wolfinbarger, supra note 76, at 1101.

79. See also Cohen v. Uniroyal, Inc., 80 F.R.D. 480 (E.D. Pa. 1978); Panter v. Marshall Field & Co., 80 F.R.D. 718 (N.D. Ill. 1978); Ohio-Sealy Mattress Mfg. Co. v. Kaplan, 90 F.R.D. 21 (N.D. Ill. 1980); Donovan v. Fitzsimmons, 90 F.R.D. 583 (N.D. Ill. 1981); In re International Sys. & Controls Corp. Sec. Litig., 693 F.2d 1235 (5th Cir. 1982).

Scope of corporate duties

One significant part of *Upjohn* that has been involved in litigation since the Supreme Court's decision is the scope of the communicating employee's corporate duties. When the communication is so made, it is said that the employee is communicating as a "personification of the corporation," that is, "as a cog in the corporate organization."[80]

In a Minnesota case, an employee witnessed an accident and gave a statement to corporate counsel. Privilege was denied.[81] In an Ohio case, the court held that the scope of the employee's duties was broad enough to encompass a communication concerning matters that occurred prior to the employee's employment with the corporation.[82] A Ninth Circuit case recognized the privilege as to communications by employees who terminated their employment before the communication.[83]

Subject matter test

There is little agreement among the decisions in establishing a rule as to when the subject matter of the communication is within the scope of the employee's corporate duties.[84]

§ 19.10. Alternatives to indemnification and D & O insurance.

Public scrutiny of corporate boards and the increased exposure of directors to lawsuits based on a variety of alleged

---

80. See Gergacz, "Attorney-Corporate Client Privilege," 37 Bus. Law. 461, 505-06 (1982).

81. Leer v. Chicago, M., S.P. & P. R.R., 308 N.W.2d 305 (Minn. 1981), cert. denied, 455 U.S. 939 (1982).

82. Baxter Travenol Lab's, Inc. v. Lemay, 89 F.R.D. 410 (S.D. Ohio 1981).

83. In re Coordinated Pretrial Proceedings in Petroleum Prods. Antitrust Litig., 658 F.2d 1355, 1361 n.7 (9th Cir. 1981), cert. denied, 455 U.S. 990 (1982).

84. E.g., Marriott Corp. v. American Academy of Psychotherapists, Inc., 157 Ga. App. 497, 277 S.E.2d 785 (1981); Consolidation Coal Co. v. Bucyrus-Erie Co. 89 Ill. 2d 103, 59 Ill. Dec. 666, 432 N.E.2d 250 (1982).

misdeeds produced a legislative response discussed in Chapters 7 and 20. Part of that response has been to extend the means by which deficiencies in indemnification and concerns about the cost and availability of D & O insurance can be overcome. In general such relief has been made available by way of insurance and noninsurance alternatives. The exclusions and coverage restrictions in many D & O policies, combined with the inflated costs, have caused corporate risk managers to go in search of such relief.

The following discussion points out that these alternatives may actually involve both indemnification and insurance. However, the indemnification alternatives are more comprehensive and seek to escape from the restrictions inherent in some statutes, and the insurance alternatives are provided by some different methods and through other entities than the carriers heretofore writing D & O insurance.

§ 19.11. Examples of alternatives.

To avoid the restrictions and limitations contained in all indemnification statutes, an alternative cast in the insurance mold should meet the definition of insurance. A primary requisite essential to a contract of insurance is the assumption of a risk of loss and an undertaking to indemnify the insured against such loss.[85] Historically and commonly insurance involves risk-shifting and risk-distributing.[86] By diffusing risks through a number of separate risk-shifting contracts, an insurer casts its lot with the law of averages.[87]

Single-parent captive insurance companies

The tax cases dealing with the deductibility of premiums paid to wholly-owned insurance affiliates generally deny such deductibility because such arrangements do not consti-

---

85. Couch on Insurance § 1.2 (2d ed. 1984).

86. Helvering v. LeGierse, 312 U.S. 531, 85 L.Ed. 996, 61 S.Ct. 646 (1941).

87. Commissioner v. Treganowan, 183 F.2d 288 (2d Cir. 1950), cert. denied, 340 U.S. 853 (1951).

tute "insurance." Thus one court declared this to be the same
as setting up reserve accounts. "The risk of loss remains with
the parent and is reflected on the balance sheet and income
statements of the parent."[88] However, in *Gulf Oil Corporation*,[88a] the Tax Court suggested that the "insurance" requirements would be met if the captive wrote a significant amount
of business unrelated to the parent corporation.

Aside from the tax aspect, the decisions suggest that a single-parent captive is merely an artifice for funding the parent's indemnification obligation and must limit its coverage
to what is permitted by the applicable indemnification statutes. Also, in bankruptcy proceedings, it has not been settled
whether creditors of the parent may reach the assets of the
captive.

Related captive insurance companies

A captive owned by an affiliate of an insured corporation
and several officers of the insured corporation was held to be
a provider of insurance in one case.[89] The court cited the
following points in support of its conclusion:

(1) The captive was formed for a legitimate business purpose;

(2) The captive was a separate and independent corporate entity;

(3) The premium charged by the captive was actuarily
based and proportionate to the risks covered;

(4) The insured was not a shareholder of the captive nor
a shareholder in any entity which had an ownership
interest in the captive;

(5) Various nonaffiliated persons or entities were also
insured by the captive, thereby enabling distribution
risks.

---

88. Mobil Oil Corp. v. United States, 8 Ct.Cl. 555 (1985).
88a. 89 T.C. No. 70 (1987).
89. Crawford Fitting Co. v. United States, 606 F. Supp. 136 (N.D. Ohio
1985). Contra Pariseau v. Commissioner, ¶85, 124 Memo TC (P-H) (1985).

Risk retention and purchasing groups

The Risk Retention Amendments of 1986[90] expanded the Risk Retention Act of 1981[91] to permit business and professional associations to form groups to purchase or insure liability coverage. The primary objective of Congress was to encourage and facilitate efficient pooling of liability risks to permit them to be insured at reasonable costs. Both groups were given broad exemptions from regulation by the states.[92]

A risk retention group is a corporation or other limited liability association, taxable as a corporation or as an insurance company, formed under the laws of any state, Bermuda, or the Cayman Islands:

(i)   whose primary activity consists of assuming and spreading all, or any portion, of the liability of its group members;

(ii)   which is organized for that primary purpose;

(iii)   which is:

(a) chartered or licensed as a liability insurance company and authorized to do business in such state, or

(b) qualified, as specified, to engage in business under the laws of Bermuda or the Cayman Islands;

(iv)   which has strict identity of its members and owners and does not exclude persons from membership to provide a competitive advantage;

(v)   whose members are engaged in business or activities similar or related to the liability to which such members are exposed by virtue of any related, similar, or common business, trade, product, services, premises or operations; and

(vi)   which meets the other statutory requirements.[93]

---

90. Pub. L. 99-563, 100 Stat. 3170-3172, 3177.

91. Pub. L. 98-193, 97 Stat. 1344.

92. Home Warranty Corp. v. Elliott, 585 F. Supp. 443, 446-47 (D. Del. 1984).

93. 15 U.S.C. § 3901(a)(4).

With specified exceptions, risk retention groups are exempted from any state law, rule, regulation or order that would make unlawful or regulate the operation or formation of such a group.[94]

A purchasing group is composed of its members whose business or activities are similar or related with respect to the liability to which such members are exposed by virtue of any related, similar, or common business, trade, product, services, premises or operation; which

(i)   has as one of its purposes the purchase of liability insurance on a group basis;

(ii)   purchases such insurance only for its group members and only to cover their similar or related liability exposure; and

(iii)   is domiciled in a state.[95]

Purchasing groups are afforded exemptions from state laws, rules and regulations similar to those for risk retention groups and with like exceptions.[96]

Group or consortium insurers

Consortium insurers are relatively new to the D & O field but are long established in the insurance picture, particularly those insurers created by trade and industry groups. In this concept the insured corporations own an equity interest in the insurer and pool their premiums and risks. Both risk-shifting and risk-distributing are accomplished.[97] Accordingly, such insurers provide insurance and may provide coverage for nonindemnifiable claims. Some such organizations brought into business in the early years of this program are the following:

---

94. Id. § 3902.
95. Id. § 3901(a)(5).
96. Id. § 3903.
97. E.g., Rev. Rul. 78-338, 1978-2 C.B. 107 (31 insureds participated); Rev. Rul. 80-102, 1980-1 C.B. 41 (5000 insureds participated); Rev. Rul. 83-172, 1983-2 C.B. 107 (40 insureds participated). See also United States v. Weber Paper Co., 320 F.2d 199 (8th Cir. 1963).

(1) American Bankers Professional and Fidelity Insurance Company Limited (ABPFIC), a mutual insurance company under Bermuda law, to reinsure risks in the D & O and financial institution bond areas written by Progressive Casualty Insurance Company for members of the American Bankers Association.

(2) American Casualty Excess Insurance Company Limited (ACE) incorporated in the Cayman Islands by thirty-three major corporations including Chase Manhattan Bank, Ford Motor Co., General Electric Co. and United States Steel Corporation. Its market was originally excess D & O coverage for companies which also purchased excess general liability coverage from the insurer.

(3) Bankers Insurance Company Limited (BICL) organized in Bermuda by some thirty large banks to provide primary and excess insurance to banks.

(4) BankInsure, Inc., formed by bankers' associations in Minnesota, North and South Dakota, Oklahoma and Wisconsin to provide primary D & O insurance to member banks in those states.

(5) Corporate Officers and Directors Assurance Limited (CODA), a Bermuda company originally writing only direct coverage, not corporate reimbursement.

(6) Directors and Officers Liability Insurance (DOLI) organized in Bermuda to provide directors and officers liability insurance for utility companies. Its initial seed capital was provided by Associated Electric & Gas Insurance Services Limited (AEGIS).

(7) Energy Insurance Mutual (EIM) providing excess D & O and general liability coverage to utility companies.

(8) University Risk Management and Insurance Association (URIMA) providing trustee and officer liability coverages for colleges and universities.

(9) X.L. Insurance Company, Ltd. providing excess D & O and general liability coverage.

Fronting insurers

Another practice new to the D & O area but of long standing in casualty insurance is the "fronting" insurer. An unrelated, duly-organized insurance company issues its policies. These risks are then covered in one of several ways, such as:

(1) The insurer establishes a special account into which all premiums are placed and from which all losses are paid, with an agreement that the insured company will hold the insurer harmless. This arrangement may not meet the requirements of the "insurance" definition because the risk may not be shifted.[98]

(2) The insurer reinsures 90% to 100% of the risk with a captive insurer wholly owned by the insured company. This arrangement may also fail to qualify as insurance.[99]

(3) Retrospective premium adjustments are made so that most, if not all, of the insurer's losses are recouped from the insured company. This plan may qualify as "insurance," depending on the facts of a particular case. If all or substantially all of the losses are recouped by the insurer through the premium adjustments, no risk shifting may occur and thus no insurance may be created.[100]

A thorough discussion of this subject is found in a 1987 Ninth Circuit decision. In that case, a corporation (Clougherty) purchased insurance from Fremont, an unrelated insurer, which reinsured the first $100,000 of each claim with Lombardy, a wholly owned subsidiary of Clougherty Packing, which was a wholly owned subsidiary of Clougherty. Lombardy engaged in no business other than the reinsuring of Clougherty business placed with it by Fremont.

---

98. Steere Tank Lines, Inc. v. United States, 577 F.2d 279 (5th Cir. 1978), cert. denied, 440 U.S. 946 (1979).

99. Carnation Co. v. Commissioner, 640 F.2d 1010 (9th Cir.), cert. denied, 454 U.S. 965 (1981); Rev. Rul. 77-316, 1977-2 C.B. 53.

100. IRS Tech. Adv. Memo 8637003 (1986).

The appropriate state agencies approved the premium charged by Fremont and the reinsurance rate charged by Lombardy.[101]

The majority of the Ninth Circuit panel found the various agreements interdependent and considered them together in deciding that there was no risk shifting. It went on to state:

> The parent of a captive insurer retains an economic stake in whether a covered loss occurs. Accordingly, an insurance agreement between parent and captive does not shift the parent's risk of loss and is not an agreement for "insurance".... Because Clougherty is the parent of the captive insurer Lombardy, the amounts paid by Clougherty to Fremont and then to Lombardy are not insurance premiums.[102]

The concurring opinion of the third panel member approved the dissent of seven judges in the Tax Court and said that the arrangement "looks like insurance, feels like insurance, and smells like insurance, but under the holding [of the majority] it isn't!"[103]

Irrevocable trust

In this plan, an irrevocable trust is created by the insured organization and funded to provide D & O coverage. Such a trust and its managers should be separated from and not dependent upon the insured organization. An illustrative case makes the point.[104] A trust was created by a medical professional corporation to provide malpractice protection for employees. The court struck down the plan and noted that the trust was not licensed as an insurance company, the corporation retained the power to amend the trust instrument, and if the trust assets were inadequate to pay all losses, the corporation was obligated to make up the difference. The court

---

101. Clougherty Packing Co. v. Commissioner, 84 T.C. 948 (1985), aff'd, 811 F.2d 1297 (9th Cir. 1987).

102. Id., 811 F.2d at 1307.

103. Id.

104. Anesthesia Serv. Med. Group, Inc. v. Commissioner, 85 T.C. 1042 (1986), aff'd, 825 F.2d 241 (9th Cir. 1987).

held that risk of loss was not shifted and that the plan did not constitute "insurance."

Self-insurance

Traditionally, self-insurance has been considered a form of indemnification. If so, it would be subject to indemnification limitations imposed by an applicable state statute. However, statutes enacted since 1986 in Arizona, Louisiana, Maryland, Nevada, New Mexico, Ohio and Pennsylvania contain provisions that afford an opportunity to avoid such limitations.[105]

Those statutes in varying terms empower a corporation to purchase or procure and maintain insurance or similar protection, including but not limited to trust funds or self-insurance, or, in Louisiana, Maryland, Nevada and Ohio, letters of credit, and, Nevada, guaranty or surety, for corporate officers, directors and others whether or not the corporation would have the power to indemnify them against such liability. Such insurance may be maintained with an insurer in which the corporation has a financial interest or, in Louisiana, owns all of its stock or securities.

Because the self-insurance that may be provided under such statutes may cover liability of directors and officers "whether or not the corporation could indemnify them against such liability," it is not limited by the restrictions in the indemnification statutes. Apparently the only limitation is the public policy inhibition generally applicable to insurance contracts, namely, that coverage for willful, intentional or malicious wrongdoing would be prohibited.

§ 19.12. Indemnification alternatives.

Alternatives to D & O insurance may be found in areas other than those which seek to provide funding for non-indemnifiable claims, although some of the alternatives mentioned supra in section 19.11 may afford some relief despite

---

105. See infra Appendix B.

not being recognized as "insurance."[106] The new legislation discussed in Chapters 7 and 20 may help restore some measure of certainty in boardrooms. The statutes which permit or provide limitations and restrictions on liability for money damages may be especially effective in this respect.

Maximizing internal indemnification

Included in the legislation discussed in Chapter 20 are some recently enacted statutes expanding the power of corporations to indemnify their directors. In Florida, Indiana, Michigan and New Jersey, for example, the amendments eliminated the restriction barring indemnification as applied to derivative actions in the case of an adverse judgment, unless ordered by a court.[107] Louisiana, North Carolina, North Dakota, Pennsylvania, Tennessee and Wisconsin[108] permit a director or officer to be indemnified against judgments and settlements as well as expenses in derivative suits, and New York[109] permits indemnification for settlements as well as expenses in such suits by court order. Other states have moved in the same direction.

At least forty-one states such as Delaware, Maryland, Michigan, New Jersey, New York, Ohio and Pennsylvania[110] now have nonexclusive provisions in their indemnification statutes. Corporations chartered in such states have the opportunity to indemnify their directors, and sometimes their officers, well beyond the statutory limits. Such expanded indemnification includes, for example, mandatory indemnification to the extent of success in the underlying proceedings, mandatory or permissive advancement of litigation expenses unless it is determined that indemnification is not permissible, as well as broader provisions for indemnification as applied to actions by or in the right of the corporation.

---

106. See supra text at notes 85 to 87.
107. See infra section 20.07 and Appendix B.
108. Id.
109. Id.
110. See infra section 20.13.

Subject to public policy limitations the courts tend to sustain such expanded indemnification as a means to encourage capable persons to serve as corporate directors, "secure in the knowledge that expenses incurred by them in upholding their honesty and integrity as directors will be borne by the corporation they serve."[111]

Indemnification contracts

Additional protection and comfort may be afforded by indemnification contracts between officers and directors, and their corporations.[112] In states where the indemnification statute is nonexclusive, such a contract may contain virtually any provisions not proscribed by public policy, and will probably be enforced by the courts.[113]

Such contracts convert directors' rights from statutory rights to contract rights and may diminish the likelihood of modification unilaterally or in case of disagreements with management or board factions. In effect such contracts make the corporation a self-insurer of the directors' liability subject only to public policy and any limitations or exclusions contained in the agreement. To provide additional protection against the insolvency of the corporation, such contracts may be funded by a trust fund, letter of credit,[114] a surety bond or similar arrangement.

Because the directors and officers who enter into such contracts clearly benefit from them, the problem of self-dealing is inherent in such undertakings. Accordingly, advance submission to and approval of such contracts by the shareholders is advantageous.[115]

---

111. Hibbert v. Hollywood Park, Inc., 457 A.2d 339, 344 (Del. 1983).

112. See discussion infra section 20.14.

113. E.g., Mooney v. Willys-Overland Motors, Inc., 204 F.2d 888 (3d Cir. 1953).

114. Under such statutes as those of Louisiana, Nevada and Ohio, such funding is expressly authorized. See text supra at note 105.

115. See Nichelson v. Duncan, 407 A.2d 211 (Del. 1979); Schreiber v. Bryan, 396 A.2d 512 (Del. Ch. 1978).

Surety bond

The National Association of Corporate Directors (NACD) and Marsh & McLennan have developed a "Director Bond" to fund indemnification of directors under circumstances stated in the bond. It is intended that the bond track the law as to both mandatory and permissible indemnity.[116] According to NACD the bond was created to supplement or complement existing insurance or as an alternative to insurance where insurance is unavailable but where the corporation qualifies for the bond.[117]

The underwriting of the bond will parallel that of any other financial guaranty obligation, in that criteria will be strict. A comprehensive application, similar to that used for D & O insurance is required. It is reported that the premium will be in the range of one to two per cent of the limit per annum, based on the net worth of the principal.

§ 19.13. Legal audits.

By the use of a "legal audit" a corporation may inspect its legal structure, look at its legal assets and liabilities, make a current evaluation of pending litigation, take inventory of potential claims, examine procedures which may result in future problems, and use preventive techniques to avoid repeating prior mistakes. Corporate directors are under constant pressure to find better means of dealing with the ever-greater responsibilities imposed upon them by regulatory agencies and the courts. A legal audit is a simple and relatively inexpensive way to keep directors better informed, up to date as to changes in law and procedure, and aware of present and potential trouble spots.

What is appropriate for a legal audit of a particular corporation will require individual analysis of its special needs.

---

116. Telex to Mr. Knepper from Michael P. Tilton, Marsh & McLennan Inc., Sept. 30, 1987.

117. NACD Insurance Announcement, Feb. 7, 1987. See also infra section 20.14.

Directors, officers, senior management, insurance representatives, accountants and attorneys all have a place in determining the nature and scope of the data-gathering process. As is apparent from that list, all significant corporate procedures will be brought into focus, financial data will be examined, and insurance policies will be reviewed and their coverages will be evaluated as part of the legal audit.

Obviously, legal counsel for the corporation, in-house as well as outside, have an important part to play in designing the data-gathering process and in the analysis of the data when it has been assembled. When legal audits take place annually, the procedures will be of an ongoing nature. Periodic meetings of legal counsel, management, and the accountants, as part of the audit process, will afford opportunities for better understanding of the concerns of each.

Legal audits review, among other things, compliance procedures, reporting procedures, control procedures and all matters relating to pending or potential legal problems. They enable legal counsel who participate in the data-gathering to make it clear that there must be complete compliance with all legal requirements at all times. Violations will result in discipline. The importance of carrying that message throughout the company cannot be overemphasized. Memoranda are not read or remembered in many instances. The legal audit affords a splendid opportunity to insist on compliance with legal requirements on a face-to-face basis.

After assembling and evaluating the data, a report of the legal audit should be presented to management. When the directors have had an opportunity to study the report, provision should be made for its discussion and to arrange to carry out such of its recommendations as are approved by the board.

In the area of litigation alone, periodic legal audits will provide means for substantial savings of money. Carrying the compliance message will help prevent errors that can result in lawsuits. Pending litigation that has become unproductive may be terminated. Potential litigation that should be compromised may be directed to the bargaining table. Alternative methods of dispute resolution may be explored. Time-consuming and expensive trials may be avoided, with the frequent result that the board can devote more time to corporate governance.

COROLLARY REFERENCES

Israels, "A New Look at Corporate Directorship," 24 Bus. Law. 727-41 (1969).

Johnston, "Developing a Protection Program for Corporate Directors and Officers," 26 Bus. Law. 445 (1970).

Knauss, "Corporate Governance — A Moving Target," 79 Mich. L. Rev. 478 (1981).

Kripke, "The SEC, Corporate Governance, and the Real Issues," 36 Bus. Law. 173 (1981).

Manning, "The Business Judgment Rule and the Director's Duty of Attention: Time for Reality," 39 Bus. Law. 1477 (1984).

Sealy, "A Reply to Professor Kripke: The Negative, Not the Positive, Is the Real Issue of Corporate Governance," 36 Bus. Law. 1655 (1981).

Veasey & Manning, "Codified Standard — Safe Harbor or Uncharted Reef? An Analysis of the Model Act Standard of Care Compared with Delaware Law," 35 Bus. Law. 919 (1980).

"The Overview Committees of the Board of Directors," A Report by the ABA Committee on Corporate Laws, 35 Bus. Law. 1335 (1980).

"The Role and Composition of the Board of Directors of the Large Publicly-Owned Corporation — Statement of the Business Roundtable," 33 Bus. Law. 2083 (1978).

Chapter 20

INDEMNIFICATION

§ 20.01. Indemnification at common law.

There was very little law on indemnification prior to the various statutory enactments. Most of the decisions were rendered in jurisdictions where indemnification statutes are now in effect, so their authoritative value is doubtful. Generally, under the common law, indemnification was not permitted unless the director or officer made a successful defense.[1] The rationale of such decisions was that a corporation was not justified in paying the expenses of an officer or director who had been derelict in his duties.[2] Even then, some courts were

---

1. E.g., Wickersham v. Crittenden, 106 Cal. 329, 39 P. 603 (1895); Hollander v. Breeze Corp., 131 N.J. Eq. 585, 26 A.2d 507 (1941), aff'd, 131 N.J. Eq. 613, 26 A.2d 522 (1942).

2. See Kansas City Operating Corp. v. Durwood, 278 F.2d 354, 358 (8th Cir. 1960).

647

reluctant to allow indemnification unless it could be proved that the litigation had been beneficial to the corporation.[3]

In New Jersey, a leading case approved indemnification on the basis that it would assist in inducing "responsible business men to accept the post of directors."[4] And in a Minnesota landmark decision, the court ruled that reimbursement was necessary for establishing a "sound public policy favorable to the development of sound corporate management as a prerequisite for responsible corporate action."[5]

Cases decided under Delaware and Illinois law have upheld the right of directors to indemnification under corporate bylaws adopted prior to enactment of indemnification statutes in those states. The Third Circuit has held that the right under the Delaware bylaw is analogous to a contract right.[6] The Second Circuit, in upholding a bylaw of an Illinois corporation, applied the Illinois indemnification statute retroactively and found that "such protection is necessary or desirable to encourage recruitment of capable management."[7] In both cases the courts deemed the enactment of indemnification statutes an expression of public policy favorable to such indemnification.

At common law it is established that an agent, who is himself guilty of no illegal conduct, is entitled to indemnification for costs of defending an action brought by third persons because of the agent's authorized conduct. Attorneys' fees are properly included in such costs.[8]

---

3. E.g., Jesse v. Four-Wheel Drive Auto Co., 177 Wis. 627, 189 N.W. 276 (1922); Griesse v. Lang, 37 Ohio App. 553, 175 N.E. 222 (1931). See also Red Bud Realty Co. v. South, 96 Ark. 281, 131 S.W. 340 (1910).

4. Solimine v. Hollander, 129 N.J. Eq. 264, 272, 19 A.2d 344, 348 (1941).

5. In re E.C. Warner Co., 232 Minn. 207, 214, 45 N.W.2d 388, 393 (1950).

6. Beneficial Indus. Loan Co. v. Smith, 170 F.2d 44, 50 (3d Cir. 1948), aff'd sub nom. Cohen v. Beneficial Indus. Loan Corp., 337 U.S. 541 (1949).

7. Wisener v. Air Express Int'l Corp., 583 F.2d 579, 583 (2d Cir. 1978).

8. Moricoli v. P & S Mgt. Co., 104 Ill. App. 3d 234, 60 Ill. Dec. 4, 432 N.E.2d 903, 908 (1982); Johnson v. Suckow, 53 Ill. App. 3d 277, 12 Ill. Dec. 846, 370 N.E.2d 650, 653-54 (1977); Virginia Corp. v. Russ, 27 Ill. App. 3d 608, 327 N.E.2d 403, 405 (1975).

§ 20.02. Indemnification and public policy.

In the enactment of statutes providing for corporate indemnification of officers and directors, legislative bodies have been confronted with the need to punish unfaithful fiduciaries and, at the same time, provide protection for aggressive corporate managers willing to undertake good faith risks in the search for profits. Likewise, in the past there has been some reluctance in the courts to approve indemnification of corporate officers and directors whose conduct gave the appearance of impropriety or unfaithfulness.

Since the beginning of the trend toward liberalized indemnification of corporate officers and directors, the public policy question has been controversial. Some commentators have questioned the propriety of such indemnification. Some statutes such as the Foreign Corrupt Practices Act of 1977 prohibit corporate indemnification when individuals are adjudged liable.[9] Most observers, however, see nothing improper in the indemnification of corporate officers and directors when they are successful in their defenses. Even in unsuccessful defenses, there are indications that indemnification for expenses would be sustained.[10] Indemnification against judgments, amounts paid in settlement, and especially fines and penalties presents a more difficult problem. Perhaps the primary question for determination is whether compensation to the wronged or the deterrence of management misconduct is the principal objective of laws imposing liability upon corporate officers and directors.

The enactment of statutes permitting (and sometimes mandating) indemnification is a demonstration of the legislative attitude toward the public policy question. Such statutes are in effect in every state, and the trend in the mid-1980's has been to liberalize and expand the scope of indemnification. A

---

9. 15 U.S.C. §§ 78ff(c)(4) and 78dd-2(b)(4).

10. See, e.g., Commissioner v. Tellier, 383 U.S. 687, 16 L.Ed.2d 185, 86 S.Ct. 1118 (1966) (permitting securities dealer to take tax deduction for cost of unsuccessful defense of criminal prosecution under Securities Act of 1933).

1983 decision in Delaware recognized that "the larger purpose" of Delaware legislation on indemnification is "to encourage capable men to serve as corporate directors, secure in the knowledge that expenses incurred by them in upholding their honesty and integrity as directors will be borne by the corporation they serve."[11]

In that decision the Delaware court interpreted a corporate bylaw permitting indemnification of one involved in "any claim, action, suit or proceeding ... as a party or otherwise." It held that the indemnitee's "role or position in the litigation is not a prerequisite to indemnification" and that the position of the indemnitees as plaintiffs was at least partly motivated by their duties as directors. The court expressly stated that a "corporation can also grant indemnification rights beyond those provided by the [Delaware] statute."[12]

In light of that rule, a majority of state legislatures have enacted nonexclusive indemnification statutes, in order that corporate shareholders may be free to liberalize indemnification of their corporate directors even beyond what the statutes now provide.[13] Public policy in favor of broad indemnification appears to be firmly established.

§ 20.03. SEC attitude toward indemnification.

Indemnification of corporate directors or officers may not be available in some matters that directly involve the SEC. For example, under Sections 11 and 12 of the Securities Act of 1933,[14] Congress' intent was "to impose a duty of competence as well as innocence"[15] and "to promote careful adherence to the statutory requirements"[16] which may be thwarted by allowing indemnification. The same problem exists when

---

11. Hibbert v. Hollywood Park, Inc., 457 A.2d 339, 344 (Del. 1983).
12. Id. at 344.
13. See infra section 20.13.
14. 15 U.S.C. §§ 77k, 77l.
15. H.R. Rep. No. 85, 73d Cong., 1st Sess. 3, 5, 9 (1933); S. Rep. No. 47, 73d Cong., 1st Sess. 5 (1933).
16. Landis, "The Legislative History of the Securities Act of 1933," 28 Geo. Wash. L. Rev. 29, 35 (1959).

liability is asserted under Section 17(a) of the 1933 Act[17] or Sections 10(b), 14(a), 14(e) or 15(c) of the Securities Exchange Act of 1934.[18]

As to the 1933 Act, the SEC has made it a condition to the acceleration of a registration statement that unless all claims for indemnification are waived, the registrant must demonstrate his cognizance that the SEC considers indemnification in certain areas to be contrary to public policy. The SEC has imposed the requirement[19] that the registrant include a brief description of any indemnifying provision in the registration statement and his cognizance of the SEC's position in substantially the following form:[20]

> Insofar as indemnification for liabilities arising under the Securities Act of 1933 may be permitted to directors, officers and controlling persons of the registrant pursuant to the foregoing provisions, or otherwise, the registrant has been advised that in the opinion of the Securities and Exchange Commission such indemnification is against public policy as expressed in the Act and is, therefore, unenforceable. In the event that a claim for indemnification against such liabilities (other than the payment by the registrant of expenses incurred or paid by a director, officer or controlling person of the registrant in the successful defense of any action, suit or proceeding) is asserted by such director, officer or controlling person in connection with the securities being registered, the registrant will, unless in the opinion of its counsel the matter has been settled by controlling precedent, submit to a court of appropriate jurisdiction the question whether such indemnification by it is against public policy as expressed in the Act and will be governed by the final adjudication of such issue.

If a director, officer, or controlling person of the registrant is also a director, officer, controlling person, or any other

---

17. 15 U.S.C. § 77g(a).

18. Id. §§ 78j(b), 78n(a) and (e), 78o(c). Cf. Tomash v. Midwest Technical Dev. Corp., 281 Minn. 21, 160 N.W.2d 273 (1968).

19. 17 C.F.R. 230.461(c); Item 512(i) of Regulation S-K, 17 C.F.R. § 229.512(i) (1985).

20. SEC Release 33-3519, October 11, 1954, 19 F.R. 6729; amended in SEC Release 33-3536, March 10, 1955, 20 F.R. 1607.

651

member of the underwriting firm, the registrant is required to make a similar statement whenever the underwriting agreement contains provisions by which indemnification against liabilities arising under the 1933 Act is made available to the underwriter or his firm.

The SEC's position on indemnification has received some support in court decisions, notably the *Globus* cases.[21] *Globus* I held that indemnification is prohibited where a defendant has violated the provisions of the securities laws with actual knowledge of the falsity of its statements or reckless disregard for the truth.[22] *Globus* II declared that indemnification for violations of the federal securities laws is a matter of federal, not state law,[23] and extended the rule of *Globus* I to apply to mere negligence under Section 12(2) of the Securities Act.[24]

In other cases in which a party seeking indemnification was found to have acted intentionally or with actual knowledge, indemnity was denied.[25] Also where the party seeking indemnity had been an "active" tortfeasor, indemnity was denied.[26] It has been held that indemnification of negligent conduct under Section 14 of the 1934 Act would be contrary to the policy of the securities law.[27]

---

21. Globus v. Law Research Serv., Inc., 287 F. Supp. 188 (S.D.N.Y. 1968), modified, 418 F.2d 1276 (2d Cir. 1969), cert. denied, 397 U.S. 913 (1970) (Globus I); Globus, Inc. v. Law Research Serv., Inc., 318 F. Supp. 955 (S.D.N.Y. 1970), aff'd per curiam, 442 F.2d 1346 (2d Cir.), cert. denied sub nom. Law Research Serv., Inc. v. Blair & Co., 404 U.S. 941 (1971) (Globus II). See also Gould v. American-Hawaiian S.S. Co., 387 F. Supp. 163, 168 (D. Del. 1974), vacated on other grounds, 535 F.2d 761 (3d Cir. 1976); Odette v Shearson Hamill & Co., 394 F. Supp. 946, 954-55 (S.D.N.Y. 1975).
22. Globus I, supra note 21, 418 F.2d at 1288.
23. Globus II, supra note 21, 318 F. Supp. at 958 n.2.
24. 15 U.S.C. § 77l(2).
25. E.g., Herzfeld v. Laventhol, Krekstein, Horwath & Horwath, 378 F. Supp. 112, 135 (S.D.N.Y. 1974), modified, 540 F.2d 27 (2d Cir. 1976).
26. State Mut. Life Assur. Co. of Am. v. Peat, Marwick, Mitchell & Co., 49 F.R.D. 202, 212 (S.D.N.Y. 1969); Odette v. Shearson, Hammill & Co., 394 F. Supp. 946, 954 & n.9 (S.D.N.Y. 1975).
27. Gould v. American-Hawaiian S.S. Co., 387 F. Supp. 163 (D. Del. 1974), vacated on other grounds, 535 F.2d 761 (3d Cir. 1976).

There has been no direct test of SEC Rule 461, although the *Leasco* litigation offered an opportunity to raise the question. However, after the 1971 decision,[28] the Leasco board determined not to seek contribution from those of its directors who had been held jointly and severally liable with it. This, of course, amounted to a determination to indemnify those officials. The corporation's motion that the court decide whether it should pay the entire judgment was unopposed, except by the SEC which moved to intervene and filed a brief. It took the position that the court would be acting contrary to public policy as expressed in Section 11 of the Securities Act if it permitted Leasco directly to indemnify those directors against their liability or indirectly to do so by failing to seek contribution from them.[29]

A different attitude appears to have been taken by the SEC in the *Baldwin-United* Chapter 11 proceedings. In an amicus curiae brief it cited the importance of outside directors of public corporations and wrote:

> Indemnification for costs incurred in the defense of the good faith exercise of their business judgment is an appropriate and necessary expense in order to attract qualified persons to serve in that capacity.[30]

The SEC treats insurance coverage differently than direct indemnification. It has declared that insurance against liabilities arising under the 1933 Act, whether the cost of such insurance is borne by the registrant, the insured, or some other person, is not a bar to acceleration and no waivers or undertakings need be furnished with respect thereto.[31]

When Wisconsin enacted a new indemnification statute in 1987, granting broad powers to indemnify corporate directors

---

28. Feit v. Leasco Data Processing Equip. Corp., 332 F. Supp. 544 (E.D.N.Y. 1971).

29. SEC Brief, p. 9, quoted in Brodsky, "Indemnity for Violations of Securities Act of 1933," N.Y.L.J., March 28, 1972.

30. In re Baldwin-United Corp., 43 B.R. 443, 447 (S.D. Ohio 1984).

31. SEC Release 33-3519, Oct. 11, 1954, 19 F.R. 6729; amended in SEC Release 33-3536, Mar. 10, 1955, 20 F.R. 1607.

and officers, it expressly declared a public policy of indemnification, allowance of expenses, and insurance for liability arising from the securities laws. The statute states:

(1) It is the public policy of this state to require or permit indemnification, allowance of expenses and insurance for any liability incurred in connection with a proceeding involving securities regulation....

(2) [These sections] apply, to the extent applicable to any other proceeding, to any proceeding involving a federal or state statute, rule or regulation regulating the offer, sale or purchase of securities, securities brokers or dealers, or investment companies or investment advisers.[32]

§ 20.04. Development of statutory indemnification.

Since the first indemnification statute in New York in 1941, legislation on this subject has been enacted in all fifty states, Puerto Rico and the Virgin Islands. All but four of the statutes bear more or less similarity to some version of the indemnification statute in the Model Business Corporation Act and even these four statutes contain language resembling what some of the Model Act versions have proposed.

The 1950 Model Act provision was the pattern for the indemnification statutes in the District of Columbia and Puerto Rico. A slight modification, found in the 1960 Model Act was the pattern for the Vermont statute. Also similar thereto was an earlier form of the Delaware statute enacted in 1949 and repealed in 1967.

The Delaware statute,[33] frequently amended since its enactment, and the 1969 Model Business Corporation Act Section 5, were substantially identical and serve as the pattern for indemnification statutes in twenty-eight jurisdictions, which are identified in Appendix B. The Delaware courts have consistently held that:

[The statute] had as its objective that capable persons would be more willing to serve as corporate officers and

32. Wis. Stat. § 180.059.
33. Del. Code tit. 8, § 145.

directors by being provided with indemnification for their expenses in defending against attacks upon their conduct as corporate officers and directors.[34]

They have cited as an additional purpose to encourage directors and officers to resist unjustified claims, "secure in the knowledge that their reasonable expenses will be borne by the corporation they have served if they are vindicated."[35]

Eighteen states pattern their statutes on the 1980 amendments of the 1969 Model Act[36] or on the 1984 Revised Model Business Corporation Act.[37]

As a general rule, internal corporate affairs are governed by the law of the state of incorporation. Such affairs relate to matters that are peculiar to the relationships between the corporation and its officers, directors and shareholders and include indemnification. The Delaware court has held that directors and officers have a significant right, under the Due Process Clause, to know what law will be applied to their actions; hence this rule.[38]

In New York, however, some provisions of the Business Corporation Law, including those relating to indemnification and insurance of corporate officers and directors, apply to some foreign corporations.[39] But foreign corporations whose shares are listed on a national securities exchange, or that derive less than a specified portion of their business income from New York state, are exempted from this requirement.[40] As to the exempted foreign corporations, the above general rule applies, and their internal affairs are governed by the law of the state of their incorporation.

At the time of the so-called D & O insurance crisis in the middle 1980's, more than half of the states amended their

---

34. E.g., Green v. Westcap Corp., 492 A.2d 260, 262-63 (Del. Super. 1985).

35. Essential Enters. Corp. v. Automatic Steel Prods., 39 Del. Ch. 371, 379, 164 A.2d 437, 441 (1960).

36. See 36 Bus. Law. 99, 103 (1980).

37. 2 Model Bus. Corp. Act Ann. §§ 8.50 to 8.57 (3d ed. 1985).

38. McDermott, Inc. v. Lewis, 531 A.2d 206 (Del. 1987).

39. N.Y. Bus. Corp. Law § 1319, reproduced in Appendix A.

40. Id. § 1320, reproduced in Appendix A.

corporation codes and expanded and liberalized their indemnification statutes and Mississippi and Virginia enacted new business corporation codes.[41]

§ 20.05. Basic statutory patterns.

There is little uniformity in the various indemnification statutes, but the basic statutory pattern is that of the Delaware Code and the 1969 Model Business Corporation Act. In this form, the subjects with which the statute deals are, in substance, the following:

(a) Empowering a corporation to indemnify in third-party actions, identifying persons covered, and statement of standards of conduct to be eligible for indemnification.

(b) Empowering a corporation to indemnify in actions by or in the right of the corporation, identifying persons covered, statement of standards of conduct to be eligible for indemnification, and provision for court ordered indemnification.

(c) Mandatory indemnification for expenses to the extent of success in action.

(d) Authorization of indemnification.

(e) Advance payment of expenses.

(f) Nonexclusivity of statutory indemnification.

(g) Empowering a corporation to purchase and maintain D & O insurance.

Sections 20.06 to 20.13 discuss the above provisions and point out how they have been amended and supplemented in various state statutes. In the case of the statutes of the District of Columbia, Puerto Rico and Vermont the indemnification is greatly limited and reference should be made to the specific laws in each case.[42]

---

41. See discussion supra section 7.01. And see infra sections 20.06 to 20.13.

42. See D.C. Code Ann. 29-304(p); P.R. Laws Ann. tit. 14, § 1202.10; Vt. Stat. Ann. tit. 11, § 1852(15). See also discussion of that statutory form in

§20.06. Persons eligible for indemnification.

The basic form of the statute permits indemnification of any person who was or is a party or is threatened to be made a party to any threatened, pending or completed action, suit or proceeding, whether civil, criminal, administrative or investigative, by reason of the fact that such person is or was a director, officer, employee or agent of the corporation. Court decisions have given considerable breadth to those provisions. For example, a former corporate officer of a Delaware corporation, licensed as a foreign corporation in New York, was held entitled to indemnification for his legal expenses incurred when subpoenaed to testify before a federal grand jury investigating antitrust activities in the copper wire industry.[43] The witness was granted "use" immunity,[44] although he had been a "target" of the investigation before being subpoenaed to testify. The court held that he was entitled to be treated as a "party," rather than a mere "information witness" and that the grand jury investigation was an "investigative proceeding" for which mandatory indemnification was provided by the Delaware statute and the corporation's certificate of incorporation.

The Southern District of New York decided an action under the Delaware statute which involved some unique indemnification problems.[45] These questions arose in an action to recover back money paid by a mutual fund to its investment advisor and other defendants to indemnify them for expenses incurred by them in SEC administrative proceedings. The court decided that the investment advisor and other defendants were agents of the fund within the meaning of subsections (a) and (f) of the Delaware Code; that a consent decree in such proceedings does not result in an adjudication against a party consenting to it; that public policy did not inhibit the

---

Essential Enters. Corp. v. Dorsey Corp., 40 Del. Ch. 343, 182 A.2d 647 (1962).

43. Stewart v. Continental Copper & Steel Indus., Inc., 67 A.D.2d 293, 414 N.Y.S.2d 910 (1979).

44. Under 18 U.S.C. § 6001 et seq.

45. Cambridge Fund, Inc. v. Abella, 501 F. Supp. 598 (S.D.N.Y. 1980).

indemnification; and that certain defendants had forfeited their right to indemnification by presenting information to the independent directors in such a one-sided and incomplete manner as to discourage any meaningful evaluation of their request.

This form of statute also makes eligible for indemnification a person who is or was serving at the request of the corporation as a director, officer, employee or agent of another corporation, partnership, joint venture, trust or other enterprise.

Thirty-two state statutes, including those in California, Delaware, Illinois, Indiana, Kansas, New Jersey, New York and North Carolina, have clarified the reference to "other enterprises" to make certain that indemnification is available to a director serving as a trustee or fiduciary for an employee benefit plan and whose liability arises under ERISA.[46] For example, the present Delaware statute contains an extensive provision clarifying this entire aspect of the indemnification process.[47] The Revised Model Business Corporation Act does so in its Sections 8.50(2) and 8.51(b).[48]

The provisions of Section 145(e) of the Delaware Code, relating to advancement of expenses, are different as to directors and officers than as to other employees or agents.

§ 20.07. Actions by or in the right of the corporation.

Most indemnification statutes differentiate between actions by or in the right of the corporation, such as derivative suits,[49] and third-party actions. The basic form of the statute does so and, as is the common practice, deals with each in a separate part of the statutory form.

---

46. See supra Chapter 9.

47. Del. Code Ann. tit. 8, § 145(i) reproduced infra Appendix A. See also Ill. Bus. Corp. Act § 8.75(j), which is substantially identical, and other statutes noted in Appendix A.

48. See also, e.g., N.Y. Bus. Corp. Law § 722(a); Ind. Code § 23-1-37-13; N.J. Stat. Ann. § 14A:3-5(b).

49. See Hydro-Dynamics, Inc. v. Pope, 146 Ariz. 586, 708 P.2d 70, 71 (1985).

In actions by or in the right of the corporation the basic form of the statute limits indemnification to expenses (including attorneys' fees) actually and reasonably incurred by the director in connection with the defense or settlement of the action or suit.

Some other indemnification statutes such as New York use the term "actually and necessarily incurred," which is a more severe standard. Anything necessary would presumably be reasonable, but an expenditure might be reasonable although not necessary.[50]

The amount paid in settlement has not usually been indemnifiable in this type action and neither have been judgments or fines. The theory of this restriction is that it will avoid circularity, namely for the corporation to recover funds directly or by derivative action and then pay them over to the director who had paid them.

Indemnification under this section of the statute is dependent on the person having acted in good faith and in a manner he reasonably believed to be in or not opposed to the best interests of the corporation. In the few states which omit "or not opposed to" the field of action of the would-be indemnitee is probably somewhat narrower. There is an additional requirement that where a person has been adjudged liable for negligence or misconduct in the performance of his duty to the corporation, there must be a finding by an appropriate court that he is fairly and reasonably entitled to indemnification. The statute provides no guidelines for the court in determining such entitlement.

In the 1986 amendment of the Delaware statute, the words "for negligence or misconduct in the performance of his duty" were deleted because the Delaware courts have established "gross negligence" as the standard of liability for directors in violating their duty of care.[51]

---

50. Tillman v. Wheaton-Haven Rec. Ass'n, 580 F.2d 1222, 1227 (4th Cir. 1978).

51. Aronson v. Lewis, 473 A.2d 805 (Del. 1984); Smith v. Van Gorkom, 488 A.2d 858 (Del. 1985).

With varying limitations, some states now permit indemnification of amounts paid in settlement and judgments in actions by or in the right of the corporation. For example, the New York statute[52] permits indemnification for amounts paid in settlement if an appropriate court determines upon application that, in view of the circumstances of the case, the person is fairly and reasonably entitled to indemnity for such portion of the settlement amount and expenses as the court deems proper. In some states, such as Illinois, no indemnification even for expenses, is permitted in this type of action unless such a court finding is made.[53] California prohibits indemnification of expenses incurred in defending a pending action which is settled without court approval.[54]

The Indiana statute makes no distinction between actions by or in the right of the corporation and third-party actions. It extends indemnification to the obligation to pay a judgment, settlement, penalty, fine (including an excise tax assessed with respect to an employee benefit plan), as well as reasonable expenses, including counsel fees.[55] The same is true of the Maine statute.[56] Other states permitting indemnification for amounts paid in settlement include Louisiana,[57] Missouri, North Carolina, Pennsylvania, and Wisconsin.[58]

Massachusetts, Minnesota, Mississippi, North Dakota, Vermont, Wyoming, and the District of Columbia neither prohibit nor require court approval for indemnification of judgments or amounts paid to settle derivative actions. In all, there are some sixteen states that have liberalized indemnification in such cases.[59]

The basic form of the statute is nonexclusive and this feature has become quite popular. Much of the recent legislation

---

52. N.Y. Bus. Corp. Law § 722(c).

53. Ill. Bus. Corp. Act § 8.75(b).

54. Cal. Corp. Code § 317(c)(3).

55. Ind. Code §§ 23-1-37-4 and 23-1-37-8.

56. Maine Rev. Stat. tit. 13A, § 719(1).

57. La. Rev. Stat. § 12:83(A).

58. Mo. Gen. & Bus. Corp. L. § 351.355; N.C. Gen. Stat. § 55.19; Wis. Stat. § 180.044.

59. See infra Appendix B.

has adopted the nonexclusive concept.[60] Assuming such legislation to be an expression of the public policy of the states enacting it, there is an apparent trend that corporations which desire to do so may amend their charters or bylaws or use indemnification agreements to provide more comprehensive indemnification as to actions by or in the right of the corporation. Decisions in Delaware, New York and Massachusetts appear to support this view.[61]

§ 20.08. Third-party actions.

The scope of indemnification in third-party actions is more comprehensive than for actions by or in the right of the corporation. The third-party action provision authorizes indemnification not only for expenses (including attorneys' fees) but also judgments, fines and amounts paid in settlement. The person indemnified must have acted in good faith and in a manner he reasonably believed to be in or not opposed to the best interests of the corporation with respect to the claim against him. As to any criminal action or proceeding, such person must have had no reasonable cause to believe his conduct was unlawful. Public policy prohibits indemnification of corporate officers for intentional illegal conduct.[62] And one who deliberately violates federal criminal law cannot be acting "in good faith."[63]

The standards for indemnification vary in different state statutes. For example, New York deletes "or not opposed to" but uses it as the standard for services undertaken for any

---

60. At least 41 states now have nonexclusivity provisions in their indemnification statutes. See discussion infra section 20.13.

61. See, e.g., Hibbert v. Hollywood Park, Inc., 457 A.2d 339 (Del. 1983); Pepsico, Inc. v. Continental Cas. Co., 640 F. Supp. 656, 660-61 (S.D.N.Y. 1986); Choate, Hall & Stewart v. SCA Servs., Inc., 22 Mass. App. 522, 495 N.E.2d 562 (1986). Cf. B & B Inv. Club v. Kleinert's, Inc., 472 F. Supp. 787, 793 (E.D. Pa. 1979).

62. Altman v. Stevens Fashion Fabrics, 441 F. Supp. 1318, 1321 n.2 (N.D. Cal. 1977).

63. Associated Milk Producers, Inc. v. Parr, 528 F. Supp. 7, 8 (E.D. Ark. 1979).

entity other than the corporation.[64] The Indiana statute is similar.[65] Maine deletes the words "not opposed to."[66]

It is explained in the Official Comment to Section 8.51 of the Revised Model Business Corporation Act[67] that the concept of good faith involves a subjective test, which would include "a mistake in judgment," even though made unwisely by objective standards. The Comment suggests that a director who failed to act with the care of an ordinarily prudent person[68] might nevertheless be indemnified if he met the indemnification standards.

Commentators have said that both the "good faith" and "reasonable belief" standards are premised on the concept of the "duty of loyalty" and not of the "duty of care."[69] The significance of that statement is pointed up by the holding in *Smith v. Van Gorkom*,[70] a class action, where the directors were found to be grossly negligent although there was no proof that they did not act in good faith or violated their duty of loyalty. Ergo, they would be eligible for indemnification under the Delaware statute despite their wrongdoing.[71]

The determination of any action, suit or proceeding by judgment, order, settlement, conviction, or upon a plea of nolo contendere or its equivalent, will not, of itself, create any presumption that the person did not act in good faith and in a manner which he reasonably believed to be in or not opposed to the best interests of the corporation, or, as to a criminal action or proceeding, had reasonable cause to believe that his conduct was unlawful. Even under such circumstances, the

---

64. N.Y. Bus. Corp. Law § 722(a).

65. Ind. Code § 23-1-37-8.

66. Maine Rev. Stat. tit. 13A, § 719(1).

67. 2 Model Bus. Corp. Act Ann. 1116 (3d ed. 1985).

68. See supra section 2.02.

69. Arsht & Stapleton, "Delaware's New General Corporation Law: Substantative Changes," 23 Bus. Law. 75, 78 (1967). See also A.C. Acquisitions Corp. v. Anderson, Clayton & Co., 519 A.2d 103, 114 (Del. Ch. 1986).

70. 488 A.2d 858, 873, 884 (1985), discussed supra sections 2.06 and 6.14.

71. Cf. Cambridge Fund, Inc. v. Abella, 501 F. Supp. 598, 613-18 (S.D.N.Y. 1980).

corporation may indemnify if the standards of "good faith" and "reasonable belief" are met.[72]

§ 20.09. Authorization of indemnification.

Permissive indemnification is not automatic but must be authorized on a case-by-case basis, unless ordered by a court, under the basic form of the indemnification statute and under most other such statutes. Such authorization requires a finding that the person seeking indemnification has met the applicable standards of conduct.[73] In Louisiana the requirement that such authorization be made in the specific case has been deleted.[74] Virginia's statute provides that the failure to make such a determination shall not create any presumption that the director is not entitled to indemnification.[75] In Wisconsin a determination is provided for, but the director or officer seeking indemnification is permitted to select the method of determination.[76]

The determination is made, under the basic form of the statute, by

    (1) a majority vote of a quorum consisting of directors who are not parties to the proceeding;
    (2) independent legal counsel; or
    (3) the shareholders.

There are various modifications of those requirements. The Model Act form permits delegation of the decision to a board committee of two or more directors, but directors who are parties to the proceeding may be involved in the delegation.[77] Several states, including Minnesota, North Dakota, Ohio and Washington define "independent legal counsel." Most states

---

72. Green v. Westcap Corp., 492 A.2d 260, 264 (Del. Super. 1985).

73. E.g., Cal. Gen. Corp. Law § 317(e); Del. Code Ann. tit. 8, § 145(d); Nev. Rev. Stat. § 78.751(4); N.Y. Bus. Corp. Law § 723(b); 42 Pa. C.S.A. § 8365.

74. E.g., La. Rev. Stat. § 12:83(C).

75. Va. Code § 13.1-700.1.

76. Wis. Stat. § 180.046.

77. Revised Model Bus. Corp. Act § 8.55(b)(2).

do not. California denies a shareholder seeking indemnification as a director, officer, employee or agent, a right to vote on authorization. The Model Act form proscribes voting of shares controlled by shareholders who are parties to the proceeding. Thus it is necessary to examine the particular statute involved in each case.

§ 20.10. Court-ordered indemnification.

The basic form of the statute provides that indemnification may be ordered by an appropriate court, upon application, even if the person seeking indemnification is adjudged liable to the corporation, when the court determines, in view of all circumstances of the case, that such person is fairly and reasonably entitled to indemnification for expenses which the court deems proper. This rule prevails in most jurisdictions.

However, in California there is a provision that the court must find that the person has met the applicable standard of conduct.[78] In New York, with court approval, amounts paid in settlements in actions by or in the right of the corporation may be indemnified.[79] Arizona's statute has a similar provision.[80] Wisconsin has a broad provision under which the court may allow expenses incurred in obtaining the court-ordered indemnification.[81]

In addition, where a person is entitled to mandatory indemnification,[82] he may enforce the right in court.[83] Some state statutes make special provision for such actions. New York[84] and Wisconsin,[85] for example, have statutory provisions for direct access to their courts for indemnification notwithstanding the failure or refusal of a corporation to provide it and, in New York, despite any contrary action by the corporation in

---

78. Cal. Corp. Code § 317(e)(4).
79. N.Y. Bus. Corp. Law § 722(c).
80. Ariz. Rev. Stat. Ann. § 10-005(B).
81. Wis. Stat. § 180.051.
82. See discussion infra section 20.11.
83. Green v. Westcap Corp., 492 A.2d 260 (Del. Super. 1985).
84. N.Y. Bus. Corp. Law § 724.
85. Wis. Stat. § 180.051.

the specific case. The New York court may order expenses, including attorneys' fees, paid during the pendency of the litigation if the defendant has raised genuine issues of fact or law.

§ 20.11. Mandatory indemnification.

Mandatory indemnification under the basic form of the statute is required to the extent that a director, officer, employee or agent of a corporation has been successful on the merits or otherwise in the defense of any action discussed above in sections 20.07 and 20.08 or in the defense of any claim, issue or matter in such an action. Mandatory indemnification is usually limited to expenses (including attorneys' fees) actually and reasonably incurred in the defense. The statutory standards for permissive indemnification do not apply when mandatory indemnification is in order. The right is absolute and the statute is self activating.[86]

There is an element of finality in the success provision of the statute. Thus indemnification was held not mandatory when a civil action was dismissed without prejudice but the claim was being litigated in other pending actions.[87] If a successful judgment is appealed, indemnification is not mandatory until the entry of a final and favorable appellate ruling.[88] The statute is broad enough to cover a termination of actions by agreement without any payment or assumption of liability.[89] It appears to be an open question whether the making of a payment — especially a so-called "nuisance value" payment — in order to bring about a dismissal of the action would defeat a claim for mandatory indemnification.

---

86. Green v. Westcap Corp., supra note 83, at 265; Penthouse North Ass'n, Inc. v. Lombardi, 436 So. 2d 184, 188 (Fla. App. 1983); Amrep Corp. v. American Home Assur. Co., 440 N.Y.S.2d 244 (1981).

87. Galdi v. Berg, 359 F. Supp. 698 (D. Del. 1973).

88. Lussies v. Mau-Van Dev., Inc. 667 P.2d 830, 833 (Haw. App. 1983).

89. Wisener v. Air Exp. Int'l Corp., 583 F.2d 579, 583 (2d Cir. 1978). Cf. B & B Inv. Club v. Kleinert's, Inc., 472 F. Supp. 787, 790-91 (E.D. Pa. 1979).

The draftsmen of the Revised Model Business Corporation Act recognized that the language "on the merits or otherwise" may result in "an occasional defendant becoming entitled to indemnification because of procedural defenses not related to the merits — e.g., the statute of limitations or disqualification of the plaintiff." Nonetheless they deemed it "unreasonable to require a defendant with a valid procedural defense to undergo a possibly prolonged and expensive trial on the merits in order to establish eligibility for mandatory indemnification."[90] However, the Model Act and the statutes following it require the defense to be "wholly successful." New York deleted "wholly" from its statute in the 1986 amendment.[91] California requires the success to be "on the merits."[92]

If the success is final, but only partial, there is authority for mandatory indemnification to that extent. In the second decision in *Merritt-Chapman and Scott Corporation v. Wolfson*[93] the court required partial indemnification of a director who successfully defended three of four counts of a criminal indictment. It should be noted, however, that this case may be distinguishable because it was decided on a by-law which created rights in addition to those contained in the statute.[94] In a 1985 decision, the same court upheld mandatory indemnification where a criminal charge was dismissed leaving a civil action pending. The court held that "indemnification must be considered as each criminal or civil proceeding arises or is concluded," and that indemnification as to the criminal case did not set any precedent for indemnification in the civil action.[95]

---

90. 2 Model Bus. Corp. Act Ann. 1121 (3d ed. 1985).
91. N.Y. Bus. Corp. Law § 723(a).
92. Cal. Corp. Code § 317(d). See also American Nat'l Bank & Trust Co. v. Schigus, 83 Cal. App. 3d 790, 148 Cal. Rptr. 116 (1978).
93. 321 A.2d 138 (Del. Super. 1974) (sometimes called "Wolfson II").
94. Id. at 142.
95. Green v. Westcap Corp., 492 A.2d 260, 265-66 (Del. Super. 1985).

§ 20.12. Advance payments.

The provision in the basic form of the statute for payment of fees and expenses in advance of the final disposition of the action has been changed in one or more particulars in most recent legislation, probably as a direct result of the amount of D & O litigation during the past decade. Before July 1, 1986, the Delaware statute, then in the basic form, permitted advancements as authorized by the board of directors in the specific case upon receipt of an undertaking by or on behalf of the director, officer, employee or agent, to repay it unless it should ultimately be determined that he was entitled to be indemnified. Delaware has now made these provisions applicable only to directors and officers, has deleted the words "as authorized by the board of directors in the specific case," and has shifted the burden by changing the obligation to repay so that it comes into being only "if it shall ultimately be determined that he is not entitled to be indemnified." There is no requirement that the undertaking to repay be secured. Several other states have followed this pattern.[96] Connecticut, however, requires only an agreement to repay.[97]

Under the present form of the Delaware statute the requirement of an undertaking to repay advancements is not applicable to employees or agents other than directors and officers. The board of directors may impose such terms and conditions, if any, as the board deems appropriate for advances to employees and agents.

The Revised Model Act added a provision for the director to furnish a written affirmation of his good faith belief that he had met the standards for indemnification. Also, the facts known must not establish that indemnification would be precluded under the statute.[98] Several states have enacted such provisions as part of their corporation codes.[99]

---

96. E.g., Kansas, Louisiana, Maryland, Michigan, New Mexico, New York, Pennsylvania, South Carolina and Utah. See also infra Appendix B.

97. Conn. Gen. Stat. Ann. § 33-320a(f).

98. Revised Model Bus. Corp. Act § 8.53(a).

99. E.g., Colorado, Indiana, Mississippi, Oregon, South Carolina, Tennessee, Texas, Virginia, Washington and Wisconsin. See also infra Appendix B.

Nevada provides for mandatory advancement if authorized by the certificate or articles of incorporation, the bylaws or an agreement.[100] Ohio's statute requires expenses of directors to be advanced unless the articles or regulations provide otherwise by specific reference to this statute, but the director's undertaking must contain an agreement to cooperate with the corporation concerning the action, suit or proceeding.[101] Ohio follows the Delaware form as to advancing expenses for a trustee, officer, employee or agent.[102]

The statutes do not usually require that the provisions for authorization of indemnification be followed as to advancements.[103] Thus an Illinois court has ruled that the statutory provisions for authorization of indemnification and for advancements are "completely independent and procedurally unrelated." The Illinois statute follows the Delaware form and there are no statutory preconditions to a board of directors authorizing the advancement of funds.[104] Another court has explained that the need for such preconditions is not present in the advancement situation. It said:

> [A]dvances under subsection (e) only become permanent obligations of the company if indemnification is later determined to be proper. Rather than director self-dealing, the primary risk posed to the company by such advances is that the officials to whom the advances are made will be unable to repay the company if they are not ultimately indemnified. The requirement that company officials undertake to repay the advances for litigation expenses is an attempt to manage this risk.[105]

§ 20.13. Exclusivity.

The Delaware indemnification statute has always been of the nonexclusive type. Since its amendment to conform sub-

---

100. Nev. Rev. Stat. § 78.751.

101. Ohio Rev. Code Ann. § 1701.13(E)(5)(a).

102. Id. § 1701.13(E)(5)(b).

103. See supra section 20.09.

104. Johnson v. Gene's Supermarket, Inc., 117 Ill. App. 3d 234, 453 N.E.2d 83, 89 (1983).

105. Security Am. Corp. v. Walsh, Case, Code, Brown & Barke, No. 82 C2953, N.D. Ill. E.D., Jan. 11, 1985 (available on Lexis and Westlaw).

stantially to Section 5 of the 1969 Model Business Corporation Act,[106] the nonexclusivity provision has preserved "any other rights to which those seeking indemnification may be entitled under any bylaw, agreement, vote of shareholders or disinterested directors or otherwise." The Delaware statute still contains those provisions broadened to include "advancement of expenses" as well as indemnification. The statute permits corporations to establish their own corporate policies for indemnification and grant indemnification rights beyond those provided by the statute.[107] In a case so holding, the Delaware court ruled that the indemnitee's role or position in the litigation is not a prerequisite to indemnification; he must only be involved "as a party or otherwise."[108]

The extent to which corporations may go in providing indemnification beyond the statute has not been established by any Delaware court decision. Knowledgeable Delaware lawyers have suggested that indemnification agreements or bylaws could provide for (i) mandatory indemnification unless prohibited by statute; (ii) mandatory advancement of expenses, which the indemnitee can, in many instances, obtain on demand; (iii) accelerated procedures for the "determination" required by section 145(d) to be made "in the specific case"; (iv) litigation "appeal" rights of the indemnitee in the event of an unfavorable determination; (v) procedures under which a favorable determination will be deemed to have been made under circumstances where the board fails or refuses to act; (vi) reasonable funding mechanisms; and (vii) certain other provisions [which are not detailed].[109]

The same commentators have questioned whether indemnification agreements or bylaws could provide for indemnifi-

---

106. See discussion supra section 20.04.

107. Hibbert v. Hollywood Park, Inc., 457 A.2d 339, 344 (Del. 1983). But cf. Hydro-Dynamics, Inc. v. Pope, 148 Ariz. 586, 708 P.2d 70, 73 (1985).

108. Cf. Cambridge Fund, Inc. v. Abella, 501 F. Supp. 598 (S.D.N.Y. 1980); Stewart v. Continental Copper & Steel Indus., Inc., 67 A.D. 293, 414 N.Y.S.2d 910 (1979).

109. Veasey, Finkelstein & Bigler, "Delaware Supports Directors with a Three-Legged Stool of Liability, Indemnification, and Insurance," 42 Bus. Law. 399, 415 (1987).

cation of judgments or amounts paid in settlement in suits by or in the right of the corporation, on the premise that the restricted statutory power of indemnification in such cases[110] may demonstrate a legislative intent to prohibit such indemnification.[111] That premise was not accepted by Judge Charles L. Brieant, in the Southern District of New York, in his analysis of the Delaware statute. He read the nonexclusivity provision as making indemnification of directors and officers "the rule rather than the exception" and declared that a corporate bylaw had supplanted the "backstop" provisions included in Sections 145(a) and (b) of the Delaware statute.[112] Also, in Massachusetts, the appellate court interpreted the same provision to say "that there may be an agreement to indemnify for legal expenses which is not founded in, or limited by the other provisions of the statute."[113] The Massachusetts court did not have the settlement sum question before it, but plainly said that the other provisions of the statute did not limit the nonexclusivity provision.

Another indication that indemnification for settlements or judgments may not be contrary to public policy is found in the trend to authorize such indemnification in recent legislation. As is noted in section 20.07, some sixteen states now do so, although Arizona and New York require court approval.

The Revised Model Business Corporation Act mandates that indemnification of directors provided by articles of incorporation, bylaws, resolutions of shareholders or directors, a contract or otherwise, be "consistent" with the statute.[114] California has changed from the "consistent" form to the "nonexclusive" form.[115] Tennessee applies the "consistent" provision

---

110. See discussion supra section 20.07.

111. Veasey, et al., supra note 109, at 405-06.

112. Pepsico, Inc. v. Continental Cas. Co., 640 F. Supp. 656, 660-61 (S.D.N.Y. 1986).

113. Choate, Hall & Stewart v. SCA Servs., Inc., 22 Mass. App. 522, 527, 495 N.E.2d 562, 565 (1986).

114. Revised Model Bus. Corp. Act § 8.58(a).

115. Cal. Corp. Code § 317(g).

only to directors.[116] The Official Comment to the Model Act points out that "consistent" is not synonymous with "exclusive" and does not preclude provisions designed to provide procedural machinery different from that in the statute or to make mandatory the permissive provisions.

There is considerable variation in the nonexclusivity provisions of the different states but the trend appears to be in the direction of expanded indemnification. In Oregon and Indiana, for example, any limitation on nonexclusivity in a corporation's articles must be consistent with the statute.[117] Virginia permits unlimited indemnification and advancement of expenses except indemnity against willful misconduct or a knowing violation of the criminal law.[118] Wisconsin prohibits indemnification of a person who (i) willfully fails to deal fairly with the corporation or its shareholders, (ii) violates a criminal law unless he believed his conduct was lawful, (iii) derives improper personal profit, or (iv) engages in willful misconduct.[119]

New York's statute, formerly requiring consistency with the statute, now permits indemnification of directors or officers and advancement of expenses on a nonexclusive basis limited only if a judgment or other final adjudication adverse to a director or officer establishes that his acts were committed in bad faith or were the result of active and deliberate dishonesty and were material to the cause so adjudicated, or that he personally gained in fact a financial profit or other advantage to which he was not legally entitled. Those provisions do not apply to any rights to indemnification held by corporate personnel other than directors or officers under a contract or otherwise.[120] Moreover, by including the words "or other advantage", the New York legislature may have prevented indemnification for director or officer acts or omissions involving breaches of loyalty.

---

116. Tenn. Code Ann. § 48-18-509.
117. Or. Rev. Stat. § 57.260; Ind. Code § 23-1-37-15.
118. Va. Code § 13.1-704(B).
119. Wis. Stat. § 180.049.
120. N.Y. Bus. Corp. Law § 721.

§ 20.14. Expanded indemnification in charter, bylaw or contract.

A majority of the states now have nonexclusive provisions in their indemnification statutes. The court decisions to date appear to support the view that the only limit on indemnification under a charter, bylaw or indemnification contract entered into pursuant to such statutes, would be a clear public policy,[121] unless the nonexclusivity provision itself contains a limitation. For example, the New York statute now is nonexclusive but the nonexclusivity provision expressly prohibits any indemnification if a judgment or other final adjudication adverse to the director or officer establishes that his acts (i) were committed in bad faith or (ii) were the result of active and deliberate dishonesty and were material to the cause of action so adjudicated, or (iii) that he personally gained in fact a financial profit or advantage to which he was not legally entitled.[122] There is no such restriction in Section 145(f) of the Delaware statute.

Whatever may be the form of such expanded indemnification, it should be contractual in nature so as to constitute a binding, enforceable agreement between the corporation and the person to be indemnified. Needless to say, it should be supported by a valid consideration. A seminal decision of the Third Circuit, under Delaware law, upheld indemnification of a corporation's former president and director pursuant to a written agreement supported by reciprocal promises of the parties. The court construed the contract as an independent undertaking to provide such indemnification.[123] That decision has been followed in upholding a contract and settlement agreement entered into pursuant to the nonexclusivity provision of the present Delaware statute.[124]

---

121. James v. Getty Oil Co., 472 A.2d 33 (Del. Super. 1983). See also cases cited supra section 20.13.

122. N.Y. Bus. Corp. Law § 721.

123. Mooney v. Willys-Cleveland Motors, 204 F.2d 888, 891, 894 (3d Cir. 1953).

124. Choate, Hall & Stewart v. SCA Servs., Inc., 22 Mass. App. 522, 527, 495 N.E.2d 562, 565 (1986).

Such contracts, bylaws or charter provisions frequently provide for indemnification "to the full extent permitted by law." That language supplants the statutory provisions for indemnification and makes irrelevant their procedures for evaluating the actions of those seeking to be indemnified.[125] This provision has been held to "provide indemnification to the greatest extent possible," unlimited by restrictions in the other sections of the statute.[126]

The charter provision or bylaw, in establishing its contractual nature, may contain a provision similar to the following:

> *Contractual rights; applicability.* The right to be indemnified or to the advancement or reimbursement of expenses (i) is a contract right based upon good and valuable considerations, pursuant to which the person entitled thereto may sue as if these provisions were set forth in a separate written contract between such person and the Corporation, and (ii) is and is intended to be retroactive and shall be available as to events occurring prior to the adoption of these provisions, and (iii) shall continue after any rescission or restrictive modification of such provisions as to events occurring prior thereto.

When such language is used in a charter provision or bylaw, or modified for use in an indemnification agreement, it should prevent unilateral modification by the corporation especially in takeover or other change of control situations. If such a contractual provision has been bargained for by the person seeking indemnification, it may have even more strength. A Second Circuit case applied a broad bylaw provision retroactively, based on a finding that the language and timing of the bylaw were persuasive that the board intended to cover the particular situation before the court.[127]

A charter provision, bylaw or indemnification agreement may track the statutory provisions, in order to establish their

---

125. E.g., Pepsico, Inc. v. Continental Cas. Co., 640 F. Supp. 656, 661 (S.D.N.Y. 1986).

126. B & B Inv. Club v. Kleinert's, Inc., 472 F. Supp. 787, 793 (E.D. Pa. 1979).

127. Wisener v. Air Express Int'l Corp., 583 F.2d 579, 583 (2d Cir. 1978).

contractual nature in this context. If it is intended to afford the broadest possible indemnification and protection, it might be drafted to contain language such as the following:

> *Expanded indemnification.* Such person shall be indemnified and held harmless by the Corporation to the full extent permitted by law, including but not limited to [identify statute], as the same exists or may hereafter be amended (but, in case of any such amendment, only to the extent that such amendment permits the Corporation to provide broader indemnification rights than the law permitted the Corporation to provide prior to the amendment) against any and all expenses, liability, loss, judgments, fines, attorneys' fees, penalties, ERISA, excise taxes, and amounts paid or to be paid in settlement, reasonably incurred or suffered by such person, in connection with or arising out of such action, suit or proceeding.

Subject to the limitations mentioned above, such a charter provision, bylaw or indemnification contract may contain substantive or procedural provisions extending beyond those contained in the statute. Some such provisions, frequently used, are the following:

- agreement is made as an inducement to obtain or retain the person's services;
- expanded description of costs, expenses and other subjects of indemnification;
- making permissive provisions mandatory;
- coordination of indemnification with D & O insurance;
- simplified or expedited procedure to determine eligibility for indemnification or advancement;
- appeal rights upon adverse determination of eligibility for indemnification or advancement;
- imposing the burden upon the corporation to prove that standards for indemnification were not met;
- requiring such proof to be by clear and convincing evidence;
- right of person seeking indemnity to bring suit to compel indemnification after a specified lapse of time following claims;

- reimbursement of person for expenses incurred in enforcing indemnification advancements under the agreement;
- mandating advancement of expenses (including attorneys' fees) and disbursements during the pendency of litigation;
- provisions for funding indemnification payments (discussed in section 20.15);
- duty of person to give notice and information to corporation when claim is made;
- duty of person seeking indemnity to cooperate in defense of claims and suits;
- right of corporation to participate in defense of claims and suits;
- right of corporation to approve selection of legal counsel by person;
- procedure to handle conflicts of interest between persons seeking indemnity and corporation;
- right of corporation to approve any proposed settlement;
- right of person seeking indemnity to approve any proposed settlement;
- subrogation of corporation to rights of person indemnified;
- provision for incorporation by reference in agreement of future statutory amendments expanding indemnification;
- provisions to modify or terminate agreement;
- binding effect of agreement on person to be indemnified, heirs and legal representatives and on corporation, its successors, assigns and transferees;
- nonexclusivity provision;
- governing law;
- severability provision.[128]

Delaware and most other states do not require shareholder approval except when the charter is amended. However, the

---

128. See other examples supra section 20.13, text at note 109. And see Appendix D-2 for form of contract under Delaware law.

inherent potential for self-interest in such matters suggests that shareholder approval may have its benefits.[129]

§ 20.15. Funding the indemnification.

Indemnification, whether statutory or pursuant to charter, bylaws or agreement, ordinarily protects directors and officers only to the extent of the corporation's available assets. If the corporation is unable to fund the indemnification because of cash flow restraints or even insolvency, some supplementary funding mechanism may be essential. As an example, in the *Baldwin-United* Chapter 11 proceedings in 1984, as the so-called D & O insurance crisis was only beginning, District Judge David S. Porter wrote:

> We do note that this entire controversy might well have been avoided had the debtors obtained directors' and officers' liability insurance, which is not only readily available to liquid corporations but which, we understand, was one of the businesses of debtors' own subsidiaries. Our decision today makes painfully apparent the importance of such insurance.[130]

When D & O insurance is not readily available, as during the D & O insurance crisis, funding of indemnification has real significance. Louisiana,[131] Nevada,[132] and Ohio[133] have expressly authorized corporations to procure and maintain insurance, or other similar arrangement, or furnish similar protection by means of trust funds, letters of credit or self-insurance for the benefit of persons indemnified by the corporation and against the liability of directors, officers, employees or agents whether or not the corporation would have the power to indemnify them. Colorado, New Jersey, New

---

129. See, e.g., Michelson v. Duncan, 407 A.2d 211 (Del. 1979); Schreiber v. Bryan, 396 A.2d 512 (Del. Ch. 1978).
130. In re Baldwin-United Corp., 43 B.R. 443, 457 (S.D. Ohio 1984).
131. La. Rev. Stat. 12:83(F).
132. Nev. Rev. Stat. § 78.752.
133. Ohio Rev. Code Ann. § 1701.13(E)(7).

Mexico and Pennsylvania have provided alternative sources of funding.[134]

Whether other states will enact similar statutes remains to be seen, but a federal district court in Illinois has ruled that trust funds could be established to fund indemnification of directors for their litigation expenses and to advance such expenses during the pendency of the litigation, pursuant to Delaware law.[135] In that case the directors adopted resolutions to pay all expenses incurred by any officer or director of the corporation in connection with an action, suit or proceeding with allegations in any way relating to a public offering of the corporation's stock pursuant to a certain prospectus, and to advance funds in such amounts and as such terms as the corporation's president should determine. Three months later, two irrevocable trusts of $100,000 each were created and funded, one to pay the expenses of the outside directors, the other to pay the expenses of the inside directors. It was conceded that the trusts were made irrevocable and unamendable to prevent a new board of directors from revoking them. New management of the corporation challenged the trusts and the use of the trust funds, but the court held the procedure proper under the Delaware indemnification statute.[136] However, the court was "troubled" by (i) the fact that one-third of the company's assets were used to fund the trusts, (ii) that the law firms defending the former directors were the trustees of the trusts, and (iii) the inability of current management to stop the advancement of litigation expenses.

As noted in section 19.12, there is presently available a surety bond that guarantees a corporation's financial responsibility to indemnify one or more directors from loss or liability attributable to their business pursuits for that corpora-

---

134. See infra Appendix B.

135. Security Am. Corp. v. Walsh, Case, Coale, Brown & Burke, No. 82 C 2953, N.D. Ill. E.D., Jan. 11, 1985 (available on Lexis and Westlaw).

136. See discussion supra section 19.12, at note 105.

tion. The Nevada statute[137] expressly provides for the use of a surety bond but no statutes prohibit such procedure. The first form of bond to be offered is intended to be coextensive with the financial and contractual obligations of the corporation. Its protection is not as broad as that afforded by D & O insurance and the bond is not intended to displace such insurance, according to its sponsors.

§ 20.16. Indemnification of national bank directors.

The Office of the Comptroller of the Currency revised Interpretive Ruling § 7.5217[138] in 1984 to permit national banks to adopt indemnification articles which substantially reflect general standards of law as evidenced by (i) the law of the state in which the bank is headquartered, (ii) the law of the state in which the bank's holding company is incorporated, or (iii) the relevant provisions of the Model Business Corporation Act, with specified limitations. The Office of the Comptroller presumes that such indemnification standards come within the bank's corporate powers,[139] and consents that such provisions may be set forth in the bank's articles of association.

The Comptroller's office further consents that a national bank may provide in its articles of association for the payment of premiums for insurance covering the liability of its directors, officers or employees to the extent that such coverage is provided for in the adopted state law or Model Act indemnification standard. However, that provision must explicitly exclude insurance coverage for a formal order assessing civil money penalties against a bank director or employee.[140]

The ruling takes cognizance of the supervisory responsibilities of the Comptroller in two respects. It denies indemnifica-

---

137. Supra note 132.

138. 12 C.F.R. § 7.5217 (1971), revised 12 C.F.R. § 7.5217 (1984), 49 Fed. Reg. 30920 (Aug. 2, 1984).

139. See 12 U.S.C. § 24.

140. Cf. National Union Fire Ins. Co. v. Seafirst Corp., 662 F. Supp. 36, 39 (W.D. Wash. 1986).

tion against expenses, penalties, or other payments incurred in any administrative proceeding or action instituted by an appropriate bank regulatory agency which results in an order either assessing civil money penalties or requiring affirmative action by one or more individuals in the form of payments to the bank. Additionally, the ruling expressly reserves the power of the Office of the Comptroller to review any threat to bank safety and soundness posed by any indemnification or for the consistency of any indemnification with the standards in the bank's articles of association. Based upon this review, the Office of the Comptroller may direct a modification of the indemnification through appropriate administrative action.

§ 20.17. Indemnification of insured savings and loan directors.

Indemnification of its directors, officers and employees by a federal association[141] is controlled by a regulation of the Federal Home Loan Bank Board (FHLBB).[142] As part of a proposed extensive revision of its regulations regarding corporate governance of such associations, the FHLBB has issued a proposal in four parts for public comment.[143] The proposed changes in the indemnification regulations are not extensive, however, and no action on them is anticipated until sometime in 1988, at the earliest.

Under the regulation now in effect, such an association is required to indemnify any present or past director, officer or employee for (1) any amount for which that person becomes liable under a judgment in an action threatened or brought because the person was a director, officer or employee of the association, and (2) reasonable costs and expenses, including

---

141. See supra sections 12.08 and 12.09.

142. 12 C.F.R. § 545.121, 48 Fed. Reg. 23058 (May 23, 1983), amended, 49 Fed. Reg. 43045 (Oct. 26, 1984).

143. The proposal would revise and relocate 12 C.F.R. § 545.121 as §§ 543.10-5 and 544.10-5. See Res. No. 85-1068, 50 Fed. Reg. 52482 (Dec. 24, 1985) and Res. No. 87-687, 52 Fed. Reg. 25870 (July 9, 1987).

reasonable attorneys' fees, actually paid or incurred in defending or settling the action, or in enforcing his rights under the regulation if he attains a favorable judgment in such enforcement action.

Unless the director, officer or employee obtains a final judgment on the merits in his favor, indemnification is conditioned upon a determination by a majority of the interested directors of the association that he was acting (i) in good faith within the scope of this employment or authority as he could reasonably have perceived it under the circumstances, and (ii) for a purpose he could reasonably have believed under the circumstances was in the best interests of the association or its members.[144]

Indemnification is further conditioned by a requirement that the association give at least sixty days notice to the FHLBB of its intention to make such indemnification, with details of the matter involved. If the FHLBB advises the association, within the notice period, of its objection, no indemnification may be made.

Expenses, including attorneys' fees, may be advanced by action of a majority of the directors and subject to an agreement to repay if it be later determined that there is no entitlement to indemnification, and on such other conditions as the directors deem warranted in the interests of the association.

The regulation permits an association to purchase D & O insurance, but it must exclude payment for losses incurred as a result of willful or criminal misconduct.

The regulation is exclusive except that "an association which has a bylaw in effect relating to indemnification [but not insurance] of its personnel shall be governed solely by that bylaw."[145]

---

144. 12 C.F.R. § 545.121(c). The proposed revision would permit disinterested stockholders to make the determination. Proposed 12 C.F.R. § 543.10-5(b)(i).

145. 12 C.F.R. § 545.121(f). The proposed revision would require that such a bylaw must have been in effect on October 1, 1969 and still be in effect. Proposed 12 C.F.R. § 543.10-5(f).

§ 20.18. Indemnification of nonprofit corporation trustees, directors and officers.

The Model Non-Profit Corporation Act[146] and several significant state enactments, such as those in Pennsylvania,[147] Delaware,[148] New York,[149] and Ohio,[150] grant powers for permissive indemnification for the protection of officers, trustees and directors of nonprofit corporations and for mandatory indemnification when they are successful in defeating claims made against them. In Delaware, the indemnification provisions of the general corporation law apply to all corporations, stock and nonstock, as well as business and nonprofit (including charitable and religious). New York and Ohio have separate nonprofit corporation laws but they virtually track the business corporation laws which is the usual pattern where separate acts govern the two types of corporations.

Several states have enacted statutes which substantially limit or eliminate the liability of persons who serve without compensation as officers, directors and trustees of nonprofit corporations.[151] For example, Nevada's statute now provides:

> No action may be brought against an officer, trustee, director or other possessor of the corporate powers of a nonprofit corporation, association or organization formed under the laws of this state based on any act or omission arising from failure in his official capacity to exercise due care regarding the management or operations of the entity unless the act or omission involves intentional misconduct, fraud or knowing violation of law.[152]

Indemnification becomes less significant when such statutes are in effect. Such limiting-of-liability enactments are frequently accompanied by expanded indemnification amendments.

---

146. Model Non-Profit Corp. Act § 5(n) and § 24A (rev. ed. 1964).
147. 42 Pa. C.S.A. § 8365.
148. Del. Code Ann. tit. 8, § 145.
149. N.Y. Not-for-Profit Corp. Law §§ 721-723.
150. See discussion supra in section 13.14.
151. See discussions supra in sections 7.03 to 7.08 and 13.14.
152. Nev. Rev. Stat. § 41.480(2).

§ 20.19. Tax considerations.

The few court decisions dealing with the tax considerations involved in payment of legal expenses by a corporation for its directors or officers distinguish between capital expenditures which become part of the depreciable value of the corporation's property and other litigation expenses deductible against ordinary income. This distinction applies to a corporation which has paid fees and expenses to plaintiff's counsel in a derivative action as well as to one which has reimbursed its directors and officers for their defense costs.

A significant tax ruling on this subject was issued by the Internal Revenue Service in 1969.[153] Its thrust was in the area of the deductibility as business expenses of premiums paid for D & O insurance protection. However, the following language in the ruling has equal applicability to the subject of funds received by way of reimbursement under an indemnification article or statute:

> The liability coverage ... is limited solely to business acts. The purpose ... is to assure the bank that its officers and directors can make banking business decisions without fear of legal entanglement .... The premiums ... are paid by the taxpayer to protect its business by limiting its liability for such wrongful acts and to assure the taxpayer that its officers and directors can make necessary corporate decisions without fear of legal entanglement. Thus, the costs are incurred for the benefit of the taxpayer rather than for the benefit of the officers.

The same principle was applied three years earlier in the leading case on the subject, *Larchfield Corporation v. United States*,[154] in which the Second Circuit characterized payment of legal fees under an indemnification bylaw as "a fringe benefit necessary to induce officers and directors to serve, deductible in any event as reasonable compensation." In Judge Henry J. Friendly's opinion he recognized the capital

---

153. Rev. Rul. 69-491, 1969-2 C.B. 22.
154. 373 F.2d 159, 167 (2d Cir. 1966).

expenditure rule[155] and the expense deduction rule,[156] but concluded that the controlling factor in the case before the court was the relief sought in the underlying litigation, which was a derivative action settled in the Supreme Court of New York. In part, that action alleged the payment of illegal and excessive bonuses; in its other parts, it sought recovery of corporate stock improperly conveyed away. So allocated, the court upheld deductibility of all costs expended in defense of objectives other than the return of specific property.

It is necessary that such expenses be incurred for business reasons and that the business be that of the corporation and not merely of the individual. Thus the Ninth Circuit denied deductibility of defense costs where a director's services were performed solely as an act of friendship for the corporation's majority shareholder and with no profit motive.[157] Where the defense costs were the personal debt of a corporation's president and sole shareholder, the Fifth Circuit refused to recognize them as necessary business expenses of the corporation. It held that the payment was a constructive dividend to the shareholder, even though his services to the corporation may have been "indispensable" to it.[158]

---

155. See, e.g., Levitt & Sons, Inc. v. Nunan, 142 F.2d 795 (2d Cir. 1944).

156. See, e.g., Hochschild v. Commissioner, 161 F.2d 817 (2d Cir. 1947).

157. De Pinto v. United States, 407 F. Supp. 1, 3 (D. Ariz. 1975), aff'd, 585 F.2d 405 (9th Cir. 1978).

158. Jack's Main. Contractors, Inc. v. Commissioner, 703 F.2d 154 (5th Cir. 1983), reversing T.C. Memo 1981-349.

COROLLARY REFERENCES

Arsht & Stapleton, "Delaware's New General Corporation Law: Substantive Changes," 23 Bus. Law. 75 (1967).

Balotli & Gentile, "Elimination or Limitation of Director Liability for Delaware Corporations," 12 Del. J. Corp. L. 5 (1987).

Block, Barton & Rodin, "Indemnification and Insurance of Corporate Officials," 13 Sec. Reg. L.J. 239 (1985).

"Delaware Amendment Relaxes Directors' Liability," 44 Wash. & Lee L. Rev. 111 (1987).

Dunlap, "New Protections for Corporate Directors," 41 Wash. St. B. News 25 (1987).

Oesterle, "Limits on a Corporation's Protection of its Directors and Officers From Personal Liability," 1983 Wis. L. Rev. 513, 33 Def. L.J. 111 (1984).

"Revising the Texas Corporation's Power to Indemnify Directors: Evaluating, Incurring and Distributing the Risk of Legal Liability," 28 S. Tex. L. Rev. 619 (1987).

Sebring, "Recent Legislative Changes in the Law of Indemnification of Directors, Officers and Others," 23 Bus. Law. 95 (1967).

Veasey, Finkelstein & Begler, "Delaware Supports Directors with Limited Liability, Indemnification and Insurance," 42 Bus. Law. 399 (1987).

Chapter 21

LIABILITY INSURANCE

§ 21.01. The need for D & O insurance.

The insurance crisis of the mid-1980's brought into focus the importance of D & O insurance in the nation's economy. When directors of major corporations, some of them troubled, found themselves confronted with expanded liability exposure, a rash of proposals for takeovers, divestitures, shareholder suits, management buyouts, proxy fights, and the like, without adequate insurance to protect their personal estates, there was a serious threat of mass defections from corporate boardrooms.[1] In this period, D & O insurance changed from being a minor coverage with very little cost to being a major issue and a major cost element in some corporations.[2]

---

1. "The Job Nobody Wants: Outside Directors Find that the Risks and Hassles Just Aren't Worth It," Business Week, Sept. 8 1986, at 56.

2. 1987 Wyatt Company Directors and Officers and Fiduciary Liability Survey 161 (hereafter Wyatt Survey). See also infra Chapter 22.

In the crisis climate it became apparent that corporate indemnification, even under the expanded state statutes enacted as a crisis relief measure, may provide inadequate financial protection for directors and officers.[3] In most states, for example, it may not be possible to indemnify against settlements and judgments in actions by or in the right of the corporation.[4] Claims under the registration and anti-fraud provisions of the federal securities acts, under the Federal Corrupt Practices Act of 1977, and under other statutes such as some antitrust laws, are not or may not be indemnifiable.[5] Indemnification may not be available for acts which do not satisfy the "good faith" and "reasonable belief" standards of most state indemnity statutes.[6] In the aftermath of a takeover an incumbent board may refuse to make a determination of eligibility for indemnification or submit the matter to independent counsel. It is likely in such instances that D & O insurance will provide protection, although each case must be considered on its particular facts.

Even in situations where a corporation proceeds under the nonexclusivity provisions of a state statute, and makes special provisions for indemnification by charter, bylaw or contract,[7] the corporation may be financially unable to fund indemnification because of cash flow restraints or even insolvency.[8]

Alternatives, such as those discussed in sections 19.11 and 19.12, may provide some benefits to the corporation and its managers, but they probably will be of less protective value than traditional D & O insurance.[9]

---

3. See discussion supra Chapter 20.

4. See supra section 20.07.

5. See supra sections 20.02 and 20.03.

6. See supra section 20.07.

7. See supra section 20.14.

8. See infra section 22.04 as to costs and losses involved in D & O litigation.

9. E.g., see In re Baldwin United Corp., 43 B.R. 443, 456-58 (1984).

§21.02. Overview of the D & O policy.

Traditional director and officer liability insurance coverage is actually two distinct coverages within one policy. The first coverage, referred to as the personal (or direct, or D & O) part of the policy, reimburses the individual directors and officers for losses for which they are not indemnified by their corporation. The second coverage, referred to as the corporate reimbursement part of the policy, reimburses the corporation for amounts which it is lawfully permitted or required to expend in indemnifying its officers and directors. Although both coverages are within the same policy, each may have its own retentions, deductibles and exclusions. The corporate reimbursement part of the policy is the one under which most claims are made.

It is important to note that these policies do not insure the liabilities or defense costs of the corporation itself.

The principal British form of D & O policy on which American policies were based was actually two policies in one, the Lloyd's of London ALS(D4)-ALS(D5), January 1974. It is still in use as is the Stewart Smith SS4 form, issued by the CNA Group and some others, which combined the two policies into one. A somewhat different form introduced by Lloyd's in 1976 and identified as Lydando No. 1[10] went nowhere in the market. The Stewart Smith SS4 form comes close to being the basis for the several D & O policies in common use today, but there is considerable divergence in those policies and their wording.[11] Those reprinted in Appendix C are fair examples of the forms in common use since about 1984.

D & O insurance is written on a claims made basis.[12] The typical policy pays for "Loss,"[13] a defined term, by reason of

10. See Hinsey, "The New Lloyd's Policy Form for Directors and Officers Liability Insurance — An Analysis," 33 Bus. Law. 1961 (1978).

11. Form 8749/8750 (6/85) of National Union Fire Insurance Company of Pittsburgh, Pa. is a two-policies-in-one form based on ALS(D4)-ALS(D5).

12. See infra section 21.04.

13. See infra section 21.07.

any "Wrongful Act,"[14] another defined term, of the directors or officers, in that capacity, arising from any claim first made during the policy period. Such payment is subject to specified exclusions and will be made in accordance with policy terms and conditions.

In the D & O policy, "costs, charges and expenses," which include attorneys' fees and other defense costs, have always been included in the policy limit. The insurer is not charged with a duty to defend, but usually may participate at its option and will have a voice in the selection of defense counsel by the insured.[15]

Most D & O policies provide for "deductibles" or "retentions," as to each individual with respect to each loss up to an aggregate deductible for all directors and officers against whom claims are made. There is a specified deductible for the corporation with respect to the corporate reimbursement coverage.

Some D & O policies also involve a co-insurance feature, whereby the insureds must bear five percent of each loss which may not be insured.

Sections 21.04 to 21.13 will consider the principal elements of the D & O policy provisions.

§ 21.03. Statutory authorization of D & O insurance.

Corporations are expressly authorized to purchase and maintain D & O insurance by the statutes of all states except Vermont. The District of Columbia and Puerto Rico have no such authorization. The amended statute in the Virgin Islands contains an authorization.[16] A similar provision is found in the Model Act.[17]

Most jurisdictions have followed the language of the Delaware statute, which provides:

---

14. See infra section 21.06.
15. See supra Chapter 17, and infra section 21.09.
16. See infra Appendix B.
17. Revised Model Bus. Corp. Act § 8.57.

A corporation shall have power to purchase and maintain insurance on behalf of any person who is or was a director, officer, employee or agent of the corporation, or is or was serving at the request of the corporation as a director, officer, employee or agent of another corporation, partnership, joint venture, trust or other enterprise against any liability asserted against him and incurred by him in any such capacity, or arising out of his status as such, whether or not the corporation would have the power to indemnify him against such liability under this section.[18]

As that language shows, it is intended that the permissible scope of protection under such a policy be of greater scope than that afforded by indemnification, although the expanded scope of indemnification now provided in many states[19] is intended to allow corporations broad discretion in protecting directors by that means. From the language of the statutes authorizing D & O insurance it appears that public policy would provide the only restriction on the protection that could be made available by insurance. Generally, public policy prohibits coverage for willful or intentional wrongdoing, fraud or knowing violation of law.[20]

New York and California limit the expansion of the right to buy insurance.[21] The New York law prohibits insurance coverage except for defense costs:

(i) if a judgment or other final adjudication adverse to the insured director or officer establishes that his acts of active and deliberate dishonesty were material to the cause of action so adjudicated, or that he personally gained in fact a financial profit or other advantage to which he was not legally entitled, or

(ii) in relation to any risk the insurance of which is prohibited under the insurance law of New York.

---

18. Del. Code tit. 8, § 145(g); as to national banks, see 12 C.F.R. § 7.5217(d).

19. See supra section 20.13.

20. See, e.g., St. Paul Fire & Marine Ins. Co. v. Weiner, 606 F.2d 864, 870 (9th Cir. 1979); Elgin Nat'l Bank v. Home Indem. Co., 583 F.2d 1281, 1284 (5th Cir. 1978).

21. N.Y. Bus. Corp. Law § 726(b) and (c); Cal. Corp. Code § 317(i).

Also, retrospective rated contracts are prohibited.

By including the words "or other advantage," the New York legislature may have prohibited insurance coverage other than for defense costs when an officer or director is adjudicated to have violated the duty of loyalty.[22]

The California law provides that a corporation may purchase and maintain D & O insurance from a company which is owned in whole or in part by the insured corporation if:

(1) the insured corporation's articles of incorporation authorize such arrangement; or

(2) the insurance company is a duly licensed and operated insurance company under applicable insurance law, the claims processing by the insurance company is not subject to the direct control of the insured corporation, and there is some manner of risk sharing between the insurance company and the insured corporation, on the one hand, and some unaffiliated person or persons on the other.

New York's statute also contains a provision of considerable significance to the validity of D & O policies, which states:

> This section is the public policy of this state to spread the risk of corporate management, notwithstanding any other general or special law of this state or of any other jurisdiction including the federal government.[23]

By establishing the public policy of the state in this manner, New York has eliminated the potential for litigation attacking D & O insurance on that ground, although the provision probably is ineffective to nullify or otherwise affect any federal statutes or regulations on that subject.

In addition to authorizing the purchase and maintenance of traditional D & O insurance, statutes enacted since 1986 in Arizona, Hawaii, Louisiana, Maryland, Nevada, New Mexico, Ohio and Pennsylvania also authorize maintenance of self

---

22. See also supra section 20.13.

23. N.Y. Bus. Corp. Law § 726(e), cited as § 727(e) and followed in Flintkote Co. v. Lloyd's Underwriters, N.Y.L.J., July 27, 1976, at 6 (N.Y. Sup. Ct. 1976), aff'd, 56 A.D.2d 743, 391 N.Y.S.2d 1005 (1977).

insurance or other forms of financial protection, of greater scope than indemnification.[24]

§ 21.04. Claims made policy.

D & O policies are written as claims made policies. The insuring clause usually states that coverage will attach to any claim or claims which are first made during the policy period. The policy will also require notice of the claim to be given to the insurer during the policy period or during any extended discovery period that may apply. The right to coverage is furnished only by the policy in effect at that time.[25] The awareness of the insured of any facts or circumstances giving reason to believe that a claim might be presented because of them would avoid coverage for that claim.[26]

In theory, at least, a claims made policy would provide unlimited retroactive coverage but not prospective coverage. However, it has become a frequent practice to deny retroactive coverage in the policy or to establish a "retroactive date" prior to which coverage will not apply.[27] Sometimes the policy will provide no retroactive coverage during the first policy year and will make the inception date of that policy the retroactive date for renewal policies.[28]

Claims made policies came into common use in the field of professional liability insurance, to which D & O insurance is more or less distantly related. They supplanted "occurrence" policies which provided unlimited prospective coverage but no retroactive coverage and confronted the insurer with a "tail" which prevented precise calculations of premiums for

---

24. See discussion supra section 19.11, text at note 105.

25. Board of Educ. v. CNA Ins. Co., 647 F. Supp. 1495, 1508 (S.D.N.Y. 1986).

26. See, e.g., F/H Indus., Inc. v. National Union Fire Ins. Co., 635 F. Supp. 60 (N.D. Ill. 1986).

27. See discussion infra section 21.14 as to disclosures in application, and section 21.10 as to discovery and notice.

28. Sparks v. St. Paul Ins. Co., 100 N.J. 325, 495 A.2d 406, 408 (1985).

losses reported long after the time when the error or wrongful act occurred.[29]

In the vast majority of cases in which claims made policies have been challenged, their validity has been upheld in state and federal courts. There are numerous decisions that such policies do not offend public policy.[30] In a case in which that statement was made, the policy provided unlimited retroactive coverage. On the same decision date, the same court construed another claims made policy which provided no retroactive coverage, and found it invalid and contrary to public policy. The court declared that the policy did not "conform to the objectively reasonable expectations of the insured" and combined "the worst features of 'occurrence' and 'claims made' policies and the best of neither."[31]

Another requirement of the claims made policy that has come under fire is that mandating the report of the claim during the policy term. In a 1984 decision,[32] the Michigan Supreme Court upheld a claims made professional liability policy which covered only claims made while the policy was in effect and required the insurer to be notified no later than sixty days after the policy terminated. The claim was made after the notice period expired. The court refused to apply the Michigan notice-of-claim statute[33] which gives relief from a policy's notice requirement, if it is not "reasonably possible to give such notice within the prescribed time." The policy provision was upheld.

A 1983 decision in the Eastern District of Michigan, relying on an unreported Michigan Court of Appeals decision in 1978, found that the notice-of-claim statute and the policy requirement were in direct conflict.[34] It cited the Stine deci-

---

29. See Zuckerman v. National Union Fire Ins. Co., 100 N.J. 304, 495 A.2d 395, 398-99 (1985).

30. Id., 495 A.2d at 400-01 and cases cited.

31. Sparks v. St. Paul Ins. Co., supra note 28, 495 A.2d at 414.

32. Stine v. Continental Cas. Co., 419 Mich. 89, 349 N.W.2d 127 (1984).

33. Michigan Ins. Code, Mich. Comp. Laws Ann. § 500.3008.

34. St. Paul Fire & Marine Ins. Co. v. Parzen, 569 F. Supp. 753 (E.D. Mich. 1983).

sion in the Court of Appeals,[35] which was reversed in the 1984 Supreme Court ruling mentioned above.

The Florida Supreme Court held in 1983 that the time stated in the policy for reporting claims could not be extended by a court. It stressed that such an extension of time, after the policy period, would be "tantamount to an extension of coverage to the insured gratis, something that the insurer [did] not bargain for."[36]

In California, where the "substantial prejudice rule" applies, the Ninth Circuit struck down the reporting requirement in a 1987 decision which was later vacated when the parties settled their differences.[37] The "substantial prejudice rule" requires an insurer to show "material and substantial prejudice" from the insured's failure to timely report a claim in order to deny liability on that basis.[38] The fact that an extended discovery and reporting period could have been purchased for an additional premium was held to be irrelevant. Also the court said it made no difference whether the reporting requirement was described as a condition precedent to liability or a coverage covenant. The "substantial prejudice rule" is in effect in only a few states;[39] accordingly, this Ninth Circuit decision was at best a minority rule.

In some states there is a statutory requirement that a claims made policy bear on its face a conspicuous legend de-

---

35. Stine v. Continental Cas. Co., 112 Mich. App. 174, 315 N.W.2d 887 (1982), rev'd, 419 Mich. 89, 349 N.W.2d 127 (1984). See also Detroit Auto. Inter-Ins. Exch. v. Leonard Underwriters, 117 Mich. App. 300, 323 N.W.2d 679 (1982).

36. Gulf Ins. Co. v. Dolan, Fertig & Curtis, 433 So.2d 512 (Fla. 1983). Cf. Gereboff v. Home Indem. Co., 383 A.2d 1024, 1026 (R.I. 1978).

37. New England Reinsurance Corp. v. National Union Fire Ins. Co., 822 F.2d 887 (9th Cir. 1987); vacation of decision reported in "Update," Business Insurance, Oct. 10, 1987, at 1, col. 4; Mt. Hawley Ins. Co. v. FSLIC, No. CV87-6MRP, C.D. Cal., Sept. 30, 1987, at 28.

38. Northwestern Title Sec. Co. v. Flack, 6 Cal. App. 3d 134, 140-41, 85 Cal. Rptr. 693, 696 (1970); Campbell v. Allstate Ins. Co., 60 Cal. 2d 303, 32 Cal. Rptr. 827 (1963).

39. See 8 Appleman, Insurance Law & Practice § 4732, at 26, and n.10 (1981).

scribing the policy as such and encouraging the insured to read it carefully.[40] Substantial compliance with that requirement has been held sufficient.[41]

§ 21.05. Insuring clauses: reimbursement; direct coverage.

There are two insuring clauses in the two policy form.[42] There is one insuring clause in two parts in the one policy form.[43]

One clause or part is the "direct" indemnification of the directors and officers and any other individual insureds against loss on account of any Wrongful Act, a defined term. The other is the corporate reimbursement part which will pay for or to the corporation amounts which it is required or permitted to pay as indemnification of the director, officer, and any other individual insureds. Although each insurer uses somewhat different wording in its insuring clauses, there will be a provision that any Wrongful Act must have been committed in their respective capacities as directors, officers or other insureds. The "claims made" language[44] may appear in the insuring clause.

Under the "direct" insuring clause, the coverage will not apply if the individual insureds are indemnified or entitled to indemnification by the corporation, but the exact language will be different in various policies.

The policy will define the individual insureds and, in rare instances, may name or categorize them. Among the questions to be considered in examining these definitions, is whether they:

   a. Cover appointed officers as well as elected officers?

---

40. E.g., Cal. Ins. Code § 11580.01.
41. Mt. Hawley Ins. Co. v. FSLIC, supra note 37, at 30.
42. Such as National Union Form 8749/8750 (6/85). See Appendix C.
43. Such as Chubb Form 14-02-0386 (Ed. 2-84) or St. Paul Form 5068 (Ed. 10-85). Aetna Cas. & Sur. Co. Independent Directors Liability Policy Form (F-1842) ED. 3-88 provides only direct coverage. See Appendix C.
44. See supra section 21.04.

b. Automatically cover all persons who become directors or officers after the inception date of the policy?

c. Cover newly created positions?

d. Cover employees with management responsibilities who are not technically officers or directors?

e. Cover all subsidiaries of the corporation or newly acquired or created subsidiaries and their respective directors and officers?

Additional insureds may be added, sometimes by payment of additional premiums, and usually must be enumerated. By definition or by an "extension" provision, the policies also extend coverage to the estates, heirs, legal representatives and assigns of the directors and officers.

The corporate reimbursement coverage usually extends to the parent company and its subsidiaries, although coverage for newly acquired subsidiaries and their directors and officers may be conditioned upon notice to the insurer of the acquisition and possibly an additional premium payment.

There is no coverage for any claims against the corporation itself. The only protection afforded the corporation by the D & O insurance policy is reimbursement for its indemnification of individuals.[44a]

A long standing question as to the scope of a D & O policy was resolved by one district court in a 1980 decision which was affirmed by the Second Circuit on appeal.[45] Continental had seated five of its directors on the board of Halliwell Mines, Limited, a supplier. By reason of their alleged breach of fiduciary duty, Continental and five dual directors were sued by Halliwell, which lost its case.[46] Continental thereupon indemnified the five directors for their legal expenses of

---

44a. Farmers & Merchants Bank v. Home Ins. Co., 514 So. 2d 825 (Ala. 1987).

45. Continental Copper & Steel Indus., Inc. v. Johnson, 491 F. Supp. 360 (S.D.N.Y. 1980), aff'd, 641 F.2d 59 (2d Cir. 1981).

46. International Halliwell Mines, Ltd. v. Continental Copper & Steel Indus., Inc., 70 Civ. 1400, District Court opinion filed Jan. 13, 1976, aff'd, 544 F.2d 105 (2d Cir. 1976).

695

$315,000 incurred in defending themselves in the Halliwell action and sought reimbursement from its D & O insurer, which covered 95% of liabilities in excess of $20,000.

The insurer contended that the claims against the five directors arose out of their duties as directors of Halliwell, not their positions as directors of Continental. However, Judge Robert W. Sweet held:

> The claim against all parties was that Continental, through its director and nominees, had dominated Halliwell and forced it to accept unfair contract terms. Although the individual defendants were serving as directors on Halliwell's board, they had gained that position only because of their responsibilities as directors of Continental.[47]

The court went on to say that the defendants were sued as agents of Continental, that there was no contention that they had acted for their personal benefit, and that there was "insufficient evidence to differentiate between the claims against the individual defendants and the claims against Continental."

On appeal, the Second Circuit affirmed and held that the directors were sued in both capacities, as Halliwell directors and officers and as directors of Continental in mismanaging Halliwell for Continental's benefit.[48]

The insurer also contended that the policy should not be extended to cover Continental directors while serving as Halliwell directors in the absence of specific language to demonstrate that intent. Judge Sweet disagreed. Noting that the policy did not expressly exclude such liability,[49] he pointed out that Section 723 of the New York Business Corporation Act expressly authorized indemnification of a director of an indemnifying corporation who served any other corporation

---

47. Continental Copper & Steel Indus., Inc. v. Johnson, supra note 45, 491 F. Supp. at 363.

48. Id., 491 F. Supp. at 363. See also 641 F.2d at 60.

49. Id., 491 F. Supp. at 364.

at the request of the indemnifying corporation.[50] He went on to state:

> The absence of an express exclusion for expenses resulting from service by Continental's directors on the boards of other corporations at Continental's request strengthens the inference that such expenses are covered....[51]

There appears to be a reasonable basis to assert, therefore, that the corporate reimbursement part of the D & O policy may cover all liabilities for which the corporation is required or permitted to indemnify its directors for actions taken by them as such, including actions as a director, officer, employee or agent of an outside entity at the request of the corporation, in the absence of an express exclusion of any such liabilities.

§ 21.06. "Wrongful Act" defined.

The defined term, Wrongful Act, is unique to D & O and fiduciary insurance. There are two parts in the definition, one relating to "conduct" and the other to "status." Wrongful Act is usually defined as:

(1) any actual or alleged error or misstatement or misleading statement or act or omission or breach of duty by directors or officers while acting in their individual or collective capacities; or

(2) any matter claimed against them solely by reason of their being directors or officers of the Company.

The significance of the two part definition is to make clear that errors, misstatements, misleading statements and so on must have occurred while the insured was acting as a director or officer. However, any matter claimed against the person solely because he or she was a director or officer is also included.

---

50. Cf. Professional Ins. Co. of N.Y. v. Barry, 60 Misc. 2d 424, 303 N.Y.S.2d 556 (1969), aff'd, 32 A.D.2d 898, 302 N.Y.S.2d 722 (1969).

51. Continental Copper & Steel Indus., Inc. v. Johnson, supra note 45, 491 F. Supp. at 365.

There are various modifications of that language in policies of different carriers. The Chubb Group form uses the term "Insured Person" instead of director or officer, and modifies its language accordingly. Of course, the policy exclusions must be read into any such definition.[52]

It is also important to bear in mind that coverage problems may arise when a director or officer acts in another capacity, as, for example, corporate attorney or even general counsel. What he does as a lawyer in his professional capacity is not done in his capacity as a director and perhaps not as an officer. Actions taken as an employee or agent, but not as an officer are not covered. To determine who is an "officer," reference to the applicable state corporation law and the corporation's bylaws or code of regulations is necessary. In some instances, executive level managers, such as a corporate comptroller, are not legally recognized "officers" and therefore may not have coverage unless it is provided by endorsement of the policy.

§ 21.07. "Loss" defined.

Under a D & O policy the insurer pays "Loss" arising from claims by reason of any "Wrongful Act." Accordingly, the definition of Loss is important and it will have some differences in the various policy forms as well as in the two parts of the two policy form.[53] In general, the term Loss means (i) any and all amounts which the individual insureds are legally obligated to pay, or the corporation shall have paid or is required or permitted to pay to one or more individuals as indemnity, (ii) for a claim or claims made against them for Wrongful Acts, (iii) and includes damages, judgments, settlements, costs, charges and expenses (excluding salaries of officers or employees of the corporation) incurred in the defense of actions, suits or proceedings and appeals therefrom, (iv) but not including fines or penalties imposed by law or mat-

---

52. Pepsico, Inc. v. Continental Cas. Co., 640 F. Supp. 656, 659 (S.D.N.Y. 1986).

53. E.g., National Union Form, supra note 42.

ters uninsurable under the law pursuant to which the policy is construed.

Because of the difficulty of predicting the insurability of punitive, exemplary,[54] or multiple damages, some recent policy forms are adding the exclusion of such damages as part of the definition of Loss. In some instances the exclusion is as to "the multiplied portion" of a multiple damages award, which may not mean what was apparently intended. In other cases all treble or multiple damages are excluded. It may be questioned whether this includes the compensatory damages before they are multiplied. Other instances of uninsurability, determinable under state law, will involve examination of both state statutes and court decisions. In New York, for example, a statute prohibits an insurance payment, other than for costs of defense, to or on behalf of a director or officer if it has been adjudicated that his acts of active and deliberate dishonesty were material to the cause of action, or that he personally gained in fact a financial profit or other advantage to which he was not legally entitled.[55] The words "or other advantage" may prevent insurance payments, other than defense costs, if the director or officer has breached the duty of loyalty.[56]

The adjudication referred to in the New York law and in similar statutes may not be made in an action seeking to establish or avoid insurance policy coverage. It must be made in the underlying litigation in order for the insurer to take advantage of it as a coverage defense.[57]

In California, the Insurance Code provides that an insurer is not liable to pay a loss caused by an insured's willful act.[58] Ohio and most other states hold that public policy prevents

---

54. E.g., Dayton Hudson Corp. v. American Mut. Liab. Ins. Co., 621 P.2d 1155 (Okla. 1980).

55. N.Y. Bus. Corp. Law § 726(b)(1).

56. See supra Chapter 3.

57. National Union Fire Ins. Co. v. Continental Ill. Corp., Nos. 85C 7080, 85C 7081, N.D. Ill., July 24, 1987 (available on Lexis and Westlaw).

58. National Union Fire Ins. Co. v. Continental Ill. Corp., supra note 57; Pepsico, Inc. v. Continental Cas. Co., supra note 52.

insurance against intentional torts.[59] However, it is not contrary to public policy for an insurance company to provide coverage unless the insured is adjudged liable for intentional misconduct in the underlying litigation.[60]

Under the Loss definition, questions may need to be determined as to the right of the corporation to indemnify directors and officers in criminal cases or similar situations. Such questions will ordinarily be decided upon the basis of the applicable indemnification statute.[61]

A Sixth Circuit decision dealt with the meaning of the word "claim" as used in the definition of Loss.[62] The court said that the policy "is speaking not of a claim that wrongdoing occurred, but a claim for some discrete amount of money owed to the claimant on account of the alleged wrongdoing." It continued:

> In context, it seems to us, the only kind of "claim or claims" that could trigger the insurer's obligations to pay would be a demand for payment of some amount of money. Thus it is that the policy defines "loss" in terms of an "amount" — i.e., an amount of money — which amount the officials are legally obligated to pay or for which amount they have been indemnified or are required to be indemnified.[63]

The corporation, in that case, had made restitution of $750,000 of fees it had received from customers for standby loan commitments in consideration that its officers would be

---

59. Wedge Prod., Inc. v. Hartford Equity Sales Co., 31 Ohio St. 3d 65, 67, 509 N.E.2d 74 (1987); Massachusetts v. American Fid. Co., 232 N.Y. 161, 165, 133 N.E. 432 (1921) (Cardozo, J.).

60. National Union Fire Ins. Co. v. Continental Ill. Corp., supra note 57, citing Gulliver's East, Inc. v. California Union Ins. Co., 118 Ill. App. 3d 589, 455 N.E.2d 264 (1983), Section III(D)(2).

61. See supra Chapter 20; Amrep Corp. v. American Home Assur. Co., 440 N.Y.S.2d 244 (App. Div. 1981); Flintkote Co. v. Lloyd's Underwriters, N.Y.L.J. July 27, 1976, at 6 (N.Y. Sup. Ct. 1976), aff'd, 56 A.D.2d 743, 391 N.Y.S.2d 1005 (1977).

62. MGIC Indem. Corp. v. Home State Sav. Ass'n, 797 F.2d 285 (6th Cir. 1986).

63. Id. at 288.

protected from the filing of criminal charges against them. Although that payment was made "for the benefit of" the individual officers, it did not constitute an amount which they were legally obligated to pay or which they had been indemnified. Moreover, the fact that there was a potential for demands against the officers for the payment of money was insufficient to meet the conditions imposed by the policy.

In another D & O case decided under California law, the court stated:

> [T]he word claim "imports the assertion, demand or challenge of something as a right; the assertion of liability to the party making it to do some service or pay a sum of money"....
> A "claim" refers to a debt due the claimant.... A "claim" is not a request for an explanation.... [citations omitted].[64]

Some D & O policies define the word "claim." Some definitions may limit the term to "a demand or suit ... for any and all sums which they may become legally obligated to pay." However, the better new forms define a claim as "a demand, suit or proceeding ... which seeks actual monetary damages or other relief."[65] That is similar to the definition in the new Lloyd's of London Market Form issued through J. H. Minet & Co. Ltd. in 1986. This is a much different form from Lydando No. 1, which made its brief appearance in early 1976.[66]

A Washington district court ruled that "loss" existed where the insureds entered into a $110 million settlement with the plaintiffs pursuant to which the plaintiffs agreed not to seek recovery of the settlement amount with the defendant D & O personally but only from the D & O's insurer. The court rejected the insurer's argument that the directors and officers

---

64. Mt. Hawley Ins. Co. v. FSLIC, No. CV87-6MRP, C.D. Cal., Sept. 30, 1987, at 26. See also Anderson v. Carlson, 171 Neb. 741, 107 N.W.2d 535 (1961). "The term 'claim' as used in the statute ... includes an action for injunctive relief."

65. E.g., DOLI Form 9100 (1/87).

66. Lloyd's new London Market Form (1986). And see supra section 21.02, text at note 10.

701

suffered no loss and were effectively released from all liability.[66a] Another new policy form in its definition of "claim" includes "(2) the institution by a federal or state regulatory agency of an injunctive or administrative proceeding arising out of a wrongful act or (3) a legal, injunctive or administrative proceeding against an Independent Director solely by reason of his or her status as a director of the Company."[66b]

Needless to say, the payment of Loss is subject to all of the provisions, conditions and exclusions of the policy and its endorsements. And, as discussed in sections 21.09 and 21.11, all elements of Loss, including defense costs and other expenses, are included in the policy limit.[67]

§ 21.08. Indemnity policy.

D & O insurance policies are labelled "liability" policies but were originally designed and have always been intended to be "indemnity" or reimbursement policies.[68] They are not liability policies in the sense that term is ordinarily used. As stated in a 1987 federal court decision in Illinois:

> [T]he insurer's obligation is to pay the insured for covered "loss" which the insured incurs in connection with the claims made against it. Furthermore, the insurance company's obligations do not accrue until the loss suffered by the insured can be ultimately determined, which is at the time the underlying claims are adjudicated or settled.[69]

In that case the court dismissed a declaratory judgment suit in which insureds under a D & O policy sought to resolve the rights and liabilities of the parties to the insurance policy during the pendency of a shareholder derivative action against the insureds. The court held:

66a. National Union Fire Ins. Co. v. Seafirst Corp., No. 685-396R, W.D. Wash., March 23, 1987.

66b. Aetna Cas. & Sur. Co. Independent Directors Liability Policy Form (F. 1842) E.D. 3-38. See Appendix C.

67. See discussion of defense costs infra section 21.09.

68. See also discussion supra section 17.03.

69. Zaborac v. American Cas. Co., 663 F. Supp. 330, 332 (C.D. Ill. 1987).

702

The insurance company's indemnification obligation must await resolution of the underlying lawsuit, so the present declaratory judgment action is premature.[70]

To the same effect is an Illinois decision holding:

A declaratory judgment action to determine an insurer's duty to indemnify its insured, brought prior to a determination of the insured's liability, is premature since the question to be determined is not then ripe for adjudication.[71]

In further support of the point that D & O policies are indemnity policies, and different from liability policies, is the statement of the Maryland court:

Provisions of the subject CNA policy relating to defense are substantially different from the duty to defend clause of a conventional liability policy. Assureds and/or the Board, not CNA, select and retain defense counsel. "Loss", whether incurred by way of judgment, settlements, or defense costs, is charged against the policy limit without distinguishing between damages and legal fees. CNA has the option, but not the obligation, to advance expenses. CNA's consent, which is not unreasonably to be withheld, is to be obtained before expenses are incurred or settlements made. If CNA advances expenses under the subject policy and "it is finally established the Insurer has no liability" under the policy, then each recipient of advances agrees to repay CNA all monies advanced on his or her behalf.[72]

A clear definition of an indemnity policy is found in a Ninth Circuit decision under New York law, namely one "under which the insurer's obligation to pay does not arise until after the insured suffers an actual monetary loss."[73] Such a

---

70. Id. at 333.

71. Maryland Cas. Co. v. Chicago & N.W. Transp. Co., 126 Ill. App. 3d 150, 466 N.E.2d 1091, 1095-96 (1984).

72. Continental Cas. Co. v. Board of Educ., 302 Md. 516, 489 A.2d 536, 543 (1985).

73. Ahmed v. American S.S. Mut. Protection & Indem. Ass'n, 640 F.2d 993, 995 (9th Cir. 1981).

703

loss may be incurred when an obligation to pay becomes fixed, even though the money has not actually been paid.

Following that principle the Southern District of New York has read a D & O policy to mean that the insurer's obligation to reimburse an insured's defense costs does not accrue until the earlier of the date of disposition of the claim against the insured or the date of determination of the insurer's liability under the policy.[74] When the insurer makes advancements prior to that time, it may reserve its rights for the return of such advancements "should the losses ultimately prove to be uncovered." In so ruling, the Ninth Circuit recognized that a D & O policy was an indemnity policy, although it called it a liability policy because of its definition of "Loss" and "the captions to the policy's declarations."[75] That decision was under Hawaii law.

A federal district court decision under California law cited the Ninth Circuit decision, but actually based its finding of a "duty to defend" on Section 2778 of the California Civil Code which imposes a duty to defend upon an indemnitor unless the indemnity agreement states a contrary intention.[76]

The California court has ruled that "indemnity against loss" is against the consequence of an event, if it should happen.[77] As both the above-cited *Okada* and the *Mt. Hawley* cases show, the D & O policies under consideration in those cases contracted to "pay Loss."[78]

---

74. Board of Educ. v. CNA Ins. Co., 647 F.2d 1495, 1507 (S.D.N.Y. 1986). See also discussion infra section 21.09.

75. Okada v. MGIC Indem. Corp., 823 F.2d 276, 284 (9th Cir. 1987), further discussed infra section 21.09.

76. Mt. Hawley Ins. Co. v. FSLIC, No. CV87-6MRP, C.D. Cal., Sept. 30, 1987, at 13, 15, 40, citing Gray v. Zurich Ins. Co., 65 Cal. 2d 263, 269, 54 Cal. Rptr. 104, 107 (1966).

77. Gribaldo, Jacobs, Jones & Assoc. v. Agrippina Versicherunges A.G., 3 Cal. 3d 434, 91 Cal. Rptr. 6, 476 P.2d 406 (1970).

78. Compare policies reproduced in Appendix C.

§21.09. Defense of actions; payment of defense costs.

No duty or obligation to defend is imposed by the typical D & O insurance policy.[79] If there ever was doubt on that point it has been dispelled by revisions of most D & O insurance policies beginning in 1984. An earlier policy form stated:

> No costs, charges and expenses shall be incurred or settlements made without the Insurer's consent, which consent shall not be unreasonably withheld; however, in the event such consent is given, the Insurer shall pay ... such costs, settlements, charges and expenses.[80]

A policy currently in use at this writing is considerably more specific. It states:

> A. The Company does not, under the terms of this policy, assume any duty to defend. Any costs, charges and expenses of defense payable by the Company are a part of and not in addition to the limit of liability. Loss as defined includes costs, charges and expenses of defense and as such is subject to the provisions of Section 3 [relating to limit and retention].
> B. Only those costs, charges, expenses and settlements consented to by the Company shall be recoverable as Loss under the terms of this policy. The Company's consent shall not be unreasonably withheld, but the Company shall be entitled to full information and all particulars it may request in order to reach a decision as to reasonableness. With respect to the settlement of any claim made against the Corporation and the Insureds, the Corporation and the Insureds and the Company agree to use their best efforts to determine a fair and proper allocation of the settlement amount as between the Corporation and the Insureds.
> C. The words "costs, charges and expenses" shall include the cost of any appeal, attachment or similar bonds.[81]

In some policies the insurer is afforded an option to take over the defense or, at its own expense, it may participate

---

79. See discussion supra sections 17.03, 17.04.

80. MGIC Indem. Corp. Form quoted in Okada v. MGIC Indem. Corp., 795 F.2d 1450, 1452 (9th Cir. 1986).

81. St. Paul Form 5068 (Ed. 10-85), Section 4. See also National Union Form quoted supra section 17.03, text at note 11.

with the insureds in the investigation, settlement and defense of claims for which indemnity is provided by the policy.[82] Such provisions afford a right, but not an obligation, to assume conduct of the defense.[83]

As is pointed out in sections 17.03 and 21.04, a D & O insurance policy is substantially different from a conventional liability policy in this respect.[84] A "duty to defend" can only result from an obligation imposed by express language in the policy.[85] There being no such expression in the D & O policy, there is no duty to defend.

In the original Ninth Circuit majority opinion in *Okada v. MGIC Indemnity Corporation,* the court held that under Hawaii law the D & O policy contained a "duty to defend."[86] That ruling was attacked by a vigorous dissent which called it "the worst form of judicial activism by a federal court."[87] The majority opinion was substantially amended and reissued a year later, with no mention of "duty to defend."[88] The amended majority opinion merely stated:

> The costs of the "defense of legal actions" are included in the definition of "Loss" in section 1(d). Thus, in the absence of other provisions, the policy demands that MGIC pay those costs when the directors become legally obligated to pay them.[89]

That statement introduces another question in the *Okada* case. It is one in which *Okada* stands in the minority of courts that have ruled upon it. The question is whether the insurer

---

82. See Appendix C.

83. Peoria v. Underwriters at Lloyd's, 290 F. Supp. 890, 892 (S.D. Ill. 1968); Outboard Marine Corp. v. Liberty Mut. Ins. Co., 536 F.2d 730, 736 (7th Cir. 1976).

84. Cf. Shapiro v. American Home Assur. Co., 616 F. Supp. 906, 910 (D. Mass. 1985).

85. All-Star Ins. Corp. v. Steel Bar, Inc., 324 F. Supp. 160, 163 (N.D. Ind. 1971).

86. 795 F.2d 1450, 1453-55 (9th Cir. 1986).

87. Id. at 1458.

88. Okada v. MGIC Indem. Corp., 823 F.2d 276 (9th Cir. 1987).

89. Id. at 280. But see Mt. Hawley Ins. Co. v. FSLIC, supra note 76, imposing a duty to defend under a California statute.

is obligated to make contemporaneous payments for legal defense of claims covered by the policy. The *Okada* majority opinion said "yes."[90]

The insurer's obligation to pay defense costs under a D & O policy is dependent upon and co-extensive with the insurer's liability to indemnify its insureds as defined in the policy.

The *Okada* dissenting opinion so stated in pointing out that the D & O policy "contemplates payment of defense costs as a loss if indemnification is required." It cites the third edition of this text to the effect that: "The [directors and officers] policy forms do not require payment of legal expenses by the insured until the legal liability of the insured has been established."[91]

The *Okada* policy contained an "option" provision that stated:

> The Insurer may at its option and upon request, advance on behalf of the Directors and Officers, or any of them, expenses which they have incurred in connection with claims made against them, prior to disposition of such claims, provided always that in the event it is finally established the Insurer has no liability hereunder, such Directors and Officers agree to repay to the Insurer, upon demand, all monies advanced by virtue of this provision.[92]

The district court held this provision ambiguous and construed the policy against the insurer.[93] The appellate court affirmed and the majority required defense costs to be paid as incurred.[94] But there is no unanimity among the courts on this subject.

---

90. Okada v. MGIC Indem. Corp., supra note 88, at 283.

91. Cynthia Holcomb Hall, C.J., dissenting, 795 F.2d at 1459 n.4.

92. 823 F.2d at 279.

93. Okada v. MGIC Indem. Corp., 608 F. Supp. 383, 386 (D. Haw. 1985).

94. 823 F.2d at 281. Cf. Little v. MGIC Indem. Corp., 649 F. Supp. 1460 (W.D. Pa. 1986), aff'd, 836 F.2d 789 (3d Cir. 1987), and American Cas. Co. of Reading v. Bank of Montana Sys., No. 4-87-48, D. Minn., Dec. 10, 1987.

Some of the courts have had trouble with the phrase "disposition of such claims."[95] In a case where the policy did not contain the above-quoted "option" provision, the court found no duty to defend but imposed a contemporaneous reimbursement duty to pay defense costs.[96] Judge Charles L. Brieant, who wrote that opinion, distinguished it three months later in a case wherein the policy did contain the "option" provisions, and stated:

> Read fairly and in accordance with its plain meaning, this [option] provision makes payable Continental's obligation to indemnify defense costs at the earlier of the date of disposition of the claim against the insured or the date of determination of the insurer's liability under the contract of insurance.[97]

A district court in Illinois has held that this provision gives the insurer "the option, but not the obligation, to advance defense costs as they are incurred." That court found Judge Hall's dissent in *Okada* "more persuasive than the majority opinion."[98] Courts in several other jurisdictions have reached similar conclusions and have held that the insurer is not obligated to pay defense costs until the claims against the insureds have been resolved and the insurer's obligation to indemnify the insureds for their losses has been determined.[99]

---

95. E.g., Western Line Consol. School Dist. v. Continental Cas. Co., 632 F. Supp. 295, 303 (N.D. Miss. 1986).

96. Pepsico, Inc. v. Continental Cas. Co., 640 F. Supp. 656 (S.D.N.Y. 1986).

97. Board of Educ. v. CNA Ins. Co., 647 F. Supp. 1495, 1507 (S.D.N.Y. 1986).

98. Zaborac v. American Cas. Co., 663 F. Supp. 330, 334 (C.D. Ill. 1987).

99. See also Amrep Corp. v. American Home Assur. Co., 440 N.Y.S.2d 244, 246 (App. Div. 1981); Bank of Commerce & Trust Co. v. National Union Fire Ins. Co., 651 F. Supp. 474 (N.D. Okla. 1986); Continental Cas. Co. v. Board of Educ., 302 Md. 516, 489 A.2d 536 (1985); Clandening v. MGIC Indem. Corp., No. CV83-2432-LIL, C.D. Cal., May 24, 1983; Enzweiler v. Fidelity & Deposit Co., No. 85-99, E.D. Ky., May 13, 1986; Luther v. Fidelity & Deposit Co., No. 85-2762 — Civ. JWK, S.D. Fla., Aug. 13, 1986; Uhlfelder v. American Cas. Co., No. 85-326031, Md. Cir. Ct., Oct. 7, 1986; American Cas. Co. v. FDIC, No. C86-4018, N.D. Iowa, Mar. 11,

Because defense costs are included in the policy limit and constitute part of "Loss," payment of defense costs depletes the funds available to pay settlements or judgments. However, creditors may not prevent payment of such costs in an action by the bankruptcy estate against the directors and officers. The bankruptcy estate does not own the insurance proceeds which are available to pay defense costs and cannot control their disposition.[99a]

It is noteworthy that a policy first issued in 1988 expressly provides for advancement of defense costs. It states:

> The underwriter shall, upon written request by an Independent Director, pay on a current basis Defense Expenses incurred by such Independent Director which are otherwise reimbursable under this Policy, except to the extent that such Defense Expenses are being paid on a current basis under the terms of any other policy or policies of insurance, or by the Company.

That policy also provides for reimbursement of such advancements by the Independent Director to the Underwriter if it is finally determined that the loss was excluded by fraud, dishonesty, criminal or willful violation of law or the gaining of an illegal personal profit or advantage.[99b]

§ 21.10. Discovery and notice; cancellation; refusal to renew.

The policy requires the individual insureds and the corporation to give written notice to the insurer as soon as practicable of any claim made against the insureds during the policy period or during the extended discovery period, if purchased. If the corporation or the insureds become aware of any circumstances which may subsequently give rise to a claim being made against the insureds, and give notice to the insurer, then the claim will be treated as having been made

---

1987. But cf. McGinnis v. Employers Reinsurance Corp., 648 F. Supp. 1263, 1271 (S.D.N.Y. 1986).

99a. In re La. World Exposition, Inc., 832 F.2d 1391 (5th Cir. 1987).

99b. Aetna Cas. & Sur. Co. Independent Directors Liability Policy Form (F-1842) ED. 3-38, reproduced in Appendix C.

during the policy period. It is generally considered that a claim is made and thus coverage attaches when such notice of claim or circumstances is given to the insurer.[100]

D & O policies usually contain a discovery clause which permits the insureds, in case the insurer cancels or refuses to renew the policy, upon payment of an additional premium, to obtain an extension of the coverage of the policy for a specified term, but only in respect of Wrongful Acts committed before the effective date of cancellation or refusal to renew, and otherwise covered by the policy. Usually the insureds must give written notice of their election to purchase the extension and pay the additional premium in full within ten days after the effective date of the cancellation or refusal to renew.

The 1986 Lloyd's form provides for termination of the extended discovery period, with pro rata refund of unearned premiums. It states:

> In the event the Optional Extension Period is purchased, it shall terminate forthwith on the effective date of any contract of insurance or indemnity which replaces the coverage afforded by this Policy through the Optional Extension Period either in whole or in part....

In recent revisions of policy forms insurers have been stating what is not intended to constitute a refusal to renew. For example, one policy recites:

> The offer by the Insurer of renewal terms, conditions, limits of liability and/or premiums different from those of the expiring policy shall not constitute refusal to renew.[101]

The Aetna form states that a renewal quotation shall not be deemed to constitute a cancellation or refusal to renew unless (i) the premium quoted is more than 25% higher, or (ii) the liability limit is less than 50% of the former limit, or (iii)

---

100. See ALS(D4)-ALS(D5) January, 1974, Section 7(a); National Union Form 8749/8750 (6/85) Section 7(a), reproduced in Appendix C.

101. National Union Form 8749/8750 (6/85), supra note 100, Section 8(a).

one or more deductibles exceeds the former corresponding deductible by more than 50%. In another form the definition applies to "renewal terms, conditions, limits of liability and/or premiums which may vary substantially from the terms and conditions of this policy."[102]

Such clauses may not accomplish their purpose, however. A California appellate court found a refusal to renew when the renewal policy increased the deductible seven-fold, reduced the term from three years to one, and raised the premium from $789.03 to $1773.90.[103] Also it may be that some state insurance departments will endeavor to restrict the use of dramatically different terms to accomplish indirectly a refusal to renew. It appears that the answer to this problem will probably depend upon the facts of a particular case.[104]

As a rule a D & O policy may be cancelled by the insureds at any time by mailing prior written notice thereof and surrendering the policy. The insurer may usually cancel by giving thirty days notice, although some policies fix longer or shorter periods, especially if the cause of cancellation is nonpayment of premium. Such provisions are valid and, generally, an insurer's motive or reason for cancellation is immaterial.[105] Wrongful cancellation, however, is a breach of contract and gives rise to causes of action for legal and equitable relief.[106]

In some instances, such as the recently issued Lloyd's London Market form (VII C(2)), cancellation or elimination of coverage for future Wrongful Acts is deemed to occur immediately upon the happening of specified events such as (i) the corporation being merged or taken over, (ii) if substantially all of its assets are acquired by another entity, (iii) if the corporation ceases to be publicly held, or (iv) there is a cumu-

---

102. Harbor Form HU8128-1 (Ed. 8-85) Section 8(A).

103. Kimmerer Eng'g Co. v. Continental Cas. Co., 253 Cal. App. 2d 188, 191, 61 Cal. Rptr. 94 (1967).

104. Cf. National Union Fire Ins. Co. v. Continental Ill. Corp., 658 F. Supp. 775, 780 (N.D. Ill. 1987).

105. 3A Appleman, Insurance Law & Practice §§ 1811-12 (1957).

106. 8B id. § 5021 (1981); 20 id. § 11251 (1980).

711

lative change of 50% or more in the personnel of the board of directors.

State statutes relating to unfair and deceptive practices by insurers, and regulations promulgated under such statutes may deal specifically with cancellations.[107] In Ohio, for example, the regulations of the Insurance Department amplify the state's unfair and deceptive practices statute[108] by prohibiting mid-term cancellation of commercial property, casualty or fire insurance policies unless the cancellation is based on (i) nonpayment of premium, (ii) discovery of fraud or material misrepresentation in procurement of the insurance or as to any claims, (iii) discovery of willful or reckless acts or omissions of the named insured increasing any hazard insured against; (iv) change in the risk insured against substantially increasing the insured hazard or (v) determination by the director of insurance that continuing the policy would create a condition hazardous to the policyholders or the public.[109]

Since June 1985 litigation in California has attacked the practices of some D & O insurers that have cancelled policies in the face of hostile takeover attempts and other change of control activities. The suits allege breaches of contracts, breach of the duty of good faith and fair dealing, violation of RICO by engaging in a pattern of racketeering activity, fraud, negligent misrepresentation and violation of the insurance code, all of which the respective defendants have consistently denied.[110]

In one of those cases, a California state appellate court ruled that the insureds properly stated a RICO cause of action against the D & O insurer by pleading with particularity that the insurer had the intent to cancel the policy at the first

---

107. 19 id. § 10558 (1982).

108. Ohio Rev. Code Ann. § 3901.21.

109. Ohio Adm. Code § 3901-1-45 (1986).

110. E.g., Unocal Corp. v. Harbor Ins. Co., No. C550-393, Cal. Super. Ct., Los Angeles, filed June 4, 1985; California Fed. of Family Day Care Ass'n v. Mission Ins. Co., No. B01637, Cal. Ct. of App., 2d Dist., Nov. 21, 1986 (available on Lexis); Berg v. First State Ins. Co., No. 87-0644 (AHS), C.D. Calif., Amended Complaint filed May 29, 1987.

sign of a hostile takeover and that such intent was concealed from the insureds.[110a] In rejecting the insurer's argument that it had the "unfettered contractual right to cancel for any reason," the court articulated the following rule:

> An insurer breaches the implied covenant of good faith and fair dealing when it cancels coverage because of circumstances that were reasonably foreseeable at the policy's inception and the risk of loss has developed to the point where it is unavoidable by the insured. A fortiori, an insurer breaches this covenant when at the time the insurance contract is executed it harbors an intent to cancel under these circumstances and with an intent to disadvantage insureds yet conceals this intent from those insureds.

Another limitation on an insurer's right to cancel is found in Chapter 11 of the Bankruptcy Code. The filing of a bankruptcy petition automatically stays cancellation of D & O policies under § 362(a)(3) of Code, because they are "property of the estate" within the meaning of § 541(a). In so holding the Ninth Circuit emphasized the fact that the corporate reimbursement part of the D & O policy "insures the debtor against claims by officers and directors" for indemnification.[111]

Sometimes a D & O policy will invoke an immediate elimination of coverage for future Wrongful Acts upon the appointment of a receiver, conservator, trustee, liquidator, rehabilitator, or similar official, for or with respect to the corporation. In light of the ineffectiveness of such a provision in the bankruptcy setting, its enforceability in other types of creditor proceedings is uncertain.

§ 21.11. Limits; retentions; co-insurance; interrelated claims.

Typically, a D & O insurer agrees to pay for Loss, a defined term, in excess of the applicable retention up to the limit of

---

110a. Unocal Corp. v. Superior Court of the State of California for the County of Los Angeles, 244 Cal. Rptr. 540 (Cal. App. 1988).

111. In re Minoco Group of Cos., Ltd., 799 F.2d 517, 519 (9th Cir. 1986).

liability stated in the declarations.[112] The limit applies to a single policy year and is the combined limit of liability for both coverages in the two policy form.[113] The limit is intended to be the maximum amount the insurer will pay in each policy year and includes all attorneys' fees, charges and all other defense costs. The limit of liability for claims made during a discovery period, if purchased, is included in that maximum amount. In some policies the limit is stated on a "per loss" or "per occurrence" basis.[114]

There are usually two elements of the personal coverage retention or deductible that are applicable to the liability of each director or officer, and an aggregate limitation on that deductible per claim or series of connected claims. There is a separate, and usually higher, retention or deductible applicable to the corporate reimbursement part for each loss.[115]

Although the co-insurance feature, discussed in section 17.07, appears in some D & O forms, it is generally losing its significance as a claim deterrent. It is frequently eliminated for losses in excess of $1 million and only sometimes applied to the personal coverage.

Losses arising out of the same act or interrelated acts of one or more insureds are considered a single loss. Only one retention is deducted from a single loss. In that context the word "act" is read "Wrongful Act." In this area, there is considerable variation in the language of different policy forms. The National Union form states:

> Loss arising out of the same Wrongful Act or interrelated, repeated or continuous Wrongful Acts of one or more of the Directors or Officers shall be considered a single Loss....[116]

The 1986 Lloyd's of London form adds some elements and states:

---

112. See supra discussion in section 17.07.

113. E.g., National Union Form 8749/8750 (6/85), reproduced in Appendix C.

114. See MGIC forms discussed in Okada v. MGIC Indem. Corp., 608 F. Supp. 383 (D. Haw. 1985), and discussion in text infra at notes 116-120.

115. See Wyatt Survey, supra note 2, at 75.

116. Supra note 113, Section 5(c).

"Interrelated Wrongful Acts" shall mean Wrongful Acts which have as a common nexus any fact, circumstance, situation, event, transaction or series of facts, circumstances, situations, events or transactions.[117]

For acts to be interrelated so that several claims would be aggregated into a single loss, it would appear that there must be an element of mutuality among the acts, namely, that those doing an act had knowledge or were conscious of the other acts. Without collusion or at least knowledge there would seem to be no interrelation.

The Chubb Group policy reprinted in the Appendix revises the customary language in a way to clarify this provision. It also allocates the loss within a specified policy year. Clause 5.1 provides:

For the purposes of this policy, all Loss arising out of all interrelated Wrongful Acts of any Insured Person(s) shall be deemed one Loss and such Loss shall be deemed to have originated in the earliest Policy Year in which a claim is made against any Insured Person alleging any such Wrongful Acts.

In supplementation and explanation of that language, the Chubb policy further states, as part of its definition of Wrongful Act in Clause 9.1, that "causally connected" errors and the like "committed or attempted by, allegedly committed or attempted by, or claimed against one or more of the Insured Persons shall be deemed interrelated Wrongful Acts." Pending judicial interpretation of that provision, it remains to be seen whether clarification has been accomplished.

Meanwhile two federal court decisions dealing with the subject have made it plain that a series of negligent acts or a series of transactions will not constitute a single loss or occurrence for purposes of determining the applicable limit of liability merely because they all contribute to a single result. In the *Okada* case, in Hawaii, that result was the collapse of the First Savings & Loan Association.[118] The various acts of the

---

117. Lloyd's new London Market Form (1986).

118. Okada v. MGIC Indem. Corp., 608 F. Supp. 383 (D. Haw. 1985), aff'd in part, rev'd in part, 795 F.2d 1450 (9th Cir. 1986), amended and corrected, 823 F.2d 276 (9th Cir. 1987).

directors and officers did not become related because they led to one overall result. "The amount of coverage was not so written as to vary depending on the effect of the losses,"[119] which were held to be multiple, not single.

A case decided in Kansas reached a similar conclusion.[120] Three different loan swap transactions were held to have constituted three separate "incidents" or "occurrences," under a D & O policy even though they all contributed to one overall result, the failure of North Kansas Savings Association. In both cases the court determined the issue with reference to the causes of the losses rather than their effect.

Courts have been more willing to aggregate related losses for purposes of determining the applicable retention. In a Fourth Circuit decision, only one retention was found applicable with respect to multiple claims involving different transactions and properties under a single loan program.[120a]

Even if multiple claims are found to be interrelated, multiple limits of liability may apply. An Illinois district court ruled that because lawsuits were filed against the insured officers in two separate policy years, the insurer was liable for twice its full policy limit, even though the claims arose out of related but not identical events.[120b] The court found the "interrelated acts" provision of the policy applicable only to determine the deductible, not the limit of liability.

§ 21.12. Exclusions usual in policy.

A D & O insurance policy "bristles with provisions governing which claims will and will not be covered, in what amounts, and under what circumstances."[121] The number and scope of exclusions have increased since 1984 and during the

---

119. 608 F. Supp. at 388.

120. North River Ins. Co. v. Huff, 628 F. Supp. 1129 (D. Kan. 1985).

120a. Atlantic Permanent Fed. Sav. & Loan v. American Cas. Co., 839 F.2d 212 (4th Cir. 1988).

120b. Harbor Ins. Co. v. Continental Ill. Corp., No. 85 C 7081, N.D. Ill. Nov. 18, 1987.

121. Mt. Hawley Ins. Co. v. FSLIC, No. CV87-6MRP, C.D. Cal., Sept. 30, 1987, at 17.

restricted D & O insurance market. In a typical policy the total of usual and optional exclusions at this writing will be at least three or four times as many as before the D & O insurance crisis. Some of the new exclusions have resulted from particular adverse experiences encountered by underwriters, such as the crushing settlements in the *Chase Manhattan, Seattle Seafirst,* and *Continental Illinois* cases, and claims made and resulting settlements in such change of control cases as *Trans Union* and *Revlon.*

Exclusions are located throughout the D & O policy and are not limited to those enumerated under the "Exclusions" label. The term "Loss," for example, excludes fines or penalties imposed by law and matters uninsurable under the law pursuant to which the policy is construed. The term "Wrongful Act" usually excludes liability of individual insureds not claimed solely by reason of their being directors or officers.[122] The insuring clause relating to the "direct" part of the policy will exclude claims for which individual insureds are indemnified or entitled to indemnification by the corporation.[123]

It is mentioned in section 21.04 that the awareness by the insured of any facts or circumstances giving reason to believe that a claim might be presented would avoid coverage. If such facts or circumstances are disclosed in the application for insurance, claims arising therefrom will be excluded. Sometimes the policy will exclude claims for acts that occurred prior to the inception date of the policy. If a retroactive date is stated in the declaration, claims for acts occurring before that date will not be covered.

The exclusions applicable to the corporation reimbursement part of the D & O policy were originally three or four in number, taking into consideration that this coverage applied only when the corporation was required or permitted to indemnify its directors and officers. Usually they excluded:

(1) Losses otherwise insured.

---

122. See supra sections 21.06 and 21.07.
123. See supra section 21.05 and Chapter 20.

(2) Liability for bodily injury, property damage, sickness or death. Some newer policy forms also exclude claims for personal injury, including emotional distress. However, one new form does not apply the bodily injury/property damage exclusion to derivative suits,[123a] which may afford significant broadening of coverage in some cases, such as those involving products liability.

(3) Liability resulting from seepage, pollution or contamination. Some policies narrowly describe this exclusion as applying to claims "for" seepage, etc., although most broadly describe the exclusion as applying to claims "based upon or arising out of" seepage, etc.

(4) Liability arising under ERISA or state laws of a similar nature. Some newer policy forms exclude claims under any state law affecting employee benefit plans, even if not "similar" to ERISA. These traditional exclusions sought to identify those risks for which the corporation could otherwise purchase insurance, thereby reflecting an underwriting intent of making the D & O policy a "backstop" protection behind all other corporate insurance policies.

In the direct or D & O part of the policy the exclusions included those mentioned above and several others. They were intended to supplant the public policy limitations contained in state indemnification statutes which affected the corporation reimbursement part of the policy but did not bear on this part. Historically, the additional exclusions included in this part applied to claims:

(5) Based upon or attributable to gaining any personal profit or advantage to which the insureds are not legally entitled.[124]

123a. Aetna Cas. & Sur. Co. Independent Directors Liability Policy Form (F-1842) ED. 3-38, reproduced in Appendix C.

124. See discussion in National Union Fire Ins. Co. v. Continental Ill. Corp., Nos. 85C 7080, 85C 7081, N.D. Ill., July 24, 1987 (available on Lexis and Westlaw).

(6) For libel or slander (which is usually covered under the commercial liability policy).

(7) For the return of any remuneration paid to the insureds without the previous approval of the shareholders of the corporation, and is thus illegal.

(8) Arising from, brought about, or contributed to by the dishonest (and, in some newer forms, fraudulent or criminal) acts of the insureds. Traditionally, this exclusion required a prior adjudication of actual and deliberate dishonesty with actual dishonest purpose and intent,[124a] although some newer forms delete that requirement. Any such adjudication must be made in the underlying litigation.[125]

(9) For short swing profits under § 16(b) of the Securities Exchange Act of 1934.

The new forms of policies usually apply those exclusions and numerous other exclusions to both parts of the policy.[126] In addition to those listed above, they will commonly exclude the following claims:[127]

Adequate insurance exclusion

(10) Based on or attributable to any failure to obtain and maintain adequate insurance.

124a. See discussion in Little v. MGIC Indem. Corp., 649 F. Supp. 1460 (W.D. Pa. 1986), aff'd on other grounds, 836 F.2d 789 (3d Cir. 1987) concerning possible unenforceability of such an exclusion because vague and ambiguous.

125. See discussion in Pepsico, Inc. v. Continental Cas. Co., 640 F. Supp. 656, 660 (S.D.N.Y. 1986); National Union Fire Ins. Co. v. Seafirst Corp., 662 F. Supp. 36, 39 (W.D. Wash. 1986); Stargatt v. Arenell, 434 F. Supp. 234 (D. Del. 1977); Elgin Nat'l Bank v. Home Indem. Co., 583 F.2d 1281, 1288 (5th Cir. 1978); Mt. Hawley Ins. Co. v. FSLIC, supra note 121; National Union Fire Ins. Co. v. Continental Ill. Corp., supra note 124; Atlantic Permanent Fed. Sav. & Loan v. American Cas. Co., supra note 120a.

126. The Chubb Group Form, however, applies exclusions separately to the two issuing clauses. See Appendix C.

127. Varying language is used in different policies, so the particular form should be reviewed in each instance.

Other insurance exclusion

(11) Insured in whole or part by other policies, except where the other insurance is primary and this is excess.

Prior notice exclusion

(12) Based on or attributable to any fact or circumstance that has been the subject of notice given under any other policy which expired before the term of this policy.

Prior litigation exclusion

(13) Arising out of any pending or prior litigation, as well as all future claims based upon the actual or alleged facts giving rise to such prior or pending litigation. This can be a deceptively broad exclusion. For example, at the inception of the D & O policy, litigation may be pending against the insured corporation or others, but not against any director or officer. Thereafter, either because of additional discovery in the lawsuit or otherwise, directors or officers may be named as additional defendants in the lawsuit. This exclusion would eliminate coverage for the claim under most of the newer D & O policies and if no notice of circumstances had been given under the prior policy, no coverage for the defendant directors and officers would exist under any policy.

Insured v. insured exclusion

(14) By or in the right of the corporation or by any insured. This is the "Insured v. Insured" exclusion, sometimes called the "Cross-Liability Exclusion," and was intended to exclude collusive actions. However, the provision is much broader than mere collusion. The National Union form states that no coverage is provided for claims:

which are brought by, or in the behalf of, any
other Insureds including but not limited to shareholders' derivative suits and/or representative
class action suits, brought by one or more past,
present or future Directors and/or Officers including their estates, beneficiaries, heirs, legal representatives, assigns and/or the Company against
one or more past, present or future Directors or
Officers.

This provision appears in different forms in various
insurance policies and the above is probably the
broadest form because it appears to exclude derivative suits as well as suits brought directly by the
corporation and other insured persons. It was sustained by a federal district court in California to
exclude claims by FSLIC as receiver for a state savings bank.[128] The court held that the provision
clearly excluded suits by the bank and that the exclusions extended to the bank's receiver. The court
cited a federal district court decision in Iowa, which
reached the same conclusion, but found that there
was a question of fact as to whether the bank and its
directors and officers had "reasonable expectations"
of coverage in this respect.[129]

A different form of this exclusion (still excluding claims
"made against the Insureds by an Insured") was held unenforceable against FDIC in a federal district court decision in
the Western District of Louisiana.[130] The court found that
"the broader policy behind" 12 U.S.C. § 1823(e) and the
D'Oench doctrine[131] would protect FDIC from this exclusion.

Another case in the Eastern District of Louisiana involved
attempted rescission and damages arising out of purchases of

---

128. Mt. Hawley Ins. Co. v. FSLIC, supra note 121. Cf. FSLIC v.
Mmahat, No. 86-5160, E.D. La. Mar. 3, 1988.

129. American Cas. Co. v. FDIC, No. C86-4018, N.D. Iowa, Mar. 11,
1987.

130. FDIC v. National Union Fire Ins. Co., 630 F. Supp. 1149, 1156-57
(W.D. La. 1986). See also FSLIC v. Mmahat, supra note 128.

131. See discussion supra section 12.05.

newly issued stock and voting trust certificates. Directors were on both sides. The court upheld the exclusion and dismissed the action as to the plaintiffs/directors,[132] holding that the exclusion applies if the plaintiff is a director at the time the claim is made even if not a director when the wrongful act occurred.

In Minnesota, a federal district court refused to apply the exclusion because the plaintiff was suing in his capacity as a former employee, not as a former officer or director. In addition the court found the exclusion ambiguous, as being susceptible to more than one reasonable interpretation, and construed it against the insurer.[133]

Nuclear energy exclusion

> (15) Resulting from the hazardous properties of nuclear material. This Nuclear Energy Liability Exclusion Endorsement (Broad Form) will be required in all appropriate cases.

§ 21.13. Optional exclusions.

Regulatory endorsement

The activity of Federal Deposit Insurance Corporation (FDIC) and Federal Savings and Loan Insurance Corporation (FSLIC) in pursuing directors and officers of financial institutions[134] has given new prominence to the "regulatory endorsement," one form of which reads:

> It is understood and agreed that the company shall not be liable to make any payment for loss in connection with any claim made against the directors or officers based upon or attributable to any claim, action or proceeding brought by or on behalf of the Federal Home Loan Bank Board, any other similar organization, or any other na-

---

132. Parker v. Watts, No. 85-4654, E.D. La., Feb. 27, 1987 (available on Lexis).

133. Conklin Co. v. National Union Fire Ins. Co., No. C4-86-860, D. Minn., Jan. 28, 1987.

134. See discussions supra sections 12.05 to 12.09.

tional or state bank, regulatory agency, whether such claim, action or proceeding is brought in the name of such regulatory agency or by or on behalf of such regulatory agency in the name of any other entity.

A federal district court in Utah held that the above endorsement "would so seriously hamper the FSLIC in carrying out its duties that public policy prevents the court from enforcing the endorsement."[135]

Another form of the same type of endorsement was considered by a federal district court in Iowa. This form read:

> It is understood and agreed that the Insurer shall not be liable to make any payment for Loss in connection with any claim made against the Directors or Officers based upon or attributable to any action or proceeding brought by or on behalf of the Federal Deposit Insurance Corporation, the Federal Savings & Loan Insurance Corporation, any other depository insurance organization, the Comptroller of the Currency, the Federal Home Loan Bank Board, or any other national or state regulatory agency (all of said organizations and agencies hereinafter referred to as "Agencies"), including any type of legal action which such Agencies have the legal right to bring as receiver, conservator, liquidator or otherwise; whether such action or proceeding is brought in the name of such Agencies or by or on behalf of such Agencies in the name of any other entity or solely in the name of any Third Party.

This court found the endorsement ambiguous because it did not clearly state that the insurer intended to exclude coverage for direct actions against the bank's officers and directors by FDIC.[136] More litigation in this area is proceeding in several courts.

---

135. FSLIC v. Oldenberg, Civil No. C-85-1418W, D. Utah, Aug. 14, 1987, appeal pending; see also FSLIC v. Mmahat, No. 86-5160, E.D. Pa. Mar. 3, 1988.

136. American Cas. Co. v. FDIC, supra note 129; FSLIC v. Mmahat, supra note 135. Cf. FDIC v. National Union Fire Ins. Co., supra note 130, and Mt. Hawley Ins. Co. v. FSLIC, No. CV87-6MRP, C.D. Cal., Sept. 30, 1987.

Exclusions involving change of control

In as many different forms as there are policies, insurers have been making liberal use of endorsements intended to exclude claims arising in the change of control context. One such exclusion relieves the insurer from liability for claims:

> arising from, attributable to or involving attempts, whether alleged or actual, successful or unsuccessful, by persons or entities to acquire securities of the Company against the opposition of the Board of Directors of the Company, nor to any claims arising from, attributable to or involving efforts, whether alleged or actual, successful or unsuccessful, by the Company and/or its Directors to resist such attempts.[137]

Another such exclusion denies coverage for:

> any attempts, whether actual or alleged, successful or unsuccessful, by any person(s) or entity(s) to acquire securities of the company and efforts, whether actual or alleged, successful or unsuccessful, by the Company and/or the assureds to resist such above-stated attempts.[138]

Such exclusions commonly deal with such subjects as:

Hostile Takeovers
Mergers and Acquisitions
Tender Offers
Going Private
Public offerings
Greenmail payments

The rule that exclusions in insurance policies are to be strictly construed has been applied to an exclusion of this type in a case in Massachusetts. Such an exclusion in a D & O policy barred recovery for claims arising from any attempt to gain control or from any gaining of control of the corporation or any claim made by a minority shareholder. The underlying litigation, by minority shareholders, had as its primary issue

---

137. National Union Form 8749/8750 (6/85), reproduced in Appendix C.
138. Home Ins. Co. Form, Section III (L).

the fairness of a transaction in which the corporation bought the assets of a company wholly owned by the corporation's chairman. The court held that the litigation did not arise out of any attempt to gain control of the corporation and refused to apply the exclusion.[139] The court considered "control" to be the essence of the exclusion, even as to claims by minority shareholders.

Securities law exclusions

The 1987 Wyatt Survey[140] reported a "surprising 25% of the participants" said they were faced with an exclusion of claims arising from SEC violations in addition to the standard Section 16(b) exclusion mentioned in section 21.12. Also reported were exclusions relating to securities transactions generally. Particularly in the case of financial institutions, some insurers make use of an exclusion of claims involving the registration, purchase or sale of securities. The Lloyd's London Market form provides for immediate cancellation if a corporation's securities representing the present right to vote for the election of directors become exempt from registration under Section 11 of the Securities Act of 1933.

Joint ventures or partnership

The Wyatt Survey[141] found that claims resulting from joint ventures or general or limited partnerships were excluded in policies reported by 12% of the participants in the survey.

Exclusions relating to law violations

The exclusion of claims arising from illegal payments or commissions was first introduced in the 1970's. The Wyatt Survey found this exclusion reported by 51% of participants in the United States and 52% in Canada. Other exclusions of

---

139. KDT Indus., Inc. v. Home Ins. Co., 603 F. Supp. 851 (D. Mass. 1985).
140. Supra note 2, at 68.
141. Id. at 69.

this type which appear from time to time relate to antitrust violations or payments that would be contrary to law.

Internal corporate matters

Some insurers make use of endorsements which exclude claims resulting from operational matters inside the corporation. Employee discrimination and wrongful discharge claims are involved in this area, as are claims arising from administration of the corporation's group life insurance, group accident or health insurance, pension plans, employee stock subscription plans, workers' compensation, unemployment insurance, social security, disability benefits, and other insurance or employee benefit programs.

Subsidiary D & O

The Lloyd's London Market form excludes coverage for Wrongful Acts of directors and officers of a subsidiary occurring prior to the time it became a subsidiary, and for Wrongful Acts occurring after that time which are related to the prior acts.

Outside directorship coverage

There is a trend to exclude coverage for outside directorships. In the Lloyd's London Market form the exclusion is absolute and applies to both parts of the policy. In another form, the coverage is excess as to any other indemnity or insurance available to the officer or director, but affords no coverage to the outside organization.[142]

§ 21.14. Application; severability.

Because the D & O policy is a claims made form, it will provide coverage for acts or omissions occurring prior to the inception date of the policy, unless otherwise excluded. Accordingly, insurers are highly interested in any prior matters which might give rise to claims under the policy.

---

142. DOLI Form 9100 (1/87).

Every applicant for D & O insurance must submit a written application which will provide an extensive history of the corporation, past and planned activities, stock ownership, annual reports, financial statements and other details to enable the insurer to determine whether to undertake the risk and on what terms. The application typically requests disclosure of all facts and circumstances known to any prospective insured that might give rise to a claim under the policy. The statements in the application, and the information furnished in its support, constitute the basis for the policy, are relied on by the insurer, and constitute representations or warranties of the applicants.

A recurring subject of concern in D & O insurance is "continuity." While it is often said to refer to "continuity of coverage," that is incorrect. It is actually "continuity of warranties" or "continuity of representations." The question usually arises when buyers change insurance carriers. If continuity is granted, the underwriter will not require a new, current identification of facts that could give rise to claims. Instead, the underwriter will review and accept the statements in the application made to the prior insurer, as if the policy were up for renewal. When the D & O market is soft, continuity increases in popularity and may be granted more frequently than in a tight or hard market. Obviously continuity reduces the likelihood that an insurer will seek to void or rescind a policy.

Not surprisingly, when a claim is made under the policy for an act or omission occurring prior to the policy's inception date, insurers often allege that the application was misleading and incomplete and therefore that the policy should be voided. A leading case, decided under Massachusetts law, is *Shapiro v. American Home Assurance Company*.[143] Applicant's president, Shapiro, signed the application for insurance, which contained the following: "Question No. 14: Does any Director or Officer have knowledge or information of any act, error or omission which might give rise to a claim under

---

143. 584 F. Supp. 1245 (D. Mass. 1984).

727

the proposed policy?" To this question, Shapiro answered, "No." The application further stated, in Item No. 17: "It is agreed that if such knowledge or information exists, any claim or action arising therefrom is excluded from the proposed coverage." Attached to the application were copies of the corporation's current financial statements, which contained fake and fraudulent statements for which Shapiro was held responsible.

Massachusetts, like a number of other states, has enacted a statute to codify the common law relating to misrepresentations made in negotiating an insurance policy. Its statute provides that

> no ... misrepresentation ... shall be deemed material or defeat or avoid the policy or prevent its attaching unless ... made with actual intent to deceive, or unless the matter represented ... increased the risk.[144]

Judge Robert E. Keeton held that Shapiro's misrepresentation increased the risk, was "material," and permitted the insurer to avoid the policy, not only as to Shapiro but also as to all others covered by the policy. In addition, he held that Item No. 17 excluded coverage for any claim arising from facts known by any director or officer at the time of the application.[145]

That decision and the rulings in *Bird v. Penn Central Company*,[146] bring into focus the problem of "innocent" directors and officers who did not participate in the application and knew nothing of the misrepresentation. *Bird v. Penn Central* held that the signer was agent for the corporation and "for each individual officer and director," and that the fraud of an

---

144. Mass. Gen. Laws ch. 175, § 186. See also, e.g., Ill. Ins. Code § 154; Ill. Rev. Stat. ch. 73, § 766; La. Rev. Stat. § 22:619; N.Y. Ins. Law § 149; Ohio Rev. Code Ann. § 3911.06 (life and health insurance); Tex. Ins. Code § 21.16; Wash. Rev. Stat. § 48.18.090(1).

145. Shapiro v. American Home Assur. Co., supra note 143, at 1252. Cf. F/H Indus., Inc. v. National Union Fire Ins. Co., 635 F. Supp. 60 (N.D. Ill. 1986).

146. 334 F. Supp. 255 (E.D. Pa. 1971), on reh'g, 341 F. Supp. 291 (E.D. Pa. 1972).

agent in inducing a contract is binding on an innocent principal.[147]

The "agency analysis" was rejected by Judge Keeton in *Shapiro*.[148] He found that Shapiro's answer misrepresented the risk incurred "in insuring all those covered by the policy," and that the insurer could avoid responsibility to all insureds on the basis of Shapiro's misrepresentation as to what he knew. The agency analysis was also rejected by Judge William K. Thomas in *Zaremba v. National Union Fire Insurance Company* as to the other officers and directors.[149] Because the misrepresentation was not a warranty, Judge Thomas found the policy voidable as to the corporation and the signer, but neither voidable nor void as to the innocent insureds.

Judge Keeton recognized that the parties could have negotiated a policy contract in which misrepresentations of the signer would not have deprived the innocent insureds of protection.[150] The solution lies in "severability," a procedure by which each insured's rights and obligations are treated separately. Judge Keeton cited and analyzed "a clear severability provision" in *Shapiro* II,[151] a companion case to his earlier decision. This clause, contained in a Securities Act Liability Policy, stated:

> [T]his Insurance shall be construed as a separate contract with each Insured so that ... as to each Insured, the reference in this Insurance to the Insured shall be construed as referring only to that particular Insured, and

---

147. Bird v. Penn Cent. Co., supra note 146, 341 F. Supp. at 294-95.

148. Shapiro v. American Home Assur. Co., supra note 143, at 1251-52. "[T]he fact that individual officers and directors relied on insurance coverages procured by Giant on their behalf cannot connect their relationship with Shapiro into one of agency, where critical elements of an agency relationship, such as control, were missing."

149. 1979 Fire & Cas. Cases (CCH) ¶1302 (N.D. Ohio 1978).

150. Shapiro v. American Home Assur. Co., supra note 143, at 1252.

151. Shapiro v. American Home Assur. Co., 616 F. Supp. 900, 902-03 (D. Mass. 1984). Cf. Atlantic Permanent Fed. Sav. & Loan v. American Cas. Co., 839 F.2d 212 (4th Cir. 1988).

the liability of the Insurer to such Insured shall be independent of its liability to any other insured.

In *Shapiro* II it was contended that coverage was barred for the same reason as in *Shapiro* I, but Judge Keeton ruled that the "clear severability provision distinguishe[d] this policy from the directors' and officers' liability policy ... which [he] previously held was voidable even as to innocent officers and directors." He went on to state that the severability clause meant that each insured must be treated as having "a separate policy."

The Aetna Independent Directors Liability Policy[151a] contains a broad severability provision stating:

> The Application shall be construed as a separate application for coverage by each of the Independent Directors. No statement in the Application or knowledge or information possessed by an Independent Director shall be imputed to any other Independent Director for the purpose of determining the availability of coverage hereunder.

That language fits Judge Keeton's definition of a "clear severability provision."

Under the California Insurance Code "[c]oncealment, whether intentional or unintentional, entitles the injured party to rescind insurance."[152] National Union Fire Insurance Company was granted rescission of a D & O policy under that rule, when the insured withheld material information relating to potential lawsuits which later ripened into litigation and were related to the underlying litigation for which the insured sought policy coverage. The circumstance that some such potential claims were disclosed suggested that no other similar potential claims existed.[153]

The type of inquiry made by an insurer and its manner and time of making may bear on the insurer's right to relief when

---

151a. Aetna Cas. & Sur. Co. Independent Directors Liability Policy Form (F-1842) ED. 3-38, reproduced in Appendix C.

152. Cal. Ins. Code § 331.

153. Jaunich v. National Union Fire Ins. Co., 647 F. Supp. 209, 214 (N.D. Cal. 1986).

information is withheld. It is the responsibility of the insurer to request the information it deems material. Under California law, for example, rescission is permitted only when an insured conceals facts he is under a duty to disclose. The insurer's questions seeking such information must be sufficiently clear to alert the insured to what is wanted.[154]

Two D & O insurance cases arising under California law resulted in denials of insurers' efforts to rescind policies because of withheld information. In both instances further inquiries by the insurer would have produced additional information.[155] Another case, involving Continental Illinois Corporation (CIC), was decided by a federal district court in Illinois with a similar result. Two insurers, when issuing policies for additional excess D & O insurance, used application forms which "supplemented" the original applications made several years earlier. Financial statements were "attached to" but not "made part of" the application. The insured was not asked to warrant the truth of the financial statements. The "supplemental" application declared that the statements in them and all other applications were true, but there was no updating of the statements in the original applications as to knowledge of facts which "could give rise to" claims against the directors and officers. The court held that the insurers

> got just what they asked for, no more, no less. This game was played with their prescribed bat and ball, and they cannot now be heard to complain CIC should have substituted better equipment.[156]

In the *Seafirst* and *Continental Illinois* litigation, insurers have endeavored to avoid liability under their D & O policies by suing their insureds for indemnity for any amounts they

---

154. Rallod Transp. Co. v. Continental Ins. Co., 727 F.2d 851, 853, 855 (9th Cir. 1984).

155. Federal Ins. Co. v. Oak Indus., Inc., Fed. Sec. L. Rep. (CCH) ¶92,519 (S.D. Cal. 1986); National Union Fire Ins. Co. v. Seafirst Corp., No. C85-396R, W.D. Wash., Mar. 19, 1986 (available on Lexis).

156. National Union Fire Ins. Co. v. Continental Ill. Corp., 643 F. Supp. 1434, 1441 (N.D. Ill. 1986).

731

might be required to pay on account of the underlying litigation. The gravamen of these suits was "postissuance" fraud
on the part of the insureds in misrepresenting the "true"
financial condition of the bank. In both cases, the courts
treated the actions as attempts to avoid the effects of the
respective state statutes relating to material misrepresentations.[157] The actions were dismissed.[158]

§ 21.15. Action against insurer.

The "new generation" D & O insurance policies which came
into the market beginning in 1984 may contain a "no action
provision" stating:

> No action shall lie against the Insurer unless, as a condi-
> tion precedent thereto, there shall have been compliance
> with all of the terms of this policy, nor until the amount
> of the Insureds' obligation to pay shall have been finally
> determined either by judgment against the Insureds af-
> ter actual trial or by written agreement of the Insureds,
> the claimant and the Insurer.[159]

Furthermore some state statutes prohibit a direct action
against a liability or indemnity insurer until a judgment has
been obtained against the insured.[160]

"No action" clauses have been upheld in some court decisions.[161] However, a federal court in Illinois was called upon

---

157. Wash. Rev. Stat. § 48.18.090(1); Ill. Ins. Code § 154; Ill. Rev. Stat.
ch. 73, § 761.

158. National Union Fire Ins. Co. v. Continental Ill. Corp., 658 F. Supp.
775 (N.D. Ill. 1987); National Union Fire Ins. Co. v. Seafirst Corp., 662 F.
Supp. 36 (W.D. Wash. 1986).

159. E.g., National Union Form 8750 (6/85), General Conditions ¶12. See
also Harbor Form HU 8128-2 (Ed. 8-85), General Conditions 8(C); Aetna
Form (F-1459-a) (Ed. 11-86), Conditions and Limitations IV(E). The language differs in various forms.

160. E.g., Ill. Rev. Stat. ch. 73, § 1000, Ill. Ins. Code § 388; Marchlik v.
Coronet Ins. Co., 40 Ill. 2d 327, 239 N.E.2d 799 (1968); 8 Appleman, Insurance Law & Practice §§ 4861-4866 (1981).

161. E.g., S.A. Compania Mexicana de Seguros Generales v. Bostrons,
347 F.2d 168, 173 (5th Cir. 1965); cf. General Cas. Co. v. Larson, 196 F.2d

to decide whether such a clause would prevent suit against an insurer after the underlying litigation had been settled. The court held that "Illinois law would treat an enforceable agreement for settlement as the equivalent of a judgment" as a basis for bringing an action against the insurer.[162] There is no apparent reason why that same rule should not be applied to a "no action provision" in a D & O insurance policy.[163]

§ 21.16. Subrogation.

Most D & O insurance policies contain a subrogation provision which usually reads:

> In the event of any payment under this policy, the Insurer shall be subrogated to the extent of such payment to all the Insureds' rights of recovery therefor, and the Insureds shall execute all papers required and shall do everything that may be necessary to secure such rights including the execution of such documents necessary to enable the Insurer effectively to bring suit in the name of the Insureds.[164]

The general rule is that an insurer, on paying a loss, is subrogated in a corresponding amount to the insured's right of action against any other person responsible for the loss. The insurer succeeds to all the procedural rights and remedies possessed by the insured.[165] But until the insurer has paid the claim under the policy, no subrogation rights accrue to it.[166] That principle was involved in a D & O insurance action in Illinois, in which the court went on to say while dismissing the action:

170, 173 (8th Cir. 1952). See also Macey v. Crum, 249 Ala. 249, 30 So. 2d 666 (1947).

162. Fowler v. Buckham, 550 F. Supp. 71, 72 (N.D. Ill. 1982), followed in National Union Fire Ins. Co. v. Continental Ill. Corp., 113 F.R.D. 527, 529-30 (N.D. Ill. 1986).

163. Cf. National Union Fire Ins. Co. v. Seafirst Corp., 662 F.2d 36, 39 (W.D. Wash. 1986).

164. E.g., National Union Form 8750 (6/85), General Conditions ¶9.

165. 6A Appleman, Insurance Law & Practice § 4051 (1972).

166. Insurance Co. of N. Am. v. Abiouness, 227 Va. 10, 313 S.E.2d 663 (1984).

Insurers' new theory is one of recovering, from defendants [insureds] who breached the insurance contract, any amounts Insurers may have to pay out to FDIC under the Policies.... Ordinarily an insurer's remedy for an insured's breach of contract is to avoid coverage under the insurance policy, thus avoiding any payout.... And under Illinois law an insurer has no right to subrogation against an insured.[167]

Another aspect of subrogation that may be available to D & O insurers is demonstrated by the facts in *First National Bank v. Hansen,* a Wisconsin case.[168] There the bank suffered losses because of the fraud of its executive vice president, Hansen. The bonding company sought subrogation to the bank's claim against its directors and officers for negligence in supervising the affairs of the bank. The court held that the bonding company had assumed the risk of such negligence, therefore lost its right of subrogation. However, the court left open the situation which would have existed if the directors had acted in bad faith or if Hansen's dishonesty had conferred some benefit upon the directors as individuals.[169]

Another question raised by commentators is whether directors and officers against whom subrogation is taken might have an individual right of indemnification against their corporation, actually or as a set-off to the subrogation claim.[170]

Litigation testing the D & O insurance subrogation provision is probably just around the corner, and should clarify the extent of usefulness of that clause.

§ 21.17. Underwriting considerations.

The legislation enacted since 1986, discussed in Chapters 7 and 20, in particular, has not been in effect long enough to

---

167. National Union Fire Ins. Co. v. Continental Ill. Corp., 658 F. Supp. 781, 794 (N.D. Ill. 1987).

168. 84 Wis. 2d 422, 267 N.W.2d 367 (1978).

169. Cf. Employers Ins. of Wausau v. Doonan, 664 F. Supp. 1220, 1223-24 (C.D. Ill. 1987).

170. See e.g., Knox, "Subrogation Rights in Fidelity Cases," 10 Forum 148 (1976); Schroeder, "Handling the Complex Fidelity or Financial Institutions Bond Claim: The Liability of the Insured's Officers and Directors and Their D & O Carrier," 21 Tort & Ins. L.J. 269, 277 n.31 (1986).

have had an appreciable effect on the market for D & O insurance. The new insurance companies, mostly policyholder formed, discussed in Chapter 19, have begun to affect the market and most observers agree that more D & O insurance is becoming available with at least a leveling and in many instances a reduction of premiums[171] and expansion of coverage terms.

Nonetheless, the underwriting of D & O insurance is complex and there is a high degree of selectivity (i) in choosing the applicants to be accepted and (ii) in fashioning the policy to be issued especially in respect of limits, retentions and exclusions.[172] The application[173] and its supporting documents will have considerable bearing on the likelihood of acceptance of the risk. Usually the supporting data will consist of (1) copies of the corporation's latest annual report; (2) copies of all proxy material sent to stockholders within the past year; (3) copies of the corporation's bylaws relating to indemnification of directors, officers, employees, and agents; (4) a listing of the directors and officers of the corporation and of all subsidiary companies (sometimes with biographical data for each); (5) a current Dun and Bradstreet report; and (6) any prospectus mentioned in the proposal or application.

The underwriting considerations governing whether to accept a particular risk include gross assets, in depth financial analysis, history of past litigation, corporate plans, examination of past annual reports, Securities and Exchange Commission filings, outstanding proxy statements and regular examination of company reports sent to stockholders.

Included also in underwriting considerations are such matters as:

(1)   The size of the corporate entity involved;
(2)   The number of directors and officers to be insured;
(3)   The deductibles and retention arrangements under the policy;

---

171. See infra section 22.05.
172. See supra sections 21.11, 21.12; infra sections 22.06, 22.07.
173. See supra section 21.14.

(4) Special coverage features, particularly negotiated exclusions;

(5) The type of company and the industry to which it belongs — certain industries have surcharges or credits applied;

(6) Companies with a high degree of acquisition activity are usually more prone to D & O claims and thus less desirable risks;

(7) Companies in diverse fields of business activity usually pay higher premiums than the general average;

(8) The nature, extent and frequency of the company's business losses in prior years;

(9) The corporate profitability;

(10) The number of subsidiaries and the degree of their control by the parent company;

(11) How the company's stock is distributed and held;

(12) Special circumstances, such as antitrust potential, political activity, adverse publicity, governmental investigations, and the like.

When considering whether to offer terms for a particular corporation, the insurer considers all aspects of the company itself and the business in which it operates. Difficulty will be encountered by a corporation evidencing such factors as erratic earnings or sale patterns, or even an extremely dramatic growth. Other negative factors could include dependence on a small number of customers, a poor "public image," or a substantial history of acquisitions or merger activity. Certain industries considered of less desirability include real estate operations, mutual funds and similar financial institutions, and speculative mining. Risks considered "politically oriented" will probably be viewed with less than complete enthusiasm.

With the possible exception of an overall financial analysis, the single most important underwriting consideration is the quality of the people involved in the management of the corporation. Any future claim under the policy will relate to alleged actions or omissions of those people. Therefore, the more experienced, capable, honest, knowledgeable and forthright is the management, the less the risk of valid claims being asserted. With more frequency, underwriters are requesting meetings with top management personnel to evaluate this intangible element. Before any such meeting, the participating managers should be thoroughly prepared by the broker and other advisors so that not only the appropriate factual information is available but also the most favorable image is properly presented.

Also, in approaching the D & O market place there is no substitute for experience. The specialists in the field and major brokers who are thoroughly familiar with the carriers and what they have to offer, can be of great help in locating and obtaining the issuance of these policies.

§ 21.18. Fiduciary liability insurance.

Fiduciary liability insurance is written to cover the fiduciaries of a corporate pension plan, profit sharing plan, thrift plan, or other employee benefit plan of any nature, against legal liability arising out of their role as fiduciaries, as well as the costs of legal defense of claims asserting such liability. Various insurers give different titles to such policies but, by whatever names they are called, they should be distinguished from

- Fidelity insurance on the trustees or administrators of such a plan, which covers only dishonesty and is solely for the benefit of the plan and its beneficiaries.
- Trust Surcharge liability policies carried by financial institutions to protect their exposures on plans handled for others.
- Employee Benefit Liability policies (or endorsements thereof on Commercial General Liability policies) which provide only limited coverage for errors and omissions in the administration of a plan, such as the

737

failure to enroll an employee, or the giving of improper advice as to benefits.[174]

As pointed out in section 21.12, a D & O insurance policy usually excludes liability for claims relating to ERISA or any form of employee benefit plan. In some instances, fiduciary liability endorsements tailored for attachment to D & O policies or bank trustee liability policies may provide adequate coverage. Generally, fiduciary liability coverage will be provided by a separate policy. The insurers of such risks are most of the same carriers that write D & O insurance.[175]

Claims made

Fiduciary liability policies are usually "claims made" policies. Coverage is afforded for claims made against the insureds during the policy period, or any extended discovery period, regardless of when the Wrongful Acts occurred.[176] This provision is subject to some qualifications:

(a) Claims resulting from Wrongful Acts which occurred prior to the effective date of a policy are excluded if the insured knew or could reasonably anticipate that claims would result from such acts;

(b) If an insured becomes aware of a potential claim during the policy period and notifies the insurer before the policy terminates, the claim will be covered although made after such termination.

(c) Only claims for Wrongful Acts which occurred before the termination of the policy may be reported during the extended discovery period;

(d) There may be a retroactive date prior to which coverage will not apply.

Insureds

Coverage will probably extend to the sponsoring organization, the plan itself, past, present or future trustees, em-

---

174. Wyatt Survey, supra note 2, at 129.
175. See infra sections 22.08 and 22.11.
176. See supra sections 21.04 and 21.10.

ployees of the trust, and their estates, heirs and legal representatives.[177]

Loss

The policy usually provides for payment of Loss, which is defined as the total amount which any Insured becomes legally obligated to pay for all claims made for Wrongful Acts, including but not limited to damages, judgments, settlements, costs and defense costs.

Wrongful Act

As to the Sponsoring Organization the Wrongful Act is a breach of its duties, responsibilities or obligations under ERISA.[178] As to other Insureds it ordinarily means matters claimed against them by reason of their serving as plan fiduciaries or any negligent act or omission in the administration of any employee benefit program.

Defense costs

Most fiduciary liability policies include defense costs as a part of Loss.[179] One policy form provides:

> The Insurer shall at all times have the right but not the obligation to take over and conduct in the name of the Insured the investigation and defense of any claims and in such event the Insured shall cooperate in every way with the Insurer.[180]

In another form, however, the Insurer undertakes the obligation of defense, although the cost is included in the policy limit as a part of Loss. That policy provides:

> 2. The Company shall have the right and duty to defend any claim for damages seeking pecuniary or nonpecuniary relief or may, at its option, give its consent to

---

177. See, e.g., Chubb Group Form 14-02-0455 (Ed. 9-84).
178. See supra Chapter 9.
179. See also discussion supra section 21.07.
180. CNA Form G-11277-A (Ed. 10/83) Section 5(D)(3).

the defense of any claim by an Insured. Coverage shall apply even if any of the allegations are groundless, false or fraudulent.

3. Defense Costs, charges and expenses incurred by the Company, or by an Insured when it is defending and investigating with the written consent of the Company, shall be paid by the Company as a part of and not in addition to the Company's liability.[181]

Exclusions

The exclusions in a fiduciary liability policy will usually deny coverage for fines or penalties imposed by law or matters uninsurable under the law pursuant to which the policy is construed. However, the policy may cover the 5% civil penalty imposed under § 502(i) of ERISA for inadvertent violations of § 406 of the Act. Other usual exclusions are:

- libel or slander
- personal injury, bodily injury and property damage
- dishonest, fraudulent or criminal acts or willful violation of any statute
- facts or circumstances which an Insured had reason to know might result in a claim
- matters as to which notice was given to another insurer
- attributable to an insured having gained any personal profit or advantage to which he was not legally entitled.

Because no two policy forms are exactly alike, it is necessary to examine the exclusions in any policy form with care, remembering that all may not be located in the section designated "Exclusions."[182]

Subrogation; recourse

Section 410 of ERISA (29 U.S.C. § 1110) permits a plan to purchase liability insurance, but such coverage must permit

---

181. Chubb Group Form, supra note 177.
182. See supra section 21.12.

recourse (or subrogation) by the insurer against a derelict fiduciary. Since the exercise of this right is not mandatory, the basic policy purchased by the trust contains a provision giving the insurer a right of recourse against a fiduciary who breaches a fiduciary duty; then, by an amendatory endorsement, the insurer may waive such right of recourse. The additional premium charged for such an amendatory endorsement cannot be paid by the trust but must be paid by the fiduciaries, by the employer, or by an employee organization such as a union.

COROLLARY REFERENCES

Block, Barton & Garfield, "Advising Directors on the D & O Insurance Crisis," 14 Sec. Reg. L. Rev. 130 (Summer 1986).

Close, "Suits Against Financial Institutions: Coverage and Considerations," 20 Forum 84 (1984).

Conard, "A Behavioral Analysis of Directors' Liability for Negligence," 1972 Duke L.J. 895.

Knepper, "Corporate Indemnification and Liability Insurance for Corporation Officers and Directors," 25 Sw. L.J. 240 (1971).

Knepper, "Officers and Directors: Indemnification and Liability Insurance — An Update," 30 Bus. Law. 951 (1975).

Knepper, "An Overview of D & O Liability for Insurance Company Directors and Officers," 45 Ins. Counsel J. 63 (1978).

Knepper, "A Primer on Bank Directors' and Officers' Indemnification and Liability Insurance," 156 The Bankers Magazine 88 (No. 3, Summer 1973).

Kroll, "Some Reflections on Indemnification Provisions and SEC Liability Insurance in Light of BarChris and Globus," 24 Bus. Law. 681 (1969).

Oettle & Howard, "D & O Insurance: Judicially Transforming a 'Duty to Pay' Policy into a 'Duty to Defend Policy,'" 22 Tort & Ins. L.J. (1987).

Oettle & Howard, "Zuckerman and Sparks: The Validity of 'Claims Made' Insurance Policies as a Function of Retroactive Coverage," 21 Tort & Ins. L.J. 619 (1986).

Olson & Morgan, "D & O Exclusions Extend to Takeover Context," Legal Times, Mar. 10, 1986, at 23, col. 1.

Schroeder, "Handling the Complex Fidelity or Financial Institutions Bond Claim: The Liability of the Insured's Officers and Directors and Their D & O Carrier," 21 Tort & Ins. L.J. 269 (1986).

Comment, "Indemnification of the Corporate Insider: Directors' and Officers' Liability Insurance," 54 Minn. L. Rev. 667 (1970).

Note, "Liability Insurance for Corporate Executives," 80 Harv. L. Rev. 648 (1967).

Note, "Practical Aspects of Directors' and Officers' Liability Insurance — Allocating and Advancing Legal Fees and the Duty to Defend," 32 UCLA L. Rev. 690 (1985).

Note, "Protecting Corporate Directors and Officers: Insurance and Other Alternatives," 40 Vand. L. Rev. 775 (1987).

Note, "Void Ab Initio: Application Fraud as Grounds for Avoiding Directors' and Officers' Liability Insurance Coverage," 74 Calif. L. Rev. (1986).

Chapter 22

LIABILITY AND FIDUCIARY SURVEYS

Section

§ 22.01. D & O liability surveys: scope and nature.

The information contained in this chapter was obtained in four comprehensive surveys conducted and announced in 1986 and 1987 for the purpose of gauging the dimensions of the D & O liability problem, learning about its effect on the quality of corporate governance, and making a comprehensive overview of claim trends, litigation, defense costs and liability insurance developments relating to directors and officers of corporations in the United States and Canada.

The 1987 Wyatt Company Director and Officers and Fiduciary Liability Survey[1] is the broadest in subject matter. It is the tenth survey of this type. There were 1,047 participating business organizations, of which 895 are organizations domiciled in the United States and 152 in Canada. Participants represented forty-seven states, the District of Columbia, and all ten Canadian provinces. The survey included 28% of the Fortune listed companies, in addition to forty-four educational institutions and sixty-five hospitals. Manufacturing companies dominated the survey, with 325 participants, followed by 112 banking and financial institutions.

Peat Marwick Mitchell & Company commissioned a survey designed by Research Strategies Corporation and conducted

---

1. Hereafter Wyatt Survey.

by Opinion Research Corporation among 7,000 chief executives in the corporate and not-for-profit sectors.[2] Respondents totaled 2,532 persons and included 570 chief executives of the 2,000 largest corporations along with executives of hospitals, municipal officials, heads of museums, symphony orchestras, national voluntary organizations, university chairpersons and presidents.[3]

A parallel study conducted by the National Association of Corporate Directors (NACD) polled 2,800 corporate directors and fifty state insurance and commerce commissioners to determine the scope and severity of the D & O situation.[4] Respondents included 370 directors representing 1,223 board seats and thirty-five state officials.[5]

Touche Ross & Company received responses to its survey from more than 1,100 directors of major United States corporations,[6] of whom 76% served on more than one board and 58% had ten or more years of board experience.

§ 22.02. Effects of increased D & O liability.

All four surveys disclosed that the seriousness of the D & O liability situation has caused increased resignations from some boards and will make more difficult the recruitment of qualified directors in the future.[7] Most participants reported increases in premiums and deductibles and reductions in coverages,[8] although in one study 7% reported broadened coverage.[9] As noted in section 22.05, the Wyatt Survey reveals that the coverage is not greatly overpriced in relation to losses.[10]

---

2. Hereafter Peat Marwick study.

3. Peat Marwick Executive Newsletter, February 9, 1987, at 1, col. 2.

4. Hereafter NACD study.

5. Director's Monthly Nov. 1986, at 3, col. 3-4.

6. Hereafter Touche Ross study.

7. Wyatt Survey 161, Peat Marwick study 7, NACD study 4, Touche Ross study 5-6.

8. Wyatt Survey 89, Peat Marwick study 6, NACD study 4.

9. Peat Marwick study 6.

10. See also Finlayson, "High D & O Premiums Here to Stay: Wyatt," Business Insurance, July 6, 1987, at 1, col. 2.

Two surveys showed that D & O liability issues have had a negative effect on corporate governance[11] and that the increased liability will create boards whose members will be less qualified or less effective than today's.[12] The NACD study found nearly half of the responding directors to be of the belief that they were "far more likely" to be sued today as compared with five years ago.

In the Peat Marwick study, all participants except CEOs were asked how great an effect the D & O liability problem was having on their organizational management. About 60% reported some effect, 10% reported a considerable effect, and 2% reported "a great deal of effect."[13]

Only the Peat Marwick study inquired about self-protective measures undertaken or under consideration. Some 55% of all participants and 70% of the CEOs reported that their boards had already improved the depth and delivery of management information to their boards; 19% more were considering or planning to do so. Fifty-four percent had formulated a conflict-of-interest policy, 17% had formed new board committees and 17% had brought in outside experts to counsel the board on legal liability. Twenty-four percent had recruited new members to add specific expertise to the board and another 26% had plans to do so or labeled it a good idea.[14]

§ 22.03. D & O claims: sources, susceptibility and frequency.

Liability claims against corporate directors and officers reviewed by Wyatt were those first made during the years 1977 through 1985.[15] More claims were made by shareholders than by any other source, although financial institutions are expe-

---

11. Peat Marwick study 4.
12. Touche Ross study 5.
13. Peat Marwick study 7.
14. Id. 11.
15. Wyatt Survey 11.

riencing a sharp growth in claim frequency, much of which can be attributed to actions taken by their customers.[16]

PERCENTAGES OF CLAIMS

Sources	United States Non-bank	United States Financial	Canadian Non-bank	Canadian Financial
Shareholders	39.5	12.6	45.8	
Employees	31.3	11.6	4.2	
Customers	8.2	53.7	4.2	84.8
Governmental	5.0	0.0	4.2	
Suppliers	3.2	1.1	4.2	3.0
Prior Owners	3.2	3.2	8.3	
Competitors	1.4	4.2	8.3	3.0
Bondholders	1.1	1.1		

In considering the nature of the allegations made by claimants in the United States,[17] the Wyatt Survey showed the following to predominate:

PERCENTAGE OF CLAIMS

Allegations	United States Non-bank	United States Financial
Misleading representations	21.0	16.8
Breach of employment contract	14.2	4.2
Breach duty — minority	13.9	2.1
Civil rights violations	13.9	11.6
Fraud	9.3	22.1
Antitrust violations	7.1	2.1
Improper expenditures	5.3	1.1
Imprudent investment	2.8	5.3
Conflict of interest	4.3	5.3

An effort was made to learn the settings in which the claims were generated. For United States corporations,[18] some of the results were:

---

16. Id. 16.
17. Wyatt Survey 31-32. For Canadian figures, see Wyatt Survey 45.
18. Wyatt Survey 36-37. For Canadian figures, see Wyatt Survey 46.

PERCENTAGE OF CLAIMS

Setting	United States Non-bank	United States Financial
Impaired employee relationship	21.4	10.5
Acquisition of another firm	10.0	4.2
Entering into a contract	8.9	8.4
Going private	6.0	1.1
Securities issue	4.6	3.2
Making a loan	0.4	16.8
Granting stock options	3.6	0.0
Denial of credit	0.0	13.7
Rejection of tender offer	2.8	3.2
Preparation of financials	4.6	3.2

Of the claims reported, 59.6% were reimbursable by the corporation (that is, they came within its power of indemnification and thus would fall under the corporate reimbursements coverage of the D & O liability insurance policy). In 26.3% of all claims the survey disclosed uncertainty as to indemnification and in 23.4% there was uncertainty as to the availability of insurance coverage.[19] The new legislation broadening the nature and scope of indemnification enacted in several states in 1986 and 1987 may have a bearing on these uncertainties in the future.[20]

The Wyatt Survey shows that claim frequency continues to exhibit a strong correlation with company size, but average claim severity appears to continue to plateau beginning with corporations having assets of $25 million.[21] Claim frequency continues to rise at an estimated rate of 15% to 20% per year. For example, the survey estimates that one out of every five Fortune listed companies will experience a D & O claim in 1987. Closely held companies have claim activity levels at about 72% of the corresponding figure for publicly held firms of equal size. Canadian firms have claim frequencies of about

---

19. Wyatt Survey 17-18.
20. See supra Chapter 20.
21. Wyatt Survey 11.

50% and claim severities of about 30% of corresponding United States firms.[22]

§ 22.04. D & O claims: disposition; loss payments; defense costs.

Claim disposition was shown in the Wyatt Survey, as follows:

Closed
by litigation	16.6%
by settlement	33.2%
dropped by claimant	12.9%

Open
still awaiting trial	33.8%
tried, but on appeal	3.4%
No information	0.7%

In the Wyatt Survey it is reported that 136 of the 232 total closed claims involved no payments to the claimants. This is 58.6% of all claims.[23] However, the average cost per claim for paid claims was $1,988,200. For all claims, including those closed without payment, the average cost was $880,800.[24]

Associated legal defense costs were reported in connection with the claims surveyed. Those reports showed that the average defense costs would be computed, as follows:[25]

Claims	Average Per Claim Cost
Closed by litigation	$488,154
Closed by settlement	313,377
Dropped by claimant	130,340
Awaiting trial	196,428
Tried, but on appeal	159,266

---

22. Id. 12.

23. Id. 15.

24. Wyatt warns that these figures may be understated because of the reluctance of some companies to report. Nine D & O claims had awards or settlements in excess of $20 million but none of the companies involved in those claims participated in the survey. Wyatt Survey 11.

25. Wyatt Survey 14, 25.

After considering the costs yet to be incurred in the last two categories, the survey calculated an average estimate of defense costs per claim of $592,000, up from $461,000 in the 1984 survey.

The average age of a claim was 4.9 years from February of 1981. Projecting a claim amounts and defense costs to increase at 10% until 1984 and 15% from 1984 to 1986, the survey calculated an average total claim cost for 1986 claims of $2,567,000.[26]

Confirming that the trend discussed in prior Wyatt studies is continuing, the 1987 survey concludes:

> Firms with assets below $25 million tend to experience smaller settlements and defense costs. Firms with greater assets seem to experience claim frequency directly related with total assets. However, they appear to share claim settlements and legal fees of similar magnitude.[27]

§ 22.05. D & O insurance: prevalence and premiums.

The Wyatt Survey showed that the percentage of companies listed on the New York Stock Exchange carrying D & O insurance was 96.8%, those on AMEX 91.1%, and the NASD companies 87.4%.[28] In the Peat Marwick study, 90% of those in the for-profit section had insurance protection, compared with 71% among those in the not-for-profit group.[29] Wyatt reports that large corporations have the greater need for such protection, in order to attract and retain directors of substance and prominence. That is borne out by the Wyatt finding that only 32% of business corporations with assets under $25 million carry D & O insurance.[30]

26. Id. 19.
27. Id. 16.
28. Id. 52.
29. Peat Marwick study 6.
30. Wyatt Survey 49.

In Canada, the percentage for large corporations was 77.8% compared to 25.9% for those having assets under $25 million.[31]

Both the Wyatt and Peat Marwick studies reported large increases in premiums for D & O liability insurance. Although simple changes in premiums do not tell the full story, because they do not reflect what was happening at the same time in terms of policy limits, deductibles, exclusions and the scope of coverage, they are enlightening. In the Wyatt study, the premium increase for 65% of the participants was in excess of 100%. It also showed that 54% of the participants had increases of more than 200%, 33% of participants had increases in excess of 500%, and 20% of participants had increases in excess of 1000%.[32]

In the Peat Marwick survey, a third of the participants reported increases of more than 300% and another 46% said that their premiums had risen up to 300%. Only 6% reported no increases.[33]

Over the nine years covered by the Wyatt studies, a premium index using the 1974 level of premiums as 100% showed the following:

Year	Average Percent
1974	100.0
1976	81.3
1978	102.6
1980	98.6
1982	71.2
1984	54.3
1987	682.4

31. Id. 51.
32. Id. 89.
33. Peat Marwick study 6.

Wyatt reports that Canadian business organizations appear to be paying about 53% of what United States firms are paying for D & O coverage.[34]

The cost of excess D & O coverage has also risen sharply. For example, in 1984 the average premium per million dollars for excess coverage attaching over a $5 million primary layer was $1,087. In 1987 that average premium amounted to $27,080, an increase of 2,491%.

Comparing the trends in indexed D & O premiums and losses, the Wyatt study charts a slight softening of the D & O market in the mid-1970's and a much more drastic softening between 1980 and 1984, the rise in premiums in 1985 and 1986, and a comparison with a loss index arbitrarily established at 100 in 1978 when it was presumed there was a reasonable relationship between losses and premiums. The survey trended the loss index from that point onward to reflect Wyatt's perception of loss frequency and severity. The conclusion:

> This chart tells us that underwriters were digging a substantial hole for themselves during the soft market, and have over-adjusted to some degree at this time, but with the present trend in losses, prices will never return to the levels of the early 1980's. Premiums should become static for a while, and may dip slightly, but this will probably not last more than a year or two before the loss index shoots past the premium index again.[35]

§ 22.06. D & O insurance: limits and deductibles.

The impact of the swift withdrawal of reinsurance support and the resulting reduction of each insurer's capacity in the D & O market reached its most severe point at the end of 1985 when 67% of all D & O liability insurance renewals were for reduced limits and the average reduction was about 50%. By the last quarter of 1986 the situation had stabilized with 30% of the renewals involving limit reductions, offset by 24% of

---

34. Wyatt Survey 91.
35. Id. 93-94.

renewals with increased limits. Exceptions to the reduction trend were companies in the smallest size bracket, where limits were low enough not to be impacted by the tight market, and the highest size bracket, where participants could avail themselves of alternative policyholder formed insurance companies.[36] In 1987 the highest reported policy limits were $141 million in the United States and $84 million in Canada.

Three of the surveys reported increases in deductibles. In the Peat Marwick study it was reported that 16% of the participants had seen deductibles go up 300%, one-fourth had experienced increases up to that figure, and about one-third said deductibles did not change.[37]

In the Wyatt Survey it was reported that personal coverage deductibles had increased an average of 44%, the increase in the aggregate maximum on personal deductibles increased by 196%, and the corporate reimbursement deductibles increased by 1,326% for business corporations from an average $51,646 in 1984 to an average of $736,290 in 1987. The survey reports that part of that increase was the result of pressure from underwriters, and part came from voluntary action on the part of corporations in entering into policyholder formed insurance companies which mandate fairly sizable corporate reimbursement deductibles.[38]

There may be a correlation between the increase in corporate reimbursement deductibles and the trend to enact legislation broadening statutory authority for corporate indemnification.[39] An effect of such laws is to shift losses to the corporate reimbursement part of the conventional D & O policy.[40]

---

36. Id. 57.

37. Peat Marwick study 6. Touche Ross study did not go into insurance. NACD study gave no details but noted the increases.

38. Wyatt Survey 75.

39. See supra Chapter 20.

40. Wyatt Survey 161.

§ 22.07. D & O insurance: policy conditions and exclusions.

The Wyatt study reports that under present market conditions insurers are not offering outside directorships coverage on as free a basis as in the past. Such coverages were reported most frequently by banks and other financial institutions which especially need this protection. Of those responding to this inquiry,[41] 41% of the participants had blanket outside directorships coverage if the outside position was held at the direction of the corporation, 29% covered only specified directorships and 30% did not insure it.[42]

The extended discovery option is being offered with some severe reductions in the extended discovery period. Now 9% have a period of 30 days or less, 15% less than 90 days, 41% have 90 days, and 42% have retained the one year which was generally available during the soft market of the early 1980's.[43]

The Wyatt Survey[44] also deals with fourteen specific exclusions found in today's D & O liability policies and details its findings by fourteen types of insureds and eighteen listed insurance companies. The development of a variety of new policy forms and new exclusions has contributed to the complexity of this part of the study. In essence, the following summarizes what is reported as to the fourteen exclusions.

- Actions by Regulatory Agencies. Intended to avoid suits by FDIC, FSLIC, insurance companies, the SEC, and other regulatory agencies, 18% of the participants reported it, chiefly banks, other financial institutions, and insurance companies.
- Failure to Maintain Insurance. Reported by only 14% in the United States and 16% in Canada in 1984; now reported by 49% in the United States and 55% in Canada.

---

41. Twenty-four percent did not respond on this point.
42. Wyatt Survey 67, 72.
43. Id. 67.
44. Id. 68-69, 73-74.

- General or Limited Partnerships. Excluded in 12% of the policies.
- Going Private. A relatively new exclusion reported by 2% of the participants.
- Illegal Payments or Commissions. Reported by 21% in the United States and 31% in Canada in 1984; now reported by 51% in the United States and 52% in Canada.
- Insured versus Insured. There are three basic forms of this exclusion:

  (1) Claims by any insured against any other insured, reported by 24%.
  (2) Claims by the corporate entity, reported by 2%.
  (3) Claims by the corporate entity and then excepting derivative actions from the exclusion, reported by 3%.

- Joint Ventures. Excluded in 12% of the policies.
- Mergers and Acquisitions. Not even considered in the 1984 survey, but reported by 13% of the 1987 participants.
- Pending or Prior Litigation. Reported by 34% in the United States and 44% in Canada in 1984; now reported by 70% of the participants in both nations.
- Pollution and Environmental Damage. Always a more or less automatic exclusion. Reported by 47% in the United States and 59% in Canada in 1984; now reported by 78% in the United States and 91% in Canada. Banks, schools, and hospitals are the only ones to avoid it in any significant way.
- Public Offerings. A recently introduced exclusion, reported by 2% of the participants.
- SEC Violations in Addition to the Standard 16(b) Exclusion. Reported by 25% of the participants. If that sampling is correct, it represents a significant erosion of coverage.
- Securities Transactions. Reported by 19% of the participants and again a serious erosion of coverage.

754

● Tender Offers or Rejections of Such Offers. Reported by 15% of the participants, three times as many in the United States as in Canada.

§ 22.08. D & O insurance: the leading carriers.

In presenting profiles of the United States market underwriting primary D & O coverage, the 1987 Wyatt Survey measured market share by (1) policy count and (2) estimated premium volume based on the information obtained from the participants in the survey. Wyatt did not have access to the data of the insurance companies themselves in these respects.

PRIMARY INSURERS

Company	Policy Count		Estimated Premiums	
	Rank	Percentage	Rank	Percentage
AIG	1	28.2%	1	41.1%
Chubb	2	24.1%	3	11.3%
CNA[45]	3	11.4%	5	3.5%
Lloyd's & Brit.	4	5.9%	4	7.7%
Continental	5	5.6%	6	2.1%
Western Emp.[46]	6	4.1%	10	1.0%
DOLI & Aegis	7	3.6%	2	24.7%
Crum & Forster	8	3.4%	9	1.3%
INA	9	2.5%	8	1.3%
St. Paul	10	1.6%	14	0.3%
Evanston	11	1.3%	11	0.8%
CODA	15	0.8%	7	1.4%

DOLI (including Aegis), and CODA are policyholder formed insurers[47] which account for 26.1% of the estimated premiums. The survey comments that while the Chubb Group drew close to AIG on a policy count basis, it was not at all close on a premium basis, making it "obvious that Chubb

---

45. CNA Group includes the MGIC book.

46. Western Employers' business has been assumed by Great American.

47. See discussion supra section 19.12.

is handling a larger portion of the small and medium size account."[48]

Wyatt measured market shares of excess insurers by policy count and estimated premium volume, with the following results.

EXCESS INSURERS

Company	Policy Count		Estimated Premiums	
	Rank	Percentage	Rank	Percentage
AIG	1	17.9%	2	18.8%
Chubb	2	15.7%	3	12.7%
A.C.E.	3	11.2%	1	18.8%
St. Paul	4	7.5%	8	3.3%
Continental	5	6.8%	10	2.6%
X.L. Ins. Co.	7	5.5%	6	7.0%
INA	8	5.3%	11	2.0%
Lloyd's & Brit.	9	4.9%	9	2.9%
DOLI & Aegis	10	4.3%	5	7.6%
Oed Republic	11	2.9%	18	0.7%
Crum & Forster	12	2.7%	19	0.7%
Electric Ins. Mut.	13	1.7%	4	8.5%
CNA	14	1.5%	15	1.0%
Western Emp.	16	1.4%	24	0.3%
BICL	17	1.2%	12	1.4%
CODA	18	1.0%	15	1.0%
Oil Cas. Ins. Co.			7	4.3%

Wyatt reports that five of the ten leading excess insurers, by premium volume, are policyholder formed insurers which account for almost 50% of the premiums on all excess policies. A.C.E. shows up as the leading excess insurer in a virtual tie with American International Group.[49]

§ 22.09. Fiduciary liability claims and payments.

The 1987 Wyatt Survey represents the seventh time information has been gathered about fiduciary liability. The claim information is for a nine-year period beginning in 1977 and

---

48. Wyatt Survey 106.
49. Id.

going through 1985. The participants in the survey made the following report on claims disposition:

> Closed
> > by litigation   21.8%
> > by settlement   37.2%
> > dropped by claimant   5.1%
> Open
> > still awaiting trial   30.8%
> > tried, but on appeal   3.8%
> No information   1.3%

The principal allegations made in the reported claims were:

> Denial of benefits   44.9%
> Administrative error   17.9%
> Improper advice or counsel   12.8%
> Misleading representation   6.4%
> Wrongful termination of plan   5.1%
> Civil rights   5.1%
> Collusion or conspiracy to   2.6%
> defraud
> Failure to fund programs   2.6%
> Conflict of interest   1.3%
> Imprudent investment   1.3%

The sources of the fiduciary liability claims were:

> Employees or former employees 96.2%
> Others   3.8%

Forty-four percent of the claims were closed without any payment to the claimant, 8% involved payments in excess of $500,000 and 2% over $1 million.

The highest defense cost reported was $327,261. The overall average defense cost was $51,561, which was about 8% of the average cost of defending a D & O claim.[50]

---

50. Id. 127.

§ 22.10. Fiduciary liability insurance: prevalence and premiums.

The Wyatt Survey points out that fiduciary liability insurance is written to cover the fiduciaries of a corporate pension plan, profit sharing plan, thrift plan, or other employee benefit plan of any nature, against legal liability arising out of their role as fiduciaries,[51] including the cost of legal defense against claims seeking to establish such liability.[52] Such insurance is carried by 79.3% of the survey participants, in some form, mostly by separate fiduciary liability policies. Only one company carried limits of $100 million and no reports of limits higher than that were made. The survey reports that limits have been reduced in the interval between the 1984 and 1987 surveys, by an average of 15%. About half of those reporting carried limits of less than $10 million.[53]

Deductibles ranged from none to $5 million with 40.8% reporting no deductible and 4.2% reporting deductibles of $100,000 or more.[54]

Premiums for fiduciary liability insurance rose sharply between 1984 and 1987 but not nearly to the extent of D & O premiums. The survey estimated the average fiduciary liability premium increase to be 264% in that period.[55] In the case of excess liability premiums for fiduciary coverage the average increase was about 587%, from an average of $617 per million in 1984 to an average of $4,235 per million in 1987.[56]

§ 22.11. Fiduciary liability insurance: the leading carriers.

The market shares of fiduciary liability insurance carriers were measured in the Wyatt Survey by reported policy count

---

51. See discussion supra in Chapter 9.
52. Wyatt Survey 129.
53. Id. 133.
54. Id. 140.
55. Id. 141.
56. Id. 142.

and by estimates of premium volume based on those reports
with the following results for primary and excess carriers.[57]

PRIMARY INSURERS

Company	Policy Count		Estimated Premiums	
	Rank	Percentage	Rank	Percentage
Chubb	1	36.2%	2	26.8%
AIG	2	20.6%	1	41.5%
Aetna	3	19.4%	4	10.8%
CNA	4	5.0%	6	1.1%
Lloyd's & Brit.	5	4.9%	5	3.1%
DOLI & Aegis	6	3.3%	3	12.8%

EXCESS INSURERS

Company	Policy Count		Estimated Premiums	
	Rank	Percentage	Rank	Percentage
Chubb	1	29.9%	2	30.3%
AIG	2	17.8%	1	31.8%
Aetna	3	16.8%	3	17.7%
DOLI-Aegis	4	5.6%	7	2.1%
Lloyd's and Brit.	5	4.7%	8	2.0%

---

57. Id. 156-57.

APPENDICES

Appendix A

SELECTED STATE STATUTES

California
Delaware
Florida
Indiana
New York
Ohio
Virginia
Wisconsin

Appendix B-1

STATUTES LIMITING DIRECTOR LIABILITY

Chart

Appendix B-2

INDEMNIFICATION STATUTES

Key
Chart

Appendix C

SELECTED INSURANCE FORMS

National Union Fire Insurance Company
   Directors and Officers Legal Liability Application
National Union Fire Insurance Company
   Directors and Officers Liability and Organization Reimbursement Appli-
   cation
National Union Fire Insurance Company
   Directors and Officers Liability and Corporation Reimbursement Policy
   American International Global Extension Endorsement
Chubb Group of Insurance Companies
   Application for Executive Liability and Indemnification Policy
Chubb Group of Insurance Companies
   Declarations; Executive Liability and Indemnification Policy
DOLI, Ltd.
   Directors and Officers Liability Insurance Policy

Appendix D-1

SAMPLE CHARTER OR BYLAW INDEMNIFICATION PROVISION

Delaware

Appendix D-2

SAMPLE INDEMNITY AGREEMENT

Delaware

Appendix E

SAMPLE STATEMENT OF SELF-INSURANCE

Ohio

Appendix A
SELECTED STATE STATUTES

CALIFORNIA

Corporations Code

§ 204. Articles of incorporation: Optional provisions.

The articles of incorporation may set forth:

***

(10) Provisions eliminating or limiting the personal liability of a director for monetary damages in an action brought by or in the right of the corporation for breach of a director's duties to the corporation and its shareholders, as set forth in Section 309, provided, however, that (A) such a provision may not eliminate or limit the liability of directors (i) for acts or omissions that involve intentional misconduct or a knowing and culpable violation of law, (ii) for acts or omissions that a director believes to be contrary to the best interests of the corporation or its shareholders or that involve the absence of good faith on the part of the director, (iii) for any transaction from which a director derived an improper personal benefit, (iv) for acts or omissions that show a reckless disregard for the director's duty to the corporation or its shareholders in circumstances in which the director was aware, or should have been aware, in the ordinary course of performing a director's duties, of a risk of serious injury to the corporation or its shareholders, (v) for acts or omissions that constitute an unexcused pattern of inattention that amounts to an abdication of the director's duty to the corporation or its shareholders, (vi) under Section 310, or (vii) under Section 316, (B) no such provision shall eliminate or limit the liability of a director for any act or omission occurring prior to the date when the provision becomes effective, and (C) no such provision shall eliminate or limit the liability of an officer for any act or omission as an officer, notwithstanding that the officer is also a director or that his or her actions, if negligent or improper, have been ratified by the directors.

(11) A provision authorizing, whether by bylaw, agreement, or otherwise, the indemnification of agents (as defined in Section 317) in excess of that expressly permitted by Section 317 for those agents of the corporation for breach of duty to the corporation and its stockholders, provided, however, that the provision may not provide for indemnification of any agent for any acts or omissions or transactions from which a director may not be relieved of liability as set forth in the exception to paragraph (10) or as to circumstances in which indemnity is expressly prohibited by Section 317.

Notwithstanding this subdivision, in the case of a close corporation any of the provisions referred to above may be validly included in a share-

763

holders' agreement. Notwithstanding this subdivision, bylaws may require for all or any actions by the board the affirmative vote of a majority of the authorized number of directors. Nothing contained in this subdivision shall affect the enforceability, as between the parties thereto, of any lawful agreement not otherwise contrary to public policy.

***

§ 204.5. Wording of provision eliminating or limiting personal liability of directors for monetary damages in action for breach of duties.

If the articles of a corporation include a provision reading substantially as follows: "The liability of the directors of the corporation for monetary damages shall be eliminated to the fullest extent permissible under California law"; the corporation shall be considered to have adopted a provision as authorized by paragraph (10) of subdivision (a) of Section 204 and more specific wording shall not be required.

(b) This section shall not be construed as setting forth the exclusive method of adopting an article provision as authorized by paragraph (10) of subdivision (a) of Section 204 and more specific wording shall not be required.

(c) This section shall not change the otherwise applicable standards or duties to make full and fair disclosure to shareholders when approval of such a provision is sought.

§ 207. Corporate powers.

Subject to any limitations contained in the articles and to compliance with other provisions of this division and any other applicable laws, a corporation shall have all of the powers of a natural person in carrying out its business activities, including, without limitation, the power to:

***

(f) Pay pensions, and establish and carry out pension, profit-sharing, share bonus, share purchase, share option, savings, thrift and other retirement, incentive and benefit plans, trusts and provisions for any or all of the directors, officers and employees of the corporation or any of its subsidiary or affiliated corporations, and to indemnify and purchase and maintain insurance on behalf of any fiduciary of such plans, trusts or provisions.

§ 309. Directors and officers to exercise powers in good faith: Liability.

(a) A director shall perform the duties of a director, including duties as a member of any committee of the board upon which the director may serve, in good faith, in a manner such director believes to be in the best interests of the corporation and with such care, including reasonable inquiry, as an ordinarily prudent person in a like position would use under similar circumstances.

(b) In performing the duties of a director, a director shall be entitled to rely on information, opinions, reports or statements, including financial statements and other financial data, in each case prepared or presented by any of the following:

(1) One or more officers or employees of the corporation whom the director believes to be reliable and competent in the matters presented.

(2) Counsel, independent accountants or other persons as to matters which the director believes to be within such person's professional or expert competence.

(3) A committee of the board upon which the director does not serve, as to matters within its designated authority, which committee the director believes to merit confidence, so long as, in any such case, the director acts in good faith, after reasonable inquiry when the need therefor is indicated by the circumstances and without knowledge that would cause such reliance to be unwarranted.

(c) A person who performs the duties of a director in accordance with subdivisions (a) and (b) shall have no liability based upon any alleged failure to discharge the person's obligations as a director. In addition, the liability of a director for monetary damages may be eliminated or limited in a corporation's articles to the extent provided in paragraph (10) of subdivision (a) of Section 204.

§ 310. Contract or transaction in which one or more directors has material financial interest: Validity: Mere common directorship as not constituting material financial interest: Quorum.

(a) No contract or other transaction between a corporation and one or more of its directors, or between a corporation and any corporation, firm or association in which one or more of its directors has a material financial interest, is either void or voidable because such director or directors or such other corporation, firm or association are parties or because such director or directors are present at the meeting of the board or a committee thereof which authorizes, approves or ratifies the contract or transaction, if

(1) The material facts as to the transaction and as to such director's interest are fully disclosed or known to the shareholders and such contract or transaction is approved by the shareholders (Section 153) in good faith, with the shares owned by the interested director or directors not being entitled to vote thereon, or

(2) The material facts as to the transaction and as to such director's interest are fully disclosed or known to the board or committee, and the board or committee authorizes, approves or ratifies the contract or transaction in good faith by a vote sufficient without counting the vote of the

interested director or directors and the contract or transactions is just and reasonable as to the corporation at the time it is authorized, approved or ratified, or

(3) As to contracts or transactions not approved as provided in paragraph (1) or (2) of this subdivision, the person asserting the validity of the contract or transaction sustains the burden of proving that the contract or transaction was just and reasonable as to the corporation at the time it was authorized, approved or ratified.

A mere common directorship does not constitute a material financial interest within the meaning of this subdivision. A director is not interested within the meaning of this subdivision in a resolution fixing the compensation of another director as a director, officer or employee of the corporation, notwithstanding the fact that the first director is also receiving compensation from the corporation.

(b) No contract or other transaction between a corporation and any corporation or association of which one or more of its directors are directors is either void or voidable because such director or directors are present at the meeting of the board or a committee thereof which authorizes, approves or ratifies the contract or transaction, if

(1) the material facts as to the transaction and as to such director's other directorship are fully disclosed or known to the board or committee, and the board or committee authorizes, approves or ratifies the contract or transaction in good faith by a vote sufficient without counting the vote of the common director or directors or the contract or transaction is approved by the shareholders (Section 153) in good faith, or

(2) As to contracts or transactions not approved as provided in paragraph (1) of this subdivision, the contract or transaction is just and reasonable as to the corporation at the time it is authorized, approved or ratified.

This subdivision does not apply to contracts or transactions covered by subdivision (a).

(c) Interested or common directors may be counted in determining the presence of a quorum at a meeting of the board or a committee thereof which authorizes, approves or ratifies a contract or transaction.

§ 316. Joint and several liability of directors approving certain corporate actions: Damages: Contributions and subrogation.

(a) Subject to the provisions of Section 309, directors of a corporation who approve any of the following corporate actions shall be jointly and severally liable to the corporation for the benefit of all the creditors or shareholders entitled to institute an action under subdivision (c):

(1) The making of any distribution to its shareholders to the extent that it is contrary to the provisions of Section 500 through 503, inclusive.

(2) The distribution of assets to shareholders after institution of dissolution proceedings of the corporation, without paying or adequately providing

for all known liabilities of the corporation, excluding any claims not filed by creditors within the time limit set by the court in a notice given to creditors under Chapters 18 (commencing with Section 1800), 19 (commencing with Section 1900) and 20 (commencing with Section 2000).

(3) The making of any loan or guaranty contrary to Section 315.

(b) A director who is present at a meeting of the board, or any committee thereof, at which action specified in subdivision (a) is taken and who abstains from voting shall be considered to have approved the action.

(c) Suit may be brought in the name of the corporation to enforce the liability (1) under paragraph (1) of subdivision (a) against any or all directors liable by the persons entitled to sue under subdivision (b) of Section 506, (2) under paragraph (2) or (3) of subdivision (a) against any or all directors liable by any one or more creditors of the corporation whose debts or claims arose prior to the time of any of the corporate actions specified in paragraph (2) or (3) of subdivision (a) and who have not consented to the corporate action, whether or not they have reduced their claims to judgment, or (3) under paragraph (3) of subdivision (a) against any or all directors liable by any one or more holders of shares outstanding at the time of any corporate action specified in paragraph (3) of subdivision (a) who have not consented to the corporate action, without regard to the provisions of Section 800.

(d) The damages recoverable from a director under this section shall be the amount of the illegal distribution or the loss suffered by the corporation as a result of the illegal loan or guaranty, as the case may be, but not exceeding the liabilities of the corporation owed to nonconsenting creditors at the time of the violation and the injury suffered by nonconsenting shareholders, as the case may be.

(e) Any director sued under this section may implead all other directors liable and may compel contribution, either in that action or in an independent action against directors not joined in that action.

(f) Directors liable under this section shall also be entitled to be subrogated to the rights of the corporation:

(1) With respect to paragraph (1) of subdivision (a), against shareholders who received the distribution.

(2) With respect to paragraph (2) of subdivision (a), against shareholders who received the distribution of assets.

(3) With respect to paragraph (3) of subdivision (a), against the person who received the loan or guaranty.

Any director sued under this section may file a cross-complaint against the person or persons who are liable to such director as a result of the subrogation provided for in this subdivision or may proceed against them in an independent action.

767

§ 317. Indemnification of agent of corporation as party to threatened, pending or completed action: Liability insurance: Inapplicability of provisions to proceeding against trustee, investment manager, etc.

(a) For the purposes of this section, "agent" means any person who is or was a director, officer, employee or other agent of the corporation, or is or was serving at the request of the corporation as a director, officer, employee or agent of another foreign or domestic corporation, partnership, joint venture, trust or other enterprise, or was a director, officer, employee or agent of a foreign or domestic corporation which was a predecessor corporation of the corporation or of another enterprise at the request of such predecessor corporation; "proceeding" means any threatened, pending or completed action or proceeding, whether civil, criminal, administrative or investigative; and "expenses" includes without limitation attorneys' fees and any expenses of establishing a right to indemnification under subdivision (d) or paragraph (3) of subdivision (e).

(b) A corporation shall have power to indemnify any person who was or is a party or is threatened to be made a party to any proceeding (other than an action by or in the right of the corporation to procure a judgment in its favor) by reason of the fact that such person is or was an agent of the corporation, against expenses, judgments, fines, settlements and other amounts actually and reasonably incurred in connection with such proceeding if such person acted in good faith and in a manner such person reasonably believed to be in the best interests of the corporation and, in the case of a criminal proceeding, had no reasonable cause to believe the conduct of such person was unlawful. The termination of any proceeding by judgment, order, settlement, conviction or upon a plea of nolo contendere or its equivalent shall not, of itself, create a presumption that the person did not act in good faith and in a manner which the person reasonably believed to be in the best interests of the corporation or that the person had reasonable cause to believe that the person's conduct was unlawful.

(c) A corporation shall have power to indemnify any person who was or is a party or is threatened to be made a party to any threatened, pending or completed action by or in the right of the corporation to procure a judgment in its favor by reason of the fact that such person is or was an agent of the corporation, against expenses actually and reasonably incurred by such person in connection with the defense or settlement of such action if such person acted in good faith, in a manner such person believed to be in the best interests of the corporation and its shareholders.

No indemnification shall be made under this subdivision for any of the following:

(1) In respect of any claim, issue or matter as to which such person shall have been adjudged to be liable to the corporation in the performance of such person's duty to the corporation and its shareholders, unless and only

to the extent that the court in which such proceeding is or was pending shall determine upon application that, in view of all the circumstances of the case, such person is fairly and reasonably entitled to indemnity for expenses and then only to the extent that the court shall determine.

(2) Of amounts paid in settling or otherwise disposing of a pending action without court approval.

(3) Of expenses incurred in defending a pending action which is settled or otherwise disposed of without court approval.

(d) To the extent that an agent of a corporation has been successful on the merits in defense of any proceeding referred to in subdivision (b) or (c) or in defense of any claim, issue or matter therein, the agent shall be indemnified against expenses actually and reasonably incurred by the agent in connection therewith.

(e) Except as provided in subdivision (d), any indemnification under this section shall be made by the corporation only if authorized in the specific case, upon a determination that indemnification of the agent is proper in the circumstances because the agent has met the applicable standard of conduct set forth in subdivision (b) or (c), by any of the following:

(1) A majority vote of a quorum consisting of directors who are not parties to such proceeding.

(2) If such a quorum of directors is not obtainable, by independent legal counsel in a written opinion.

(3) Approval of the shareholders (Section 153), with the shares owned by the person to be indemnified not being entitled to vote thereon.

(4) The court in which such proceeding is or was pending upon application made by the corporation or the agent or the attorney or other person rendering services in connection with the defense, whether or not such application by the agent, attorney or other person is opposed by the corporation.

(f) Expenses incurred in defending any proceeding may be advanced by the corporation prior to the final disposition of such proceeding upon receipt of an undertaking by or on behalf of the agent to repay such amount if it shall be determined ultimately that the agent is not entitled to be indemnified as authorized in this section.

(g) The indemnification provided by this section shall not be deemed exclusive of any other rights to which those seeking indemnification may be entitled under any bylaw, agreement, vote of shareholders or disinterested directors or otherwise, both as to action in an official capacity and as to action in another capacity while holding such office, to the extent such additional rights to indemnification are authorized in the articles of the corporation. The rights to indemnity hereunder shall continue as to a person who has ceased to be a director, officer, employee, or agent and shall inure to the benefit of the heirs, executors, and administrators of the person. Nothing contained in this section shall affect any right to indemnification to which persons other than such directors and officers may be entitled by contract or otherwise.

(h) No indemnification or advance shall be made under this section, except as provided in subdivision (d) or paragraph (3) of subdivision (e), in any circumstance where it appears:

(1) That it would be inconsistent with a provision of the articles, bylaws, a resolution of the shareholders or an agreement in effect at the time at the accrual of the alleged cause of action asserted in the proceeding in which the expenses were incurred or other amounts were paid, which prohibits or otherwise limits indemnification.

(2) That it would be inconsistent with any condition expressly imposed by a court in approving a settlement.

(i) A corporation shall have power to purchase and maintain insurance on behalf of any agent of the corporation against any liability asserted against or incurred by the agent in such capacity or arising out of the agent's status as such whether or not the corporation would have the power to indemnify the agent against such liability under the provisions of this section. The fact that a corporation owns all or a portion of the shares of the company issuing a policy of insurance shall not render this subdivision inapplicable if either of the following conditions are satisfied: (1) if authorized in the articles of the corporation, any policy issued is limited to the extent provided by subdivision (d) of Section 204; or (2) (A) the company issuing the insurance policy is organized, licensed, and operated in a manner that complies with the insurance laws and regulations applicable to its jurisdiction of organization, (B) the company issuing the policy provides procedures for processing claims that do not permit that company to be subject to the direct control of the corporation that purchased that policy, and (C) the policy issued provides for some manner of risk sharing between the issuer and purchaser of the policy, on one hand, and some unaffiliated person or persons, on the other, such as by providing for more than one unaffiliated owner of the company issuing the policy or by providing that a portion of the coverage furnished will be obtained from some unaffiliated insurer or reinsurer.

(j) This section does not apply to any proceeding against any trustee, investment manager or other fiduciary of an employee benefit plan in such person's capacity as such, even though such person may also be an agent as defined in subdivision (a) of the employer corporation. A corporation shall have power to indemnify such a trustee, investment manager or other fiduciary to the extent permitted by subdivision (f) of Section 207.

DELAWARE

General Corporation Law (Title 8)

§ 102. Contents of certificate of incorporation.

(a) The certificate of incorporation shall set forth:

* * *

(b) In addition to the matters required to be set forth in the certificate of incorporation by subsection (a) of this section, the certificate of incorporation may also contain any or all of the following matters:

* * *

(7) A provision eliminating or limiting the personal liability of a director to the corporation or its stockholders for monetary damages for breach of fiduciary duty as a director, provided that such provision shall not eliminate or limit the liability of a director: (i) For any breach of the director's duty of loyalty to the corporation or its stockholders; (ii) for acts or omissions not in good faith or which involve intentional misconduct or a knowing violation of law; (iii) under section 174 of this title; or (iv) for any transaction from which the director derived an improper personal benefit. No such provision shall eliminate or limit the liability of a director for any act or omission occurring prior to the date when such provision becomes effective. All references in this subsection to a director shall also be deemed to refer to a member of the governing body of a corporation which is not authorized to issue capital stock.

§ 144. Interested directors; quorum.

(a) No contract or transaction between a corporation and 1 or more of its directors or officers, or between a corporation and any other corporation, partnership, association, or other organization in which 1 or more of its directors or officers, are directors or officers, or have a financial interest, shall be void or voidable solely for this reason, or solely because the director or officer is present at or participates in the meeting of the board or committee which authorizes the contract or transaction, or solely because his or their votes are counted for such purpose, if:

(1) The material facts as to his relationship or interest and as to the contract or transaction are disclosed or are known to the board of directors or the committee, and the board or committee in good faith authorizes the contract or transaction by the affirmative votes of a majority of the disinterested directors, even though the disinterested directors be less than a quorum; or

(2) The material facts as to his relationship or interest and as to the contract or transaction are disclosed or are known to the shareholders

771

entitled to vote thereon, and the contract or transaction is specifically approved in good faith by vote of the shareholders; or

(3) The contract or transaction is fair as to the corporation as of the tie it is authorized, approved or ratified, by the board of directors, a committee or the shareholders.

(b) Common or interested directors may be counted in determining the presence of a quorum at a meeting of the board of directors or of a committee which authorizes the contract or transaction.

§ 145. Indemnification ***; insurance.

(a) A corporation may indemnify any person who was or is a party or is threatened to be made a party to any threatened, pending or completed action, suit or proceeding, whether civil, criminal, administrative or investigative (other than an action by or in the right of the corporation) by reason of the fact that he is or was a director, officer, employee or agent of the corporation, or is or was serving at the request of the corporation as a director, officer, employee or agent of agent of another corporation, partnership, joint venture, trust or other enterprise, against expenses (including attorneys' fees), judgments, fines and amounts paid in settlement actually and reasonably incurred by him in connection with such action, suit or proceeding if he acted in good faith and in a manner he reasonably believed to be in or not opposed to the best interests of the corporation, and, with respect to any criminal action or proceeding, had no reasonable cause to believe his conduct was unlawful. The termination of any action, suit or proceeding by judgment, order, settlement, conviction, or upon a plea of nolo contendere or its equivalent, shall not, of itself, create a presumption that the person did not act in good faith and in a manner which he reasonably believed to be in or not opposed to the best interests of the corporation, and, with respect to any criminal action or proceeding, had reasonable cause to believe that his conduct was unlawful.

(b) A corporation may indemnify any person who was or is a party or is threatened to be made a party to any threatened, pending or completed action or suit by or in the right of the corporation to procure a judgment in its favor by reason of the fact that he is or was a director, officer, employee or agent of the corporation, or is or was serving at the request of the corporation as a director, officer, employee or agent of another corporation, partnership, joint venture, trust or other enterprise against expenses (including attorneys' fees) actually and reasonably incurred by him in connection with the defense or settlement of such action or suit if he acted in good faith and in a manner he reasonably believed to be in or not opposed to the best interests of the corporation and except that no indemnification shall be made in respect of any claim, issue or matter as to which such person shall have been adjudged to be liable to the corporation unless and only to the extent that the Court of Chancery or the court in which such action or suit

772

was brought shall determine upon application that, despite the adjudication of liability but in view of all the circumstances of the case, such person is fairly and reasonably entitled to indemnity for such expenses which the Court of Chancery or such other court shall deem proper.

(c) To the extent that a director, officer, employee or agent of a corporation has been successful on the merits or otherwise in defense of any action, suit or proceeding referred to in subsections (a) and (b) of this section, or in defense of any claim, issue or matter therein, he shall be indemnified against expenses (including attorneys' fees) actually and reasonably incurred by him in connection therewith.

(d) Any indemnification under subsections (a) and (b) of this section (unless ordered by a court) shall be made by the corporation only as authorized in the specific case upon a determination that indemnification of the director, officer, employee or agent is proper in the circumstances because he has met the applicable standard of conduct set forth in subsections (a) and (b) of this section. Such determination shall be made (1) by the board of directors by a majority vote of a quorum consisting of directors who were not parties to such action, suit or proceeding, or (2) if such a quorum is not obtainable, or, even if obtainable a quorum of disinterested directors so directs, by independent legal counsel in a written opinion, or (3) by the stockholders.

(e) Expenses incurred by an officer or director in defending a civil or criminal action suit or proceeding may be paid by the corporation in advance of the final disposition of such action, suit or proceeding upon receipt of an undertaking by or on behalf of such director or officer to repay such amount if it shall ultimately be determined that he is not entitled to be indemnified by the corporation as authorized in this section. Such expenses incurred by other employees and agents may be so paid upon such terms and conditions, if any, as the board of directors deems appropriate.

(f) The indemnification and advancement of expenses provided by, or granted pursuant to, the other subsections of this section shall not be deemed exclusive of any other rights to which those seeking indemnification or advancement of expenses may be entitled under any bylaw, agreement, vote of stockholders or disinterested directors or otherwise, both as to action in his official capacity and as to action in another capacity while holding such office.

(g) A corporation shall have power to purchase and maintain insurance on behalf of any person who is or was a director, officer, employee or agent of the corporation, or is or was serving at the request of the corporation as a director, officer, employee or agent of another corporation, partnership, joint venture, trust or other enterprise against any liability asserted against him and incurred by him in any such capacity, or arising out of his status as such, whether or not the corporation would have the power to indemnify him against such liability under this section.

773

(h) For purposes of this section, references to "the corporation" shall include, in addition to the resulting corporation, any constituent corporation (including any constituent of a constituent) absorbed in a consolidation or merger which, if its separate existence had continued, would have had power and authority to indemnify its directors, officers, and employees or agents, so that any person who is or was a director, officer, employee or agent of such constituent corporation, or is or was serving at the request of such constituent corporation as a director, officer, employee or agent of another corporation, partnership, joint venture, trust or other enterprise, shall stand in the same position under this section with respect to the resulting or surviving corporation as he would have with respect to such constituent corporation if its separate existence had continued.

(i) For purposes of this section, references to "other enterprises" shall include employee benefit plans; references to "fines" shall include any excise taxes assessed on a person with respect to any employee benefit plan; and references to "serving at the request of the corporation" shall include any service as a director, officer, employee or agent of the corporation which imposes duties on, or involves services by, such director, officer, employee, or agent with respect to an employee benefit plan, its participants or beneficiaries; and a person who acted in good faith and in a manner he reasonably believed to be in the interest of the participants and beneficiaries of an employee benefit plan shall be deemed to have acted in a manner "not opposed to the best interests of the corporation" as referred to in this section.

(j) The indemnification and advancement of expenses provided by, or granted pursuant to, this section shall, unless otherwise provided when authorized or ratified, continue as to a person who has ceased to be a director, officer, employee or agent and shall inure to the benefit of the heirs, executors and administrators of such a person.

§ 174. Liability of directors for unlawful [distributions], etc.

(a) In case of any willful or negligent violation of § 160 or 173 of this title, the directors under whose administration the same may happen shall be jointly and severally liable, at any time within 6 years after paying such unlawful dividend or after such unlawful stock purchase or redemption, to the corporation, and to its creditors in the event of its dissolution or insolvency, to the full amount of the dividend unlawfully paid, or to the full amount unlawfully paid for the purchase or redemption of the corporation's stock, with interest from the time such liability accrued. Any director who may have been absent when the same was done, or who may have dissented from the act or resolution by which the same was done, may exonerate himself from such liability by causing his dissent to be entered on the books containing the minutes of the proceedings of the directors at the time the same was done, or immediately after he has notice of the same.

(b) Any director against whom a claim is successfully asserted under this section shall be entitled to contribution from the other directors who voted for or concurred in the unlawful dividend, stock purchase or stock redemption.

(c) Any director against whom a claim is successfully asserted under this section shall be entitled, to the extent of the amount paid by him as a result of such claim, to be subrogated to the rights of the corporation against stockholders who received the dividend on, or assets for the sale or redemption of, their stock with knowledge of facts indicating that such dividend, stock purchase or redemption was unlawful under this chapter, in proportion to the amounts received by such stockholders respectively.

FLORIDA

General Corporation Act

§ 607.014. Indemnification of officers, directors, employees, and agents.

(1) A corporation shall have power to indemnify any person who was or is a party to any proceeding (other than an action by, or in the right of, the corporation), by reason of the fact that he is or was a director, officer, employee, or agent of the corporation or is or was serving at the request of the corporation as a director, officer, employee, or agent of another corporation, partnership, joint venture, trust, or other enterprise against liability incurred in connection with such proceeding, including any appeal thereof, if he acted in good faith and in a manner he reasonably believed to be in, or not opposed to, the best interests of the corporation and, with respect to any criminal action or proceeding, had no reasonable cause to believe his conduct was unlawful. The termination of any proceeding by judgment, order, settlement, or conviction or upon a plea of nolo contendere or its equivalent shall not, of itself, create a presumption that the person did not act in good faith and in a manner which he reasonably believed to be in, or not opposed to, the best interests of the corporation or, with respect to any criminal action or proceeding, had reasonable cause to believe that his conduct was unlawful.

(2) A corporation shall have power to indemnify any person, who was or is a party to any proceeding by or in the right of the corporation to procure a judgment in its favor by reason of the fact that he is or was a director, officer, employee, or agent of the corporation or is or was serving at the request of the corporation as a director, officer, employee, or agent of another corporation, partnership, joint venture, trust, or other enterprise, against expenses and amounts paid in settlement not exceeding, in the judgment of the board of directors, the estimated expense of litigating the proceeding to conclusion, actually and reasonably incurred in connection with the defense or settlement of such proceeding, including any appeal thereof. Such indemnification shall be authorized if such person acted in good faith and in a manner he reasonably believed to be in, or not opposed to, the best interests of the corporation, except that no indemnification shall be made under this subsection in respect of any claim, issue, or matter as to which such person shall have been adjudged to be liable unless, and only to the extent that, the court in which such proceeding was brought, or any other court of competent jurisdiction, shall determine upon application that, despite the adjudication of liability but in view of all circumstances of the case, such person is fairly and reasonably entitled to indemnity for such expenses which such court shall deem proper.

(3) To the extent that a director, officer, employee, or agent of a corporation has been successful on the merits or otherwise in defense of any pro-

776

ceeding referred to in subsection (1) or subsection (2), or in defense of any claim, issue, or matter therein, he shall be indemnified against expenses actually and reasonably incurred by him in connection therewith.

(4) Any indemnification under subsection (1) or subsection (2), unless pursuant to a determination by a court, shall be made by the corporation only as authorized in the specific case upon a determination that indemnification of the director, officer, employee, or agent is proper in the circumstances because he has met the applicable standard of conduct set forth in subsection (1) or subsection (2). Such determination shall be made:

(a) By the board of directors by a majority vote of a quorum consisting of directors who were not parties to such proceeding;

(b) If such a quorum is not obtainable or, even if obtainable, by majority vote of a committee duly designated by the board of directors (in which directors who are parties may participate) consisting solely of two or more directors not at the time parties to the proceeding;

(c) By independent legal counsel:

1. Selected by the board of directors prescribed in paragraph (a) or the committee prescribed in paragraph (b); or

2. If a quorum of the directors cannot be obtained for paragraph (a) and the committee cannot be designated under paragraph (b), selected by majority vote of the full board of directors (in which directors who are parties may participate); or

(d) By the shareholders by a majority vote of a quorum consisting of shareholders who were not parties to such proceeding or, if no such quorum is obtainable, by a majority vote of shareholders who were not parties to such proceeding.

(5) Evaluation of the reasonableness of expenses and authorization of indemnification shall be made in the same manner as the determination that indemnification is permissible. However, if the determination of permissibility is made by independent legal counsel, persons specified by paragraph (4)(c) shall evaluate the reasonableness of expenses and may authorize indemnification.

(6) Expenses incurred by an officer or director in defending a civil or criminal proceeding may be paid by the corporation in advance of the final disposition of such proceeding upon receipt of an undertaking by or on behalf of such director or officer to repay such amount if he is ultimately found not to be entitled to indemnification by the corporation pursuant to this section. Expenses incurred by other employees and agents may be paid in advance upon such terms or conditions that the board of directors deems appropriate.

(7) The indemnification and advancement of expenses provided pursuant to this section are not exclusive, and a corporation may make any other or further indemnification or advancement of expenses of any of its directors, officers, employees, or agents, under any bylaw, agreement, vote of shareholders or disinterested directors, or otherwise, both as to action in his

official capacity and as to action in another capacity while holding such office. However, indemnification or advancement of expenses shall not be made to or on behalf of any director, officer, employee, or agent if a judgment or other final adjudication establishes that his actions, or omissions to act, were material to the cause of action so adjudicated and constitute.

(a) A violation of the criminal law, unless the director, officer, employee, or agent had reasonable cause to believe his conduct was lawful or had no reasonable cause to believe his conduct was unlawful;

(b) A transaction from which the director, officer, employee, or agent derived an improper personal benefit;

(c) In the case of a director, a circumstance under which the liability provisions of s. 607.144 are applicable; or

(d) Willful misconduct or a conscious disregard for the best interests of the corporation in a proceeding by or in the right of the corporation to procure a judgment in its favor or in a proceeding by or in the right of a shareholder.

(8) Indemnification and advancement of expenses as provided in this section shall continue as, unless otherwise provided when authorized or ratified, to a person who has ceased to be a director, officer, employee, or agent and shall inure to the benefit of the heirs, executors, and administrators of such a person, unless otherwise provide when authorized or ratified.

(9) Unless the corporation's articles of incorporation provide otherwise, notwithstanding the failure of a corporation to provide indemnification, and despite any contrary determination of the board or of the shareholders in the specific case, a director, officer, employee, or agent of the corporation who is or was a party to a proceeding may apply for indemnification or advancement of expenses, or both, to the court conducting the proceeding, to the circuit court, or to another court of competent jurisdiction. On receipt of an application, the court, after giving any notice that it considers necessary, may order indemnification and advancement of expenses, including expenses incurred in seeking court-ordered indemnification or advancement of expenses, if it determines that:

(a) The director, officer, employee, or agent is entitled to mandatory indemnification under subsection (3), in which case the court shall also order the corporation to pay the director reasonable expenses incurred in obtaining court-ordered indemnification or advancement of expenses;

(b) The director, officer, employee, or agent is entitled to indemnification or advancement of expenses, or both, by virtue of the exercise by the corporation of its power pursuant to subsection (7); or

(c) The director, officer, employee, or agent is fairly and reasonably entitled to indemnification or advancement of expenses, or both, in view of all the relevant circumstances, regardless of whether such person met the standard of conduct set forth in subsection (1), subsection (2), or subsection (7).

(10) For purposes of this section, the term "corporation" includes, in addition to the resulting corporation, any constituent corporation (including any constituent of a constituent) absorbed in a consolidation or merger, so that any person who is or was a director, officer, employee, or agent of a constituent corporation, or is or was serving at the request of a constituent corporation as a director, officer, employee, or agent of another corporation, partnership, joint venture, trust, or other enterprise, is in the same position under this section with respect to the resulting or surviving corporation as he would have with respect to such constituent corporation if its separate existence had continued.

(11) For purposes of this section:

(a) The term "other enterprises" includes employee benefit plans;

(b) The term "expenses" includes counsel fees, including those for appeal;

(c) The term "liability" includes obligations to pay a judgment, settlement, penalty, fine (including an excise tax assessed with respect to any employee benefit plan), and expenses actually and reasonably incurred with respect to a proceeding;

(d) The term "proceeding" includes any threatened, pending, or completed action, suit, or other type of proceeding, whether civil, criminal, administrative, or investigative and whether formal or informal;

(e) The term "agent" includes a volunteer;

(f) The term "serving at the request of the corporation" includes any service as a director, officer, employee, or agent of the corporation that imposes duties on such persons, including duties relating to an employee benefit plan and its participants or beneficiaries; and

(g) The term "not opposed to the best interest of the corporation" describes the actions of a person who acts in good faith and in a manner he reasonably believes to be in the best interests of the participants and beneficiaries of an employee benefit plan.

(12) A corporation shall have power to purchase and maintain insurance on behalf of any person who is or was a director, officer, employee, or agent of the corporation or is or was serving at the request of the corporation as a director, officer, employee, or agent of another corporation, partnership, joint venture, trust, or other enterprise against any liability asserted against him and incurred by him in any such capacity or arising out of his status as such, whether or not the corporation would have the power to indemnify him against such liability under the provisions of this section.

(13) If any expenses or other amounts are paid by way of indemnification otherwise than by court order or action by the shareholders or by an insurance carrier pursuant to insurance maintained by the corporation, the corporation shall, not later than the time of delivery to shareholders of written notice of the next annual meeting of shareholders, unless such meeting is held within 3 months from the date of such payment, and, in any event, within 15 months from the date of such payment, deliver either

personally or by mail to each shareholder of record at the time entitled to vote for the election of directors a statement specifying the persons paid, the amounts paid, and the nature and status at the time of such payment of the litigation or threatened litigation.

§ 607.111. Board of directors; exercise of corporate powers.

(1) All corporate powers shall be exercised by or under the authority of, and the business and affairs of a corporation shall be managed under the direction of, a board of directors, except as may be otherwise provided in this chapter or in the articles of incorporation. If any such provision is made in the articles of incorporation, the powers and duties conferred or imposed upon the board of directors by this chapter shall be exercised or performed to such extent and by such person or persons as shall be provided in the articles of incorporation.

***

(4) A director shall perform his duties as a director, including his duties as a member of any committee of the board upon which he may serve, in good faith, in a manner he reasonably believes to be in the best interests of the corporation, and with such care as an ordinarily prudent person in a like position would use under similar circumstances.

(5) In performing his duties, a director shall be entitled to rely on information, opinions, reports, or statements, including financial statements and other financial data, in each case prepared or presented by:

(a) One or more officers or employees of the corporation whom the director reasonably believes to be reliable and competent in the matters presented.

(b) Counsel, public accountants, or other persons as to matters which the director reasonably believes to be within such persons' professional or expert competence.

(c) A committee of the board upon which he does not serve, duly designated in accordance with a provision of the articles of incorporation or the bylaws, as to matters within its designated authority, which committee the director reasonably believes to merit confidence.

(6) A director shall not be considered to be acting in good faith if he has knowledge concerning the matter in question that would cause such reliance described in subsection (5) to be unwarranted.

(7) A person who performs his duties in compliance with this section shall have no liability by reason of being or having been a director of the corporation.

(8) A director of a corporation who is present at a meeting of its board of directors at which action on any corporate matter is taken shall be presumed to have assented to the action taken, unless he votes against such

780

action or abstains from voting in respect thereto because of an asserted conflict of interest.

§ 607.124. Director conflicts of interest.

(1) No contract or other transaction between a corporation and one or more of its directors or any other corporation, firm, association, or entity in which one or more of its directors are directors or officers or are financially interested shall be either void or voidable because of such relationship or interest, because such director or directors are present at the meeting of the board of directors or a committee thereof which authorizes, approves, or ratifies such contract or transaction, or because his or their votes are counted for such purpose, if:

(a) The fact of such relationship or interest is disclosed or known to the board of directors or committee which authorizes, approves, or ratifies the contract or transaction by a vote or consent sufficient for the purpose without counting the votes or consents of such interested directors;

(b) The fact of such relationship or interest is disclosed or known to the shareholders entitled to vote and they authorize, approve, or ratify such contract or transaction by vote or written consent; or

(c) The contract or transaction is fair and reasonable as to the corporation at the time it is authorized by the board, a committee, or the shareholders.

(2) Common or interested directors may be counted in determining the presence of a quorum at a meeting of the board of directors or a committee thereof which authorizes, approves, or ratifies such contract or transaction.

§ 607.144. Liabilities of directors in certain cases.

(1) In addition to any other liabilities, a director shall be liable in the following circumstances, unless he complies with the standard provided in this chapter for the performance of the duties of directors:

(a) A director of a corporation who votes for or assents to the declaration of any dividend or other distribution of the assets of a corporation to its shareholders contrary to the provisions of this chapter or contrary to any restrictions contained in the articles of incorporation shall be liable to the corporation, jointly and severally with all other directors so voting or assenting, for the amount of such dividend which is paid or the value of such assets which are distributed in excess of the amount of such dividend or distribution which could have been paid or distributed without a violation of the provisions of this chapter or the restrictions in the articles of incorporation, to the extent that any creditor or shareholder of the corporation has suffered damage as a result thereof.

(b) A director of a corporation who votes for or assents to the purchase of the corporation's own shares contrary to the provisions of this chapter shall be liable to the corporation, jointly and severally with all other directors so voting or assenting, for the amount of the consideration paid for such shares which is in excess of the maximum amount which could have been paid therefor without a violation of the provisions of this chapter, to the extent that any creditor or shareholder of the corporation has suffered damage as a result thereof.

(c) A director who votes for or assents to any distribution of assets of a corporation to its shareholders during the liquidation of the corporation without the payment and discharge of, or making adequate provision for, all known debts, obligations, and liabilities of the corporation shall be liable to the corporation, jointly and severally with all other directors so voting or assenting, for the value of such assets which are distributed, to the extent that such debts, obligations, and liabilities of the corporation are not thereafter paid and discharged.

(2) Any director against whom any claim shall be asserted under or pursuant to this section for the payment of a dividend or other distribution of assets of a corporation and who shall be held liable thereon shall be entitled to contribution from the shareholders who accepted or received any such dividends or assets knowing such dividend or distribution to have been made in violation of this chapter, in proportion to the amounts received by them respectively.

(3) Any director against whom any claim shall be asserted under or pursuant to this section shall be entitled to contribution from the other directors who voted for or assented to the action upon which the claim is asserted.

§ 607.1645. Liability of directors.

(1) A director is not personally liable for monetary damages to the corporation or any other person for any statement, vote, decision, or failure to act, regarding corporate management or policy, by a director, unless:

(a) The director breached or failed to perform his duties as a director; and

(b) The director's breach of, or failure to perform, those duties constitutes:

1. A violation of the criminal law, unless the director had reasonable cause to believe his conduct was lawful or had no reasonable cause to believe his conduct was unlawful. A judgment or other final adjudication against a director in any criminal proceeding for a violation of the criminal law estops that director from contesting the fact that his breach, or failure to perform, constitutes a violation of the criminal law; but does not estop the director from establishing that he had reasonable cause to believe that his conduct was lawful or had no reasonable cause to believe that his conduct was unlawful;

2. A transaction from which the director derived an improper personal benefit, either directly or indirectly;

3. A circumstance under which the liability provisions of s. 607.144 are applicable;

4. In a proceeding by or in the right of the corporation to procure a judgment in its favor or by or in the right of a shareholder, conscious disregard for the best interest of the corporation, or willful misconduct; or

5. In a proceeding by or in the right of someone other than the corporation or a shareholder, recklessness or an act or omission which was committed in bad faith or with malicious purpose or in a manner exhibiting wanton and willful disregard of human rights, safety, or property.

(2) For the purposes of this section, the term "recklessness" means the action, or omission to act, in conscious disregard of risk:

(a) Known, or so obvious that it should have been known, to the director; and

(b) Known to the director, or so obvious that it should have been known, to be so great as to make it highly probable that harm would follow from such action or omission.

§ 607.165. Director deemed not to have derived improper personal benefit.

(1) For purposes of ss. 607.014 and 607.1645, a director is deemed not to have derived an improper personal benefit from any transaction if the transaction and if the transaction and the nature of any personal benefit derived by the director are not prohibited by state or federal law or regulation and, without further limitation:

(a) In an action other than a derivative suit regarding a decision by the director to approve, reject, or otherwise affect the outcome of an offer to purchase the stock of, or to effect a merger of, the corporation, the transaction and the nature of any personal benefits derived by a director are disclosed or known to all directors voting on the matter, and the transaction was authorized, approved, or ratified by at least two directors who comprise a majority of the disinterested directors (whether or not such disinterested directors constitute a quorum);

(b) The transaction and the nature of any personal benefits derived by a director are disclosed or known to the shareholders entitled to vote, and the transaction was authorized, approved, or ratified by the affirmative vote or written consent of such shareholders who hold a majority of the shares, the voting of which is not controlled by directors who derived a personal benefit from other otherwise had a personal interest in the transaction; or

(c) The transaction was fair and reasonable to the corporation at the time it was authorized by the board, a committee, or the shareholders, notwithstanding that a director received a personal benefit.

783

(2) Common or interested directors may be counted in determining the presence of a quorum at a meeting of the board of directors which authorizes, approves, or ratifies such a transaction.

(3) The circumstances set forth in subsection (1) are not exclusive and do not preclude the existence of other circumstances under which a director will be deemed not to have derived an improper benefit.

(4) The provisions of this section shall also apply to officers of nonprofit organizations as provided in s. 617.0285.

§ 627.9122. Officers' and directors' liability claims; reports by insurers.

(1) Each insurer providing coverage for officers' and directors' liability coverage shall report to the Department of Insurance any claim or action for damages claimed to have been caused by error, omission, or negligence in the performance of the officer's or director's services, if the claim resulted in:

(a) A final judgment in any amount.

(b) A settlement in any amount.

(c) A final disposition not resulting in payment on behalf of the insured. Reports shall be filed with the department no later than 60 days following the occurrence of any event listed in paragraphs (a), (b), or (c).

(2) The reports required by subsection (1) shall contain:

(a) The name, address, and position held by the insured, and the type of corporation or organization, including classifications as provided in section 501 (c) of the Internal Revenue Code of 1986, as amended.

(b) The insured's policy number.

(c) The date of the occurrence which created the claim.

(d) The date the claim was reported to the insurer.

(e) The name of the injured person. This information shall be privileged and confidential and shall not be disclosed by the department without the consent of the injured person. This information may be used by the department for purposes of identifying multiple or duplicate claims arising out of the same occurrence.

(f) The date of suit, if filed.

(g) The total number and names of all defendants involved in the claim.

(h) The date and amount of judgment or settlement, together with a copy of the settlement or judgment.

(i) In the case of a settlement, such information as the department may require with regard to the claimant's anticipated future losses.

(j) The loss adjustment expense paid to defense counsel, and all other allocated loss adjustment expenses paid.

(k) The date and reason for final disposition, if no judgment or settlement.

(l) A summary of the occurrence which created the claim, which shall include:

1. Whether the injuries claimed were the result of physical damage to the claimant, were the result of damage to the reputation of the claimant, were based on self-dealing by the defendant, or were in the nature of a shareholder dispute.

2. A description of the type of activity which caused the injury.

3. The steps taken by the officers or directors to assure that similar occurrences are less likely in the future.

(m) Any other information required by the department to analyze and evaluate the nature, causes, costs, and damages involved in officers' and directors' liability cases.

(3) The department shall include a summary of this information in its annual report.

INDIANA

General Corporation Act

CHAPTER 35

STANDARDS OF CONDUCT FOR DIRECTORS

§ 23-1-35-1. Enumeration of conduct standards which avert personal liability.

(a) A director shall, based on facts then known to the director, discharge the duties as a director, including the director's duties as a member of a committee:

(1) In good faith;

(2) With the care an ordinarily prudent person in a like position would exercise under similar circumstances; and

(3) In a manner the director reasonably believes to be in the best interests of the corporation.

(b) In discharging the director's duties a director is entitled to rely on information, opinions, reports, or statements, including financial statements and other financial data, if prepared or presented by:

(1) One (1) or more officers or employees of the corporation whom the director reasonably believes to be reliable and competent in the matters presented;

(2) Legal counsel, public accountants, or other persons as to matters the director reasonably believes are within the person's professional or expert competence; or

(3) A committee of the board of directors of which the director is not a member if the director reasonably believes the committee merits confidence.

(c) A director is not acting in good faith if the director has knowledge concerning the matter in question that makes reliance otherwise permitted by subsection (b) unwarranted.

(d) A director may, in considering the best interests of a corporation, consider the effects of any action on shareholders, employees, suppliers, and customers of the corporation, and communities in which offices or other facilities of the corporation are located, and any other factors the director considers pertinent.

(e) A director is not liable for any action taken as a director, or any failure to take any action, unless:

(1) The director has breached or failed to perform the duties of the director's office in compliance with this section; and

(2) The breach or failure to perform constitutes willful misconduct or recklessness.

786

§ 23-1-35-2. Conflict of interest.

(a) A conflict of interest transaction is a transaction with the corporation in which a director of the corporation has a direct or indirect interest. A conflict of interest transaction is not voidable by the corporation solely because of the director's interest in the transaction if any one (1) of the following is true:

(1) The material facts of the transaction and the director's interest were disclosed or known to the board of directors or a committee of the board of directors and the board of directors or committee authorized, approved, or ratified the transaction.

(2) The material facts of the transaction and the director's interest were disclosed or known to the shareholders entitled to vote and they authorized, approved, or ratified the transaction.

(3) The transaction was fair to the corporation.

(b) For purposes of this section, a director of the corporation has an indirect interest in a transaction if:

(1) Another entity in which the director has a material financial interest or in which the director is a general partner is a party to the transaction; or

(2) Another entity of which the director is a director, officer, or trustee is a party to the transaction and the transaction is, or is required to be, considered by the board of directors of the corporation.

(c) For purposes of subsection (a)(1), a conflict of interest transaction is authorized, approved, or ratified if it receives the affirmative vote of a majority of the directors on the board of directors (or on the committee) who have no direct or indirect interest in the transaction, but a transaction may not be authorized, approved, or ratified under this section by a single director. If a majority of the directors who have no direct or indirect interest in the transaction vote to authorize, approve, or ratify the transaction, a quorum is present for the purpose of taking action under this section. The presence of, or a vote cast by, a director with a direct or indirect interest in the transaction does not affect the validity of any action taken under subsection (a)(1) if the transaction is otherwise authorized, approved, or ratified as provided in that subsection.

(d) For purposes of subsection (a)(2), shares owned by or voted under the control of a director who has a direct or indirect interest in the transaction, and shares owned by or voted under the control of an entity described in subsection (b), may be counted in a vote of shareholders to determine whether to authorize, approve, or ratify a conflict of interest transaction.

§ 23-1-35-4. Liability based on violation of conduct standards.

(a) Subject to section 1 (e) [23-1-35-1(e)] of this chapter, a director who votes for or assents to a distribution made in violation of this article or the articles of incorporation is personally liable to the corporation for the

787

amount of the distribution that exceeds what could have been distributed without violating this article or the articles of incorporation.

(b) A director held liable for an unlawful distribution under subsection (a) is entitled to contribution:

(1) From every other director who voted for or assented to the distribution, subject to section 1 (e) of this chapter; and

(2) From each shareholder for the amount the shareholder accepted.

CHAPTER 37

INDEMNIFICATION

§ 23-1-37-1. "Corporation" defined.

As used in this chapter, "corporation" includes any domestic or foreign predecessor entity of a corporation in a merger or other transaction in which the predecessor's existence ceased upon consummation of the transaction.

§ 32-1-37-2. "Director" defined.

As used in this chapter, "director" means an individual who is or was a director of a corporation or an individual who while a director of a corporation, is or was serving at the corporation's request as a director, officer, partner, trustee, employee, or agent of another foreign or domestic corporation, partnership, joint venture, trust, employee benefit plan, or other enterprise, whether for profit or not. A director is considered to be serving an employee benefit plan at the corporation's request if the director's duties to the corporation also impose duties on, or otherwise involve services by, the director to the plan or to participants in or beneficiaries of the plan. "Director" includes, unless the context requires otherwise, the estate or personal representative of a director.

§ 23-1-37-3. "Expenses" defined.

As used in this chapter, "expenses" include counsel fees.

§ 23-1-37-4. "Liability" defined.

As used in this chapter, "liability" means the obligation to pay a judgment, settlement, penalty, fine (including an excise tax assessed with respect to an employee benefit plan), or reasonable expenses incurred with respect to a proceeding.

§ 23-1-37-5. "Official capacity" defined.

As used in this chapter, "official capacity" means:

(1) When used with respect to a director, the office of director in a corporation; and

(2) When used with respect to an individual other than a director, as contemplated in section 13 [23-1-37-13] of this chapter, the office in a corporation held by the officer or the employment or agency relationship undertaken by the employee or agent on behalf of the corporation.

"Official capacity" does not include service for any other foreign or domestic corporation or any partnership, joint venture, trust, employee benefit plan, or other enterprise, whether for profit or not.

§ 23-1-37-6. "Party" defined.

As used in this chapter, "party" includes an individual who was, is, or is threatened to be made a named defendant or respondent in a proceeding.

§ 23-1-37-7. "Proceeding" defined.

As used in this chapter, "proceeding" means any threatened, pending, or completed action, suit, or proceeding, whether civil, criminal, administrative, or investigative and whether formal or informal.

§ 23-1-37-8. Basis.

(a) A corporation may indemnify an individual made a party to a proceeding because the individual is or was a director against liability incurred in the proceeding if:

(1) The individual's conduct was in good faith; and

(2) The individual reasonably believed:

(A) In the case of conduct in the individual's official capacity with the corporation, that the individual's conduct was in its best interests; and

(B) In all other cases, that the individual's conduct was at least not opposed to its best interests; and

(3) In the case of any criminal proceeding, the individual either:

(A) Had reasonable cause to believe the individual's conduct was lawful; or

(B) Had no reasonable cause to believe the individual's conduct was unlawful.

(b) A director's conduct with respect to an employee benefit plan for a purpose the director reasonably believed to be in the interests of the participants in and beneficiaries of the plan is conduct that satisfies the requirement of subsection (a)(2)(B).

(c) The termination of a proceeding by judgment, order, settlement, conviction, or upon a plea of nolo contendere or its equivalent is not, of itself, determinative that the director did not meet the standard of conduct described in this section.

§ 23-1-37-9. Authorized.

Unless limited by its articles of incorporation, a corporation shall indemnify a director who was wholly successful, on the merits or otherwise, in the defense of any proceeding to which the director was a party because the director is or was a director of the corporation against reasonable expenses incurred by the director in connection with the proceeding.

§ 23-1-37-10. Before final disposition of proceedings.

(a) A corporation may pay for or reimburse the reasonable expenses incurred by a director who is a party to a proceeding in advance of final disposition of the proceeding if:

(1) The director furnishes the corporation a written affirmation of the director's good faith belief that the director has met the standard of conduct described in section 8 [23-1-37-8] of this chapter;

(2) The director furnishes the corporation a written undertaking, executed personally or on the director's behalf, to repay the advance if it is ultimately determined that the director did not meet the standard of conduct; and

(3) A determination is made that the facts then known to those making the determination would not preclude indemnification under this chapter.

(b) The undertaking required by subsection (a)(2) must be an unlimited general obligation of the director but need not be secured and may be accepted without reference to financial ability to make repayment.

(c) Determinations and authorizations of payments under this section shall be made in the manner specified in section 12 [23-1-37-12] of this chapter.

§ 23-1-37-11. Judicial order.

Unless a corporation's articles of incorporation provide otherwise, a director of the corporation who is a party to a proceeding may apply for indemnification to the court conducting the proceeding or to another court of competent jurisdiction. On receipt of an application, the court after giving any notice the court considers necessary may order indemnification if it determines:

(1) The director is entitled to mandatory indemnification under section 9 [23-1-37-9] of this chapter, in which case the court shall also order the corporation to pay the director's reasonable expenses incurred to obtain court-ordered indemnification; or

(2) The director is fairly and reasonably entitled to indemnification in view of all the relevant circumstances, whether or not the director met the standard of conduct set forth in section 8 [23-1-37-8] of this chapter.

§ 23-1-37-12. Procedure for determining amount.

(a) A corporation may not indemnify a director under section 8 [23-1-37-8] of this chapter unless authorized in the specific case after a determination has been made that indemnification of the director is permissible in the circumstances because the director has met the standard of conduct set forth in section 8 of this chapter.

(b) The determination shall be made by any one (1) of the following procedures:

(1) By the board of directors by majority vote of a quorum consisting of directors not at the time parties to the proceeding.

(2) If a quorum cannot be obtained under subdivision (1), by majority vote of a committee duly designated by the board of directors (in which designation directors who are parties may participate), consisting solely of two (2) or more directors not at the time parties to the proceeding.

(3) By special legal counsel:

(A) Selected by the board of directors or its committee in the manner prescribed in subdivision (1) or (2); or

(B) If a quorum of the board of directors cannot be obtained under subdivision (1) and a committee cannot be designated under subdivision (2), selected by majority vote of the full board of directors (in which selection directors who are parties may participate).

(4) By the shareholders, but shares owned by or voted under the control of directors who are at the time parties to the proceeding may not be voted on the determination.

(c) Authorization of indemnification and evaluation as to reasonableness of expenses shall be made in the same manner as the determination that indemnification is permissible, except that if the determination is made by special legal counsel, authorization of indemnification and evaluation as to reasonableness of expenses shall be made by those entitled under subsection (b)(3) to select counsel.

§ 23-1-37-13. Officers, employees or agents.

Unless a corporation's articles of incorporation provide otherwise:

(1) An officer of the corporation, whether or not a director, is entitled to mandatory indemnification under section 9 [23-1-37-9] of this chapter, and is entitled to apply for court-ordered indemnification under section 11 [23-1-37-11] of this chapter, in each case to the same extent as a director;

(2) The corporation may indemnify and advance expenses under this chapter to an officer, employee, or agent of the corporation, whether or not a director, to the same extent as to a director; and

(3) A corporation may also indemnify and advance expenses to an officer, employee, or agent, whether or not a director, to the extent, consistent with

public policy, that may be provided by its articles of incorporation, bylaws, general or specific action of its board of directors, or contract.

§ 23-1-37-14. Insurance.

A corporation may purchase and maintain insurance on behalf of an individual who is or was a director, officer, employee, or agent of the corporation, or who, while a director, officer, employee, or agent of the corporation, is or was serving at the request of the corporation as a director, officer, partner, trustee, employee, or agent of another foreign or domestic corporation, partnership, joint venture, trust, employee benefit plan, or other enterprise, against liability asserted against or incurred by the individual in that capacity or arising from the individual's status as a director, officer, employee, or agent, whether or not the corporation would have power to indemnify the individual against the same liability under section 8 or 9 [23-1-37-8 or 23-1-37-9] of this chapter.

§ 23-1-37-15. Remedy not exclusive of other rights.

(a) The indemnification and advance for expenses provided for or authorized by this chapter does not exclude any other rights to indemnification and advance for expenses that a person may have under:

(1) A corporation's articles of incorporation or bylaws;

(2) A resolution of the board of directors or of the shareholders; or

(3) Any other authorization, whenever adopted, after notice, by a majority vote of all the voting shares then issued and outstanding.

(b) If the articles of incorporation, bylaws, resolutions of the board of directors or of the shareholders, or other duly adopted authorization of indemnification or advance for expenses limit indemnification or advance for expenses, indemnification and advance for expenses are valid only to the extent consistent with the articles, bylaws, resolution of the board of directors or of the shareholders, or other duly adopted authorization of indemnification or advance for expenses.

(c) This chapter does not limit a corporation's power to pay or reimburse expenses incurred by a director, officer, employee, or agent in connection with the person's appearance as a witness in a proceeding at a time when the person has not been made a named defendant or respondent to the proceeding.

NEW YORK

Business Corporation Law

§ 402. Certificate of incorporation; contents.

***

(b) The certificate of incorporation may set forth a provision eliminating or limiting the personal liability of directors to the corporation or its shareholders for damages for any breach of duty in such capacity, provided that no such provision shall eliminate or limit:

(1) the liability of any director if a judgment or other final adjudication adverse to him establishes that his acts or omissions were in bad faith or involved intentional misconduct or a knowing violation of law or that he personally gained in fact a financial profit or other advantage to which he was not legally entitled or that his acts violated section 719, or

(2) the liability of any director for any act or omission prior to the adoption of a provision authorized by this paragraph.

***

§ 713. Interested directors.

(a) No contract or other transaction between a corporation and one or more of its directors, or between a corporation and any other corporation, firm, association or other entity in which one or more of its directors are directors or officers, or have a substantial financial interest, shall be either void or voidable for this reason alone or by reason alone that such director or directors are present at the meeting of the board, or of a committee thereof, which approves such contract or transaction, or that his or their votes are counted for such purpose:

(1) If the material facts as to such director's interest in such contract or transaction and as to any such common directorship, officership or financial interest are disclosed in good faith or known to the board or committee, and the board or committee approves such contract or transaction by a vote sufficient for such purpose without counting the vote of such interested director or, if the votes of the disinterested directors are insufficient to constitute an act of the board as defined in section 708 (Action by the board), by unanimous vote of the disinterested directors; or

(2) If the material facts as to such director's interest in such contract or transaction and as to any such common directorship, officership or financial interest are disclosed in good faith or known to the shareholders entitled to vote thereon, and such contract or transaction is approved by vote of such shareholders.

(b) If such good faith disclosure of the material facts as to the director's interest in the contract or transaction and as to any such common directorship, officership or financial interest is made to the directors or share-

793

holders, or known to the board or committee or shareholders approving such contract or transaction, as provided in paragraph (a), the contract or transaction may not be avoided by the corporation for the reasons set forth in paragraph (a). If there was no such disclosure or knowledge, or if the vote of such interested director was necessary for the approval of such contract or transaction at a meeting of the board or committee at which it was approved, the corporation may avoid the contract or transaction unless the party or parties thereto shall establish affirmatively that the contract or transaction was fair and reasonable as to the corporation at the time it was approved by the board, a committee or the shareholders.

(c) Common or interested directors may be counted in determining the presence of a quorum at a meeting of the board or of a committee which approves such contract or transaction.

(d) The certificate of incorporation may contain additional restrictions on contracts or transactions between a corporation and its directors and may provide that contracts or transactions in violation of such restrictions shall be void or voidable by the corporation.

(e) Unless otherwise provided in the certificate of incorporation or the by-laws, the board shall have authority to fix the compensation of directors for services in any capacity.

§ 717. Duty of directors.

(a) A director shall perform his duties as a director, including his duties as a member of any committee of the board upon which he may serve, in good faith and with that degree of care which an ordinarily prudent person in a like position would use under similar circumstances. In performing his duties, a director shall be entitled to rely on information, opinions, reports or statements including financial statements and other financial data, in each case prepared or presented by:

(1) one or more officers or employees of the corporation or of any other corporation of which at least fifty percentum of the outstanding shares of stock entitling the holders thereof to vote for the election of directors is owned directly or indirectly by the corporation, whom the director believes to be reliable and competent in the matters presented,

(2) counsel, public accountants or other persons as to matters which the director believes to be within such person's professional or expert competence, or

(3) a committee of the board upon which he does not serve, duly designated in accordance with a provision of the certificate of incorporation or the by-laws, as to matters within its designated authority, which committee the director believes to merit confidence, so long as in so relying he shall be acting in good faith and with such degree of care, but he shall not be considered to be acting in good faith if he has knowledge concerning the matter in question that would cause such reliance to be unwarranted. A

person who so performs his duties shall have no liability by reason of being or having been a director of the corporation.

(b) In taking action, including, without limitation, action which may involve or relate to a change or potential change in the control of the corporation, a director shall be entitled to consider, without limitation, both the long-term and the short-term interests of the corporation and its shareholders. For this purpose, "control" shall mean the possession, directly or indirectly, of the power to direct or cause the direction of the management and policies of the corporation, whether through the ownership of voting stock, by contract, or otherwise.

§ 719. Liability of directors in certain cases.

(a) Directors of a corporation who vote for or concur in any of the following corporate actions shall be jointly and severally liable to the corporation for the benefit of its creditors or shareholders, to the extent of any injury suffered by such persons, respectively, as a result of such action:

(1) The declaration of any dividend or other distribution to the extent that it is contrary to the provisions of paragraphs (a) and (b) of section 510 (Dividends or other distributions in cash or property).

(2) The purchase of the shares of the corporation to the extent that it is contrary to the provisions of section 513 (Purchase or redemption by a corporation of its own shares).

(3) The distribution of assets to shareholders after dissolution of the corporation without paying or adequately providing for all known liabilities of the corporation, excluding any claims not filed by creditors within the time limit set in a notice given to creditors under articles 10 (Nonjudicial dissolution) or 11 (Judicial dissolution).

(4) The making of any loan contrary to section 714 (Loans to directors).

(b) A director who is present at a meeting of the board, or any committee thereof, when action specified in paragraph (a) is taken shall be presumed to have concurred in the action unless his dissent thereto shall be entered in the minutes of the meeting, or unless he shall submit his written dissent to the person acting as the secretary of the meeting before the adjournment thereof, or shall deliver or send by registered mail such dissent to the secretary of the corporation promptly after the adjournment of the meeting. Such right to dissent shall not apply to a director who voted in favor of such action. A director who is absent from a meeting of the board, or any committee thereof, when such action is taken shall be presumed to have concurred in the action unless he shall deliver or send by registered mail his dissent thereto to the secretary of the corporation or shall cause such dissent to be filed with the minutes of the proceedings of the board or committee within a reasonable time after learning of such action.

(c) Any director against whom a claim is successfully asserted under this section shall be entitled to contribution from the other directors who voted for or concurred in the action upon which the claim is asserted.

(d) Directors against whom a claim is successfully asserted under this section shall be entitled, to the extent of the amounts paid by them to the corporation as a result of such claims:

(1) Upon payment to the corporation of any amount of an improper dividend or distribution, to be subrogated to the rights of the corporation against shareholders who received such dividend or distribution with knowledge of facts indicating that it was not authorized by section 510, in proportion to the amounts received by them respectively.

(2) Upon payment to the corporation of any amount of the purchase price of an improper purchase of shares, to have the corporation rescind such purchase of shares and recover for their benefit, but at their expense, the amount of such purchase price from any seller who sold such shares with knowledge of facts indicating that such purchase of shares by the corporation was not authorized by section 513.

(3) Upon payment to the corporation of the claim of any creditor by reason of a violation of subparagraph (a) (3), to be subrogated to the rights of the corporation against shareholders who received an improper distribution of assets.

(4) Upon payment to the corporation of the amount of any loan made contrary to section 714, to be subrogated to the rights of the corporation against a director who received the improper loan.

(e) A director shall not be liable under this section if, in the circumstances, he performed his duty to the corporation under paragraph (a) of section 717.

(f) This section shall not affect any liability otherwise imposed by law upon any director.

§ 720. Action against directors and officers for misconduct.

(a) An action may be brought against one or more directors or officers of a corporation to procure a judgment for the following relief:

(1) Subject to any provision of the certificate of incorporation authorized pursuant to paragraph (b) of section 402, to compel the defendant to account for his official conduct in the following cases:

(A) The neglect of, or failure to perform, or other violation of his duties in the management and disposition of corporate assets committed to his charge.

(B) The acquisition by himself, transfer to others, loss or waste of corporate assets due to any neglect of, or failure to perform, or other violation of his duties.

(2) To set aside an unlawful conveyance, assignment or transfer of corporate assets, where the transferee knew of its unlawfulness.

(3) To enjoin a proposed unlawful conveyance, assignment or transfer of corporate assets, where there is sufficient evidence that it will be made.

(b) An action may be brought for the relief provided in this section, and in paragraph (a) of section 719 (Liability of directors in certain cases) by a corporation, or a receiver, trustee in bankruptcy, officer, director or judgment creditor thereof, or, under section 626 (Shareholders' derivative action brought in the right of the corporation to procure a judgment in its favor), by a shareholder, voting trust certificate holder, or the owner of a beneficial interest in shares thereof.

(c) This section shall not affect any liability otherwise imposed by law upon any director or officer.

§ 721. Nonexclusivity of statutory provisions for indemnification of directors and officers.

The indemnification and advancement of expenses granted pursuant to, or provided by, this article shall not be deemed exclusive of any other rights to which a director or officer seeking indemnification or advancement of expenses may be entitled, whether contained in the certificate of incorporation or the by-laws or, when authorized by such certificate of incorporation or by-laws, (i) a resolution of shareholders, (ii) a resolution of directors, or (iii) an agreement providing for such indemnification, provided that no indemnification may be made to or on behalf of any director or officer if a judgment or other final adjudication adverse to the director or officer establishes that his acts were committed in bad faith or were the result of active and deliberate dishonesty and were material to the cause of action so adjudicated, or that he personally gained in fact a financial profit or other advantage to which he was not legally entitled. Nothing contained in this article shall affect any rights to indemnification to which corporate personnel other than directors and officers may be entitled by contract or otherwise under law.

§ 722. Authorization for indemnification of directors and officers.

(a) A corporation may indemnify any person made, or threatened to be made, a party to an action or proceeding (other than one by or in the right of the corporation to procure a judgment in its favor), whether civil or criminal, including an action by or in the right of any other corporation of any type or kind, domestic or foreign, or any partnership, joint venture, trust, employee benefit plan or other enterprise, which any director or officer of the corporation served in any capacity at the request of the corporation, by reason of the fact that he, his testator or intestate, was a director or officer of the corporation, or served such other corporation, partnership, joint venture, trust, employee benefit plan or other enterprise in any capacity, against judgments, fines, amounts paid in settlement and reasonable expenses, including attorneys' fees actually and necessarily incurred as a result of such action or proceeding, or any appeal therein, if such director or

797

officer acted, in good faith, for a purpose which he reasonably believed to be in, or, in the case of service for any other corporation or any partnership, joint venture, trust, employee benefit plan or other enterprise, not opposed to, the best interests of the corporation and, in criminal actions or proceedings, in addition, had no reasonable cause to believe that his conduct was unlawful.

(b) The termination of any such civil or criminal action or proceeding by judgment, settlement, conviction or upon a plea of nolo contendere, or its equivalent, shall not in itself create a presumption that any such director or officer did not act, in good faith, for a purpose which he reasonably believed to be in, or, in the case of service for any other corporation or any partnership, joint venture, trust, employee benefit plan or other enterprise, not opposed to, the best interests of the corporation or that he had reasonable cause to believe that his conduct was unlawful.

(c) A corporation may indemnify any person made, or threatened to be made, a party to an action by or in the right of the corporation to procure a judgment in its favor by reason of the fact that he, his testator or intestate, is or was a director or officer of the corporation, or is or was serving at the request of the corporation as a director or officer of any other corporation of any type or kind, domestic or foreign, of any partnership, joint venture, trust, employee benefit plan or other enterprise, against amounts paid in settlement and reasonable expenses, including attorneys' fees, actually and necessarily incurred by him in connection with the defense or settlement of such action, or in connection with an appeal therein, if such director or officer acted, in good faith, for a purpose which he reasonably believed to be in, or, in the case of service for any other corporation or any partnership, joint venture, trust, employee benefit plan or other enterprise, not opposed to, the best interests of the corporation, except that no indemnification under this paragraph shall be made in respect of (1) a threatened action, or a pending action which is settled or otherwise disposed of, or (2) any claim, issue or matter as to which such person shall have been adjudged to be liable to the corporation, unless and only to the extent that the court in which the action was brought, or, if no action was brought, any court of competent jurisdiction, determines upon application that, in view of all the circumstances of the case, the person is fairly and reasonably entitled to indemnity for such portion of the settlement amount and expenses as the court deems proper.

(d) For the purpose of this section, a corporation shall be deemed to have requested a person to serve an employee benefit plan where the performance by such person of his duties to the corporation also imposes duties on, or otherwise involves services by, such person to the plan or participants or beneficiaries of the plan; excise taxes assessed on a person with respect to an employee benefit plan pursuant to applicable law shall be considered fines; and action taken or omitted by a person with respect to an employee benefit plan in the performance of such person's duties for a purpose reasonably believed by such person to be in the interest of the participants and beneficiaries of the plan shall be deemed to be for a purpose which is not opposed to the best interests of the corporation.

§ 723. Payment of indemnification other than by court award.

(a) A person who has been successful, on the merits or otherwise, in the defense of a civil or criminal action or proceeding of the character described in section 722 shall be entitled to indemnification as authorized in such section.

(b) Except as provided in paragraph (a), any indemnification under section 722 or otherwise permitted by section 721, unless ordered by a court under section 724 (Indemnification of directors and officers by a court), shall be made by the corporation, only if authorized in the specific case:

(1) By the board acting by a quorum consisting of directors who are not parties to such action or proceeding upon a finding that the director or officer has met the standard of conduct set forth in section 722 or established pursuant to section 721, as the case may be, or,

(2) If a quorum under subparagraph (1) is not obtainable or, even if obtainable, a quorum of disinterested directors so directs;

(A) By the board upon the opinion in writing of independent legal counsel that indemnification is proper in the circumstances because the applicable standard of conduct set forth in such sections has been met by such director or officer, or

(B) By the shareholders upon a finding that the director or officer has met the applicable standard of conduct set forth in such sections.

(c) Expenses incurred in defending a civil or criminal action or proceeding may be paid by the corporation in advance of the final disposition of such action or proceeding upon receipt of an undertaking by or on behalf of such director or officer to repay such amount as, and to the extent, required by paragraph (a) of section 725.

§ 724. Indemnification of directors and officers by a court.

(a) Notwithstanding the failure of a corporation to provide indemnification, and despite any contrary resolution of the board or of the shareholders in the specific case under section 723 (Payment of indemnification other than by court award), indemnification shall be awarded by a court to the extent authorized under section 722 (Authorization for indemnification of directors and officers), and paragraph (a) of section 723. Application therefor may be made, in every case, either:

(1) In the civil action or proceeding in which the expenses were incurred or other amounts were paid, or

(2) To the supreme court in a separate proceeding, in which case the application shall set forth the disposition of any previous application made

799

to any court for the same or similar relief and also reasonable cause for the failure to make application for such relief in the action or proceeding in which the expenses were incurred or other amounts were paid.

(b) The application shall be made in such manner and form as may be required by the applicable rules of court or, in the absence thereof, by direction of a court to which it is made. Such application shall be upon notice to the corporation. The court may also direct that notice be given at the expense of the corporation to the shareholders and such other persons as it may designate in such manner as it may require.

(c) Where indemnification is sought by judicial action, the court may allow a person such reasonable expenses, including attorneys' fees, during the pendency of the litigation as are necessary in connection with his defense therein, if the court shall find that the defendant has by his pleadings or during the course of the litigation raised genuine issues of fact or law.

§ 725. Other provisions affecting indemnification of directors and officers.

(a) All expenses incurred in defending a civil or criminal action or proceeding which are advanced by the corporation under paragraph (c) of section 723 (Payment of indemnification other than by court award) or allowed by a court under paragraph (c) of section 724 (Indemnification of directors and officers by a court) shall be repaid in case the person receiving such advancement or allowance is ultimately found, under the procedure set forth in this article, not to be entitled to indemnification or, where indemnification is granted, to the extent the expenses so advanced by the corporation or allowed by the court exceed the indemnification to which he is entitled.

(b) No indemnification, advancement or allowance shall be made under this article in any circumstance where it appears:

(1) That the indemnification would be inconsistent with the law of the jurisdiction of incorporation of a foreign corporation which prohibits or otherwise limits such indemnification;

(2) That the indemnification would be inconsistent with a provision of the certificate of incorporation, a by-law, a resolution of the board or of the shareholders, an agreement or other proper corporate action, in effect at the time of the accrual of the alleged cause of action asserted in the threatened or pending action or proceeding in which the expenses were incurred or other amounts were paid, which prohibits or otherwise limits indemnification; or

(3) If there has been a settlement approved by the court, that the indemnification would be inconsistent with any condition with respect to indemnification expressly imposed by the court in approving the settlement.

(c) If any expenses or other amounts are paid by way of indemnification, otherwise than by court order or action by the shareholders, the corporation shall, not later than the next annual meeting of shareholders unless such meeting is held within three months from the date of such payment, and, in any event, within fifteen months from the date of such payment, mail to its shareholders of record at the time entitled to vote for the election of directors a statement specifying the persons paid, the amounts paid, and the nature and status at the time of such payment of the litigation or threatened litigation.

(d) If any action with respect to indemnification of directors and officers is taken by way of amendment of the by-laws, resolution of directors, or by agreement, then the corporation shall, not later than the next annual meeting of shareholders, unless such meeting is held within three months from the date of such action, and, in any event, within fifteen months from the date of such action, mail to its shareholders of record at the time entitled to vote for the election of directors a statement specifying the action taken.

(e) The provisions of this article relating to indemnification of directors and officers and insurance therefor shall apply to domestic corporations and foreign corporations doing business in this state, except as provided in section 1320 (Exemption from certain provisions).

§ 726. Insurance for indemnification of directors and officers.

(a) Subject to paragraph (b), a corporation shall have power to purchase and maintain insurance:

(1) To indemnify the corporation for any obligation which it incurs as a result of the indemnification of directors and officers under the provisions of this article, and

(2) To indemnify directors and officers in instances in which they may be indemnified by the corporation under the provisions of this article, and

(3) To indemnify directors and officers in instances in which they may not otherwise be indemnified by the corporation under the provisions of this article provided the contract of insurance covering such directors and officers provides, in a manner acceptable to the superintendent of insurance, for a retention amount and for co-insurance.

(b) No insurance under paragraph (a) may provide for any payment, other than cost of defense, to or on behalf of any director or officer:

(1) if a judgment or other final adjudication adverse to the insured director or officer establishes that his acts of active and deliberate dishonesty were material to the cause of action so adjudicated, or that he personally gained in fact a financial profit or other advantage to which he was not legally entitled, or

(2) in relation to any risk the insurance of which is prohibited under the insurance law of this state.

(c) Insurance under any or all subparagraphs of paragraph (a) may be included in a single contract or supplement thereto. Retrospective rated contracts are prohibited.

(d) The corporation shall, within the time and to the persons provided in paragraph (c) of section 725 (Other provisions affecting indemnification of directors or officers), mail a statement in respect of any insurance it has purchased or renewed under this section, specifying the insurance carrier, date of the contract, cost of the insurance, corporate positions insured, and a statement explaining all sums, not previously reported in a statement to shareholders, paid under any indemnification insurance contract.

(e) This section is the public policy of this state to spread the risk of corporate management, notwithstanding any other general or special law of this state or of any other jurisdiction including the federal government.

§ 1317. Liabilities of directors and officers of foreign corporations.

(a) Except as otherwise provided in this chapter, the directors and officers of a foreign corporation doing business in this state are subject, to the same extent as directors and officers of a domestic corporation, to the provisions of:

(1) Section 719 (Liability of directors in certain cases) except subparagraph (a) (3) thereof, and

(2) Section 720 (Action against directors and officers for misconduct.)

(b) Any liability imposed by paragraph (a) may be enforced in, and such relief granted by, the courts in this state, in the same manner as in the case of a domestic corporation.

§ 1318. Liability of foreign corporations for failure to disclose required information.

(a) A foreign corporation doing business in this state shall, in the same manner as a domestic corporation, disclose to its shareholders of record who are residents of this state the information required under paragraph (c) of section 510 (Dividends or other distributions in cash or property), paragraphs (f) and (g) of section 511 (Share distributions and changes), paragraph (d) of section 515 (Reacquired shares), paragraph (c) of section 516 (Reduction of stated capital in certain cases), subparagraph (a) (4) of section 517 (Special provisions relative to surplus and reserves) or paragraph (f) of section 519 (Convertible shares and bonds), and shall be liable as provided in section 520 (Liability for failure to disclose required information) for failure to comply in good faith with these requirements.

(b) For the purposes of this section, an authorized foreign corporation may by board action determine the amount of its earned surplus before the declaration of its first dividend after either (1) the effective date of this chapter or (2) the date of filing of its application for authority under this chapter, whichever is later; and such determination if made in good faith shall be conclusive. Thereafter such foreign corporation may determine the amount or availability of its earned surplus in the same manner as a domestic corporation.

§ 1319. Applicability of other provisions.

(a) In addition to articles 1 (Short title; definitions; application; certificates; miscellaneous) and 3 (Corporate name and service of process) and the other sections of article 13, the following provisions, to the extent provided therein, shall apply to a foreign corporation doing business in this state, its directors, officers and shareholders:

(1) Section 623 (Procedure to enforce shareholder's right to receive payment for shares).

(2) Section 626 (Shareholders' derivative action brought in the right of the corporation to procure a judgment in its favor).

(3) Section 627 (Security for expenses in shareholders' derivative action brought in the right of the corporation to procure a judgment in its favor).

(4) Sections 721 (Exclusivity of statutory provisions for indemnification of directors and officers) through 727 (Insurance for indemnification of directors and officers), inclusive.

(5) Section 808 (Reorganization under act of congress).

(6) Section 907 (Merger or consolidation of domestic and foreign corporations).

§ 1320. Exemption from certain provisions.

(a) Notwithstanding any other provision of this chapter, a foreign corporation doing business in this state which is authorized under this article, its directors, officers and shareholders, shall be exempt from the provisions of paragraph (e) of section 1316 (Voting trust records), subparagraph (a) (1) of section 1317 (Liabilities of directors and officers of foreign corporations), section 1318 (Liability of foreign corporations for failure to disclose required information) and subparagraph (a) (4) of section 1319 (Applicability of other provisions) if when such provision would otherwise apply:

(1) Shares of such corporation were listed on a national securities exchange, or

(2) Less than one-half of the total of its business income for the preceding three fiscal years, or such portion thereof as the foreign corporation was in existence, was allocable to this state for franchise tax purposes under the tax law.

OHIO

General Corporation Law

§ 1701.13. Authority of corporation.

***

(E)(1) A corporation may indemnify or agree to indemnify any person who was or is a party or is threatened to be made a party, to any threatened, pending, or completed action, suit, or proceeding, whether civil, criminal, administrative, or investigative, other than an action by or in the right of the corporation, by reason of the fact that he is or was a director, officer, employee, or agent of the corporation, or is or was serving at the request of the corporation as a director, trustee, officer, employee, or agent of another corporation, domestic or foreign, nonprofit or for profit, partnership, joint venture, trust, or other enterprise, against expenses, including attorney's fees, judgments, fines, and amounts paid in settlement actually and reasonably incurred by him in connection with such action, suit, or proceeding if he acted good faith and in a manner he reasonably believed to be in or not opposed to the best interests of the corporation, and with respect to any criminal action or proceeding, had no reasonable cause to believe his conduct was unlawful. The termination of any action, suit, or proceeding by judgment, order, settlement, or conviction, or upon a plea of nolo contendere or its equivalent, shall not, of itself, create a presumption that the person did not act in good faith and in a manner he reasonably believed to be in or not opposed to the best interests of the corporation and, with respect to any criminal action or proceeding, he had reasonable cause to believe that his conduct was unlawful.

(2) A corporation may indemnify or agree to indemnify any person who was or is a party or is threatened to be made a party, to any threatened, pending, or completed action or suit by or in the right of the corporation to procure a judgment in its favor by reason of the fact that he is or was a director, officer, employee, or agent of the corporation, or is or was serving at the request of the corporation as a director, trustee, officer, employee, or agent of another corporation, domestic or foreign, nonprofit or for profit, partnership, joint venture, trust, or other enterprise, against expenses, including attorney's fees, actually and reasonably incurred by him in connection with the defense or settlement of such action or suit if he acted in good faith and in a manner he reasonably believed to be in or not opposed to the best interests of the corporation, except that no indemnification shall be made in respect of any of the following:

(a) Any claim, issue, or matter as to which such person is adjudged to be liable for negligence or misconduct in the performance of his duty to the corporation unless, and only to the extent that the court of common pleas or the court in which such action or suit was brought determines upon appli-

804

cation that, despite the adjudication of liability, but in view of all the circumstances of the case, such person is fairly and reasonably entitled to indemnity for such expenses as the court of common pleas or such other court shall deem proper;

(b) Any action or suit in which the only liability asserted against a director is pursuant to section 1701.95 of the Revised Code.

(3) To the extent that a director, trustee, officer, employee, or agent has been successful on the merits or otherwise in defense of any action, suit, or proceeding referred to in divisions (E)(1) and (2) of this section, or in defense of any claim, issue, or matter therein, he shall be indemnified against expenses, including attorney's fees, actually and reasonably incurred by him in connection with the action, suit, or proceeding.

(4) Any indemnification under divisions (E)(1) and (2) of this section, unless ordered by a court, shall be made by the corporation only as authorized in the specific case upon a determination that indemnification of the director, trustee, officer, employee, or agent is proper in the circumstances because he has met the applicable standard of conduct set forth in divisions (E)(1) and (2) of this section. Such determination shall be made as follows:

(a) By a majority vote of a quorum consisting of directors of the indemnifying corporation who were not and are not parties to or threatened with any such action, suit, or proceeding;

(b) If the quorum described in division (E)(4)(a) of this section is not obtainable or if a majority vote of a quorum of disinterested directors so directs, in a written opinion by independent legal counsel other than an attorney, or a firm having associated with it an attorney, who has been retained by or who has performed services for the corporation or any person to be indemnified within the past five years;

(c) By the shareholders;

(d) By the court of common pleas or the court in which such action, suit, or proceeding was brought.

Any determination made by the disinterested directors under division (E)(4)(a) or by independent legal counsel under division (E)(4)(b) of this section shall be promptly communicated to the person who threatened or brought the action or suit by or in the right of the corporation under division (E)(2) of this section, and within ten days after receipt of such notification, such person shall have the right to petition the court of common pleas or the court in which such action or suit was brought to review the reasonableness of such determination.

(5)(a) Unless at the time of a director's act or omission that is the subject of an action, suit, or proceeding referred to in divisions (E)(1) and (2) of this section, the articles or the regulations of a corporation state by specific reference to this division that the provisions of this division do not apply to the corporation and unless the only liability asserted against a director in an action, suit, or proceeding referred to in divisions (E)(1) and (2) of this section is pursuant to section 1701.95 of the Revised Code, expenses, in-

805

cluding attorney's fees, incurred by a director in defending the action, suit, or proceeding shall be paid by the corporation as they are incurred, in advance of the final disposition of the action, suit, or proceeding upon receipt of an undertaking by or on behalf of the director in which he agrees to do both of the following:

(i) Repay such amount if it is proved by clear and convincing evidence in a court of competent jurisdiction that his action or failure to act involved an act or omission undertaken with deliberate intent to cause injury to the corporation or undertaken with reckless disregard for the best interests of the corporation;

(ii) Reasonably cooperate with the corporation concerning the action, suit, or proceeding.

(b) Expenses, including attorney's fees, incurred by a director, trustee, officer, employee, or agent in defending any action, suit, or proceeding referred to in divisions (E)(1) and (2) of this section, may be paid by the corporation as they are incurred, in advance of the final disposition of the action, suit, or proceeding as authorized by the directors in the specific case upon receipt of an undertaking by or on behalf of the director, trustee, officers, employee, or agent to repay such amount, if it ultimately is determined that he is not entitled to be indemnified by the corporation.

(6) The indemnification authorized by this section shall not be exclusive of, and shall be in addition to, any other rights granted to those seeking indemnification under the articles or the regulations or any agreement, vote of shareholders or disinterested directors, or otherwise, both as to action in his official capacity and as to action in another capacity while holding such office, and shall continue as to a person who has ceased to be a director, trustee, officer, employee, or agent and shall inure to the benefit of the heirs, executors, and administrators of such a person.

(7) A corporation may purchase and maintain insurance or furnish similar protection, including but not limited to trust funds, letters of credit, or self-insurance, on behalf of or for any person who is or was a director, officer, employee, or agent of the corporation, or is or was serving at the request of the corporation as a director, trustee, officer, employee, or agent of another corporation, domestic or foreign, nonprofit or for profit, partnership, joint venture, trust, or other enterprise, against any liability asserted against him and incurred by him in any such capacity, or arising out of his status as such, whether or not the corporation would have the power to indemnify him against such liability under this section. Insurance may be purchased from or maintained with a person in which the corporation has a financial interest.

(8) The authority of a corporation to indemnify persons pursuant to divisions (E)(1) and (2) of this section does not limit the payment of expenses as they are incurred, indemnification, insurance, or other protection that may be provided pursuant to divisions (E)(5), (6), and (7) of this section. Divisions (E)(1) and (2) of this section do not create any obligation to repay or

return payments made by the corporation pursuant to divisions (E)(5), (6), or (7).

(9) As used in this division, references to "corporation" includes all constituent corporations in a consolidation or merger and the new or surviving corporation, so that any person who is or was a director, officer, employee, or agent of such a constituent corporation, or is or was serving at the request of such constituent corporation as a director, trustee, officer, employee, or agent of another corporation, domestic or foreign, nonprofit or for profit, partnership, joint venture, trust, or other enterprise, shall stand in the same position under this section with respect to the new or surviving corporation as he would if he had served the new or surviving corporation in the same capacity.

***

§ 1701.59. Authority of directors; bylaws; standard of care.

***

(B) A director shall perform his duties as a director, including his duties as a member of any committee of the directors upon which he may serve, in good faith, in a manner he reasonably believes to be in or not opposed to the best interests of the corporation, and with the care that an ordinarily prudent person in a like position would use under similar circumstances. In performing his duties, a director is entitled to rely on information, opinions, reports, or statements, including financial statements and other financial data, that are prepared or presented by:

(1) One or more directors, officers, or employees of the corporation who the director reasonably believes are reliable and competent in the matters prepared or presented;

(2) Counsel, public accountants, or other persons as to matters that the director reasonably believes are within the person's professional or expert competence;

(3) A committee of the directors upon which he does not serve, duly established in accordance with a provision of the articles or the regulations, as to matters within its designated authority, which committee the director reasonably believes to merit confidence.

(C) For purposes of division (B) of this section:

(1) A director shall not be found to have violated his duties under division (B) of this section unless it is proved by clear and convincing evidence that the director has not acted in good faith, in a manner he reasonably believes to be in or not opposed to the best interests of the corporation, or with the care than an ordinarily prudent person in a like position would use under similar circumstances, in any action brought against a director, including actions involving or affecting any of the following:

(a) A change or potential change in control of the corporation;

807

(b) A termination or potential termination of his service to the corporation as a director;

(c) His service in any other position or relationship with the corporation.

(2) A director shall not be considered to be acting in good faith if he has knowledge concerning the matter in question that would cause reliance on information, opinions, reports, or statements that are prepared or presented by the persons described in divisions (B)(1) to (3) of this section to be unwarranted.

(3) Nothing contained in this division limits relief available under section 1701.60 of the Revised Code.

(D) A director shall be liable in damages for any action he takes or fails to take as a director only if it is proved by clear and convincing evidence in a court of competent jurisdiction that his action or failure to act involved an act or omission undertaken with deliberate intent to cause injury to the corporation or undertaken with reckless disregard for the best interests of the corporation. Nothing contained in this division affects the liability of directors under section 1701.95 of the Revised Code or limits relief available under section 1701.60 of the Revised Code. This division does not apply if, and only to the extent that, at the time of a director's act or omission that is the subject of complaint, the articles or the regulations of the corporation state by specific reference to this division that the provisions of this division do not apply to the corporation.

(E) For purposes of this section, a director, in determining what he reasonably believes to be in the best interests of the corporation, shall consider the interests of the corporation's shareholders and, in his discretion, may consider any of the following:

(1) The interests of the corporation's employees, suppliers, creditors, and customers;

(2) The economy of the state and nation;

(3) Community and societal considerations;

(4) The long-term as well as short-term interests of the corporation and its shareholders, including the possibility that these interests may be best served by the continued independence of the corporation.

(F) Nothing contained in division (C) or (D) of this section affects the duties of either of the following:

(1) A director who acts in any capacity other than his capacity as a director;

(2) A director of a corporation that does not have issued and outstanding shares that are listed on a national securities exchange or are regularly quoted in an over-the-counter market by one or more members of a national or affiliated securities association, who votes for or assents to any action taken by the directors of the corporation that, in connection with a change in control of the corporation, directly results in the holder or holders of a majority of the outstanding shares of the corporation receiving a greater consideration for their shares than other shareholders.

808

§ 1701.60. Contract, action or transaction not voidable; directors to fix compensation.

(A) Unless otherwise provided in the articles or the regulations:

(1) No contract, action, or transaction shall be void or voidable with respect to a corporation for the reason that it is between or affects the corporation and one or more of its directors or officers, or between or affects the corporation and any other person in which one or more of its directors or officers are directors, trustees, or officers, or have a financial or personal interest, or for the reason that one or more interested directors or officers participate in or vote at the meeting of the directors or a committee of the directors that authorizes such contract, action, or transaction, if in any such case any of the following apply:

(a) The material facts as to his or their relationship or interest and as to the contract, action, or transaction are disclosed or are known to the directors or the committee and the directors or committee, in good faith reasonably justified by such facts, authorizes the contract, action, or transaction by the affirmative vote of a majority of the disinterested directors, even though the disinterested directors constitute less than a quorum of the directors or the committee;

(b) The material facts as to his or their relationship or interest and as to the contract, action, or transaction are disclosed or are known to the shareholders entitled to vote thereon and the contract, action, or transaction is specifically approved at a meeting of the shareholders held for such purpose by the affirmative vote of the holders of shares entitling them to exercise a majority of the voting power of the corporation held by persons not interested in the contract, action, or transaction; or

(c) The contract, action, or transaction is fair as to the corporation as of the time it is authorized or approved by the directors, a committee of the directors, or the shareholders;

(2) Common or interested directors may be counted in determining the presence of a quorum at a meeting of the directors, or of a committee of the directors that authorizes the contract, action, or transaction;

(3) The directors, by the affirmative vote of a majority of those in office, and irrespective of any financial or personal interest of any of them, shall have authority to establish reasonable compensation, that may include pension, disability, and death benefits, for services to the corporation by directors and officers, or to delegate such authority to one or more officers or directors.

(B) Nothing contained in divisions (A)(1) and (2) of this section shall limit or otherwise affect the liability of directors under section 1701.95 of the Revised Code.

(C) For purposes of division (A) of this section, a director is not an interested director solely because the subject of the contract, action, or transaction may involve or affect a change in control of the corporation or his continuation in office as a director of that corporation.

(D) For purposes of this section, "action" means a resolution adopted by the directors or a committee of the directors of a corporation.

§ 1701.95. Unlawful loans, dividends, distribution of assets.

(A) In addition to any other liabilities imposed by law upon directors of a corporation and except as provided in division (B) of this section, directors who vote for or assent to any of the following:

(1) The payment of a dividend or distribution, the making of a distribution of assets to shareholders, or the purchase or redemption of the corporation's own shares, contrary in any such case to law or the articles;

(2) A distribution of assets to shareholders during the winding up of the affairs of the corporation, on dissolution or otherwise, without the payment of all known obligations of the corporation, or without making adequate provision for their payment;

(3) The making of loans, other than in the usual course of business, to an officer, director, or shareholder of the corporation, except in the case of a building and loan association or a corporation engaged in banking or in the making of loans generally; shall be jointly and severally liable to the corporation as follows: in cases under division (A)(1) of this section up to the amount of such dividend, distribution, or other payment, in excess of the amount that could have been paid or distributed without violation of law or the articles but not in excess of the amount that would inure to the benefit of the creditors of the corporation if it was insolvent at the time of the payment or distribution or there was reasonable ground to believe that by such action it would be rendered insolvent, plus the amount that was paid or distributed to holders of shares of any class in violation of the rights of holders of shares of any other class; and in cases under division (A)(2) of this section, to the extent that the obligations of the corporation that are not otherwise barred by statute are not paid, or for the payment of which adequate provision has not been made; and in cases under division (A)(3) of this section, for the amount of the loan with interest on it at the rate of six per cent per annum until such amounts has been paid.

(B)(1) A director shall not be liable under division (A)(1) or (2) of this section if, in determining the amount available for any such dividend, purchase, redemption, or distribution to shareholders, he in good faith relied on a financial statement of the corporation prepared by an officer or employee of the corporation in charge of its accounts or certified by a public accountant or firm of public accountants, or in good faith he considered the assets to be of their book value, or he followed what he believed to be sound accounting and business practice.

(2) A director is not liable under division (A)(3) of this section for making any loan to, or guaranteeing any loan to or other obligation of, an employee

stock ownership plan, as defined in section 4975(e)(7) of the Internal Revenue Code of 1954, 68A Stat. 3, 26 U.S.C. 1, as amended.

(C) A director who is present at a meeting of the directors or a committee of the directors at which action on any matter is authorized or taken and who has not voted for or against such action shall be presumed to have voted for the action unless his written dissent from the action is filed either during the meeting or within a reasonable time after the adjournment of the meeting, with the person acting as secretary of the meeting or with the secretary of the corporation.

(D) A shareholder who knowingly receives any dividend, distribution, or payment made contrary to law or the articles shall be liable to the corporation for the amount received by him which is in excess of the amount which could have been paid or distributed without violation of law or the articles.

(E) A director against whom a claim is asserted under or pursuant to this section and who is held liable on the claim shall be entitled to contribution, on equitable principles, from other directors who also are liable. In addition, any director against whom a claim is asserted under or pursuant to this section or who is held liable shall have a right of contribution from the shareholders who knowingly received any dividend, distribution, or payment made contrary to law or the articles, and such shareholders as among themselves also shall be entitled to contribution in proportion to the amounts received by them respectively.

(F) No action shall be brought by or on behalf of a corporation upon any cause of action arising under division (A)(1) or (2) of this section at any time after two years from the day on which the violation occurs.

(G) Nothing contained in this section shall preclude any creditor whose claim is unpaid from exercising such rights as he otherwise would have by law to enforce his claim against assets of the corporation paid or distributed to shareholders.

VIRGINIA

Stock Corporation Act

ARTICLE 9

DIRECTORS AND OFFICERS

§ 13.1-690. General standards of conduct for director.

A. A director shall discharge his duties as a director, including his duties as a member of a committee, in accordance with his good faith business judgment of the best interests of the corporation.

B. Unless he has knowledge or information concerning the matter in question that makes reliance unwarranted, a director is entitled to rely on information, opinions, reports or statements, including financial statements and other financial data, if prepared or presented by:

1. One or more officers or employees of the corporation whom the director believes, in good faith, to be reliable and competent in the matters presented;

2. Legal counsel, public accountants, or other persons as to matters the director believes, in good faith, are within the person's professional or expert competence; or

3. A committee of the board of directors of which he is not a member if the director believes, in good faith, that the committee merits confidence.

C. A director is not liable for any action taken as a director, or any failure to take any action, if he performed the duties of his office in compliance with this section.

D. A person alleging a violation of this section has the burden of proving the violation.

§ 13.1-691. Director conflict of interests.

A. A conflict of interests transaction is a transaction with the corporation in which a director of the corporation has a direct or indirect personal interest. A conflict of interests transaction is not voidable by the corporation solely because of the director's interest in the transaction if any one of the following is true:

1. The material facts of the transaction and the director's interest were disclosed or known to the board of directors or a committee of the board of directors and the board of directors or committee authorized, approved, or ratified the transaction;

2. The material facts of the transaction and the director's interest were disclosed to the shareholders entitled to vote and they authorized, approved, or ratified the transaction; or

3. The transaction was fair to the corporation.

812

B. For the purposes of this section, a director of the corporation has an indirect personal interest in a transaction if:

1. Another entity in which he has a material financial interest or in which he is a general partner is a party to the transaction; or

2. Another entity of which he is a director, officer or trustee is a party to the transaction and the transaction is or should be considered by the board of directors of the corporation.

C. For purposes of paragraph 1 of subsection A of this section, a conflict of interests transaction is authorized, approved, or ratified if it receives the affirmative vote of a majority of the directors on the board of directors, or on the committee, who have no direct or indirect personal interest in the transaction. A transaction shall not be authorized, approved, or ratified under this section by a single director. If a majority of the directors who have no direct or indirect personal interest in the transaction vote to authorize, approve or ratify the transaction, a quorum is present for the purpose of taking action under this section. The presence of, or a vote cast by, a director with a direct or indirect personal interest in the transaction does not affect the validity of any action taken under paragraph 1 of subsection A of this section if the transaction is otherwise authorized, approved or ratified as provided in that subsection.

D. For purposes of paragraph 2 of subsection A of this section, a conflict of interests transaction is authorized, approved, or ratified if it receives the vote of a majority of the shares entitled to be counted under this subsection. Shares owned by or voted under the control of a director who has a direct or indirect personal interest in the transaction, and shares owned by or voted under the control of an entity described in paragraph 1 of subsection B of this section, may not be counted in a vote of shareholders to determine whether to authorize, approve, or ratify a conflict of interests transaction under paragraph 2 of subsection A of this section. The vote of those shares, however, shall be counted in determining whether the transaction is approved under other sections of this chapter. A majority of the shares, whether or not present, which are entitled to be counted in a vote on the transaction under this subsection constitutes a quorum for the purpose of taking action under this section.

§ 13.1-692. Liability for unlawful distributions.

A. Unless he complies with the applicable standards of conduct described in § 13.1-690, a director who votes for or assents to a distribution made in violation of this chapter or the articles of incorporation is personally liable to the corporation and its creditors for the amount of the distribution that exceeds what could have been distributed without violating this chapter or the articles of incorporation.

B. A director held liable for an unlawful distribution under subsection A of this section is entitled to contribution:

1. From every other director who voted for or assented to the distribution without complying with the applicable standards of conduct described in § 13.1-690; and

2. From the shareholders who received the unlawful distribution in proportion to the amounts of such unlawful distribution received by them respectively.

C. No suit shall be brought against any director for any liability imposed by this section except within two years after the right of action shall accrue.

§ 13.1-692.1. Limitation on liability of officers and directors; exception.

A. In any proceeding brought by a shareholder in the right of a corporation or brought by or on behalf of shareholders of the corporation, the damages assessed against an officer or director arising out of a single transaction, occurrence or course of conduct shall not exceed the lesser of:

1. The monetary amount specified in the articles of incorporation or, if approved by the shareholders, in the bylaws as a limitation on the liability of the officer or director; or

2. The greater of (i) $100,000 or (ii) the amount of cash compensation received by the officer or director from the corporation during the twelve months immediately preceding the act or omission for which liability was imposed.

B. The liability of an officer or director shall not be limited as provided in this section if the officer or director engaged in willful misconduct or a knowing violation of the criminal law or of any federal or state securities law, including, without limitation, any claim of unlawful insider trading or manipulation of the market for any security.

ARTICLE 10

INDEMNIFICATION

§ 13.1-696. Definitions.

In this article:

"Corporation" includes any domestic or foreign predecessor entity of a corporation in a merger or other transaction in which the predecessor's existence ceased upon consummation of the transaction.

"Director" means an individual who is or was a director of a corporation or an individual who, while a director of a corporation, is or was serving at the corporation's request as a director, officer, partner, trustee, employee, or agent of another foreign or domestic corporation, partnership, joint venture, trust, employee benefit plan, or other enterprise. A director is considered to be serving an employee benefit plan at the corporation's request if his duties to the corporation also impose duties on, or otherwise involve

814

services by, him to the plan or to participants in or beneficiaries of the plan. "Director" includes, unless the context requires otherwise, the estate or personal representative of a director.

"Expenses" includes counsel fees.

"Liability" means the obligation to pay a judgment, settlement, penalty, fine, including any excise tax assessed with respect to an employee benefit plan, or reasonable expenses incurred with respect to a proceeding.

"Official capacity" means, (i) when used with respect to a director, the office of director in a corporation; or (ii) when used with respect to an individual other than a director, as contemplated in § 13.1-702, the office in a corporation held by the officer or the employment or agency relationship undertaken by the employee or agent on behalf of the corporation. "Official capacity" does not include service for any other foreign or domestic corporation or any partnership, joint venture, trust, employee benefit plan, or other enterprise.

"Party" includes an individual who was, is, or is threatened to be made a named defendant or respondent in a proceeding.

"Proceeding" means any threatened, pending, or completed action, suit, or proceeding, whether civil, criminal, administrative or investigative and whether formal or informal.

§ 13.1-697. Authority to indemnify.

A. Except as provided in subsection D of this section, a corporation may indemnify an individual made a party to a proceeding because he is or was a director against liability incurred in the proceeding if:

1. He conducted himself in good faith; and

2. He believed:

a. In the case of conduct in his official capacity with the corporation, that his conduct was in its best interests; and

b. In all other cases, that his conduct was at least not opposed to its best interests; and

3. In the case of any criminal proceeding, he had no reasonable cause to believe his conduct was unlawful.

B. A director's conduct with respect to an employee benefit plan for a purpose he believed to be in the interests of the participants in and beneficiaries of the plan is conduct that satisfies the requirement of paragraph 2 b of subsection A of this section.

C. The termination of a proceeding by judgment, order, settlement or conviction is not, of itself, determinative that the director did not meet the standard of conduct described in this section.

D. A corporation may not indemnify a director under this section:

1. In connection with a proceeding by or in the right of the corporation in which the director was adjudged liable to the corporation; or

815

2. In connection with any other proceeding charging improper personal benefit to him, whether or not involving action in his official capacity, in which he was adjudged liable on the basis that personal benefit was improperly received by him.

E. Indemnification permitted under this section in connection with a proceeding by or in the right of the corporation is limited to reasonable expenses incurred in connection with the proceeding.

§ 13.1-698. Mandatory indemnification.

Unless limited by its articles of incorporation, a corporation shall indemnify a director who entirely prevails in the defense of any proceeding to which he was a party because he is or was a director of the corporation against reasonable expenses incurred by him in connection with the proceeding.

§ 13.1-699. Advance for expenses.

A. A corporation may pay for or reimburse the reasonable expenses incurred by a director who is a party to a proceeding in advance of final disposition of the proceeding if:

1. The director furnishes the corporation a written statement of his good faith belief that he has met the standard of conduct described in § 13.1-697;

2. The director furnishes the corporation a written undertaking, executed personally or on his behalf, to repay the advance if it is ultimately determined that he did not meet the standard of conduct; and

3. A determination is made that the facts then known to those making the determination would not preclude indemnification under this article.

B. The undertaking required by paragraph 2 of subsection A of this section shall be an unlimited general obligation of the director but need not be secured and may be accepted without reference to financial ability to make repayment.

C. Determinations and authorizations of payments under this section shall be made in the manner specified in § 13.1-701.

§ 13.1-700.1. Court orders for advances, reimbursement or indemnification.

A. An individual who is made a party to a proceeding because he is or was a director of a corporation may apply to a court for an order directing the corporation to make advances or reimbursement for expenses or to provide indemnification. Such application may be made to the court conducting the proceeding or to another court of competent jurisdiction.

B. The court shall order the corporation to make advances and/or reimbursement for expenses or to provide indemnification if it determines that the director is entitled to such advances, reimbursement or indemnification

816

and shall also order the corporation to pay the director's reasonable expenses incurred to obtain the order.

C. With respect to a proceeding by or in the right of the corporation, the court may (i) order indemnification of the director to the extent of his reasonable expenses if it determines that, considering all the relevant circumstances, the director is entitled to indemnification even though he was adjudged liable to the corporation and (ii) also order the corporation to pay the director's reasonable expenses incurred to obtain the order of indemnification.

D. Neither (i) the failure of the corporation, including its board of directors, its independent legal counsel and its shareholders, to have made an independent determination prior to the commencement of any action permitted by this section that the applying director is entitled to receive advances and/or reimbursement nor (ii) the determination by the corporation, including its board of directors, its independent legal counsel and its shareholders, that the applying director is not entitled to receive advances and/or reimbursement or indemnification shall create a presumption to that effect or otherwise of itself be a defense to that director's application for advances for expenses, reimbursement or indemnification.

§ 13.1-701. Determination and authorization of indemnification.

A. A corporation may not indemnify a director under § 13.1-697 unless authorized in the specific case after a determination has been made that indemnification of the director is permissible in the circumstances because he has met the standard of conduct set forth in § 13.1-697.

B. The determination shall be made:

1. By the board of directors by a majority vote of a quorum consisting of directors not at the time parties to the proceeding;

2. If a quorum cannot be obtained under paragraph 1 of this subsection, by majority vote of a committee duly designated by the board of directors (in which designation directors who are parties may participate), consisting solely of two or more directors not at the time parties to the proceeding;

3. By special legal counsel:

a. Selected by the board of directors or its committee in the manner prescribed in paragraph 1 or 2 of this subsection; or

b. If a quorum of the board of directors cannot be obtained under paragraph 1 of this subsection and a committee cannot be designated under paragraph 2 of this subsection, selected by majority vote of the full board of directors, in which selection directors who are parties may participate; or

4. By the shareholders, but shares owned by or voted under the control of directors who are at the time parties to the proceeding may not be voted on the determination.

C. Authorization of indemnification and evaluation as to reasonableness of expenses shall be made in the same manner as the determination that

817

indemnification is permissible, except that if the determination is made by special legal counsel, authorization of indemnification and evaluation as to reasonableness of expenses shall be made by those entitled under paragraph 3 of subsection B of this section to select counsel.

§ 13.1-702. Indemnification of officers, employees and agents.

Unless limited by a corporation's articles of incorporation,

1. An officer of the corporation is entitled to mandatory indemnification under § 13.1-698, and is entitled to apply for court-ordered indemnification under § 13.1-700, in each case to the same extent as a director; and

2. The corporation may indemnify and advance expenses under this article to an officer, employee, or agent of the corporation to the same extent as to a director.

§ 13.1-703. Insurance.

A corporation may purchase and maintain insurance on behalf of an individual who is or was a director, officer, employee, or agent of the corporation, or who, while a director, officer, employee, or agent of the corporation, is or was serving at the request of the corporation as a director, officer, partner, trustee, employee, or agent of another foreign or domestic corporation, partnership, joint venture, trust, employee benefit plan, or other enterprise, against liability asserted against or incurred by him in that capacity or arising from his status as a director, officer, employee, or agent, whether or not the corporation would have power to indemnify him against the same liability under § 13.1-697 or § 13.1-698.

§ 13.1-704. Application of article.

A. Unless the articles of incorporation or bylaws expressly provide otherwise, any authorization of indemnification in the articles of incorporation or bylaws shall not be deemed to prevent the corporation from providing the indemnity permitted or mandated by this article.

B. Any corporation shall have power to make any further indemnity, including indemnity with respect to a proceeding by or in the right of the corporation, and to make additional provision for advances and reimbursement of expenses, to any director, officer, employee or agent that may be authorized by the articles of incorporation or any bylaw made by the shareholders or any resolution adopted, before or after the event, by the shareholders, except an indemnity against (i) his willful misconduct, or (ii) a knowing violation of the criminal law. Unless the articles of incorporation, or any such bylaw or resolution expressly provide otherwise, any determination as to the right to any further indemnity shall be made in accordance with § 13.1-701 B. Each such indemnity may continue as to a person who has ceased to have the capacity referred to above and may inure to the benefit of the heirs, executors and administrators of such a person.

WISCONSIN

Business Corporation Law

§ 180.303. Reliance by directors or officers.

(1) Unless the director or officer has knowledge that makes reliance unwarranted, a director or officer, in discharging his or her duties to the corporation, may rely on information, opinions, reports or statements, any of which may be written or oral, formal or informal, including financial statements and other financial data, if prepared or presented by any of the following:

(a) An officer or employee of the corporation whom the director or officer believes in good faith to be reliable and competent in the matters presented.

(b) Legal counsel, public accountants or other persons as to matters the director or officer believes in good faith are within the person's professional or expert competence.

(c) In the case of reliance by a director, a committee of the board of directors of which the director is not a member if the director believes in good faith that the committee merits confidence.

(2) This section does not apply to a director's reliance under s. 180.40(3).

§ 180.305. Consideration of interests in addition to shareholders' interests.

In discharging his or her duties to the corporation and in determining what he or she believes to be in the best interests of the corporation, a director or officer may, in addition to considering the effects of any action on shareholders, consider the following:

(1) The effects of the action on employes, suppliers and customers of the corporation.

(2) The effects of the action on communities in which the corporation operates.

(3) Any other factors the director or officer considers pertinent.

§ 180.307. Limited liability of directors to corporation and shareholders.

(1) Except as provided in subs. (2) and (3), a director is not liable to the corporation, its shareholders, or any person asserting rights on behalf of the corporation or its shareholders, for damages, settlements, fees, fines, penalties or other monetary liabilities arising from a breach of, or failure to perform, any duty resulting solely from his or her status as a director, unless the person asserting liability proves that the breach or failure to perform constitutes any of the following:

820

(a) A wilful failure to deal fairly with the corporation or its shareholders in connection with a matter in which the director has a material conflict of interest.

(b) A violation of criminal law, unless the director had reasonable cause to believe his or her conduct was lawful or no reasonable cause to believe his or her conduct was unlawful.

(c) A transaction from which the director derived an improper personal profit.

(d) Wilful misconduct.

(2) This section does not apply to the liability of a director under s. 180.40(1).

(3)(a) A corporation may limit the immunity provided under this section as follows:

1. If the corporation is incorporated on or after the effective date of this subdivision ... [revisor inserts date], by the articles of incorporation, including any amendments or restatements of the articles of incorporation.

2. If the corporation was incorporated before the effective date of this subdivision ... [revisor inserts date], by an amendment to, or restatement of, the articles of incorporation which becomes effective only after the effective date of this subdivision ... [revisor inserts date].

(b) A limitation under par. (a) applies if the cause of action against a director accrued while the limitation is in effect.

§ 180.355. Interested directors.

No contract or other transaction between a corporation and one or more of its directors or any other corporation, firm, association, or entity in which one or more of its directors are directors or officers or are financially interested, shall be either void or voidable because of such relationship or interest or because such director or directors are present at the meeting of the board of directors or a committee thereof which authorizes, approves or ratifies such contract or transaction or because his or their votes are counted for such purpose, if (1) the fact of such relationship or interest is disclosed or known to the board of directors or committee which authorizes, approves or ratifies the contract or transaction by a vote or consent sufficient for the purpose without counting the votes or consents of such interested directors; (2) the fact of such relationship or interest is disclosed or known to the shareholders entitled to vote and they authorize, approve or ratify such contract or transaction by vote or written consent; or (3) the contract or transaction is fair and reasonable to the corporation. Common or interested directors may be counted in determining the presence of a quorum at a meeting of the board of directors or a committee thereof which authorizes, approves or ratifies such contract transaction.

821

§ 180.40. Unlawful distributions.

(1) In addition to any other liabilities imposed by law upon directors of a corporation:

(a) Directors of a corporation who vote for or assent to the declaration of any dividend or other distribution of the assets of a corporation to its shareholders contrary to the provisions of this chapter or contrary to any restrictions contained in the articles of incorporation, shall be jointly and severally liable to the corporation for the amount of such dividend which is paid or the value of such assets which are distributed in excess of the amount of such dividend or distribution which could have been paid or distributed without a violation of the provisions of this chapter or the restrictions in the articles of incorporation.

(b) Directors of a corporation who vote for or assent to the purchase of its own shares contrary to the provisions of this chapter or contrary to any restrictions contained in the articles of incorporation, shall be jointly and severally liable to the corporation for the amount of consideration paid for such shares which is in excess of the maximum amount which could have been paid therefor, without a violation of the provisions of this chapter or any restrictions in the articles of incorporation.

(c) Directors of a corporation who vote for or assent to any distribution of assets of a corporation to its shareholders during the liquidation of the corporation without the payment and discharge of, or making adequate provision for, all known debts, obligations, and liabilities of the corporation shall be jointly and severally liable to the corporation for the value of such assets which are distributed, to the extent that such debts, obligations and liabilities of the corporation are not thereafter paid, discharged or barred by statute.

(d) Directors of a corporation who vote for or assent to the making of a loan to an officer or director of the corporation shall be jointly and severally liable to the corporation for the amount of such loan until the repayment thereof, unless such directors shall sustain the burden of proof that such loan was made for a proper business purpose.

(2) A director of a corporation who is present at a meeting of its board of directors or a committee thereof of which he is a member at which action on any corporation matter is taken shall be presumed to have assented to the action taken unless his dissent is entered in the minutes of the meeting or unless he files his written dissent to such action with the person acting as the secretary of the meeting before the adjournment thereof or forwards such dissent by registered mail to the secretary of the corporation immediately after the adjournment of the meeting. Such right to dissent shall not apply to a director who voted in favor of such action.

(3) A director shall not be liable under subsection (1)(a), (b) or (c) if he relied and acted in good faith upon financial statements of the corporation represented to him to be correct by the president or the officer of such

822

corporation having charge of its books of account, or stated in a written report by an independent public or certified public accountant or firm of such accountants to fairly reflect the financial condition of such corporation, nor shall he be so liable if in good faith in determining the amount available for any such dividend or distribution he considered the assets to be of their book value.

(4) Any director against whom a claim shall be asserted under or pursuant to this section shall be entitled to contribution from the other directors who voted for or assented to the action upon which the claim is asserted.

(4m) Sections 180.303 and 180.307 do not apply to the liability of a director under sub. (1) or the reliance of a director under sub. (3).

(5) In addition to any other liabilities imposed by law upon shareholders of a corporation:

(a) Any director against whom a claim shall be asserted under or pursuant to this section for the payment of a dividend or other distribution of assets of a corporation and who shall be held liable thereon, shall be entitled to contribution from the shareholders who accepted or received any such dividend or assets, knowing such dividend or distribution to have been made in violation of this chapter, in proportion to the amounts received by them respectively.

(b) Any shareholder receiving any dividend or distribution of the assets of the corporation which dividend is paid or distribution is made contrary to the provisions of this chapter or contrary to any restrictions contained in the articles of incorporation, shall be liable to the corporation for the amount received by said shareholder which is paid or distributed in excess of the amount which could have been paid or distributed without a violation of the provisions of this chapter or any restrictions in the articles of incorporation.

(6) The shareholders of every corporation, other than railroad corporations, shall be personally liable to an amount equal to the par value of shares owned by them respectively, and to the consideration for which their shares without par value was issued, for all debts owing to employees of the corporation for services performed for such corporation, but not exceeding 6 months' service in any one case.

§ 180.042. Definitions applicable to indemnification and insurance provisions.

In ss. 180.042 to 180.059:

(1) "Corporation" means a domestic corporation and any domestic or foreign predecessor of a domestic corporation where the predecessor corporation's existence ceased upon the consummation of a merger or other transaction.

(2) "Director or officer" means any of the following:

(a) A natural person who is or was a director or officer of a corporation.

(b) A natural person who, while a director or officer of a corporation, is or was serving at the corporation's request as a director, officer, partner, trustee, member of any government or decision-making committee, employe or agent of another corporation or foreign corporation, partnership, joint venture, trust or other enterprise.

(c) A natural person who, while a director or officer of a corporation, is or was serving an employe benefit plan because his or her duties to the corporation also impose duties on, or otherwise involve services by, the person or to participants in or beneficiaries of the plan.

(d) Unless the context requires otherwise, the estate or personal representative of a director or officer.

(3) "Expenses" include fees, costs, charges, disbursements, attorney fees and any other expenses incurred in connection with a proceeding.

(4) "Liability" includes the obligation to pay a judgment, settlement, penalty, assessment, forfeiture or fine, including an excise tax assessed with respect to an employe benefit plan, and reasonable expenses.

(5) "Party" includes a natural person who was or is, or who is threatened to be made, a named defendant or respondent in a proceeding.

(6) "Proceeding" means any threatened, pending or completed civil, criminal, administrative or investigative action, suit, arbitration or other proceeding, whether formal or informal, which involves foreign, federal, state or local law and which is brought by or in the right of the corporation or by any other person.

§ 180.044. Mandatory indemnification.

(1) A corporation shall indemnify a director or officer, to the extent he or she has been successful on the merits or otherwise in the defense of a proceeding, for all reasonable expenses incurred in the proceeding if the director or officer was a party because he or she is a director or officer of the corporation.

(2)(a) In cases not included under sub. (1), a corporation shall indemnify a director or officer against liability incurred by the director or officer in a proceeding to which the director or officer was a party because he or she is a director or officer of the corporation, unless liability was incurred because the director or officer breached or failed to perform a duty he or she owes to the corporation and the breach or failure to perform constitutes any of the following:

1. A wilful failure to deal fairly with the corporation or its shareholders in connection with a matter in which the director or officer has a material conflict of interest.

2. A violation of criminal law, unless the director or officer had reasonable cause to believe his or her conduct was lawful or no reasonable cause to believe his or her conduct was unlawful.

824

3. A transaction from which the director or officer derived an improper personal profit.

4. Wilful misconduct.

(b) Determination of whether indemnification is required under this subsection shall be made under s. 180.046.

(c) The termination of a proceeding by judgment, order, settlement or conviction, or upon a plea of no contest or an equivalent plea, does not, by itself, create a presumption that indemnification of the director or officer is not required under this subsection.

(3) A director or officer who seeks indemnification under this section shall make a written request to the corporation.

(4)(a) Indemnification under this section is not required to the extent limited by the articles of incorporation under s. 180.048.

(b) Indemnification under this section is not required if the director or officer has previously received indemnification or allowance of expenses from any person, including the corporation, in connection with the same proceeding.

§ 180.046. Determination of right to indemnification.

Unless otherwise provided by the articles of incorporation or bylaws or by written agreement between the director or officer and the corporation, the director or officer seeking indemnification under s. 180.044 (2) shall select one of the following means for determining his or her right to indemnification:

(1) By a majority vote of a quorum of the board of directors consisting of directors not at the time parties to the same or related proceedings. If a quorum of disinterested directors cannot be obtained, by majority vote of a committee duly appointed by the board of directors and consisting solely of 2 or more directors not at the time parties to the same or related proceedings. Directors who are parties to the same or related proceedings may participate in the designation of members of the committee.

(2) By independent legal counsel selected by a quorum of the board of directors or its committee in the manner prescribed in sub. (1) or, if unable to obtain such a quorum or committee, by a majority vote of the full board of directors, including directors who are parties to the same or related proceedings.

(3) By a panel of 3 arbitrators consisting of one arbitrator selected by those directors entitled under sub. (2) to select independent legal counsel, one arbitrator selected by the director or officer seeking indemnification and one arbitrator selected by the 2 arbitrators previously selected.

(4) By an affirmative vote of shares as provided in s. 180.28. Shares owned by, or voted under the control of, persons who are at the time parties to the same or related proceedings, whether as plaintiffs or defendants or in any other capacity, may not be voted in making the determination.

825

(5) By a court under s. 180.051.

(6) By any other method provided for in any additional right to indemnification permitted under s. 180.049.

§ 180.047. Allowance of expenses as incurred.

Upon written request by a director or officer who is a party to a proceeding, a corporation may pay or reimburse his or her reasonable expenses as incurred if the director or officer provides the corporation with all of the following:

(1) A written affirmation of his or her good faith belief that he or she has not breached or failed to perform his or her duties to the corporation.

(2) A written undertaking, executed personally or on his or her behalf, to repay the allowance and, if required by the corporation, to pay reasonable interest on the allowance to the extent that it is ultimately determined under s. 180.046 that indemnification under s. 180.044 (2) is not required and that indemnification is not ordered by a court under s. 180.051 (2)(b). The undertaking under this subsection shall be an unlimited general obligation of the director or officer and may be accepted without reference to his or her ability to repay the allowance. The undertaking may be secured or unsecured.

§ 180.048. Corporation may limit indemnification.

(1) A corporation's obligations to indemnify under s. 180.044 may be limited as follows:

(a) If the corporation is incorporated on or after the effective date of this paragraph ... [revisor inserts date], by the articles of incorporation, including any amendments or restatements of the articles of incorporation.

(b) If the corporation was incorporated before the effective date of this paragraph ... [revisor inserts date], by an amendment to, or restatement of, the articles of incorporation which becomes effective on or after the effective date of this paragraph ... [revisor inserts date].

(2) A limitation under sub. (1) applies if the first alleged act of a director or officer for which indemnification is sought occurred while the limitation was in effect.

§ 180.049. Additional rights to indemnification and allowance of expenses.

(1) Except as provided in sub. (2), ss. 180.044 and 180.047 do not preclude any additional right to the indemnification or allowance of expenses that a director or officer may have under any of the following:

(a) The articles of incorporation or bylaws.

(b) A written agreement between the director or officer and the corporation.

826

(c) A resolution of the board of directors.

(d) A resolution, after notice, adopted by a majority vote of all of the corporation's voting shares then issued and outstanding.

(2) Regardless of the existence of an additional right under sub. (1), the corporation may not indemnify a director or officer, or permit a director or officer to retain any allowance of expenses unless it is determined by or on behalf of the corporation that the director or officer did not breach or fail or perform a duty he or she owes to the corporation which constitutes conduct under s. 180.044 (2)(a) 1, 2, 3 or 4. A director or officer who is a party to the same or related proceeding for which indemnification or an allowance of expenses is sought may not participate in a determination under this subsection.

(3) Sections 180.042 to 180.059 do not affect a corporation's power to pay or reimburse expenses incurred by a director or officer in any of the following circumstances:

(a) As a witness in a proceeding to which he or she is not a party.

(b) As a plaintiff or petitioner in a proceeding because he or she is or was an employe, agent, director or officer of the corporation.

§ 180.051. Court-ordered indemnification.

(1) Except as provided otherwise by written agreement between the director or officer and the corporation, a director or officer who is a party to a proceeding may apply for indemnification to the court conducting the proceeding or to another court of competent jurisdiction. Application shall be made for an initial determination by the court under s. 180.046 (5) or for review by the court of an adverse determination under s. 180.046 (1), (2), (3), (4) or (6). After receipt of an application, the court shall give any notice it considers necessary.

(2) The court shall order indemnification if it determines any of the following:

(a) That the director or officer is entitled to indemnification under s. 180.044 (1) or (2). If the court also determines that the corporation unreasonably refused the director's or officer's request for indemnification, the court shall order the corporation to pay the director's or officer's reasonable expenses incurred to obtain the court-ordered indemnification.

(b) That the director or officer is fairly and reasonably entitled to indemnification in view of all the relevant circumstances, regardless of whether indemnification is required under s. 180.044 (2).

§ 180.056. Indemnification and allowance of expenses of employes and agents.

A corporation may indemnify and allow reasonable expenses of an employe or agent who is not a director or officer to the extent provided by the

827

articles of incorporation or bylaws, by general or specific action of the board of directors or by contract.

§ 180.058. Insurance.

A corporation may purchase and maintain insurance on behalf of an individual who is an employe, agent, director or officer of the corporation against liability asserted against or incurred by the individual in his or her capacity as an employe, agent, director or officer or arising from his or her status as an employe, agent, director or officer, regardless of whether the corporation is required or authorized to indemnify or allow expenses to the individual against the same liability under ss. 180.044, 180.047, 180.049 and 180.056.

§ 180.059. Indemnification and insurance against securities law claims.

(1) It is the public policy of this state to require or permit indemnification, allowance of expenses and insurance for any liability incurred in connection with a proceeding involving securities regulation described under sub. (2) to the extent required or permitted under ss. 180.042 to 180.058.

(2) Sections 180.042 to 180.058 apply, to the extent applicable to any other proceeding, to any proceeding involving a federal or state statute, rule or regulation regulating the offer, sale or purchase of securities, securities brokers or dealers, or investment companies or investment advisers.

Appendix B-1

STATUTES LIMITING DIRECTOR LIABILITY

(as of April 30, 1988)

STATE	CITATION	SELF ENACTING	FOLLOWS DELAWARE	LESS THAN DELAWARE LIABILITY
Arizona	§ 10-054(9)	No	Yes	
Arkansas	§ 4-27-202(B)(3)	No	Yes	
California	Corps. Code § 204(10)	No	Yes	
Colorado	§ 7-3-101(1)(u)	No	Yes	
Delaware	Tit.8 § 102(b)(7)	No	Yes	
Florida	§§ 607.1645; 607.165	Yes		Yes
Georgia	§ 14-2-171(b)	No		Yes
Idaho	§ 30-1-54(2)	No	Yes	
Indiana	§ 23-1-35-1(e)	Yes		Yes
Iowa	§ 496A.49(13)	No	Yes	
Kansas	§ 17-6002(b)(8)	No	Yes	
Louisiana	§ 12-24C(4)	No	Yes	
Maryland	Corps. & Ass'ns §§ 2-104(b)(8); 2-405.2(a)			
Massachusetts	Ch. 156B § 13	No	Yes	
Michigan	§ 450.1209(c)	No	Yes	
Minnesota	§§ 302A.251(4); 302A.111(4)(u)	No	Yes	
Montana	§ 35-1-202(2)(e)	No	Yes	
Nevada	§ 78.036	No		Yes
New Jersey	§§ 14A:2-7(3); 14A:6-14	No	Yes	
New Mexico	§ 53-12-2(E)	No		Yes
New York	Bus. Corp. § 402(b)	No		Yes
North Carolina	§ 55-7	No		Yes
Ohio	§ 1701.59(D)	Yes		Yes
Oklahoma	Tit.18 § 1006B(7)	No	Yes	
Oregon	§ 16(2)(c)	No	Yes	
Pennsylvania	42 PS § 8364	No		Yes
Rhode Island	§ 7-1.1-48(a)(6)	No	Yes	
South Dakota	§ 47-2-58.8	No	Yes	
Tennessee	§ 48-12-102(b)(3)	No	Yes	
Texas	Civ. Stat. Art. 1302-7.06	No	Yes	
Utah	§ 16-10-49.1	No	Yes	
Virginia	§ 13.1-692.1	Yes		Yes
Washington	§ 23A.12.020	No		Yes
Wisconsin	§ 180.307	Yes		Yes
Wyoming	§ 17-1-202(c)	No	Yes	

Appendix B-2

KEY TO INDEMNIFICATION CHART

A   Similar to § 5 of 1969 Model Act/Delaware form.

B   Similar to § 4(o) of 1950 Model Act form.

C   Similar to 1980 or 1984 Model Act form.

D   Person who is or was or is threatened to be a party to any civil, criminal, investigative or administrative action, suit or proceeding, by reason of being a director, officer, employee or agent, or serving at corporation's request in another entity. Mandatory indemnification if successful on the merits or otherwise. Corporation may purchase and maintain D & O insurance.

E   Other entity includes employee benefit plans.

F   Settlements indemnified in direct/derivative actions.

G   Settlements or judgments in direct/derivative actions.

H   Mandatory subject to compliance with standards.

I   Mandatory if wholly successful.

J   Court may order indemnification of expenses.

K   Court may order indemnification of expenses and settlement.

L   Advance payment of expenses — undertaking or promise to repay.

M   Notice or report to be given shareholders.

N   Nonexclusive, directors and others.

O   Indemnification must be consistent with statute.

P   Corporation may establish trust fund, letters of credit, self-insurance, etc.

Q   Corporation may own interest in insurer.

R   Indemnification extends to heirs and representatives.

FOOTNOTES

1. Insurance includes retrospectively rated and self-insured programs.
2. Mandatory only if successful on the merits.
3. No indemnification for employees or agents.
4. State banks, savings and loan associations and credit unions may indemnify only by insurance.
5. Extent of indemnification in articles or bylaw of shareholders.
6. Notice must be given to plaintiff in direct or derivative actions.
7. Does not include administrative or investigative proceedings.
8. Purchase of D & O insurance not authorized.

Appendix B-2

CHART OF INDEMNIFICATION STATUTES

(as of April 30, 1988)

STATE	CITATION	A	B	C	D	E	F	G	H	I	J	K	L	M	N	O	P	Q	R
Alabama	§ 10-2A-21 (1980)	A			D						J		L		N				R
Alaska	§ 10.05.010 (1970)	A			D						J		L		N				R
Arizona[1]	§ 10-005 (1987)	A			D		F					K	L		N		P		R
Arkansas	§§ 4-26-814; 4-27-850; 4-27-1621 (1987)	A			D						J		L	M	N				R
California[2]	Corps. Code § 317 (1987)	A			D	E	F				J		L			O		Q	R
Colorado	§ 7-3-101.5 (1987)			C	D	E				I	J		L	M		O		Q	R
Connecticut[2]	§ 33-320a (1982)				D	E					J		L						R
Delaware	Tit.8 § 145 (1986)	A			D	E					J		L		N				R
Dist. Col.[3-7-8]	§ 29-304(16) (1963)		B												N				
Florida	§ 607.014 (1987)	A			D	E	F				J		L	M	N				R
Georgia	§ 14-2-156 (1987)	A			D						J		L	M	N				R
Hawaii	§ 415-5 (1987)			C	D	E					J		L		N			Q	R
Idaho[4]	§ 30-1-5 (1987)	A			D						J		L						R
Illinois	Ch.32 § 8.75 (1983)	A			D	E					J		L	M	N				R
Indiana	§§ 23-1-37-1 to 15 (1986)			C	D	E	F			I		K	L		N				
Iowa	§ 496A.4A (1987)			C	D	E				I	J		L	M	N				R
Kansas	§ 17-6305 (1987)	A			D	E					J		L		N				R
Kentucky	§ 271A.026 (1982)			C	D	E				I			L	M	N				R
Louisiana	§ 12:83 (1986)	A			D		F	G			J		L		N		P	Q	R
Maine	Tit.13A § 719 (1975)	A			D			G		I	J		L		N				
Maryland	Corps. & Ass'ns § 2-418 (1988)			C	D	E		G			J		L		N		P	Q	
Massachusetts[5-7]	Ch. 156B § 67 (1983)				D	E							L		N				
Michigan	§§ 450.1561 to 450.1569 (1987)	A			D		F				J		L		N				R
Minnesota	§ 302A.521 (1987)				D	E	F		H	I			L	M					
Mississippi	§§ 79-4-8.50 to 79-4-8.58 (1988)			C	D	E				I	J		L		N				R
Missouri	§ 351.355 (1986)	A			D	E	F				J		L		N				R
Montana	§ 35-1-414 (1981)			C	D	E				I	J		L	M		O			
Nebraska	§ 21-2004(15) (1981)	A			D	E					J		L	M		O			
Nevada	§ 78.751 (1987)	A			D		F				J		L		N		P	Q	R
New Hampshire	§ 293-A:5 (1982)	A			D						J		L		N				R
New Jersey	§ 14A:3-5 (1987)			C	D	E	F				J		L		N		P		
New Mexico	§ 53-11-4.1 (1987)			C	D	E				I	J		L	M	N		P		R
New York[3]	Bus. Corp. §§ 721 to 726 (1986)	A			D	E	F					K	L		N				R
North Carolina	§§ 55-19 to 55-21 (1986)	A				E				I		K		M	N				
North Dakota	§ 10-19.1-91 (1985)			C	D	E		G	H			K	L						R
Ohio[6]	§ 1701.13(E) (1986)	A			D				H		J		L		N		P	Q	R
Oklahoma	Tit.18 § 1031 (1986)			C	D	E				I	J		L		N				R

831

A   Similar to § 5 of 1969 Model Act/Delaware form.
B   Similar to § 4(o) of 1950 Model Act form.
C   Similar to 1980 or 1984 Model Act form.
D   Person who is or was or is threatened to be a party to any civil, criminal, investigative or administrative action, suit or proceeding, by reason of being a director, officer, employee or agent, or serving at corporation's request in another entity. Mandatory indemnification if successful on the merits or otherwise. Corporation may purchase and maintain D & O insurance.
E   Other entity includes employee benefit plans.
F   Settlements indemnified in direct/derivative actions.
G   Settlements or judgments in direct/derivative actions.
H   Mandatory subject to compliance with standards.
I   Mandatory if wholly successful.
J   Court may order indemnification of expenses.
K   Court may order indemnification of expenses and settlement.
L   Advance payment of expenses — undertaking or promise to repay.
M   Notice or report to be given shareholders.
N   Nonexclusive, directors and others.
O   Indemnification must be consistent with statute.
P   Corporation may establish trust fund, letters of credit, self-insurance, etc.
Q   Corporation may own interest in insurer.
R   Indemnification extends to heirs and representatives.

FOOTNOTES

1. Insurance includes retrospectively rated and self-insured programs.
2. Mandatory only if successful on the merits.
3. No indemnification for employees or agents.
4. State banks, savings and loan associations and credit unions may indemnify only by insurance.
5. Extent of indemnification in articles or bylaw of shareholders.
6. Notice must be given to plaintiff in direct or derivative actions.
7. Does not include administrative or investigative proceedings.
8. Purchase of D & O insurance not authorized.

STATE	CITATION	ELEMENTS INCLUDED IN STATUTE
Oregon	§§ 94 to 102 (1987)	A D J L N R
Pennsylvania	15 PS § 1410; 42 PS § 8365 (1987)	A D F G J L N P R
Puerto Rico [3-7-8]	Tit.14 § 1202(10) (1968)	B N
Rhode Island	§ 7-1.1-4.1 (1986)	C D E I J L M O
South Carolina	§ 33-13-180 (1981)	C D E I J L M O
South Dakota	§§ 47-2-58.1 to 47-2-58.7 (1987)	A D E J L N R
Tennessee	§ 48-18-501 to 48-18-509 (1988)	C D E G I J L N R
Texas	Bus. Corp. Act Art. 2.02-1 (1987)	C D E I J L O
Utah	§ 16-10-4(2) (1987)	A D J L N R
Vermont [3-7-8]	Tit.11 § 1852(15) (1971)	B N
Virginia	§§ 13.1-696 to 13.1-704 (1987)	C D E I J L N R
Virgin Islands	Tit.13 § 67a (1984)	A D J L N R
Washington	§ 23A.08.025 (1980)	C D E I J L N R
West Virginia	§ 31-1-9 (1975)	A D J L N R
Wisconsin	§§ 180.042 to 180.059 (1987)	C D E G H J L N
Wyoming	§ 17-1-105.1 (1987)	A D G N

833

Appendix C

SELECTED INSURANCE FORMS

NATIONAL UNION
FIRE INSURANCE COMPANY
OF PITTSBURGH, PA.

A CAPITAL STOCK COMPANY
ADMINISTRATIVE OFFICES
70 PINE STREET, NEW YORK, N.Y. 10270

DIRECTORS AND OFFICERS LEGAL LIABILITY APPLICATION

IF A POLICY IS ISSUED, IT WILL BE ON A CLAIMS-MADE BASIS

NOTICE: THE POLICY PROVIDES THAT THE LIMIT OF LIABILITY AVAILABLE TO PAY JUDGEMENTS OR SETTLE-MENTS SHALL BE REDUCED BY AMOUNTS INCURRED FOR LEGAL DEFENSE. FURTHER NOTE THAT AMOUNTS INCURRED FOR LEGAL DEFENSE SHALL BE APPLIED AGAINST THE RETENTION AMOUNT.

1. (a) Corporation Name:
   (b) State of Incorporation:

2. Address:

3. Amount of Insurance Requested $_____.
   Self Insured Retention (Each Loss) $_____

4. (a) Nature of Business
   (b) Annual Sales
   (c) Net Worth
   (d) Total Assets

5. Corporation has continually been in business since _____

6. Attach copies of the following:
   (a) Latest annual report
   (b) Latest 10-K report filed with the SEC (if the Company is publicly traded)
   (c) Latest Dun & Bradstreet report
   (d) Latest interim financial statement available
   (e) Latest copy of the Notice of Annual Meeting of Stockholders
   (f) Latest proxy statement
   (g) Copy (certified by Corporate Secretary) of the indemnification provisions of the by-laws.

7. Stock ownership
   (a) Total number of common shares outstanding _____
   (b) Total number of common stock shareholders _____
   (c) Total number of common shares owned by its Directors (direct and benefical) _____
   (d) Total number of common shares owned by its Officers (direct and benefical) not Directors _____
   (e) In the event any shareholder owns 5 percent or more of the common shares directly or beneficially, designate name and percentage of holdings:

   (f) Please designate if there are any other securities convertible to common stock. If so, describe fully.

8760 (6/85)

—1—

8. Complete list of all Directors of parent company by name and affiliation with other Corporations.

9. Complete list of all Officers of parent company by name and affiliation with other Corporations.

10. (a) List of subsidiary companies

Name	Business or Type of Operation	Percentage of Ownership	Date Acquired	Domestic or Foreign

(b) Coverage to include all subsidiaries   Yes_____   No_____
If "yes", include complete list of Directors and Officers of each subsidiary.

11. (a) Are any plans for merger, acquisition or consolidation being considered?

(b) If so, have they been approved by the board of directors?

(c) If so, have they been submitted to the shareholders for approval?

12. Does the corporation anticipate any new public offering of securities or any registration of securities under the Securities Act of 1933 or qualification of securities under Regulation A within the next year? (If "yes", give details and submit prospectus)

13. There has not been nor is there now pending any claim(s) against any person proposed for insurance in their capacity of either Director or Officer of the above Corporation and its subsidiaries except as follows: (attach complete details) (if no such claims, check here:_____NONE).

14. No Director or Officer has knowledge or information of any act, error, or omission which might give rise to a claim under the proposed policy except as follows: (attach complete details) (if they have no such knowledge or information, check here:_____NONE).

15. Has the Corporation or any of its Directors and Officers been involved in or have any knowledge of any fact or circumstance involving the following which may give rise to a claim under the proposed policy?

(a) Anti-trust, copyright or patent litigation? _____

(b) Been charged in any civil or criminal action or administrative proceeding with a violation of any federal or state security law or regulation? _____

(c) Been charged in any civil or criminal action or administrative proceeding with a violation of any federal or state anti-trust or Fair Trade Law? _____

(d) Been involved in any representative actions, class actions or derivative suits? _____
(If any of the above are answered "yes", attach full details.)

16. It is agreed with respect to questions #14 and #15 above, that if such knowledge or information exists any claim or action arising therefrom is excluded from this proposed coverage.

17. It is agreed that the Directors and Officers will give the Insurer the right to associate with them in the defense and settlement of any claim that appears reasonably likely to involve the Insurer and the Directors and Officers will cooperate with the Insurer in the defense of such claim.

18. It is agreed that a Director(s) or Officer(s) may elect not to appeal a judgement in excess of the retained limits, however, the Insurer shall have the right to make such appeal at its own cost and expense.

—2—

8760 (6/85)

19. It is agreed that all Directors and Officers shall furnish the Insurer with copies of investigations, pleadings, and all other papers relating to an occurrence which could give rise to a possible claim under the proposed policy.

20. It is agreed that the Corporation will file with National Union Fire Insurance Company of Pittsburgh, Pa., as soon as the same become available, a copy of each registration statement and annual or interim report which the Corporation may from time to time file with the Securities and Exchange Commission.

21. Previous Directors and Officers Legal Liability Insurance (Answer each item)

   Name of Company:

   (a) Limit _____.   Self Insured Retention _____.

   Policy Expiration _____.

   (b) Premium _____ (indicate annual or three year).

22. Has any carrier refused or cancelled coverage? (If cancelled, date of cancellation) _____

   Loss Experience _____

THE UNDERSIGNED AUTHORIZED OFFICER OF THE CORPORATION DECLARES THAT THE STATEMENTS SET FORTH HEREIN ARE TRUE. THE UNDERSIGNED AUTHORIZED OFFICER AGREES THAT IF THE INFORMATION SUPPLIED ON THIS APPLICATION CHANGES BETWEEN THE DATE OF THIS APPLICATION AND THE EFFECTIVE DATE OF THE INSURANCE, HE/SHE (UNDERSIGNED) WILL IMMEDIATELY NOTIFY THE INSURER OF SUCH CHANGES, AND THE INSURER MAY WITHDRAW OR MODIFY ANY OUTSTANDING QUOTATIONS AND/OR AUTHORIZATION OR AGREEMENT TO BIND THE INSURANCE.

SIGNING OF THIS APPLICATION DOES NOT BIND THE APPLICANT NOR THE INSURER TO COMPLETE THE INSURANCE, BUT IT IS AGREED THAT THIS FORM SHALL BE THE BASIS OF THE CONTRACT SHOULD A POLICY BE ISSUED, AND IT WILL BE ATTACHED TO AND BECOME PART OF THE POLICY.

NOTICE TO NEW YORK APPLICANTS: ANY PERSON WHO KNOWINGLY AND WITH INTENT TO DEFRAUD ANY INSURANCE COMPANY OR OTHER PERSON FILES AN APPLICATION FOR IN-SURANCE CONTAINING ANY FALSE INFORMATION, OR CONCEALS FOR THE PURPOSE OF MIS-LEADING INFORMATION CONCERNING ANY FACT MATERIAL THERETO, COMMITS A FRAUDULENT INSURANCE ACT, WHICH IS A CRIME.

Signed: _____

Date: _____

Title: _____
   Must Be Signed By Chairman
   of the Boards or President

Attest:

_____

Broker: _____

Address: _____

Corporation _____

(Corporate Seal)

IF AN ORDER IS RECEIVED, THE APPLICATION IS ATTACHED TO THE POLICY SO IT IS NECESSARY THAT ALL QUESTIONS BE ANSWERED IN DETAIL.

IMPORTANT — NEW YORK APPLICANTS — SEE REVERSE SIDE

—3—

8760 (6/85)

NEW YORK APPLICANTS: PLEASE READ THE FOLLOWING STATEMENT CAREFULLY AND SIGN BELOW WHERE INDICATED. IF A POLICY IS ISSUED, NEW YORK INSURANCE DEPARTMENT REGULATIONS REQUIRE THAT THIS SIGNED STATEMENT BE ATTACHED TO THE POLICY.

The insured hereby acknowledges that he/she/it is aware that the limit of liability contained in this policy shall be reduced and may be completely exhausted, by the costs of legal defense and, in such event, the Insurer shall not be liable for the costs of legal defense or for the amount of any judgement or settlement to the extent that such exceeds the limit of liability of this policy.

The insured hereby further acknowledges that he/she/it is aware that legal defense costs that are incurred shall be applied against the retention amount.

Signed: _____

Date: _____

TITLE: _____

Must Be Signed By Chairman
of the Board or President

8760 (6/85)

—4—

838

NATIONAL UNION
FIRE INSURANCE COMPANY
OF PITTSBURGH, PA.

A CAPITAL STOCK COMPANY

ADMINISTRATIVE OFFICES
70 PINE STREET, NEW YORK, N.Y. 10270

DIRECTORS AND OFFICERS LIABILITY AND
ORGANIZATION REIMBURSEMENT APPLICATION

IF A POLICY IS ISSUED, IT WILL BE ON A CLAIMS-MADE BASIS

NOTICE: THE POLICY PROVIDES THAT THE LIMIT OF LIABILITY AVAILABLE TO PAY JUDGEMENTS OR SETTLEMENTS SHALL BE REDUCED BY AMOUNTS INCURRED FOR LEGAL DEFENSE. FURTHER NOTE THAT AMOUNTS INCURRED FOR LEGAL DEFENSE SHALL BE APPLIED AGAINST THE RETENTION AMOUNT.

1. (a) Name of Organization
   (b) State of Incorporation or charter
   (c) Chartered or Incorporated as a_____.

2. Address:

3. Amount of Insurance $_____ Self Insured Retention $_____.

4. Nature of Operations:

5. Organization has continually been operating since _____.

6. Attach copies of latest Annual Report and Balance Sheet.

7. If a Corporation, attach a copy (Certified by Corporate Secretary) of the By Laws of the organization and current amendments.

8. Stock (a) Total number of common stock shareholders_____.
   (b) Total number of common shares outstanding_____.
   (c) Total number of common shares owned by its Directors (direct and beneficial)_____.
   (d) Total number of common shares owned by its Officers (direct and beneficial) not Directors_____.

9. (a) Annual election date of Directors_____.
   (b) Compulsory retirement age for Directors_____; Officers_____.

—1—

8759 (6/85)

10. List of all subsidiary corporations, associations and fraternities.

11. Complete list of all Directors by name and affiliation with other associations, etc.

12. Complete list of all Officers by name and affiliations with other associations, etc.

13. Has this organization merged with any other organization within the last ten years?   Yes_____   No_____
    If so, please list dates and names of such organizations.

14. Previous Directors and Officers Legal Liability Insurance (Answer Each Item)
    (a) Name of company.
    (b) Limit   Self Insured Retention
    (c) Premium (indicate annual or three year).
    (d) Has any carrier refused or cancelled coverage?
    (e) Loss experience.

15. There has not been nor is there now pending any claim against any person proposed for insurance in their
    capacity of either Director or Officer or Trustee of the above Organization except as follows:
    (attach complete details) (if no such claims, check here: _____ NONE)

16. No Director or Officer has knowledge or information of any act, error or omission which might give rise to
    a claim under the proposed policy except as follows: (attach complete details) (if they have no such
    knowledge or information, check here: _____ NONE)

17. It is agreed with respect to question #16 above, that if such knowledge or information exists any claim or
    action arising therefrom is excluded from this proposed coverage.

18. It is agreed that the Directors and Officers will give the Insurer the right to associate with them in the
    defense and settlement of any claim that appears reasonably likely to involve the Insurer and the Directors
    and Officers will cooperate with the Insurer in the defense of such claim.

19. It is agreed that the Director(s) or Officer(s) may elect not to appeal a judgement in excess of the retained
    limits, however, the Insurer shall have the right to make such appeal at its own cost and expense.

20. It is agreed that all Directors and Officers shall furnish the Insurer with copies of investigations, pleadings,
    and all other papers relating to an occurrence which could give rise to a possible claim under the proposed
    policy.

—2—

8759 (6/85)

THE UNDERSIGNED AUTHORIZED OFFICER OF THE ORGANIZATION DECLARES THAT THE STATEMENTS SET FORTH HEREIN ARE TRUE. THE UNDERSIGNED AUTHORIZED OFFICER AGREES THAT IF THE INFORMATION SUPPLIED ON THIS APPLICATION CHANGES BETWEEN THE DATE OF THIS APPLICATION AND THE EFFECTIVE DATE OF THE INSURANCE, HE/SHE (UNDERSIGNED) WILL IMMEDIATELY NOTIFY THE INSURER OF SUCH CHANGES, AND THE INSURER MAY WITHDRAW OR MODIFY ANY OUTSTANDING QUOTATIONS AND/OR AUTHORIZATION OR AGREEMENT TO BIND THE INSURANCE.

SIGNING OF THIS APPLICATION DOES NOT BIND THE APPLICANT NOR THE INSURER TO COMPLETE THE INSURANCE, BUT IT IS AGREED THAT THIS FORM SHALL BE THE BASIS OF THE CONTRACT SHOULD A POLICY BE ISSUED, AND IT WILL BE ATTACHED TO AND BECOME PART OF THE POLICY.

NOTICE TO NEW YORK APPLICANTS: ANY PERSON WHO KNOWINGLY AND WITH INTENT TO DE- FRAUD ANY INSURANCE COMPANY OR OTHER PERSON FILES AN APPLICATION FOR INSURANCE CONTAINING ANY FALSE INFORMATION, OR CONCEALS FOR THE PURPOSE OF MISLEADING, INFORMATION CONCERNING ANY FACT MATERIAL THERETO, COMMITS A FRAUDULENT IN- SURANCE ACT, WHICH IS A CRIME.

Signed: _____

Date: _____

Title: _____
Must Be Signed By Chairman
of the Board or President

Attest

_____

Broker: _____   Corporation _____

Address: _____

_____   (Corporate Seal)

IF AN ORDER IS RECEIVED, THE APPLICATION IS ATTACHED TO THE POLICY SO IT IS NECESSARY THAT ALL QUESTIONS BE ANSWERED IN DETAIL.

NEW YORK APPLICANTS: PLEASE READ THE FOLLOWING STATEMENT CAREFULLY AND SIGN BELOW WHERE INDICATED. IF A POLICY IS ISSUED, NEW YORK INSURANCE DEPARTMENT REGULATIONS REQUIRE THAT THIS SIGNED STATEMENT BE ATTACHED TO THE POLICY.

The insured hereby acknowledges that he/she/it is aware that the limit of liability contained in this policy shall be reduced, and may be completely exhausted, by the costs of legal defense and, in such event, the Insurer shall not be liable for the costs of legal defense or for the amount of any judgement or settlement to the extent that such exceeds the limit of liability of this policy.

The insured hereby further acknowledges that he/she/it is aware that legal defense costs that are incurred shall be applied against the retention amount.

Signed: _____

Date: _____

TITLE: _____
MUST BE SIGNED BY PRESIDENT OR CHAIRMAN OF THE BOARD

—3—

8759 (6/86)

841

NATIONAL UNION
FIRE INSURANCE COMPANY
OF PITTSBURGH, PA.
A CAPITAL STOCK COMPANY

Administrative Offices
70 PINE STREET, NEW YORK, N.Y. 10270

DIRECTORS AND OFFICERS LIABILITY AND CORPORATION REIMBURSEMENT

THIS IS A CLAIMS-MADE POLICY — PLEASE READ CAREFULLY

NOTICE: THE LIMIT OF LIABILITY AVAILABLE TO PAY JUDGEMENTS OR SETTLEMENTS SHALL BE REDUCED BY AMOUNTS INCURRED FOR LEGAL DEFENSE. FURTHER NOTE THAT AMOUNTS INCURRED FOR LEGAL DEFENSE SHALL BE APPLIED AGAINST THE RETENTION AMOUNT.

DECLARATIONS

ITEM 1.   NAMED INSURED: The Directors and Officers of

          MAILING ADDRESS:

          STATE OF INCORPORATION OF THE COMPANY NAMED ABOVE:

ITEM 2.   POLICY PERIOD: From   to
          (12:00 Noon Standard Time at the address stated in Item 1)

ITEM 3.   LIMIT OF LIABILITY: $_____ each Policy Year and this shall be the combined limit of liability for both policy forms 8750 and 8749 which attach hereto and form a part hereof.

ITEM 4.   RETENTIONS:
          A. Corporation Reimbursement: $_____ per Loss

          B. Directors and Officers Liability
             $_____ per Director or Officer, subject to a maximum of
             $_____ per Loss.

ITEM 5.   PREMIUM: 3 Year Premium Prepaid $_____
                    3 Year Installments
                    payable each anniversary
                        1st $_____ Inception
                        2nd $_____
                        3rd $_____

_____
AUTHORIZED REPRESENTATIVE

_____   _____
COUNTERSIGNATURE DATE   COUNTERSIGNED AT

In consideration of the premiums and statements made to the Insurer by application together with its attachments, a copy of which is attached and made a part hereof, this Declarations page with policy form 8749 and/or policy form 8750 together with the completed and signed application, constitute the contract, and the National Union Fire Insurance Company of Pittsburgh, Pa., herein call the "Insurer" agrees as follows:

8749/8750 (6/85)   Order by 42614 (7/85)

NATIONAL UNION FIRE INSURANCE COMPANY OF PITTSBURGH, PA.

CORPORATION REIMBURSEMENT

1. INSURING CLAUSE

This policy shall, subject to its terms, conditions and limitations as hereinafter provided, pay on behalf of the Company named in Item 1 of the Declarations (herein called the "Company") Loss (as herein defined) arising from any claim or claims which are first made during the policy period against each and every person, jointly or severally, who was or now is or may hereafter be a Director or Officer (as herein defined) of the Company, by reason of any Wrongful Act (as herein defined) in their respective capacities as Directors or Officers of the Company, but only when the Directors or Officers (herein individually or collectively sometimes called the "Insureds") shall have been indemnified by the Company for damages, judgments, settlements, costs, charges or expenses incurred in connection with the defense of any action, suit or proceeding or any appeal therefrom to which the Directors or Officers may be a party or with which they may be threatened, pursuant to law, common or statutory, or the Charter or By-Laws of the Company duly effective under such law which determines and defines such rights of indemnity.

2. DEFINITIONS

(a) The term "Director or Officer" shall mean:

    (i) Any duly elected Director or duly elected or appointed Officer of the Company. Coverage will automatically apply to all newly created Directors and Officers after the inception date of this policy, subject to:

        a) Written notice of all such changes to the Insurer, within thirty (30) days after each anniversary date, or the termination date, and

        b) payment of any additional premium required.

(b) The term "Policy Year" shall mean a period of one year, within the policy period, commencing each year on the day and hour first named in Item 2 of the Declarations, or if the time between the effective date or anniversary and termination of the policy is less than one year, then such lesser period.

(c) The term "Loss" shall mean any amount the Company shall have paid to a Director or Officer as indemnity for a claim or claims arising out of those matters set forth in the Insuring Clause above whether actual or asserted and subject to the applicable limits and conditions of this policy, shall include damages, judgments, settlements, costs, charges and expenses (excluding salaries of Officers or employees of the Company) incurred in the defense of actions, suits or proceedings and appeals therefrom for which payment by the Company may be required or permitted according to applicable law, common or statutory, or under provisions of the Company's Charter or By-Laws effective pursuant to such law; provided always that such subject of Loss shall not include fines or penalties imposed by law, punitive or exemplary damages, or matters which may be deemed uninsurable under the law pursuant to which this policy shall be construed.

(d) The term "Wrongful Act" shall mean any breach of duty, neglect, error, misstatement, misleading statement, omission or other act done or wrongfully attempted by the Directors or Officers or any of the foregoing so alleged by any claimant or any matter claimed against them solely by reason of their being such Directors or Officers.

(e) The term "Subsidiary Company" shall mean a company of which the Company named in Item 1 of the Declarations owns more than 50% of the voting stock. This policy shall automatically insure any Subsidiary Company acquired or created after the inception of this policy, but only for Wrongful Acts occurring subsequent to such creation or acquisition, and only if the Company has provided the Insurer with full particulars of the Subsidiary Company and paid the additional premium required not later than ninety (90) days after said acquisition or creation.

3. EXTENSIONS

Subject otherwise to the terms hereof, this policy shall cover the Company for Loss arising from any claims made against the estates, heirs, or legal representatives of deceased Directors or Officers who were Directors or Officers at the time the Wrongful Acts upon which such claims are based were committed, and the legal representatives of Directors or Officers in the event of their incompetency, insolvency or bankruptcy.

4. EXCLUSIONS

The Insurer shall not be liable to make any payment for Loss in connection with any claim or claims made against the Insureds:

(a) which result in a finding of personal profit, gain or advantage;

(b) for the return by the Insureds of any remuneration paid to the Insureds without the previous approval of the stockholders of the Company, which payment without such previous approval shall be held by the courts to have been illegal;

(c) for an accounting of profits in fact made from the purchase or sale by the Insureds of securities of the Company within the meaning of Section 16(b) of the Securities Exchange Act of 1934 and amendments thereto or similar provisions of any state statutory law;

(d) brought about or contributed to by the fraudulent, dishonest or criminal acts of the Insureds; however the provisions of this exclusion shall not apply unless a judgment or other final adjudication thereof adverse to the Insureds shall establish fraud, dishonesty or criminal acts;

(e) arising from, attributable to or involving attempts, whether alleged or actual, successful or unsuccessful, by persons or entities to acquire securities of the Company against the opposition of the Board of Directors of the Company, nor to any claims arising from, attributable to or involving efforts, whether alleged or actual, successful or unsuccessful, by the Company and/or its Directors to resist such attempts;

(f) based on or attributable to any failure or omisssion on the part of the Insureds to effect and maintain insurance;

(g) which is insured by any other policy or policies, except in respect of any excess beyond the amounts of the limits of liability of such other policy or policies;

(h) arising from any circumstances of which notice has been given under any policy of which this policy is a renewal or replacement or which it may succeed in time;

(i) which are brought by, or on the behalf of, any other Insureds including but not limited to shareholders' derivative suits and/or representative class action suits, brought by one or more past, present or future Directors and/or Officers including their estates, beneficiaries, heirs, legal representatives, assigns and/or the Company against one or more past, present or future Directors or Officers;

(j) for violation of any of the responsibilities, obligations or duties imposed upon fiduciaries by the Employee Retirement Income Security Act of 1974 or amendments thereto or any similar provisions of state statutory law or common law;

(k) arising from any pending or prior litigation as of the inception date of this policy, as well as all future claims or litigation based upon the pending or prior litigation or derived from the same or essentially the same facts (actual or alledged) that gave rise to the prior or pending litigation;

(l) for bodily injury, sickness, disease, death, or emotional distress of any person, or for damage to or destruction of any tangible property, including the loss of use thereof, or for oral or written publication of a libel or slander or of other defamatory or disparaging material or of material that violates a person's right of privacy;

(m) arising from charges of seepage, pollution or contamination and based upon or attributed to violation or alleged violation of any federal, state, municipal or other governmental statute, regulation or ordinance prohibiting or providing for the control or regulation of emissions or effluents of any kind into the atmosphere or any body of land, water, waterway or watercourse or arising from any action or proceeding brought for enforcement purposes by any public official, agency, commission, or board of pollution control adminstration pursuant to any such statutes, regulations or ordinances or arising from any suits alleging seepage, pollution or contamination based upon common law nuisance or trespass.

5. LIMIT AND RETENTION

(a) The Insurer shall be liable to pay 95% of Loss excess of the amount stated in (c) below up to the amount here-inafter stated, it being warranted that the remaining 5% of each and every Loss shall be carried by the Company at its own risk and uninsured.

(b) Subject to the foregoing, the Insurer's liability for Loss shall be the amount stated in Item 3 of the Declarations which shall be the maximum liability of the Insurer in each Policy Year. The limit of liability of the Insurer in the Discovery Period shall be part of, and not in addition to, the limit of liability of the Insurer in the Policy Year which terminates at the inception of the Discovery Period.

(c) This policy is only to pay the excess over the retention amount stated in Item 4.A. of the Declarations in respect of each and every Loss hereunder, including costs, charges and expenses as described in Clause 6, and such retention amount is to be borne by the Company and is not to be insured. Loss arising out of the same Wrongful Act or interrelated, repeated or continuous Wrongful Acts of one or more of the Directors or Officers shall be con-sidered a single Loss and only one retention amount shall be deducted from the aggregate amount of such Loss.

(d) Loss arising out of claims for the same Wrongful Act or interrelated, repeated or continuous Wrongful Acts of one or more of the Directors or Officers shall be deemed Loss in the Policy Year in which the first such claim or Wrong-ful Act is first reported to the Insurer.

(e) The foregoing provisions shall apply to this policy and the Directors and Officers Liability policy attached hereto as though they constitute a single policy and the Insurer's maximum liability under both policies together shall not exceed the limits and retention set out in this Clause 5.

6. DEFENSE COSTS, CHARGES AND EXPENSES AND SETTLEMENTS, (INCLUDED IN THE LIMIT OF LIABILITY)

(a) The Insurer does not, under the terms of this policy, assume any duty to defend, nor are the costs, charges and expenses of defense payable by the Insurer in addition to the limit of liability. Costs, charges and expenses of defense are part of Loss insured under this policy and as such are subject to the provisions of Clause 5.

(b) Only those costs, charges, expenses and settlements consented to by the Insurer shall be recoverable as Loss under the terms of this policy. The Insurer's consent shall not be unreasonably withheld, but the Insurer shall be entitled to full information and all particulars it may request in order to reach a decision as to reasonableness.

With respect to the settlement of any claim made against the Company and the Insureds, the Company and the Insureds and the Insurer agree to use their best efforts to determine a fair and proper allocation of the settlement amount as between the Company and the Insureds.

(c) The words "costs, charges and expenses" shall include the cost of any appeal, attachment or similar bonds.

7. LOSS PROVISIONS

(a) The time when a Loss shall be incurred for purposes of determining the application of Clause 5(b) shall be the date on which the Company shall give written notice to the Insurer as hereinafter provided.

(b) The Company shall as a condition precedent to its right to be indemnified under this policy give to the Insurer notice in writing of any claim made against the Directors or Officers as soon as practicable during the policy period or during the Discovery Period, if effective in accordance with Clause 8(a).

(c) If during the policy period or during the Discovery Period, if effective in accordance with Clause 8(a), the Company shall become aware of any circumstances which may subsequently give rise to a claim being made against the Insureds and shall give written notice of the circumstances and the reasons for anticipating a claim, with full partic-ulars as to dates and persons involved, then any claim which is subsequently made against the Insureds asrising out of such circumstances shall be treated as a claim made during the currency hereof.

(d) Notice hereunder shall be given to the Insurer, 70 Pine Street, New York, N.Y. 10270.

8749 (6/85)   -3-

845

(e) The Company shall give the Insurer such information and cooperation as it may reasonably require and as shall be in the Company's power.

8. GENERAL CONDITIONS

(a) DISCOVERY CLAUSE

If the Insurer shall cancel or refuse to renew this policy the Company shall have the right, upon payment of the additional premium of 25% of the three year premium hereunder, to an extension of the cover granted by this policy in respect of any claim or claims which are made against the Directors or Officers during the period of twelve calendar months after the effective date of such cancellation or non-renewal, herein called the Discovery Period, but only in respect of any Wrongful Act committed before the effective date of such cancellation or non-renewal and otherwise covered by this policy. This right shall terminate, however, unless written notice of such election together with payment of the additional premium due is received by the Insurer within ten (10) days after the effective date of cancellation or non-renewal. The offer by the Insurer of renewal terms, conditions, limits of liability and/or premiums different from those of the expiring policy shall not constitute refusal to renew. This Clause and the rights granted herein to the Company shall not apply to any cancellation resulting from non-payment of premium.

(b) CANCELLATION CLAUSE

This policy may be cancelled by the Company at any time only by mailing written prior notice to the Insurer or by surrender of this policy to the Insurer or its authorized agent. This policy may also be cancelled by or on behalf of the Insurer by delivering to the Company or by mailing to the Company, by registered, certified, or other first class mail, at the Company's address as shown in Item 1 of the Declarations, written notice stating when, not less than thirty (30) days thereafter, the cancellation shall be effective. The mailing of such notice as aforesaid shall be sufficient proof of notice. The policy period terminates at the date and hour specified in such notice, or at the date and time of surrender.

If this policy shall be cancelled by the Company, the Insurer shall retain the customary short rate proportion of the premium hereon.

If this policy shall be cancelled by the Insurer, the Insurer shall retain the pro rata proportion of the premium hereon.

Payment or tender of any unearned premium by the Insurer shall not be a condition precedent to the effectiveness of cancellation but such payment shall be made as soon as practicable.

If the period of limitation relating to the giving of notice is prohibited or made void by any law controlling the construction thereof, such period shall be deemed to be amended so as to be equal to the minimum period of limitation permitted by such law.

9. SUBROGATION

In the event of any payment under this policy, the Insurer shall be subrogated to the extent of such payment to all the Company's rights of recovery therefor, and the Company shall execute all papers required and shall do everything that may be necessary to secure such rights including the execution of such documents necessary to enable the Insurer effectively to bring suit in the name of the Company.

10. NOTICE AND AUTHORITY

It is agreed that the Company shall act on behalf of all Insureds with respect to the giving and receiving of notice of claim or cancellation, the payment of premiums and the receiving of any return premiums that may become due under this policy, the receipt and acceptance of any endorsements issued to form a part of this policy, and the exercising or declining to exercise any right to a Discovery Period.

11. ASSIGNMENT

This policy and any and all rights hereunder is not assignable without the written consent of the Insurer.

8749 (6/85)   -4-

12. ACTION AGAINST INSURER

No action shall lie against the Insurer unless, as a condition precedent thereto, there shall have been full compliance with all of the terms of this policy, nor until the amount of the Company's obligation to pay shall have been finally determined either by judgement against an Insured after actual trial or by written agreement of the Company, the claimant and the Insurer.

Any person or organization or the legal representative thereof who has secured such judgement or written agreement shall thereafter be entitled to recover under this policy to the extent of the insurance afforded by this policy. No person or organization shall have any right under this policy to join the Insurer as a party to any action against the Company and/or Insureds to determine the Company's liability, nor shall the Insurer be impleaded by the Company and/or Insureds or their legal representatives. Bankruptcy or insolvency of the Company or of the Company's estate shall not relieve the Insurer of any of its obligations hereunder.

IN WITNESS WHEREOF, the Insurer has caused this policy to be signed by its President and a Secretary and counter-signed on the Declarations Page by a duly authorized agent of the Insurer.

Secretary

President

847

NATIONAL UNION FIRE INSURANCE COMPANY OF PITTSBURGH, PA.

DIRECTORS AND OFFICERS LIABILITY

1. INSURING CLAUSE

    This policy shall, subject to its terms, conditions and limitations as hereinafter provided, pay on behalf of each and every person who was or now is or may hereafter be a Director or Officer (who are herein individually or collectively sometimes called the "Insureds") of the Company named in Item 1 of the Declarations (herein called the "Company") Loss (as herein defined) arising from any claim or claims which are first made against the Insureds, jointly or severally, during the policy period by reason of any Wrongful Act (as herein defined) in their respective capacities as Directors or Officers.

2. DEFINITIONS

    (a) The term "Director or Officer" shall mean:

        (i) Any duly elected Director or duly elected or appointed Officer of the Company. Coverage will automatically apply to all newly created Directors and Officers after the inception date of this policy, subject to:

            a) Written notice of all such changes to the Insurer, within thirty (30) days after each anniversary date, or the termination date, and

            b) payment of any additional premium required.

    (b) The term "Policy Year" shall mean a period of one year, within the policy period, commencing each year on the day and hour first named in Item 2 of the Declarations, or if the time between the effective date or anniversary and termination of the policy is less than one year, then such lesser period.

    (c) The term "Loss" shall mean any amount which the Insureds are legally obligated to pay for a claim or claims for Wrongful Acts, and shall include damages, judgments, settlements, costs, charges and expenses (excluding salaries of officers or employees of the Company) incurred in the defense of actions, suits or proceedings and appeals therefrom; provided always that such subject of Loss shall not include fines or penalties imposed by law, punitive or exemplary damages, or matters which may be deemed uninsurable under the law pursuant to which this policy shall be construed.

    (d) The term "Wrongful Act" shall mean any breach of duty, neglect, error, misstatement, misleading statement, omission or other act done or wrongfully attempted by the Insureds or any of the foregoing so alleged by any claimant or any matter claimed against them solely by reason of their being such Directors or Officers of the Company.

    (e) The term "Subsidiary Company" shall mean a company of which the Company named in Item 1 of the Declarations owns more than 50% of the voting stock. This policy shall automatically insure the Directors and Officers of any Subsidiary Company acquired or created after the inception of this policy, but only for Wrongful Acts occurring subsequent to such creation or acquisition, and only if the Company has provided the Insurer with full particulars of the Subsidiary Company and paid the additional premium required not later than ninety (90) days after said acquisition or creation.

8750 (6/85)   -1-

3. EXTENSIONS

Subject otherwise to the terms hereof, this policy shall cover Loss arising from any claims made against the estates, heirs, or legal representatives of deceased Insureds who were Directors or Officers at the time the Wrongful Acts upon which such claims are based were committed, and the legal representatives of Directors or Officers in the event of their incompetency, insolvency or bankruptcy.

4. EXCLUSIONS

The Insurer shall not be liable to make any payment for Loss in connection with any claim or claims made against the Insureds:

(a) which result in a finding of personal profit, gain or advantage;

(b) for the return by the Insureds of any remuneration paid to the Insureds without the previous approval of the stockholders of the Company, which payment without such previous approval shall be held by the courts to have been illegal;

(c) for an accounting of profits in fact made from the purchase or sale by the Insureds of securities of the Company within the meaning of Section 16(b) of the Securities Exchange Act of 1934 and amendments thereto or similar provisions of any state statutory law;

(d) brought about or contributed to by the fraudulent, dishonest or criminal acts of the Insureds; however the provisions of this exclusion shall not apply unless a judgment or other final adjudication thereof adverse to the Insureds shall establish fraud, dishonesty or criminal acts;

(e) arising from, attributable to or involving attempts, whether alleged or actual, successful or unsuccessful, by persons or entities to acquire securities of the Company against the opposition of the Board of Directors of the Company, nor to any claims arising from, attributable to or involving efforts, whether alleged or actual, successful or unsuccessful, by the Company and/or its Directors to resist such attempts;

(f) based on or attributable to any failure or omission on the part of the Insureds to effect and maintain insurance;

(g) which is insured by any other policy or policies, except in respect of any excess beyond the amounts of the limits of liability of such other policy or policies;

(h) arising from any circumstances of which notice has been given under any policy of which this policy is a renewal or replacement or which it may succeed in time;

(i) which are brought by, or on the behalf of, any other Insureds including but not limited to shareholders' derivative suits and/or representative class action suits, brought by one or more past, present or future Directors and/or Officers including their estates, beneficiaries, heirs, legal representatives, assigns and/or the Company against one or more past, present or future Directors or Officers;

(j) for violation of any of the responsibilities, obligations or duties imposed upon fiduciaries by the Employee Retirement Income Security Act of 1974 or amendments thereto or any similar provisions of state statutory law or common law;

(k) arising from any pending or prior litigation as of the inception date of this policy, as well as all future claims or litigation based upon the pending or prior litigation or derived from the same or essentially the same facts (actual or alleged) that gave rise to the prior or pending litigation;

(l) for bodily injury, sickness, disease, death, or emotional distress of any person, or for damage to or destruction of any tangible property, including the loss of use thereof, or for oral or written publication of a libel or slander or of other defamatory or disparaging material or of material that violates a person's right of privacy;

8750 (6/85)   -2-

850

(m) arising from charges of seepage, pollution or contamination and based upon or attributed to violation or alleged violation of any federal, state, municipal or other governmental statute, regulation or ordinance prohibiting or providing for the control or regulation of emissions or effluents of any kind into the atmosphere or any body of land, water, waterway or watercourse or arising from any action or proceeding brought for enforcement purposes by any public official, agency, commission, or board of pollution control administration pursuant to any such statutes, regulations or ordinances or arising from any suits alleging seepage, pollution or contamination based upon common law nuisance or trespass;

(n) for which the Directors and/or Officers are indemnified by, or are entitled to indemnification by, the Company.

NOTE: The Wrongful Act of any Director or Officer shall not be imputed to any other Director or Officer for the purpose of determining the applicability of the foregoing Exclusions enumerated in this Clause 4 (a), (b), (c) and (d).

5. LIMIT AND RETENTION

(a) The Insurer shall be liable to pay 95% of Loss excess of the amount stated in (c) below up to the amount hereinafter stated, it being warranted that the remaining 5% of each and every Loss shall be carried by the Insureds at their own risk and uninsured.

(b) Subject to the foregoing, the Insurer's liability for Loss shall be the amount stated in Item 3 of the Declarations which shall be the maximum liability of the Insurer in each Policy Year. The limit of liability of the Insurer in the Discovery Period shall be part of, and not in addition to the limit of liability of the Insurer in the Policy Year which terminates at the inception of the Discovery Period.

(c) This policy is only to pay the excess over the retention amounts stated in Item 4. B. of the Declarations in respect of each and every Loss hereunder, including costs, charges and expenses as described in Clause 6. The retention amounts stated in Item 4. B. of the Declarations are to be borne by the Insureds and are not to be insured. Loss arising out of the same Wrongful Act or interrelated, repeated or continuous Wrongful Acts of one or more of the Insureds shall be considered a single Loss. The amount stated as the retention "per Director or Officer" in Item 4. B. of the Declarations applies separately to each Director or Officer per each such Loss, subject to the maximum retention "per Loss" as stated in Item 4. B. of the Declarations. In such cases where the maximum retention "per Loss" applies, the retention shall be pro-rated among the Insureds in proportion to their respective Loss.

(d) Loss arising out of claims for the same Wrongful Act or interrelated, repeated or continuous Wrongful Acts of one or more of the Directors or Officers shall be deemed Loss in the Policy Year in which the first such claim or Wrongful Act is first reported to the Insurer.

(e) The foregoing provisions shall apply to this policy and the Corporation Reimbursement policy attached hereto, as though they constitute a single policy and the Insurer's maximum liability under both policies together shall not exceed the limits and retention set out in this Clause 5.

6. DEFENSE COSTS, CHARGES AND EXPENSES AND SETTLEMENTS, (INCLUDED IN THE LIMIT OF LIABILITY)

(a) The Insurer does not, under the terms of this policy, assume any duty to defend, nor are the costs, charges and expenses of defense payable by the Insurer in addition to the limit of liability. Costs, charges and expenses of defense are part of Loss insured under this policy and as such are subject to the provisions of Clause 5.

(b) Only those costs, charges, expenses and settlements consented to by the Insurer shall be recoverable as Loss under the terms of this policy. The Insurer's consent shall not be unreasonably withheld, but the insurer shall be entitled to full information and all particulars it may request in order to reach a decision as to reasonableness.

With respect to the settlement of any claim made against the Company and the Insureds, the Company and the Insureds and the Insurer agree to use their best efforts to determine a fair and proper allocation of the settlement amount as between the Company and the Insureds.

(c) the words "costs, charges and expenses" shall include the cost of any appeal, attachment or similar bonds.

8750 (6/85)   -3-

851

7. LOSS PROVISONS

(a) The time when a Loss shall be incurred for purpose of determining the application of Clause 5(b) shall be the date on which the Company or the Insureds shall give written notice to the Insurer as hereinafter provided.

(b) The Company or the Insureds shall as a condition precedent to the Insureds' right to be indemnified under this policy give to the Insurer notice in writing of any claim made against the Insureds as soon as practicable during the policy period or during the Discovery Period, if effective in accordance with Clause 8(a).

(c) If during the policy period or during the Discovery Period, if effective in accordance with Clause 8(a), the Insured(s) shall become aware of any circumstances which may subsequently give rise to a claim being made against the Insureds and shall give written notice of the circumstances and the reasons for anticipating a claim, with full particulars as to dates and persons involved, then any claim which is subsequently made against the Insureds arising out of such circumstances shall be treated as a claim made during the currency hereof.

(d) Notice hereunder shall be given to the Insurer, 70 Pine Street, New York, New York 10270.

(e) The Insureds shall give the Insurer such information and cooperation as it may reasonably require and as shall be in the Insureds' power.

8. GENERAL CONDITIONS

(a) DISCOVERY CLAUSE

If the Insurer shall cancel or refuse to renew this policy the Insureds shall have the right, upon payment of the additional premium of 25% of the three year premium hereunder, to an extension of the cover granted by this policy in respect of any claim or claims which are made against the Insureds during the period of twelve calendar months after the effective date of such cancellation or non-renewal, herein called the Discovery Period, but only in respect of any Wrongful Act committed before the effective date of such cancellation or non-renewal and otherwise covered by this policy. This right shall terminate, however, unless written notice of such election together with payment of the additional premium due is received by the Insurer within ten (10) days after the effective date of cancellation or non-renewal. The offer by the Insurer of renewal terms, conditions, limits of liability and/or premiums different from those of the expiring policy shall not constitute refusal to renew. This Clause and the rights granted herein to the Insureds shall not apply to any cancellation resulting from non-payment of premium.

(b) CANCELLATION CLAUSE

This policy may be cancelled by the Company or the Insureds at any time only by mailing written prior notice to the Insurer or by surrender of this policy to the Insurer or its authorized agent. This policy may also be cancelled by or on behalf of the Insurer by delivering to the Company or by mailing to the Company, by registered, certified, or other first class mail, at the Company's address as shown in Item 1 of the Declarations, written notice stating when, not less than thirty (30) days thereafter, the cancellation shall be effective. The mailing of such notice as aforesaid shall be sufficient proof of notice. The policy period terminates at the date and hour specified in such notice. or at the date and time of surrender.

If this policy shall be cancelled by the Company or the Insureds, the Insurer shall retain the customary short rate proportion of the premium hereon.

If this policy shall be cancelled by the Insurer, the Insurer shall retain the pro rata proportion of the premium hereon.

Payment or tender of any unearned premium by the Insurer shall not be a condition precedent to the effectiveness of cancellation but such payment shall be made as soon as practicable.

If the period of limitation relating to the giving of notice is prohibited or made void by any law controlling the construction thereof, such period shall be deemed to be amended so as to be equal to the minimum period of limitation permitted by such law.

9. SUBROGATION

In the event of any payment under this policy, the Insurer shall be subrogated to the extent of such payment to all the Insureds' rights of recovery therefor, and the Insureds shall execute all papers required and shall do everything that may be necessary to secure such rights including the execution of such documents necessary to enable the Insurer effectively to bring suit in the name of the Insureds.

10. NOTICE AND AUTHORITY

It is agreed that the Company shall act on behalf of all Insureds with respect to the giving and receiving of notice of claim or cancellation, the payment of premiums and the receiving of any return premiums that may become due under this policy, the receipt and acceptance of any endorsements issued to form a part of this policy, and the exercising or declining to exercise any right to a Discovery Period.

11. ASSIGNMENT

This policy and any and all rights hereunder is not assignable without the written consent of the Insurer.

12. ACTION AGAINST INSURER

No action shall lie against the Insurer unless, as a condition precedent thereto, there shall have been full compliance with all of the terms of this policy, nor until the amount of the Insureds' obligation to pay shall have been finally determined either by judgment against the Insureds after actual trial or by written agreement of the Insureds, the claimant and the Insurer.

Any person or organization or the legal representative thereof who has secured such judgment or written agreement shall thereafter be entitled to recover under this policy to the extent of the insurance afforded by this policy. No person or organization shall have any right under this policy to join the Insurer as a party to any action against the Insureds to determine the Insureds' liability, nor shall the Insurer be impleaded by the Insureds or their legal representatives. Bankruptcy or insolvency of the Insureds or of the Insureds' estate shall not relieve the Insurer of any of its obligations hereunder.

IN WITNESS WHEREOF, the Insurer has caused this policy to be signed by its President and a Secretary and countersigned on the Declarations page by a duly authorized agent of the Insurer.

Secretary   President

SELECTED INSURANCE FORMS

AMERICAN INTERNATIONAL GLOBAL
EXTENSION ENDORSEMENT

In consideration of the premium charged, it is hereby understood and agreed that such coverage as is provided under this Policy shall include coverage Worldwide.

It is further understood and agreed that with regard to any claim made or suit instituted outside of the United States of America, its territories or possessions and Canada and reported under the Provisions of Policy Form 8750 the Insurer shall, when requested to do so in writing by the Parent Company designated in Item 1 of the Declarations:

a) undertake the investigation, settlement and defense of claims or suits against Directors and Officers and the Insureds shall cooperate in the investigation and defense of such claims and suits as may be required by the Insurer;

b) pay on behalf of the Directors and Officers:

   (i) all sums for damages arising from liability imposed upon the Directors and Officers by reason of a final judgment under law by a court of competent jurisdiction by reason of a Wrongful Act (as defined in this Policy) to which this insurance applies, and;

   (ii) all reasonable expenses incurred in connection with the investigation, settlement or defense of such claims or suits to which this Endorsement applies, and;

   (iii) all sums for settlements negotiated by the Insurer with the approval of the Insureds provided that if the Insureds refuse to consent to a settlement recommended by the Insurer, the Insurer's liability under this Endorsement for defense under Section (a) above shall terminate and the Insurer's liability for payment under this section (b) shall not exceed the amount of the settlement recommended and the expenses under (ii) above as of the time of the refusal to consent.

The amounts due under b(i), (ii) and (iii) shall be included in and not in addition to the Limit of Liability set forth in Item 3 of the Declarations and shall be subject to the applicable Policy Retentions. The amounts due under this Endorsement shall be paid in the currency of the Country in which the final adjudication was made, the expenses incurred and/or the settlement negotiated.

It is further understood and agreed that the Insurer shall not be held responsible for any delay or failure to perform its obligations hereunder due to National, Federal, State, or Municipal action or regulation, strikes or other labor troubles; acts of God, war, riot, insurrection or mutiny; or any other causes, contingencies, or circumstances without the United States not subject to the Insurer's control which make the fulfillment of this agreement impracticable; any of which shall, without liability, excuse the Insurer from the defense obligation set forth in this Endorsement.

Chubb Group of Insurance Companies

15 Mountain View Road, Warren, New Jersey 07060

**APPLICATION
EXECUTIVE LIABILITY AND
INDEMNIFICATION POLICY**

**UNDERWRITTEN IN FEDERAL INSURANCE COMPANY, TEXAS PACIFIC INDEMNITY COMPANY, OR
NORTHWESTERN PACIFIC INDEMNITY COMPANY**

1. **General Information**

   Parent Organization _____
   Principal Address _____
   State of Incorporation _____
   Established _____
   Nature of Business _____
   Total Assets (consolidated) _____ Total Sales/Revenues _____
   Subsidiaries: Do you want to include all subsidiaries? ☐ Yes ☐ No.

Name	Business	% Owned	Date Acq./Created

   Attach list or refer to Annual Reports or Form 10-K.

2. **Coverage Requested**

   Limits: (a) Each **Loss** $ _____
                    (b) Each **Policy Year** $ _____

   Deductible Amounts: (a) Each **Insured Person** $ _____
                         (b) All **Insured Persons** $ _____
                         (c) **Insured Organization** $ _____

3. **Policy Period**

   From _____ To _____ both days at 12:01 a.m. at the principal address

4. **Insured Persons**

   Is coverage requested for managers or supervisory personnel who are not officers and/or directors of the **Parent
   Organization** and/or any subsidiary? ☐ Yes ☐ No. If yes, please explain and describe the positions for which
   you want coverage. _____

5. **Stock Ownership**

   Privately held? ☐ Yes ☐ No. Closely held? ☐ Yes ☐ No. If yes to either of these, please indicate if
   more than one member of the family controlling the stock is an officer and/or director, and complete distribution
   of ownership questions.

   _____
   _____

   Distribution of Ownership:

   Common shares outstanding _____ Common stock shareholders _____
   Common stock owned directly and beneficially by directors _____
   Common stock owned directly and beneficially by officers who are not directors _____
   Name and percentage of holdings of any shareholder who owns 10% or more of the common shares directly or
   beneficially _____
   Describe fully any other securities convertible to common stock _____

Form 14-03-0024 (Rev. 4-84)

P-40978 (20M)   PRINTED IN U.S.A.

6. Outside Directorships

Is coverage requested for outside positions (for example, directorships or trusteeships in other organizations) held by executives of the **Insured Organization** at its request? ☐ Yes ☐ No. If yes, list the executives and their outside positions:

Executive	Outside Organization	Position With Outside Organization	Year Position Assumed

7. Announced Changes

Has the **Parent Organization** publicly revealed that it now has under consideration any acquisitions, tender offers or mergers? ☐ Yes ☐ No. If yes, attach details.
Has the **Parent Organization** publicly announced any new public offering of securities pursuant to the Securities Act of 1933 or exempt from registration under Regulation A within the next year? ☐ Yes ☐ No. If yes, attach a statement of full details including the prospectus.

8. Past Activities

Has the **Parent Organization**, its directors, officers and/or other **Insured Persons** been involved in any of the following:
    Any antitrust, copyright or patent litigation? ☐ Yes ☐ No.
    Any civil or criminal action or administrative proceeding charging a violation of any federal or state security law or regulation? ☐ Yes ☐ No.
    Any representative actions, class actions or derivative suits? ☐ Yes ☐ No.
If yes to any of these, attach a statement of full details.

9. Prior Insurance

Has your **Parent Organization** or any subsidiary had previous directors and officers liability insurance?
☐ Yes ☐ No. If no, skip to Question 10 and answer the warranty statement.
Have any loss payments been made under any directors and officers liability policy or similar insurance?
☐ Yes ☐ No. If yes, attach full details.
Has the **Parent Organization** or any **Insured Person(s)** given written notice under the provisions of any prior or current directors and officers liability insurance of specific facts or circumstances which might give rise to a claim being made against any **Insured Person(s)**? ☐ Yes ☐ No. If yes, attach full details.
Details of previous insurance:

Insurer	Limits	Period	Deductibles	Premium
(Expiring)				
(Previous)				
(Earliest)				

Continuity With Prior Coverage:

Note: This section applies only if you currently have coverage and request continuity of coverage.

The proposed policy is to replace existing insurance, and continuity of coverage is requested. It is understood that if continuity of coverage is not granted the Company may require the completion of the Warranty Statement in Question 10 prior to binding coverage. Before granting continuity of coverage, the Company will require complete copies of all prior and current policies, with which continuity of coverage is to be maintained, including all applications and proposals submitted to previous Insurers. In granting continuity of coverage, the Company will be relying upon the declarations and statements contained in the previous applications and proposals and those declarations and statements shall be considered to be incorporated in and form a part of the policy of the Company. Details of the previous are included above.

Note: The continuity date is the effective date of your earliest previous D&O coverage and/or the date on which you last signed a warranty statement.

10. Prior Knowledge

*Note: This section also applies if you have requested continuity of coverage and your request has not been ac-
cepted or granted.*

It is important that you fill in the blank in this paragraph. No person proposed for coverage is aware of any facts
or circumstances which (a) he or she has reason to suppose might afford valid grounds for any future claim(s)
that would fall within the scope of the proposed coverage or (b) indicate the probability of any future claim(s) except: *(If no exceptions please state)_____.
It is agreed that if facts or circumstances exist any claim or action arising from them is excluded from this proposed
coverage.*

1. Additional Material

As part of this application, please attach the following (where applicable):

*   Latest audited Annual Report (including balance sheet and income statement).
*   Latest Form 10-K and 10-Q reports filed with the S.E.C.
*   Latest interim financial statement.
*   A complete list of proposed **Insured Persons** by name, position and, if an outside director, affiliation with
    other organizations.
*   A copy of the indemnification provisions of the by-laws; if a non-profit organization, also attach the complete
    by-laws, charter or articles of incorporation and brochures descriptive of operations and purpose.

False Information

**Any person who, knowingly and with intent to defraud any insurance company or other person, files an ap-
plication for insurance containing any false information, or conceals for the purpose of misleading, information concerning any fact material thereto, commits a fraudulent insurance act, which is a crime.**

Defense Cost Provision

**Please note that the Defense Cost provision of this policy stipulates that the Limits of Liability may be com-
pletely exhausted by the cost of legal defense. Any deductible or retention may be similarly reduced or exhausted by legal defense costs.**

Declaration and Signature

The undersigned declares that to the best of his or her knowledge and belief the statements set forth herein are true.
Although the signing of this application does not bind the undersigned on behalf of the **Parent Organization** or its
directors, officers or **Insured Persons** to effect insurance, the undersigned agrees that this application and its attachments shall be the basis of the contract should a policy be issued and shall be attached to and form part of the
policy. The Company is hereby authorized to make any investigation and inquiry in connection with this application
that it deems necessary.

Date _____ Signed _____ Title _____
                                                                        Chairman of the Board
                                                                            or President

857

	CHUBB GROUP of Insurance Companies	DECLARATIONS
C CHUBB	15 Mountain View Road, Warren, NJ 07060	**EXECUTIVE LIABILITY AND INDEMNIFICATION POLICY**

Item 1. **Parent Organization:**   Policy Number

Item 2. **Principal Address:**   **FEDERAL INSURANCE COMPANY**
                                                            Incorporated under the laws of New Jersey
                                                            a stock insurance company, herein called the Company

THIS IS A CLAIMS MADE POLICY. Except as otherwise provided herein, this policy covers only claims first made against the insured during the Policy Period. Please read carefully.

Item 3. Limits of Liability: (a) Each **Loss** $
                                   (b) Each **Policy Year** $

Item 4. Coinsurance Percent:

Item 5. Deductible Amounts:

         Insuring Clause 1   (a) Each **Insured Person** $
                                   (b) All **Insured Persons** $
         Insuring Clause 2   (c) The **Insured Organization** $

Item 6. **Insured Organization:**

Item 7. **Insured Persons:**

Item 8. Policy Period: From 12:01 a.m.
                          To   12:01 a.m.
                          Local time at the address shown in Item 2.

Item 9. Extended Reporting Period: (a) Additional Premium:
                                     (b) Additional Period:

Item 10. Endorsement(s) Effective at Inception:

Item 11. Termination of Prior Policy(ies):

In witness whereof, the Company issuing this policy has caused this policy to be signed by its authorized officers, but it shall not be valid unless also signed by a duly authorized representative of the Company.

FEDERAL INSURANCE COMPANY

Henry A Aulcic   _Henry L Harder_
Secretary   President

_____   _____
Authorized Representative   Date

INSURING CLAUSES

In consideration of payment of the required premium and subject to the declarations, the limitations, conditions, provisions and other terms of this policy, the Company agrees as follows:

EXECUTIVE LIABILITY COVERAGE—INSURING CLAUSE 1

1.1   The Company shall pay on behalf of each of the **Insured Persons** all **Loss** for which the **Insured Person** is not indemnified by the **Insured Organization** and which the **Insured Person** becomes legally obligated to pay on account of any claim first made against him, individually or otherwise, during the **Policy Period** or, if exercised, during the Extended Reporting Period for a **Wrongful Act** committed, attempted, or allegedly committed or attempted, by the **Insured Person(s)** before or during the **Policy Period.**

EXECUTIVE INDEMNIFICATION COVERAGE—INSURING CLAUSE 2

1.2   The Company shall pay on behalf of the **Insured Organization** all **Loss** for which the **Insured Organization** grants indemnification to each **Insured Person**, as permitted or required by law, which the **Insured Person** has become legally obligated to pay on account of any claim first made against him, individually or otherwise, during the **Policy Period** or, if exercised, during the Extended Reporting Period for a **Wrongful Act** committed, attempted, or allegedly committed or attempted, by such **Insured Person(s)** before or during the **Policy Period.**

ESTATES AND LEGAL REPRESENTATIVES

2.1   Subject otherwise to all the terms and conditions of this policy, coverage shall extend to claims for the **Wrongful Acts** of **Insured Persons** made against the estates, heirs, legal representatives or assigns of **Insured Persons** who are deceased or against the legal representatives or assigns of **Insured Persons** who are incompetent, insolvent or bankrupt.

TERRITORY

2.2   Subject otherwise to all the terms and conditions of this policy, coverage shall extend to claims made anywhere in the world against **Insured Persons** for **Wrongful Acts** wherever committed, attempted, or allegedly committed or attempted.

EXTENDED REPORTING PERIOD

2.3   If the Company terminates or refuses to renew this policy, the **Parent Organization** and the **Insured Persons** shall have the right, upon payment of the additional premium in item 9(a) of the declarations, to an extension of the coverage granted by this policy for the period in item 9(b) of the declarations following the effective date of termination, but only for any **Wrongful Act** committed, attempted, or allegedly committed or attempted, prior to the effective date of termination. This right of extension shall lapse unless written notice is given to the Company within 30 days following the effective date of nonrenewal or termination. If the **Parent Organization** terminates or declines to accept renewal, the Company may, if requested, at its sole option, grant an Extended Reporting Period. The offer of renewal terms and conditions or premiums different from those in effect prior to renewal shall not constitute refusal to renew.

EXCLUSIONS

3.1   The Company shall not be liable under this policy to make any payment for **Loss** in connection with any claim(s) made against any **Insured Person(s):**

   (a)   arising from any circumstance if written notice of such circumstance has been given under any policy, the term of which has expired prior to or upon the inception of this policy, and if such prior policy affords coverage (or would afford such coverage except for the exhaustion of its limits of liability) for such **Loss**, in whole or in part, as a result of such notice;

(b) based upon an actual or alleged violation of the responsibilities, obligations or duties imposed upon fiduciaries by the Employee Retirement Income Security Act of 1974 and amendments thereto or similar provisions of any federal, state or local statutory law or common law;

(c) for bodily injury, sickness, disease or death of any person, or for damage to or destruction of any tangible property including loss of use thereof; or

(d) for seepage, pollution or contamination and based upon or attributable to violation or alleged violation of any federal, state, municipal or other governmental statute, regulation or ordinance prohibiting or providing for the control or regulation of emissions or effluents of any kind into the atmosphere or any body of land, water, waterway or watercourse or arising from any action or proceeding brought for enforcement purposes by any public official, agency, commission, board or pollution control administration pursuant to any such statutes, regulations or ordinances or arising from any claims alleging seepage, pollution or contamination based upon common law nuisance or trespass.

3.2   The Company shall not be liable under Insuring Clause 1 to make any payment for **Loss** in connection with any claim(s) made against any of the **Insured Person(s)**:

(a) for libel or slander;

(b) for the return by any such **Insured Person** of any remuneration paid in fact to him without the previous approval of the stockholders of the **Insured Organization** if it shall be determined by a judgment or other final adjudication that such remuneration is in violation of law or if such remuneration is to be repaid to the **Insured Organization** under a settlement agreement;

(c) for an accounting of profits made from the purchase or sale by such **Insured Person** of securities of the **Insured Organization** within the meaning of Section 16(b) of the Securities Exchange Act of 1934 and amendments thereto or similar provisions of any federal, state or local statutory law or common law;

(d) brought about or contributed to by the dishonesty of such **Insured Person** if a judgment or other final adjudication adverse to such **Insured Person** establishes that acts of active and deliberate dishonesty were committed or attempted by such **Insured Person** with actual dishonest purpose and intent and were material to the cause of action so adjudicated; or

(e) based upon or attributable to such **Insured Person** having gained any personal profit or advantage to which he was not legally entitled regardless of whether or not (1) a judgment or other final adjudication adverse to such **Insured Person** establishes that such **Insured Person** in fact gained such personal profit or other advantage to which he was not entitled, or (2) the **Insured Person** has entered into a settlement agreement to repay such unentitled personal profit or advantage to the **Insured Organization**.

3.3   With respect to the exclusions in section 3, no fact pertaining to or knowledge possessed by any **Insured Person(s)** shall be imputed to any other **Insured Person(s)** for the purpose of determining the availability of coverage for, or with respect to claims made against, any **Insured Person(s)**.

REPORTING AND NOTICE

4.1   The **Insureds** shall, as a condition precedent to exercising their rights under this policy, give to the Company written notice as soon as practicable of any claim made against any of them for an identifiable **Wrongful Act** and shall give the Company such information and cooperation as it may reasonably require, including but not limited to, the nature of the **Wrongful Act**, the alleged injury, the names of claimants, and the manner in which the **Insured** first became aware of the claim.

4.2   If during the **Policy Period** or Extended Reporting Period (if exercised), any **Insured** becomes aware of circumstances which could give rise to a claim and written notice of such circumstance(s) is given to the Company as outlined in paragraph 4.1, then any claims subsequently arising from such circumstances shall be considered to have been reported during the **Policy Period** or the Extended Reporting Period in which the circumstances were reported.

4.3   Notice hereunder shall be given to the Company at its address shown on the declarations page.

LIMIT OF LIABILITY, DEDUCTIBLE AND COINSURANCE

5.1 For the purposes of this policy, all **Loss** arising out of all interrelated **Wrongful Acts** of any **Insured Person(s)** shall be deemed one **Loss**, and such **Loss** shall be deemed to have originated in the earliest **Policy Year** in which a claim is made against any **Insured Person** alleging any such **Wrongful Acts.**

5.2 The total limit of the Company's liability to pay any **Loss** hereunder, whether covered under Insuring Clause 1 or Insuring Clause 2 or both, shall not exceed the amount(s) set forth in item 3 of the declarations page.

5.3 The Company's liability hereunder shall apply only to that part of each **Loss** which is excess of the deductible amount specified in item 5 of the declarations, and such deductible amount shall be borne by the **Insureds** uninsured and at their own risk.

5.4 The deductible amount applicable to each **Loss** under Insuring Clause 1 shall be the amount set forth in item 5(a) of the declarations for each of the **Insured Persons** against whom claim is made, but not more than the amount set forth in item 5(b) of the declarations for all such **Insured Persons.** The deductible amount applicable to each **Loss** under Insuring Clause 2 shall be the amount set forth in item 5(c) of the declarations.

5.5 If a single **Loss** is covered in part under Insuring Clause 1 and in part under Insuring Clause 2, the maximum deductible amount applicable to such **Loss** shall be the amount set forth in item 5(c) of the declarations.

5.6 With respect to all **Loss** (excess of applicable deductible amounts) originating in any one **Policy Year**, the **Insureds** shall bear uninsured and at their own risk that percent of all such **Loss** specified as the Coinsurance Percent in item 4 of the declarations, and the Company's liability hereunder shall apply only to the remaining percent of all such **Loss.**

DEFENSE AND SETTLEMENT

6.1 No **Defense Costs** shall be incurred or settlements made without the Company's consent, which shall not be unreasonably withheld. The Company shall not be liable for any settlements or **Defense Costs** to which it has not consented. If the **Insured Organization** is a defendant in a legal action along with any **Insured Person** and the Company shall unconditionally consent to the incurring of **Defense Costs**, then the Company may, at its sole option, advance such **Defense Costs** on behalf of all **Insureds** until an appropriate allocation of **Defense Costs** among the **Insured Person**(s) and the **Insured Organization** is agreed to by the Company and the **Insured.** If the Company shall unconditionally consent to the incurring of **Defense Costs**, the Company shall advance **Defense Costs** periodically during the course of legal proceedings.

6.2 An **Insured Person** shall not be required to contest any legal proceedings unless counsel (to be mutually agreed upon by such **Insured Person** and the Company) shall advise that such proceedings should be contested by the **Insured Person** and the **Insured Person** consents thereto, which consent shall not be unreasonably withheld.

6.3 If **Insured Person(s)** are so required to contest legal proceedings, the Company, subject to the provisions of items 3, 4 and 5 of the declarations, will pay that portion of **Loss** relating to the costs, charges and expenses in connection therewith.

REPRESENTATIONS AND SEVERABILITY

7.1 In granting coverage under this policy to any one of the **Insureds**, the Company has relied upon the declarations and statements in the written application for coverage. All such declarations and statements are the basis of such coverage and shall be considered as incorporated in and constituting part of the policy.

7.2 The written application for coverage shall be construed as a separate application for coverage by each of the **Insured Persons.** With respect to the declarations and statements contained in such written application for coverage, no statement in the application or knowledge possessed by any **Insured Person(s)** shall be imputed to any other **Insured Person(s)** for the purpose of determining the availability of coverage with respect to claims made against any **Insured Persons(s)** whether or not the **Insured Organization** grants indemnification.

OTHER INSURANCE

8.1 If any **Loss** arising from any claim made against any **Insured Person(s)** is insured under any other valid policy(ies), prior or current, then this policy shall cover such **Loss**, subject to its limitations, conditions, provisions and other terms, only to the extent that the amount of such **Loss** is in excess of the amount of payment from such other insurance whether such other insurance is stated to be primary, contributory, excess, contingent or otherwise, unless such other insurance is written only as specific excess insurance over the limits provided in this policy.

CHANGES IN EXPOSURE

8.2 If the **Insured Organization** acquires more than 50 percent of the voting stock of another entity, coverage shall extend to the **Insured Persons** of the acquired entity and to the acquired **Insured Organization** but only with respect to **Wrongful Acts** committed or attempted, or allegedly committed or attempted, after such acquisition unless the Company agrees, after presentation of a complete application and all appropriate information, to provide coverage, by endorsement, for **Wrongful Acts** committed or attempted, or allegedly committed or attempted, prior to such acquisition. The **Parent Organization** shall give written notice of such acquisition to the Company as soon as practicable thereafter together with such information as the Company may require and shall pay any reasonable additional premium required by the Company.

8.3 If the **Insured Organization** creates a new entity or makes any other acquisition not described in paragraph 8.2, coverage shall be afforded without reporting or payment of additional premium to the extent that the description of the **Insured Organization** in item 6 of the declarations provides.

OUTSIDE DIRECTORSHIPS

8.4 If any **Outside Directorship** held by an **Insured Person** is included within the description of such person's **Insured Capacity** in item 7 of the declarations or is included by endorsement during the **Policy Period**, any coverage under this policy resulting from such inclusion shall be subject to the following:

    (a) such coverage shall not be construed to extend to the outside organization in which such **Outside Directorship** is held or to any of the other officers, directors, or employees of such organization;

    (b) such coverage shall be specifically excess of any other indemnity or insurance available to such **Insured Person** by reason of serving in such **Outside Directorship**; and

    (c) such coverage shall apply only if the Company is given specific written application, together with any information it may require, at the inception of this policy or as soon as practicable (but not more than 120 days) after the commencement of such **Outside Directorship** that such **Insured Person** is serving in such **Outside Directorship** at the specific request of the **Insured Organization**. Such coverage shall be subject to and shall not become effective until the date of written approval by the Company and the payment of any reasonable additional premium required by the Company.

ALTERATION & ASSIGNMENT

8.5 No change in, modification of, or assignment of interest under this policy shall be effective except when made by written endorsement to this policy signed by an authorized employee of Chubb & Son Inc.

SUBROGATION

8.6 If any payment is made under this policy, the Company shall be subrogated to the extent of such payment to all the **Insureds'** rights of recovery. In such case the **Insureds** shall execute all papers required and shall do everything necessary to secure and preserve such right, including the execution of such documents necessary to enable the Company effectively to bring suit in the name of the **Insureds**.

TERMINATION OF POLICY

8.7 This policy shall terminate at the earliest of the following times:

    (a) 60 days after receipt by the **Parent Organization** at the address designated in item 2 of the declarations of a written notice of termination from the Company, or, if a later time is specified in such notice, at such later time;

    (b) upon receipt by the Company of written notice of termination from the **Parent Organization**, or, if a later time is specified in such notice, at such later time;

    (c) at such other time as may be agreed upon by the Company and the **Parent Organization**, or

    (d) upon expiration as set forth in item 8 of the declarations.

The Company shall refund any unearned premium computed at customary short rates if the policy is terminated by the **Parent Organization**. Under any other circumstances the refund shall be computed prorata.

TERMINATION OF PRIOR POLICY(IES)

8.8   The taking effect of this policy shall terminate, if not already terminated, any policy(ies) of the Chubb Group of Insurance Companies specified in item 11 of the declarations.

AUTHORIZATION CLAUSE

8.9   By acceptance of this policy, the **Parent Organization** agrees to act on behalf of all **Insureds** with respect to the giving and receiving of notice of claim or of termination, the payment of premiums, the receiving of any return premiums that may become due under this policy, the acceptance of endorsements, and the giving or receiving of any other notice provided for in this policy; and the **Insureds** agree that the **Parent Organization** shall act on their behalf.

DEFINITIONS

9.1   When used in this policy:

Defense Costs means that part of **Loss** consisting of costs, charges and expenses (other than regular or over-time wages, salaries or fees of the directors, officers or employees of the **Insured Organization**) incurred in defending, investigating or monitoring legal actions, claims, or proceedings and appeals therefrom and the cost of appeal, attachment or similar bonds.

Insured(s) means the **Insured Organization** and/or any **Insured Person(s)**.

Insured Capacity(ies) means the position or capacity designated in item 7 of the declarations held by any **Insured Person**.

Insured Organization means, collectively, those organizations designated in item 6 of the declarations.

Insured Person(s) means any of those persons designated in item 7 of the declarations.

Loss means the total amount which any **Insured Person(s)** becomes legally obligated to pay on account of each claim and for all claims in each **Policy Year** made against them for **Wrongful Acts** for which coverage applies, including, but not limited to, damages, judgments, settlements, costs and **Defense Costs**. **Loss** does not include fines or penalties imposed by law or matters uninsurable under the law pursuant to which this policy is construed.

Outside Directorship means the executive position held by an **Insured Person** at the specific request of the **Insured Organization** in any corporation, joint venture, partnership, trust or other enterprise which is not included in the definition of **Insured Organization**.

Parent Organization means the organization designated in item 1 of the declarations.

Policy Period means the period from the inception of this policy until its termination, in accordance with paragraph 8.7.

Policy Year means the period of one year following the inception of this policy or any anniversary, or, if the time between inception or any anniversary and the termination of the policy is less than one year, the lesser period. If the Extended Reporting Period is exercised, then it shall be part of the last **Policy Year** and not an additional period.

Subsidiary(ies) means any organization controlled by any entity included in the **Insured Organization** through ownership of more than 50 percent of the outstanding voting stock.

Wrongful Act means any error, misstatement, misleading statement, act, omission, neglect, or breach of duty committed, attempted, or allegedly committed or attempted, by any **Insured Person**, individually or otherwise, in his **Insured Capacity**, or any matter claimed against him solely by reason of his serving in such **Insured Capacity**. All such causally connected errors, statements, acts, omissions, neglects or breaches of duty or other such matters committed or attempted by, allegedly committed or attempted by, or claimed against one or more of the **Insured Persons** shall be deemed interrelated **Wrongful Acts**.

Form 14-02-0386 (Ed. 2-84)   Page 6 of 6

Chubb Group of Insurance Companies

ENDORSEMENT

15 Mountain View Road, Warren, New Jersey 07060

Company:

Effective date of
this endorsement:

Endorsement No:

To be attached to and form part of
Policy No.

Issued to:

PENDING OR PRIOR LITIGATION

It is agreed that the Company shall not be liable to make any payment under this policy in connection wth any claim(s) arising from:

(A)   any litigation occurring prior to, or pending as of _____, including (but not limited to) claims, demands, causes of action, legal or quasi-legal proceedings, decrees or judgements against any Insured(s) of which any Insured(s) had received notice or otherwise had knowledge as or such date;

(B)   any subsequent litigation arising from, or based on substantially the same matters as alleged in the pleadings of such prior or pending litigation; or

(C)   any act of any Insured(s) which gave rise to such prior or pending litigation.

ALL OTHER TERMS AND CONDITIONS REMAIN UNCHANGED.

_____
Authorized Employee

_____
Date

Form 14-02-227 (Ed. 11-80) (Reprint 1-81)   P-80287 (4M)   PRINTED IN USA

865

SELECTED INSURANCE FORMS

INSURED VS. INSURED

It is agreed that:

Item 3.1, Exclusions, shall be amended by adding the following:

"() By an Insured Person, by the Insured Organization or by the Parent Organization except a claim made on behalf of the Insured Organization or Parent Organization by one or more claimants who are not Insured Persons.

ALL OTHER TERMS AND CONDITIONS REMAIN UNCHANGED.

DIRECTORS AND OFFICERS LIABILITY
INSURANCE POLICY

THIS IS A "CLAIMS-FIRST-MADE" INSURANCE POLICY. PLEASE READ IT CAREFULLY.

Words and phrases which appear in all capital letters have the special meanings set forth in Section II–DEFINITIONS

DIRECTORS & OFFICERS
LIABILITY INSURANCE, LTD.
HAMILTON, BERMUDA

DECLARATIONS

POLICY NO.

DECLARATION NO.

Item 1: This POLICY provides indemnification with respect to the DIRECTORS and OFFICERS of:

Item 2: POLICY PERIOD: from the

both days at 12:01 A.M. Standard Time at the address of the

COMPANY

Item 3: RETROACTIVE DATE: the   at 12:01 A.M. Standard Time
at the address of the COMPANY.

Item 4: A. FLAT PREMIUM: $
         B. MINIMUM PREMIUM: $

Item 5: Limits of Liability:
         A. $ Each WRONGFUL ACT
         B. $ Aggregate Limit of Liability for the POLICY PERIOD.

Item 6: UNDERLYING LIMITS:
         This POLICY is written as   Insurance.
                                (Primary or Excess)
         A. If this POLICY is written as Primary Insurance with respect to Insuring Agreement I(AX2) only:
             (1) $ Each WRONGFUL ACT not arising from NUCLEAR
                                       OPERATIONS
             (2) $ Each WRONGFUL ACT arising from NUCLEAR
                                       OPERATIONS

9000 (1/88)   (1 OF 2)

867

DØLÎ

DECLARATIONS
continued

POLICY NO.

DECLARATION NO.

B. If this POLICY is written as Excess Insurance:
   (1) (a) $ Each WRONGFUL ACT
         (b) $ In the Aggregate for all WRONGFUL ACTS
   (2) $ Each WRONGFUL ACT not covered under Underlying
                                      Insurance
   (3) In the Event of Exhaustion of the UNDERLYING LIMIT stated in Item 6(B)(1)(b) above with
        respect to Insuring Agreement I(A)(2) only:
        (a) $ Each WRONGFUL ACT not arising from NUCLEAR
                                      OPERATIONS
        (b) $ Each WRONGFUL ACT arising from NUCLEAR
                                      OPERATIONS

Item 7: Any notice to be provided or any payment to be made hereunder to the COMPANY shall be
        made to:

        NAME
        TITLE
        ADDRESS

Item 8: Any notice to be provided or any payment to be made hereunder to the INSURER shall be
        made to:

        NAME   Michael Hardy
        TITLE   Assistant Treasurer
        ADDRESS   Directors & Officers Liability Insurance, Ltd.
                      Argus Insurance Building, 12 Wesley Street,
                      P.O. Box HM 1064, Hamilton 5, Bermuda

ENDORSEMENTS ATTACHED AT POLICY ISSUANCE:

Countersigned at   Hamilton, Bermuda

on: _____

Directors & Officers Liability Insurance, Ltd.

By _____
                Authorized Representative

9000 (1/88)   (2 OF 2)

POLICY OF DIRECTORS AND OFFICERS LIABILITY INSURANCE EFFECTED
WITH DIRECTORS & OFFICERS LIABILITY INSURANCE, LTD.
HAMILTON, BERMUDA
(hereinafter referred to as the "POLICY")

THIS IS A "CLAIMS-FIRST-MADE" INSURANCE POLICY. PLEASE READ IT CAREFULLY.

Words and phrases which appear in all capital letters have the special meanings set forth in Section II-DEFINITIONS

In consideration of the payment of premium, and in reliance upon all statements made and information furnished to Directors & Officers Liability Insurance, Ltd. (hereinafter referred to as the "INSURER") by the Application attached hereto which is hereby made a part hereof, and subject to all the terms hereinafter provided, the INSURER agrees as follows:

I. **INSURING AGREEMENT**

(A) *Indemnity*

(1) The INSURER shall indemnify the DIRECTORS and OFFICERS for any and all sums which they shall become legally obligated to pay as ULTIMATE NET LOSS for which the COMPANY has not provided reimbursement, by reason of any WRONGFUL ACT which takes place during the COVERAGE PERIOD and is actually or allegedly caused, committed or attempted by the DIRECTORS or OFFICERS while acting in their respective capacities as DIRECTORS or OFFICERS, provided such ULTIMATE NET LOSS arises from a CLAIM first made against the DIRECTORS or OFFICERS during the POLICY PERIOD or during the DISCOVERY PERIOD, if purchased.

(2) The INSURER shall indemnify the COMPANY for any and all sums required to reimburse it for ULTIMATE NET LOSS it has incurred, as required or permitted by applicable common or statutory law or under provisions of the COMPANY'S Charter or Bylaws effected pursuant to such law, to indemnify DIRECTORS or OFFICERS for ULTIMATE NET LOSS which they are legally obligated to pay by reason of any WRONGFUL ACT which takes place during the COVERAGE PERIOD and is actually or allegedly caused, committed or attempted by such DIRECTORS or OFFICERS while acting in their respective capacities as DIRECTORS or OFFICERS, provided the ULTIMATE NET LOSS arises from a CLAIM first made against the DIRECTORS or OFFICERS during the POLICY PERIOD or during the DISCOVERY PERIOD, if purchased.

(B) *Limits of Liability*

(1) The INSURER shall only be liable hereunder for the amount of ULTIMATE NET LOSS in excess of the UNDERLYING LIMITS as stated in Item 6 of the Declarations as a result of each WRONGFUL ACT covered under Insuring Agreement I(A)(1) or I(A)(2) or both, and then only up to the Limit of Liability stated in Item 5A of the Declarations and further subject to the aggregate Limit of Liability stated in Item 5B of the Declarations as the maximum amount payable hereunder in the aggregate for all CLAIMS first made against the DIRECTORS or OFFICERS during both:

(a) the POLICY PERIOD and

(b) the DISCOVERY PERIOD, if purchased.

Notwithstanding the foregoing, in the event that the INSURER cancels or refuses to renew this POLICY, and a DISCOVERY PERIOD extension is purchased by the COMPANY, then the aggregate Limit of Liability stated in Item 5B of the Declarations shall be reinstated but only with respect to CLAIMS first made against the DIRECTORS or OFFICERS during such DISCOVERY PERIOD.

9100 (1/88) [1 of 11]

DØLI

(2)   Multiple CLAIMS arising out of the same WRONGFUL ACT, even if made against different DIRECTORS or OFFICERS, shall be deemed to be a single CLAIM arising from a single WRONGFUL ACT and to have been reported during the POLICY PERIOD or, if purchased, during the DISCOVERY PERIOD in which the first of such multiple CLAIMS is made against any of the DIRECTORS or OFFICERS. The Limits of Liability and UNDERLYING LIMITS, stated in Items 5 and 6 of the Declarations respectively, shall apply only once regardless of the number of CLAIMS arising out of the same WRONGFUL ACT. All interrelated acts shall be deemed to be a single WRONGFUL ACT.

(3)   The inclusion herein of more than one DIRECTOR or OFFICER, or the application of both Insuring Agreements I(AX1) and I(AX2), shall not operate to increase the INSURER'S Limits of Liability as stated in Item 5 of the Declarations.

(C) *UNDERLYING LIMITS*

(1)   If this POLICY is written as Primary Insurance with respect to Insuring Agreement I(AX2), the UNDERLYING LIMIT for the COMPANY for each WRONGFUL ACT shall be as stated in Item 6A(1) of the Declarations, unless it is based upon, arises out of or is attributable to NUCLEAR OPERATIONS, in which event it shall be as stated in Item 6A(2) of the Declarations;

(2)   If this POLICY is written as Excess Insurance:

(a)   with respect to Insuring Agreements I(AX1) and I(AX2), the UNDERLYING LIMIT for each WRONGFUL ACT shall be as stated in Item 6B(1Xa) of the Declarations and the maximum UNDERLYING LIMIT for all WRONGFUL ACTS shall be as stated in Item 6B(1Xb) of the Declarations;

(b)   with respect to ULTIMATE NET LOSS covered hereunder:

(i)   in the event of reduction- of the underlying aggregate limit as stated in Item 6B(1Xb), the UNDERLYING LIMIT shall be such reduced underlying aggregate limit; or

(ii)   in the event of exhaustion of the underlying aggregate limit as stated in Item 6B(1Xb), the UNDERLYING LIMIT shall be as stated in Item 6B(3) of the Declarations;

(c)   with respect to any WRONGFUL ACT covered hereunder but not covered under such Underlying Insurance, the UNDERLYING LIMIT shall be as stated in Item 6B(2) of the Declarations; and

(d)   nothing herein shall make this POLICY subject to the terms and conditions of any Underlying Insurance.

(3)   Only payment of indemnity or defense expenses which, except for the amount thereof, would have been indemnifiable under this POLICY, may reduce or exhaust an UNDERLYING LIMIT.

(4)   In the event that both Insuring Agreement I(AX1) and I(AX2) are applicable to INDEMNITY and DEFENSE COST resulting from a WRONGFUL ACT then:

(a)   If this POLICY is written as Primary Insurance, the UNDERLYING LIMIT applicable to such WRONGFUL ACT shall be the UNDERLYING LIMIT stated in Item 6A of the Declarations; and

(b)   If this POLICY is written as Excess Insurance and the UNDERLYING LIMIT has been exhausted, the UNDERLYING LIMIT applicable to such WRONGFUL ACT shall be the UNDERLYING LIMIT stated in Item 6B(3);

and there shall be no UNDERLYING LIMIT applicable with respect to coverage provided under Insuring Agreement I(AX1).

[2 of 11]

870

(5) The UNDERLYING LIMITS stated in Item 6 of the Declarations applicable to Insuring Agreement I(AX2) shall apply to all INDEMNITY and/or DEFENSE COST for which indemnification of the DIRECTORS and/or OFFICERS by the COMPANY is legally permissible, whether or not such indemnification is granted by the COMPANY.

II. DEFINITIONS

(A) CLAIM: The term "CLAIM" shall mean:

(1) any demand, suit or proceeding against any DIRECTORS and/or OFFICERS during the POLICY PERIOD or during the DISCOVERY PERIOD, if purchased, which seeks actual monetary damages or other relief and which may result in any DIRECTORS and/or OFFICERS becoming legally obligated to pay ULTIMATE NET LOSS by reason of any WRONGFUL ACT actually or allegedly caused, committed or attempted during the COVERAGE PERIOD by the DIRECTORS and/or OFFICERS while acting in their capacity as such; or

(2) written notice to the INSURER during the POLICY PERIOD or during the DISCOVERY PERIOD, if purchased, by the DIRECTORS , OFFICERS and/or the COMPANY, describing with the specificity set forth in Condition (C) hereof, circumstances of which they are aware involving an identifiable WRONGFUL ACT actually or allegedly caused, committed or attempted during the COVERAGE PERIOD by the DIRECTORS and/or OFFICERS while acting in their capacity as such, which circumstances are likely to give rise to a demand, suit or proceeding being made against such DIRECTORS and/or OFFICERS.

A CLAIM shall be deemed to be first made against a DIRECTOR or OFFICER at the earlier of the time at which a demand, suit or proceeding is first made against the DIRECTOR or OFFICER, as set forth in section (1) of this Definition or the time at which written notice is given to the INSURER, as set forth in section (2) of this Definition.

Multiple demands or suits arising out of the same WRONGFUL ACT or interrelated acts shall be deemed to be a single "CLAIM".

(B) COMPANY: The term "COMPANY" shall mean the organization(s) named in Item 1 of the Declarations and, subject to Condition (A) hereof, any SUBSIDIARIES of such organization(s).

(C) COVERAGE PERIOD: The term "COVERAGE PERIOD" shall mean the period of time from the RETROACTIVE DATE to the termination of the POLICY PERIOD.

(D) DEFENSE COST: The term "DEFENSE COST" shall mean all expenses incurred by or on behalf of the DIRECTORS, OFFICERS or the COMPANY, where reimbursable under I(AX2), in the investigation, negotiation, settlement and defense of any CLAIM except all salaries, wages and benefit expenses of DIRECTORS, OFFICERS or the COMPANY.

(E) DIRECTOR and OFFICER: The terms "DIRECTOR" and "OFFICER" as used herein, either in the singular or plural, shall mean:

(1) any person who was, is now, or shall be a director, officer or trustee of the COMPANY and any other employee of the COMPANY who may be acting in the capacity of a director, officer or trustee of the COMPANY with the express authorization of a director, officer or trustee of the COMPANY;

(2) any director, officer or trustee of the COMPANY who is serving or has served at the specific request of the COMPANY as a director, officer or trustee of any outside NOT—FOR—PROFIT ORGANIZATION; or

(3) the estates, heirs, legal representatives or assigns of deceased persons who were directors, officers or trustees of the COMPANY at the time the WRONGFUL ACTS upon which such CLAIMS were based were committed, and the legal representatives or assigns of directors, officers or trustees of the COMPANY in the event of their incompetency, insolvency or bankruptcy;

9100 (1/88)   [3 of 11]

DØLÎ

provided, however, that the terms "DIRECTOR" and "OFFICER" shall not include a trustee appointed pursuant to Title 11, United States Code, or pursuant to the Securities Investor Protection Act, a receiver appointed for the benefit of creditors by Federal or State courts, as assignee for the benefit of creditors or similar fiduciary appointed under Federal or State laws for the protection of creditors or the relief of debtors.

(F) DISCOVERY PERIOD: The term "DISCOVERY PERIOD" shall mean the period of time set forth in Condition (L).

(G) INDEMNITY: The term "INDEMNITY" shall mean all sums which the DIRECTORS, OFFICERS or COMPANY, where reimbursable under I(AX2), shall become legally obligated to pay as damages either by adjudication or compromise with the consent of the INSURER, after making proper deduction for the UNDERLYING LIMITS and all recoveries, salvages and other valid and collectible insurance.

(H) INSURER: The term "INSURER" shall mean Directors & Officers Liability Insurance, Ltd., Hamilton, Bermuda, a non-assessable mutual insurance company.

(I) NOT—FOR—PROFIT ORGANIZATION: The term "NOT—FOR—PROFIT ORGANIZATION" shall mean an organization, no part of the income or assets of which are distributable to its owners, stockholders or members and which is formed and operated for a purpose other than for the pecuniary profit or financial gain of its owners, stockholders or members.

(J) NUCLEAR OPERATIONS: The term "NUCLEAR OPERATIONS" shall mean the design, engineering, financing, construction, operation, maintenance, use, ownership, conversion or decommissioning of any "nuclear facility" as defined in the Broad Form Nuclear Energy Liability Exclusion, which is endorsed hereto.

(K) POLICY: The term "POLICY" shall mean this insurance policy, including the Application, the Declarations and any endorsements issued by the INSURER to the organization first named in Item 1 of the Declarations for the POLICY PERIOD listed in Item 2 of the Declarations.

(L) POLICY PERIOD: The term "POLICY PERIOD" shall mean the period of time stated in Item 2 of the Declarations.

(M) RETROACTIVE DATE: The term "RETROACTIVE DATE" shall mean the date stated in Item 3 of the Declarations.

(N) SUBSIDIARIES: The term "SUBSIDIARY" shall mean any entity more than fifty (50) percent of whose outstanding securities representing the present right to vote for election of directors are owned by the COMPANY and/or one or more of its "SUBSIDIARIES".

(O) ULTIMATE NET LOSS: The term "ULTIMATE NET LOSS" shall mean the total INDEMNITY and DEFENSE COST with respect to each WRONGFUL ACT to which this POLICY applies.

(P) UNDERLYING LIMITS: The term "UNDERLYING LIMITS" shall mean the amounts stated in Item 6 of the Declarations.

(Q) WRONGFUL ACT: The term "WRONGFUL ACT" shall mean any actual or alleged breach of duty, neglect, error, misstatement, misleading statement or omission actually or allegedly caused, committed or attempted by any DIRECTOR or OFFICER while acting individually or collectively in their capacity as such, claimed against them solely by reason of their being DIRECTORS or OFFICERS.

All such interrelated breaches of duty, neglects, errors, misstatements, misleading statements or omissions actually or allegedly caused, committed or attempted by or claimed against one or more of the DIRECTORS or OFFICERS shall be deemed to be a single "WRONGFUL ACT".

9100 (1/88)

[4 of 11]

872

III. EXCLUSIONS

The INSURER shall not be liable to make any payment for ULTIMATE NET LOSS arising from any CLAIM(S) made against any DIRECTOR or OFFICER:

(A) (1) for any fines or penalties imposed in a criminal suit, action or proceeding;

    (2) for any fines or penalties imposed in conjunction with political contributions, payments, commissions or gratuities; or

    (3) for any other fines or penalties imposed by final adjudication of a court of competent jurisdiction or any agency or commission possessing quasi—judicial authority; or

    (4) where, at inception of the POLICY PERIOD, such DIRECTOR or OFFICER had knowledge of a fact or circumstance which was likely to give rise to such CLAIM(S) and which such DIRECTOR or OFFICER failed to disclose or misrepresented in the Application or in the process of preparation of the Application, other than in a Renewal Application; provided, however, that this exclusion shall not apply to such CLAIM(S) made against any DIRECTOR or OFFICER other than such DIRECTOR or OFFICER who failed to disclose or misrepresented such fact or circumstance; provided further that this exclusion shall not limit the INSURER'S right to exercise any remedy available to it with respect to such failure to disclose or misrepresentation other than the remedy provided for in this Exclusion.

(B) with respect to Insuring Agreement I(AX 1) only:

    (1) based upon, arising out of or attributable to such DIRECTOR or OFFICER having gained any personal profit or advantage to which such DIRECTOR or OFFICER was not legally entitled if:

        (a) a judgment or other final adjudication adverse to such DIRECTOR or OFFICER establishes that he in fact gained such personal profit or other advantage; or

        (b) such DIRECTOR or OFFICER has entered into a settlement agreement to repay such personal profit or advantage to the COMPANY;

    (2) for the return by such DIRECTOR or OFFICER of any remuneration paid to such DIRECTOR or OFFICER without the previous approval of the shareholders of the COMPANY which payment without such previous approval shall be held by the courts to have been illegal;

    (3) for an accounting of profits made from the purchase or sale by such DIRECTOR or OFFICER of securities of the COMPANY within the meaning of Section 16(b) of the Securities Exchange Act of 1934 and amendments thereto or similar provisions of any other federal or state statutory or common law;

    (4) brought about or contributed to by the dishonest, fraudulent, criminal or malicious act or omission of such DIRECTOR or OFFICER if a final adjudication establishes that acts of active and deliberate dishonesty were committed or attempted with actual dishonest purpose and intent and were material to the cause of action so adjudicated; or

    (5) where such payment would be contrary to applicable law.

(C) for bodily injury, mental anguish, mental illness, emotional upset, sickness or disease sustained by any person, death of any person or for physical injury to or destruction of tangible property or the loss of use thereof.

(D) for injury based upon, arising out of or attributable to:

    (1) false arrest, wrongful detention or wrongful imprisonment or malicious prosecution;

    (2) wrongful entry, wrongful eviction or other invasion of the right of private occupancy;

    (3) discrimination or sexual harassment;

9100 (1/88)   [5 of 11]

873

DØLÎ

(4) publication or utterance:

    (a) of a libel or slander or other defamatory or disparaging material; or

    (b) in violation of an individual's right of privacy; or

(5) with respect to the COMPANY'S advertising activities: piracy, plagiarism, unfair competition, idea misappropriation under implied contract, infringement of copyright, title or slogan, registered trademark, service mark, or trade name.

(E) based upon, arising out of or attributable to the violation of any responsibility, obligation or duty imposed upon fiduciaries by the Employee Retirement Income Security Act of 1974 or amendments thereto or by similar common or statutory law of the United States of America or any state or other jurisdiction therein.

(F) based upon, arising out of or attributable to:

(1) the rendering of advice with respect to;

(2) the interpreting of; or

(3) the handling of records in connection with the enrollment, termination or cancellation of employees under the COMPANY'S group life insurance, group accident or health insurance, pension plans, employee stock subscription plans, workers' compensation, unemployment insurance, social security, disability benefits and any other employee benefit programs.

(G) based upon, arising out of or attributable to any failure or omission on the part of the DIRECTORS, OFFICERS and/or the COMPANY to effect and maintain insurance(s) of the type and amount which is customary with companies in the same or similar business.

(H) (1) arising from any circumstances, written notice of which has been given under any policy or any DISCOVERY PERIOD thereof, which policy expired prior to or upon the inception of this POLICY; or

(2) which is one of a number of CLAIMS arising out of the same WRONGFUL ACT, if any CLAIM of such multiple CLAIMS was made against the DIRECTORS or OFFICERS during any policy or any DISCOVERY PERIOD thereof, which policy expired prior to or upon the inception of this POLICY.

(I) if any other policy or policies also afford(s) coverage in whole or in part for such CLAIM(S); except, this exclusion shall not apply:

(1) to the amount of ULTIMATE NET LOSS with respect to such CLAIM(S) which is in excess of the limit of liability of such other policy or policies and any applicable deductible or retention thereunder; or

(2) with respect to coverage afforded such CLAIM(S) by any other policy or policies purchased or issued specifically as insurance underlying or in excess of the coverage afforded under this POLICY;

provided always that nothing herein shall be construed to cause this POLICY to contribute with any other policy or policies or to make this POLICY subject to any of the terms of any other policy or policies.

(J) for any WRONGFUL ACTS which took place prior to the RETROACTIVE DATE.

(K) by, on behalf of, in the right of, at the request of, or for the benefit of, any security holder of the COMPANY, any DIRECTOR or OFFICER, or the COMPANY, unless such CLAIM is:

(1)   made derivatively by any shareholder of the COMPANY for the benefit of the COMPANY
      and such shareholder is:

      (a)   acting totally independent of, and totally without the suggestion, solicitation, direction,
            assistance, participation, or intervention, of any DIRECTOR or OFFICER, the COMPANY,
            or any affiliate of the COMPANY; and

      (b)   not an affiliate of the COMPANY nor any entity within the definition of the term
            COMPANY; or

(2)   made non-derivatively by a security holder who is not

      (a)   a DIRECTOR or OFFICER; or

      (b)   an affiliate of the COMPANY or any entity within the definition of the term COMPANY.

(L)   where such CLAIM(S) arise out of such DIRECTOR'S or OFFICER'S activities as a director, officer
      or trustee of any entity other than:

      (1)   the COMPANY; or

      (2)   any outside NOT-FOR-PROFIT ORGANIZATION as provided in Section II(EX2).

IV. CONDITIONS

(A) *Acquisition, Merger and Dissolution*

If, after inception of the POLICY PERIOD, the COMPANY or any of its SUBSIDIARIES:

(1)   forms or acquires any SUBSIDIARY, the COMPANY shall report such formation or acquisition
      within thirty (30) days thereafter and, if so reported, the INSURER shall provide coverage
      for the DIRECTORS and OFFICERS of such newly formed or acquired SUBSIDIARY from the
      date of its formation or acquisition respectively, upon payment of an additional premium
      and upon such terms as may be required by the INSURER; or

(2)   is acquired by or merged with any other entity, or is dissolved, coverage under this POLICY
      shall continue only with respect to the DIRECTORS and OFFICERS of the COMPANY or its
      SUBSIDIARIES who were serving as such prior to such acquisition, merger or dissolution
      and only with respect to WRONGFUL ACTS actually or allegedly caused, committed or
      attempted prior to such acquisition, merger or dissolution.

(B) *Non-Duplication of Limits*

To avoid the duplication of the INSURER'S Limits of Liability stated in Item 5 of the Declarations,
the DIRECTORS, OFFICERS and COMPANY agree that:

(1)   in the event the INSURER provides INDEMNITY or DEFENSE COSTS for any WRONGFUL
      ACT under this POLICY, neither the DIRECTORS, OFFICERS nor the COMPANY shall have any
      right to additional INDEMNITY or DEFENSE COSTS for such WRONGFUL ACT under any
      other policy issued by the INSURER to the DIRECTORS, OFFICERS or COMPANY that
      otherwise would apply to such WRONGFUL ACT; and

(2)   in the event the INSURER provides INDEMNITY or DEFENSE COSTS for any WRONGFUL
      ACT under any policy issued by the INSURER to the DIRECTORS, OFFICERS, or COMPANY,
      neither the DIRECTORS, OFFICERS nor the COMPANY shall have any right to additional
      INDEMNITY or DEFENSE COSTS for such WRONGFUL ACT under this POLICY.

9100 (1/88)   [7 of 11]

875

DØLÎ

(C) *Notice of Claim*

As a condition precedent to any rights under this POLICY, the DIRECTORS, OFFICERS and/or the COMPANY, shall give written notice to the INSURER as soon as practicable of any CLAIM, which notice shall include the nature of the WRONGFUL ACT, the alleged injury, the names of the claimants, and the manner in which the DIRECTOR, OFFICER or COMPANY first became aware of the CLAIM, and shall cooperate with the INSURER and give such additional information as the INSURER may reasonably require.

The Application or any information contained therein for this POLICY shall not constitute a notice of CLAIM.

(D) *Cooperation and Settlements*

In the event of any WRONGFUL ACT which may involve this POLICY, the DIRECTORS, OFFICERS or COMPANY without prejudice as to liability, may proceed immediately with settlements which in their aggregate do not exceed the UNDERLYING LIMITS. The COMPANY shall notify the INSURER of any such settlements made.

The INSURER shall not be called upon to assume charge of the investigation, settlement or defense of any demand, suit or proceeding, but the INSURER shall have the right and shall be given the opportunity to associate with the DIRECTORS, OFFICERS and COMPANY or any underlying insurer, or both, in the investigation, settlement, defense and control of any demand, suit or proceeding relative to any WRONGFUL ACT where the demand, suit or proceeding involves or may involve the INSURER. At all times, the DIRECTORS, OFFICERS and COMPANY and the INSURER shall cooperate in the investigation, settlement and defense of such demand, suit or proceeding.

The DIRECTORS, OFFICERS and COMPANY and their underlying insurer(s) shall, at all times, use diligence and prudence in the investigation, settlement and defense of demands, suits or other proceedings.

(E) *Appeals*

In the event that the DIRECTORS, OFFICERS, COMPANY or any underlying insurer elects not to appeal a judgment in excess of the UNDERLYING LIMITS, the INSURER may elect to conduct such appeal at its own cost and expense and shall be liable for any taxable court costs and interest incidental thereto, but in no event shall the total liability of the INSURER, exclusive of the cost and expense of appeal exceed its Limits of Liability stated in Item 5 of the Declarations.

(F) *Subrogation*

In the event of any payment under this POLICY, the INSURER shall be subrogated to the extent of such payment to all rights of recovery thereof, and the DIRECTORS, OFFICERS and COMPANY shall execute all papers required and shall do everything that may be necessary to enable the INSURER to bring suit in the name of the DIRECTORS, OFFICERS or COMPANY.

(G) *Bankruptcy or Insolvency*

Bankruptcy or insolvency of the COMPANY shall not relieve the INSURER of any of its obligations hereunder.

9100 (1/88)   [8 of 11]

(H) *Uncollectibility of Underlying Insurance*

Notwithstanding any of the terms of this POLICY which might be construed otherwise, if this POLICY is written as excess over any Underlying Insurance, it shall drop down only in the event of reduction or exhaustion of any aggregate limits contained in such Underlying Insurance and shall not drop down for any other reason including, but not limited to, uncollectibility (in whole or in part) because of the financial impairment or insolvency of an underlying insurer. The risk of uncollectibility of such Underlying Insurance (in whole or in part) whether because of financial impairment or insolvency of an underlying insurer or for any other reason, is expressly retained by the DIRECTORS, OFFICERS and the COMPANY and is not in any way or under any circumstances insured or assumed by the INSURER.

(I) *Maintenance of UNDERLYING LIMITS*

If this POLICY is written as Excess Insurance, it is a condition of this POLICY that any UNDERLYING LIMITS stated in Item 6 of the Declarations shall be maintained in full force and effect, except for reduction or exhaustion of any underlying aggregate limits of liability, during the currency of this POLICY. Failure of the COMPANY to comply with the foregoing shall not invalidate this POLICY but in the event of such failure, without the agreement of the INSURER, the INSURER shall only be liable to the same extent as it would have been had the COMPANY complied with this Condition.

(J) *Changes and Assignment*

The terms of this POLICY shall not be waived or changed, nor shall an assignment of interest be binding, except by an endorsement to this POLICY issued by the INSURER.

(K) *Outside NOT-FOR-PROFIT ORGANIZATION*

If any DIRECTOR or OFFICER is serving or has served at the specific request of the COMPANY as a DIRECTOR or OFFICER of an outside NOT—FOR—PROFIT ORGANIZATION, the coverage afforded by this POLICY:

(1) shall be specifically excess of any other indemnity or insurance available to such DIRECTOR or OFFICER by reason of such service; and

(2) shall not be construed to extend to the outside NOT—FOR—PROFIT ORGANIZATION in which the DIRECTOR or OFFICER is serving or has served, nor to any other director, officer or employee of such outside NOT—FOR—PROFIT ORGANIZATION.

(L) *DISCOVERY PERIOD*

(1) In the event of cancellation or nonrenewal of this POLICY, the COMPANY shall have the the right, upon execution of a warranty that all known CLAIMS and facts or circumstances likely to give rise to a CLAIM have been reported to the INSURER and payment of an additional premium to be determined by the INSURER which shall not exceed two hundred (200) percent of the Flat Premium stated in Item 4 of the Declarations, to an extension of the coverage afforded by this POLICY with respect to any CLAIM first made against any DIRECTOR or OFFICER during the period of twelve (12) months after the effective date of such cancellation or nonrenewal, but only with respect to any WRONGFUL ACT committed during the COVERAGE PERIOD. This right of extension shall terminate unless written notice of such election is received by the INSURER within thirty (30) days after the effective date of cancellation or nonrenewal.

The offer by the INSURER of renewal on terms, conditions or premiums different from those in effect during the POLICY PERIOD shall not constitute cancellation or refusal to renew this POLICY.

9100 (1/88)

DØLÎ

(2) In the event of renewal on terms and conditions different from those in effect during the POLICY PERIOD, the COMPANY shall have the right, upon execution of a warranty that all known CLAIMS and facts or circumstances likely to give rise to a CLAIM have been reported to the INSURER and payment of an additional premium to be determined by the INSURER which shall not exceed two hundred (200) percent of the Flat Premium stated in Item 4 of the Declarations, to an extension of the original terms and conditions with respect to any CLAIM first made against any DIRECTOR or OFFICER during the period of twelve (12) months after the effective date of renewal, but only with respect to any WRONGFUL ACT committed during the COVERAGE PERIOD and not covered by the renewal terms and conditions. This right of extension shall terminate unless written notice of such election is received by the INSURER within thirty (30) days after the effective date of renewal.

(M) *Cancellation*

This POLICY may be cancelled:

(1) at any time by the COMPANY by mailing written notice to the INSURER stating when thereafter cancellation shall be effective; or

(2) at any time by the INSURER by mailing written notice to the COMPANY stating when, not less than ninety (90) days from the date such notice was mailed, cancellation shall be effective, except in the event of cancellation for nonpayment of premiums, such cancellation shall be effective ten (10) days after the date notice thereof is mailed.

The proof of mailing of notice to the address of the COMPANY stated in Item 7 of the Declarations or the address of the INSURER stated in Item 8 of the Declarations shall be sufficient proof of notice and the insurance under this POLICY shall end on the effective date and hour of cancellation stated in the notice. Delivery of such notice either by the COMPANY or by the INSURER shall be equivalent to mailing.

With respect to all cancellations, the premium earned and retained by the INSURER shall be the sum of (a) the Minimum Premium stated in Item 4B of the Declarations plus (b) the pro-rata proportion, for the period this POLICY has been in force, of the difference between (i) the FLAT Premium stated in Item 4A of the Declarations and (ii) the Minimum Premium stated in Item 4B of the Declarations.

The offer by the INSURER of renewal on terms, conditions or premiums different from those in effect during the POLICY PERIOD shall not constitute cancellation or refusal to renew this POLICY.

(N) *Currency*

All amounts stated herein are expressed in United States Dollars and all amounts payable hereunder are payable in United States Dollars.

(O) *Sole Agent*

The COMPANY first named in Item 1 of the Declarations shall be deemed the sole agent of each DIRECTOR and OFFICER for the purpose of requesting any endorsement to this POLICY, making premium payments and adjustments, receipting for payments of INDEMNITY and receiving notifications, including notice of cancellation from the INSURER.

(P) *Acts, Omissions or Warranties*

The acts, omissions or warranties of any DIRECTOR or OFFICER shall not be imputed to any other DIRECTOR or OFFICER with respect to the coverages applicable under this POLICY.

9100 (1/88)   [10 of 11]

(Q) *Arbitration/Service of Suit*

Any controversy or dispute arising out of or relating to an interpretation or breach of this POLICY, shall be settled by binding arbitration in accordance with the Rules of the American Arbitration Association and judgment upon the award rendered by the arbitrator(s) may be entered in any court having jurisdiction thereover. The arbitration process shall be governed by and conducted in accordance with the laws of the State of New York. The terms of this POLICY are to be construed in an evenhanded fashion as between the DIRECTORS, OFFICERS or COMPANY and the INSURER in accordance with the laws of the jurisdiction in which the situation forming the basis for this controversy arose. Where the language of this POLICY is deemed to be ambiguous or otherwise unclear, the issue shall be resolved in a manner most consistent with the relevant terms of the POLICY without regard to authorship of the language and without any presumption or arbitrary interpretation or construction in favor of either the DIRECTORS, OFFICERS or COMPANY or the INSURER. In reaching any decision the arbitrators shall give due consideration for the customs and usages of the insurance industry.

In the event of a judgment entered against the INSURER on an arbitration award, the INSURER at the request of the DIRECTORS, OFFICERS or COMPANY, shall submit to the jurisdiction of any court of competent jurisdiction within the United States of America, and shall comply with all requirements necessary to give such court jurisdiction and all matters relating to such judgment and its enforcement shall be determined in accordance with the law and practice of such court.

Service of process in such suit or any other suit against the INSURER, may be made upon Messrs. LeBoeuf, Lamb, Leiby & MacRae, 520 Madison Avenue, New York, New York 10022, and, in any suit instituted against it under this POLICY, the INSURER will abide by the final decision of such court or of any appellate court in the event of any appeal.

Messrs. LeBoeuf, Lamb, Leiby & MacRae are authorized and directed to accept service of process on behalf of the INSURER in any such suit and, upon the DIRECTORS, OFFICERS or COMPANY'S request, to give a written undertaking to the DIRECTORS, OFFICERS or COMPANY that they will enter a general appearance on the INSURER'S behalf in the event such suit is instituted.

(R) *Severability*

In the event that any provision of this POLICY shall be declared or deemed to be invalid or unenforceable under any applicable law, such invalidity or unenforceability shall not affect the validity or enforceability of the remaining portion of this POLICY.

(S) *Non-assessability*

The COMPANY (and, accordingly, any DIRECTOR or OFFICER for whom the COMPANY acts as agent) shall only be liable under this POLICY for:

(1) the premium stated in Item 4 of the Declarations; and

(2) any premium collectable pursuant to the Retrospective Premium Endorsement.

Neither the COMPANY nor any DIRECTOR or OFFICER for whom the COMPANY acts as agent shall be subject to any contingent liability or be required to pay any dues or assessments in addition to the premium described in (1) and (2) above.

IN WITNESS WHEREOF, Directors & Officers Liability Insurance, Ltd. has caused this POLICY to be signed by its President at Hamilton, Bermuda. However, this POLICY shall not be binding upon the INSURER unless countersigned on the Declaration Page by a duly authorized representative of the INSURER.

Robert R. Fortune
Robert R. Fortune, President

9100 (1/88)

**APPLICATION FOR
INDEPENDENT DIRECTORS' LIABILITY POLICY**

NOTICE: THE POLICY FOR WHICH APPLICATION IS MADE APPLIES, SUBJECT TO ITS TERMS, ONLY TO ANY "CLAIM" (AS DEFINED IN THE POLICY) FIRST MADE OR DEEMED MADE AGAINST THE "INDEPENDENT DIRECTORS" (AS DEFINED IN THE POLICY) DURING THE "POLICY PERIOD" (AS DEFINED IN THE POLICY). THE LIMIT OF LIABILITY AVAILABLE TO PAY DAMAGES OR SETTLEMENTS SHALL BE REDUCED BY "DEFENSE EXPENSES" (AS DEFINED IN THE POLICY) AND "DEFENSE EXPENSES" SHALL BE APPLIED AGAINST THE RETENTION. THE POLICY DOES NOT PROVIDE FOR ANY DUTY BY THE UNDERWRITER TO DEFEND ANY PERSON.

Complete and correct information must be supplied by the **Parent Corporation** whether or not such information is deemed confidential by the **Parent Corporation**.

A.   1.   a) Name of **Parent Corporation:** _____

           b) Principal address: _____

           _____

           c) State of incorporation or charter: _____

    2.   If permitted under state law or statute, have the **Parent Corporation** and its' **Subsidiaries** adopted a provision eliminating or limiting the personal liability of their directors to the broadest extent permitted at present?   ☐ Yes   ☐ No

B.   Identify the **Independent Directors** for which this coverage is sought:

    _____   _____   _____

    _____   _____   _____

    _____   _____   _____

    1.   Do the **Independent Directors** listed above have independent legal counsel, other than counsel for the **Parent Corporation,** regularly available for consultation?   ☐ Yes   ☐ No

       If so, give details: _____

       _____

    2.   Has the **Parent Corporation** or any **Subsidiary** changed its outside auditors within the last 36 months? If so, give details: _____

       _____

    3.   Does the **Parent Corporation** have an Audit Committee?   ☐ Yes   ☐ No

       If so, state whether any persons other than **Independent Directors** are members of such committee, and identify any such persons.   ☐ Yes   ☐ No

       _____   _____

       State how often the Audit Committee has met within the last 12 months: _____

    4.   Has the board of directors established formal, written policies and procedures for reporting claims against directors or officers of the **Parent Corporation** and its **Subsidiaries**?   ☐ Yes   ☐ No

    5.   Are such policies and procedures for reporting claims periodically reviewed?   ☐ Yes   ☐ No

C.   1.   a) Please give details of the following insurance carried by the **Parent Corporation** and its **Subsidiaries** (if the answer is none, so state):

	LIMIT	RETENTION	CARRIER	POLICY PERIOD	PREMIUM
Directors and Officers Liability	____	_____	_____	____ to ____	_____
Fiduciary Liability	____	_____	_____	____ to ____	_____
Fidelity Bond	____	_____	_____	____ to ____	_____

       Advise what directors' and/or officers' coverage will be carried on renewal (If "as exp.," so state):

(F-1841) ED. 3-88

THIS IS A CLAIMS MADE INDEMNITY POLICY WITH
EXPENSES INCLUDED IN THE LIMIT OF LIABILITY.
PLEASE READ THE ENTIRE POLICY CAREFULLY.

THE ÆTNA CASUALTY AND SURETY COMPANY

DECLARATIONS

INDEPENDENT DIRECTORS' LIABILITY POLICY

POLICY NUMBER:

NOTICE: THIS IS A CLAIMS MADE INDEMNITY POLICY WHICH APPLIES ONLY TO ANY "CLAIM" FIRST MADE DURING
THE "POLICY PERIOD" AGAINST THE "INDEPENDENT DIRECTORS" FOR A "WRONGFUL ACT." THE LIMIT OF
LIABILITY AVAILABLE TO PAY DAMAGES OR SETTLEMENTS SHALL BE REDUCED BY "DEFENSE EXPENSES," AND
"DEFENSE EXPENSES" SHALL BE APPLIED AGAINST THE RETENTION. THIS POLICY DOES NOT PROVIDE FOR ANY
DUTY BY THE UNDERWRITER TO DEFEND ANY PERSON. THE COVERAGE AFFORDED BY THIS POLICY DIFFERS IN
SOME RESPECTS FROM THAT AFFORDED BY MOST OTHER POLICIES. PLEASE READ CAREFULLY.

ITEM 1. **PARENT CORPORATION** NAME AND PRINCIPAL ADDRESS: State of Incorporation _____	ITEM 2. **POLICY PERIOD:** (a) Inception Date: _____ (b) Expiration Date:_____ at 12:01 a.m. Standard Time both dates at the Principal Address in ITEM 1.

ITEM 3.   LIMIT OF LIABILITY (Inclusive of **Defense Expenses**):

$ _____. maximum aggregate Limit of Liability for the **Policy Period.**

ITEM 4.   RETENTIONS:

$ _____ each **Independent Director** each **Claim,** not to exceed
$ _____ in the aggregate, each **Claim.**

ITEM 5.   PREMIUM:

$ _____ prepaid premium.

ITEM 6. **OTHER DIRECTORS AND OFFICERS** **LIABILITY INSURANCE:** Insurer: _____ Policy No: _____	ITEM 7. **NOTICE REQUIRED TO BE GIVEN TO THE** **UNDERWRITER SHALL BE ADDRESSED TO:**

ITEM 8.   ENDORSEMENTS ATTACHED AT ISSUANCE:

**These Declarations, the completed signed Application and the Policy with Endorsements shall constitute the contract
between the Company, the Independent Directors and the Underwriter.**

THE ÆTNA CASUALTY AND SURETY COMPANY By (Attorney-in-Fact)

(F-1842) ED. 3-88

SAMPLE COPY

2. a) No claims have been made against any person(s) proposed for this insurance in their capacity as a director or officer of any corporation, except as follows (include loss payment and defense costs; if answer is "none", so state): _____

_____

b) No person or entity proposed for this insurance is cognizant of any act, error, or omission which they have reason to suppose might afford valid grounds for any **Claim** such as would fall within the scope of the proposed insurance, except as follows (if answer is "none," so state): _____

_____

_____

If any such person has knowledge of any such claim, act, error or omission whether or not disclosed, it is understood and agreed that there will be no coverage for such person under the proposed insurance in respect of any **Claim** arising therefrom.

3. As part of this application, please submit the following documents with respect to the **Parent Corporation**:

    a) Last 2 annual reports, including audited financial statements with all notes and schedules.
    b) Latest 10-K, and any 10-Q and 8-K reports filed subsequent to the latest annual report.
    c) Most recent prospectus.
    d) Last 2 notices of shareholders' meetings with accompanying proxy statements.
    e) Indemnification provisions in the **Parent Corporation's** certificate of incorporation or by-laws, or indemnification agreements or contracts with the **Independent Directors**.
    f) Any provisions in the **Parent Corporation's** certificate of incorporation or by-laws eliminating or limiting personal liability of directors.
    g) Copies of all directors' and/or officers' policies that will be continued or renewed if the insurance requested in this application is purchased.

IT IS REPRESENTED THAT THE PARTICULARS AND STATEMENTS CONTAINED IN THE APPLICATION FOR THE PROPOSED POLICY AND ANY MATERIALS SUBMITTED HEREWITH (WHICH SHALL ALSO BE ON FILE WITH THE UNDERWRITER AND BE DEEMED ATTACHED TO THE POLICY AS IF PHYSICALLY ATTACHED) ARE TRUE AND COMPLETE AND ARE THE BASIS FOR THE PROPOSED POLICY AND ARE TO BE CONSIDERED AS INCORPORATED INTO AND CONSTITUTING A PART OF THE PROPOSED POLICY.

THE UNDERSIGNED AUTHORIZED AGENT OF THE COMPANY AND OF THE INDIVIDUALS PROPOSED FOR COVERAGE UNDER THE INSURANCE CONTRACT FOR WHICH APPLICATION IS MADE UNDERSTAND THAT:

    (A) THE POLICY, SUBJECT TO ITS TERMS, APPLIES ONLY TO ANY "CLAIM" FIRST MADE OR DEEMED MADE AGAINST THE "INDEPENDENT DIRECTORS" DURING THE "POLICY PERIOD;"

    (B) THE LIMIT OF LIABILITY AVAILABLE TO PAY DAMAGES OR SETTLEMENTS SHALL BE REDUCED BY "DEFENSE EXPENSES" AND "DEFENSE EXPENSES" SHALL BE APPLIED AGAINST THE RETENTION;

    (C) THE POLICY DOES NOT PROVIDE FOR ANY DUTY BY THE UNDERWRITER TO DEFEND ANY PERSON.

NOTICE TO NEW YORK APPLICANTS: ANY PERSON WHO KNOWINGLY AND WITH INTENT TO DEFRAUD ANY INSURANCE COMPANY OR OTHER PERSON FILES AN APPLICATION FOR INSURANCE CONTAINING ANY FALSE INFORMATION, OR CONCEALS FOR THE PURPOSE OF MISLEADING, INFORMATION CONCERNING ANY FACT MATERIAL THERETO, COMMITS A FRAUDULENT INSURANCE ACT, WHICH IS A CRIME.

APPLICANT		
BY *(Chairman and/or President Signature)*	TITLE	DATE

NOTE: This application must be signed by the chairman and/or president of the **Parent Corporation** acting as the authorized agent of the Company and of the persons proposed for this insurance.

SUBMITTED BY *(Insurance Agency)*	INSURANCE AGENCY TAX PAYER ID OR SOCIAL SECURITY NO.
ADDRESS *(No., Street, City, State and Zip Code)*	

2

THIS IS A CLAIMS MADE INDEMNITY POLICY WITH
EXPENSES INCLUDED IN THE LIMIT OF LIABILITY.
PLEASE READ THE ENTIRE POLICY CAREFULLY.

THE ÆTNA CASUALTY AND SURETY COMPANY

INDEPENDENT DIRECTORS' LIABILITY POLICY

The Ætna Casualty And Surety Company (the "Underwriter"), the Independent Directors and the Company,
subject to all of the terms, conditions and limitations of this Policy, agree as follows:

I. INSURING AGREEMENT

The Underwriter will pay on behalf of the **Independent Directors Loss** from **Claims** first made during the **Policy Period**,
including **Defense Expenses** which, subject to IV. Condition (A)(2), will be paid on a current basis, except for such
Loss which the **Company** pays to or on behalf of the **Independent Directors** as indemnification.

II. DEFINITIONS

Whenever used in this Policy:

(A) **"Application"** means the application attached to and forming part of this Policy, including any materials submitted
therewith, which materials shall be on file with the Underwriter and deemed a part hereof and attached hereto,
as if physically attached;

(B) **"Claim"** means (1) written notice received by an **Independent Director** or the **Company** from or on behalf of
any person or entity that it is the intention of such person or entity to hold one or more of the **Independent Directors**
responsible for a **Wrongful Act,** (2) the institution by a federal or state regulatory agency of an injunctive or
administrative proceeding arising out of a **Wrongful Act** or (3) a legal, injunctive or administrative proceeding
against an Independent Director solely by reason of his or her status as a director of the Company.

(C) **"Company"** means the **Parent Corporation** and/or any **Subsidiary**;

(D) **"Defense Expenses"** means reasonable legal fees and expenses incurred by an **Independent Director** in
defense of a **Claim**; provided, however, that **Defense Expenses** shall not include remuneration, overhead or benefit
expenses associated with directors, officers or employees of the **Company**;

(E) **"Independent Directors"** means only those past and present directors of the **Company** not otherwise employed
by the **Company** who are identified by endorsement to this Policy or were identified as such in any predecessor
Independent Directors' Liability Policy issued by the Underwriter to the **Parent Corporation**; and, in the event of
the death, incapacity or bankruptcy of an **Independent Director**, the estate, heirs, legal representatives or assigns
of such individual;

(F) **"Loss"** means any amount, including **Defense Expenses**, in excess of the applicable retention and not exceeding
the Limit of Liability which an **Independent Director** is legally obligated to pay as a result of a **Claim**; provided,
however, that **Loss** shall not include matters which are uninsurable;

(G) **"Parent Corporation"** means the entity named in ITEM 1 of the Declarations;

(H) **"Policy Period"** means the period from the inception date of the Policy to the expiration date of the Policy, as
set forth in ITEM 2 of the Declarations, or to any earlier cancellation date pursuant to IV. Condition (L); provided,
however, that the Discovery Period under IV. Condition (E), shall be part of and not in addition to the **Policy Period**;

(I) **"Subsidiary"** means any entity of whose outstanding securities representing the present right to vote for the
election of directors more than fifty percent (50%) are owned by the **Parent Corporation** and/or one or more
of its **Subsidiaries**;

(J) **"Wrongful Act"** means any actual or alleged error, omission, misstatement, misleading statement or breach of
duty by an **Independent Director** while serving as such and solely in his or her capacity as a director of the
Company.

(F-1843) ED. 3-88

883

III. EXCLUSIONS

    (A) Except for **Defense Expenses**, which will be paid on a current basis subject to IV. Condition (A)(2), the Underwriter shall not be liable to make any payment for **Loss** in connection with any **Claim** made against an **Independent Director:**

        (1) brought about or contributed to in fact (a) by any dishonest or fraudulent act or omission or any criminal act or omission or any willful violation of any statute, rule or law by such **Independent Director** or (b) by such **Independent Director** gaining any personal profit, remuneration or advantage to which he or she was not legally entitled; provided, however, that for the purposes of determining the applicability of this exclusion, no **Wrongful Act** pertaining to any of the **Independent Directors** shall be imputed to any other **Independent Director;**

        (2) by or at the behest of the **Company** or any director or officer thereof, or by any security holder of the **Company** whether directly or derivatively unless such security holder is acting independently of, and without the solicitation, assistance, participation or intervention of the **Company** or any director or officer thereof; provided, however, that this exclusion shall not apply to any **Claim** (a) by a director or officer of the Company in the form of a claim for contribution or indemnity which results directly from a Claim not otherwise excluded under this Policy or (b) arising out of the actual or alleged tort of wrongful termination.

    (B) The Underwriter shall not be liable to make any payment for **Loss**, including **Defense Expenses,** in connection with any **Claim** made against any of the **Independent Directors** for bodily injury, sickness, mental anguish, emotional distress, disease or death of any person, or for any damage to or destruction of any tangible property including loss of use thereof; provided, however, that this exclusion shall not apply to any derivative **Claim** made by any security holder of the **Company** acting independently of, and without the solicitation, assistance, participation or intervention of the **Company** or any director or officer thereof.

IV. CONDITIONS

    (A) **NO DUTY TO DEFEND; ADVANCEMENT OF DEFENSE EXPENSES:**

        (1) It shall be the duty of the **Independent Directors** and not the duty of the Underwriter to defend **Claims.** No **Defense Expenses** shall be incurred and no settlement of any **Claim** shall be made without the Underwriter's consent, such consent not to be unreasonably withheld.

        (2) The Underwriter shall, upon written request by an **Independent Director,** pay on a current basis **Defense Expenses** incurred by such **Independent Director** which are otherwise reimbursable under this Policy, except to the extent that such **Defense Expenses** are being paid on a current basis under the terms of any other policy or policies of insurance, or by the **Company.** Each **Independent Director** agrees that, in the event it is finally established that, by reason of III, Exclusion (A)(1), the Underwriter has no liability for **Loss** such **Independent Director** will repay the Underwriter, upon demand, all **Defense Expenses** so paid.

    (B) **OTHER INSURANCE:**

        Subject to the Underwriter's obligation to pay **Defense Expenses** on a current basis under IV. Condition (A)(2) above, this Policy shall be excess of and not contribute with other valid and collectible insurance, including but not limited to the policy or policies identified in ITEM 6 of the Declarations and any replacement, renewal or policy excess thereof, other than insurance specifically in excess of this Policy. Nothing herein shall be construed to make this Policy subject to the terms of any other insurance.

    (C) **LIMIT OF LIABILITY; PAYMENT OF LOSS:**

        (1) The amount stated in ITEM 3 of the Declarations shall be the maximum aggregate Limit of Liability of the Underwriter under the Policy for all **Loss** resulting from all **Claims,** regardless of the time of payment by the Underwriter. **Defense Expenses** shall be part of and not in addition to such Limit of Liability, and payment of **Defense Expenses** by the Underwriter shall reduce such Limit of Liability.

        (2) All **Claims** based on, arising out of, directly or indirectly resulting from, in consequence of, or in any way involving the same or related facts, circumstances, situations, transactions or events or the same or related series of facts, circumstances, situations, transactions or events shall be deemed to be a single **Claim,** which shall be deemed to have been made at the time the earliest such **Claim** was first made, or at the time notice thereof was first given under IV. Condition (F), whichever occurred first.

        (3) Except as provided in IV. Condition (A)(2) above, the Underwriter shall pay or reimburse **Loss,** including **Defense Expenses,** only upon the final disposition of any **Claim.**

2

884

(D) **COOPERATION; SUBROGATION:**

In the event of a **Claim**, the **Independent Directors** and the **Company** will provide the Underwriter with all information, assistance and cooperation that the Underwriter reasonably requests, and will do nothing that may prejudice the Underwriter's position or potential or actual rights of recovery. In the event of payment under this Policy, the Underwriter shall be subrogated to all of the rights of recovery therefor of the **Independent Directors**, including without limitation their rights of recovery (1) under any other valid and collectible insurance, including but not limited to the policy or policies identified in ITEM 6 of the Declarations and any replacement, renewal or policy excess thereof, other than insurance specifically in excess of this Policy, and (2) against the **Company** for nonpayment of indemnification. For purposes hereof, all relevant corporate documents shall be deemed to have been adopted or amended to provide indemnification to the **Independent Directors** and to limit liability to the fullest extent permitted by law. The **Independent Directors** shall execute all papers required and shall do everything that may be necessary to secure such rights, including the execution of such documents as may be necessary to enable the Underwriter effectively to bring suit in their name.

(E) **DISCOVERY PERIOD:**

If the policy is cancelled by mutual written agreement in accordance with IV. Condition (L), or is not renewed by the Parent Corporation or the Underwriter, the coverage granted by this policy shall be extended for a period of 365 days after the expiration date of the policy, but only with respect to any **Wrongful Act** committed before such date.

(F) **NOTICE OF CLAIM OR CIRCUMSTANCES:**

(1) If during the **Policy Period** any **Claim** is first made against an **Independent Director**, the **Independent Directors** or the **Company**, as a condition precedent to the right of the **Independent Directors** to payment under this Policy, shall give the Underwriter written notice of any such **Claim** as soon as practicable after such **Claim** is first made, by certified mail to the address specified in ITEM 7 of the Declarations.

(2) If during the **Policy Period** an **Independent Director** or the **Company** first becomes aware of any circumstances which may subsequently give rise to a **Claim** being made against one or more of the **Independent Directors** and, as soon as practicable thereafter but in any event prior to the expiration or cancellation of the Policy, gives the Underwriter written notice of such circumstances with full particulars of the specific **Wrongful Act** involved, by certified mail to the address specified in ITEM 7 of the Declarations, then any **Claim** subsequently made against an **Independent Director** arising out of such **Wrongful Act** which is not otherwise excluded by the terms of this Policy shall be deemed made during the **Policy Period**.

(G) **REPRESENTATIONS; SEVERABILITY:**

The **Independent Directors** and the **Company** represent that the particulars and statements contained in the **Application** are true and agree that: (1) those particulars and statements are the basis of this Policy and are to be considered as incorporated into and constituting a part of this Policy; (2) those particulars and statements are material to the acceptance of the risk assumed by the **Underwriter**; and (3) this Policy is issued in reliance upon the truth of such representations. The **Application** shall be construed as a separate application for coverage by each of the **Independent Directors**. No statement in the **Application** or knowledge or information possessed by an **Independent Director** shall be imputed to any other **Independent Director** for the purpose of determining the availability of coverage hereunder.

(H) **NO ACTION AGAINST UNDERWRITER:**

(1) No action shall be taken against the Underwriter unless, as a condition precedent thereto, there shall have been full compliance with all of the terms of this Policy and until the amount of the obligation of the **Independent Directors** to pay shall have been finally determined either by judgment against the **Independent Directors** after adjudicatory proceedings, or by written agreement of the **Independent Directors**, the claimant and the Underwriter.

3

(2) No person or organization shall have any right under this Policy to join the Underwriter as a party to any **Claim** against an **Independent Director** to determine the liability of such **Independent Director;** nor shall the Underwriter be impleaded by an **Independent Director** or his or her legal representative in any such **Claim.** Bankruptcy or insolvency of any of the **Independent Directors** or of any of their estates shall not relieve the Underwriter of any of its obligations hereunder.

(I) AUTHORIZATION AND NOTICES:

By acceptance of this Policy, the **Independent Directors** and the **Company** agree that the **Parent Corporation** shall act on behalf of the **Independent Directors** and the **Company** with respect to receiving all notice from the Underwriter and any return premiums that may become due.

(J) CHANGES:

Notice to any agent or knowledge possessed by any agent or other person acting on behalf of the Underwriter shall not effect a waiver or change in any part of this Policy or estop the Underwriter from asserting any right under the terms, conditions and limitations hereof; nor shall the terms, conditions and limitations hereof be waived or changed except by written endorsement issued to form a part of this Policy.

(K) ASSIGNMENT:

Assignment of interest under this Policy shall not bind the Underwriter unless its consent is endorsed hereon.

(L) CANCELLATION:

This Policy may be cancelled by mutual written agreement among the **Parent Corporation** and all of the **Independent Directors** upon such terms and conditions as the parties may agree and, in such event, the earned premium shall be computed in accordance with the customary short rate table and procedure. The Policy may be cancelled by the Underwriter for failure to pay a premium when due by mailing or delivering to the **Parent Corporation** written notice stating when, not less than ten (10) days thereafter, such cancellation shall be effective. If this Policy is cancelled by the Underwriter, earned premium shall be computed pro rata. Premium adjustment may be made either at the time cancellation is effective or as soon as practicable after cancellation becomes effective, but payment or tender of unearned premium is not a condition of cancellation.

(M) EXHAUSTION:

In the event that the Limit of Liability is exhausted by the payment of **Loss**, including **Defense Expenses**, any and all obligations of the Underwriter hereunder shall be deemed to be completely fulfilled and extinguished, and the Underwriter shall have no further obligations hereunder of any kind or nature whatsoever.

(N) ACCEPTANCE:

By acceptance of this Policy, the **Independent Directors** and the **Company** agree that this Policy (including the **Application)** and any written endorsements attached hereto constitute the entire agreement existing between them and the Underwriter or any of its agents relating to this insurance.

(O) HEADINGS:

The descriptions in the headings and sub-headings of this Policy are solely for convenience, and form no part of the terms and conditions of coverage.

In witness whereof the Underwriter has caused this Policy to be executed on the Declarations Page.

4

Appendix D-1

SAMPLE CHARTER OR BYLAW
INDEMNIFICATION PROVISION

Delaware

(a) *Right to Indemnification.* Each person who was or is a party or is threatened to be made a party to or is involved in any threatened, pending or completed action, suit or proceeding, whether civil, criminal, administrative or investigative ("Proceeding"), by reason of the fact that he or she, or a person of whom he or she is the legal representative, is or was a director or officer of the Corporation or, as a director or officer of the Corporation, is or was serving at the request of the Corporation as a director, officer, employee or agent of another corporation, partnership, joint venture, trust or other enterprise, including service with respect to employee benefit plans, whether the basis of such Proceeding is alleged action in an official capacity as a director, officer, trustee, employee or agent or in any other capacity, shall be indemnified and held harmless by the Corporation to the fullest extent authorized by law, including but not limited to the Delaware General Corporation Law, as the same exists or may hereafter be amended (but, in the case of any such amendment, only to the extent that such amendment permits the Corporation to provide broader indemnification rights than said Law permitted the Corporation to provide prior to such amendment), against all expenses, liability and loss (including attorney's fees, judgments, fines, ERISA excise taxes or penalties and amounts paid or to be paid in settlement) reasonably incurred or suffered by such person in connection therewith; provided, however, that the Corporation shall indemnify any such person seeking indemnity in connection with an action, suit or proceeding (or part thereof) initiated by such person only if such action, suit or proceeding (or part thereof) initiated by such person was authorized by the board of directors of the Corporation. Such right shall include the right to be paid by the Corporation expenses, including attorney's fees, incurred in defending any such Proceeding in advance of its final disposition; provided, however, that the payment of such expenses in advance of the final disposition of such Proceeding shall be made only upon delivery to the Corporation of an undertaking, by or on behalf of such director or officer, in which such director or officer agrees to repay all amounts so advanced if it should be ultimately determined that such person is not entitled to be indemnified under this Section or otherwise.

(b) *Right of Claimant to Bring Suit.*

(i) If a claim under paragraph (a) is not paid in full by the Corporation within thirty days after a written claim therefor has been received by the Corporation, the claimant may any time thereafter bring suit against the Corporation to recover the unpaid amount of the claim and, if successful in

887

whole or in part, the claimant shall be entitled to be paid also the expense of prosecuting such claim. It shall be a defense to any such action (other than an action brought to enforce a claim for expenses incurred in defending any proceeding in advance of its final disposition where the required undertaking has been tendered to the Corporation) that the claimant has not met the standards of conduct which make it permissible under the applicable law for the corporation to indemnify the claimant for the amount claimed, but the burden of proving such defense shall be on the Corporation.

(ii) Neither the failure of the Corporation (including its Board of Directors, independent legal counsel, or its shareholders) to have made a determination prior to the commencement of such action that indemnification of the claimant is proper in the circumstances because he or she has met the applicable standard of conduct, nor an actual determination by the Corporation (including its Board of Directors, independent legal counsel, or its shareholders) that the claimant has not met such applicable standard of conduct, shall be a defense to the action or create a presumption that the claimant has not met the applicable standard of conduct.

(c) *Contractual Rights; Applicability.* The right to be indemnified or to the reimbursement or advancement of expenses pursuant hereto (i) is a contract right based upon good and valuable consideration, pursuant to which the person entitled thereto may bring suit as if the provisions hereof were set forth in a separate written contract between the Corporation and the director or officer, (ii) is intended to be retroactive and shall be available with respect to events occurring prior to the adoption hereof, and (iii) shall continue to exist after the rescission or restrictive modification hereof with respect to events occurring prior thereto.

(d) *Requested Service.* Any director or officer of the Corporation serving, in any capacity, (i) another corporation of which a majority of the shares entitled to vote in the election of its directors is held by the Corporation, or (ii) any employee benefit plan of the Corporation or of any corporation referred to in clause (i), shall be deemed to be doing so at the request of the Corporation.

(e) *Non-Exclusivity of Rights.* The rights conferred on any person by paragraphs (a) and (b) shall not be exclusive of and shall be in addition to any other right which such person may have or may hereafter acquire under any statute, provision of the Articles of Incorporation, Code of Regulations, bylaw, agreement, vote of shareholders or disinterested directors or otherwise.

(f) *Insurance.* The Corporation may maintain insurance, at its expense, to protect itself and any such director, officer, employee or agent of the Corporation or another corporation, partnership, joint venture, trust or other enterprise against such expense, liability or loss, whether or not the corporation would have the power to indemnify such person against such expense, liability or loss under the Delaware General Corporation Law.

888

Appendix D-2

SAMPLE INDEMNITY AGREEMENT

Delaware

This Agreement is made as of the _____ day of _____, 19____, by and between _____, a Delaware corporation (the "Corporation"), and _____ (the "Indemnitee"), a Director and/or Officer of the Corporation.

WHEREAS, it is essential to the Corporation to retain and attract as Directors and Officers the most capable persons available, and

WHEREAS, the substantial increase in corporate litigation subjects Directors and Officers to expensive litigation risks at the same time that the availability of and coverage provided by directors' and officers' liability insurance has become uncertain, and

WHEREAS, it is now and has been the express policy of the Corporation to indemnify its Directors and Officers so as to provide them, with the maximum possible protection permitted by law, and

WHEREAS, the Corporation does not regard the protection available to Indemnitee as adequate in the present circumstances, and realizes that Indemnitee may not be willing to serve as a Director or Officer without adequate protection, and the Corporation desires Indemnitee to serve in such capacity;

NOW, THEREFORE, in consideration of Indemnitee's service as a director or officer after the date hereof the parties agree as follows:

1. *Definitions.* As used in this Agreement:

(a) The term "Proceeding" shall include any threatened, pending or completed action, suit or proceeding, whether brought by or in the right of the Corporation or otherwise and whether of a civil, criminal, administrative or investigative nature.

(b) The term "Expenses" shall include, but is not limited to, expenses of investigations, judicial or administrative proceedings or appeals, damages, judgments, fines, amounts paid in settlement by or on behalf of Indemnitee, attorneys fees and disbursements and any expenses of establishing a right to Indemnification under this Agreement.

(c) The term "Director" and "Officer" shall include Indemnitee's service at the request of the corporation as a director, officer, employee or agent of another corporation, partnership, joint venture, trust or other enterprise as well as Director or Officer of the Corporation.

(d) For purposes of Section 3 and 4, the phrase "decided in a Proceeding" shall mean a decision by a court, arbitrator(s), hearing officer or other judicial agent having the requisite legal authority to make such a decision which decision has become final and from which no appeal or other review proceeding is permissible.

889

2. *Indemnity of Director or Officer.* Subject only to the limitations set forth in Section 3, Corporation will pay on behalf of the Indemnitee all Expenses actually and reasonably incurred by Indemnitee because of any claim or claims made against him in a Proceeding by reason of the fact that he is or was a Director and/or Officer.

3. *Limitations on Indemnity.* Corporation shall not be obligated under this Agreement to make any payment of Expenses to the Indemnitee:

(a) the payment of which is prohibited by applicable law;

(b) for which and to the extent payment is actually and unqualifiedly made to the Indemnitee under an insurance policy or otherwise;

(c) resulting from a claim in a Proceeding decided adversely to the Indemnitee based upon or attributable to the Indemnitee gaining in fact any personal profit or advantage to which he was not legally entitled.

4. *Advance Payment of Costs.* Expenses incurred by Indemnitee in defending a claim against him in a Proceeding shall be paid by the Corporation as incurred and in advance of the final disposition of such Proceeding. Indemnitee hereby agrees and undertakes to repay such amounts advanced if it shall be decided in a Proceeding that he is not entitled to be indemnified by the Corporation pursuant to this Agreement or otherwise.

5. *Enforcement.* If a claim under this Agreement is not paid by Corporation, or on its behalf, within thirty days after a written claim has been received by Corporation, the Indemnitee may at any time thereafter bring suit against Corporation to recover the unpaid amount of the claim and if successful in whole or in part, the Indemnitee shall be entitled to be paid also the Expenses of prosecuting such claim.

6. *Subrogation.* In the event of payment under this Agreement, Corporation shall be subrogated to the extent of such payment to all of the rights of recovery of the Indemnitee, who shall execute all papers required and shall do everything that may be necessary to secure such rights, including the execution of such documents necessary to enable Corporation effectively to bring suit to enforce such rights.

7. *Notice.* The Indemnitee, as a condition precedent to his right to be indemnified under this Agreement, shall give to Corporation notice in writing as soon as practicable of any claim made against him for which indemnity will or could be sought under this Agreement. Notice to Corporation shall be given at its principal office and shall be directed to the Corporate Secretary (or such other address as Corporation shall designate in writing to the Indemnitee); notice shall be deemed received if sent by prepaid mail properly addressed, the date of such notice being the date postmarked. In addition, the Indemnitee shall give Corporation such information and cooperation as it may reasonably require.

8. *Saving Clause.* If this Agreement or any portion thereof shall be invalidated on any ground by any court of competent jurisdiction, the Corporation shall nevertheless indemnify Indemnitee to the full extent permitted

by any applicable portion of this Agreement that shall not have been invalidated or by any other applicable law.

9. *Indemnification Hereunder Not Exclusive.* Nothing herein shall be deemed to diminish or otherwise restrict the Indemnitee's right to indemnification under any provision of the Certificate of Incorporation or Bylaws of the Corporation or under Delaware law.

10. *Applicable Law.* This Agreement shall be governed by and construed in accordance with Delaware law.

11. *Counterparts.* This Agreement may be executed in any number of counterparts, each of which shall constitute the original.

12. *Successors and Assigns.* This Agreement shall be binding upon the Corporation and its successors and assigns.

13. *Continuation of Indemnification.* The indemnification under this Agreement shall continue as to Indemnitee even though he may have ceased to be a Director and/or Officer and shall inure to the benefit of the heirs and personal representatives of Indemnitee.

14. *Coverage of Indemnification.* The indemnification under this Agreement shall cover Indemnitee's service as a Director and/or Officer and all of his acts in such capacity, whether prior to or on or after the date of the Agreement.

IN WITNESS WHEREOF, the parties hereto have caused this Agreement to be duly executed and signed as of the day and year first above written.

INDEMNITEE   CORPORATION

By: _____   By: _____

891

Appendix E

SAMPLE STATEMENT OF SELF-INSURANCE

Ohio

DIRECTORS AND OFFICERS LIABILITY

_____, an Ohio corporation, hereby establishes this Statement of Self-Insurance pursuant to authority expressly granted by Section 1701.13(E)(7), Ohio Revised Code. The rights of directors and officers under this Statement of Self-Insurance are contract rights based upon good and valuable consideration and shall be enforceable the same as if the provisions hereof were set forth in a separate written contract between the **Self-Insured** and the director or officer. Any amendment or termination of this Statement of Self-Insurance shall not affect any such rights which have accrued prior to the effective date of such amendment or termination. The provisions of this Statement of Self-Insurance are as follows:

I. _Self-Insured:_ _____.

II. _Insured Persons:_ Any person who was, is or hereafter may be a director or officer of the **Self-Insured** or was, is or hereafter may be serving at the request of the **Self-Insured** as a director, trustee, officer, employee or agent of another corporation, domestic or foreign, non-profit or for-profit, partnership, joint venture, trust or other enterprise, including service with respect to employee benefit plans.

Any person who has served, is serving or hereafter may serve as a director or officer of another corporation of which a majority of the shares entitled to vote in the election of its directors is held by the **Self-Insured** at the time of such service shall be deemed to have served or be serving at the request of the **Self-Insured.**

III. _Period of Coverage:_ Commencing at 12:01 A.M. _____ and ending at 12:01 A.M. _____. Such **Period of Coverage** shall be automatically extended for a period of one (1) year on each _____ thereafter, subject to the right of the **Self-Insured,** in its sole and absolute discretion, to terminate this Statement of Self-Insurance as of any _____, subject to the provisions hereof relating to the **Extended Discovery Period.** Each such period of one (1) year shall constitute a separate **Insurance Year** for the purposes of this Statement of Self-Insurance.

IV. _Limit of Self-Insurance:_ The total limit of the **Self-Insured's** liability to pay any **Loss** resulting from all claims first made during any one **Insurance Year** or during the **Extended Discovery Period** shall be $_____, regardless of the time of payment by the **Self-Insured.**

893

V. *Coverage:* Subject to the **Limit of Self-Insurance** and all other provisions of this Statement of Self-Insurance, the **Self-Insured** will pay to or on behalf of any **Insured Person** all **Loss** which the **Self-Insured** does not indemnify and which arises out of any claim first made against the **Insured Person,** individually or otherwise, during the **Period of Coverage** for a **Wrongful Act** committed, attempted or allegedly committed or attempted by the **Insured Person** before or during the **Period of Coverage.** Such **Coverage** shall extend to claims for the **Wrongful Acts** of **Insured Persons** when made against the estates, heirs or legal representatives of **Insured Persons** who are deceased, incompetent, insolvent or bankrupt.

VI. *Extended Discovery Period:* If the **Self-Insured** terminates this Statement of Self-Insurance pursuant to Section III hereof, the **Period of Coverage** shall be automatically and irrevocably extended for an additional two (2) year period from the effective date of such termination, but only with respect to any **Wrongful Act** committed, attempted or allegedly committed or attempted prior to the effective date of such termination.

VII. *Exclusions:* The **Self-Insured** shall not be liable hereunder to make any payment for **Loss** in connection with any claim(s) made against any **Insured Person(s)**:

(a) for the return by any such **Insured Person** of any remuneration paid in fact to him if (1) a judgment or other final adjudication adverse to such **Insured Person** establishes that such remuneration is in violation of law, or (2) the **Insured Person** has entered into a settlement agreement to repay such remuneration to the **Self-Insured**;

(b) for an accounting of profits made from the purchase or sale by such **Insured Person** of securities of the **Self-Insured** within the meaning of Section 16(b) of the Securities Exchange Act of 1934 and amendments thereto or similar provisions of any federal, state or local statutory law or common law;

(c) based upon or attributable to such **Insured Person** having gained any personal profit or advantage to which he was not legally entitled if (1) a judgment or other final adjudication adverse to such **Insured Person** establishes that such **Insured Person** in fact gained such personal profit or other advantage to which he was not entitled, or (2) the **Insured Person** has entered into a settlement agreement to repay such unentitled personal profit or advantage to the **Self-Insured**;

(d) based upon or attributable to the dishonesty of such **Insured Person** if a judgment or other final adjudication adverse to such **Insured Person** establishes that acts of active and deliberate dishonesty were committed or attempted by such **Insured Person**

894

with actual dishonest purpose and intent and were material to the cause of action so adjudicated;

(e) if such **Loss** arises from any claim made against any **Insured Person(s)** which is insured under any other valid policy(ies), prior or current; provided, however, this exclusion shall not apply to the extent that the amount of such **Loss** is in excess of the amount of payment from such other insurance whether such other insurance is stated to be primary, contributory, excess, contingent or otherwise, unless such other insurance is written only as specific excess insurance over the limits provided herein; or

(f) to the extent that such **Loss** is indemnified by any other person, corporation, partnership, joint venture, trust or other enterprise.

With respect to the exclusions set forth herein, no fact pertaining to or knowledge possessed by any **Insured Person(s)** shall be imputed to any other **Insured Person(s)** for the purpose of determining the availability of coverage for, or with respect to claims made against, any **Insured Person(s)**.

VIII. *Notice:* The **Insured Persons** shall, as a condition precedent to exercising their rights under this Statement of Self-Insurance, give to the **Self-Insured** written notice as soon as practicable of any claim made against any of them for a **Wrongful Act.** If during the **Period of Coverage,** including any **Extended Discovery Period,** any **Insured Person** becomes aware of any circumstance(s) which could give rise to a claim for a **Wrongful Act** and written notice of such circumstance(s) is given to the **Self-Insured,** then all claims subsequently arising from such circumstance(s) shall be considered to have been made during the **Insurance Year** or the **Extended Discovery Period** in which such written notice was given.

Claims arising out of the same act or interrelated acts of one or more **Insured Persons** shall be considered made during the **Insurance Year** or the **Extended Discovery Period** in which the first of such claims is made.

The time when a claim is made shall be the date on which written notice is given to the **Self-Insured** as herein provided.

The **Insured Person** shall give the **Self-Insured** such information and cooperation as it may reasonably require, including but not limited to, the nature of the alleged **Wrongful Act,** the alleged injury and the names of all claimants and witnesses known to the **Insured Persons.**

IX. *Defense and Settlement:* No **Defense Costs** shall be incurred or settlements made without the **Self-Insured** consent, which shall not be unreasonably withheld. The **Self-Insured** shall not be liable to make any payments on account of any settlements or **Defense Costs** to which it has not consented. The **Self-Insured** shall advance reasonable **Defense Costs,**

895

including attorney's fees, periodically during the course of legal proceedings.

An **Insured Person** shall not be required to contest any legal proceedings unless counsel (to be mutually agreed upon by such **Insured Person** and the **Self-Insured**) shall advise that such proceedings should be contested by the **Insured Person** and the **Insured Person** consents thereto, which consent shall not be unreasonably withheld.

X. *Subrogation:* If any payment is made under this policy, the **Self-Insured** shall be subrogated to the extent of such payment to the **Insured Persons'** rights of recovery. In such case the **Insured Persons** shall execute all papers required and shall do everything necessary to secure and preserve such rights, including the execution of such documents necessary to enable the **Self-Insured** effectively to bring suit in the name of the **Insured Persons.**

XI. *Definitions:* When used herein:

Defense Costs means that part of **Loss** consisting of costs, charges and expenses incurred in defending, investigating or monitoring legal actions, claims, or proceedings and appeals therefrom and the cost of appeal, attachment or similar bonds.

Loss means the total amount which any **Insured Person(s)** becomes legally obligated to pay by reason of any **Wrongful Act** and, subject to all other terms, conditions, definitions, exclusions and limitations of this Statement of Self-Insurance, shall include damages, judgments, settlements, and **Defense Costs** but shall not include matters uninsurable under Ohio law.

Wrongful Act means any error, misstatement, misleading statement, act, omission, neglect, or breach of duty committed, attempted, or allegedly committed or attempted, by any **Insured Person,** individually or otherwise, in his capacity as an **Insured Person,** or any matter claimed against him by reason of his serving in such capacity. All causally connected errors, misstatements, misleading statements, acts, omissions, neglects, or breaches of duty committed or attempted by, allegedly committed or attempted by, or claimed against one or more of the **Insured Persons** shall be deemed interrelated **Wrongful Acts.**

XII. *Non-Exclusive:* The **Coverage** provided by this Statement of Self-Insurance shall not be deemed exclusive of or in any way to limit any other rights to which any **Insured Person** may be or become entitled as a matter of law, by the articles, bylaws or regulations of the **Self-Insured,** agreements, insurance, vote of shareholders or directors or otherwise.

Index

899

900

903

919

EDGAR V. MITE, §15.09.
Self-interest in takeover situations, §15.01.

EDUCATIONAL INSTITUTIONS.
Nonprofit and charitable organizations generally.
See NONPROFIT AND CHARITABLE ORGANIZATIONS.

ELECTRONIC DATA PROCESSING.
Nonuse or misuse of computers, §2.13.

EMPLOYEES, §2.10.
Actions.
Wrongful discharge, §10.10.
Benefit plans.
ERISA liability generally.
See ERISA LIABILITY.
Fiduciary liability insurance.
See LIABILITY INSURANCE.
Criminal liability generally.
See CRIMES AND OFFENSES.
Discrimination against.
Discriminatory work environment, §10.12.
Generally, §10.09.
Race discrimination, §10.11.
Enforcement of liability, §2.15.
Indemnification.
Eligibility, §20.06.
Generally.
See INDEMNIFICATION OF DIRECTORS AND OFFICERS.
Inside information.
Misuse by outsiders, §16.07.
Insider trading.
Civil liability of employer, §16.09.
Liability generally, §10.09.
Reliance on, §2.06.
Safety.
Occupational Safety and Health Act (OSHA), §10.08.
Stock ownership plans under ERISA, §§9.08, 9.09.
Workers' compensation, §2.10.
Wrongful discharge, §10.10.

EMPLOYMENT RETIREMENT SECURITY ACT OF 1974, §§9.01 to 9.09.
See ERISA LIABILITY.

ENVIRONMENTAL LAWS.
Civil liability, §10.01.
Clean Air Act, §10.04.
Clean Water Act, §10.05.
Comprehensive Environmental Response Compensation and Liability Act of 1980 (CERCLA), §10.03.
Conflict of laws, §10.02.

ENVIRONMENTAL LAWS—Cont'd
Criminal liability generally, §8.07.
  Basis of individual liability, §10.01.
Resource Conservation and Recovery Act of 1976 (RCRA), §10.07.
Superfund Act, §10.03.
Superfund Amendments and Reauthorization Act of 1986 (SARA), §10.03.
Toxic Substances Control Act of 1976 (TSCA), §10.06.

EQUITY FUNDING LITIGATION, §11.10.

ERISA LIABILITY, §§9.01 to 9.09.
Corporate control, §9.09.
Delinquent contributions, §9.07.
Employee stock ownership plans, §§9.08, 9.09.
Fiduciaries.
  Corporate officers and directors, §9.06.
  Generally, §9.03.
Fiduciary liability insurance, §§21.18, 22.10, 22.11.
Indemnification of directors and officers, §20.06.
Nature of ERISA, §9.01.
Parties in interest, §9.04.
Preemption provisions, §9.02.
Prohibited transactions, §9.05.
Takeovers, mergers and buyouts, §15.08.

ERNST & ERNST V. HOCHFELDER.
Allegation of scienter, §§11.06, 11.15.

ESOPS, §§9.08, 9.09.

EVIDENCE.
Advice of counsel.
  Reliance on, §2.04.
Burden of proof.
  Business judgments.
    Directors' burden if presumption rebutted, §6.11.
  Compensation.
    Reasonableness of compensation, §4.10.
  Conflicts of interest, §§3.02, 3.05.
    Corporate control.
      Use of corporate powers to maintain control, §3.06.
    Voting by interested directors, §3.17.
  Corporate control.
    Use of corporate powers to maintain control, §3.06.
  Majority shareholders.
    Fair dealing, §3.21.
  Self-dealing, §3.02.
Business judgments.
  Burden of proof.
    Directors' burden if presumption rebutted, §6.11.

921

924

925

926

938

946